INTERNATIONAL LILAC SOCIETY

International Register and Checklist of Cultivar Names in the Genus *Syringa* L. (Oleaceae)

As of March 5, 2021

Edited by Mark L. DeBard, MD, Registrar

International Lilac Society

International Lilac Society

International Register and Checklist of Cultivar Names in the Genus *Syringa* L. (Oleaceae)
("Work-in-Progress" Lilac Register)

Copyright © 2021 Mark L. DeBard, MD, Registrar & International Lilac Society
Freek Vrugtman, Registrar Emeritus
Assistant Registrars: Claire Fouquet, David Gressley, Tatyana Polyakova

Photos © 2017 Mark L. DeBard

Cover: Montreal Botanical Gardens
Back cover photos: I 'John Kennedy', Royal Botanical Gardens (RBG), Hamilton, Ontario, Canada 2017; II 'Square Deal' (FC 09), Highland Park, Rochester, New York, USA, 2018; III 'Madame Charles Souchet', St. Petersburg Botanical Garden (SPBG or Komarov Institute of the Russian Academy of Sciences), St. Petersburg, Russia, 2018; IV 'Mollie Ann', RBG, 2017; V 'Dr Masters', RBG, 2017; VI 'Lady Lindsay', SPBG, 2018; VII 'Marshal Sokolovskiĭ, SPBG, 2018

Book and cover design by Kitty Werner, RSBPress

For information on title, copyright, address, table of content, acknowledgements, historical overview and introduction see the online Introductory Pages.

RELEASE NOTE: This printed Lilac (*Syringa*) Register & Checklist of Cultivar Names is the first one in twenty years. It has 3561 entries and includes 1223 registered lilacs, 640 more with established but non-registered names, and 669 more with non-established names, as well as 1025 more with synonyms or with rejected and unacceptable names. Errors are inevitable and corrections are welcomed by the Registrar at:
registrar@internationallilacsociety.org.

The online version of this file includes flower and bud color information for over 1450 cultivars, as well as a sortable Excel file and multiple appendices. It is available at: https://www.internationallilacsociety.org/public-register/

Printed Release Date: March 5, 2021

ISBN 978-1-7362935-0-8 tradepaper
ISBN 978-1-7362935-1-5 hardcover

Introductory notes concerning the entries in the Register and Checklist

The Register and Checklist contains all cultivar names known to the Registrar, and many designations that may be interpreted erroneously as being cultivar names.

The name of a cultivar or Group consists of the name of the genus or lower taxonomic unit to which it is assigned together with a cultivar or Group epithet. The name may be written in a variety of equivalent ways (ICNCP-2016, Article 8.1). *Syringa* 'Excel', *Syringa* ×*hyacinthiflora* 'Excel', lilac 'Excel', sering 'Excel' (in Dutch), lilas 'Excel' (in French), and Flieder 'Excel' (in German) are names for the same cultivar.

A trade designation is not a name but is a device that is usually used for marketing a cultivar or Group in place of its accepted name when the accepted name is not considered suitable for marketing purposes (ICNCP-2016, Article 13)[1]. Trade designations, including trademarks, appear in small capital letters (e.g. LUDWIG SPAETH). Trade designations, including trademarks, must be distinguished typographically with no quotes and are always to be cited together with, or in juxtaposition to, the accepted name (ICNCP-2016, Article 17) (e.g. *Syringa* LUDWIG SPAETH ['Andenken an Ludwig Späth'], or TINKERBELLE™ ['Bailbelle']).

Diacritical marks are an integral part of certain languages such as French, German, Latvian and Swedish, where they affect pronunciation. Neglecting umlauts is simply an orthographic error and changes the pronunciation of a name or word; neglecting diacritical marks is unnecessary and awkward, although sometimes convenient for an English keyboard.

Cultivar names originally published in Cyrillic script have been transliterated. In accordance with Article 33 of the *International Code of Nomenclature for Cultivated Plants-2016* transliterations in this publication are based on the 1997 edition, 2012 revision, of the *ALA-LC Romanization Tables*[2]. Certain Cyrillic characters are transliterated to English by using two or more Latin characters, such as я = ya; ю = yu; ш = sh; ч = ch, and so on. Whenever this is the case the Latin characters have been underlined. For example, the Latin ya will transliterate to the Cyrillic я, rather than to the individual characters ы and a. The Latin transliteration of the Cyrillic character щ is underlined twice: shch, distinguishing it from ш = sh and ч = ch appearing side by side. This convention has been adopted from Charles Dragutin Holetich, *Lilacs - Special Issue* 11(2):1, International Lilac Society; 1982.

Each entry in the Register follows this pattern

1st line:

Cultivar epithet followed by Group epithet if applicable and/or taxonomic unit.

Registered cultivar epithets appear in bold type (e.g. **'Michel Buchner'**); non-registered epithets appear in normal type (e.g. 'Prairie Gem'). Cultivar names originally published in Cyrillic and Chinese have been transliterated (romanized) or appear in pinyin, respectively.

Group names appear in round brackets (Villosae Group). This is the only Group name established, accepted and registered in the genus *Syringa*. For the definition of Villosae Group see Appendix F, summary of classification, Series Villosae (online only).

Botanical names, here referred to as the "lower taxonomic unit", appear in italics. This may vary from simply *S.* (for *Syringa*, the genus), to *S. vulgaris* (genus and specific epithet, together the species), *S. oblata* subsp. *dilatata* (species and subspecies), *S. vulgaris* var. *purpurea* (species and botanical variety), and *S.* ×*hyacinthiflora* (named interspecific hybrid or nothospecies).

Cultivar names originally published in Cyrillic, Chinese, or Japanese script have been recorded on an additional line (first added April 12, 2016).

2nd and 3rd lines:

(May be preceded by the original language name). Originator and year followed by the 1953 Wister Color Code (for explanations see below). The color is usually chosen by the originator and may not be accurate. About 10% of colors include two or more colors. No bud colors are yet included.

---

[1] The International Code of Nomenclature for Cultivated Plants, 9th edition 2016 may be electronically downloaded from http://www.ishs.org/scripta-horticulturae/international-code-nomenclature-cultivated-plants-ninth-edition

[2] The *American Library Association - Library of Congress Romanization Tables* may be electronically downloaded from http://lcweb.loc.gov/catdir/cpso/roman.html

Nota bene: The "year" is not always a reliable date; revisions are frequent, depending on information available.

Subsequent lines may provide information on:
- parentage: { × }
- synonymy: syn. - (more accurately, any other designations used for this cultivar in the past).
- literature citations
- photo on Jorgovani/Lilacs 2015 DVD–This notation indicates that one or more photographs of the cultivar can be found on the DVD, second, revised and expanded edition, compiled by Želimir Borzan and Charles Holetich.
  Disclaimer: The identity of the cultivars photographed may or may not have been confirmed.
- name: Notation on etymology, derivation or meaning of the cultivar name.
- awards: notation on awards received (RHS = Royal Horticultural Society, UK; KMTP = Royal Society of Horticulture and Botany, NL.)
- notation on establishment, acceptance and registration of the cultivar name.
- notation if it is known as a lilac for forcing.
- other notations

1953 Wister Color Code
Abbreviations:
S - Single flowers   D - Double flowers

Colors
I   white   V pink or pinkish
II violet   VI magenta
III blue or bluish VII purple
IV lilac

&   bicolor [*e.g. VII & I for purple and white*]
/ - color combinations [*e.g. III/VII for bluish-purple; V-VI for pinkish to magenta*]
*   cultivar with variegated and/or golden foliage
?   information incomplete

Cultivar names appearing in **bold type** have been registered

Abréviations:
S - fleur simple   D - fleur double

Couleurs
I   blanc   V rose ou rosâtre
II violet   VI magenta
III bleu ou bleuâtre VII pourpre
IV lilas

&   bicolore [*par exemple VII & I pour pourpre et blanc*]
/ - combinaison de couleurs [*par exemple III/VII pour bleuâtre-pourpre; V-VI pour rosâtre à magenta*]
*   cultivar avec feuillage panaché et/ou doré
?   information incomplète

Épithètes de cultivars en **caractères gras** ont été enregistrées

Abkürzungen:
S - einfache Blüten   D - gefüllte Blüten

Farben
I   weiß   V rosa oder rötlich
II violett   VI magentarot
III bläu oder bläulich VII purpurrot
IV lila

&   zweifarbig [z.B. VII & I für purpurrot und weiß]
/ - Übergangsfarben [z.B. III/VII für bläulich-purpurrot; V-VI für blaßrosa bis magentarot]
*   Sorte (Cultivar) mit panaschierter und/oder goldfarbiger Belaubung
?   Information unvollständig

Fett gedruckte Sortennamen sind registriert

Сокращения:
S - простые цветки   D - махровые цветки

Окраска
I   белая   V розовая или розоватая
II фиолетовая   VI мажентовая
III голубая и голубоватая VII пурпурная
IV лиловая

&   двухцветная [например, VII и I для пурпурной и белой]
/ - цветовые комбинации [например, III / VII для голубовато-пурпурного цвета; V-VI от розоватого до мажентового]
* сорт с пёстрой и / или золотистой листвой
? информация неполная

Названия сортов, выделенные жирным шрифтом, зарегистрированы

List of Registered, Established, Accepted, or other Names of *Syringa* Cultivars

'Abel Carrière', *Syringa vulgaris*
  Lemoine 1896; D III
  common name: Abel Carriere
  Lemoine, Cat. No. 134, 9 [1896]; McKelvey, The Lilac, 249 [1928]; Wister, Lilacs for America, 43 [1942], 24 [1953]; Photo on Jorgovani/Lilacs 2015 DVD.
  Named for Élie Abel Carrière, 1818-1896, French horticulturist and author.
  Cultivar name presumed registered 1953; name established and accepted.

Abel Chatney - see **'Mme Abel Chatenay'**.

'A. B. Lamberton', S. vulgaris
  Dunbar 1916; D VII
  syn. - Dunbar No. 201
  {'Marie Legraye' × ? }
  Dunbar, Hort. 26:35 [1917] - name only, 27:534, 553 & frontispiece [1918]; McKelvey, The Lilac, 249 [1928]; Wister, Lilacs for America, 43 [1942], 24 [1953]; Photo on Jorgovani/Lilacs 2015 DVD.
  Named for Alexander B. Lamberton, 1839- x, president of the board of park commissioners, 1902-1918, Rochester, New York, USA.
  Cultivar name registered presumed 1953; name established and accepted.

A. Buckner - see **'Mme Antoine Buchner'**.

Abundance - see **'Izobilie'**.

'Abundant Bloomer', S. vulgaris
  Klager 1928; S V
  Cooley, Cat. 1928-29, 8 [1928]; McKelvey, The Lilac, 559 [1928]; Stand. Pl. Names, 614 [1942] - erroneously as common name for 'City of Kelso'; Wister, Lilacs for America, 43, 45 [1942], 24, 27 [1953] - erroneously as common name for 'City of Kelso', D V; Anon., ILS Newsletter 14(4):3-4 [1988]; Photo on Jorgovani/Lilacs 2015 DVD.
  Cultivar name presumed registered 1953; name established and accepted.

'Ada', *S. ×hyacinthiflora*
  Preston 1953; S VI
  {*S. ×hyacinthiflora* 'Muriel' × *S. ×hyacinthiflora* 'Patricia'}
  Wister, Lilacs for America, 24 [1953]
  Cultivar name presumed registered 1953; name established and accepted.

'Adam Mickiewicz', *S. vulgaris*
  Karpow-Lipski 1958; D IV
  syn. - KL 34, Siewka nr 23
  Karpow-Lipski, Arboretum Kórnickie, 3:105 [1958]; Wister & Oppe, Arnoldia 31(3):125 [1971]; Anon., Lista odmian roślin ozdobnych 1971, 17 & 1973, 25 - syn.: 'KL 34', as II; Photo on Jorgovani/Lilacs 2015 DVD.
  Named for Adam Mickiewicz, 1798-1855, national poet of Poles and Lithuanians.
  Cultivar name registered 1970; name established and accepted.

'Addie Tischler', *S. vulgaris*
  Tischler 1981; D V
  Peterson, Lilacs - Proceedings 16(1):17 [1987] - name only; Vrugtman, Lilacs -Quart. Jour. 32(4):149 [2003] - as D V.
  Cultivar name established and accepted.

'Addie V. Hallock', *S. vulgaris*
  Boice; S I
  Wister, Arnoldia 23(4):80 [1963]
  Cultivar name registered 1963;
  Cultivar not reported in cultivation.

'Adelaide Dunbar', *S. vulgaris*
  Dunbar 1916; D VII
  syn. - Dunbar no. 200
  {'Aline Mocqueris' × ? }
  Dunbar, Hort. 26:35 [1917], 27:534 [1918]; McKelvey, The Lilac, 249 [1928]; Wister, Lilacs for America, 43 [1942], 24 [1953]; Lilacs - Quart. Jour. 21(4): back cover ill. [1992]; Photo on Jorgovani/Lilacs 2015 DVD.
  Named for Adelaide (Addie) Marie Davis, 1868- x, wife of John Dunbar.
  Cultivar name presumed registered 1953; name established and accepted.

'Adelina', *S. vulgaris*
  'Аделина'
  Aladin, S., Aladina, O., Polyakova, T., and Akimova, S. 2011; S V
  {'Nevesta' × OP}
  Registered with the State Commission of the Russian Federation for Testing and Protection of Selection Achievements, No. 8853112, 2011; Питомник-частный сад (Pitomnik i chastnyi sad; Nursery and private garden) 3/2015:14-22 (in Russian) ; Приусадебное хозяйство (Annex to the magazine Homestead farming: "Flowers in the garden and at home. Brushes and paints"), 08/2015: 5-14; Вестник АППМ (Catalog in Vestnik APPM (Planting material association) magazine) 1/2018: 59-72.
  Named for Adelina Veniaminovna Kondratieva (Abramson) Аделина Вениаминовна Кондратьева, 1917-2012; fighter in the Spanish Civil War and author of publications about the International Brigade.
  Statutory registration, Russia, State Register No. 8853112 (2011).
  Cultivar name established and accepted; name registered.

'Admiral Farragut', *S. vulgaris*
    Dunbar 1923; S IV
    syn. - Dunbar no. 306
    {'Gilbert' × ? }
    Wister, Nat. Hort. Mag. 6(1):1-16 [1927] - as S V; McKelvey, The Lilac, 250 [1928]; Wister, Lilacs for America, 43 [1942] - as S VII; Wister, Lilacs for America, 24 [1953]; Photo on Jorgovani/Lilacs 2015 DVD.
    Named for David Glasgow Farragut, 1801-1870, American naval commander.
    Cultivar name presumed registered 1953; name established and accepted.

'Admiral Kuznetsov', *S. vulgaris*
    'Адмирал Кузнецов'
    Aladin, S., Aladina, O. and Polyakova, T. 2015; D VII/II
    {elite form 10-182 × 'Maximowicz'}
    Вестник АППМ (Catalog in Vestnik APPM (Planting material association) magazine) 1/2018: 59-72 (in Russian); Приусадебное хозяйство (Annex to the magazine Homestead farming: "Flowers in the garden and at home. Brushes and paints") 08/2015: 5-14; Питомник-частный сад (Pitomnik i chastnyi sad; Nursery and private garden) 2/2015: 32-38; Садовник (Gardener) magazine, 05 (141)/2017 :16-22.
    Named for Nikolay Gerasimovich Kuznetsov (Николай Герасимович Кузнецов), 1904-1974, Soviet fleet Admiral, 1920-1956, Hero of the Soviet Union.
    Cultivar name established and accepted.

'Admiral Nakhimov', *S. vulgaris*
    'Адмирал Нахимов'
    Aladin, S., Aladina, O., Polyakova, T., and Aladina, A. 2016; S VI
    {'Indiya' × OP}
    Садовник (Gardener) magazine, 05 (141)/2017 :16-22; Вестник АППМ (Catalog in Vestnik APPM (Planting material association) magazine) 1/2018: 59-72 (in Russian).
    Named for Pavel Stepanovich Nakhimov (Павел Степанович Нахимов), 1802-1855, Admiral of the Imperial Russian Navy, defender of Sevastopol.
    Cultivar name established and accepted.

Adolf Vaigla – see 'Kivi Ats'

'Adriana', *S.* (Villosae Group), *S.* ×*prestoniae*
    Preston 1928; S IV
    syn. - 'Adrianna', 'Adrianne', Preston No. 20-14-02
    {*S. villosa* subsp. *villosa* × *S. komarowii* subsp. *komarowii*}
    Macoun, Rep. Dom. Hort. 1928, p. 55 [1930] - name only; Wister, Lilacs for America, 64 [1942], 24, 48 [1953] - as 'Adrianna' and 'Adrianne'; Photo on Jorgovani/Lilacs 2015 DVD.
    Named for the Wife of Antipholus of Ephesus in Shakespeare's *Comedy of Errors*.
    Cultivar name presumed registered 1953; name established and accepted.

'A. Eizyk', *S. vulgaris*
    Karpow-Lipski; D V
    syn. - Siewka nr 150
    Karpow-Lipski, Arboretum Kórnickie, 3:107 [1958]
    Named for Aron Eizyk, nurseryman and grower of roses in Kutno, central Poland, 1930s to 1950s.
    Cultivar name established and accepted.

'Aėlita', *S. vulgaris*
    'Аэлита'
    Vekhov 1952; S IV-VII
    {'Vestale' × ? }
    Rubtzov et al. 1980. Vidy i sorta sireni, kul'tiviruemye v SSSR. Kiev; Naukova Dumka. – in Russian; Holetich, C.D. 1982. Lilac species and cultivars in cultivation in USSR. Lilacs 11(2):1-38. - translation of Rubtzov et al. 1982; Photo on Jorgovani/Lilacs 2015 DVD.
    Named for Aėlita or The Decline of Mars, a 1923 science fiction novel by the Russian author Alekseĭ Nikolayevich Tolstoĭ.
    Cultivar name established and accepted.

À fleurs d'oranger, *S. vulgaris*
    origin not known pre-1917; S I
    Harzer Baumschulen, Cat. 1917-18, p. 83 [1917] - as gelblichweiß.
    Probably not a cultivar name.

'Afrodita', *S. vulgaris*
    'Афродита'
    Aladin, S., Aladina, O., and Polyakova, T. 2016; D V
    {'Zhemchuzhina' × ? }= {Obtained from open pollinated 'Zhemchuzhina' cultivar}.
    Садовник (Gardener) magazine 04 (140)/2017 :18-25; Вестник АППМ (Catalog in Vestnik APPM (Planting material association) magazine) 1/2018: 59-72 (in Russian).
    Named for Aphrodite, the Greek goddess of beauty and love.
    Cultivar name established and accepted.

'Agata', *S.* (Villosae Group) *S.* ×*prestoniae*
    Bugała pre-1970; S IV
    syn. - 'Diana' (Bugała) (not 'Diana', Preston)
    Bugała, Arboretum Kórnickie 15:61-70 [1970] - as 'Diana', in Polish, for summary see ILS Newsletter 2(1):15-16 [1973]; Wister & Oppe, Arnoldia 31(3):121-126 [1971] - as 'Diana'; Vrugtman, AABGA Bull. 15(3):72 [1981] - registration changed to 'Agata'; Bugała, Lilacs - Quart. Jour. 24(4):90-91 [1995] - erroneously as 'Diana', see: Vrugtman, Lilacs - Quart. Jour. 25(2):38 [1996]
    Named for Mrs Agata Bugała, mother of the originator.
    Cultivar name registered 1970; name established and accepted.

'Agidel", *S. vulgaris*
    'Агидель'
    Sakharova 1973; S I
    syn. - Sakharova No. 2414

{'Mme Lemoine' × 'Marie Legraye'}
Sakharova, Introduktsiya i selektsiya dekorativnykh rasteniĭ v Bashkirii, 32 [1978] - in Russian; Rubtzov et al. 1980. Vidy i sorta sireni, kul'tiviruemye v SSSR. Kiev; Naukova Dumka. – in Russian; Holetich, C.D. 1982. Lilac species and cultivars in cultivation in USSR. Lilacs 11(2):1-38. - translation of Rubtzov et al. 1982; Photo on Jorgovani/Lilacs 2015 DVD.
Named after the main waterway of Bashkortostan, the White river.
Cultivar name established and accepted.

'Agincourt Beauty', *S. vulgaris*
Slater 1970; S II
{'Frank Paterson' × 'Dr Brethour'}
Registered with COPF in 1971; Wister & Oppe, Arnoldia 31(3):121 [1971]; Anon., ILS Newsletter 1(4):11 [1972]; Sheridan Nurseries, Cat., 82 [1973] - as "very deep purple'; Anon., Landscape Canada 10(7):19 & front cover ill. [1973]; Slater, US Plant Patent No. 3694 [May 15, 1975 - statutory registration]; Lilacs - Quart. Jour. 21(1): back cover ill. [1992]; Photo on Jorgovani/Lilacs 2015 DVD.
Named for Agincourt, Ontario, Canada, hometown of the originator.
Cultivar name registered 1970; name established and accepted.

'Agnes Smith', *S.* (Villosae Group)
Rogers 1970; S I
{'James Macfarlane' × OP }
syn. - R63-1, 'Miss USA'; probably also: New Hampshire, white; marketed in Germany as *S. ×prestoniae* Miss USA™ (No. 302008033734; G. & J. Rosskamp) and Miss America
Anon., Technical Sheet, University of New Hampshire [n.d., probably 1970] - as *S. ×prestoniae*, but corrected to *S. ×josiflexa*; Wister & Oppe, Arnoldia 31(3):121 [1971] - no affiliation listed; Fiala, Lilacs, 220 [1988] - erroneously as *S. ×prestoniae*; Rogers, Lilacs - Quart. Jour. 23(4):107 [1994] - parentage; J. Bentley, Lilacs 42(2):57, ill. Back cover [2013];
<http://www.park-der-gaerten.de/Pflanzenliste1.pdf> - as 'Miss USA"; Photo on Jorgovani/Lilacs 2015 DVD.
Named for Agnes Greene Smith, 1883-1969; school teacher; 1st president of the New Hampshire Federation of Garden Clubs.
Cultivar name registered 1970; name established and accepted.

AGS 2281, *S. tomentella* subsp. *yunnanensis*
origin not known ? ?
listed in NCCPG Collection, UK [1997]
Probably not a cultivar name.

'Ahonen', *S.* (Villosae Group)
Ahonen 2012; S IV
<www.ahosentaimisto.fi/product/901/ahosen_syreeni>
seen 24 March 2012

Name: Ahonen is a Finnish family name; we don't know for whom this cultivar was named.
Cultivar name not established.

'Aïgul", *S. vulgaris*
'Айгуль'
Sakharova 1973; D IV-V
syn. - 'Ajgul', Sakharova No. 1276
{'Mme Lemoine' × 'Capitaine Baltet'}
Sakharova, Introduktsiya i selektsiya dekorativnykh rasteniĭ v Bashkirii, 30-31 [1978] - in Russian; Rubtzov et al. 1980. Vidy i sorta sireni, kul'tiviruemye v SSSR. Kiev; Naukova Dumka. – in Russian; Holetich, C.D. 1982. Lilac species and cultivars in cultivation in USSR. Lilacs 11(2):1-38. - translation of Rubtzov et al. 1982; Photo on Jorgovani/Lilacs 2015 DVD.
Name: In Bashkir and Farsi "lunar flower"; also a female name.
Cultivar name established and accepted.

'Aino', *S. vulgaris*
Vaigla 1970; S II-III (S IV-VI per Semenov)
{parentage not known}
Vrugtman, HortScience 26(5): 476-477 [1991]; Kivistik, Maakodu 1997(5):22-23 (ill.) [1997] - in Estonian; I. Semenov, Lilacs 48(2): 65, 63 (photo) [2019]
Cultivar name registered 1990; name accepted and established.

'Ainola', *S.* (Villosae Group), *S. ×henryi*
Uosukainen ca 2001; S II
Wickmans Plantskola http://www.tawi.fi/~wiplant/uddamod.html [Jul.18/07] - name only; MTT (Agrifood Research Finland) cat. Varmennetun taimituotannon emokasvihinnasto vuonna 2010, p. 53; F. Moro, Lilacs 42(3):88 (photo)
Named for Ainola, Kuokkala, the city of Jyväskylä, Middle-Finland, where the original plant was found.
Cultivar name established and accepted.

A. J. Klettenberg - see **'Madame A. J. Klettenberg'**.

'Akademik E.M. Primakov', *S. vulgaris*
Академик Е.М. Примаков
Dyagilev B & Degtev V. 2020; D II/VII
(Международная научная конференция "Syringa L.: коллекции, выращивание, использование")
"International Scientific Conference "Syringa L.: collections, cultivation, using" / Collection of Scientific Articles of Botanical Institute named after V.L. Komarov, Botanical Garden of Peter the Great BIN RAS. - St. Petersburg. -2020.- pp.23-27 (in Russian).
Named for the USSR Academy of Sciences academician, politician, and statesman.
Cultivar name established and accepted.

'Akademik Burdenko', *S. vulgaris*
'Академик Бурденко'
Kolesnikov 1941; D III-IV
syn. - 'Academic Burdenko', 'Arademik Surdenko'
{parentage not known}

Date of creation and description in the book by N.K. Vekhov "Lilacs" 1953.
Rubtzov et al. 1980. Vidy i sorta sireni, kul'tiviruemye v SSSR. Kiev; Naukova Dumka. – in Russian; Holetich, C.D. 1982. Lilac species and cultivars in cultivation in USSR. Lilacs 11(2):1-38. - translation of Rubtzov et al. 1982; USDA-ARS GRIN database, PI No. 26776.
Creation date and description in "Lilacs" by N.K. Vekhov, 1953.
Named for Academician Nikolaĭ Nilovich Burdenko, 1876–1946; neurosurgeon; Surgeon-General of the Red Army; Hero of Socialist Labour; Russia and Soviet Union.
Cultivar name established and accepted.

'Akademik Kurchatov', *S. vulgaris*
 'Академик Курчатов'
 Aladin, S., Aladina, O., and, Polyakova, T. 2016; S VII
 {'Buffon' × OP}
 Садовник (Gardener) magazine 04 (140)/2017 :18-25; Вестник АППМ (Catalog in Vestnik APPM (Planting material association) magazine) 1/2018: 59-72 (in Russian)
 Named for Academician Igor Vasilyevich Kurchatov (Игорь Васильевич Курчатов), 1903-1960, Soviet nuclear physicist, director of the Soviet atomic bomb project.
 Cultivar name established and accepted.

'Akademik Maksimov', *S. vulgaris*
 'Академик Максимов'
 Kolesnikov pre-1953; D VII/V
 Rubtzov et al. 1980. Vidy i sorta sireni, kul'tiviruemye v SSSR. Kiev; Naukova Dumka. – in Russian; Holetich, C.D. 1982. Lilac species and cultivars in cultivation in USSR. Lilacs 11(2):1-38. - translation of Rubtzov et al. 1982; Vrugtman, Lilacs -Quart. Jour. 32(4):149 [2003] - plants in cultivation in North America under this name with single, white flowers (S I) are not true to name.
 Named for Academician Аркадий Леонидович Максимов, Arkadiĭ Leonidovich Maksimov, Director of the Scientific Research Centre "Arktika", Far Eastern Branch of the Russian Academy of Sciences (Magadan, Russia).
 Cultivar name established and accepted.

'Akademik Sakharov', *S. vulgaris*
 'Академик Сахаров'
 Dyagilev 1989; D I
 {'Mme Abel Chatenay' '' × OP}
 Dyagilev, Lilacs - Quart. Jour.22(1):19 [1993] - as D I; Pikaleva, Lilacs - Quart. Jour. 23(4):84 [1994] - as S I. (Международная научная конференция "Syringa L.: коллекции, выращивание, использование") "International Scientific Conference "Syringa L.: collections, cultivation, using" / Collection of Scientific Articles of Botanical Institute named after V.L. Komarov, Botanical Garden of Peter the Great BIN RAS. - St. Petersburg. -2020.- pp.23-27 (in Russian) as D I.
 Named for Academician Andrei Dimitrievich Sakharov, 1921-1989, Russian physicist and human rights activist.
 Cultivar name established and accepted.

Akademik Surdenko - see 'Akademik Burdenko'
 Q No. 26776 [= in quarantine, USDA] - as Aradmik Surdenko.

'Akatombo', *S. pubescens* subsp. *pubescens*
 '赤蜻蛉'
 Ihara 2004; S VII
 syn. - seedling no. 20040520001#13.
 {*S. pubescens* subsp. *pubescens* 'Palibin' × *S. pubescens* subsp. *pubescens* 'Palibin'}
 (Vrugtman, Cultivated Plant Diversity ... 2017)
 Name: Japanese for red dragonfly.
 Cultivar name registered 2017; name established and accepted.

'Akkila', *S. vulgaris*
 origin not known ca 2002; S II
 distributed by Wickmans Plantskola http://www.tawi.fi/~wiplant/uddamod.html [Apr.3/01] - name only
 Cultivar name not established.

'Akku', *S. vulgaris*
 'Акку'
 Sagitova & Dzevitski 1994; S I
 varietal denomination registered 1994, No. 10, State Register of Selected Achievements in Republic of Kazakhstan.
 Cultivar name not established.

'Aladdin', *S.* (Villosae Group)
 origin not known pre-1960; S V
 {probably derived from *S. josikaea*, *S. komarowii* subsp. *komarowii* and *S. villosa* subsp. *villosa*}
 Wister, Arnoldia 23(4):80 [1963] - as *S. villosa* hybrid
 Cultivar name registered 1963; name established and accepted.

'Ala-Tau', *S. vulgaris*
 'Ала-Тау'
 Sagitova 1968; D V-VII
 {'Vesnovka' × mixed pollen of Nos 76(4) & 88}
 Named for the Ala-Tau, several mountain ranges of the Tien Shan in eastern Kyrgyzstan and southeast Kazakhstan.
 Cultivar name not established.

'Alba' or *alba*, *S.* ×*chinensis* - see 'Correlata'.
 Photo on Jorgovani/Lilacs 2015 DVD.

'Alba', *S.* (Villosae Group), *S.* ×*henryi*
 Lemoine 1934; S V
 syn. - 'Henryi alba', *henryi alba*
 Lemoine, Cat. No. 210, 25 [1936]; Wister, Lilacs for America, 43, 49 [1942] - as S I; Wister, Lilacs for America, 24, 31 [1953]
 Cultivar name presumed registered 1953; name established and accepted.

Alba, *S. josikaea* - see 'Holger'.

'Alba', *S. komarowii* subsp. *reflexa*
  Upton 1933; S I
  syn. - *reflexa* f. *alba*
  common - white nodding lilac
  Upton, Horticulture 11(4):59 [1933] - as *S. reflexa* f. *alba*; Woody Plant Register, AAN, No. 26 [1949]; Wister, Lilacs for America, 43, 57 [1942], 24, 40 [1953]
  Cultivar name presumed registered 1953; name established and accepted.

Alba, *S. pubescens* subsp. *pubescens* - see **'Palibin Pearl'**
  Anon., Lilacs - Quart. Jour. 21(4):105 [1992] - in cultivation at Arnold Arboretum (AA number 266-88-A), name only.

'Alba', *S. oblata* subsp. *oblata*
  Origin not known pre-1902; S I
  syn. - *S. affinis* L. Henry, *S. oblata* var. *affinis* Lingelsheim, *S. oblata* var. *alba* (Hort.) ex Rehder
  Rehder, in Bailey, Cycl. Am Hort. 4:1763 [1902]; P. S. Green, The Plantsman 6:12-13 [1984]; Anon. *Syringa*. Flora of China 15:285 [1996]
  Cultivar name established and accepted.

'Alba', *S.* ×*persica*
  origin not known pre-1770; S I
  syn. - *S.* ×*persica* var. *alba* Weston
  Weston, Bot. Univ. 1:289 [1770]; Wister, Lilacs for America, 38 [1953]
  Awards: RHS Award of Garden Merit 1993.
  Cultivar name presumed registered 1953; name established and accepted.

'Alba', *S. pubescens* subsp. *microphylla*
  pre-1920; S I
  (not *S. pubescens* subsp. *microphylla* 'Alba', Upton)
  syn. - Farrer 309
  {from seed coll. by Reginald Farrer}
  Cox, The Plant Introductions of Reginald Farrer, 51 [1930]; Bean, Hand-List of Trees and Shrubs (excluding Conifers) Cultivated in the Royal Botanic Gardens, Kew, 4th ed., 331 [1934].
  Cultivar name established and accepted.

'Alba', *S. pubescens* subsp. *microphylla*
  (not *S. pubescens* subsp. *microphylla* 'Alba', Farrer)
  Upton; S I
  Wister, Lilacs for America, 32 [1953]
  Cultivar name not established; epithets may not be used more than once (Art. 17.2).

'Alba', *S. villosa* subsp. *villosa*
  origin not known pre-1942; S I
  Wister, Lilacs for America, 43, 60 [1942], 24, 42 [1953]; Hillier, Trees and Shrubs, 136 [1950]
  Cultivar name presumed registered 1953; name established and accepted.

alba, *S. vulgaris* - see *S. vulgaris* var. *alba* Weston

'Alba', *S. vulgaris*
  origin not known pre-2006; S I
  <http://www.smts.fi/> (Finnish Society of Agricultural Sciences) name only, seen Dec. 6, 2006 (no longer listed, April 24, 2016)
  Cultivar name not established.

'Alba', *S. tomentella* subsp. *yunnanensis*
  Hillier ca 1946; S I
  Hillier, Hillier's Manual of Trees & Shrubs, 391 & 573 [1971].

'Alba Albo-variegata', *S. vulgaris*
  pre-1730; S I *
  McKelvey, The Lilac, 250 [1928] - confused name.

Alba Bertha, Alba Bertha Dammann - see **'Frau Bertha Dammann'**.

'Alba Grandiflora', *S. vulgaris*
  perhaps Dauvesse pre-1832; S I
  syn. - 'Grandiflora Alba'
  common name - Great White
  Stand. Pl. Names, 485, 486 [1923] - as Great White; McKelvey, The Lilac, 250-251 [1928]; Wister, Lilacs for America, 43 [1942], 24 [1953]; Photo on Jorgovani/Lilacs 2015 DVD.
  Cultivar name presumed registered 1953; name established and accepted.

'Alba Luteo-variegata', *S. vulgaris*
  pre-1730; S I *
  McKelvey, The Lilac, 251 [1928] - confused name.

'Alba Magna', *S. vulgaris*
  origin not known pre-1887; S I
  McKelvey, The Lilac, 251 [1928].

'Alba Major', *S. vulgaris*
  Origin not known pre-1923; S I
  common name: - Large White
  Loddiges, Cat. [1823]; Stand. Pl. Names, 485, 486 [1923] - as Large White; McKelvey, The Lilac, 252 [1928] - probably scarcely different from 'Alba Grandiflora' and 'Alba Magna'.

'Alba Plena', *S. vulgaris*
  pre-1823; D I
  Loddiges, Cat., 35 [1823]; McKelvey, The Lilac, 252 [1928] - confused name; Photo on Jorgovani/Lilacs 2015 DVD.
  Cultivar name not established.

Alba Pyramidalis - see **'Pyramidalis Alba'**.

'Alba Sanguinea', *S. vulgaris*
  pre-1925; S I
  Gracewood, Cat. [1941]; Wister, Lilacs for America, 36 & 43 [1942], 24 [1953] - as doubtful name
  Cultivar name not established, not recorded in cultivation in 1953.

'Alba Virginalis', *S. vulgaris*
    origin not known pre-1841; S I
    syn. - 'Virginal', 'Virginalis'
    common name: Virgin, Blanc Virginal, White Virgin
    Oudin, Cat. [1841]; Stand. Pl. Names, 488 [1923] - as Virgin; McKelvey, The Lilac, 252-253 [1928]; Wister, Lilacs for America, 43 [1942], 24 [1953]; Photo on Jorgovani/Lilacs 2015 DVD.
    Cultivar name presumed registered 1953; name established and accepted.

'Albert F. Holden', *S. vulgaris*
    Fiala 1980; S II-VII
    syn. - 'Al Holden', 'Albert Holden'
    {'Sarah Sands' × 'Réaumur'}
    Knight, Lilacs-Proceedings 9:8 [1981] - a deep purple with a silver reverse; Vrugtman, AABGA Bull. 16(4):131 [1982] - name only, as 'Albert Holden'; Fiala, Lilacs, 93, 105, 107, 108 & Pl. 82 [1988]; Lilacs - Quart. Jour. 18(3): front cover ill [1989]; Photo on Jorgovani/Lilacs 2015 DVD.
    Named for Albert Fairchild Holden, 1877-1913, geologist and metallurgist, who initiated the establishment of an institution for botanical education, known today as the Holden Arboretum, Kirtland, Ohio, USA.
    Cultivar name established and accepted.

'Albert the Good', *S. vulgaris*
    Dougall 1874; S VII
    Dougall (Windsor Nurs.) Cat. 1874; Mckelvey, The Lilac, 253 [1928]; Wister, Lilacs for America, 43 [1942], 24 [1953]
    Named for Prince Albert of Saxe-Coburg and Gotha (Francis Albert Augustus Charles Emmanuel), 1819-1861, Prince Consort of Queen Victoria.
    Cultivar name presumed registered 1953; name established and accepted.

'Albida', *S.* (Villosae Group)
    Lemoine 1930; S I
    {*S. tomentella* subsp. *sweginzowii* × *S. tomentella* subsp. *tomentella*}
    syn. - 'Pink Pearl', *S. sweginzowii albida*
    Lemoine, Cat. No. 204, 26 [1930] - as *S. sweginzowii albida*; Wister, Lilacs for America, 43, 59 [1942], 24, 42 [1953]; Pringle, Baileya 20(2):51 [1977]; Photo on Jorgovani/Lilacs 2015 DVD.
    Cultivar name presumed registered 1953; name established and accepted.

albiflora, *S. microphylla*, f. (forma)
    Gorb 1975; S I
    seedling selected as a cultivar
    Gorb 1989 Сирени на Украина, p. 51-52
    Cultivar name not established; after 1958 cultivar names in Latin form are not established.

albiflora, *S. villosa* subsp. *villosa*, f. (forma)
    Gorb 1979; S I
    bud mutation selected as a cultivar
    Gorb 1989 Сирени на Украина, p. 51-52
    Cultivar name not established; after 1958 cultivar names in Latin form are not established.

'Albīns', *S. vulgaris*
    Kārkliņš 2003; D I
    Strautiņa & Kaufmane, Dobeles ceriņi, pp. 13-14, 92 [2011]; Semënov, I., and S. Stautiņa, Lilacs 42(2):53-55, ill. [2013]; Photo on Jorgovani/Lilacs 2015 DVD.
    Obtained from seedlings from wild lilacs in Riga, Latvia per Igor Semenov (personal communication 7-18-2019).
    Name: Latvian for albino.
    Cultivar name established and accepted.

'Albo-coerulea', *S. vulgaris*
    origin not known ? ?
    McKelvey, The Lilac, 253 [1928]
    Cultivar name not established.

'Albo-marginata', *S. vulgaris*
    pre-1899; ? ? *
    Rehder, Möller's Deutsche Gärtn.-Zeit. XIV. 206 [1899]; McKelvey, The Lilac, 254 [1928] - confused name
    Cultivar name not established.

'Albo-rosea', *S. vulgaris*
    origin not known pre-1903; ? ?
    McKelvey, The Lilac, 254 [1928]
    Cultivar name not established.

'Albo-variegata', *S. vulgaris*
    pre-1809; ? ? *
    Wiegers, Cat. 1809, 119; McKelvey, The Lilac, 254 [1928]
    Cultivar name not established.

Album, *S. vulgaris*
    origin not known; S I
    <www.westonnurseries.com/plantname/Syringa-vulgaris-Album>
    Rejected name
    Cultivar name not established.

'Aleksandr Blok', *S. vulgaris*
    'Александр Блок'
    Aladin, S., Aladina, O., and Polyakova, T. 2012; D IV
    {'Vechernyaya Moskva' × OP}
    Садовник (Gardener) magazine 04 (140)/2017 :18-25; http://floribunda.ru/?a=390 - seen March 13, 2018 - as S IV-IV/V; Вестник АППМ (Catalog in Vestnik АРРМ (Planting material association) magazine) 1/2018: 59-72 (in Russian).
    Named for Aleksandr Aleksandrovich Blok (Александр Александрович Блок), 1880-1921, Russian poet, writer, publicist, playwright, translator, literary critic.
    Cultivar name established and accepted.

'Aleksandr Matrosov', *S. vulgaris*
    'Александр Матросов'
    Kolesnikov
    Polyakova, 2010, Istoriya Russkoĭ Sireni, p. 43, 154; name only.

Named for Aleksandr Matveevich Matrosov, 1924-1943; Hero of the Soviet Union.
Cultivar name not established.

'Aleksandr Prokhorenko', *S. vulgaris*
'Александр Прохоренко'
Aladin, S., Aladina, O., Polyakova, T., and Aladina, A. 2016; D II-IV&V
{'Violetta' × OP}
Садовник (Gardener) magazine, 05 (141)/2017 :16-22; Вестник АППМ (Catalog in Vestnik APPM (Planting material association) magazine) 1/2018: 59-72 (in Russian).
Named for Senior Lieutenant Aleksandr Aleksandrovich Prokhorenko (Александр Александрович Прохоренко), 1990-2016, Hero of the Russian Federation, who died in the battles for Palmyra, Syria.
Cultivar name established and accepted.

'Aleksandr Pushkin', *S. vulgaris*
'Александр Пушкин'
Potutova 1971; S II
syn. - 'Alexander Puschcin'
Rubtzov et al. 1980. Vidy i sorta sireni, kul'tiviruemye v SSSR. Kiev; Naukova Dumka. – in Russian; Holetich, C.D. 1982. Lilac species and cultivars in cultivation in USSR. Lilacs 11(2):1-38. - translation of Rubtzov et al. 1982.
Named for Aleksandr Sergevich Pushkin, 1799-1837, Russian poet.
Cultivar name established and accepted.

'Aleksandra Pakhmutova', *S. vulgaris*
'Александра Пахмутова'
Aladin, S., Aladina, O., Polyakova, T., and Aladina, A. 2018; D V
{'Anabel' × OP}
IX International Scientific Conference (IX Международная научная конференция "Цветоводство: история, теория, практика") " Floriculture: history, theory, practice" , St. Petersburg, Botanical Garden of Peter the Great BIN RAS, September 7-13, 2019 (in Russian)
Named for Pakhmutova Aleksandra Nikolaevna (Пахмутова Александра Николаевна), 1929 -, one of the most famous Soviet composers.
Cultivar name established and accepted.

'Aleksandrs Čaks', *S.*
(no information); D II
In cultivation at Dobele, Latvia, in litt. Natalia Savenko to Mark DeBard, September 2018.

'Alekseĭ Mares'ev', *S. vulgaris*
'Алексей Маресьев'
Kolesnikov 1951; S III-IV
syn. - 'Aleksej Mares'ev', 'Aleksei Mares'ev', Aleksei Mares'iev', 'Alexei Maresyev', 'Alexey Mares'ev', 'Alexey Maressyev', 'Alexi Maresiev', 'Alexi Maresyev', Alexej Maresjev, Kolesnikov No. 443
{'Gastello' × ('Fürst Bülow' × Kolesnikov No. 105)}
Howard, Arnoldia 19(6-7):31-35 [1959]; Gromov, Siren', 99 [1963]; Gromov, AABGA Quart. Newsl. No. 64, 17-21 [1965]; Bilov et al., Siren', 117 [1974] - in Russian; ILS Proceedings 2(4):17 [1974]; Rubtzov et al. 1980. Vidy i sorta sireni, kul'tiviruemye v SSSR. Kiev; Naukova Dumka. – in Russian; Holetich, C.D. 1982. Lilac species and cultivars in cultivation in USSR. Lilacs 11(2):1-38. - translation of Rubtzov et al. 1982 ; Photo on Jorgovani/Lilacs 2015 DVD.
Named for Second World War fighter pilot major Alekseĭ Mares'ev, 1916-2001, Hero of the Soviet Union.
Cultivar name established and accepted.

'Alenushka', *S. vulgaris*
'Алёнушка'
Shtan'ko & Mikhaĭlov 1956; S V
syn. - 'Aljonuschka'
{'Maximowicz' × ? }
Bilov et al., Siren', 32 [1974] - in Russian; Rubtzov et al. 1980. Vidy i sorta sireni, kul'tiviruemye v SSSR. Kiev; Naukova Dumka. – in Russian; Holetich, C.D. 1982. Lilac species and cultivars in cultivation in USSR. Lilacs 11(2):1-38. - translation of Rubtzov et al. 1982; Photo on Jorgovani/Lilacs 2015 DVD.
Named for Mikhaĭlov's younger daughter.
Cultivar name established and accepted.

'Alesha', *S. vulgaris*
'Алёша'
Sakharova 1973; S VI
syn. - Sakharova No. 79
{'Andenken an Ludwig Späth' × 'Marie Legraye'}
Sakharova, Introduktsiya i selektsiya dekorativnykh rasteniĭ v Bashkiriĭ, 29-30 [1978] - in Russian; Rubtzov et al. 1980. Vidy i sorta sireni, kul'tiviruemye v SSSR. Kiev; Naukova Dumka. – in Russian; Holetich, C.D. 1982. Lilac species and cultivars in cultivation in USSR. Lilacs 11(2):1-38. - translation of Rubtzov et al. 1982; Photo on Jorgovani/Lilacs 2015 DVD.
Name: Diminutive of the name Alexey, pronounced "Alyosha".
Cultivar name established and accepted.

'Alessandro', *S. tomentella* subsp. *tomentella*
Moro, F. ?; S I
{'Royal Crown' × ? }
Select Plus web page - name only (seen Nov 4, 2016).
Named for Alessandro [1999 -], son of Frank and Sara Moro.
Cultivar name not established.

Alex.. - see also Aleks..

Alexander de Croncels - see '**De Croncels**'.

Alexander de Humboldt -see '**De Humboldt**'.

'**Alexander Hamilton**', *S. vulgaris*
Dunbar 1923; D VI

syn. - Dunbar no. 334
{'A. B. Lamberton' × ? }
Dunbar, Florist Exchange, 831 [Sept. 22, 1923]; McKelvey, The Lilac, 254 [1928]; Wister, Lilacs for America, 43 [1942], 24 [1953]; Photo on Jorgovani/Lilacs 2015 DVD.
Named for Alexander Hamilton, 1757-1804, American soldier, statesman, secretary of the treasury, 1789-1795.
Cultivar name presumed registered 1953; name established and accepted.

'Alexander's Advance', *S.* (Villosae Group)
Alexander Sr; ? ?
{*S.* ×*josiflexa* 'James Macfarlane' × *S.* ×*prestoniae* 'Ethel M. Webster'}
Wister, Arbor. Bot. Gard. Bull. 1(2):20 [1967] - name only
Cultivar name registered 1967;
Cultivar not reported in cultivation.

'Alexander's Aristocrat', *S.* (Villosae Group)
Alexander Sr; S V
{*S.* ×*josiflexa* 'James Macfarlane' × *S.* ×*prestoniae* 'Ethel M. Webster'}
Wister, Arbor. Bot. Gard. Bull. 1(2):20 [1967] - name only; Photo on Jorgovani/Lilacs 2015 DVD.
Cultivar name registered 1967; name established and accepted.

'Alexander's Attraction', *S.* ×*hyacinthiflora*
Alexander Sr 1968; S I
{parentage not known}
Wister & Oppe, Arnoldia 31(3):121 [1971] - name only
Cultivar name registered 1970; not recorded in cultivation.

'Alexander's Late', *S.* (Villosae Group)
Alexander Sr; S V
{'Ethel M. Webster' × (*S.* ×*josiflexa* 'James Macfarlane' × *S.* ×*prestoniae* 'Ethel M. Webster')}
Alexander Sr, Cat. sheets [n.d.; received Jan. 1970]
Cultivar name not established.

'Alexander's Perfection', *S.* (Villosae Group)
Alexander Sr; S V
{*S.* ×*josiflexa* 'James Macfarlane' × *S.* ×*prestoniae* 'Ethel M. Webster'}
Alexander Sr, Cat. sheets [n.d.; received March 1969]
Cultivar name not established.

'Alexander's Pink', *S.* (Villosae Group)
Alexander Sr 1967; S V
{*S.* ×*josiflexa* 'James Macfarlane' × *S.* ×*prestoniae* 'Ethel M. Webster'}
Wister, Arbor. Bot. Gard. Bull. 1(2):20 [1967] - name only; Alexander Sr, Cat. sheets [n.d.; received January 1970]
Cultivar name registered 1967; name established and accepted.

Alexander's Rose Red - see **'Jack Alexander'**.

'Alexander's Variegated', *S.* (Villosae Group)
Alexander Sr 1968; S V *
{*S.* ×*josiflexa* 'James Macfarlane' × *S.* ×*prestoniae* 'Ethel M. Webster'}
Wister & Oppe, Arnoldia 31(3):21 [1971] - name only
Cultivar name registered 1970;
Cultivar not reported in cultivation.

'Alexander I', *S. vulgaris*
origin not known pre-1886; ? ?
Lemoine, Cat. No. 103, 28 [1886]; McKelvey, The Lilac, 254 [1928]
Named, probably, for Alexander I, Александр Павлович, Aleksandr Pavlovich Romanov, 1777-1825, emperor of Russia.
Cultivar name not established.

'Alexandra', *S. pubescens* subsp. *pubescens*
Unknown; S VII
Seen September 2019 at www.plantsandpictures.com
Cultivar name not established.

'Alfa', *S. vulgaris*
Kārkliņš 2003; D I
In cultivation at Dobele, Latvia, in litt. Natalia Savenko to Mark DeBard, September 2018. Photo in 2020 ILS Photo Database. Noted to be a Kārkliņš selection by Semenov (personal communication, July 2018).
Cultivar name not established.

'Alfi', *S. pubescens* subsp. *microphylla*
origin not known pre-2008?; ? ?
<www.piccoplant.de/htm/english/produkte.htm> seen December 7, 2008; probably a selection of 'Superba'
Cultivar name not established.

'Alf. Neuner' or **'Alfred Neuner'**, *S. vulgaris*
origin not known pre-1892; D ?
McKelvey, The Lilac, 255 [1928] - confused name, not a Lemoine, introduction
Cultivar name not established.

'Alice', *S.* (Villosae Group), *S.* ×*prestoniae*
Preston 1928; S VII
syn. - Preston No. 20-14-140
{*S. villosa* subsp. *villosa* × *S. komarowii* subsp. *reflexa*}
Macoun, Rep. Dom. Hort. 1928, 55 [1930]; Wister, Lilacs for America, 43, 64 [1942], 24, 48 [1953] - name only; Photo on Jorgovani/Lilacs 2015 DVD.
Named for the Attendant on Princess Katharine in Shakespeare's *King Henry V*.
Cultivar name presumed registered 1953; name established and accepted.

'Alice', *S. vulgaris*
Klager 1928; S IV
Cooley, Cat.1928-1929, 7 [1928]; McKelvey, The Lilac, 559 [1928]; Wister, Lilacs for America, 43 [1942], 24 [1953] - as "discard".
Cultivar name presumed registered 1953; name established and accepted.

'Alice Adams', *S. vulgaris*
Alverson pre-2014; S IV
Grown from OP seed by Alice Mae Alverson.
Seen by the Registrar at Cherry Valley Lilacs, Cherry Valley NY USA June 2019.
Information provided by Charle-Pan Dawson, email to Registrar 6/9/2019
Named: for family member, possibly the breeder's mother.

'Alice Case', *S. vulgaris*
Case ca 1930; D VI
Wister, Lilacs for America, 43 [1942] & 24 [1953]
Cultivar name presumed registered 1953; name established and accepted.

'Alice Chieppo', *S.* ×*hyacinthiflora*
Fiala 1984; D IV
{*S. oblata* subsp. *dilatata* × 'Rochester'}
Clark, Lilacs - Proceedings 15(1):4 [1986] - name only; Fiala, Lilacs, 95, 224, Pl. 82 [1988]; Photo on Jorgovani/Lilacs 2015 DVD.
Cultivar name established and accepted.

'Alice Christianson', *S. vulgaris*
Klager; D VII
syn. - 'Alice Christenson'
Anon., ILS Newsletter 14(4):3-4 [1988]; Microplant Nurseries, 1994-1995 Wholesale Price list, p.6 - as 'Alice Christenson', triple, lavender
Cultivar name not established.

'Alice Eastwood', *S.* ×*hyacinthiflora*
Clarke 1943; D VI
{parentage not known}
Clarke, Cat. vol. 16, 6 [1949]; Woody Plant Register, AAN, No. 183 [1949]; Wister, Lilacs for America, 43 [1942] - as D V; Wister, Lilacs for America, 24 [1953] - as D VI; Photo on Jorgovani/Lilacs 2015 DVD.
Named for Alice Eastwood, 1859-1953; Canadian-American botanist.
Cultivar name presumed registered 1953; name established and accepted.

'Alice Franklin', *S. vulgaris*
Barnes, F.L. & A.G. ca 1928; S VII
{seedling of unknown parentage}
Wister & Oppe, Arnoldia 31(3):121 [1971]; (Vrugtman, Cultivated Plant Diversity (2017)
Named for Alice and Franklin Barnes, parents of Franklin Lockwood ("Woody") Barnes, Jr.
Cultivar name registered 1970; name established and accepted.

Alice Harding - see **'Souvenir d'Alice Harding'**.

'Alice Klager', *S. vulgaris*
Klager; D VII
Anon., ILS Newsletter 14(4):3-4 [1988] - as double, lavender
Cultivar name not established.

'Alice Mills', *S. vulgaris*
Klager; S IV
Wister, Lilacs for America, 24 [1953] - name only; Heard Gardens, lilac stock plants list [Apr. 4, 1975]; Anon., ILS Newsletter 14(4):3-4 [1988]
Cultivar name not established.

'Alice Rose Foster', *S.* (Villosae Group)
Alexander Sr 1968; S V
{*S.* ×*josiflexa* 'James Macfarlane' × *S.* ×*prestoniae* 'Ethel M. Webster'}
Alexander Sr, Cat. sheets [n.d.; received Jan. 1970]; Wister & Oppe, Arnoldia 31(3):121 [1971]; Photo on Jorgovani/Lilacs 2015 DVD.
Cultivar name registered 1970; name established and accepted.

'Alice Schiewe', *S. vulgaris*
Klager; D VII
Anon., ILS Newsletter 14(4):3-4 [1988] - as triple and lavender
Cultivar name not established.

'Alice Stofer', *S. vulgaris*
Rankin; S IV
{parentage not known}
Wister, Arnoldia 23(4):80 [1963]
Cultivar name registered 1963; not reported in cultivation.

Aline Macqueris - see **'Aline Mocqueris'**.

Aline Macquery - see **'Aline Mocqueris'**.

'Aline Mocqueris', *S. vulgaris*
Dauvesse 1872; S VII
syn. - 'Aline Macquery', 'Halia Mocqueris', 'Aline Maqueris'
Dauvesse, Cat. No. 36, 46 [1872]; Ottolander et al., Ned. flora en pomona, ill. Vol. 2, Plate 2 [1876-1879] by A.J. Wendel (1826-1915); Moore, Lilacs, 154 [1903] - as 'Aline Macquery'; McKelvey, The Lilac, 255, 563 [1928]; Wister, Lilacs for America, 43 [1942] - as S VI ; Wister, Lilacs for America, 24 [1953] - as S VII ; Photo on Jorgovani/Lilacs 2015 DVD.
Cultivar name presumed registered 1953; name established and accepted.

'Aliya', *S. vulgaris*
'Алия'
Sagitova & Dzevitski; S IV
{parentage not known}
Cultivar name not established.

"Aliya Moldagulova', *S. vulgaris*
'Алия Молдагулова'
Dyagilev 2020; D V-IV
Selected from Dyagilev's seedlings and received variety status and name in 2020.
(Международная научная конференция "Syringa

L.: коллекции, выращивание, использование")
"International Scientific Conference "Syringa L.: collections, cultivation, using" / Collection of Scientific Articles of Botanical Institute named after V.L. Komarov, Botanical Garden of Peter the Great BIN RAS. - St. Petersburg. -2020.- pp.23-27 (in Russian).
Named for the sniper heroine of the Soviet Union during World War II.
Cultivar name established and accepted.

Aljonuschka - see 'Alenushka'.

'Allene', *S. vulgaris*
Klager; S V
Anon., ILS Newsletter 14(4):3-4 [1988]
Cultivar name not established.

'Allison Gray', *S. vulgaris*
Havemeyer; S II
Wister, Lilacs for America, 43 [1942], 24 [1953]; Eickhorst, ILS Lilac Newsletter 4(1):4-5 [1978]; Photo on Jorgovani/Lilacs 2015 DVD.
Cultivar name presumed registered 1953; name established and accepted.

'Al Lumley', *S.* (affiliation not known)
Peterson 2004; D I-II
Anon., Lilacs - Quart. Jour. 33(1):11 [2004]
Three private collectors verified as a double (JJ Miller email to Registrar 6/3/20)
Cultivar name not established.

'Alma', *S. vulgaris*
Klager 1932; S VII
Wister, Lilacs for America, 43 [1942], 24 [1953]
Cultivar name presumed registered 1953; name established and accepted.

'Almaatinka', *S. vulgaris*
'Алмаатинка'
Sagitova & Dzevitski 1994; D III/VII
varietal denomination registered 1994, No. 11, State Register of Selected Achievements in Republic of Kazakhstan.
Cultivar name not established.

'Alma-Atinskaya', *S. vulgaris*
'Алма-Атинская'
Mel'nik 1972; S II
syn. - 'Alma-Atinskaja'
{'Volcan' × OP}
Syn. - seedling No. 141
Rubanik, V. G. et al., Siren' - *Syringa* L., publishing house "Kaĭnar", Alma-Ata page 57 [1977] - in Russian; Rubtzov et al. 1980. Vidy i sorta sireni, kul'tiviruemye v SSSR. Kiev; Naukova Dumka. – in Russian; Holetich, C.D. 1982. Lilac species and cultivars in cultivation in USSR. Lilacs 11(2):1-38. - translation of Rubtzov et al. 1982.
Cultivar name established and accepted.

'Alma G', *S. vulgaris*
Klager; S VI *
Anon., ILS Newsletter 14(4):3-4 [1988]
Cultivar name not established.

'Aloise', *S. vulgaris*
Fiala 1986; S I
{'Flora 1953' × 'Flora 1953'}
Fiala, Lilacs, 91, 136, 223, & Pl. 82 [1988] - as induced tetraploid; Photo on Jorgovani/Lilacs 2015 DVD.
Named by John Fiala for his mother.
Cultivar name established.

'Alpenglow', *S. vulgaris* (?)
Ballreich pre-2004; D V
syn. - 'Pink Diamond'
Anon., Tentative list of lilacs for auction. Lilacs - Quart. Jour. 33(1):11 [2004] - as 'Pink Diamond'; marketed by Select Plus Nursery, Mascouche, Quebec, Canada as 'Alpenglow'
Named for Alpenglow Lilac Gardens of Garry Parton at Idyllwild, California, USA.
Cultivar name not established.

Alphonse Bouvier - see **'Alphonse Lavallée'**
Wister, Lilacs for America, 24 [1953] - as D VI; Wister, Lilac Registrations (mimeogr. list), p.4 [n.d.; ca 1968] - as misspelling of 'Alphonse Lavallée'.

'Alphonse Lavallée', *S. vulgaris*
Lemoine 1885; D IV
syn. - 'Alfons Lavallée'; see also: 'Sunol', Clarke 1936
Lemoine, Cat. No. 101, 8 [1885]; McKelvey, The Lilac, 255-256 [1928]; Starcs, Mitt. D. Dendrol. Ges. 1928, 43 [1928] - as 'Alfons Lavallée'; Wister, Lilacs for America, 43 [1942], 24 [1953]; Photo on Jorgovani/Lilacs 2015 DVD.
Named for Pierre Alphonse Martin Lavallée, 1836-1884, French botanist and general secretary of the Central Horticultural Society of France.
Awards: RHS Award of Merit 1893.
Cultivar name presumed registered 1953; name established and accepted.

'Altayskaya Rozovaya', *S. vulgaris*
'Алтайская Розовая'
Luchnik 1984; S V
Pikaleva, Lilacs - Quart. Jour. 23(4):84 [1994]; Lyakh, Lilacs - Quart. Jour. 36(1):18 [2007] - name only; Sinogeykina, G. E. 2014. Evaluation of parental winter hardiness and ornamental varieties and hybrids of Syringa vulgaris L. in the steppe of the Altai Region (PhD thesis).
Name: Russian for Altai pink.
Cultivar name established and accepted.

'Alvan R. Grant', *S. vulgaris*
Fenicchia 1995; S VII
syn. - 'Alvan Grant', RAF No. 185

{'Rochester' × 'Madame Charles Souchet'}
Vrugtman, HortScience 31(3):327 [1996]; in litt., Hoepfl to Vrugtman [Nov.29/2003] - Fiala, Lilacs, Pl. 79, lilac No. 185 [1988]; K. Millham, Lilacs - Quart. Jour. 42(2):59[2013]
Named for Alvan Roger Grant, 1916-2007, horticulturist, Rochester, New York, USA, who discovered the 'Rochester' cultivar. 8-10' height, no suckering.
Cultivar name registered 1995; name established and accepted.

Alvatar - see 'Veera'.

amaena - see **'Amoena'**.

'Amanda Bergen', *S. vulgaris*
Berdeen; ? II
Vrugtman, AABGA Bulletin 16(4):131 [1982]; King & Coggeshall, Lilacs - Quart. Jour. 27(2):49-50 [1998] - name only
Named for the daughter of Berdeen's friend and neighbor.
Cultivar name not established.

'Ambassadeur', *S. vulgaris*
Lemoine 1930; S III
Lemoine, Cat. No. 204, 25 [1930]; Wister, Lilacs for America, 43 [1942], 24 [1953]; Photo on Jorgovani/Lilacs 2015 DVD.
Awards: Certificate of Merit 1932 (KMTP).
Cultivar name presumed registered 1953; name established and accepted.

'A. M. Brand', *S. vulgaris*
Brand 1940; S VII
Brand Peony Farms, Cat. 24 [1953] - as rich rose-red; Wister, Lilacs for America, 24 [1953]; anon., Lilacs - Quart. Jour. 29(3):92 [2000] - reprinted from 1940; Photo on Jorgovani/Lilacs 2015 DVD.
Named for Archie Mack Brand, 1871-1953, American lawyer and horticulturist.
Cultivar name presumed registered 1953; name established and accepted.

'Ambroise Verschaffelt', *S. vulgaris*
Brahy-Ekenholm pre-1863; S IV
syn. - 'Ambrose Verschaffelt', 'Ambrosius Verschaffelt'; see also 'Verschaffeltii'
Lemaire, Ill. Hort. x.t. 357 [1863]; McKelvey, The Lilac, 256 [1928]; Starcs, Mitt. D. Dendrol. Ges. 1928, 40-42 [1928] - as 'Ambrosius Verschaffelt'; Wister, Lilacs for America, 43 [1942], 24 [1953]
Named for Ambroise Colette Alexandre Verschaffelt, 1825-1886, third generation of the Belgian Verschaffelt florist dynasty, and founder of *L'illustration horticole*, 1854-1896.
Cultivar name presumed registered 1953; name established and accepted.

amena - see **'Amoena'**.

'Amethyst', *S. vulgaris*
Späth 1887; S V
{chance seedling of unknown parentage}
Späth, Cat. No. 69, 4 [1887]; McKeley, The Lilac, 256-257 [1928]; Späth, Späth-Buch, 110, [1930]; Wister, Lilacs for America, 43 [1942], 24 [1953]; Photo on Jorgovani/Lilacs 2015 DVD.
Cultivar name presumed registered 1953; name established and accepted.

'Amethyst Purple', *S. vulgaris*
probably Kelly Brothers pre-1987; S VII-IV
Peterson, Lilacs - Proceedings 16(1):17 [1987] - name only; in litt. Max Peterson to F. Vrugtman [Jun.06/2002], plants purchased from Kelly Brothers Nursery, 'Amethyst Purple' was offered by Kelly Brothers Nursery for two years only.
Cultivar name not established.

'Ametist 2', *S. vulgaris*
'Аметист 2'
Shtan'ko & Mikhaïlov 1956; S III-IV
{'Prince de Beauvau' × ? }
Rubtzov et al. 1980. Vidy i sorta sireni, kul'tiviruemye v SSSR. Kiev; Naukova Dumka. – in Russian; Holetich, C.D. 1982. Lilac species and cultivars in cultivation in USSR. Lilacs 11(2):1-38. - translation of Rubtzov et al. 1982; Pikaleva, Lilacs - Quart. Jour. 23(4):84 [1994] - as S VI; Photo on Jorgovani/Lilacs 2015 DVD.
Cultivar name established and accepted.

'Ametistovaya', *S. vulgaris*
'Аметистовая'
Kravchenko 1970; S V
{ 'Congo' × OP }
Kravchenko L. Culture of lilacs in Uzbekistan. Publishing house "Uzbekistan", Tashkent, 1970 p. 13.
Name: Russian for amethyst color.
Cultivar name established and accepted.

'Amigo', *S. ×chinensis*
Esveld pre-2004; S VII
{parentage not given}
syn. - pre-2015 as 'Ellen' (see KVBC - 2015)
listed by Fa C. Esveld nurseries, Plant of the Month May 2016. <https://twitter.com/esveldboskoop/status/730069213432385536> seen July 15, 2018;
Awards: KVBC Bronze Award (8 May 2015).
Cultivar name established and accepted.

'Ami Schott', *S. vulgaris*
Lemoine 1933; D III
Wister, Lilacs for America, 43 [1942], 24 [1953]; Kammerer, Morton Arb. Bull. Pop. Info. 36(6):27-29 [1961]; Photo on Jorgovani/Lilacs 2015 DVD.
Cultivar name presumed registered 1953; name established and accepted.

'Amoena', *S. vulgaris*
Oudin pre-1846; S V
syn. - amena, *amaena*
Oudin, Cat. 1846-1847, 17 - name only; Wister, Nat. Hort. Mag. 6(1):8 [1927] - as single, blue; McKelvey, The Lilac, 257 [1928] - as S V; Starcs, Mitt. D. Dendrol. Ges. 1928, 40-41 [1928] - as single, pink; Späth, Späth-Buch, 303 [1930] - as S V; Wister, Lilacs for America, 43 [1942] - as S V; Wister, Lilacs for America, 24 [1953] - erroneously as D VI; Rogers, Tentative International Register, 4 [1976] - erroneously as D V; Vrugtman, Lilac Newsletter 4(10):13 [1978] - true identity of plants in cultivation in North America not resolved; Photo on Jorgovani/Lilacs 2015 DVD.
Cultivar name presumed registered 1953; name established and accepted.

'Amor', *S. vulgaris*
Löbner pre-1947; S VI
Meyer, Flieder, 72 [1952] - as wine red; Wister, Lilacs for America, 24 [1953]; Vrugtman, Lilacs - Quart. Jour. 22(3):90-92 [1993]; Photo on Jorgovani/Lilacs 2015 DVD.
Cultivar name presumed registered 1953; name established and accepted.

'Amors', *S. vulgaris*
Kārkliņš 2003; D VII/II
Strautiņa & Kaufmane, Dobeles ceriņi, p. 92 [2011]
Name: Latvian for Cupid.
Cultivar name established and accepted.

amurensis argentea - see **'Argentea'**.

'Amurensis Korea', *S.* (species affiliation not known, probably *S. reticulata* subsp. *reticulata*)
origin not known pre-1974; S I
Lilac Land list, [n.d., pre-1974]
Cultivar name not established.

'Anabel', *S.* ×*hyacinthiflora*
Hawkins 1956; D V
syn. - 'Annabel', 'Annabelle'
{*S. oblata* subsp. *dilatata* × ? }
Wister, Lilacs for America, 25 [1953] - as 'Annabel', name only; Wister, Lilac Registrations (mimeogr. list), 4 [n.d.; ca 1968] - as 'Anabel', D I?; Linn County Nurseries, Cat. Spring 1956, 16; Lilacs - Quart. Jour. 23(3): front cover ill. [1994]; Photo on Jorgovani/Lilacs 2015 DVD.
Named for Mrs Annabelle Hawkins, wife of the originator; see also: Vrugtman, Lilacs - Quart. Jour. 24(3):68-70 [1995].
Cultivar name presumed registered 1953; name established and accepted.

'Anabella', *S. vulgaris*
Kārkliņš 2003; S VII
(no information yet)
Photo on Jorgovani/Lilacs 2015 DVD.
Name: A woman's name.
Cultivar name not established.

'Anastasia', *S.*
Moro, F. 1996; S VI
{'Josée' × ? }
Select Plus, Cat. Spring 2000
Cultivar name established and accepted.

'Anastasiya', *S. vulgaris*
'Анастасия'
Aladin, S., Aladina, O., and Polyakova, T. 2016; D III/IV
{elite form 12-94 × elite form 11-301}
Садовник (Gardener) magazine 04 (140)/2017 :18-25; Вестник АППМ (Catalog in Vestnik APPM (Planting material association) magazine) 1/2018: 59-72 (in Russian).
Named for Anastasiya Aladina (Анастасия Сергеевна Аладина), artist, contemporary Russian lilac breeder, member of the creative breeding group "Russian Lilac", Moscow
Cultivar name established and accepted.

'Anastasiya Shirinskaya', *S. vulgaris*
'Анастасия Ширинская'
Aladin, S., Aladina, O., and Polyakova, T. 2015; D V & VII
{'Zhemchuzhina' × OP}
Садовник (Gardener) magazine 04 (140)/2017 :18-25; Вестник АППМ (Catalog in Vestnik APPM (Planting material association) magazine) 1/2018: 59-72 (in Russian).
Named for Anastasiya Shirinskaya (Анастасия Александровна Ширинская), 1912-2009, devoted to preserving the memory of the sailors of the Russian Imperial Fleet in Bizerta (Tunisia).
Cultivar name established and accepted.

'Andenken an Ludwig Späth', *S. vulgaris*
Späth 1883; S VII
syn. - 'Andenken an Ludwig Spaeth', Ludwig Spath, 'Ludwig Späth', 'Souv. de Ludwig Spaeth', Ludwig Spath (trade designation used for cut flowers of this cultivar) marketed in North America as Ludwig Spaeth
common name: Ludwig Spaeth in Stand. Pl. Names, 614 [1942]
{chance seedling of unknown parentage}
Späth, Cat., 3 [1883]; Stand. Pl. Names, 485, 496 [1923] - as Ludwig Spaeth [1923]; Kache, Gartenschönheit 5:82 [1924]; McKelvey, The Lilac, 257-258 [1928]; Späth, Späth-Buch, 110, 303 [1930]; Wister, Lilacs for America, 43, 52 [1942], 25, 34 [1953]; Photo on Jorgovani/Lilacs 2015 DVD.
Named for Johann Ludwig Carl Späth, 1793-1883, German nurseryman, Berlin.
Awards: Certificate of Merit 1966 (KMTP); RHS Award of Garden Merit 1993.
Cultivar name presumed registered 1953; name established and accepted.
Forcing cultivar in the Netherlands.

Anderson nana - see **'Mount Domogled'**.

Andre Czizic - see **'André Csizik'**.

'André Csizik', *S. vulgaris*
Eveleens Maarse 1950; S VI
syn. - 'Andre Csizik', 'Andre Czizic'
{'Ambassadeur' × 'Hugo de Vries'}
Wister, Lilacs for America, 25 [1953]; Eveleens Maarse, Dendron 1(1):12 [1954];
Photo on Jorgovani/Lilacs 2015 DVD.
Awards: Award of Merit 1950 (KMTP).
Cultivar name presumed registered 1953; name established and accepted.

'André Laurent', *S. vulgaris*
Nollent 1908; S VII
Stepman-Demessemaeker, Suppl. Gen. Cat. [1908?];
McKelvey, The Lilac 258 [1928]; Wister, Lilacs for America, 25 [1953]
Cultivar name presumed registered 1953; name established and accepted.

'Andres', *S. vulgaris*
Vaigla 1969; S IV/V (II-V per Semenov)
{parentage not known}
Semenov, I., Lilacs 48(2):65 [2019].
Cultivar name not established.

'Andrew Dupont', *S. vulgaris*
origin unknown ca 1922; ? ?
McKelvey, The Lilac, 258-259 [1928] - name only
Cultivar name not established; not reported in cultivation.

'Andrey', *S.* (Villosae Group)
origin unknown pre-2019; S V
photo by Ole Heide from Denmark seen in ILS 2020 Photo DVD.
Cultivar name not established.

'Andromache', *S.* (Villosae Group), *S.* ×*prestoniae*
Preston date not known; ? ?
syn. - Preston ? 20-14-02
{*S. villosa* subsp. *villosa* × *S. komarowii* subsp. *komarowii*}
Preston, List of varieties of ornamental plants, originated in the Division of Horticulture, Central Experimental Farm, Ottawa, showing their respective parentage; undated typed list, p. 2 - name only.
Named for Andromache, Wife to Hector in Shakespeare's *Troilus and Cressida.*
Cultivar name not established and accepted; not know in cultivation.

'Andryusha Gromov', *S. vulgaris*
'Андрюша Громов'
Kolesnikov pre-1953; D III-IV
syn. - 'Andrjusha Gromov'
Rubtzov et al. 1980. Vidy i sorta sireni, kul'tiviruemye v SSSR. Kiev; Naukova Dumka. – in Russian; Holetich, C.D. 1982. Lilac species and cultivars in cultivation in USSR. Lilacs 11(2):1-38. - translation of Rubtzov et al. 1982; Photo on Jorgovani/Lilacs 2015 DVD.
Cultivar name established and accepted.

'Anemonaeflora', *S. vulgaris*
origin not known pre-1885; ? ?
McKelvey, The Lilac, 259 [1928]
Cultivar name not established; not reported in cultivation.

'Angel White', *S.* ×*hyacinthiflora*
Lammerts 1971; S I
syn. - 'White Angel'
{'Lavender Lady' × ? }
Monrovia Cat., 80 [1971] - as *S.* hybrid 'Angel White'
Cultivar name established and accepted.
Nota bene: Since this cultivar appears to be of 'Lavender Lady' ancestry see also: Pringle, Lilacs - Quart. Jour. 24(4):97-99 [1995]; and Vrugtman, HortScience 31(3):328 [1996]; Photo on Jorgovani/Lilacs 2015 DVD.

'Anite Duke', *S. vulgaris*
origin not known ca 1922; ? ?
McKelvey, The Lilac, 259 [1928]
Cultivar name not established.

'Anna', *S. vulgaris*
Klager; S IV
Wister, Lilacs for America, 43 [1942], 25 [1953]
Cultivar name presumed registered 1953;
Cultivar not reported in cultivation.

'Anna Akhmatova', *S. vulgaris*
'Анна Ахматова'
Aladin, S., Aladina, O., Polyakova, T., and Aladina, A. 2016; S II
{elite form 11-112* x 'Frank Paterson'}
*elite form 11-112 was obtained from open pollinated seeds of 'Stefan Makowiecki'.
(Международная научная конференция "Syringa L.: коллекции, выращивание, использование")
"International Scientific Conference "Syringa L.: collections, cultivation, using" / Collection of Scientific Articles of Botanical Institute named after V.L. Komarov, Botanical Garden of Peter the Great BIN RAS. - St. Petersburg. -2020.- pp.3-7 (in Russian); Photo exhibition of all varieties of the creative breeding group "Russian Lilac" at the Festival "Lilac February", St. Petersburg, Botanical Garden of Peter the Great BIN RAS, February 22-24, 2020.
The cultivar is dedicated to the great Russian poet of the Silver Age Anna Andreevna Akhmatova (1912-1965).
Cultivar name established and accepted.

'Anna Amhoff', *S.* (Villosae Group), *S.* ×*josiflexa*
Yeager 1961; S I
{*S.* ×*josiflexa* 'Royalty' × ? }
Yeager, New Hampsh. Agri. Exp. Sta. Bull. No. 461, 12 [1959] - as pink in bud, white in full bloom; Wister, Arnoldia 23(4):80 [1963]; J. Bentley, Lilacs 42(2):57 [2013].
Named for Mrs Anna Evans Amhoff, x-1951, flower show judge and president of the Portsmouth Garden Club, New Hampshire, USA.
Cultivar name registered 1963; name established and accepted.

Annabel - see **'Anabel'**.

'Anna Elisabeth Jaquet', *S. vulgaris*
Piet 1907; S VII
syn. - 'Anna Elizabeth Jacquet', 'Jaquet'
Felix & Dijkhuis, Trade Letter, July 25, 1924; McKelvey, The Lilac, 259 [1928]; Wister, Lilacs for America, 25 & 32 [1953] - as 'Anna Elizabeth Jacquet' and 'Jaquet'; Photo on Jorgovani/Lilacs 2015 DVD.
Named for Anna Elisabeth Jaquet, 1874-1962, the second wife of Willem Piet, 1866-1956, nurseryman and florist, Aalsmeer, The Netherlands.
Cultivar name presumed registered 1953; name established and accepted.

'Anna Karpow', *S. vulgaris*
Karpow-Lipski 1958; D I
syn. - Siewka nr 84
Karpow-Lipski, Arboretum Kórnickie 3:105 [1958]; Wister & Oppe, Arnoldia 31(3):125 [1971]
Named for the mother (or grandmother?) of the originator.
Cultivar name registered 1970; name established and accepted.

'Anna Nickles', *S. vulgaris*
Stone 1963; S IV
syn. - 'Anna Nickels'
Wister, Arnoldia 23(4):80 [1963]; Photo on Jorgovani/Lilacs 2015 DVD.
Cultivar name registered 1963; name established and accepted.

'Anne Shiach', *S. vulgaris*
Havemeyer & Michie 1943; S VII
syn. - 'Anne Schiach'
Wister, Lilacs for America, 44 [1943] - as S VI; Wister, Lilacs for America, 25 [1953]; Kammerer, Morton Arb. Bull. Pop. Info. 36(6):27-29 [1961] - as 'Anne Schiach'; Eickhorst, ILS Lilac Newsletter 4(1):4-5 [1978]; Photo on Jorgovani/Lilacs 2015 DVD.
Named for Anne Shiach, mother of Alex Michie.
Cultivar name presumed registered 1953; name established and accepted.

'Anne Tighe', *S. vulgaris*
Yeager 1945; D VII
{'Volcan' × ? }
Woody Plant Register, AAN, No. 63 [1949]; Yeager, New Hampsh. Agri. Exp. Sta. Bull. No. 383, 14 [1950]; Wister, Lilacs for America, 25 [1953]; J. Bentley, Lilacs 42(2):57 [2013]; Photo on Jorgovani/Lilacs 2015 DVD.
Named for Mrs Anne (Annie) Sullivan Tighe, 1884-1945, teacher, active member of the Community Garden Club, Salmon Falls, New Hampshire, and the New Hampshire Federation of Garden Clubs.
Cultivar name presumed registered 1953; name established and accepted.

'Annie Ouwerkerk', *S. vulgaris*
Ouwerkerk 1946; S V
{parentage not known}
syn. - 'Annie van Ouwerkerk', 'Mevr. Annie Ouwerkerk'
VKC/VBN-Produktenregistratie 02-106610
Named for Antje (Annie) van Ouwekerk-Maarsen, wife of the originator.
Cultivar name established and accepted.

'Annys200809', *S. pubescens* subsp. *pubescens*
van Nijnatten 2013, S VII
{'Pink Perfume' × OP}
Flower color RHS 75A, bud color RHS 72B.
marketed in European Union as FLOWERFESTA® PURPLE, PRB EU No. 20132647
USPP 31300 in 2019.
Cultivar name registered by statute; name established and accepted.

'Annys200810', *S. pubescens* subsp. *pubescens*
Nijnatten 2013, S I
{*S. pubescens* subsp. *pubescens* seedling}
marketed in European Union as FLOWERFESTA® WHITE, PRB EU No. 20132165
Cultivar name registered by statute; name established and accepted.

'Annys200817', *S. pubescens* subsp. *pubescens*
Nijnatten 2013, S VII
{*S. pubescens* subsp. *pubescens* seedling}
marketed in European Union as FLOWERFESTA® PINK, PRB EU No. 20132164
Cultivar name registered by statute; name established and accepted.

Antoine Buchner - see **'Mme Antoine Buchner'**.

'Antonina Mel'nik', *S. vulgaris*
'Антонина Мельник'
Mel'nik, Rubanik & Dyagilev 1972; D IV/V
{'Katherine Havemeyer' × OP}
Syn. - 'Zailiĭskaya', N83
Rubanik, V. G. et al., Siren' - Syringa L., publishing house "Kaĭnar", Alma-Ata [1977] page 56 - in Russian.
Dyagilev, Lilacs - Quart. Jour. 22(1):19 [1993]; Pikaleva, Lilacs - Quart. Jour. 23(4):84 [1994].
Detailed description given in "Lilacs of the Central Botanical Garden of Kazakhstan", SV Biryukova, published in (Международная научная конференция "Syringa L.: коллекции, выращивание, использование") "International Scientific Conference "Syringa L.: collections, cultivation, using" / Collection of Scientific Articles of Botanical Institute named after V.L. Komarov, Botanical Garden of Peter the Great BIN RAS. - St. Petersburg. -2020.- pp.23-27 (in Russian).
Cultivar name established and accepted.

'Antuan de Sent-Ėkzyuperi', *S. vulgaris*
'Антуан де Сент Экзюпери'
Aladin, S., Aladina, O., and Polyakova, T. 2015; D V

{'Mrs Edward Harding' × OP}
Приусадебное хозяйство (Annex to the magazine Homestead farming: "Flowers in the garden and at home. Brushes and paints") 08/2015: 5-14; Садовник (Gardener) magazine, 05 (141)/2017 :16-22; Вестник АППМ (Catalog in Vestnik APPM (Planting material association) magazine) 1/2018: 59-72 (in Russian).
Named for Antoine de Saint-Exupéry, 1900-1944, French aristocrat, writer, poet, and pioneering aviator.
Cultivar name established and accepted.

Arbutus Pink - see '**Lustrous**'.

Archduke John - see '**Erzherzog Johann**'.

'Archevêque', *S. vulgaris*
Lemoine 1923; D VII
syn. - 'Archeveque'
Lemoine, Cat. No. 197, 19 [1923]; McKelvey, The Lilac, 259 [1928]; Wister, Lilacs for America, 44 [1942], 25 [1953] as 'Archeveque'; Photo on Jorgovani/Lilacs 2015 DVD.
Cultivar name presumed registered 1953; name established and accepted.

'Archiduchesse Charlotte', *S. vulgaris*
Brahy-Ekenholm 1861; S V
{'Charles X' × 'Noisette'}
Duvivier, Jour. Hort. Pratique Belgique, sér. 2, 5:241, XIX. fig. 3 [1861]; McKelvey, The Lilac, 259-260 [1928]; Wister, Lilacs for America, 44 [1942], 25 [1953]
Named for Charlotte, 1840-1927, daughter of the King Léopold I of Belgium, and future empress of Mexico.
Cultivar name presumed registered 1953; name established and accepted.

'Architekt Fr. J. Thomayer', *S. vulgaris*
Thomayer 1932; S VII
{parentage not known}
Thomayerovy Stromové Školky, Cat., p. 37 [n.d.]
Named for František Thomayer, 1856-1938, Czech landscape architect, pomologist and nurseryman.
Cultivar name not established.

'Arch McKean', *S. vulgaris*
Fiala 1984; S VI
syn. - 'Archibald McKean'
{'Agincourt Beauty' × 'Rochester'}
Fiala, Lilacs, 102, 223 & Pl. 82 [1988]; Vrugtman, HortScience 24(3):435 [1989];
Photo on Jorgovani/Lilacs 2015 DVD.
Named for Arch McKean, 189?-2003, Grand Beach, Michigan, USA.
Cultivar name registered 1988; name established and accepted.

'Argentea', *S. reticulata* subsp. *reticulata*
Temple 1890; S I *
syn. - *amurensis argentea*, *japonica argentea*
L.H. Bailey, Annals of hort. in North America for the year 1890 [1891] - as *S. japonica* var. *argentea*
- originated at Shady Hill Nurs., Cambridge, Mass.; McKelvey, The Lilac, 489 [1928]; Wister, Lilacs for America, 42 [1942]
Cultivar name not established; not reported in cultivation in 1953.

'Argentea', *S. vulgaris*
origin not known ? ? *
Wister, Lilacs for America, 36, 44 [1942] - as doubtful name
Cultivar name not established, not reported in cultivation in 1953.

'Ariel', *S.* (Villosae Group), *S.* ×*prestoniae*
Preston 1942; S II
Wister, Lilacs for America, 44 [1942] - name only; Wister, Lilacs for America, 25 [1953]; Alexander Sr, Cat. sheets [n.d., received 1964]
Named for An Airy Spirit in Shakespeare's *The Tempest*.
Cultivar name presumed registered 1953; name established and accepted.

'Ariya', *S.* ×*hyacinthiflora*
'Ария'
Mikhaĭlov & Rybakina 2002; S III/IV
{'Kosmos' × 'Esther Staley'}
Chapman, Lilacs - Quart. Jour. 32(1):17-18 [2003]
- translated from N. L. Mikhaĭlov in Tsvetovodstvo, May-June issue (in Russian); Photo on Jorgovani/Lilacs 2015 DVD.
Cultivar name established and accepted.

'Arlene Welch', *S. vulgaris*
Berdeen 1983; D V
King & Coggeshall, Lilacs - Quart. Jour. 27(2):49-50 [1998] - name only
in cultivation at Picoplant Microvermehrungen GmbH (seen Dec. 2016)
Cultivar name not established.

Arnold Dwarf (as *S. pubescens* subsp. *patula*) - see Dwarf Arnold

'Arnold Pukk', *S.vulgaris*
Mägi pre-2018; S VII
Semenov, I., Lilacs 48(2):69 (photo) [2019].
Cultivar name not established.

'Artek', *S. vulgaris*
'Артек'
Aladin, S., Aladina, O., Polyakova, T., and Aladina, A. 2016; S VI
{elite form 12-247 × OP}
Садовник (Gardener) magazine 04 (140)/2017 :18-25; Вестник АППМ (Catalog in Vestnik APPM (Planting material association) magazine) 1/2018: 59-72 (in Russian).
Named for "Artek", the international children's center located on the southern coast of the Crimea in the village of Gurzuf.
Cultivar name established and accepted.

'Arthur William Paul', *S. vulgaris*
Lemoine 1898; D VII
Lemoine, Cat. No. 140, 10 [1898]; Kache, Gartenschönheit 5:82 [1924]; McKelvey, The Lilac, 260 [1928]; Wister, Lilacs for America, 44 [1942], 25 [1953]; Photo on Jorgovani/Lilacs 2015 DVD.
Named for Arthur William Paul, 1870s-1910s, nurseryman in the United Kingdom.
Cultivar name presumed registered 1953; name established and accepted.

'Arved', *S. ×hyacinthiflora*
Vaigla; S ?
Cultivar name not established.

'Arvid Vilms', *S. ×hyacinthiflora*
Vaigla ca 1955; S IV (VI/IV per Semenov)
syn. - 'Arvid Films'
{'Clarke's Giant' × ? }
Vrugtman, HortScience 26(5):476 [1991]; Kivistik, Maakodu 1997(5):22-23 [1997] - in Estonian; I. Semenov, Lilacs 48(2):62,65,63 (photo) [2019].
Cultivar name registered 1990; name established and accepted.

'Asessippi', *S. ×hyacinthiflora*
Skinner 1932; S IV
syn. - frequently misspelled 'Assessippi'
Woody Plant Register, AAN, No. 16 [1949] - as 'Assessippi'; Skinner, Hort. Horizons, 109 [1966]; Wister, Lilacs for America, 44 [1942], 25 [1953] - as 'Assessippi'; Lilacs - Quart. Jour. 22(4): front & back cover ill. [1993] - as 'Assessippi'; Photo on Jorgovani/Lilacs 2015 DVD.
Named for Asessippi Parkland, the 800-square-mile region in western Manitoba, between the western slopes of Riding Mountain National Park and the Saskatchewan border, Canada.
Cultivar name presumed registered 1953; name established and accepted.

'Ashes of Roses', *S. vulgaris*
Klager 1930; S V
Wister, Lilacs for America, 44 [1942], 25 [1953]
Cultivar name presumed registered 1953;
Cultivar not reported in cultivation.

'Astra', *S. vulgaris*
Scott; S IV
Wister, Lilacs for America, 44 [1942]; 25 [1953]; Photo on Jorgovani/Lilacs 2015 DVD.
Cultivar name presumed registered 1953; name established and accepted.

Atceries Mani - see **'Dobeles Sapņotājs'**.

'Atheline Wilbur', *S. vulgaris*
Fiala 1979; D VI
{('Rochester' × 'Edward J. Gardner') × 'Rochester'}
Knight, Lilacs-Proceedings 9:8 [1981] - a multipetaled bluish lavender-rose; Fiala, Lilacs, 102, 108, 223 & Pl. 22 [1988]; Vrugtman, HortScience 35(4):549 [2000]; Photo on Jorgovani/Lilacs 2015 DVD.
Named for Mrs John Wilbur (Atheline Wilbur).
Cultivar name registered 1999 by Charles Tubesing of the Holden Arboretum; name established and accepted.

'Atlant', *S. vulgaris*
Strekalov no dates, S III?
seen 21 January 2018 on <http://www.piccoplant.de/en/assortment/lilacs>D:\Documents\Lilacs\Lilac Register\ILS Register 2019\Vrugtman\Register\<http:\www.piccoplant.de\en\assortment\lilacs> - name and picture only.
Cultivar name not established.

'Atmiņu Maurs', *S. vulgaris*
Upītis 1950; D II
Kalniņš, Dārs un drava 1986, No. 6, 13-15 - in Latvian; in litt. S. Strautiņa to F. Vrugtman [21 Dec. 2007] - 1950, D II
Name: Latvian for lawn of memory.
Cultivar name established and accepted; cultivar may be extinct.

Atrosanguinea - see **'Saugeana'** (×*chinensis*)

'Aucubaefolia', *S. vulgaris*
Gouchault 1919; D III *
syn. - 'Acubaeifolia', 'Aucutiloba', 'Président Grévy foliis variegatis', *variegata gouchaultii*
{mutation of 'Président Grévy' with variegated foliage, flush pinkish, turning yellow-green}
Chenault, Cat. 15 [1919]; McKelvey, The Lilac, 260-261 [1928]; Wister, Lilacs for America, 44 [1942], 25 [1953]; Photo on Jorgovani/Lilacs 2015 DVD.
Cultivar name presumed registered 1953; name established and accepted.

'Audrey', *S.* (Villosae Group), *S. ×prestoniae*
Preston 1928; S V
syn. - Preston No. 20-14-195
{*S. villosa* subsp. *villosa* × *S. komarowii* subsp. *reflexa*}
Macoun, Rep. Dom. Hort. 1928, 55 [1930]; Davis, Rep. Dom Hort., Progress Report 1934-1948, 147, [1950]; Wister, Lilacs for America, 44, 64 [1942], 25, 48 [1953]; Photo on Jorgovani/Lilacs 2015 DVD.
Named for A Country Wench in Shakespeare's *As You Like It*.
Awards: RHS Award of Merit 1939.
Cultivar name presumed registered 1953; name established and accepted.

'Augerius de Busbek', *S. vulgaris*
'Аугериус д'Бусбек'
Dyagilev 1992, D IV-III
{'Katherine Havemeyer' x OP}
Syn. - 'Ogier de Busbecq'
Dyagilev, Lilacs - Quart. Jour. 22(1):19 [1993]; Pikaleva, Lilacs - Quart. Jour. 23(4):84 [1994]
Named for Augerius (Ogier) de Busbecq, 1522-1592, ambassador of Emperor Ferdinand I to the court of Sultan Soliman I at Constantinople; Busbecq and his

physician Quakelbeen, when returning to Vienna, are said to have brought with them plants of *Syringa*.
Cultivar name established and accepted.

'Aurea', *S. emodi*
origin not known pre-1886; S I *
syn. - *emodi* var. *aurea*, 'Emodi Aurea'
Carrière in Rev. Hort. 547 [1886]; McKelvey, The Lilac, 25-26 [1928]; Wister, Lilacs for America, 44, 47 [1942], 25, 29 [1953]; Photo on Jorgovani/Lilacs 2015 DVD.
Cultivar name presumed registered 1953; name established and accepted.

'Aurea', *S. villosa* subsp. *villosa*
origin not known pre-1942; S V *
syn. - 'Aurea villosa'
(not *S. villosa* var. *aurea* Simon-Louis ex Rehder)
Wister, Lilacs for America, 44, 60 [1942]; Wister, Lilacs for America, 25, 43 [1953] - name only; in cultivation at Royal Botanical Gardens, Burlington, Ontario, Canada, in 1998 (RBG 790588 & 81524).
Cultivar name established and accepted.

'Aurea', *S. vulgaris*
origin not known pre-1880; S II *
Baudriller, Cat. No. 43 (1880); McKelvey, The Lilac, 261 [1928]; Wister, Lilacs for America, 44 [1942]; Plants 6(3):119 [2001] - name only.

'Aurea Cucullata', *S. vulgaris*
Ordnung 1892; ? ? *
Anon., Wiener Ill. Gart.-Zeitung 17:76 [1892]; McKelvey, The Lilac, 262 [1928]
Cultivar name not established; not reported in cultivation.

'Aurea Joreauensis', *S. vulgaris*
Baudriller pre-1889; ? ? *
Späth, Cat. No. 76, 122 [1889]; McKelvey, The Lilac, 262 [1928]
Cultivar name not established.

Aurea Tomentella - see **'Kum-Bum'**.

Aurelianensis - see **'Triomphe d'Orléans'**.

Aureo-marginata - see **'Elegantissima'** (*emodi*).

Aureo-variegata, Aureovariegata - see **'Variegata'** (*emodi*).

Aureo-variegata, *S. vulgaris*
origin not known 1867; ? ? *
L. van Houtte, Cat. No. 117, 12 [1867] - name only; McKelvey, The Lilac, 262 [1928] - confused name.
Cultivar name not established.

'Aurore', *S. vulgaris*
Klettenberg 1930; S V
Klettenberg, Cat., 17 [1930]; Wister, Lilacs for America, 25 [1953]
Cultivar name presumed registered 1953; name established and accepted.

'Avalanche', *S. vulgaris*
Fiala 1983; S I
{'Flora 1953' × 'Carley'}
Fiala, Lilacs, 91, 223, & Pl. 9 [1988]; Chapman, Lilacs - Quart. Jour. 34(2):37 [2005]; Photo on Jorgovani/Lilacs 2015 DVD.
Cultivar name established and accepted.

'Avon', *S. vulgaris*
Lederman ca 1930; S I
Wister, Lilacs for America, 44 [1942], 25 [1953]
Cultivar name presumed registered 1953; name established and accepted.

'Azhigali', *S. vulgaris*
'Ажигали'
Dyagilev, B & Degtev, V. 2020; S VII/II
Selected from Dyagilev's seedlings and received name in 2020.
(Международная научная конференция "Syringa L.: коллекции, выращивание, использование")
"International Scientific Conference "Syringa L.: collections, cultivation, using" / Collection of Scientific Articles of Botanical Institute named after V.L. Komarov, Botanical Garden of Peter the Great BIN RAS. - St. Petersburg. -2020.- pp.23-27 (in Russian).
Named for Azhigali Serik Yeskendiruly - Kazakh ethnologist, archaeologist, doctor of historical sciences, professor of orientalism.
Cultivar name established and accepted.

'Azhurnaya', *S. vulgaris*
'Ажурная'
Mel'nik 1967; S VII
syn. - 'Azhurnaja'
{'Mechta' × ? }
Rubanik, V. G. et al., Siren' - *Syringa* L., publishing house "Kaĭnar", Alma-Ata p. 54 [1977] - in Russian; Rubtzov et al. 1980. Vidy i sorta sireni, kul'tiviruemye v SSSR. Kiev; Naukova Dumka. – in Russian; Holetich, C.D. 1982. Lilac species and cultivars in cultivation in USSR. Lilacs 11(2):1-38. - translation of Rubtzov et al. 1982.
The cultivar name means lacy, openwork.
Cultivar name established and accepted.

Azure - see 'Golubaya'.

'Azurea Plena', *S. vulgaris*
Libert-Darimont 1843; D III
syn. - 'flore duplo Liberti', 'flore pleno Liberti'
common name: blue lilac, Double Azuré, lilas double de Libert
C.F.A. Morren, Bull. Acad. Roy. Sci. Lettres, Beaux-arts Belg. ser. I, 273 [1853] - as 'flore pleno Liberti'; Gartenflora 3:60 [1854] - as 'Azurea Plena'; Stand. Pl. Names, 485, 486 [1923] - as Double Azure; McKelvey, The Lilac, 262-265, [1928]; Wister, Lilacs for America, 44 [1942], 25 [1953]; D. De Meyere, Belgische Dendrologie Belge 1998, p. 41 [1999]; Photo on Jorgovani/Lilacs 2015 DVD.
Cultivar name presumed registered 1953; name established and accepted.

'Azuré de Gathoye', *S. vulgaris*
   Gathoye 1851; S IV
   C.F.A. Morren, Belg. Hort. 1:420 [1851]; McKelvey, The Lilac, 265 [1928]; Wister, Lilacs for America, 25 [1953]
   Cultivar name presumed registered 1953; name established and accepted.

A1 - see '**Robuste Albert**'

A2, *S. vulgaris*
   Maarse & Keessen 1990.
   {a rootstock selection made 50 to 60 years ago at the Fa Eveleens & Maarse}
   Sytsema, Proefbeschrijving [1990]; Rijsewijk, De Boomkwekerij, 45:24-25 [1994]
   Cultivar name not established.

A3, *S. vulgaris*
   Maarse & Keessen 1990.
   {a rootstock selection made 50 to 60 years ago at the Fa Eveleens & Maarse}
   Sytsema, Proefbeschrijving [1990]; Rijsewijk, De Boomkwekerij, 45:24-25 [1994]
   Cultivar name not established.

A20, *S. vulgaris*
   Origin not known; S VI
   Hauta-aho, Lilacs - Quart. Jour. 35(4):119 & ill. inside back cover (2006)
   unidentified old selection growing near Villa Anneberg, Helsinki region, Finland.
   Cognomen, not a cultivar name.

Baardse - see '**G. J. Baardse**'.

'Baby Blue', *S. vulgaris*
   Yeager; ? ?
   Cultivar name not established; selection not introduced.

'Baby Doll', *S. vulgaris*
   Clarke pre-1947; ? ?
   AAN "registered without release" [n.d.]; Wister, Lilacs for America, 25 [1953] - name only, sales discontinued in 1947
   Cultivar name presumed registered 1953 without description; not reported in cultivation.

'Bacio di Amore', *S. vulgaris*
   Moro, F. 2010; S VI
   {'Pixie' × ?}
   Vrugtman, Hanburyana 7:28 [2013].
   Name: Italian for kiss of love.
   Cultivar name registered 2012; name established and accepted.

'Bad Frankenhausen', *S. vulgaris*
   Haase 2017; S VII/II
   seen <http://fliedertraum.de/raritaeten/syringa-vulgaris-bad-frankenhausen>
   <http://blog.fliedertraum.de/2017/05/16/ich-taufe-dich-auf-den-namen/>
   Named for Bad Frankenhausen (officially: Bad Frankenhausen/Kyffhäuser) a spa town in the German state of Thuringia, known for its annual lilac festival.
   Cultivar name established and accepted.

'Baĭkal', *S. vulgaris*
   'Байкал'
   Kolesnikov pre-1953; S III
   {parentage not known}
   Description in the book "Lilacs" by N.K. Vekhov, 1953.
   T. Polyakova , 2018, Мастер Сиреневой Кисти (Master of the Lilac Brush), p. 108 - photo only; the only plant known of this selection grows in the garden of the Smolsky Institute, a museum dedicated to Lenin, in St Petersburg, Russian Federation.

'Baikonur', *S. vulgaris*
   'Байконур'
   Mel'nik, Rubanik & Dyagilev 1986; S VII
   syn. - 'Baykonur', 'Boiconur'
   {'Volcan' × OP }
   certificate of authorship No. 4872, 1989.
   Reported growing in C. Chapman collection, UK, August 2009; at Piccoplant January 2018.
   (Международная научная конференция "Syringa L.: коллекции, выращивание, использование")
   "International Scientific Conference "Syringa L.: collections, cultivation, using" / Collection of Scientific Articles of Botanical Institute named after V.L. Komarov, Botanical Garden of Peter the Great BIN RAS. - St. Petersburg. -2020.- pp.23-27 (in Russian).
   Named after the Baikonur Cosmodrome.
   Cultivar name established and accepted.

'Bailbelle', *S.* (Pubescentes Series)
   Holland pre-1999; S V
   syn. - No. 85-1, Tinkerbelle®, No. 75847303
   {*S. pubescens* subsp. *pubescens* 'Palibin' × *S. pubescens* subsp. *microphylla* 'Superba'}
   Fairytale® Series
   marketed in Europe also as 'Tincabell'
   Bailey Nurs. Cat. pp. 91 & 164, ill. inside front cover [1999] - first introduction in their Fairytale® Series; Landscape Trades 21(9):9 [1999]; Anon., COPF News 12(1):3 [2000]; COPF, New Plant Introductions, Tinkerbelle™, [Dec. 2000]; Vrugtman, Lilacs - Quart. Jour. 35(3):94-95; Photo on Jorgovani/Lilacs 2015 DVD.
   United States Plant Patent No. 12,294 [Dec. 18, 2001]; Canadian Plant Breeders' Rights registration No. 1204, effective 2002-07-08 to 2020-07-08.
   Cultivar name established and accepted; statutory registration.

'Bailbridget', *S.* ×*hyacinthiflora*
   Selinger 2007; D II
   syn. - Marketed in the United States by Bailey Nurseries as Virtual Violet® (U.S. trademark #5327451 registered 7 November 2017).
   {*S. vulgaris* 'Charles Joly' × *S.* ×*hyacinthiflora* 'Declaration' or 'Old Glory'}

United States Plant Patent No. 30,286 [March 12, 2019]; statutory registration.
Cultivar name established and accepted.

'Baildust', *S.* (Pubescentes Series)
Holland 2001; S V
{*S. pubescens* subsp. *pubescens* 'Palibin' × *S. pubescens* subsp. *microphylla* 'Superba'}
syn. - No. 85.4, Fairy Dust™, (TM No. 76125803, applied for Sept. 2000; abandoned Nov. 2002).
Fairytale® Series
Anon., American Nurseryman 193(12):38 [June 15, 2001]: Vrugtman, Lilacs - Quart. Jour. 35(3):94-95.
United States Plant Patent No. 15,152 [Sept. 21, 2004]; statutory registration.
Cultivar name established and accepted.

'Bailina', *S.* (Pubescentes Series)
Holland 2004; S V
syn. - Thumbelina™ (TM No. 76387841, expired)
{*S. pubescens* subsp. *pubescens* 'Palibin' × *S. pubescens* subsp. *microphylla* 'Superba'}
Fairytale® Series
Vrugtman, Lilacs - Quart. Jour. 35(3):94-95.
United States Plant Patent No. 16,662 [June 13, 2006]; statutory registration.
Cultivar name established and accepted.

'Bailming', *S.* (Pubescentes Series)
Holland 2004; S V
syn. - No. 92-1, Prince Charming™ (TM No. 76387842, expired)
{*S. pubescens* subsp. *pubescens* 'Palibin' × *S. pubescens* subsp. *microphylla* 'Superba'}
Fairytale® Series
Song Sparrow Nursery, Cat. 53, ill. [2004]; Vrugtman, Lilacs - Quart. Jour. 35(3):94-95.
United States Plant Patent No. 16,349 [March 14, 2006]; statutory registration.
Cultivar name established and accepted.

'Bailnce', *S. reticulata* subsp. *reticulata*
Bailey 2007; S I
syn. - Snow Dance (Snowdance™, expired)
United States Plant Patent No. 20,458 [November 10, 2009] - statutory registration; Stoven, Lilacs 38(4):133 [2009]; Vrugtman, Hanburyana 5:5-6 [2011].
Cultivar name established and accepted.

'Bailsugar', *S.* (Pubescentes Series)
Holland 2003; S V/IV
syn. - No. 81.3, Sugar Plum Fairy™ (TM No. 76387840, expired)
{*S. pubescens* subsp. *pubescens* 'Palibin' × *S. pubescens* subsp. *microphylla* 'Superba'}
Fairytale® Series
Song Sparrow Nursery, Cat. 53, ill. [2004]; Vrugtman, Lilacs - Quart. Jour. 35(3):94-95.
United States Plant Patent No. 15,588 [Feb. 22, 2005]; statutory registration.
Cultivar name established and accepted.

'Bakhut', *S. vulgaris*
'Бахут'
Sagitova; D VI
{parentage not known}
Name: Kazakh for happiness.
Cultivar name not established.

'Baldishol', *S. villosa* subsp. *villosa*
Horntvedt; S II/V
syn. - klon 319
Lønø, Norsk Hagetident, 7-8/85, pp. 395-397 [1985]; Kjær, Gartneryrket (G.Y.) 1987:274; Bjerkestrand & Sandved, Grøntanleggsplanter utvalgt for norske forhold 1986-1987-1988, 25-26 [1989]; Vrugtman, Lilacs - Quart. Jour. 25(2):41-42 [1996].
Cultivar name established and accepted.

'Bal'zak', *S. vulgaris*
'Бальзак'
Kolesnikov; D VI
Rubtzov et al. 1980. Vidy i sorta sireni, kul'tiviruemye v SSSR. Kiev; Naukova Dumka. – in Russian; Holetich, C.D. 1982. Lilac species and cultivars in cultivation in USSR. Lilacs 11(2):1-38. - translation of Rubtzov et al. 1982.
Named for Honoré de Balzac, 1799-1850, French novelist and playwright.
Cultivar name established and accepted.

Banner of Lenin - see **'Znamya Lenina'**.

'Banquise', *S. vulgaris*
Lemoine 1905; D I
Lemoine, Cat. No. 161, 28 [1905]; McKelvey, The Lilac, 265 [1928]; Wister, Lilacs for America, 44 [1942], 25 [1953]; Photo on Jorgovani/Lilacs 2015 DVD.
Cultivar name presumed registered 1953; name established and accepted.

'Bardwell', *S. vulgaris*
Erickson pre-1981; S III/V
{'President Lincoln' × ?}
In lit. Giles Waines to Mark Debard, 11 Nov. 2017 - name only; Lilacs - Quart. Jour. 47(1):11 [2018] - name only; in lit. Waines to Vrugtman 27 March 2018 - as S III/V, perhaps {'President Lincoln' × 'Romance'}.
Cultivar name not established and accepted.

'Barnes Foundation', *S. vulgaris*
Barnes, L.L.; S IV
Wister, Lilacs for America, 25 [1953]
Named for the Barnes Foundation, an educational institution teaching classes in its galleries and Arboretum at Merion, Pennsylvania, USA.
Cultivar name presumed registered 1953; not reported in cultivation.

'Baron Dietrich de Val Duchesse', *S. vulgaris*
  Klettenberg 1934; D V
  Klettenberg, Cat. 20 [1934]; Wister, Lilacs for America, 25 [1953]
  Named for Charles Henri Dietrich, Baron de Val Duchesse, 1865-1939, Auderghem, Belgium.
  Cultivar name presumed registered 1953; name established and accepted.

'Bary<u>sh</u>nya–Kres'ty<u>a</u>nka', *S. vulgaris*
  'Барышня-Крестьянка'
  Aladin, S., Aladina, O., Polyakova, T., and Aladina, A. 2017; D I/V/IV-V
  {'Madame Antoine Buchner' × OP}
  Statutory registration, Russia, State Register and Plant Patent No. 80047/8058577 (2019)
  (Международная научная конференция "Syringa L.: коллекции, выращивание, использование") "International Scientific Conference "Syringa L.: collections, cultivation, using" / Collection of Scientific Articles of Botanical Institute named after V.L. Komarov, Botanical Garden of Peter the Great BIN RAS. - St. Petersburg. -2020.- pp. 7-13 (in Russian); Photo exhibition of all varieties of the creative breeding group "Russian Lilac" at the Festival "Lilac February", St. Petersburg, Botanical Garden of Peter the Great BIN RAS, February 22-24, 2020.
  Named after the romantic heroine of the famous story by A.S. Pu<u>sh</u>kin. Name means young peasant lady.
  Cultivar name established and accepted.

'Basia', *S.* (Villosae Group), *S.* ×*prestoniae*
  Bugała pre-1970; S V
  Syn.—'Busia' (a wrong spelling).
  Bugała, Arboretum Kórnickie 15:61-70 [1970] - in Polish; Wister & Oppe, Arnoldia 31(3):121 [1971]; Bugała, Lilacs - Quart. Jour. 24(4):90-91 [1995]; Photo on Jorgovani/Lilacs 2015 DVD.
  Cultivar name registered 1970; name established and accepted.

BEACH PARTY™
  trademark for a series of "low-chill" *S.* ×*hyacinthiflora* cultivars originated by John Schoustra. See: 'Rosie' and 'Snowy'.

'Beacon', *S.* (Villosae Group), *S.* ×*prestoniae*
  Preston & Leslie 1937; S VI
  {parentage not known}
  Wister, Lilacs for America, 25 [1953]; Cumming, Agric. Canada Public. 1628, p. 17 [1977] - as introduced in 1937, and "obsolete"; Photo on Jorgovani/Lilacs 2015 DVD.
  Cultivar name presumed registered 1953; name established and accepted.

'Beatrice', *S.* (Villosae Group), *S.* ×*prestoniae*
  Preston 1928; S V
  syn. - Preston No. 20-14-150
  {*S. villosa* subsp. *villosa* × *S. komarowii* subsp. *reflexa*}
  Macoun, Rep. Dom. Hort. 1928, 55 [1930] - name only; Wister, Lilacs for America, 44, 64 [1942] - name only; Wister, Lilacs for America, 25, 48 [1953] - as discard
  Named for the niece of Leonato in Shakespeare's *Much Ado About Nothing*.
  Cultivar name presumed registered 1953; name established and accepted.

'Beautiful Susan', *S. komarowii* subsp. *reflexa*
  Slavin & Millham 2011; S V
  syn. - BHS #6
  Lilacs 40(1):6 - erroneously as *S. pubescens* subsp. *reflexa*; Millham, Lilacs 40(2):47, ill. back cover; Vrugtman, Hanburyana 7:
  Named for Susan Taskett Millham, 1951-2007, wife of Kent Millham [Lilacs 36(3):91-92].
  Cultivar name registered 2011; name established and accepted.

BEAUTY OF FRANKFURT - see 'Hermann Eilers'.

'Beauty of Heaven', *S. vulgaris*
  Klager (?); S III
  Peterson, Lilacs - Proceedings 16(1):17 [1987] - name only
  Cultivar name not established.

BEAUTY OF MOSCOW - trade designation for 'Krasavi<u>ts</u>a Moskvy'.

'Beckwith', *S. vulgaris*
  Speirs 2007; D III
  {parentage not known}
  Original plant selected and collected 2007 by Speirs and Lilac Team, Friends of the Central Experimental Farm, Ottawa, on property of Claude and Cora Nolan (Park Lot-1), Franktown, Ontario, Canada.
  Speirs, J., Friends of the Central Experimental Farm, Newsletter 28(2):6 [2016].
  Named for the township of Beckwith in which the town of Franktown is located.
  Cultivar name established and accepted.

BEIJING GOLD™ - see 'Zhang Zhiming'.

Bei Jing Huang - see 'Jin Yuan'.

'Belaya Noch', *S. vulgaris*
  'Белая Ночь'
  Vek<u>h</u>ov 1952; D V
  Rub<u>tz</u>ov et al. 1980. Vidy i sorta sireni, kul'tiviruemye v SSSR. Kiev; Naukova Dumka. – in Russian; Holetich, C.D. 1982. Lilac species and cultivars in cultivation in USSR. Lilacs 11(2):1-38. - translation of Rub<u>tz</u>ov et al. 1982; Photo on Jorgovani/Lilacs 2015 DVD.
  Name: Russian for white nights.
  Cultivar name established and accepted.

'Bel<u>a</u>ya Vetka' – see 'Vetka Mira'

'Bella Donna Sara', *S. vulgaris*
  Moro, F.; 2008; S I

{'Excellent' × ?}
F. Moro, Lilacs - Quart. Jour. 41(2):55, ill. p. 56 [2012]; Vrugtman, Hanburyana 7:28 [2013].
Named for Sara Moro [1966 -], wife of the originator.
Cultivar name registered 2012; name established and accepted.

'Belle d'Elewyt', *S. vulgaris*
Draps (?); S I
Wister, Lilacs for America, 25 [1953]
Cultivar name not established, not reported in cultivation in 1953.

BELLE DE MOSCOU - see **'Krasavi<u>ts</u>a Moskvy'**.

'Belle de Nancy', *S. vulgaris*
Lemoine 1891; D V
Lemoine, Cat. No. 119, 10 [1891]; McKelvey, The Lilac, 266 [1928]; Wister, Lilacs for America, 44 [1942], 25 [1953]; Photo on Jorgovani/Lilacs 2015 DVD.
Cultivar name presumed registered 1953; name established and accepted.

'Bellicent', *S.* (Villosae Group), *S.* ×*josiflexa*
Preston 1937; S V
syn. - Preston No. 24.02.05; 'Беллисент'; probably MISS JAPAN
{*S.* ×*josiflexa* 'Guinevere' × ? }
Wister, Lilacs for America, 44, 64 [1942]; Wyman, Arnoldia 8(7):31 [1948]; Davis, Rep. Dom. Hort., Progress Report 1934-1948, 149 [1950]; Wister, Lilacs for America, 25, 48 [1953]; Buckley, Arboretum Notes 16:22 - as planted 1922 (?); Davidson et al, Landscape Plants at the Morden Arboretum [1994] - received at Morden Research Station in 1937; Registered with the State Commission of the Russian Federation for Testing and Protection of Selection Achievements, No. 9810217, 2001, as 'Беллисент'; Photo on Jorgovani/Lilacs 2015 DVD.
Named for Queen Bellicent, character from Idylls of the King, poem by Alfred, Lord Tennyson, 1809-1892.
Awards: RHS First Class Certificate 1946; RHS Award of Garden Merit 1993.
Cultivar name presumed registered 1953; name established and accepted.

'Belomor'e', *S. vulgaris*
'Беломорье'
Aladin, S., Aladina, O., and Polyakova, T. 2016; D I
{elite form 9-131 × OP}
Садовник (Gardener) magazine 04 (140)/2017 :18-25; Вестник АППМ (Catalog in Vestnik APPM (Planting material association) magazine) 1/2018: 59-72 (in Russian).
Named for the Russian White Sea coast.
Cultivar name established and accepted.

'Belorusskie Zori', *S. vulgaris*
'Белорусские Зори'
Smol'skiĭ & Bibikova 1964; S IV-V
syn. - 'Byelorusskie Zori', ZORIE (trade designation used for cut flowers of this cultivar)
{'Andenken an Ludwig Späth' × 'Hyazinthenflieder'}
Rub<u>tz</u>ov et al. 1980. Vidy i sorta sireni, kul'tiviruemye v SSSR. Kiev; Naukova Dumka. – in Russian; Holetich, C.D. 1982. Lilac species and cultivars in cultivation in USSR. Lilacs 11(2):1-38. - translation of Rub<u>tz</u>ov et al. 1982; Semenov, Igor, Lilacs - Quart. Jour. 43(3):85-87 [2014]; Photo on Jorgovani/Lilacs 2015 DVD.
Name: Russian for Belorussian dawns.
Cultivar name established and accepted.
Forcing lilac in the Netherlands.

'Belosne<u>zh</u>ka', *S. vulgaris*
'Белоснежка' (not Mel'nik, Rubanik & D<u>y</u>agilev)
Sagitova 1985; ? I
syn. - S-106S
{'Akku' × ? }
Name: Russian for Snow White.
Cultivar name not established.

'Belosne<u>zh</u>ka', *S. vulgaris*
'Белоснежка' (not Sagitova) (not Makedonska<u>ya</u>)
Mel'nik, Rubanik & D<u>y</u>agilev pre-1994; D I
Pikaleva, Lilacs - Quart. Jour. 23(4):84 [1994]
Name: Russian for Snow White.
Cultivar name not established.

'Belosnezhka', *S. vulgaris*
'Белоснежка'
Makedonska<u>ya</u> 2018; S I (not Mel'nik, Rubanik & D<u>y</u>agilev) (not Sagitova)
{open pollinated seedling}
Statutory registration with the State Inspection for testing and protection of plant varieties of the Republic of Belarus. Makedonska<u>ya</u> N. 'Assortment of lilac varieties for landscaping cities and towns of Belarus' pp 85-89 "International Scientific Conference "Syringa L.: collections, cultivation, using" / Collection of Scientific Articles of Botanical Institute named after V.L. Komarov, Botanical Garden of Peter the Great BIN RAS. - St. Petersburg. -2020 (in Russian).
Name: Russian for Snow White.
Cultivar name established and accepted

'Benita', *S. vulgaris*
Kārkliņš 2003; D VII/II
Strautiņa & Kaufmane, Dobeles ceriņi, pp. 14, 92 [2011]; Photo on Jorgovani/Lilacs 2015 DVD.
Named for the wife of the originator.
Cultivar name established and accepted.

'Béranger', *S. vulgaris*
Simon-Louis pre-1867; S VI
L. van Houtte, Cat. No. 121, 41-42 [1867]; McKelvey, The Lilac, 266 [1928]; Wister, Lilacs for America, 44 [1942] - as S III; Wister, Lilacs for America, 25 [1953]
Named for Pierre Jean Béranger, 1780-1857, French poet.
Cultivar name presumed registered 1953; name established and accepted.

'Berdeen's Chocolate', *S. vulgaris*
    Berdeen; S VI
    Wister, Arnoldia 23(4):80 [1963]; Vrugtman, Lilac Newsletter 4(11):7 [1978]; King & Coggeshall, Lilacs - Quart. Jour. 27(2):49-50 [1998] - name only
    Cultivar name registered 1963; name established and accepted.

Berdeen's Unnamed Single Blue, *S. vulgaris*
    Berdeen pre-1990; S III
    Anon., Lilacs - Quart. Jour. 19(3):63 [1990] - name only
    Cognomen, not a cultivar name.

Berdeen's Unnamed Single Red, *S. vulgaris*
    Berdeen pre-1990; S ?
    Anon., Lilacs - Quart. Jour. 19(3):63 [1990] - name only
    Cognomen, not a cultivar name.

Berdeen Hybrids No. 1 through 8, *S. vulgaris*
    Berdeen; ? ?
    Anon., Lilacs - Quart. Jour. 21(4):93 [1992] - no information, reported in cultivation at Philip Hodgdon Memorial Lilac Garden
    Cognomen, not cultivar names, but code names used in P. Hodgdon Mem. Lilac Garden.

'Bergen', *S. vulgaris*
    origin not known ? ?
    Farr, Cat., 59 [1922]; McKelvey, The Lilac, 266 [1928] - probably a misnomer; Wister, Lilacs for America, 44 [1942] - probably misspelling of 'Berryer'
    Cultivar name not established, not reported in cultivation in 1953.

Beri - see **'Berryer'**.

Be Right Back™ - see 'GARlisabzar'

'Bernard Harkness', *S. vulgaris*
    Ruliffson; S VII
    {'C. B. van Nes' × 'Jeanne d'Arc'}
    Wister, Lilacs for America, 25 [1953]
    Named for Bernard Emerson Harkness, 1907-1980, plant taxonomist with Monroe County Department of Parks, 1940s-1967, Rochester, New York, USA.
    Cultivar name presumed registered 1953; name established and accepted.

'Bernard Slavin', *S. vulgaris*
    Fenicchia 1972; S I
    syn. - 'Barney Slavin', 'Bernard H. Slavin', R 18
    {'Rochester' × ? }
    Clark, ILS Newsletter, Convention Issue, 6-7 [May 1972]; Clark, Arnoldia 32(3):133-135 [1972]; Hoepfl & Rogers, Lilac Newsletter 14(7):5 [1988]; Fiala, Lilacs, 91, 219 [1988]; Vrugtman, HortScience 32(4):587 [1997]; K. Millham, Lilacs- Quart. Jour. 42(2):60 & ill. 62 [2013]; Photo on Jorgovani/Lilacs 2015 DVD.
    Named for Bernard H. Slavin, 1874-1960, horticulturist, Monroe County Parks, 1890-1942, Rochester, New York, USA.
    Cultivar name registered 1996; name established and accepted.

Berrier - see **'Berryer'**.

'Berryer', *S.* ×*hyacinthiflora*
    Lemoine 1913; D V
    syn. - 'Berger', 'Beri', 'Berrier'; see also - 'Bergen'
    Lemoine, Cat. No. 185, 41 [1913-1914]; McKelvey, The Lilac 196 [1928]; Wister, Lilacs for America, 44 [1942], 25 [1953]; Photo on Jorgovani/Lilacs 2015 DVD.
    Named for Pierre Antoine Berryer, 1790-1868, French statesman and orator.
    Cultivar name presumed registered 1953; name established and accepted.

'Bertha Child', *S. vulgaris*
    Child; S VII-V
    {parentage not known}
    Vrugtman, Lilacs - Proceedings 6(1):15 [1978]; Vrugtman, AABGA Bull. 13(4):105 [1979]; Photo on Jorgovani/Lilacs 2015 DVD.
    Named for Bertha Child, 1899-1986, wife of the originator.
    Cultivar name registered 1976; name established and accepted.

Bertha Dammann - see **'Frau Bertha Dammann'**.

'Bertha Dunham', *S. vulgaris*
    Rankin; D II
    {parentage not known}
    Wister, Lilacs for America, 25 [1953]
    Cultivar name presumed registered 1953; name established and accepted.

'Bertha Phair', *S. vulgaris*
    Phair; D VII
    {'Paul Thirion' × ? }
    Wister, Arnoldia 23(4):80 [1963]; Photo on Jorgovani/Lilacs 2015 DVD.
    Cultivar name registered 1963; name established and accepted.

'Bertha Van Damme', *S.* Villosae Group
    Aelbrecht 2009; S VII
    in cultivation at Zilverspar nursery; no additional information available.
    Cultivar name not established.

'Bērzes Krasts', *S. vulgaris*
    Upītis ca 1970; S V/II
    syn. - 'Beerzes Krasts'
    Kalniņš, Dārzs un drava 1986, No. 12, 13-15; in litt. S. Strautiņa to F. Vrugtman [22 Jan. 2008] - ca 1970, S V/II
    Named for the bank of river Berze.
    Cultivar name established and accepted.

'Beskonechnost" (Infinity), *S.* × *hyacinthiflora*
    'Бесконечность'
    Aladin, S., Aladina, O., Polyakova, T., and Aladina, A. 2015; S II-IV

{'Buffon' × OP}
(Международная научная конференция "Syringa L.: коллекции, выращивание, использование") "International Scientific Conference "Syringa L.: collections, cultivation, using" / Collection of Scientific Articles of Botanical Institute named after V.L. Komarov, Botanical Garden of Peter the Great BIN RAS. - St. Petersburg. -2020.- pp.3-7 (in Russian); Photo exhibition of all varieties of the creative breeding group "Russian Lilac" at the Festival "Lilac February", St. Petersburg, Botanical Garden of Peter the Great BIN RAS, February 22-24, 2020.
The flower petals form a characteristic "eight" - a sign of infinity.
Cultivar name established and accepted.

'Best Blue', *S. vulgaris*
origin not known pre-1939; ? III
Howell, Cat. [1939]; Wister, Lilacs for America, 36 & 44 [1942] - doubtful name
Cultivar name not established, not reported in cultivation in 1953.

'Beth', *S. vulgaris*
Peterson 1999; D I
{open pollinated F2 seedling from irradiated seed of unknown origin; the same irradiated seed lot also gave rise to 'Prairie Petite'}
Vrugtman, HortScience 35(4):549 [2000]
Cultivar name registered 1999; name established and accepted.

'Beth Morrison', *S. vulgaris*
Berdeen 1998; S IV
Vrugtman, AABGA Bulletin 16(4):131 [1982]; King & Coggeshall, Lilacs - Quart. Jour. 27(2):49-50 [1998] - name only
Named for the granddaughter of the local doctor in Kennebunk, Maine.
Cultivar name not established.

'Beth Turner', *S. vulgaris*
Clarke, J. 1968; S V
J. Clarke Nursery Co., Wholesale Price List 1968-1969, p. 8; Photo on Jorgovani/Lilacs 2015 DVD.
Cultivar name established and accepted.

'Betsy Bowman', *S. vulgaris*
Berdeen 2005; S VII
King & Coggeshall, Lilacs - Quart. Jour. 27(2):49-50 [1998] - name only; Vrugtman, Encyclopedia, 312 [2008]
Named for Betsy Bowman, teacher in Ipswich, Maine.
Cultivar name established and accepted.

'Betsy Ross', *S.* ×*hyacinthiflora*
Egolf & Pooler 1992; S I
syn. - NA 62973, PI 596517
{?(Highland Park unidentified *Syringa*) × *S. oblata* NA 36751, PI 391403, coll. in China in 1974}
USDA-ARS Notice of Release [July 21, 2000]; American Nurseryman 192(12):46 [2000]; USNA Pl Introduction [Aug. 2000]; Vrugtman, HortScience 37(7):1145 [2002]; Pooler, HortScience 43(2):544–545 [2008]; Photo on Jorgovani/Lilacs 2015 DVD.
Named for Betsy Ross, née Elizabeth Griscom, 1752-1836, a flag maker, who may have sewn the first American flag. Named by Pooler.
Nomenclatural standard deposited at United States National Arboretum Herbarium (NA); NA-0035725; Hanburyana 4:56 [2009].
Cultivar name registered 2001; name established and accepted.

'Betty Louise', *S. vulgaris*
Klager; S V
Wister, Lilacs for America, 44 [1942], 25 [1953]
Cultivar name presumed registered in 1953;
Cultivar not reported in cultivation.

'Betty Opper', *S. vulgaris*
Rankin; D V
{parentage not known}
Wister, Arnoldia 23(4):80 [1963]; Photo on Jorgovani/Lilacs 2015 DVD.
Cultivar name registered 1963; name established and accepted.

'Betty Stone', *S. vulgaris*
Stone 1963; S IV
Wister, Arnoldia 23(4):80 [1963]
Cultivar name registered 1963; name established and accepted.

BHS #5, *S. komarowii* subsp. *reflexa*
Slavin; S V
Fiala, Lilacs, 71 [1988] - Fiala proposes the epithet 'Slavin'; Kent Millham, in litt. Feb.22/05 - awaiting evaluation
Breeder's designation, not a cultivar name.

BHS #6 – see **'Beautiful Susan'**.

'Biała Anna', *S. vulgaris*
'Biała Anna'
Karpow-Lipski 1971; S I
syn. - 'Biały Hiacyntowy', KL 21,
Anon., Lista odmian roślin ozdobnych 1971, 17 & 1973, 25; Photo on Jorgovani/Lilacs 2015 DVD.
Name: Polish for white Anna; probably named in honour of Anna Karpow.
Varietal denomination registered COBORU 1971;
Cultivar name established and accepted.

Biały Hiacyntowy - see **Biała Anna**.

'Bianca', *S.* (Villosae Group), *S.* ×*prestoniae*
Preston; S ?
syn. - Preston No. 20-14-08
{*S. villosa* subsp. *villosa* × *S. komarowii* subsp. *reflexa*}

Macoun, Rep. Dom. Hort. 1928, 55 [1930] - name only; USDA Plant Inventory No. 101, 20 (PI 81990) [Apr. 1931] - name only; Wister, Lilacs for America, 64 [1942], 48 [1953] - not in cultivation, no plants distributed
Named for the Sister of Katherine in Shakespeare's *Taming of the Shrew*.
Cultivar name not established.

'Bicentennial', *S. vulgaris*
Fenicchia 1988; S III
syn. - 'Monroe Centennial', R333RAF433
{'Rochester' × 'Dusk'}
Anon., ILS Pipeline 3(3):8 [1977]; Vrugtman, AABGA Bull. 17(3):69 [1984] - as 'Monroe Centennial'; Vrugtman, HortScience 24(3):435 [1989]; K. Millham, Lilacs -Quart. Jour. 42(2):60 & ill. 63 [2013]; Photo on Jorgovani/Lilacs 2015 DVD.
Named for the bicentennial of the USA, 1976.
Cultivar name registered 1988; name established and accepted.

'Bicolor', *S. ×chinensis*
Lemoine 1853; S I & VII
syn. - *S. chinensis* nothof. *bicolor* (Lemoine) Jäger.
Jäger, Ziergehölze, p. 528 [1865]; McKelvey, The Lilac, 418-419 [1928]; Wister, Lilacs for America, 44 [1942], 26 [1953]; Photo on Jorgovani/Lilacs 2015 DVD.
Cultivar name established and accepted.

'Bicolor', *S. vulgaris*
origin not known pre-1864; S II
syn. - Flore Bicolor, flore bicolor
Petzold & Kirchner, Arb. Muscav. 494 [1864]; McKelvey, The Lilac, 266-267 [1928] - descriptions vary, confused name; Wister, Lilacs for America, 44, 48 [1942] - as S III; Wister, Lilacs for America, 25, 29 [1953] - as S VI
Cultivar name not established; plants in cultivation may not be true to name.

'Big Blue', *S. ×hyacinthiflora*
Lammerts 1953; S III
{(Lammerts C 112 × 'Lamartine' seedling) × (Lammerts 42-109-4 × ?)}
Lammerts, US Plant Patent No. 3895 [Aug. 15, 1976]; Vrugtman, Lilacs - Proceedings 6(1):17 [1978]; Vrugtman, AABGA Bull. 13(4):107 [1979]; see also Vrugtman, Lilacs-Quart. Jour. 28(4):99-100 [1999] - description, p.93, and plate 77 in Fiala, Lilacs-The Genus Syringa [1988] are incorrect
Cultivar name registered 1976; name established and accepted.
Nota bene: Since this cultivar appears to be of 'Lavender Lady' ancestry see also: Pringle, Lilacs - Quart. Jour. 24(4):97-99 [1995]; and Vrugtman, HortScience 31(3):328 [1996].

'Bill Heard', *S. vulgaris*
Peterson 2004; D VI
{'Beth' × OP}
Anon., Lilacs - Quart. Jour. 33(1):11 [2004]; also in private collection (KA) in USA per `email to Registrar 10-4-19.
Named for the nurseryman, crabapple expert, and horticulture author who planted trees at the White House during the Reagan administration.
Cultivar name not established.

'Bill Horman', *S.vulgaris*
Peterson 2003; ? VII/VI
In private collection (KA) in USA per email to Registrar 10-4-19.
Named for lifelong friend and fellow lilac enthusiast from Michigan, USA.
Cultivar name not established.

Bill Utley, *S.*
origin not known pre-2007; ? ?
Kilcoyne, Lilacs-Quart. Jour. 36(2):82 [2007] - name only
Cultivar name not established.

Bill Wiley, *S.*
origin not known pre-2007; ? ?
Kilcoyne, Lilacs-Quart. Jour. 36(2):82 [2007] - name only
Cultivar name not established.

Billy Mills - see **'Wm. K. Mills'**.

'Billy Woollatt', *S. vulgaris*
Paterson; ? ?
Anon., *Evening Telegram*, Toronto, June 6, 1939 - name only
Cultivar name not established.

BILTZ – *S. vulgaris*
ca 1970; S VII
Known to be growing on Biltz family farm on Lynn Rd. in Rootstown, Ohio USA since 1970, dug up in 2000 and since marketed by Peter Schneider
Seen on September 29, 2019 at http://www.combinedroselist.com/freedom-gardens.html
More information from Peter Schneider in September 28, 2019 email to Mark DeBard
Cognomen, not a cultivar name; possibly an old cultivar vs OP seedling.

'Birchwood', *S. oblata* subsp. *dilatata*
Clark; S V
Anon., Lilacs - Proceedings 17(1):26 [1988] - name only; Fiala, Lilacs, 62 [1988] - selected for fine autumn coloration; Lilacs - Quart. Jour. 22(3): back cover ill. [1993]
Cultivar name established and accepted.

'Bishop McQuaid', *S. vulgaris*
Fenicchia 1972; S VII
syn. - 'Bishop Bernard McQuaid', 'Bishop Bernard J. McQuaid', R 63
{'Rochester' × ? }
Clark, ILS Newsletter, Convention Issue, 6-7 [May 1972]; Clark, Arnoldia 32(3):133-135 [1972]; Fiala, Lilacs, 105,

219 [1988]; Vrugtman, HortScience 32(4):587 [1997]; K. Millham, Lilacs - Quart. Jour. 42(2):63 ill. [2013]; Photo on Jorgovani/Lilacs 2015 DVD.
Named for the Rt. Rev. Bernard J. McQuaid, DD, 1829(?)-1909, rector of St Patrick's Cathedral, Rochester, New York, USA.
Cultivar name registered 1996; name established and accepted.

'Blanca Beltran', *S. vulgaris*
Margaretten; D I
{'Mme Lemoine' × ? }
Cultivar name not established; not reported in cultivation.

'Blanc de Carrière', *S. vulgaris*
origin not known pre-1912; S I
Criadero de Árboles de "Santa Ines", Catálogo Jeneral No. 5, 356 [año 24 = 1912]; McKelvey, The Lilac, 267 (1928).
Cultivar name established and accepted.

'Blanch', *S.* (Villosae Group), *S.* ×*prestoniae*
Preston; S IV
syn. - Preston No. 20-14-156
{*S. villosa* subsp. *villosa* × *S. komarowii* subsp. *reflexa*}
Macoun, Rep. Dom. Hort. 1928, 55 [1930]; Wister, Lilacs for America, 64 [1942], 48 [1953] - name only, plants never distributed.
Named for the Niece of King John in Shakespeare's *King John*.
Cultivar name not established, probably extinct.

'**Blanche Sweet**', *S.* ×*hyacinthiflora*
Fiala 1988; S III
{('Rochester' × *S. oblata* subsp. *dilatata*) × 'Rochester'}
Vrugtman, HortScience 24(3):435 [1989]; Knight Hollow Nursery, 1996 Cultured cutting and liner descriptive list; Photo on Jorgovani/Lilacs 2015 DVD.
Named for Sarah Blanche Sweet (also known as Daphne Wayne), [1895-1986], American silent film actress and film historian.
Cultivar name registered 1988; name established and accepted.

Blanc Pyramidal - see '**Pyramidalis Alba**'.

blandii, *S. vulgaris*
Bland 1853; S VII
Gardener's Chronicle 16 (1856): 675 - as *S. vulgaris* var. *blandii*.
Cultivar name not established; probably extinct.

'Blāzma', *S. vulgaris*
Kārkliņš 2003; S VII/II
Strautiņa & Kaufmane, Dobeles ceriņi, p. 92 [2011]
Name: Latvian for glow.
Cultivar name established and accepted.

'**Bleuâtre**', *S. vulgaris*
Baltet 1894; S III
syn. - 'Bleuatre'

Henry, Jardin 8:175 [1894]; McKelvey, The Lilac, 267-268 [1928]; Wister, Lilacs for America, 44 [1942], 25 [1953]
Cultivar name presumed registered 1953; name established and accepted.

'Blizzard', *S. vulgaris*
Peterson 2001; D II
Parentage unknown.
In private collection (KA) in USA per email to Registrar 10-4-19.
Cultivar name not established.

'**Bloemenlust**', *S. vulgaris*
Piet 1956; S I
Wister, Arnoldia 23(4):80 [1963]; Bunnik/Stapel, in litt. January 3, 2000 - no longer in cultivation; Cornelis van Dam, in litt. January 11, 2000.
Named for "Bloemenlust", an Aalsmeer flower auction house.
Awards: Certificate of Merit 1956; First Class Certificate 1958 (KMTP).
Formerly a forcing cultivar in the Netherlands.
Cultivar name registered 1963; name established and accepted.

BLOOMERANG® - Trademark registered by Spring Meadow Nursery, Inc., covering several reblooming/remontant cultivars. Registration No. 3655456, July 14, 2009.
BLOOMERANG® DARK PURPLE - see '**SMSJBP7**'.
BLOOMERANG® DWARF PINK - see '**SMNJRPI**'.
BLOOMERANG® DWARF PURPLE - see '**SMNJRPU**'.
BLOOMERANG® PINK PERFUME - see '**PINK PERFUME**'.
BLOOMERANG® PURPLE - see '**PENDA**'.

'**Blue Angel**', *S. vulgaris*
Havemeyer & Eaton 1954; S III
Wister, Lilacs for America, 25 [1953]; Lilac Land, Cat. 1954; Eickhorst, ILS Lilac Newsletter 4(1):4-5 [1978]
Cultivar name presumed registered 1953; name established and accepted.

Blue Beard - see 'Bluebird'.

'Bluebird', *S. vulgaris*
Fiala 1969; S III
syn. - 'Blue Beard'
{'Gismonda' × 'Rustica'}
Clark, Lilacs - Proceedings 15(1):4 [1986]; Fiala, Lilacs, 96, 97 [1988]
Cultivar name established and accepted.

'**Blue Boy**', *S.* ×*hyacinthiflora*
Sobeck (not Sass & Peterson); S III
Wister, Arnoldia 26(3):13 [1966]
Cultivar name registered 1966; name established and accepted.
Nota bene: Since this cultivar appears to be of 'Lavender Lady' ancestry see also: Pringle, Lilacs - Quart. Jour. 24(4):97-99 [1995]; and Vrugtman, HortScience 31(3):328 [1996].

'Blue Boy', *S. vulgaris*
    Sass, H. E., & Peterson 2004 (not Sobeck); S III
    syn. - 'Blueboy'
    Anon., Lilacs - Quart. Jour. 33(1):10 & back cover ill. [2004] - as S III; in litt. M. Peterson to F. Vrugtman [March 05, 2004] - as S III
    rejected name (the proposed cultivar name is already in use).

'Blue Danube', *S. vulgaris*
    Fiala 1986; S III
    {'Rochester' × 'True Blue'}
    Fiala, Lilacs, 96, 97, Pl. 14 [1988]; Photo on Jorgovani/Lilacs 2015 DVD.
    Cultivar name established and accepted.

'Blue Delft', *S. vulgaris*
    Fiala 1982; S III
    syn. - 'Delft Blue'
    {'Mrs A. Belmont' × 'Rochester'}
    Fiala, Lilacs, 96, 97, 108 [1988]; Lilacs - Quart. Jour. 25(3): back cover ill. [1996]
    Cultivar name established and accepted.

'Blue Delight', *S. vulgaris*
    Castle 1969; S III
    Wister & Oppe, Arnoldia 31(3):122 [1971]; Photo on Jorgovani/Lilacs 2015 DVD.
    Cultivar name registered 1970; name established and accepted.

'Blue Diamond', *S. vulgaris*
    Fenicchia; S III
    syn. - R 164-168
    {'Rochester' × 'Madame Charles Souchet'}
    Hoepfl & Rogers, Lilac Newsletter 14(7):6 [1988]; Vrugtman, HortScience 33(4):588-589 [1998]; K. Millham, Lilacs - Quart. Jour. 42(2):60 [2013].
    Cultivar name registered 1997; name established and accepted.

blue dream - see 'Lan Meng'.

'Blue Eyes', *S. vulgaris*
    Schneider S. 2009; S III
    {'Albert F. Holden × OP}
    Seen Sept. 29, 2019 at: http://www.combinedroselist.com/freedom-gardens.html
    Additional information per Sept 28, 2019 email from Peter Schneider to Mark DeBard
    Cultivar name not established.

'Blue Giant', *S. vulgaris*
    Fiala 1977; S III
    {'Flora 1953' × 'True Blue'}
    Clark, Lilacs - Proceedings 15(1):5 [1986]; Fiala, Lilacs, 97, 223 [1988]
    Cultivar name established and accepted.

'Blue Heaven', *S.*
    Peterson pre-2019; ?
    In private collection (KA) in USA per email to Registrar 10-4-19.
    Cultivar name not established.

'Blue Hills', *S. vulgaris*
    Kawahara 2000; S II/III
    {parentage not known}
    Named for Little Rock Hills, the English Garden, B&B and restaurant establishment, Iwamizawa, Hokkaido, Japan <http://littlerockhills.com/>.
    <http://www.068.jp/products/pdt_2/0031a.html>
    (Vrugtman, Cultivated Plant Diversity ... 2017)
    Cultivar name registered 2016; name established and accepted.

'Blue Hyacinth', *S.* ×*hyacinthiflora*
    Clarke 1943; S III
    {parentage not known}
    Clarke, Cat. vol. 16, 7 [1949]; Woody Plant Register, AAN, No. 184 [1949]; Wister, Lilacs for America, 44 [1942], 25 [1953]
    Cultivar name presumed registered 1953; name established and accepted.

'Blue Ice', *S. vulgaris*
    Oakes 1996; S III
    Photo on Jorgovani/Lilacs 2015 DVD.
    Cultivar name not established.

'Blue Jay' – noted by Freek Vrugtman in LILACS, Spring 1996, p. 44 to not belong to *Syringa*.

BLUE LAGOON - trade designation used for cut flowers of *S.* ×*hyacinthiflora* 'Excel'.

blue lilac - see **'Azurea Plena'**.

'Blue Mist', *S. vulgaris*
    Origin not known; S III
    Peterson, Lilacs - Proceedings 16(1):17 [1987] - name only
    Cultivar name not established.

BLUE MOON - trade designation used for cut flowers of *S. vulgaris* 'Pam<u>yat</u>' o S. M. Kirove'.

'Blue Mountain', *S.* ×*hyacinthiflora*
    Sobeck; S III
    Wister, Arnoldia 26(3):13 [1966]
    Cultivar name registered 1966; name established and accepted.
    Nota bene: Since this cultivar appears to be of 'Lavender Lady' ancestry see also: Pringle, Lilacs - Quart. Jour. 24(4):97-99 [1995]; and Vrugtman, HortScience 31(3):328 [1996].

'Blue Pixie', *S. vulgaris*
    Origin not known; D III
    reportedly in cultivation at Descanso Gardens since 1998; Photo on Jorgovani/Lilacs 2015 DVD.
    Note: Probably not related to either 'Pixie' or 'Red Pixie'
    Cultivar name not established.

Blue Porcelain - see 'Porcelain Blue'.

'Blue Revery', *S. vulgaris*
Fiala 2000; S III
syn. - 'Blue Reverie', 'Blue Reverly'
Select Plus Cat. [2000] - erroneously as 'Blue Reverly';
Anon., Lilacs for the convention, Lilacs - Quart. Jour
2991):19 [2000] - erroneously as 'Blue Reverly'; Anon.,
Lilacs - Quart. Jour. 33(1):11 [2004] - as 'Blue Reverie'
Cultivar name not established.

BLUE SKIES® - see **'Monore'**.

'Bluets', *S. vulgaris*
Fiala 1979; S III
{'General Sherman' × 'Mrs A. Belmont'}
Fiala, Lilacs, 223, Pl. 14 [1988]
Cultivar name established and accepted.

BLUE YANNY - see **'JN Upright Select'**.

'Blushing Nova', *S.vulgaris*
Moro, F. before 2016; S I
http://www.pepinierelemay.com:7779/portal/
page?_pageid=237,214506,237_214576:237_214580&_
dad=ptldb&_schema=PORTALDB&23123_
PRODUCT_1_201019.search_product_
name2=blushing%20nova
<http://www.spi.8m.com/> seen October 25, 2016,
photo only
Seen in Phytoclone company catalog September 15, 2019
in private email from Claire Fouquet to Mark DeBard
Cultivar name not established.

'Blūzs', *S. vulgaris*
Kārkliņš 2003; S II/V-I
Strautiņa & Kaufmane, Dobeles ceriņi, p. 92 [2011];
Photo on Jorgovani/Lilacs 2015 DVD.
Name: Latvian for blues.
Cultivar name established and accepted.

'Bob Tischler', *S. vulgaris*
Tischler; S II
Peterson, Lilacs - Proceedings 16(1):17 [1987] - name
only; Vrugtman, Lilacs - Quart. Jour. 32(4):149 [2003] -
as S II; Photo on Jorgovani/Lilacs 2015 DVD.
Cultivar name established and accepted.

Boerner, Boerner Selection, or Boerner Strain, *S. pekinensis*
S I
United Information Systems Inc., Datascape Botanical
Index, 112 [1995], 655 [2001] - as 'Boerner', name only;
Select Plus Nursery, e-Cat. p. 27 [Spring 2000] - name
only; in litt. M. Zautke to F. Vrugtman [February 3, 2003]
- Milwaukee County Parks accessions 82-7A & 82-7B
were grown from seed of *S. pekinensis* received from
Univ. of Minnesota Landscape Arboretum in 1982, but
plants no longer extant;
Cognomen, not a cultivar name; plants grown under this
name are indistinguishable from *S. pekinensis*.

'Bogdan Khmel'nitskiĭ', *S. vulgaris*
'Богдан Хмельницкий'
Rubtzov, Zhogoleva, Lyapunova 1954; D V
syn. - 'Bogdan Chmelnyckyj', 'Bogdan Khmel'nickij',
'Bogdan Khmelnizky', 'Bogdan Khmelnytskii'
{'Maréchal Foch' × ? }
Rubtzov et al. 1980. Vidy i sorta sireni, kul'tiviruemye
v SSSR. Kiev; Naukova Dumka. – in Russian; Holetich,
C.D. 1982. Lilac species and cultivars in cultivation in
USSR. Lilacs 11(2):1-38. - translation of Rubtzov et al.
1982; Photo on Jorgovani/Lilacs 2015 DVD.
Named for Bogdan Khmel'nitskiĭ, 1595-1657, Ukrainian
leader in the War of Liberation of the Ukrainian People
of 1648–54
Cultivar name established and accepted.

'Bogdan Przyrzykowski', *S. vulgaris*
Karpow-Lipski 1961; D VI
Wister & Oppe, Arnoldia 31(3):125 [1971]; Photo on
Jorgovani/Lilacs 2015 DVD.
Cultivar name registered 1970; name established and
accepted.

'Bohdan Kaminský', *S. vulgaris*
Thomayer; S II/VII
{parentage not known}
Thomayerovy Stromové Školky, Cat., p. 38 [n.d.]
Named for Bohdan Kaminský, 1859-1929, Czech poet.
Cultivar name not established.

'Boiconur'-- misspelling of 'Baikonur'

'Bol'shevik', *S. vulgaris*
'Большевик'
Kolesnikov 1938; D II/V
Rubtzov et al. 1980. Vidy i sorta sireni, kul'tiviruemye v
SSSR. Kiev; Naukova Dumka. – in Russian; Holetich, C.D.
1982. Lilac species and cultivars in cultivation in USSR.
Lilacs 11(2):1-38. - translation of Rubtzov et al. 1982.
Name: Russian for Bolshevik, or "One of the Majority".
Cultivar name established and accepted.

'Bonnie S. Polin', *S. vulgaris*
Polin; S VII
Cultivar name not established.

'Botaniste Pauli', *S. vulgaris*
Klettenberg 1935; S VI
Klettenberg, Cat. 26[1935]; Wister, Lilacs for America,
25 [1953]
Named for Johan Pauli, 1732-1804, botanist.
Cultivar name presumed registered 1953; name
established and accepted.

'Boule Azurée', *S. vulgaris*
Lemoine 1919; S III
syn. - 'Boule Azure', 'Boule Azuree'
Lemoine, Cat. No. 193, 22 [1919]; McKelvey, The Lilac,
268 [1928]; Wister, Lilacs for America, 44 [1942], 25
[1953]; Photo on Jorgovani/Lilacs 2015 DVD.

Cultivar name presumed registered 1953; name
established and accepted.

'Boulevard', *S. reticulata*
origin not known; S
https://plants.cannoredmonton.ca/11050017/
Plant/16746/Boulevard_Japanese_Tree_Lilac
Listed by Cannor Nurseries, Edmonton, Alberta, Canada

'Bountiful', *S.* ×*hyacinthiflora*
Clarke 1949; S V
Clarke, Cat. vol. 16, 7 [1949]; Wister, Lilacs for America,
25 [1953]; Photo on Jorgovani/Lilacs 2015 DVD.
Cultivar name presumed registered 1953; name
established and accepted.

'Boussingault', *S. vulgaris*
Lemoine 1896; D V
Lemoine, Cat. No. 134, 14 [1896]; McKelvey, The Lilac,
268 [1928]; Wister, Lilacs for America, 44 [1942], 25
[1953]; Photo on Jorgovani/Lilacs 2015 DVD.
Named for Jean Baptiste Boussingault, 1802-1887,
French agricultural chemist.
Cultivar name presumed registered 1953; name
established and accepted.

'Brenda Parker', *S. vulgaris*
Moro, F. 2010; S V/VI-I/VI (?)
{'Edward J. Gardner' × ?}
in litt. Moro to Vrugtman 8 August 2013.
Named for Ms Brenda Parker, Quincy, Massachusetts, USA.
Cultivar name not established.

'Brent Beauty', *S.*
Origin not known pre-2019; ?
In private collection (KA) in USA per email to Registrar
10-4-19.
Cultivar name not established.

'Brent Sirois', *S. vulgaris*
Berdeen 2005; D VI
Vrugtman, AABGA Bulletin 16(4):131 [1982]; Peterson,
Lilacs - Proceedings 16(1):17 [1987] - name only; King
& Coggeshall, Lilacs - Quart. Jour. 27(2):49-50 [1998] -
name only; Vrugtman, Encyclopedia, 312 [2008]
Named for Ken Berdeen's grandson.
Cultivar name established and accepted.

Bretschneider, *bretschneideri* - see 'Dr Bretschneider' and *S.
villosa* subsp. *villosa* Vahl.

'Bridal Memories', *S. vulgaris*
Peterson 1993; S I
{'Rochester' × 'Vestale'}
Briggs Nurseries, 1993/94 Liner List, 23; Vrugtman,
HortScience 29(9):972 [1994];
Photo on Jorgovani/Lilacs 2015 DVD.
Cultivar name registered 1993; name established and
accepted.

'Bridal Wreath', *S.* (affiliation not known)
origin not known; S I
Vrugtman, Lilacs - Quart. Jour. 32(4):149 [2003] - as S I.
Cultivar name not established.

'Bright Centennial', *S. vulgaris*
Robinson 1967; S VI
Robinson, Cat., 7 [1968]; Wister & Oppe, Arnoldia
31(3):122 [1971]; Photo on Jorgovani/Lilacs 2015 DVD.
Named for the Centennial of Canadian Confederation, 1967.
Cultivar name registered 1970; name established and
accepted.

'Brilliant', *S. vulgaris*
'Бриллиант'
Dyagilev 1986; S IV
Dyagilev, Lilacs - Quart. Jour. 22(1):20 [1993]; Pikaleva,
Lilacs - Quart. Jour. 23(4):84 [1994].
Cultivar name not established.

broadleaf lilac - see *S. oblata* Lindl.

Brodyaga - see 'Radzh Kapur'.

'Brougnartii', *S. vulgaris*
Oudin pre-1849; ? ?
Oudin, Cat.1849-1850, 11; McKelvey, The Lilac, 268
[1928] - confused name
Cultivar name not established.

Bruxelles - see **'Bruxelles 1935'**.

'Bruxelles 1935', *S. vulgaris*
Klettenberg 1935; S VII
syn. - 'Bruxelles'
Klettenberg, Cat. 25 [1935]; Wister, Lilacs for America,
25 [1953]
Named for L'Exposition Universelle et Internationale de
Bruxelles 1935, Belgium.
Cultivar name presumed registered 1953; name
established and accepted.

'Buffon', *S.* ×*hyacinthiflora*
Lemoine 1921; S V
Lemoine, Cat. No. 195, 18 [1921]; McKelvey, The Lilac,
197 [1928]; Wister, Lilacs for America, 44 [1942], 26
[1953]; Photo on Jorgovani/Lilacs 2015 DVD.
Named for Georges-Louis Leclerc, Comte de Buffon,
1707-1788, French naturalist and director of the Jardin
du Roi.
Awards: RHS Award of Merit 1961.
Cultivar name presumed registered 1953; name
established and accepted.

BUGALA'S No.4, –*S.*
Bugala ?; S VII
selection in cultivation for evaluation; Kornik
Arboretum, Poland; Photo on Jorgovani/Lilacs 2015
DVD.
Not a cultivar name.

Bugala's No.7, *S.*
Bugala ?; S VII
selection in cultivation for evaluation; Kornik Arboretum, Poland; Photo on Jorgovani/Lilacs 2015 DVD.
Not a cultivar name.

'Burgemeester Loggers', *S. vulgaris*
Eveleens Maarse 1960; S II
{'Maréchal Foch' × 'Ambassadeur'}
Wister, Arnoldia 23(4):80 [1963]; Photo on Jorgovani/Lilacs 2015 DVD.
Named for Gerrit Gesinus Loggers, 1900- x, mayor of Aalsmeer, The Netherlands, 1954-1965.
Awards: Certificate of Merit 1960 (KMTP).
Cultivar name registered 1963; name established and accepted.

'Burgemeester Voller', *S. vulgaris*
Eveleens Maarse 1948; S II
syn. - 'Burgomeester Voller'
{'Excellent' × 'Johan Mensing'}
Wister, Lilacs for America, 26 [1953]; Eveleens Maarse, Dendron 1(1):12 [1954]
Awards: Certificate of Merit 1948 (KMTP).
Named for Dirk Henri Pereboom Voller, 1911- x, mayor of Aalsmeer, The Netherlands, 1946-1954.
Cultivar name presumed registered 1953; name established and accepted.

Burgundy Queen® - see 'LECburg'

'Burvis', *S. vulgaris*
Kārkliņš pre-2005; D VII
Strautiņa & Kaufmane, Dobeles ceriņi, p. 92 [2011]; Photo on Jorgovani/Lilacs 2015 DVD.
Name: Latvian for magician.
Cultivar name established and accepted.

'Busia' – misspelling of 'Basia'

Byelorusskie Zori - see 'Belorusskie Zori'.

cadenza - see 'Hua Cai'.

Caerulea Superba - see '**Coerulea Superba**'.

'Caerulescens', *S. vulgaris* (?)
origin not known pre-1845; ? ?
Oudin, Cat. 1845-46, 6 - name only; McKelvey, The Lilac, 268 [1928] - a doubtful plant, possibly another name for *S. vulgaris*
Cultivar name not established.

'Caliban', *S.* (Villosae Group), *S.* ×*prestoniae*
Preston 1938; S V
{parentage not known}
Wister, Lilacs for America, 44, 64 [1942], 26, 48 [1953]; Davidson et al, Landscape Plants at the Morden Arboretum [1994] - received at Morden Research Station in 1938; Photo on Jorgovani/Lilacs 2015 DVD.
Named for A Savage and Deformed Slave in Shakespeare's *The Tempest*.
Cultivar name presumed registered 1953; name established and accepted.

'California Rose', *S.* ×*hyacinthiflora*
Sobeck pre-1966; S V
Wister, Arnoldia 26(3):13 [1966]; Photo on Jorgovani/Lilacs 2015 DVD.
Cultivar name registered 1966; name established and accepted.
Forcing cultivar in the Netherlands.
Nota bene: Since this cultivar appears to be of 'Lavender Lady' ancestry see also: Pringle, Lilacs - Quart. Jour. 24(4):97-99 [1995]; and Vrugtman, HortScience 31(3):328 [1996].

'Calphurnia', *S.* (Villosae Group), *S.* ×*prestoniae*
Preston pre-1942; S IV
syn. - 'Calphürnia', 'Calpurnia', Preston No. 20-15-18; corrected to 'Calphurnia' because of the derivation of the name.
Davis, Rep. Dom. Hort., Progress Report 1934-1948, 148 [1950]; Wister, Lilacs for America, 44, 64 [1942], 26, 48 [1953] - as 'Calpurnia'; Photo on Jorgovani/Lilacs 2015 DVD.
Named for the Wife of Cæsar in Shakespeare's *Julius Cæsar*.
Cultivar name presumed registered 1953; name established and accepted.

'Calvin C. Laney', *S. vulgaris*
Dunbar 1923; S VII
syn. - Dunbar no. 308
{'Monge' × ? }
Wister, Nat. Hort. Mag. 6(1):1-16 [1927]; McKelvey, The Lilac, 268-269 [1928]; Wister, Lilacs for America, 44 [1942], 26 [1953]; Photo on Jorgovani/Lilacs 2015 DVD.
Named for Calvin C. Laney, 1850-1941, civil engineer, superintendent of Highland Park, naturalist; served on Park Commission 1889-1926; Rochester, New York, USA.
Cultivar name presumed registered 1953; name established and accepted.

'Cameo's Jewel', *S. reticulata* subsp. *reticulata*
Moro, F. 1995; S I *
{'Ivory Silk' × ? }
Select Plus, Price List, no pagination [1995]
Named for Cameo Moro [1992 -], daughter of the originator.
Cultivar name established and accepted.

'Cameo's Passion', *S. vulgaris*
Moro, F. 2013; S V
{'Belle de Nancy' × ?}
Lilacs - Quart. Jour. 42(3):85 [2013]
Named for Cameo Moro [1992 -], daughter of the originator; "much like her character, passionate and delicate".
Cultivar name established and accepted.

Camille de Rohan - see **'Princesse Camille de Rohan'**.

'Campsie', *S.* ×*hyacinthiflora*
Wallace 1963; S IV
{parentage not known}
Beaverlodge Nursery, Cat. 1964, p.20; Photo on Jorgovani/Lilacs 2015 DVD.
Named for Campsie, Alberta, the location of the original Wallace family farm.
Cultivar name established and accepted.

Canada Gem, *S.* (Villosae Group), *S.* ×*prestoniae*
pre-1968; S II
Vrugtman, International Lilac Soc. Pipeline 2(9):2 [1976] and Newsletter 8(8):8 [1982]; still listed by the J. W. Jung Seed Co. of Randolph, Wisconsin, in 2006.
Cognomen for an unknown cultivar; probably 'Royalty' or less likely 'Isabella' per letter from John C. Jung to Freek Vrugtman. Personal inspection by Registrar shows no resemblance to 'Royalty', but perfect resemblance to 'Isabella'.

'Canadensis', *S. vulgaris*
origin not known pre-1922; D I
McKelvey, The Lilac, 269 (1928)
Cultivar name not established.

'Canadian Blue', *S.* (Villosae Group), *S.* ×*prestoniae*
origin not known pre-1999; S III
H.-J. Albrecht, Garten Zeitung 5/99 [1999], p.11 - ill. and name only
Cultivar name not established.

Canadian Tree lilac
J. W. Jung Seed Co. of Randolph, Wisconsin, [1972]; Lilac Land list, [n.d., pre-1974] - as S I; Vrugtman, ILS Pipeline 2(9):2 [1976] and ILS Newsletter 8(8):8 [1982];
Not a cultivar and not a clone.

'Candeur', *S. vulgaris*
Lemoine 1931; S I
Lemoine, Cat., 24 [1933]; Wister, Lilacs for America, 44 [1943], 26 [1953]; Photo on Jorgovani/Lilacs 2015 DVD.
Cultivar name presumed registered 1953; name established and accepted.

'C. & E. Wilson', *S. vulgaris*
Klager; S VII
Anon., ILS Newsletter 14(4):3-4 [1988]
Cultivar name not established.

'Candidissima', *S. vulgaris*
pre-1886; S I
Dammann, Cat. No. 34, 28 [1886-1887]; McKelvey, The Lilac, 269 [1928].
Cultivar name established and accepted.

'Capitaine Baltet', *S. vulgaris*
Lemoine 1919; S VI
syn. - 'Captain Baltet'
Lemoine, Cat. No. 193, 22 [1919]; McKelvey, The Lilac, 269 [1928]; Wister, Lilacs for America, 44 [1942], 26 [1953]; Photo on Jorgovani/Lilacs 2015 DVD.
Named for Lucien Baltet, x -1915, killed in World War I, son of Charles Baltet, nurseryman of Troyes, France.
Cultivar name presumed registered 1953; name established and accepted.

'Capitaine Baltet' (dwarf sport of); *S. vulgaris*
S VI
Melrose, Lilacs - Proceedings 7(1):21 [1978] - name only.
Cultivar name not established.

'Capitaine Perrault', *S. vulgaris*
Lemoine 1925; D V
Lemoine, Cat. No. 199, 19 [1925]; McKelvey, The Lilac, 269 [1928]; Wister, Lilacs for America, 44 [1942], 26 [1953]; Photo on Jorgovani/Lilacs 2015 DVD.
Cultivar name presumed registered 1953; name established and accepted.

Capitan Gastello - see 'Gastello'.

Cardinal - see **'Kardynał'**.

'Carl Cole', *S. vulgaris*
Peterson 2003; S I
{'Beth' × OP}
In private collection (KA) in USA per email to Registrar 10-4-19.
Named for the developer's father-in-law.
Cultivar name not established.

'Carley', *S. vulgaris*
Havemeyer pre-1942; S I
Wister, Lilacs for America, 44 [1942], 26 [1953]
Named for Carley H. Wagner a grand-niece of T. A. & K. Havemeyer.
Cultivar name presumed registered 1953; name established and accepted.

'Carlsruhensis', *S. vulgaris*
origin not known pre-1864; S IV
syn. - 'Karlsruhensis'
common - Flieder von Carlsruhe, lilas commun de Karlsruhe
Petzold & Kirchner, Arb. Muscav. 494 [1864]; McKelvey, The Lilac, 269-270 [1928]
Named for the city of Karlsruhe, Germany.
Cultivar name established and accepted.

'Carlton', *S.* (Villosae Group), *S.* ×*swegiflexa*
Preston 1948; S V
{*S. komarowii* subsp. *reflexa* × *S. tomentella* subsp. *sweginzowii*}
Wyman, Arnoldia 8(7):32 [1948]; Wister, Lilacs for America, 26 [1953]
Cultivar name presumed registered 1953; name established and accepted.

'Carmen', *S. vulgaris*
   Lemoine 1918; D V
   Lemoine, Cat. No. 192, 23 [1918-1919]; McKelvey, The Lilac, 270 [1928]; Wister, Lilacs for America, 44 [1942], 26 [1953]; Photo on Jorgovani/Lilacs 2015 DVD.
   Named for the heroine of Bizet's opera "Carmen".
   Cultivar name presumed registered 1953; name established and accepted.

'Carmine', *S. vulgaris*
   Klager 1928; S VI
   syn. - 'Mrs R. W. Mills'
   Wister, Lilacs for America, 44 [1942] - as S VII, syn. 'Mrs R. W. Mills'; Wister, Lilacs for America, 26 [1953] - syn. 'Mrs R. W. Mills'; Photo on Jorgovani/Lilacs 2015 DVD.
   Synonym name was for Hulda Klager's daughter, Elizabeth, wife of Roy Wilson Mills (aka Rody Mills).
   Cultivar name presumed registered 1953; name established and accepted.

'Carnea', *S.* ×*chinensis*
   origin not known pre-1831; S I/V
   syn. - *S.* ×*chinensis* f. *carnea* Audibert
   Common name - Carné de Chine
   Audibert, Cat. 1831-1832, 51 [1831]; McKelvey, The Lilac, 419 [1928] - confused name, probably not a single clone, if still in cultivation
   Cultivar name not established.

'Carola', *S.* (species affiliation not known)
   origin not known ? ?
   Moore, Lilacs, 153 [1903]
   Cultivar name not established.

Caroli - see **'Charles X'**
   Prince, Cat. 1844-1845, 70; McKelvey, The Lilac, 274 [1928]; Wister, Lilacs for America, 44 [1942], 26 [1953] - "but not identical in some collections"
   Cultivar name not established.

'Caroline Foley', *S. vulgaris*
   Rankin; S VI
   {parentage not known}
   Wister, Arnoldia 23(4):80 [1963]; Fiala, Lilacs, p. 207 [1988] - re. use as standard for grafting
   Cultivar name registered 1963; name established and accepted.

'Carolyn Bergen', *S. vulgaris*
   Berdeen 2005; D V
   King & Coggeshall, Lilacs - Quart. Jour. 27(2):49-50 [1998] - name only; Vrugtman, Encyclopedia, 312 [2008]
   Named for the wife of Berdeen's friend and neighbor.
   Cultivar name established and accepted.

'Carolyn Howland', *S. vulgaris*
   Berdeen 1976; S III&VI
   {'Firmament' × 'Capitaine Baltet'}
   Nieds, in litt. to Vrugtman [Apr.5/76]; Vrugtman, Lilacs - Proceedings 7(1):36 [1979]; Vrugtman, Bulletin - AABGA 13(4):108 [1979]
   Named for a friend of Ken Berdeen.
   Cultivar name registered 1977; name established and accepted.

'Carolyn Mae', *S. vulgaris*
   Sass, J. 1942; D IV-V
   syn. - 'Caroline Mae', 'Carolin Mae Nelson', 'Carolin Mae Nelson', 'Carol Mae Nelson', 'Carolyne Mae', 'Carolyn Mae Nelson'
   {perhaps 'Leon Gambetta' × ? }
   Wister, Lilacs for America, 44 [1942], 26 [1953]; Photo on Jorgovani/Lilacs 2015 DVD.
   Named for Mrs Carolyn Mae Nelson [no information].
   Cultivar name presumed registered 1953; name established and accepted.

CARPE DIEM® - see **'Evert de Gier'**.

'Case's Frilled Pink', *S. vulgaris*
   Case; D V
   Wister, Lilacs for America, 26 [1953]
   Cultivar name presumed registered 1953; name established and accepted.

Casimir Périer, Casimir Perrier - see **'Mme Casimir Périer'**.

'Cassandra', *S.* (Villosae Group), *S.* ×*prestoniae*
   Preston 1928; S V
   syn. - Preston No. 20-14-135
   {*S. villosa* subsp. *villosa* × *S. komarowii* subsp. *reflexa*}
   Macoun, Rep. Dom. Hort. 1928, 67 [1930] - name only; Macoun, Rep. Dom. Hort. 1930, 67 [1931]; Wister, Lilacs for America, 44, 64 [1942], 26, 48 [1953] - as discard
   Named for the Daughter of Priam in Shakespeare's *Troilus and Cressida*.
   Cultivar name presumed registered 1953; name established and accepted.

'Catawba Pink', *S. vulgaris*
   Utley 1980; D V
   {parentage not known; originated at Jackson & Perkins, Newark, NY}
   Fiala, Lilacs, 100, 217 & Pl.20 [1988]; Lilacs - Proceedings 17(1): front cover ill. [1988]; Photo on Jorgovani/Lilacs 2015 DVD.
   Cultivar name established and accepted.

'Catherine', *S. vulgaris*
   Orchard, between 1912 & 1940s; ? ?
   Named for the daughter of the originator.
   No report of being in cultivation
   http://www.mhs.mb.ca/docs/people/orchard_h.shtml
   http://www.manitobaaghalloffame.com/ahofmember/orchard-harold/

Catherine Bruchet - see **'Mme Catherine Bruchet'**.

'Catinat', *S.* ×*hyacinthiflora*
Lemoine 1922; S V
syn. - praecox 'Catinat'
Lemoine, Cat. No. 196, 19 [1922]; McKelvey, The Lilac, 197 [1928]; Späth, Späth Buch, 302 [1930]; Wister, Lilacs for America, 45 [1942], 26 [1953]; Photo on Jorgovani/Lilacs 2015 DVD.
Named for Nicholas Catinat, 1637-1712, French soldier, marshal of France.
Cultivar name presumed registered 1953; name established and accepted.

'Catskill', *S. vulgaris*
Lape; S VII
{'Kapriz' × ? }
Vrugtman, AABGA Bull. 17(3):67 [1984]
Named for the Catskill region in south-east New York State, USA.
Cultivar name registered 1982;
Cultivar not reported in cultivation.

'Cavour', *S. vulgaris*
Lemoine 1910; S II
Lemoine, Cat. No. 176, 7 [1910]; McKelvey, The Lilac, 270-271 [1928]; Wister, Lilacs for America, 45 [1942], 26 [1953]; Photo on Jorgovani/Lilacs 2015 DVD.
Named for Count Camillo Benso di Cavour, 1810-1861, Italian statesman and restorer of Italian nationality.
Cultivar name presumed registered 1953; name established and accepted.

'C. B. van Nes', *S. vulgaris*
Van Nes 1901; S VII
syn. - 'C. B. van Nees', 'Mrs E. Van Nes', 'Mrs van Nes'
André, Rev. Hort. 102 [1904]; McKelvey, The Lilac, 271 [1928]; Wister, Lilacs for America, 37, 45 [1942] - as S II; Wister, Lilacs for America, 26 [1953].; Tromp, Boskoops Koninklijke (1861-1986), 195 [1986]
Named for Cornelius B. van Nes, x -1922, nurseryman, rhododendron breeder and founder of the nursery C. B. van Nes en Zn, Boskoop, The Netherlands.
Cultivar name presumed registered 1953; name established and accepted.

'Celestial Blue', *S. vulgaris*
Klager 1930; S III
Wister, Lilacs for America, 45 [1942], 26 [1953]; ILS Newsletter 14(4):3-4 [1988]
Cultivar name presumed registered 1953; name established and accepted.

'Celia', *S.* (Villosae Group), *S.* ×*prestoniae*
Preston 1928; S IV
syn. - Preston No. 20-14-176
{*S. villosa* subsp. *villosa* × *S. komarowii* subsp. *reflexa*}
Macoun, Rep. Dom. Hort. 1928, 67 [1930] - name only; Davis, Rep. Dom. Hort. 1934-1948, 147-148 [1950], Progress Report 1934-1948, 147-148 [1950]; Wister, Lilacs for America, 45, 64 [1942], 26, 48 [1953];
Registered with the State Commission of the Russian Federation for Testing and Protection of Selection Achievements, No. 9810215, 2001; Photo on Jorgovani/Lilacs 2015 DVD.
Named for the Daughter of Frederick in Shakespeare's *As You Like It*.
Cultivar name presumed registered 1953; name established and accepted.

'Centenaire de la Linneenne', *S. vulgaris*
Klettenberg 1936; S IV
Wister, Lilacs for America, 26 [1953]
Cultivar name presumed registered 1953; name established and accepted.

Centennial - see '**Sesquicentennial**'.

'Ceriņu Laiks', *S.*
Upītis 1970; S II
In cultivation at Dobele, Latvia, in litt. Natalia Savenko to Mark DeBard, September 2018.

Chad 1417, *S. emodi*
origin not known pre-1997; ? ?
in cultivation in NCCPG Collection, United Kingdom
perhaps a breeder's code; may not be a clone.

Chadwick - see '**Doctor Chadwick**'.

'Chamaethyrsus', *S. vulgaris*
Machet & Josem 1894; S VII
{dwarf mutant, probably of *S. vulgaris* var. *purpurea* Weston}
André, Rev. Hort. 370 [1894]; McKelvey, The Lilac, 271-272 [1928].
Cultivar name established and accepted.

'Champlain', *S. vulgaris*
Lemoine 1930; D II
Lemoine, Cat. No. 204 [1930]; Wister, Lilacs for America, 45 [1942], 26 [1953]; Photo on Jorgovani/Lilacs 2015 DVD.
Named for Samuel de Champlain, 1567-1635, French explorer, founder of Québec, Canada.
Cultivar name presumed registered 1953; name established and accepted.

'Chang Tong Bai', *S. oblata*
Zang & Fan 1984; S I
syn. - 'Changtongbai'
Zang & Fan, Pl. Introd. Acclimatization 3:117-121 [1983] - in Chinese; Vrugtman, HortScience 33(4):588-589 [1998]; Anon., Beijing Bot. Garden 2006:24 - as Changtongbai; Photo on Jorgovani/Lilacs 2015 DVD.
Cultivar name registered 1997; name established and accepted.

'Chantilly Lace', *S. reticulata* subsp. *reticulata*
Herrmann ca 1990; S I *
{mutation of *S. reticulata* subsp. *reticulata*}
Vrugtman, HortScience 23(3):485 [1988] & 24(3):436

[1989]; Photo on Jorgovani/Lilacs 2015 DVD.
Cultivar name registered 1986; name established and accepted.

'Charisma', S. (Villosae Group), S. ×prestoniae
Boughen pre-2002; S VII
{reportedly propagated from a witches'-broom on 'Royalty' caused by phytoplasmas}
originally listed as a S. ×prestoniae cultivar; see 'Royalty' for nomenclature.
Cultivar name not established.
Nota bene: The presence of phytoplasma in plants of 'Charisma' has been confirmed (in litt. D. Thompson to F. Vrugtman, December 8, 2003). Vrugtman 2005, Lilacs - Quart. Jour. 34(4):106. Willis, Landscape Trades, Spring 2005 - Special Edition, p. 35.
See also: Green, M.J., E.L. Dally, and R.E. Davis. 2015. The Lilac Cultivar Syringa 'Charisma' is a New Host for '*Candidatus* Phytoplasma pruni', the Group 16SrIII, Subgroup A, Phytoplasma. Plant Disease 99(6):886.
And: https://www.ars.usda.gov/research/publications/publication/?seqNo115=312114.

'Charivnist', S.
Tereshchenko pre 2007; S IV
{'Lavoisier' × ?}
Tereshchenko S. "A Souvenir from Donetsk", article in the magazine "Vestnik Tsvetovoda" №10 (78), 2007 (in Russian).
Name: Ukrainian for enchantment
Cultivar name established and accepted.

'**Charlemagne**', S. vulgaris
Brahy-Ekenholm pre-1854; S VII
syn. - 'Charlemberg' (?), 'Charlembourg' (?), 'Charlemburg' (?), 'Charlesmagne', common name: Lilas Charlemagne
C.F.A. Morren, Belg. Hort. 4:69 [1854]; McKelvey, The Lilac, 272-273 [1928]; Wister, Lilacs for America, 45 [1942], 26 [1953]; Photo on Jorgovani/Lilacs 2015 DVD.
Named for Charlemagne (Carolus magnus, Charles the Great), 747-814, king of the Franks and Christian emperor of the West.
Cultivar name presumed registered 1953; name established and accepted.

'Charlemberg', S. vulgaris
origin not known pre-1867; S VII & V
'Charlembourg', 'Charlemburg' - see also 'Charlemagne'
Ellwanger & Barry, Cat. No. 2, 43 [1867]; McKelvey, The Lilac, 272-273 [1928]

'**Charles Baltet**', S. vulgaris
Lemoine 1893; D IV
Lemoine, Cat. No. 125, 9 [1983]; McKelvey, The Lilac, 273 [1928]; Wister, Lilacs for America, 45 [1942], 26 [1953]; Photo on Jorgovani/Lilacs 2015 DVD.
Named for Charles Appolinaire Baltet, 1830-1908, horticulturist and nurseryman of Troyes, France.

Cultivar name presumed registered 1953; name established and accepted.

Charles Dix - see '**Charles X**'.

'**Charles Hepburn**', S. villosa subsp. *villosa*
origin not known pre-1934; S V
Bobbink & Atkins, price list, 1934-1935, p.6.; Wister, Lilacs for America, 45, 60 [1942], 26 [1953] - name only; Wyman, Arnoldia 8(7):34 [1948] - as S. villosa × ?
Cultivar name presumed registered 1953; name established and accepted.

'Charles Holetich', S. vulgaris
Margaretten; S IV
{'Mme Lemoine' × ?}
reported in cultivation at Royal Botanical Gardens, Ontario, Canada
Named for Charles Dragutin Holetich, Arboriculturist, 1963-1995, Royal Botanical Gardens, Hamilton, Canada.
Cultivar name not established.

'**Charles Joly**', S. vulgaris
Lemoine 1896; D VII
syn. - 'Chas Joly'
Lemoine, Cat. No. 134, 9 [1896]; Kache, Gartenschönheit 5:82 [1924]; McKelvey, The Lilac, 273 [1928]; Wister, Lilacs for America, 45 [1942] - as D VI; Wister, Lilacs for America, 26 [1953]; Photo on Jorgovani/Lilacs 2015 DVD.
Named for Victor Charles Joly, 1818-1902, French physician, hotelier, and writer on horticultural subjects.
Awards: RHS Award of Garden Merit 1993.
Cultivar name presumed registered 1953; name established and accepted.

'Charles Joy', S. vulgaris
origin not known ? ?
Melrose, Lilacs - Proceedings 7(1):21 [1978] - name only (perhaps 'Charles Joly').
Cultivar name not established.

'**Charles Lindbergh**', S. vulgaris
Fenicchia 1988; S II-III
syn. - 'Charles Lindberg', RF 2
{'Rochester' × 'Madame Charles Souchet'}
Hoepfl & Rogers, Lilac Newsletter 14(7):6 [1988]; Vrugtman, HortScience 24(3):435 [1989], 31(3):328 [1996]; K. Millham, Lilacs - Quart. Jour. 42(2):60 [2013]; Photo on Jorgovani/Lilacs 2015 DVD.
Named for Charles Augustus Lindbergh, 1902-1974, American aviator.
Cultivar name registered 1988; name established and accepted.

Charlesmagne - see '**Charlemagne**'.

'**Charles Nordine**', S. ×hyacinthiflora
Skinner pre-1953; S III
syn. - 'Charles Nordline'
Wister, Lilacs for America, 26 [1953]; Skinner, Hort.

Horizons, 109 [1966]; Photo on Jorgovani/Lilacs 2015 DVD.
Cultivar name presumed registered 1953; name established and accepted.

'Charles Sargent', *S. vulgaris*
Lemoine 1905; D III
Lemoine, Cat. No. 161, 8 [1905]; Kache, Gartenschönheit 5:82 [1924]; McKelvey, The Lilac, 273-274 [1928]; Wister, Lilacs for America, 45 [1942], 26 [1953]; Photo on Jorgovani/Lilacs 2015 DVD.
Named for Charles Sprague Sargent, 1841-1927, American botanist and author, founder of the Arnold Arboretum of Harvard University, Jamaica Plain, Massachusetts, USA.
Cultivar name presumed registered 1953; name established and accepted.

Charles the Tenth - see **'Charles X'**.

'Charles X', *S. vulgaris*
origin not known pre-1830; S VI
syn. - 'Charles Dix', 'Charles the Tenth', 'Charlex X', 'Rubra' (*S. vulgaris*), 'Rubra Major', 'Caroli' (?), 'Karl X', etc.
Audibert, Cat. 1831-1832; McKelvey, The Lilac, 274-276 [1928] - descriptions vary; Wister, Lilacs for America, 44, 45 [1942], 26 [1953]; Photo on Jorgovani/Lilacs 2015 DVD.
Named for Charles X, 1757-1836, king of France and of Navarre, 1824-1830.
Cultivar name presumed registered 1953; name established and accepted.
Nota bene: Plants in cultivation show variations that are not true-to-name.
Formerly a forcing cultivar in the Netherlands.

'Charlet', *S. vulgaris*
origin not known pre-1900; S ?
syn. - 'Lina Charlet'
Baltet, Cat. 28 [1900]; Wister, Nat. Hort. Mag. 6(1):1-16 [1927]; McKelvey, The Lilac, 276 [1928] - doubtful plant, possibly error for 'Charles X'; Wister, Lilacs for America, 26 [1953]
Cultivar name not established.

'Charlotte Morgan', *S. vulgaris*
Seabury ca 1928; D VI
Stand. Pl. Names, 614 [1942] - perhaps identical to 'Mrs Morgan'; Wister, Lilacs for America, 45 [1942] - as D VII; Wister, Lilacs for America, 26 [1953]; Photo on Jorgovani/Lilacs 2015 DVD.
Cultivar name presumed registered 1953; name established and accepted.

'Charm', *S. vulgaris*
Havemeyer pre-1941; S V
Wister, Lilacs for America, 45 [1942], 26 [1953]; Kammerer, Morton Arb. Bull. Pop. Info. 36(6):27-29 [1961]; Eickhorst, ILS Lilac Newsletter 4(1):4-5 [1978]; Photo on Jorgovani/Lilacs 2015 DVD.
Nota bene: Some plants sold under this name are D V and not true-to-name.
Cultivar name presumed registered 1953; name established and accepted.

'Charmant', *S. vulgaris*
origin not known pre-1975; D I
Wayside Gardens, Cat. 34 [1975]; Wayside Gardens purchased this cultivar from Gulf Stream Nursery (in litt. J. E. Elsley to F. Vrugtman, May 3, 1984); Photo on Jorgovani/Lilacs 2015 DVD.
Cultivar name established and accepted.

Charmhin - see **'Charmian'**.

'Charmian', *S.* (Villosae Group), *S.* ×*prestoniae*
Preston 1928; S IV
syn. - 'Charmaine', 'Charmhin', Preston No. 20-14-176
{*S. villosa* subsp. *villosa* × *S. komarowii* subsp. *reflexa*}
Macoun, Rep. Dom. Hort. 1928, 55 [1930]; Wister, Lilacs for America, 45, 64 [1942], 26, 48 [1953]; Photo on Jorgovani/Lilacs 2015 DVD.
Named for the Attendant on Cleopatra in Shakespeare's *Antony and Cleopatra*.
Cultivar name presumed registered 1953; name established and accepted.

'Charming Chihorin', *S. pubescens* subsp. *microphylla*
Ihara 2004; S VII
syn. - seedling no. 20040520002#1.
{*S. pubescens* subsp. *microphylla* 'Superba' × *S. pub.* subsp. *micr.* 'Superba'}
(Vrugtman, Cultivated Plant Diversity … 2017)
Named for Chiho Ihara [2006 -], first daughter of Rimi and Hideo Ihara.
Cultivar name registered 2017; name established and accepted.

'Charoit', *S. vulgaris*
'Чароит'
Aladin, S., Aladina, O., Polyakova, T., and Aladina, A. 2016; D IV
{'Katherine Havemeyer' × OP}
(Международная научная конференция "Syringa L.: коллекции, выращивание, использование")
"International Scientific Conference "Syringa L.: collections, cultivation, using" / Collection of Scientific Articles of Botanical Institute named after V.L. Komarov, Botanical Garden of Peter the Great BIN RAS. - St. Petersburg. -2020.- pp.3-7 (in Russian); Photo exhibition of all varieties of the creative breeding group "Russian Lilac" at the Festival "Lilac February", St. Petersburg, Botanical Garden of Peter the Great BIN RAS, February 22-24, 2020.
This cultivar resembles the miracle of Siberia, a unique and rare gem of Charoite.
Cultivar name established and accepted.

'Cheerbenbough', *S. vulgaris*
origin not known ? ?

B. O. Case & Son, Cat. [ca 1937]; Upton Scrapbook 1:35 [1980]
Cultivar name not established; doubtful name.

'Cheerbenburg', *S. vulgaris*
Origin not known; S IV
doubtful name, perhaps '**Charlemagne**'?
Stand. Pl. Names, 614 [1942] - name only; Wister, Lilacs for America, 26 [1953]
Cultivar name not established.

'Chenbolt', *S. vulgaris*
origin not known pre-1931; D IV
syn. - 'Chenbault'
B. O. Case & Son, Cat. [ca 1937]; Stand. Pl. Names, 614 [1942] - doubtful name; Wister, Lilacs for America, 36 & 45 [1942] - doubtful name; Upton Scrapbook 1:35 [1980]
Cultivar name not established; not reported in cultivation in 1953.

Chengtu lilac - see *S. tomentella* subsp. *sweginzowii* Koehne & Lingelsh.

'Cheyenne', *S. oblata* subsp. *dilatata*
Dorsett & Morse, Hildreth 1971; S III
syn. - Cheyenne Stn. Sel. 52-6, 'Dr Hildreth', 'Hildreth', Wyoming No. 6
{*S. oblata* subsp. *dilatata* seedling}
USDA Plant Inventory No. 105, pp.62-63, PI 90671 [Oct. 1932] - as *S. oblata* Lindl., grown from seed coll. by Dorsett & Morse (No. 6513) in Manchuria; in litt. Howard to Niedz Jan. 13, 1970, and Howard to Wister Jun. 12, 1970 - as Wyoming No. 6 (Sel. 52-6); Anon., American Nurseryman 134(3):74 [1971]; Anon., W. Canad. Soc. Hort. Proc. 1972, p. 110; Vrugtman, Lilac Newsletter 6(4):11-13 [1980]; http://www.botanic.org/Plants_of_the_Arboretum.asp [May 25, 2004]; Photo on Jorgovani/Lilacs 2015 DVD.
Named for the United States Department of Agriculture Horticultural Field Station at Cheyenne, Wyoming.
Cultivar name established and accepted.

'Chicago Tower' - see '**Morton**'.

'Chiffon', *S.* ×*hyacinthiflora*
Sobeck; S IV
Wister, Arnoldia 26(3):13 [1966]; Photo on Jorgovani/Lilacs 2015 DVD.
Cultivar name registered 1966; name established and accepted.
Nota bene: Since this cultivar appears to be of 'Lavender Lady' ancestry see also: Pringle, Lilacs - Quart. Jour. 24(4):97-99 [1995]; and Vrugtman, HortScience 31(3):328 [1996].

'China Gold', *S. reticulata*
Fiala; S I *
{*S. reticulata* subsp. *reticulata* × ? ; seed colchicine treated}
Vrugtman, HortScience 26(5):476 [1991]
Cultivar name registered 1990; name established and accepted.

China Snow™ - see '**Morton**'.
×*chinensis alba* Rehder - 'Correlata'.
×*chinensis* nothof. *bicolor* (Lemoine) Jäger - see 'Bicolor'.
×*chinensis* f. *carnea* Audibert - see 'Carnea'.
×*chinensis* f. *duplex* (Lemoine) Rehder - see '**Duplex**'.
×*chinensis* f. *fructiferum* (Gorb) – see 'Fructiforum'
×*chinensis* f. *metensis* Simon-Louis - see '**Metensis**'.
×*chinensis* f. *saugeana* (Loudon) Hort. - see '**Saugeana**'.

'Chinese Magic', *S.*
Fiala 1978; S I
syn. - Seedling 9415B
{*S. pekinensis* × *S. reticulata* subsp. *amurensis*; corrected parentage in litt. Fiala to Vrugtman, May 1989}
Anon., ILS seed exchange list - as Seedling 9415B; Clark, Lilacs - Proceedings 15(1):6 [1986]; Fiala, Lilacs, 93, 224, Pl. 61 [1988] - conflicting parentage and introduction date information
Cultivar name established and accepted.

Chinese Rouen hybrid lilac - see *S.* ×*chinensis* Schmidt ex Willd.

'Chinook', *S.* (Villosae Group) ×*prestoniae*
Moro unknown date; S I
Seen September 2016 at www.spi.8m.com/select_plus_introductions.html
Cultivar name not established

'Chistaya Voda', *S. vulgaris*
'Чистая вода'
Aladin, S., Aladina, O., Aladina, A., and Polyakova, T. 2017; D IV-III
{elite form 12-94 × elite form 11-301}
Садовник (Gardener) magazine 04 (140)/2017 :18-25; Вестник АППМ (Catalog in Vestnik APPM (Planting material association) magazine) 1/2018: 59-72 (in Russian).
Name: Russian for pure water.
Cultivar name established and accepted

'Chmurka', *S. vulgaris*
Karpow-Lipski ca 1971; S VI
{'Maréchal Foch' × ? }
syn - 'Zhmurka'
Anon., Lista odmian roślin ozdobnych 1971, 17 - name only; Lista .. 1973, p.25; Lista . . . 1980, 150; Anon., Lilak Pospolity - COBO Informator 8/78 1976; Pikaleva, Lilacs - Quart. Jour. 23(4):89 [1994] - erroneously as 'Zhmurka'
Name: Polish for little cloud.
Varietal denomination registered COBORU 1971; Cultivar name established and accepted; statutory registration.

'Chokan Valikhanov', *S. vulgaris*
'Чокан Валиханов'
Mel'nik, Rubanik & Dyagilev pre-1994 D IV
Pikaleva, Lilacs - Quart. Jour. 23(4):84.
(Международная научная конференция "Syringa

L.: коллекции, выращивание, использование") "International Scientific Conference "Syringa L.: collections, cultivation, using" / Collection of Scientific Articles of Botanical Institute named after V.L. Komarov, Botanical Garden of Peter the Great BIN RAS. - St. Petersburg. -2020.- pp.23-27 (in Russian).
Named for Chokan Valikhanov (real name Muhammed-Hanafiyah), 1835-1865, Kazakh scholar, ethnographer and historian.
Cultivar name established and accepted.

'Chrestensens', S. vulgaris
Origin not known; D IV-VI
Flieder-Sortiment, Oberlausitzer Baum- und Rosenschulen GmbH, Cat. [n.d., ca 1992]
Cultivar name not established.

'Chris', S. vulgaris
Berdeen 1963; S VII
Wister, Arnoldia 23(4):80 [1963]; Alexander Sr, Rare Lilacs, 1 [n.d., received Mar. 17, 1969 - plants not true to name (in litt. J. H. Alexander Sr to Vrugtman, Dec. 4, 1971); Photo on Jorgovani/Lilacs 2015 DVD.
Named for Ken Berdeen's Norwegian friend of Kennebunk, Maine.
Cultivar name registered 1963; name established and accepted.
Nota bene: Plants grown under this name may not be true to name.

'Christa Vu', S. vulgaris
origin not known ? VI-II
Kilcoyne, Lilacs - Quart. Jour. 32(3): 112 [2003] - lavender to violet bicolor.
Cultivar name not established.

'Christine's Butterfly Dance', S. ×hyacinthiflora
Moro, F. 2013; ? ?
{'Silver King' × ? }
In lit. Moro to Vrugtman July 13, 2013. Also seen at www.spi.8m.com/select_plus_introductions.html Sept 2016.
Named for Christine Beaudet, a friend of the Moro family.
Cultivar name not established.

'Christophe Colomb', S. vulgaris
Lemoine 1905; S IV
syn. - 'Christoph Colomb', 'Christophe Colombe', 'Christophe Columb'
common name: Christopher Columbus
Lemoine, Cat. No. 161, 30 [1905]; Stand. Pl. Names, 485 [1923] - as Christopher Columbus; Kache, Gartenschönheit 5:82 [1924]; McKelvey, The Lilac, 276 [1928]; Wister, Lilacs for America, 45 [1942], 26 [1953]; Photo on Jorgovani/Lilacs 2015 DVD.
Named for Christophe Colomb, 1452-1506, the Portuguese circum-navigator.
Cultivar name presumed registered 1953; name established and accepted.

Christopher Columbus - see **'Christophe Colomb'**.

'Chrystle', S. vulgaris
Klager; S I
syn. - 'Crystal'
Anon., ILS Newsletter 14(4):3-4 [1988]; Anon., Lilacs - Quart. Jour. 22(2):32 [1993] - name only, as 'Crystal'
Cultivar name not established.

'Chun Ge', S. vulgaris
Zang & Fan 1984; D V-VII
syn. - 'Chunge'
Zang & Fan, Pl. Introd. Acclimatization 3:117-121 [1983] - in Chinese; Vrugtman, HortScience 33(4):588-589 [1998] - as 'Chunge'
Cultivar name registered 1997; name established and accepted.

'Churchill', S. ×hyacinthiflora
Skinner 1945; S V
Woody Plant Register, AAN, No. 58 [1949]; Wister, Lilacs for America, 26 [1953]; Skinner, Hort. Horizons, 49 & 109 [1966]; Photo on Jorgovani/Lilacs 2015 DVD.
Named for Sir Winston Leonard Spencer Churchill, 1874-1965, British statesman.
Cultivar name presumed registered 1953; name established and accepted.

'Cinderella', S. pubescens subsp. *patula*
Moro, F. 1998; S V
<http://www.spi.8m.com/prestoncat.html> [seen Feb. 27, 2007]; Photo on Jorgovani/Lilacs 2015 DVD.
Named for Cinderella, principal character in *The Little Glass Slipper*, a classic folk tale.
Cultivar name established and accepted.

'Citriflora', S. vulgaris
origin not known ca 1880; S I
Baudriller, Cat. No. 43, 141 [1880]; McKelvey, The Lilac, 277 [1928]
Cultivar name not established.

'City of Chehalis', S. vulgaris
Klager; S V
Wister, Lilacs for America, 45 [1942], 26 [1953]; Eickhorst et al, Woody Pl. Morton Arb., 210 [1972]; Dvorak, Lilac Study 21 (1N), 23 (C-8) (line drawings) [1978]
Named for the City of Chehalis, Washington State, USA.
Cultivar name presumed registered in 1953; name established and accepted.

'City of Gresham', S. vulgaris
Klager 1915; S VII
syn. - 'Klager Dark Purple', 'Klager's Dark Purple'
Wister, Lilacs for America, 45 [1942], 27, 33 [1953]; ILS Newsletter 14(4):3-4 [1988]; Photo on Jorgovani/Lilacs 2015 DVD.
Named for the City of Gresham, Oregon, USA.
Cultivar name presumed registered 1953; name established and accepted.

'City of Hillsboro', *S. vulgaris*
original name not known; S I
Wister, Lilacs for America, 27 [1953] - "old variety renamed by Mrs Klager"
Named for the City of Hillsboro, Oregon, USA.
Cultivar name not established.

'City of Kalama', *S. vulgaris*
Klager 1915; S VII
syn. - 'Kalama'
Wister, Lilacs for America, 45 [1942], 27 [1953]; Anon., ILS Newsletter 14(4):3-4 [1988]; Photo on Jorgovani/Lilacs 2015 DVD.
Named for the City of Kalama, Washington State, USA.
Cultivar name presumed registered 1953; name established and accepted.

'City of Kelso', *S. vulgaris*
Klager; D V
Stand. Pl. Names, 615 [1942] - syn. 'Abundant Bloomer' is in error; Wister, Lilacs for America, 43, 45 [1942], 24, 27 [1953] - syn. 'Abundant Bloomer' is in error
Named for the City of Kelso, Washington State, USA.
Cultivar name presumed registered 1953; name established and accepted.

'City of Lancaster', *S. vulgaris*
Margaretten; S IV & I
{'Mme Lemoine' × ?}
Named for the City of Lancaster, California, USA.
Not reported in cultivation
Cultivar name not established.

'City of Longview', *S. vulgaris*
Klager 1930; D V
syn. - 'Longview'
Cooley, Cat., 7 [1930]; Wister, Lilacs for America, 45 [1942], 27 [1953]; Photo on Jorgovani/Lilacs 2015 DVD.
Named for the City of Longview, Washington State, USA.
Cultivar name presumed registered 1953; name established and accepted.

'City of Olympia', *S. vulgaris*
Klager 1934; S IV
syn. - 'Olympia'
Wister, Lilacs for America, 45 [1942], 27 [1953]
Named for the City of Olympia, Washington State, USA.
Cultivar name presumed registered 1953; name established and accepted.

'City of Palmdale', *S. vulgaris*
Margaretten; S III
{'Mme Lemoine' × ?}
Not reported in cultivation
Named for the City of Palmdale, California, USA.
Cultivar name not established.

'City of Toronto', *S. reticulata* subsp. *reticulata*
Kircher ca. 2000; S I
syn. - *S. vulgaris* 'City of Toronto'
{seedling selection}
Kircher Baumschulen, Cat. 2002/2003, p. 2 - as cream-colored; KIRCHER COLLECTION® p. 20, ill., undated publication by Baumschule Rosskamp GmbH & Co. KG.
Named for the City of Toronto, Ontario, Canada.
Cultivar name established and accepted.

'City of Vancouver', *S. vulgaris*
Klager 1930; S VII
Wister, Lilacs for America, 45 [1942], 27 [1953]
Named for the City of Vancouver, Washington State, USA.
Cultivar name presumed registered in 1953;
Cultivar not reported in cultivation.

City of Woodland - see **'Woodland'**.

'C. J. Gardner', *S. vulgaris*
Gardner; ? ?
syn. - Gardner No. 442
Cultivar name not established.

'Clara', *S. vulgaris*
Klager 1928; S V
Cooley, Cat. 1928-1929, 7 [1928]; McKelvey, The Lilac, 559 [1928]; Wister, Lilacs for America, 45 [1942], 27 [1953] - as S VI; Photo on Jorgovani/Lilacs 2015 DVD.
Cultivar name presumed registered 1953; name established and accepted.

'Clara Cochet', *S. vulgaris*
Cochet 1855; S V
{seedling of unknown parentage}
Petit-Coq, Jour. des Roses, 176 [1885]; McKelvey, The Lilac, 277 [1928]; Wister, Lilacs for America, 45 [1942], 27 [1953]; Photo on Jorgovani/Lilacs 2015 DVD.
Named for Clara Cochet, daughter of the originator.
Cultivar name presumed registered 1953; name established and accepted.

Clara No. 2 or Clara # 2 - see **'Dresden China'**.

'Clara Wilke', *S. vulgaris*
Klager; S V-VI
Anon., ILS Newsletter 4(4):3-4 [1988]
Cultivar name not established.

'Clarence D. Van Zandt', *S. vulgaris*
Dunbar 1923; S VII
syn. - Dunbar no. 236
{'Aline Mocqueris' × ?}
McKelvey, The Lilac, 277-278 [1928]; Wister, Lilacs for America, 45 [1942], 27 [1953]; Photo on Jorgovani/Lilacs 2015 DVD.
Named for Clarence D. Van Zandt, mayor, 1922-1926, of Rochester, New York, USA.
Cultivar name presumed registered 1953; name established and accepted.

'Clarinet', *S.* (Villosae Group), *S.* ×*prestoniae*
  origin not known ? ?
  Cultivar name not established.

Clarke No. C112, *S. vulgaris*
  Clarke; S III
  Wister, Lilacs for America, 45 [1942]
  Breeder's designation, not a cultivar name; not reported as being in cultivation in 1953.

Clarke No. 114, *S. vulgaris*
  Clarke; S VII
  Wister, Lilacs for America, 45 [1942]
  Not a cultivar name, but breeder's designation or cognomen; not reported as being in cultivation in 1953.

Clarke No. 117, *S. vulgaris*
  Clarke; S III
  Wister, Lilacs for America, 45 [1942]
  Not a cultivar name, but breeder's designation or cognomen; not reported as being in cultivation in 1953.

Clarke No. 119, *S. vulgaris*
  Clarke; S III
  Wister, Lilacs for America, 45 [1942]
  Not a cultivar name, but breeder's designation or cognomen; not reported as being in cultivation in 1953.

'Clarke's Double White', *S. vulgaris*
  Clarke, J. 1968; D I
  J. Clarke Nursery Co., Wholesale Price List 1968-1969, 8; Photo on Jorgovani/Lilacs 2015 DVD.
  Cultivar name established and accepted.

'Clarke's Giant', *S.* ×*hyacinthiflora*
  Clarke 1948; S III
  syn. - 'Clark's Giant'
  {unnamed double seedling × ? }
  Clarke, US Plant Patent No. 754 [Aug. 26, 1947] - as *S. vulgaris*; Clarke, Cat. vol. 15, 8 [1948]; Woody Plant Register, AAN, No. 65 [1949]; Wister, Lilacs for America, 27 [1953]; Photo on Jorgovani/Lilacs 2015 DVD.
  Awards: RHS Award of Merit 1958.
  Cultivar name presumed registered 1953; name established and accepted.

'Claude Bernard', *S.* ×*hyacinthiflora*
  Lemoine 1915; D V
  syn. - 'Claud Bernard'
  Lemoine, Cat. No. 189, 23 [1915]; McKelvey, The Lilac, 197 [1928]; Wister, Lilacs for America, 45 [1942], 27 [1953]; Photo on Jorgovani/Lilacs 2015 DVD.
  Named for Claude Bernard, 1813-1878, French physiologist, who studied the effects of anesthetics on plants and animals (ether and chloroform were later used in breaKing flower-bud dormancy when forcing lilacs).
  Cultivar name presumed registered 1953; name established and accepted.

'Claude de Lorrain', *S. vulgaris*
  Lemoine 1889; S VII & V
  syn. - 'Claude le Lorrain', 'Claude Lorraine'
  Lemoine, Cat. No. 113, 9 [1889]; McKelvey, The Lilac, 278 [1928]; Wister, Lilacs for America, 45 [1942], 27 [1953] - as S V
  Named for Claude de Lorrain, first Duke of Guise, 1527, grandfather of Marie Stuart, queen of Scots, great grandfather of James II of England.
  Cultivar name presumed registered 1953; name established and accepted.

'Claudia Berdeen', *S. vulgaris*
  Berdeen; ? ?
  King & Coggeshall, Lilacs - Quart. Jour. 27(2):49-50 [1998] - name only
  Named for Ken Berdeen's daughter-in-law.
  Cultivar name not established.

'Cleaves', *S. pekinensis*
  Cleaves 2000; S I
  syn. - 'Cleaves Select' (rejected name), 'Celeve'
  Arbor Village Farm Nursery, Cat. 2000/2001 p.51 [2000]; Hirshfeld http://www.plantations.cornell.edu/publications/IthacaJournalArticles/Little_Known_Lilacs.cfm - as 'Celeve' [June 22, 2005]
  Cleaves verbal conversation 3/19/19 reports this selection taken from *S. pekinensis* 'Pendula' in Camden, Maine, identified as such by Douglas Johnson, arborist with TreeKeepers, so that it is not a new cultivar as originally believed.
  Not a cultivar name.

'Cleopatra', *S.* (Villosae Group), *S.* ×*prestoniae*
  Preston 1937; S VI
  Wister, Lilacs for America, 45, 64 [1942], 27, 48 [1953]; Davidson et al. Landscape Plants at the Morden Arboretum [1994] - received at Morden Research Station, Morden, Manitoba, Canada, in 1937.
  Named for the queen of Egypt in Shakespeare's *Antony and Cleopatra*.
  Cultivar name presumed registered 1953; name established and accepted.

'Clyde Heard', *S. vulgaris*
  Heard 1984; S VI
  Heard Gardens Ltd., 1984 Lilac List; Vrugtman, HortScience 31(3):327 [1996]; Photo on Jorgovani/Lilacs 2015 DVD.
  Named for Clyde Heard, 1889-1982, nurseryman (Heard Gardens), father of the originator, De Moines, Iowa, USA.
  Cultivar name registered 1995; name established and accepted.

'Clyde Lucie', *S. vulgaris*
  origin not known pre-1975; S V
  syn. - distributed for a period by Jackson & Perkins, Newark, NY, under the name 'Lucie Baltet', but discontinued by 1990

{mutation or seedling of 'Lucie Baltet'}
Anon., Lilacs - Proceedings 17(1):26 [1988] - name only, this selection was named 'Clyde Lucie' by William A. Utley, Grape Hill Gardens, Clyde, New York; Fiala, Lilacs, 100, 115 & 217 [1988]; Vrugtman, Lilacs - Quart. Jour. 23(3):75-76 [1994] - selection with unstable characteristics; may not be distinct from 'Lucie Baltet'
Cultivar name not established.

coerulea - see *S. vulgaris* var. *coerulea* Weston - included in *S. vulgaris* L.

'Coerulea Superba', *S. vulgaris*
Ellwanger & Barry 1868; S III
syn. - 'Caerulea Superba', 'Coerulea' (not *S. v.* var. *coerulea* Weston)
common name: Royal Blue
Ellwanger & Barry Cat. No. 2, 38 [1869]; Stand. Pl. Names, 485, 487 [1923] - as Royal Blue; McKelvey, The Lilac, 278 [1928]; Wister, Lilacs for America, 46, 58 [1942], 27, 41 [1953]; Photo on Jorgovani/Lilacs 2015 DVD.
Cultivar name presumed registered 1953; name established and accepted.

'Colbert', *S. vulgaris*
Lemoine 1899; D VI
syn. - 'Maxima Colbert' (?)
Lemoine, Cat. No. 143, 22 [1899]; McKelvey, The Lilac, 278-279 [1928]; Wister, Lilacs for America, 46, 53 [1942], 27, 35 [1953] - as 'Maxima Colbert', D IV; Photo on Jorgovani/Lilacs 2015 DVD.
Named for Jean Baptiste Colbert, 1619-1683, French statesman, chief minister of Louis XIV.
Cultivar name presumed registered 1953; name established and accepted.

'Colby's Rainbow', *S. pubescens* subsp. *patula*
Moro, F. ?; ? ?
{parentage not listed}
Select Plus web page http://www.spi.8m.com/select_plus_introductions.html - name only (seen November 4, 2016).
Named for Colby Moro [2002 -], son of Sara and Frank Moro.
Cultivar name not established.

'Colby's Starburst', *S. pubescens* subsp. *patula*
Moro, F. 2010; S I
{'Excellens' × ?}
Vrugtman, Hanburyana 7:30 [2013].
Named for Colby Moro [2002 -], son of Sara and Frank Moro.
Cultivar name established and accepted; name registered 2012.

'Colby's Twinkling Little Star', *S. pubescens* subsp. *patula*
Moro, F. 2009; S VII
Vrugtman, Hanburyana 5:6 [2011].
Named for Colby Moro [2002 -], son of Sara and Frank Moro.
Cultivar name established and accepted; name registered 2009.

'Colby's Wishing Star', *S.*
Moro, F. 2003; S V
{'Josée' × ?}
F. Moro, Lilacs - Quart. Jour. 32(2):144 [2003] - erroneously as seedling offspring of *S. microphylla* × *S. pubescens* subsp. *pubescens* 'Palibin'; Moro, Lilacs - Quart. Jour. 32(3):114 [2003] - corrected parentage as seedling of *S.* 'Josée'; Giguère & Moro, Les Lilas, p. 301 [2005].
Named for Colby Moro, born 30 April 2002 with Down syndrome, son of Sara and Frank Moro.
Cultivar name established and accepted.

'Cole', *S. reticulata*
Cole 1977; S I
syn. - 'Cole's Selection'(rejected name)
Cole, Cat. 1977; Fiala, Lilacs, 85, 93 [1988]
Cultivar name not established.

'Colmariensis', *S. vulgaris*
origin not known ca 1840; S III
syn. - 'Colmarensis'
common name: Colmar
Prévost, Ann. Fl. Pomone, sér. 2, 4:253 [1846]; Stand. Pl. Names, 485 [1923] - as Colmar; McKelvey, The Lilac, 279-280 [1928]; Wister, Lilacs for America, 46 [1942], 27 [1953]; Photo on Jorgovani/Lilacs 2015 DVD.
Named, presumably, for the city of Colmar, Alsace, France.
Cultivar name presumed registered 1953; name established and accepted.

'Columbiana', *S. vulgaris*
International Exhibition, 1876, US Centennial Commission, Volume 11, p. 309 - name only.
Cultivar name not established.

'Columnare', *S. reticulata*
origin not known ? ?
Plant America (Internet) listing, 1998.
Cultivar name not established.

'Columnaris', *S. vulgaris*
origin not known pre-1953; ? ?
Wister, Lilacs for America, 43 [1953]
Cultivar name not established.

'Col. Wm. R. Plum', *S. vulgaris*
Brand pre-1942; S VII
syn. - 'Colonel William R. Plum', 'Col. William R. Plum'
Wister, Lilacs for America, 46 [1942], 27 [1953]; Photo on Jorgovani/Lilacs 2015 DVD.
Named for Colonel William Rattle Plum, 1845-1927, lawyer and attorney, founder and benefactor of Lilacia Park and its lilac collection, Lombard, Illinois, USA.
Cultivar name presumed registered 1953; name established and accepted.

COMMEMORATION OF S. M. KIROV - see 'Pam<u>yat</u>' o S. M. Kirove'.

'Compacta', *S. vulgaris* (?)
origin not known pre-1826; S I
Miller (Bristol Nursery), Cat., 14 [1826]; McKelvey, The Lilac, 280 [1928].
Cultivar name not established.

Comsomolka - see 'Komsomolka'.

'**Comte Adrien de Montebello**', *S. vulgaris*
Lemoine 1910; D IV
syn. - 'Comte Adrian de Montebelle', 'Comte de Montebello', 'Montebello'
Lemoine, Cat. No. 176, 7 [1910]; McKelvey, The Lilac, 280 [1928]; Wister, Lilacs for America, 46 [1942], 27 [1953]; Photo on Jorgovani/Lilacs 2015 DVD.
Cultivar name presumed registered 1953; name established and accepted.

'**Comte de Kerchove**', *S. vulgaris*
Lemoine 1899; D VI
syn - 'Comte de Kerkove'
Lemoine, Cat. No. 143, 10 [1899]; McKelvey, The Lilac, 280 [1928]; Wister, Lilacs for America, 46 [1942], 27 [1953]
Named for Oswald Charles Eugene, Comte de Kerchove de Denterghem, 1844-1906, Belgian politician, member of East-Flanders provincial council, amateur botanist and author.
Cultivar name presumed registered 1953; name established and accepted.

'**Comte de Smet de Naeyer**', *S. vulgaris*
Mathieu pre-1917; S III
Wister, Lilacs for America, 27 [1953]
Named for Count Paul de Smet de Naeyer, 1843-1913; Belgian politician, banker and head of Société générale de Belgique.
Cultivar name presumed registered 1953;
Cultivar not reported in cultivation.

'Comte de Paris', *S. vulgaris*
origin not known pre-1893; S VII
Froebel, Cat. No. 116, 17 [1893]; McKelvey, The Lilac, 281 [1928].
Cultivar name not established.

'**Comte Horace de Choiseul**', *S. vulgaris*
Lemoine 1887; D V
syn. - 'Comte de Choiseul'
Lemoine, Cat. No. 107, 8 [1887]; McKelvey, The Lilac, 281 [1928]; Wister, Lilacs for America, 46 [1942], 27 [1953]; Photo on Jorgovani/Lilacs 2015 DVD.
Named for Comte Eugene Antoine Horace de Choiseul-Praslin, French statesman and noted amateur horticulturist.
Cultivar name presumed registered 1953; name established and accepted.

'**Comte Osw[ald] de Kerchove de Denterghem**', *S. vulgaris*
Klettenberg 1934; S IV
Klettenberg, Cat., 20 [1934]; Wister, Lilacs for America, 27 [1953]
Named for Oswald Charles Eugene, Comte de Kerchove de Denterghem [1844-1906], Belgian politician, member of East-Flanders provincial council, amateur botanist and author.
Cultivar name presumed registered 1953; name established and accepted.

'**Comtesse d'Harcourt**', *S. vulgaris*
Bellion 1995; S I
syn. - 'Contesse D'Accourt', 'Contesse d'Harcourt'
{'Jeanne d'Arc' × ? }
Minier, Les arbres ont des idées [n.d. prob. 1994]; Vrugtman, HortScience 31(3):327 [1996]; Photo on Jorgovani/Lilacs 2015 DVD.
Cultivar name registered 1995; name established and accepted.

'**Comtesse Horace de Choiseul**', *S. vulgaris*
Lemoine 1891; D V
Lemoine, Cat. No. 119, 10 [1891]; McKelvey, The Lilac, 281 [1928]; Wister, Lilacs for America, 46 [1942], 27 [1953]; Photo on Jorgovani/Lilacs 2015 DVD.
Named for the wife of Comte Eugene Antoine Horace de Choiseul-Praslin, French statesman and noted amateur horticulturist.
Cultivar name presumed registered 1953; name established and accepted.

'**Condorcet**' (Europe, Montreal, Brooklyn NY), *S. vulgaris*
Lemoine 1888; D III
Lemoine, Cat. No. 110, 13 [1888]; McKelvey, The Lilac, 281-282 [1928]; Wister, Lilacs for America, 46 [1942] - as D V; Wister, Lilacs for America, 27 [1953]; Photo on Jorgovani/Lilacs 2015 DVD.
Named for Marie Jean Antoine Nicholas de Caritat, Marquis de Condorcet, 1743-1794, French mathematician, philosopher and political scientist.
Cultivar name presumed registered 1953; name established and accepted.

'**Condorcet**' (North America), *S. vulgaris*
Lemoine 1888; D VI
Lemoine, Cat. No. 110, 13 [1888]; McKelvey, The Lilac, 281-282 [1928]; (original North American plant received at Arnold Arboretum 1889, cuttings taken 1895 and called 'Concordat' in 1897; color noted as magenta to purple as are all North American plants noted since 1928, not true to original name); Wister, Lilacs for America, 46 [1942] - as D V; Wister, Lilacs for America, 27 [1953]; Photo on Jorgovani/Lilacs 2015 DVD.
Named for Marie Jean Antoine Nicholas de Caritat, Marquis de Condorcet, 1743-1794, French mathematician, philosopher and political scientist.
Cultivar name presumed registered 1953; name established and accepted.

'**Congo**', *S. vulgaris*
   Lemoine 1896; S VI
   syn. - 'Kongo'
   Lemoine, Cat. 134, 11 [1896]; Kache, Gartenschönheit 5:82 [1924]; McKelvey, The Lilac, 282 [1928]; Wister, Lilacs for America, 46 [1942], 27 [1953]; Photo on Jorgovani/Lilacs 2015 DVD.
   Named for Congo red, the dye developed by Paul Böttiger in 1883; originally used to dye cotton it gained importance as a histologic stain.
   Cultivar name presumed registered 1953; name established and accepted.

'**Conquête**', *S. vulgaris*
   origin not known pre-1940; S VI
   syn. - 'Conquette', 'Coquette'
   Wister, Lilacs for America, 46 [1942], 27 [1953] - originally from France; Photo on Jorgovani/Lilacs 2015 DVD.
   Cultivar name presumed registered 1953; name established and accepted.

Conseiller Heyder - see '**Geheimrat Heyder**'.

Conseiller Singelmann - see '**Geheimrat Singelmann**'.

'**Constance**', *S.* (Villosae Group), *S.* ×*prestoniae*
   Preston 1928; S VII
   syn. - Preston No. 20-14-168
   {*S. villosa* subsp. *villosa* × *S. komarowii* subsp. *reflexa*}
   Macoun, Rep. Dom. Hort. 1928, 56 [1930] - name only; Wister, Lilacs for America, 64 [1942], 27 [1953] - name only; Brand Peony Farm, Cat., 18 [1975] - as light pink
   Named for the Mother of Arthur in Shakespeare's *King John*.
   Cultivar name presumed registered 1953; name established and accepted.

'**Constantinopolitana**', *S. vulgaris*
   International Exhibition, 1876, US Centennial Commission, Volume 11, p. 310 - name only.
   Cultivar name not established.

Copper Curls® - see '**SunDak**' (*S. pekinensis*).

'**Cora Brandt**', *S. vulgaris*
   Clarke 1947; D I
   syn. - 'Cora Brand'
   {parentage not known}
   Clarke, Cat. vol. 14, 8 [1947]; Woody Plant Register, AAN, No. 66 [1949]; Lilacs for America, 27 [1953]; Photo on Jorgovani/Lilacs 2015 DVD.
   Named for Cora Brandt, Secretary of California Horticultural Society.
   Cultivar name presumed registered 1953; name established and accepted.

'**Coral**', *S.* (Villosae Group), *S.* ×*prestoniae*
   Preston & Leslie 1936; S V
   {parentage not known}
   Wister, Lilacs for America, 46, 64 [1942], 27, 48 [1953]; Alexander Sr, Cat. sheets [n.d.; received Feb. 1964]; Buckley, Greenh. - Garden - Grass, 8(3):3-4 [1969]; Cumming, Agric. Canada Publication 1628, 17, fig. 19 [1977] - as introduced in 1936; Photo on Jorgovani/Lilacs 2015 DVD.
   Cultivar name presumed registered 1953; name established and accepted.

'**Cora Lyden**', *S. vulgaris*
   Lyden ca 1966; D V
   Wister, Arnoldia 23(4):80 [1963]; Alexander Sr, Rare Lilacs, 1 [n.d. received March 1969]; Photo on Jorgovani/Lilacs 2015 DVD.
   Cultivar name registered 1963; name established and accepted.

'**Cora McCormack**', *S. vulgaris*
   Klager; S VII
   Stand. Pl. Names, 615 [1942] - name only; Wister, Lilacs for America, 46 [1942], 27 [1953]
   Cultivar name presumed registered 1953;
   Cultivar not reported in cultivation.

'**Cordelia**', *S.* (Villosae Group), *S.* ×*prestoniae*
   Preston; S V/VII
   syn. - Preston No. 20-14-157
   {*S. villosa* subsp. *villosa* × *S. komarowii* subsp. *reflexa*}
   Macoun, Rep. Dom. Hort. 1928, 67 [1930] - name only; Macoun, Rep. Dom. Hort. 1930, 67 [1931]; Wister, Lilacs for America, 64 [1942], 48 [1953] - name only, not in cultivation, no plants distributed
   Named for the Daughter of Lear in Shakespeare's *King Lear*.
   Cultivar name presumed registered 1953; not recorded in cultivation.

'**Corinna's Mist**', *S.* ×*hyacinthiflora*
   Moro, F. 2001; S V *
   {variegated mutant of 'California Rose'}
   in litt. email F. Moro to Vrugtman, Mar.30/99; Cat. Select Plus 2000.
   Named for Corinna Moro [1989 -], daughter of the originator.
   Cultivar name established and accepted.

'**Corinne**', *S. vulgaris*
   Baltet pre-1900; S VI
   Baltet, Cat. 1900-1901, 28; McKelvey, The Lilac, 282 [1928]; Wister, Lilacs for America, 46 [1942] - as S IV; Wister, Lilacs for America, 27 [1953]; Photo on Jorgovani/Lilacs 2015 DVD.
   Cultivar name presumed registered 1953; name established and accepted.

'**Correlata**', *S.*
   prob. Wolfhagen pre-1873; S I(-IV)
   {*S.* ×*chinensis* + *S. vulgaris*}; a graft chimera
   syn. - *S.* +*correlata* A. Braun (pro sp.); *S. chinensis* var. *alba* (Kirchn.) Rehder; see also McKelvey, The Lilac, 412-418 [1928], and Rehder, Bibliography, 567-568 [1949].

common name: White Chinese
Braun, Sitzungsber. Ges. Naturf. Freunde Berlin, 1873:69 [1873]; Anon., Verh. Bot. Vereins Prov. Brandenburg 16:12 [1874]; Stand. Pl. Names, 264, 488 [1923] - White Chinese; McKelvey, The Lilac, 415-415 [1928]; Hjelmqvist, Hereditas 33:367-376 [1947]; Photo on Jorgovani/Lilacs 2015 DVD - plant incorrectly labelled.
Note: Few plants, if any, in cultivation under this name appear to be true to name.
Cultivar name established and accepted.

'Corrie', S. (Pubescentes Series)
Nijnatten 1994; S II
{S. pubescens subsp. pubescens × S. pubescens subsp. microphylla 'Superba'}
Van Suchtelen, Deutsche Baumschule 8/1994, 380; André van Nijnatten, Prijslijst 1995-1996, 1 [1995]; Vrugtman, Lilacs - Quart. Jour. 25(2):40 [1996].
Named for Corrie van Nijnatten, wife of the originator.
Cultivar name established and accepted.

'Countess Irene', S. vulgaris
Klager; S VII
Anon., ILS Newsletter 14(4):3-4 [1988]
Cultivar name not established.

C. Perier - see **'Mme Casimir Périer'**.

CP 13 DS 730
Origin unknown (donor Conard-Pyle Co.); S II
on trial at JC Raulston Arboretum, Raleigh, North Carolina, USA, seen 31 March 2019 at <https://jcra.ncsu.edu/resources/photographs/results.php?search=syringa+cp>
Photo seen online 6/21/19; email info Andrew Pais, North Carolina State University.
Cognomen, not a cultivar name.

CP 13 DS 734
Origin unknown (donor Conard-Pyle Co.); S I
on trial at JC Raulston Arboretum, Raleigh, North Carolone, USA, seen 31 March 2019 at https://jcra.ncsu.edu/resources/photographs/results.php?search=syringa+cp photo seen online 6/21/19; email info Andrew Pais, North Carolina State University.
Cognomen, not a cultivar name.

'Crampel', S. vulgaris
Lemoine 1899; S III
Lemoine, Cat. No. 143, 24 [1899]; McKelvey, The Lilac, 282 [1928]; Wister, Lilacs for America, 46 [1942], 27 [1953]; Photo on Jorgovani/Lilacs 2015 DVD.
Named for Paul Crampel, 1864-1891, French explorer who died in Africa.
Cultivar name presumed registered 1953; name established and accepted.

'Crayton Red', S. (Villosae Group), S. ×henryi
origin not known pre-1931; S VII
syn. - 'Crayton'
Howell's Descriptive Cat. and Price List, 36 [1931?]; Wister, Lilacs for America, 46 [1942], 27 [1953] - as ×chinensis, S VI; Peterson, Lilacs 16(1):24 [1987] - as S. ×prestoniae and p.25 as ×chinensis; Meyer et al., Catalog of cultivated woody plants of the Southeastern United States, 199 [1994] - as S. villosa; Vrugtman, Lilacs - Quart. Jour. 25(2):38-40 [1996] - corrected to S. ×henryi.
Cultivar name presumed registered 1953; name established and accepted.

'Crépuscule', S. vulgaris
Lemoine 1928; S III
syn. - 'Crepuscle'
Lemoine, Cat. No. 203, 23 [1928]; Wister, Lilacs for America, 46 [1942], 27 [1953];
Photo on Jorgovani/Lilacs 2015 DVD.
Name: French for twilight.
Cultivar name presumed registered 1953; name established and accepted.

'Cressida', S. (Villosae Group), S. ×prestoniae
Preston 1928; S V
syn. - Preston No. 20-14-164
{S. villosa subsp. villosa × S. komarowii subsp. reflexa}
Macoun, Rep. Dom. Hort. 1928, 56 [1930] - name only; Wister, Lilacs for America, 46, 64 [1942], 27, 48 [1952]
Named for the Daughter of Calchas in Shakespeare's *Troilus and Cressida*.
Cultivar name presumed registered 1953; name established and accepted.

'Crimson Brilliant', S. vulgaris
origin not known ? ?
Cultivar name not established.

CRIMSON DOLL™ - see 'Grecrimdol'.

'Cristalli di Cortina', S. vulgaris
Moro, F. 2010; S I
{'White Lace' × ? }
Vrugtman, Hanburyana 7:28-29 [2013]
Name: Italian for crystals of Cortina; Cortina d'Ampezzo is the name of the town in the Dolomite Mountains of the Southern Alps of Italy.
Cultivar name registered 2012; name established and accepted.

'Croix de Brahy', S. vulgaris
Brahy-Ekenholm 1853; S V
syn. - 'Crux Brahy', 'Croix de Broby'
C.F.A. Morren, Belg. Hort. 1:419 [1850]; McKelvey, The Lilac, 282-283 [1928]; Wister, Lilacs for America, 46 [1942], 27 [1953]; Photo on Jorgovani/Lilacs 2015 DVD.
Name: French for cross of Brahy.
Cultivar name presumed registered 1953; name established and accepted.

Crux Brahy - see **'Croix de Brahy'**.

Crystal - see 'Chrystle'.

'Crystal White', *S. vulgaris*
  Daniels & Ludekens 1985; S I
  {*S. vulgaris* var. *alba* seedling}
  marketed in the USA as Crystal White™ Lilac
  L. E. Cooke Co. Cat. 44 [2009]; Nursery Management & Production 26(4):16; ill. [2010]
  <www.lecooke.com/cms/images/news/nmpro-april2010-lec.pdf> - erroneously as 'Chrystal White'.
  Cultivar name established and accepted.

'Cussie', *S. vulgaris*
  Margaretten; D III
  {'Mme Lemoine' × ?}
  Named for Tita Margaretten's cat.
  Cultivar name not established.

'Cynthia', *S. vulgaris*
  Berdeen 1971; S V
  Wister & Oppe, Arnoldia 31(3):122 [1971]; King & Coggeshall, Lilacs - Quart. Jour. 27(2):49-50 [1998] - name only; Photo on Jorgovani/Lilacs 2015 DVD.
  Named for the daughter of the originator.
  Cultivar name registered 1970; name established and accepted.

Č. 18., *S. vulgaris*
  probably Thomayer; D V
  {parentage not known}
  Thomayerovy Stromové Školky, Cat., p. 37 [n.d.]
  Breeder's code, not a cultivar name; not reported in cultivation.

Č. 19., *S. vulgaris*
  probably Thomayer; D IV/V-II/VII
  {parentage not known}
  Thomayerovy Stromové Školky, Cat., p. 37 [n.d.]
  Breeder's code, not a cultivar name; not reported in cultivation.

Č. 20., *S. vulgaris*
  probably Thomayer; S VI
  {parentage not known}
  Thomayerovy Stromové Školky, Cat., p. 37 [n.d.]
  Breeder's code, not a cultivar name; not reported in cultivation.

Č. 21., *S. vulgaris*
  probably Thomayer; D IV/V-III
  {parentage not known}
  Thomayerovy Stromové Školky, Cat., p. 38 [n.d.]
  Breeder's code, not a cultivar name; not reported in cultivation.

Č. 22., *S. vulgaris*
  probably Thomayer; D IV/VII
  {parentage not known}
  Thomayerovy Stromové Školky, Cat., p. 38 [n.d.]
  Breeder's code, not a cultivar name; not reported in cultivation.

Č. 23., *S. vulgaris*
  probably Thomayer; D V
  {parentage not known}
  Thomayerovy Stromové Školky, Cat. p. 38 [n.d.]
  Breeder's code, not a cultivar name; not reported in cultivation.

'Dafna', *S. vulgaris*
  `Дафна`
  Luchnik and Semenyuk 1994; S VI
  Pikaleva, Lilacs - Quart. Jour. 23(4):84 [1994] - reported in cultivation at the Dendrarium of the Science-Research Institute, Barnaul, Altai, Russia; Registered with the State Commission of the Russian Federation for Testing and Protection of Selection Achievements, No. 8506272, 1994; Lyakh, Lilacs - Quart. Jour. 36(3):116 [2007] - name and originator only; Chapman, Lilacs - Quart. Jour. 36(1):19 [2007]; Sinogeĭkina, G. E. (Синогейкиаг, Галина Эдуардовна) 2014. Evaluation of parental winter hardiness and ornamental varieties and hybrids of *Syringa vulgaris* L. in the steppe of the Altai Region (PhD thesis).
  Name: Russian for daphne (not to be confused with *S.* ×*hyacinthiflora* 'Daphne Pink').
  Cultivar name registered, established and accepted.

'Daiga', *S. vulgaris*
  Kārkliņš 2003; S V/II
  Strautiņa & Kaufmane, Dobeles ceriņi, p. 92 [2011]; Photo on Jorgovani/Lilacs 2015 DVD.
  Named for the daughter of the originator.
  Cultivar name established and accepted.

'Daisy G', *S. vulgaris*
  Klager; D VII
  Anon., ILS Newsletter 14(4):3-4 [1988]
  Cultivar name not established.

'Daisy Wolcott', *S.* ×*hyacinthiflora*
  Moro, F. 2009; S III
  {'Forrest Kresser Smith' × ?}
  <http://www.spi.8m.com/hyacinthifloracdncat.html>
  Named for Daisy Wolcott (1879-1955) who created The Lilac Gardens in Kent, Ohio, USA.
  Cultivar name established and accepted.

'D'Alger', *S. vulgaris*
  origin not known pre-1898; ? ?
  Dauthenay, Rev. Hort., 58 [1898]; McKelvey, The Lilac, 283 [1928]
  Cultivar name not established.

'Dalia', *S. vulgaris*
  Klager; S V
  Anon., ILS Newsletter 14(4):3-4 [1988]
  Cultivar name not established.

'Dal'nevostochnitsa', *S.* ×*hyacinthiflora*
  `Дальневосточница`
  Pshennikova 2018; D VII

{'Olimpiada Kolsnikova' × OP}
Russian Patent No. 10698.
Name: Russian for a woman living in the Far East.
Cultivar name established and accepted.

'Dame Blanche', *S. vulgaris*
Lemoine 1903; D I
Lemoine, Cat. No. 155, 29 [1903]; McKelvey, The Lilac, 283 [1928]; Wister, Lilacs for America, 46 [1942], 27 [1953]
Named for leading role in the opera *La Dame Blanche*, 1825, by François Adrien Boïeldieu, 1775-1834.
Cultivar name presumed registered 1953; name established and accepted.

'Dana Horton', *S. vulgaris*
Berdeen; D VII
King & Coggeshall, Lilacs - Quart. Jour. 27(2):49-50 [1998] - name only.
Photo seen by Claire Fouquet from The Lilac Museum, Saint-Georges, Quebec, Canada in the ILS 2020 Photo DVD.
Cultivar growing at Cherry Valley Lilacs in Cherry Valley, NY USA
Seen September 14, 2019 on ILS Facebook page posted by Charle-Pan Dawson
Cultivar name not established.

'Dancing Druid', *S.* (Villosae Group)
Fiala 1968; S VI
{presumably: (*S. tomentella* subsp. *yunnanensis* × *S. tomentella* subsp. *tomentella*) × (*S. komarowii* subsp. *komarowii* × [*S. tomentella* subsp. *sweginzowii* × *S. tomentella* subsp. *tomentella*])}
Fiala, Lilacs, 104, 124, 224 [1988] - as *S. ×quatrobrida* J.Fiala (hybrid name not validly published), parentage not clearly defined; Vrugtman, Lilacs - Quart. Jour. 27(3):88; Pringle, Lilacs - Quart. Jour. 29(3):86-89 [2000]; Anon., Lilacs - Quart. Jour. 33(1):11 [2004] - erroneously as S IV; Photo on Jorgovani/Lilacs 2015 DVD.
Cultivar name established and accepted.

DANTE'S INFERNO, *S.*
Chapman ?, ? ?
Chapman, Lilacs - Quart. Jour. 38(3):83[2009] - name only.
Cultivar name not established.

'Danton', *S. vulgaris*
Lemoine 1911; S VII
Lemoine, Cat. 179, 5 [1911]; McKelvey, The Lilac, 283-284 [1928]; Wister, Lilacs for America, 46 [1942], 27 [1953]; Photo on Jorgovani/Lilacs 2015 DVD.
Named for Georges Jaques Danton, 1759-1794, French revolutionary leader.
Cultivar name presumed registered 1953; name established and accepted.

'Danusia', *S.* (Villosae Group), *S. ×prestoniae*
Bugała pre-1970; S V
Bugała, Arboretum Kórnickie 15:61-70 [1971]; Wister & Oppe, Arnoldia 31(3):122 [1971]; Bugała, Lilacs - Quart. Jour. 24(4):90-91 [1995]; Photo on Jorgovani/Lilacs 2015 DVD.
Cultivar name registered 1970; name established and accepted.

'Daphne', *S. vulgaris*
origin not known ? ?
Anon., Lilacs - Proceedings 17(1):26 [1988] - name only, listed as growing at Grape Hill Gardens (Wm. Utley; now defunct), probably a misidentification.
Cultivar name not established; probably no longer in cultivation.

'Daphne' - see 'Daphne Pink'
Nota bene: The notation: "Daphne (syn. of *S. microphylla superba*)" appeared in Wister, Arnoldia 23(4):80 [1963] as a new registration; it is now believed that this is an erroneous entry. Vrugtman, HortScience 31(3):328 [1996].

'Daphne Pink', *S. ×hyacinthiflora*
Skinner 1959; S V
F2 hybrid of *S. vulgaris* × *S. oblata dilatata*
syn. - 'Daphne'
Skinner, Dropmore, Cat., 11 [1959] - as 'Daphne'; in lit. F.L. Skinner to D. Wyman, 28 Dec. 1964 - name changed to 'Daphne Pink' in compliance with the ICNCP; Wister, Registrations 1965 [mimeographed], p. 4 - as 'Daphne Pink', "name not approved"; Skinner, Hort. Horizons, 49, 109, Pl. 29 [1966] - as 'Daphne Pink'; Skinner, Dropmore, Cat., 11 [1968] - as 'Daphne Pink'; Photo on Jorgovani/Lilacs 2015 DVD.
Cultivar name established and accepted.
Nota bene: Although originally published as 'Daphne' the registered epithet 'Daphne Pink' is in general use and should be retained.

'Dappled Dawn', *S. vulgaris*
Hauck & Payne 1966; S III *
{mutation of *S. vulgaris*; no cultivar name provided}
Hauck, US Plant Patent No. 2614 [Mar. 22, 1966] - as purple-mauve, S or D not given; Wister & Oppe, Arnoldia 31(3):122 [1971] - name only; Rogers, Tent. Int. Reg. genus *Syringa* [1976] - as S VI; Vrugtman, AABGA Bull. 15(3):72 [1981] - correction to S III *; in lit. Jeff Payne to Mark DeBard (30 June 2017) S III * confirmed; DeBard & Vrugtman, Lilacs - Quart. Jour. 47(1):33-37 [2018], see **NOTE**; Photos on Jorgovani/Lilacs 2015 DVD, show florets to be D, the photos appear to be of 'Aucubaefolia' (FV 1 July 2017).
Cultivar name registered 1970; name established and accepted.
Note: We believe that all plants marketed in the past and at present as 'Dappled Dawn' which are double blues, are in fact 'Aucubaefolia'. It is also likely that such plants which have single light blue florets are not 'Dappled Dawn' (which has single dark blue florets).

'Darimonti', *S. vulgaris*
  origin not known pre-1875; ? ?
  L. van Houtte, Cat. No. 165-LL, 18 [1875] - name only;
  McKelvey, The Lilac, 284 [1928] - confused name.
  Cultivar name not established.

'Dark Blue', *S. vulgaris*
  origin not known ca 1875; S VII/III
  McKelvey, The Lilac, 284, 563 [1928].

Dark Dense Truss - see **'Klager Dark Dense Truss'**.

Dark Knight - see **'Dark Night'**.

'Dark Koster', *S. vulgaris*
  prob. J. Eveleens 1930s; S III
  syn. - 'Donkere Koster'
  {mutation of 'Hugo Koster'; perhaps not one single clone}
  Vakblad v d Bloemisterij 17 [1990]: VKC/VBN-Produktenregistratie deel 10, p. 4; Jongkind, Seringensortiment voor de trek, p.4 [1997] - name only; http://www.syringa.nl/assortment.htm [Aug.21/00]; Photo on Jorgovani/Lilacs 2015 DVD.
  Cultivar name established and accepted.
  Forcing cultivar in the Netherlands since the mid-1980s.

'Dark Night', *S. ×hyacinthiflora*
  Sobeck; S VII
  syn. - 'Dark Knight', ELFE
  marketed in Germany as ELFE™ (No. 399487824; K. Kircher)
  Wister, Arnoldia 26(3):13 [1966]; Photo on Jorgovani/Lilacs 2015 DVD.
  Cultivar name registered 1966; name established and accepted.
  Nota bene: Since this cultivar appears to be of 'Lavender Lady' ancestry see also: Pringle, Lilacs - Quart. Jour. 24(4):97-99 [1995]; and Vrugtman, HortScience 31(3):328 [1996]; ForesFarm Cat. p.244 [1997], p.308 [1998-1999], p.308 [2000] - as 'Dark Knight'.

'Dark Purple', *S. villosa* subsp. *villosa*
  Origin not known; S VII
  McKay Nursery Co., Cat., 25 [1989]
  Cultivar name not established.

Dark Purple (*S. vulgaris*) - see 'Hulda'.

'Darlene', *S. vulgaris*
  Peterson 1996; D V
  Peterson, Lilacs - Proceedings 16(1):18 [1987] - name only; Anon., Lilacs - Quart. Jour. 33(1):11 [2004] - as D V; Photo on Jorgovani/Lilacs 2015 DVD.
  Cultivar name not established.

'Daudzpusīgais Zemzaris', *S. vulgaris*
  Upītis 1963; S II
  {parentage not known}
  syn. - 'Daudzpusiigais Zemzaris', Upītis No. 3143
  Rubtzov et al. 1980. Vidy i sorta sireni, kul'tiviruemye v SSSR. Kiev; Naukova Dumka. – in Russian; Holetich, C.D. 1982. Lilac species and cultivars in cultivation in USSR. Lilacs 11(2):1-38. - translation of Rubtzov et al. 1982; Kalniņš, Ceriņu jaunšķirnes Dobelē, Dārs un drava 1986 (12):13-15 - in Latvian; Strautiņa, S. 1992. Ceriņi Dārzs un Drava. No. 6, pp. 12-13; Strautiņa, S. 2002. Ceriņu un jasmīnu avīze. LA, R., p. 62; Vrugtman, HortScience 31(3):327 [1996]; in litt. S. Strautiņa to F. Vrugtman [21 Dec. 2007] - 1963, S II; Photo on Jorgovani/Lilacs 2015 DVD.
  Name: Latvian for versatile Zemzaris.
  Cultivar name registered 1995; name established and accepted.

'David Gilfillan', *S. ×hyacinthiflora*
  Descanso Gardens ca 1965; S II
  {open pollinated seedling, possibly of 'Lavender Lady'}
  Vrugtman, AABGA Bull. 13(4):109-110 [1979]
  Named for David Inglis Gilfillan, 1889-1979, horticulturist, garden writer and radio personality in Southern California, USA.
  Cultivar name registered 1978; name established and accepted.

'Dawn', *S.* (Villosae Group), *S. ×prestoniae*
  Preston & Leslie 1937; S V-I
  {parentage not known}
  Stand. Pl. Names, 615 [1942] - name only; Wister, Lilacs for America, 46 [1942], 27 [1953] - as S V; Cumming, Agric. Canada Public. 1628, 17 [1977] - as S V-I, Introduced in 1937; Photo on Jorgovani/Lilacs 2015 DVD.
  Cultivar name presumed registered 1953; name established and accepted.

'Dawn', *S. vulgaris*
  Havemeyer pre-1942 (not Klager); S III
  Lilac Land, Cat. [1954]; Wister, Lilacs for America, 46 [1942] - as S IV; Wister, Lilacs for America, 27 [1953]; Eickhorst, ILS Lilac Newsletter 4(1):4-5 [1978]
  Cultivar name presumed registered 1953; name established and accepted.
  Nota bene: 'Dawn' (Havemeyer) and 'Dawn' (Klager) may have become confused and mixed in cultivation.

'Dawn', *S. vulgaris*
  Klager (not Havemeyer); S IV
  Wister, Lilacs for America, 46 [1942], 27 [1953]
  Cultivar name presumed registered 1953; reported in cultivation at Highland Park, Rochester NY USA.
  Nota bene: 'Dawn' (Havemeyer) and 'Dawn' (Klager) may have become confused and mixed in cultivation.

DAWN OF COMMUNISM - see **'Zarya Kommunizma'**.

'Dazzle', *S. vulgaris*
  Havemeyer & Eaton 1954; D I
  Lilac Land, Cat. [1954]; Eickhorst, ILS Lilac Newsletter 4(1):4-5 [1978]
  Cultivar name established and accepted.

'D-Dream', *S. vulgaris*
   Weening 1990s; S V
   {mutation of 'Hugo Koster'}
   syn. - *S. vulgaris* ROZE (first marketed under this trade designation in 2016 by Kwekerij Hulsbos, Aalsmeer, Netherlands; in lit. Jan & Irma Hulsbos to Marco Hoffman 24 October 2016); listed: https://www.floraxchange.nl/Artikel/Info/335425/D-Dream
   Cultivar name established and accepted.
   Nota bene: The trade designation *S. vulgaris* ROZE appears to have been used in the nursery trade for more than one lilac selection.

'De Belder', *S. pubescens* subsp. *patula*
   De Belder & Fiala 1988; S IV
   syn. - *S. debelderorum* R.B.Clark & J.L.Fiala (*S. debelderi*)
   Fiala, Lilacs, 48, Pl. 31 [1988] - as *S. debelderi*; P. S. Green, Kew Magaz. 6(2):90-92 [1989] - corrected to *S. debelderorum*; Vrugtman, F. 2004. Lilacs Quart. Journ. 33(4):123 - as 'De Belder'.
   Named for Robert De Belder, 1921-1995 and his wife Jelena De Belder-Kovačič, 1925-2003, amateur horticulturists, Arboreta Kalmthout and Domain Hemelrijk (Essen), Belgium.
   Cultivar name established and accepted.

'Debija', *S. vulgaris*
   Kārkliņš 2003; S VII ?
   Photo on Jorgovani/Lilacs 2015 DVD.
   Cultivar name established.

'Decaisne', *S. vulgaris*
   Lemoine 1910; S III
   syn. - 'Descaisne', 'Deken'
   Lemoine, Cat. No. 176, 31 [1910]; Kache, Gartenschönheit 5:82 [1924]; McKelvey, The Lilac, 284 [1928]; Wister, Lilacs for America, 46 [1942], 27 [1953]; Photo on Jorgovani/Lilacs 2015 DVD.
   Named for Joseph Decaisne, 1807-1882, Belgian botanist and horticulturist, founder and director of his "jardin fruitier du muséum".
   Cultivar name presumed registered 1953; name established and accepted.

Deceiver - see 'Obman<u>shchitsa</u>'.

'Declaration', *S.* ×*hyacinthiflora*
   Egolf & Pooler 2006; S VI-VII
   syn. - NA62975, PI641804
   {*S.* ×*hyacinthiflora* 'Sweet Charity' × *S.* ×*hyacinthiflora* 'Pocahontas'}
   USDA-ARS Notice of Release [March 24, 2006]; Pooler, HortScience 43(2):544–545 [2008]; Photo on Jorgovani/Lilacs 2015 DVD.
   The name refers to the U. S. Declaration of Independence, 4 July 1776.
   Nomenclatural standard deposited at United States National Arboretum Herbarium (NA); NA-0041457; Hanburyana 4:56 [2009].
   Cultivar name registered 2007; name established and accepted.

'Decorative', *S. vulgaris*
   origin not known pre-1922; D III
   McKelvey, The Lilac, 284 [1928]; Wister, Lilacs for America, 36 & 46 [1942]
   Cultivar name not established, not recorded in cultivation in 1953.

'De Croncels', *S. vulgaris*
   Baltet pre-1876; S VII
   syn. - 'Alexander de Croncels', 'Alexandre de Croncels', 'Gloire de Croncels'
   L. Leroy, Cat., 72 [1876]; McKelvey, The Lilac, 284-285 [1928]; Wister, Lilacs for America, 46, 49 [1942] - as S VI; Wister, Lilacs for America, 27 [1953]; Photo on Jorgovani/Lilacs 2015 DVD.
   Named for Croncels, the hometown of the Baltet nursery, near Troyes, France.
   Cultivar name presumed registered 1953; name established and accepted.

Defontaines - see '**Desfontaines**'.

'De Humboldt', *S. vulgaris*
   Lemoine 1892; D II
   syn. - 'Alexander de Humboldt', 'Graf von Humboldt', 'Humboldt'
   common name: Alexander Humboldt
   Lemoine, Cat. No. 122, 15 [1892]; Stand. Pl. Names, 486 [1923] - as Alexander Humboldt; Kache, Gartenschönheit 5:82 [1924]; McKelvey, The Lilac, 285 [1928]; Wister, Lilacs for America, 46 [1942] - as D III; Wister, Lilacs ;for America, 27 [1953]; Photo on Jorgovani/Lilacs 2015 DVD.
   Named for Friedrich Heinrich Alexander, Baron von Humboldt, 1769-1859, German naturalist and traveller.
   Cultivar name presumed registered 1953; name established and accepted.

'De Jussieu', *S. vulgaris*
   Lemoine 1891; D IV
   Lemoine, Cat. No. 119, 13 [1891]; McKelvey, The Lilac, 285-286 [1928]; Wister, Lilacs for America, 46 [1942], 27 [1953]; Photo on Jorgovani/Lilacs 2015 DVD.
   Named for Antoine Laurent de Jussieu, 1748-1836, French botanist, professor at the Jardin des Plantes, Paris, 1793-1826.
   Cultivar name presumed registered 1953; name established and accepted.

Deken - see '**Decaisne**'.

de Laurel - see '**Lavaliensis**'.

De Laval - see '**Lavaliensis**'.

'Delepine', *S. vulgaris*
   origin not known pre-1855; S VII

syn - 'Delepin', 'Delépine, 'Délépine', 'De Lépine'
William Prince, Cat. 1856-1857 - name only, as *Syringa Delepine*; McKelvey, The Lilac, 286 [1928]; Lilacs for America, 28 [1953]
Cultivar name presumed registered 1953; name established and accepted.

Delft Blue - see 'Blue Delft'.

'Delia', *S. vulgaris*
Klager; S V
Anon., ILS Newsletter 14(4):3-4 [1988]
Cultivar name not established.

'De Louvain', *S. vulgaris* (not 'Louvain', *S. ×hyacinthiflora*)
origin not known pre-1855; S V
syn. - 'Lavanensis', 'Louvainiensis', 'Lovanensis', 'Lovaniensis'
common name: Louvain
Dauvesse, Cat. No. 20, 24 [1855] - as Lilas de Louvain, name only; Stand. Pl. Names, 486 [1923] - as Louvain (common name); McKelvey, The Lilac, 286-287 [1928]; Wister, Lilacs for America, 46 [1942], 27 [1953] - as S IV; Wister, Arnoldia 23(4):81 [1963] - erroneously as 'Louvin'; Photo on Jorgovani/Lilacs 2015 DVD.
Named for the town of Louvain, capital of the province of Flemish Brabant, Belgium (French: Louvain; Flemish: Leuven; German: Löwen).
Cultivar name presumed registered 1953; name established and accepted.

'Delphinium', *S. vulgaris*
Klager 1920; S VII
Wister, Lilacs for America, 46 [1942], 28 [1953]
Cultivar name presumed registered 1953; not reported in cultivation.

'Delreb', *S. vulgaris*
Delbard 1992; D III
syn. - 'Delreble'
marketed in France as Rêve Bleu™; marketed in Europe also as 'Rêve Bleu'
André Briant Jeunes Plantes, 1992-93 Internat. ed., 71; Photo on Jorgovani/Lilacs 2015 DVD.
Cultivar name established and accepted.

De Marley, De Marly - see 'Marlyensis'; see also 'Lake Bled'.

'De Miribel', *S. vulgaris*
Lemoine 1903; S II
syn. - 'De Mirabel'
Lemoine, Cat. No. 155, 31 [1903]; Kache, Gartenschönheit 5:82 [1924]; McKelvey, The Lilac, 287 [1928]; Wister, Lilacs for America, 46 [1942], 28 [1953]; Photo on Jorgovani/Lilacs 2015 DVD.
Derivation of the name uncertain.
Cultivar name presumed registered 1953; name established and accepted.

'Den' Pobedy', *S. vulgaris*
'День Победы'
Aladin, S., Arkhangel'skii, V., Polyakova, T., and Aladina, O. 2011; S VII
{'Monge' × OP}
Registered with the State Commission of the Russian Federation for Testing and Protection of Selection Achievements, No. 8853118, 2011; Lilacs Quart. Journ. 40(2):42 [2011]- name only; Питомник -частный сад (Pitomnik i chastnyi sad; Nursery and private garden) 2/2015:32-40 (in Russian); Садовник (Gardener) magazine, 05 (141)/2017 :16-22; Вестник АППМ (Catalog in Vestnik APPM (Planting material association) magazine) 1/2018: 59-72 (in Russian); Photo on Jorgovani/Lilacs 2015 DVD.
Name: Russian for Victory Day.
Cultivar name established and accepted; name registered.

'Densiflora', *S. tomentella* subsp. *sweginzowii*
Lemoine 1933; S V
Lemoine, Cat. No. 210, 26 [1936]; Wister, Lilacs for America, 46, 59 [1942], 28, 42 [1953]
Cultivar name presumed registered 1953; name established and accepted.

'De Oirsprong', *S. ×chinensis*
Origin not known; S IV-V
listed by Esveld nursery http://www.esveld.nl/htmldia/s/sycdoi.htm [July 23, 2005] - in cultivation at PlantenTuin de Oirsprong, Oirschot, The Netherlands.
Cultivar name not established.

'De Saussure', *S. vulgaris*
Lemoine 1903; D VII
syn. - 'De Saussaure'
Lemoine, Cat. No. 152, 32 [1902]; McKelvey, The Lilac, 287 [1928]; Wister, Lilacs for America, 46 [1942], 28 [1953]; Photo on Jorgovani/Lilacs 2015 DVD.
Named for Horace Bénédict de Saussure, 1740-1799, Swiss physicist and geologist.
Cultivar name presumed registered 1953; name established and accepted.

Descaisne - see 'Decaisne'.

'Descanso Beauty', *S. ×hyacinthiflora*
Sobeck; S IV
Wister, Arnoldia 26(3):13 [1966]
Cultivar name registered 1966; name established and accepted.
Nota bene: Since this cultivar appears to be of 'Lavender Lady' ancestry see also: Pringle, Lilacs - Quart. Jour. 24(4):97-99 [1995]; and Vrugtman, HortScience 31(3):328 [1996].

'Descanso Giant', *S. ×hyacinthiflora*
Sobeck; S IV
Wister, Arnoldia 26(3):13 [1966]; LASCA Leaves 20(4): cover ill. [1970]
Cultivar name registered 1966; name established and accepted.

Nota bene: Since this cultivar appears to be of 'Lavender Lady' ancestry see also: Pringle, Lilacs - Quart. Jour. 24(4):97-99 [1995]; and Vrugtman, HortScience 31(3):328 [1996].

'Descanso King', *S.* ×*hyacinthiflora*
Sobeck 1966; S III
Wister, Arnoldia 26(3):13 [1966]; Photo on Jorgovani/Lilacs 2015 DVD.
Cultivar name registered 1966; name established and accepted.
Nota bene: Since this cultivar appears to be of 'Lavender Lady' ancestry see also: Pringle, Lilacs - Quart. Jour. 24(4):97-99 [1995]; and Vrugtman, HortScience 31(3):328 [1996].

'Descanso Princess', *S.* ×*hyacinthiflora*
Sobeck; S IV
Wister, Arnoldia 26(3):13 [1966]; Photo on Jorgovani/Lilacs 2015 DVD.
Cultivar name registered 1966; name established and accepted.
Nota bene: Since this cultivar appears to be of 'Lavender Lady' ancestry see also: Pringle, Lilacs - Quart. Jour. 24(4):97-99 [1995]; and Vrugtman, HortScience 31(3):328 [1996].

'Descanso Spring', *S.* ×*hyacinthiflora*
Sobeck; S VI
syn. - 'Spring in Descanso'
Wister, Arnoldia 26(3):13 [1966]
Cultivar name registered 1966; name established and accepted.
Nota bene: Since this cultivar appears to be of 'Lavender Lady' ancestry see also: Pringle, Lilacs - Quart. Jour. 24(4):97-99 [1995]; and Vrugtman, HortScience 31(3):328 [1996].

'Descartes', *S.* ×*hyacinthiflora*
Lemoine 1916; S V
Lemoine, Cat. No. 190, 25 [1916]; McKelvey, The Lilac, 197- 198 [1928]; Wister, Lilacs for America, 46 [1942], 28 [1953]; Photo on Jorgovani/Lilacs 2015 DVD.
Named for René Descartes, 1596-1650, French mathematician.
Cultivar name presumed registered 1953; name established and accepted.

'Deschanel' - see **'Paul Deschanel'**.
listed by Longwood Gardens, L.2376, 11/1998.

'Desdemona', *S.* (Villosae Group), *S.* ×*prestoniae*
Preston 1927; S III
syn. - Preston No. 20-14-179
{*S. villosa* subsp. *villosa* × *S. komarowii* subsp. *reflexa*}
Macoun, Rep. Dom. Hort. 1928, 56 [1930]; Wister, Lilacs for America, 46, 64 [1942], 28, 48 [1953]; Photo on Jorgovani/Lilacs 2015 DVD.
Named for the Wife of Othello in Shakespeare's *Othello*.
Cultivar name presumed registered 1953; name established and accepted.

'Desfontaines', *S. vulgaris*
Lemoine 1906; D VI
syn. - 'Defontaines'
Lemoine, Cat. No. 164, 28 [1906]; McKelvey, The Lilac, 287 [1928]; Wister, Lilacs for America, 46 [1942] - as D IV; Wister, Lilacs for America, 28 [1953]; Photo on Jorgovani/Lilacs 2015 DVD.
Named for René Louiche Desfontaines, 1750-1833, French botanist.
Cultivar name presumed registered 1953; name established and accepted.

'Desponda', *S. vulgaris*
origin not known ? ?
Cultivar name not established.

De Trianon - see **'Rouge de Trianon'**.

'De<u>t</u>stvo', *S. vulgaris*
'Детство'
Krav<u>ch</u>enko 1970; D V
{'Congo' × 'Belle de Nancy'}
Krav<u>ch</u>enko L. Culture of lilacs in Uzbekistan. Publishing house "Uzbekistan", Tashkent, 1970 p. 16.
Name: Russian for childhood.
Cultivar name established and accepted.

'Deuil d'Émile Gallé', *S. vulgaris*
Lemoine 1904; D V
syn. - 'Deuil d'Emile Galle'
Lemoine, Cat. No. 158, 8 [1904]; McKelvey, The Lilac, 287-288 [1928]; Wister, Lilacs for America, 46 [1942], 28 [1953]; Photo on Jorgovani/Lilacs 2015 DVD.
Named in memory of Émile Gallé, 1846-1904, French designer and glass maker whose work was influenced by his studies of botany.
Cultivar name presumed registered 1953; name established and accepted.

'Devi<u>ch</u>'e S<u>ch</u>ast'e', *S. vulgaris*
'Девичье Счастье'
Klimenko, V. & Z., & Grigor'ev 1955; S V-VII
Rub<u>tz</u>ov et al. 1980. Vidy i sorta sireni, kul'tiviruemye v SSSR. Kiev; Naukova Dumka. – in Russian; Holetich, C.D. 1982. Lilac species and cultivars in cultivation in USSR. Lilacs 11(2):1-38. - translation of Rub<u>tz</u>ov et al. 1982.
Name: Russian for maiden happiness.
Cultivar name established and accepted.

Diana, Bugała (not Preston) - see **'Agata'**, *S.* (Villosae Group), *S.* ×*prestoniae*.

'Diana', *S.* (Villosae Group), *S.* ×*prestoniae*
Preston (not Bugała) 1928; S IV-V
syn. - Preston No. 20-03-01
{*S. komarowii* subsp. *reflexa* × *S. villosa* subsp. *villosa*}
Macoun, Rep. Dom. Hort. 1928, 56 [1930] - name only; Wister, Lilacs for America, 46, 64 [1942] - as S VI, only seedling of reciprocal cross; Wister, Lilacs for America, 28, 48 [1953] - as S VI; Photo on Jorgovani/Lilacs 2015 DVD.

Named for the Daughter to Widow in Shakespeare's *All's Well that Ends Well*.
Cultivar name presumed registered 1953; name established and accepted.

'Dianah Abbott', *S. vulgaris*
Berdeen 1976; S VII
syn. - 'Diana Abbott'
{probably open pollinated seedling}
Berdeen, in litt. to O. M. Rogers [May 19/76] - as 'President Roosevelt' × 'Massena'; W. W. Oakes, in litt. to Vrugtman [Mar.2/79] - as seed parent unknown, pollen parent 'Violetta'; Vrugtman, AABGA Bull. 13(4):110 [1979]
Named for a friend of the Berdeen family.
Cultivar name registered 1978; name established and accepted.

'Diane', *S. vulgaris*
Nelson, Caspar 1933; S VI
{parentage not known}
Woody Plant Register, AAN, No. 67 [1949]; Wister, Lilacs for America, 28 [1953]
Named for one of the originator's granddaughters.
Cultivar name presumed registered 1953; name established and accepted.

'Diderot', *S. vulgaris*
Lemoine 1915; S VII
Lemoine, Cat. No. 189, 22 [1915]; McKelvey, The Lilac, 288 [1928]; Wister, Lilacs for America, 46 [1942], 28 [1953]; Photo on Jorgovani/Lilacs 2015 DVD.
Named for Denis Diderot, 1713-1784, French philosopher, encyclopedist and man-of-letters.
Cultivar name presumed registered 1953; name established and accepted.

'Dillia', *S. vulgaris*
Klager 1915; D I
Wister, Lilacs for America, 46 [1942], 28 [1953]; Photo on Jorgovani/Lilacs 2015 DVD.
Cultivar name presumed registered 1953; name established and accepted.

'Dingle Variegated', *S. vulgaris*
Dingle pre-1995; ? ? *
RHS Plant Finder / PFRL 1995/96
Cultivar name not established.

'Diplomate', *S. vulgaris*
Lemoine 1930; S III
Lemoine, Cat. No. 204, 25 [1930]; Wister, Lilacs for America, 47 [1942], 28 [1953];
Photo on Jorgovani/Lilacs 2015 DVD.
Cultivar name presumed registered 1953; name established and accepted.

'Directeur Doorenbos', *S. vulgaris*
Eveleens Maarse 1955; S IV
syn. - 'Directeur Dorenbos'
{'Excellent' × 'Johan Mensing'}
Wister, Arnoldia 23(4):81 [1963]; Photo on Jorgovani/Lilacs 2015 DVD.
Named for Siemon Godfried Albert Doorenbos, 1891-1980, horticulturist, director of parks, The Hague, The Netherlands.
Awards: Certificate of Merit 1955 (KMTP).
Cultivar name registered 1963; name established and accepted.

'Directeur Général Van Orshoven', *S. vulgaris*
Klettenberg 1936; S VI
Wister, Lilacs for America, 28 [1953]
Cultivar name presumed registered 1953; name established and accepted.

'Director General van de Plassche', *S. vulgaris*
Eveleens Maarse 1961; S VI
syn. - 'Director General Van Der Plassche', 'Ir. A. W. van de Plassche', 'Jr. Am Van de Plassche'
{'G. J. Baardse' × 'Excellent'}
Wister, Arnoldia 23(4):81 [1963] - as 'Director General Van Der Plassche'
Named for Dr Ir Andries Willem van de Plassche [1896-1988], horticulturist and educator, Director General for Agriculture, 1952-1961, The Hague, The Netherlands.
Awards: Certificate of Merit 1961 (KMTP).
Cultivar name registered 1963; name established and accepted.

'Dixie', *S. vulgaris*
Speirs 2007; D V
{parentage not known}
original plant selected and collected 2007 by Speirs and Lilac Team, Friends of the Central Experimental Farm, Ottawa, on property of Claude and Cora Nolan (Park Lot-1), Franktown, Ontario, Canada.
Speirs, J., Friends of the Central Experimental Farm, Newsletter 28(2):6 [2016].
Named Dixie for Dixina (Pierce) McLellan, former co-owner of the property.
Cultivar name established and accepted.

D. Nehru - see 'Dzhavakharlal Neru'.

'Dobeles Meitene', *S. vulgaris*
Upītis 1980; S I
syn. - Upītis No. 66-37
Kalva, Ceriņi (Lilac), 165-166 [1980] - in Latvian; Kalniņš, Ceriņu jaunšķirnes Dobelē, Dārs un drava 1986 (12):13-15 - in Latvian; in litt. S. Strautiņa to F. Vrugtman [21 Dec. 2007] - 1980, S I; Semenov, Igor, Lilacs - Quart. Jour. 44(2):49, ill. 54 [2015]; Photo on Jorgovani/Lilacs 2015 DVD.
Name: Latvian for a girl from Dobele.
Cultivar name established and accepted.

'Dobeles Sapņotājs', *S. vulgaris*
Upītis 1950; D VII/II
syn. - 'Atceries Mani', 'Dobeles Sapnjotaajs', 'Dobeles Sapnotaīs'

{parentage not known}
Kalniņš, Ceriņu jaunšķirnes Dobelē, Dārs un drava 1986 (12):13-15 - in Latvian; Vrugtman, HortScience 31(3):327 [1996]; Strautiņa, S. 2002. Ceriņu un jasmīnu avīze. LA, R., p. 62; in litt. S. Strautiņa to F. Vrugtman [21 Dec. 2007] - 1950, D VII/II; Semenov, Igor, Lilacs - Quart. Jour. 44(2):50, ill. 56 [2015] - as II fading to II with a pearl tint; Photo on Jorgovani/Lilacs 2015 DVD.
Name: Latvian for Dobele dreamer.
Cultivar name registered 1995; name accepted and established.

'Do<u>ch</u>' Tamara', *S. vulgaris*
'Дочь Тамара'
Kolesnikov & Mironovich 1986; S V
syn. - 'Doch Tamara'
Pikaleva, Lilacs - Quart. Jour. 23(4):91 [1994]; Registered with the State Commission of the Russian Federation for Testing and Protection of Selection Achievements, No. 8803544, 1998; Polyakova, 2010, Istoriya Russkoĭ Sireni, p. 78; Photo on Jorgovani/Lilacs 2015 DVD.
Name: daughter Tamara, Tamara Kolesnikova, daughter of Leonid A. Kolesnikov.
Cultivar name established and accepted; name registered.

Docteur ... - see also: Doctor ..., Dr ...

'Docteur Charles Jacobs', *S. vulgaris*
Stepman-Demessemaeker pre-1906; S VII
syn. - 'Doctor Charles Jacobs', 'Dr Charles Jacob', 'Dr Charles Jacobs'
{'Dr Lindley' × 'Marie Legraye'}
Fl. Stepman-Demessemaeker, Cat. 2 [1908]; McKelvey, The Lilac 288 [1928]; Wister, Lilacs for America, 47 [1942], 28 [1953]; Photo on Jorgovani/Lilacs 2015 DVD.
Named for Charles Jacobs, 1862-1924, Belgian gynecologist. Dokter Jacobsstraat / Rue Docteur Jacobs, Anderlecht (Brussels), was named for him.
Cultivar name presumed registered 1953; name established and accepted.

'Docteur Louis Delattre', *S. vulgaris*
Klettenberg 1935; S IV
syn. - 'Dr Louis Delattre'
Klettenberg, Cat., 26 [1935]; Wister, Lilacs for America, 28 [1953] - as 'Dr Louis Delattre.
Named for Louis Delattre, 1870-1938; Belgian physician and naturalist, "un écologiste précoce"; author of "Le Jardin du docteur", 1911; member of l'Académie royale de langue et de littérature françaises de Belgique.
Cultivar name presumed registered 1953; name established and accepted.

Doctor ... - see also: Docteur ..., Dr ...

Doctor Brethour - see '**Dr Brethour**'.

'**Doctor Chadwick**', *S.* ×*hyacinthiflora*
Skinner pre-1963; S III
syn. - 'Chadwick', 'Dr Chadwick'
Wister, Arnoldia 23(4):81 [1963]; Skinner, Hort. Horizons, 108-109 [1966]; Photo on Jorgovani/Lilacs 2015 DVD.
Named for Lewis Charles Chadwick, 1902-1993, horticulturist, Ohio State University, USA.
Cultivar name registered 1963; name established and accepted.

Doctor Charles Jacobs - see '**Docteur Charles Jacobs**'

'Doctor Frederick Margaretten', *S. vulgaris*
Margaretten; ? ?
Cultivar name not established.

'Doctor Ilizarov', *S. vulgaris*
'И Доктор лизаров'
Aladin, S., Aladina, O., Polyakova, T., and Aladina, A. 2018; D I
{'Edith Cavell' × OP}
IX International Scientific Conference (IX Международная научная конференция "Цветоводство: история, теория, практика") " Floriculture: history, theory, practice" , St. Petersburg, Botanical Garden of Peter the Great BIN RAS, September 7-13, 2019 (in Russian).
Named for Academician Gavriil Abramovich Ilizarov (Гавриил Абрамович лизаров), 1921 – 1992, Soviet physician, known for inventing the Ilizarov apparatus for lengthening limb bones and for the method of surgery named after him, the Ilizarov surgery.
Cultivar name established and accepted.

Doctor Joel Margaretten - see 'Dr Joel Margaretten'.

'Doctor John', *S. vulgaris*
origin not known pre-1988; ? ?
Anon., Lilacs - Proceedings 17(1):26 [1988] - name only

Doctor John Rankin - see 'Dr John Rankin'.

Doctor Lemke - see 'No. 71', Lemke.

Doctor Nobbe - see '**Dr Nobbe**'.

'Doctor Nobbe Foliis Maculatis', *S. vulgaris*
Baudriller pre-1880; S IV *
{mutation of 'Dr Nobbe'}
Baudriller, Cat. No. 43, 142 [1880]; McKelvey, The Lilac, 291 [1928]
Cultivar name not established.

'**Donald Wyman**', *S.* (Villosae Group), *S.* ×*prestoniae*
Skinner 1944; S VII
Woody Plant Register, AAN, No. 23 [1949]; Wister, Lilacs for America, 47 [1942], 28 [1953]; Skinner, Hort. Horizons, 49, 107 109 [1966]; Photo on Jorgovani/Lilacs 2015 DVD.
Named for Donald Wyman, 1904-1993, horticulturist of the Arnold Arboretum of Harvard University, 1935-1970, Jamaica Plain, Massachusetts, USA.
Cultivar name presumed registered 1953; name established and accepted.

'Donaldii', *S. oblata* subsp. *dilatata*
  Egolf & Fiala 1988; S VII
  Fiala & Vrugtman, Syringa - A Gardener's Encyclopedia, 80-81 [2008]
  Named for Donald R. Egolf, 1928-1990, plant breeder, US National Arboretum, Washington, DC, USA.
  Cultivar name established and accepted.

'Donetskie Zori', *S. vulgaris*
  'Донецкие Зори'
  Tereshchenko 2002; D V
  {'Bogdan Khmel'nitskii' × ? }
  Tereshchenko, Lilacs in the South-East of Ukraine, p. 112-113, ill. back cover lower right [2002]; Chapman & Semyonova, Lilacs - Quart. Jour. 33(1):15 [2003] - translated from Tereshchenko, 2002
  Name: Russian for dawns of Donetsk, the city where this lilac was originated.
  varietal denomination registered UANA 2002;
  Cultivar name established and accepted.

'Donetskiï Suvenir', *S. vulgaris*
  'Донецкий Сувенир'
  Tereshchenko 2002; S IV
  {'Volcan' × ? }
  Tereshchenko, Lilacs in the South-East of Ukraine, p. 113-114, ill. back cover upper left [2002]; Chapman & Semyonova, Lilacs - Quart. Jour. 33(1):15-16 [2003] - as 'Donetsky Souvenir', translated from Tereshchenko, 2002
  Name: Russian for souvenir or memento of Donetsk, the city where this lilac was originated.
  Statutory registration UANA 2002;
  Cultivar name established and accepted.

Donkere Koster - see 'Dark Koster'.

'Don Wedge', *S. vulgaris*
  Margaretten; D IV
  {'Mme Lemoine' × ? }
  reported in cultivation at Royal Botanical Gardens, Ontario, Canada; Photo on Jorgovani/Lilacs 2015 DVD.
  Named for Donald Wedge, ca 1912 -2008, nurseryman, Albert Lea, Minnesota, USA.
  Cultivar name not established.

'Dorcas', *S.* (Villosae Group), *S.* ×*prestoniae*
  Preston 1930; S IV
  syn. - Preston No. 20-14-19
  Macoun, Rep. Dom. Hort. 1930, 67 [1931]; Wister, Lilacs for America, 47, 64 [1942], 28, 48 [1953]; Photo on Jorgovani/Lilacs 2015 DVD.
  Named for A Shepherdess in Shakespeare's *Winter's Tale*.
  Cultivar name presumed registered 1953; name established and accepted.

'Dorembos' - prob. **'Directeur Doorenbos'**.

'Doroga Zhizni', *S. vulgaris*
  'Дорога Жизни'
  Aladin, S., Aladina, O., and Polyakova, T. 2014; S I
  {'Flora 1953' × OP}
  Питомник-частный сад (Pitomnik i chastnyi sad; Nursery and private garden) 3/2015:14-22 (in Russian); ; Приусадебное хозяйство (Annex to the magazine Homestead farming: "Flowers in the garden and at home. Brushes and paints") 08/2015: 5-14; Садовник (Gardener) magazine, 05 (141)/2017 :16-22; Вестник АППМ (Catalog in Vestnik APPM (Planting material association) magazine) 1/2018: 59-72 (in Russian).
  Named for Дорога жизни, Doroga Zhizni or Road of Life, the ice road winter transport route across the frozen Lake Ladoga, which provided the only access to the besieged city of Leningrad 1941-1944.
  Cultivar name established and accepted.

'Dorothy', *S. vulgaris*
  Orchard between 1912 & 1940; ? ?
  Named for the daughter of the originator.
  No report of being in cultivation
  http://www.mhs.mb.ca/docs/people/orchard_h.shtml
  http://www.manitobaaghalloffame.com/ahofmember/orchard-harold/

'Dorothy Ramsden', *S. vulgaris*
  Alexander Sr ca 1980; S VII
  {'Mrs W. E. Marshall' × ? }
  in litt. J. H. Alexander Sr to F. Vrugtman, Dec. 16, 1971 - as *S. vulgaris* 'La Place' × 'Monge'; in litt. J. H. Alexander III [Sept. 24, 1976] - as open pollinated 'Mrs W. E. Marshall' seedling; RBG Hamilton, List of Lilacs [1995] - name only; Photo on Jorgovani/Lilacs 2015 DVD.
  Cultivar name not established.

Double Azure - see **'Azurea Plena'**.

Double Common (*S. vulgaris*) in Stand. Pl. Names, 615 [1942] - (?).
  Probably not a cultivar name.

Double Hyacinth - see **'Hyacinthiflora Plena'**.

Double Lemoine - see **'Lemoinei'**.

Double Rubella - see **'Rubella Plena'**.

'Double Sweetheart', *S. vulgaris*
  Origin not known; D V
  Spring Hill N., Wholesale Cat. 7 [1974] - as "creamy coral pink".

'Dove', *S. vulgaris*
  Rankin; D II
  {parentage not known}
  Fiala, Lilacs, p. 208 [1988] - as gray-purple, slate-gray
  Cultivar name established and accepted.

'**Downfield**', *S. vulgaris*
  Havemeyer pre-1942; D VI
  Wister, Lilacs for America, 47 [1942], 28 [1953]; Eickhorst, ILS Lilac Newsletter 4(1):4-5 [1978]; Photo on Jorgovani/Lilacs 2015 DVD.

Cultivar name presumed registered 1953; name established and accepted.

'Doyen Keteleer', *S. vulgaris*
Lemoine 1895; D IV
Lemoine, Cat. No. 131, 10 [1895]; McKelvey, The Lilac, 292 [1928].; Wister, Lilacs for America, 47 [1942] - as D III; Wister, Lilacs for America, 28 [1953]; Photo on Jorgovani/Lilacs 2015 DVD.
Cultivar name presumed registered 1953; name established and accepted.

Dr . . . - see also: Docteur . . . , Doctor . . .

'Dr Brethour', *S. vulgaris*
Paterson 1960; S VII
syn. - 'Doctor Brethour', 'Dr F. G. Brethour'
Ellesmere Nurseries, Cat. 15 [1960]; Wister, Arnoldia 23(4):81 [1963] - as 'Doctor Brethour'; Photo on Jorgovani/Lilacs 2015 DVD.
Named for Dr Frederick G. Brethour, Canadian peony breeder of the 1920s and 30s.
Cultivar name registered 1963; name established and accepted.

'Dr Bretschneider', *S. villosa* subsp. *villosa*
pre-1890; S V
syn. - 'Breitschneideri', *S. bretschneideri* Lemoine, *S. villosa bretschneideri*
Lemoine, Cat. No. 115, 19 [1890] - as *S. bretschneideri*; E. Lemoine, Garden 39:91, ill. [1891] - as *S. bretschneideri*; McKelvey, The Lilac, 82, 88-95 [1928] - included in *S. villosa*; Clarke Nursery, Garden Aristocrats, 12 [1937] - as 'Dr Breitschneider'; Wister, Lilacs for America, 44, 47, 60 [1942], 25, 28, 43 [1953] - as *villosa bretschneideri*; A.Rehder, Bibl. Cult. Trees and Shrubs p. 565a [1949] - as *S. villosa*
May not be distinct from *S. villosa* subsp. *villosa* Vahl.; Photo on Jorgovani/Lilacs 2015 DVD.
Named for Emil Vasilievic Bretschneider, 1833-1901, Russian physician, botanist and orientalist.
Cultivar name presumed registered 1953; name established and accepted.

Dr Bugała - see **'Dr W. Bugała'**.

Dr Chadwick - see **'Doctor Chadwick'**.

Dr Charles Jacobs - see **'Docteur Charles Jacobs'**.

'Dr Donald R. Egolf', *S. vulgaris*
Margaretten; D IV
{'Mme Lemoine' × ? }
Named for Donald R. Egolf, 1928-1990, plant breeder, US National Arboretum, Washington, DC, USA.
Cultivar name not established; not reported in cultivation.

DREAM - see **'Mechta'**

DREAM CLOUD™ - see 'Pink Flower Select' (*S. pubescens* subsp. *patula*)

'Dr Edward Mott Moore', *S. vulgaris*
Fenicchia 1972; S II
syn. - 'Doctor Edward Mott Moore', R 88
{'Rochester' F2}
Clark, The Newsletter, ILS, Convention Issue, pp. 6-7 [May 1972]; Clark, Arnoldia 32(3):133-135 [1972]; Fiala, Lilacs, pp. 94, 107, 219 [1988]; K. Millham, Lilacs -Quart. Jour. 42(2):62 [2013].
Named for Edward Mott Moore, 1814-1902, physician, "Father of the Park System" and first president of Park Commission of Rochester, New York, USA.
Cultivar name not established; no plants reported in cultivation, probably extinct.

'Dresden China', *S. vulgaris*
Klager 1930; S IV
syn. - Clara No. 2, Clara #2
Wister, Lilacs for America, 45, 47 [1942], 26, 28 [1953] - as Clara No. 2
Cultivar name presumed registered 1953; name established and accepted.

'Dr Frederick Margaretten', *S. vulgaris*
Margaretten; S VI
{'Mme Lemoine' × ? }
Not reported in cultivation
Cultivar name not established.

Dr Gaspard Callot - see **'Souvenir de Gaspard Callot'**.

Dr Hildreth - see 'Cheyenne'.

'Dr Hoffman', *S. vulgaris*
Klager; S V
Anon., ILS Newsletter 14(4):3-4 [1988]; Macore Co. Inc. photo library [Nov.28, 1999] http://www.macore.com/photolib.htm
Cultivar name not established.

'Drifting Dream', *S. vulgaris*
Fiala 1985; D II
{'Rochester' × 'Rochester' seedling}
Fiala, Lilacs, 223 [1988]; Photo on Jorgovani/Lilacs 2015 DVD.
Cultivar name established.

'Dr Joel Margaretten', *S. vulgaris*
Fiala 1983; S VII
syn. - 'Doctor Joel Margaretten'
{'Prodige' × 'Rochester'}
Fiala, Lilacs, 223 [1988]
Named for Joel Margaretten, 1910-1998, dentist and amateur lilac breeder, Leona Valley, California, USA.
Cultivar name established and accepted.

'Dr John', *S. vulgaris*
origin not known ? ?
anon., Lilacs - Quart. Jour. 17(1):26 [1988] - name only
Cultivar name not established.

'Dr John Rankin', *S. vulgaris*
Fiala 1985; S II
syn. - 'Doctor John Rankin'
{'Glory' × 'Flora 1953'}
Fiala, Lilacs, 94, 223 [1988]
Named for John Paul Rankin, 1891-1967, physician, collector and selector of lilacs, Elyria, Ohio, USA.
Cultivar name established and accepted.

'Dr John Wister', *S. vulgaris*
Margaretten; S V
{'Mme Lemoine' × ?}
Named for John Caspar Wister, 1887-1982, American landscape architect, garden writer and plantsman, editor of Lilacs for America, 1942, 1943 and 1953.
Cultivar name not established; not reported in cultivation.

'Dr Kirkhaven', *S. vulgaris*
pre-1958; D II
John G. Stropkey and Sons Nurseries, Cat. 4 [1972].

'Dr Lemke' - see No. 71, Lemke.

'Dr Lindley', *S. vulgaris*
Darimont 1858; S IV
syn. - 'Doctor Lindley', 'Lindley', 'Lindleyi', 'Lindleyana' (also 'Louis van Houtte' according to Wister, 1953)
{parentage not known}
L. van Houtte in Fl. Serres, 14:237, t. 1481-1482 [1861]; McKelvey, The Lilac, 289 [1928]; Wister, Lilacs for America, 47 [1942], 28 [1953]; Photo on Jorgovani/Lilacs 2015 DVD.
Named for John Lindley, 1799-1865, British botanist.
Cultivar name presumed registered 1953; name established and accepted.

'Dr Lyals', *S. vulgaris*
origin not known ? ?
McKelvey, The Lilac, 289 [1928]
Cultivar name not established.

'Dr Mahaux', *S. vulgaris*
Vandendriessche 1922; S VI
Wister, Lilacs for America, 28 [1953]
Cultivar name presumed registered 1953; name established and accepted.

'Dr Maillot', *S. vulgaris*
Lemoine 1895; D IV
syn. - 'Doctor Maillot'
Lemoine, Cat. No. 131, 12 [1895]; McKelvey, The Lilac, 290 [1928]; Wister, Lilacs for America, 47 [1942], 28 [1953]; Photo on Jorgovani/Lilacs 2015 DVD.
Cultivar name presumed registered 1953; name established and accepted.

'Dr Masters', *S. vulgaris*
Lemoine 1898; D V
syn. - 'Doctor Masters'
Lemoine, Cat. No. 140, 10 [1898]; Kache, Gartenschönheit 5:82 [1924]; McKelvey, The Lilac, 290 [1928]; Wister, Lilacs for America, 47 [1942] - as D III; Wister, Lilacs for America, 28 [1953]; Photo on Jorgovani/Lilacs 2015 DVD.
Named for Maxwell Tylden Masters, M.D., 1833-1907, editor of *Gardeners Chronicle*, United Kingdom.
Cultivar name presumed registered 1953; name established and accepted.

'Dr Nobbe', *S. vulgaris*
Eichler 1862; S IV
syn. - 'Doctor Nobbe', 'Dr Noble'
{'Marlyensis' × ?}
Eichler, Garten-Nachr. 7:27 [1862] in Wochenschr. Ver. Beförd. Gartenb. Preuss. [1862]; Anon., Hamburger Garten- und Blumenzeitung 392-393 [1862]; McKelvey, The Lilac, 290-291, 559-560, 563 [1928]; Wister, Lilacs for America, 47 [1942], 28 [1953]; Photo on Jorgovani/Lilacs 2015 DVD.
Named for Johann Christian Friedrich Nobbe, 1830-1922; botanist and seed specialist; founder of the world's first seed testing station; Forstakademie Tharandt, Saxony, Germay.
Cultivar name presumed registered 1953; name established and accepted.

Drouot - see **'Général Drouot'**.

Dr Regel - see **'Dr von Regel'**.

'Dr Troyanowsky', *S. vulgaris*
Lemoine 1901; D IV
syn. - 'Doctor Troyanowsky'
Lemoine, Cat. No. 149, 8 [1901]; Kache, Gartenschönheit 5:82 [1924]; McKelvey, The Lilac, 291 [1928]; Wister, Lilacs for America, 47 [1942], 28 [1953]; Photo on Jorgovani/Lilacs 2015 DVD.
Cultivar name presumed registered 1953; name established and accepted.

'Druzhba', *S.* ×*hyacinthiflora*
'Дружба'
Kopp 2013; D V
Syn. – 'Drushba Gisela'; seen on 12/9/20 at www.fliedertraum/de/syringa-hyacinthiflora-drushba
Nordwest Zeitung 06 May 2013
http://www.nwzonline.de/wirtschaft/weser-ems/gaeste-hinterlassen-rosafarbene-drushba_a_5,1,1551917979.html
Name: Russian for friendship; named and first planted May 2013 at the memorial cemetery for Russian prisoners of war at Wilhelmshaven, Germany.
Cultivar name established and accepted.

'Druzhba Narodov', *S. vulgaris*
'Дружба Народов'
Kolesnikov pre 1960; D VII
Syn - No. 205
Polyakova, 2018, "Master of the Lilac Inflorescence", p. 118; cultivar passport.
Name: Russian for friendship of nations.
Cultivar name established and accepted.

'Dr von Regel', *S. vulgaris*
Späth 1883; S V
syn. - 'Doctor von Regel', 'Dr Regel', 'Dr von Regal', Dr Von Regel
{chance seedling of unknown parentage}
Späth, Cat., 2 [1883]; Kache, Gartenschönheit 5:82 [1924]; McKelvey, The Lilac, 291-292 [1928]; Späth, Späth-Buch, 110 [1930]; Wister, Lilacs for America, 47 [1942], 28 [1953]; Photo on Jorgovani/Lilacs 2015 DVD.
Named for Eduard August von Regel, 1815-1892, German botanist, director of St Petersburg botanical garden, Russia.
Cultivar name presumed registered 1953; name established and accepted.

'Dr W. Bugała', *S. vulgaris*
Karpow-Lipski 1962; S V
syn. - 'Dr Bugała'
Wister & Oppe, Arnoldia 31(3):125 [1971] - as 'Dr W Bugała'
Named for Władysław Bugała 1924-2008, Polish horticulturist and hybridizer, director of Kórnik Arboretum and Institute for Dendrology, 1980-1995.
Cultivar name registered 1970; name established and accepted.

'DTR 124', *S. pekinensis*
Wandell 1992; S I
marketed in North America as SUMMER CHARM™
{parentage not known}
Discov-Tree R & D, flyer [n.d.] - as SUMMER CHARM™, 'DTR 124'; Handy Nursery Co., Cat., 6 [1992] - as 'Summer Charm', name only; United Information Systems Inc., Datascape Botanical Index, 106 [1994] - as 'Summer Charm', name only;
United States Plant Patent No. 8,951 [Oct. 18, 1994] - as SUMMER CHARM; statutory registration
Cultivar name established and accepted.

dubia 'Président Hayes' - see **'Président Hayes'**.

dubia rosea - see **'Mme Jeanne Cornu'**.

dubia rubra - see **'Saugeana'**.

'Dubrava', *S. vulgaris*
origin not known ? ? *
Listed at Nat'l Bot. G., Salaspils, Latvia 2/2000 - prob. 'Aucubaefolia'
Cultivar name not established.

'Duc de Nassau', *S. vulgaris*
Anon., The lilacs at Highland Park, Rochester, N.Y., 1912. p. 9.
Perhaps a misspelling of **'Duc de Massa'**.

'Duc de Massa', *S. vulgaris*
Lemoine 1905; D III
Lemoine, Cat. No. 161, 8 [1905]; Kache, Gartenschönheit 5:82 [1924]; McKelvey, The Lilac, 292 [1928]; Wister, Lilacs for America, 47 [1942], 28 [1953]; Photo on Jorgovani/Lilacs 2015 DVD.
Cultivar name presumed registered 1953; name established and accepted.

'Duc de Rohan', *S. vulgaris*
origin not known pre-1875; S V
Hartwig & Rümpler, Vilmorin's ill. Blumengärtnerei, part 3 (suppl.), 560 [1875].
Cultivar name established and accepted.

'Duchesse de Brabant', *S. vulgaris*
Brahy-Ekenholm 1860; S V
{'Charles X' × 'Noisette'}
Duvivier, Journ. Hort. Pratique Belg., ser. 2, 5:241, t. XIX fig. 2 [1861]; McKelvey, The Lilac, 293 [1928]; Wister, Lilacs for America, 47 [1942], 28 [1953]
Awards: Médaille de Vermeil, 1860 (Société royale des Conférences horticoles of Liège).
Named for Marie-Henriette, duchesse de Brabant, 1836-1902; born Maria-Henrietta von Habsburg-Lorreinen, Erzherzogin von Österreich, who married crown prince Léopold of Belgium in 1853, the future King Léopold II.
Cultivar name presumed registered 1953; name established and accepted.

'Duchesse de Nemours', *S. vulgaris*
origin not known pre-1845; S VII
McKelvey, The Lilac, 293 [1928].

'Duchesse d'Orléans', *S. vulgaris*
origin not known pre-1846; S VI
McKelvey, The Lilac, 293 [1928]; Wister, Lilacs for America, 47 [1942], 28 [1953]
Cultivar name presumed registered 1953; name established and accepted.

'Dunbar', *S. vulgaris*
origin not known pre-1998; ? ?
perhaps identical to one of the following: 'Adelaide Dunbar', 'Joan Dunbar' or 'John Dunbar'
Girard Nurs., Cat. p.23 [1998] as listed in Andersen Hort. Libr. Source List of Plants and Seeds, 5th ed., p.282 [2000] - no response to request for additional information.
Cultivar name not established.

'Duplex', *S. ×chinensis*
Lemoine 1897; D IV
syn. - many, see McKelvey, The Lilac, 419-420 (1928]
common name: Polumakhrovaya (Russian)
Lemoine, Cat. No. 134, 9 [1896] - as *S. varina duplex*; McKelvey, The Lilac, 419-420 [1928] - as *S. chinensis* f. *duplex* (Lemoine) Rehder; Wister, Lilacs for America, 47 [1942], 28 [1953]; Bean, Trees and Shrubs 4:540 [1980]; Gorb, Lilacs in the Ukraine, p.32 [1989] - as Polumakhrovaya; Photo on Jorgovani/Lilacs 2015 DVD.
Cultivar name presumed registered 1953; name established and accepted.

'Duplex', *S. vulgaris*
pre-1867; D III
Kuntze, Taschen-Flora, Leipzig, 82 [1867]; McKelvey, The Lilac, 293 [1928].

'Dusk', *S. vulgaris*
Havemeyer pre-1942; S VII
Wister, Lilacs for America, 47 [1942], 28 [1953]; Eickhorst, ILS Lilac Newsletter 4(1):4-5 [1978]
Cultivar name presumed registered 1953; name established and accepted.

Dwarf Arnold, *S. pubescens* subsp. *pubescens*
Origin not known; S V
also: Arnold Dwarf
photo seen by Claire Fouquet at The Lilac Museum, Saint-Georges, Quebec Canada in the ILS 2020 Photo DVD.
Lambert & Fricke, Lilacs - Quart. Jour. 26(2):57 [1997] - name only; see also in litt. Koller to Vrugtman of Jul.29/92 - material may be AA 1251-71 or AA 1252-71, compact clones grown as *S. velutina* at Arnold Arboretum.
Cognomen, not a cultivar name.

dwarf littleleaf lilac - see **'Palibin'** (*S. pubescens* subsp. *pubescens*).

'Dwarf Princess', *S. vulgaris*
origin not known ? ?
{'Rochester' × ? }
Fiala, Lilacs, 115 [1988] - name only
Cultivar name not established.

'Dwight D. Eisenhower', *S. vulgaris*
Fenicchia 1969; S III
syn. - 'Dwight Eisenhower', R164 RAF102
{'Rochester' × ? }
Wister & Oppe, Arnoldia 31(3):122 [1971]; Clark, The Newsletter, ILS, Convention Issue, pp. 6-7 [May 1972]; Hoepfl & Rogers, Lilac Newsletter 14(7):5 [1988]; in litt., Hoepf to Vrugtman [Nov.29/2003] - Fiala, Lilacs, Pl. 79, upper right, Fenicchia with 'Dwight Eisenhower' [1988]; K. Millham, Lilacs - Quart. Jour. 42(2):60 & ill. 64[2013]; Photo on Jorgovani/Lilacs 2015 DVD.
Named for Dwight David Eisenhower, 1890-1969, soldier and 34th president of the USA. Good multipetaling.
Cultivar name registered 1970; name established and accepted.

'Dymka', *S. vulgaris*
'Димка'
Kravchenko 1970; S V
{'Lamartine' x OP}
Kravchenko L. Culture of lilacs in Uzbekistan. Publishing house "Uzbekistan", Tashkent, 1970 p. 14.
Name: Russian for boy's name.
Cultivar name established and accepted.

'Dymok', *S. vulgaris*
'Дымок'
Dyagilev pre-1992, D III
Syn. - seedling 970
{'Katherine Havemeyer' × OP}
Dyagilev, Lilacs - Quart. Jour. 22(1): 19; Pikaleva, Lilacs - Quart. Jour. 23(4):84 [1994]
Name: Russian for plume of smoke.
Cultivar name not established.

D. Z. 5, *S.* (species affiliation not known)
origin not known pre-1998; ? ?
in cultivation at Ole Heide collection, Thisted, DK.
Probably a breeder's code; not a cultivar name.

'Dzhambul', *S. vulgaris*
'Джамбул'
Kolesnikov 1921; S II with I margin
syn. - 'Dzhambul', 'Jambul'
{'Andenken an Ludwig Späth' × 'Marie Legraye'}
Kolesnikov, Lilac, 26 [1955]; Howard, Arnoldia 19(6-7):31-35 [1959]; AABGA Quart. Newsl. No. 64, 17-21 [1965]; Luneva et al., Siren', 75-76 [1989] - in Russian; Photo on Jorgovani/Lilacs 2015 DVD.
Named for the Kazakh Soviet poet Dzhambul Dzhabayev (1846-1945).
Cultivar name established and accepted.

'Dzhavakharlal Neru', *S. vulgaris*
'Джавахарлал Неру'
Kolesnikov 1952; S VII
syn. - 'D. Nehru', 'D. Neru', Kolesnikov No. 724
{('Andenken an Ludwig Späth' × Kolesnikov No. 110) × Kolesnikov No. 105}
Gromov, Lilacs - Proceedings 2(4):17 [1974]; Rubtzov et al. 1980. Vidy i sorta sireni, kul'tiviruemye v SSSR. Kiev; Naukova Dumka. – in Russian; Holetich, C.D. 1982. Lilac species and cultivars in cultivation in USSR. Lilacs 11(2):1-38. - translation of Rubtzov et al. 1982; Photo on Jorgovani/Lilacs 2015 DVD.
Named for Jawaharlal Nehru, 1889-1964, Indian statesman, also known as Pandit Nehru.
Cultivar name established and accepted.

'Earliest', *S. oblata* subsp. *dilatata*
Clarke 1944; S V
{*S. oblata* subsp. *dilatata* seedling selected for early bloom}
Woody Plant Register, AAN, No. 79 [1949]; Wister, Lilacs for America, 28 [1953]
Cultivar name presumed registered 1953; name established and accepted.

Earliest Evangeline - see **'Evangeline'**.

'Earl Rousseau', *S. vulgaris*
origin not known ? ?
Peterson, Lilacs - Proceedings 16(1):18 [1987] - name only, obtained from Hulda Klager Lilac Garden, Woodland, Washington, USA, but does not appear on their list of lilacs, Lilacs - Quart. Jour. 20(2):41 [1991]
Cultivar name not established.

'Early Bird', *S.* ×*hyacinthiflora*
Sobeck; S V
Wister, Arnoldia 26(3):13 [1966]
Cultivar name registered 1966; name established and accepted.
Nota bene: Since this cultivar appears to be of 'Lavender Lady' ancestry see also: Pringle, Lilacs - Quart. Jour. 24(4):97-99 [1995]; and Vrugtman, HortScience 31(3):328 [1996].

'Early Double White', *S. vulgaris*
Clarke 1944; D I
syn. - 'Earliest Double White'
Clarke, Cat. vol. 16, 7 [1949]; Woody Plant Register, AAN, No. 78 [1949]; Wister, Lilacs for America, 28 [1953]; Photo on Jorgovani/Lilacs 2015 DVD.
Cultivar name presumed registered 1953; name established and accepted.

EARLY DWARF, *S.* (species affiliation not known)
origin not known ? ?
Prairie Regional Trials 1959-1993 - name only
Cognomen; not a cultivar name.

East, *S. villosa* subsp. *villosa*
Origin not known; S V
Peterson, Lilacs - Proceedings 16(1):25[1987] - name only, received from Heard Gardens Ltd (W. R. Heard) as Villosa East, which appears to be a location designation
Not a cultivar name.

'Eaton Red', *S. vulgaris*
Eaton 1960; ? ?
Wister & Oppe, Arnoldia 31(3):122 [1971] - name only
Cultivar name registered 1970, but without description;
Not reported in cultivation.

'Eburonensis', *S. vulgaris*
origin not known pre-1875; S IV
L. van Houtte, Cat. No. 165-LL, 18 [1875] - name only; McKelvey, The Lilac, 294 [1928]; Lilacs for America, 28 [1953]
Cultivar name presumed registered 1953; name established and accepted.

Eckenholm - see **'Ekenholm'**.

Ed Andrea - see **'Edouard André'**.

EDDY, *S.*
Origin not known;
Cognomen. Seen on Facebook page of Cordetta Valthauser on May 17, 2020.
Named for Ed Kowalik of Drums, PA who originated starts of this unknown cultivar.

'Eden', *S. vulgaris*
Oliver 1939; S VI
Wister, Lilacs for America, 47 [1942], 28 [1953]
Cultivar name presumed registered 1953; name established and accepted.'

'Ede Upītis', *S. vulgaris*
Upītis 1963; S I
syn. - 'Maate Ede Upiitis', 'Mate Ede Upītis', 'Mate Ede Upītis', Upītis No. 66-77
statutory epithet Ede Upitis
{parentage not known}
Kalva, V., Ceriņi (Lilac), 165-166 [1980] - in Latvian; Rub<u>t</u>zov et al. 1980. Vidy i sorta sireni, kul'tiviruemye v SSSR. Kiev; Naukova Dumka. – in Russian; Holetich, C.D. 1982. Lilac species and cultivars in cultivation in USSR. Lilacs 11(2):1-38. - translation of Rub<u>t</u>zov et al. 1982; Kalniņš, L., Ceriņu jaunšķirnes Dobelē, Dārs un drava 1986 (12):13-15 - in Latvian; Strautiņa, S. 1992. Ceriņi Dārzs un Drava. No. 6, pp.12-13; Strautiņa, S. 1996. Characteristics and propagation of lilacs obtained by P. Upītis. Problems of fruit plant breeding I. Jelgava. pp. 32-38; Strautiņa, S. 2002. Ceriņu un jasmīnu avīze. LA., R., p. 62; Vrugtman, HortScience 31(3):328 [1996]; in litt. S. Strautiņa to F. Vrugtman [21 Dec. 2007] - 1963, S I; Photo on Jorgovani/Lilacs 2015 DVD.
Named for the mother of the originator.
Statutory registration (breeder's rights) Nr. 299, CER-6, in Latvia [2004 - 2029] with the statutory epithet Ede Upitis
Cultivar name registered 1995; name established and accepted.

'Ed Frolich', *S. vulgaris*
Margaretten; S III
{Mme Lemoine' × ? }
reported in cultivation at University of Utah, USA.
Cultivar name not established.

'Edgar T. Robinson', *S. vulgaris*
Lyden; D IV
Wister, Arnoldia 23(4):81 [1963]
Cultivar name registered 1963;
Cultivar not reported in cultivation.

EDITH, *S.* - trade designation used for cut flowers of *S. vulgaris* 'Edith Braun'.

'Edith Braun', *S. vulgaris*
Rankin 1968; S VII
syn. - EDITH (trade designation used for cut flowers of this cultivar).
{parentage not known}
Fiala, Lilacs, 105, 207 [1988] - as rich magenta red-purple; Photo on Jorgovani/Lilacs 2015 DVD.
Named for Edith Braun, bride-to-be of the originator.
Cultivar name established and accepted.
Forcing lilac in the Netherlands.

'Edith Cavell', *S. vulgaris*
Lemoine 1916; D I
Lemoine, Cat. No. 190, 24 [1916]; McKelvey, The Lilac, 294 [1928]; Wister, Lilacs for America, 47 [1942], 28 [1953]; Photo on Jorgovani/Lilacs 2015 DVD.
Named for Edith Louisa Cavell, 1865-1915, WWI British army nurse executed in Belgium by German military for

treason on October 12.
Cultivar name presumed registered 1953; name established and accepted.

'Edith Groneau', S. vulgaris
Origin not known; S VII
Caprice Farm Nursery inventory system, A. Rogers, 05/07/84; Photo on Jorgovani/Lilacs 2015 DVD.
Cultivar name not established.

'Ed Kwolek', S.
Origin not known pre-2019; ?
In private collection (KA) in USA per email to Registrar 10-4-19.
Cultivar name not established.

'Edmond About', S. vulgaris
Lemoine 1908; D VI
syn. - 'Edmund About'
Lemoine, Cat. No. 170, 8 [1908]; Starcs, Mitt. Deutsche Dendrol. Ges. 40:44 [1928] - as 'Edmund About'; McKelvey, The Lilac, 294 [1928]; Wister, Lilacs for America, 47 [1942], 28 [1953]; Photo on Jorgovani/Lilacs 2015 DVD.
Named for Edmond François Valentin About, 1828-1885, French author.
Cultivar name presumed registered 1953; name established and accepted.

'Edmond Boissier', S. vulgaris
Lemoine 1906; S VII
syn. - 'Edmund Boissier', 'Edouard Boissier'
Lemoine, Cat. No. 164, 30 [1906]; Starcs, Mitt. Deutsche Dendrol. Ges. 40:41 [1928] - as 'Edmund Boissier'; McKelvey, The Lilac, 284-295 [1928]; Wister, Lilacs for America, 47 [1942], 28 [1953]; Photo on Jorgovani/Lilacs 2015 DVD.
Named for Edmond Boissier, 1810-1885, French botanist.
Cultivar name presumed registered 1953; name established and accepted.

'Edna Dunham', S. vulgaris
Rankin; S I
syn. - 'Edna'
{parentage not known}
Wister, Lilacs for America, 28 [1953]
Cultivar name presumed registered 1953; probably never introduced.

'Edouard André', S. vulgaris
Lemoine 1900; D V
syn. - 'Ed Andrea', 'Edward Andre'
Lemoine, Cat. No. 146, 11 [1900]; Kache, Gartenschönheit 5: opp. 82 - color ill. [1924]; McKelvey, The Lilac, 295 [1928]; Wister, Lilacs for America, 47 [1942], 28 [1953]; Photo on Jorgovani/Lilacs 2015 DVD.
Named for Edouard André, 1840-1911, French landscape architect.
Cultivar name presumed registered 1953; name established and accepted.

Edward Andre - see 'Edouard André'.

'Edward A. Schmidt', S. vulgaris
Ruliffson 1940; D VI
Wister, Lilacs for America, 47 [1942] & 28 [1953]
Cultivar name presumed registered 1953; not recorded in cultivation.

'Edward J. Gardner', S. vulgaris
Gardner pre-1950; D V
syn. - 'Ed J. Gardner', 'Edward Gardner', 'Edward J. Gardener', 'Edw. J. Gardner', Gardner No. 443, 'Flamingo' marketed in Germany as FLAMINGO™ (No. 305349856; G. & J. Rosskamp)
Edw. J. Gardner Nursery, Price list, 3 [1950]; Gardner, US Plant Patent No. 1086 [Apr. 22, 1952]; Wister, Lilacs for America, 28 [1953]; Lilacs - Quart. Jour. 20(4): front cover ill. [1991] & 22(4): back cover ill. [1993]; Photo on Jorgovani/Lilacs 2015 DVD.
Named for Edward J. Gardner, 1891-1952, nurseryman, Horicon, Wisconsin, USA.
Cultivar name presumed registered 1953; name established and accepted.

'Efrim Zimbaslist', S. vulgaris
Rankin; S IV
{parentage not known}
Cultivar name not established; probably extinct.

'Ekenholm', S. vulgaris
Brahy-Ekenholm pre-1854; S IV
syn. - 'Eckeholm', 'Eckenholm', 'Ekenholme'
C.F.A. Morren, Belg. Hort. 4:67, t. XI. fig. I [1854]; Moore, Lilacs, 132 [1903] - as 'Eckenholm'; McKelvey, The Lilac, 295 [1928]; Wister, Lilacs for America, 47 [1942], 29 [1953]; Photo on Jorgovani/Lilacs 2015 DVD.
Cultivar name presumed registered 1953; name established and accepted.

'Eksotika', S. vulgaris
Kārkliņš 2003; D VI ?
(no information; listed by T. Polyakova, 2014); Photo on Jorgovani/Lilacs 2015 DVD.
Name: Latvian for exotic.
Cultivar name not established.

'Ekwanok', S. vulgaris
originator not know; pre-1990?; D IV
said to have been discovered at the Ekwanok Country Club, Manchester Village, Vermont; For sale at: Equinox Valley Nursery, Manchester, Vermont.
<mail@equinoxvalleynursery.com>
<http://www.equinoxvalleynursery.com/nursery.html>
Also grown in the Lilac Trials, University of Vermont (Dr Leonard Perry)
<http://www.uvm.edu/pss/ppp/wplilacs.html>
Probably a new name for an old cultivar
Cultivar name not established and accepted.

'**Elaine**', *S.* (Villosae Group), *S.* ×*josiflexa*
Preston 1948; S I
syn. - Preston No. 30-01-47
{*S.* ×*josiflexa* 'Guinevere' × ? }
Davis, Rep. Dom. Hort., Progress Report 1934-1948, 149 [1950]; Wister, Lilacs for America, 29, 48 [1953]; Buckley, Greenhouse-Garden-Grass 8(3) [1969]; Photo on Jorgovani/Lilacs 2015 DVD.
Cultivar name presumed registered 1953; name established and accepted.

'**Elaire Brown Alexander**', *S.* ×*hyacinthiflora*
Alexander Sr; D V
{parentage not known}
Wister & Oppe, Arnoldia 31(3);122 [1971]
Cultivar name registered 1970;
Cultivar not reported in cultivation.

'El'brus', *S. vulgaris*
'Эльбрус'
Aladin, S., Polyakova, T., and Aladina, O. 2016; S I
{'Lebedushka' × OP}
Садовник (Gardener) magazine 04 (140)/2017 :18-25; Вестник АППМ (Catalog in Vestnik APPM (Planting material association) magazine) 1/2018: 59-72 (in Russian).
Named for Mount Elbrus, stratovolcano in the Caucasus; with 5,642 m above sea level the highest mountain peak in Russia and Europe.
Cultivar name established and accepted.

'Elda Beltran', *S. vulgaris*
Margaretten; D IV
{'Mme Lemoine' × ? }
Not reported in cultivation
Cultivar name not established.

'**Eleanor Berdeen**', *S. vulgaris*
Berdeen 1979; S III & V
syn. - 'Eleanor Furbish Berdeen', 'Eleanore Berdeen', 'Eleanov Gerdeen'
{mutation of 'René Jarry-Desloges'}
Vrugtman, Lilacs - Proceedings 7(1):36 [1979]; Vrugtman, AABGA Bull. 13(4):108 [1979]; Fiala, Lilacs, 97, 217, Pl. 76 [1988] - also as 'Eleanore Berdeen'
Named for the originator's wife.
Cultivar name registered 1977; name established and accepted.

'**Elegantissima**', *S. emodi*
van der Bom 1876; S I *
syn. - 'Aureo-marginata'
Ottolander, Sieboldia 2:191 [1876]; McKelvey, The Lilac, 26-27 [1928]; Wister, Lilacs for America, 47 [1942], 29 [1953]
Cultivar name presumed registered 1953; name established and accepted.

'Elena Anzhuĭskaya', *S. vulgaris*
'Елена Анжуйская'
Aladin, S., Aladina, O., Polyakova, T., and Aladina A. 2017; D V
{elite form 8-926 × 'Lavoisier'}
Садовник (Gardener) magazine 04 (140)/2017 :18-25; Вестник АППМ (Catalog in Vestnik APPM (Planting material association) magazine) 1/2018: 59-72 (in Russian).
Named for Elena of Anjou, 1236-1314, queen of Serbia who, according to legend, brought the lilacs to the Ibar River Valley.
Name established and accepted.

'Elena Rosse', *S.* ×*hyacinthiflora*
'Елена Россе'
Mikhaĭlov & Rybakina 2002; S IV-V
{'Esther Staley × 'Lucie Baltet'}
Chapman, Lilacs - Quart. Jour. 32(1):17-18 [2003]
- translated from N. L. Mikhaĭlov in Tsvetovodstvo, May-June issue (in Russian); Photo on Jorgovani/Lilacs 2015 DVD.
Named for Elena Rosse [no dates], Russian choreographer who worked with the Bolshoi and other Russian theatres.
Cultivar name established and accepted.

'Elena Vekhova', *S. vulgaris*
'Елена Вехова'
Vekhov 1952; D I
syn. - 'Elena Vechova', 'Jelena Vekhova', 'Pamyati Eleni Vekhovoy'*
{'Vestale' × ? }
*Synonym referenced in the magazine 'Tsvetovodstvo' ("floriculture"), No. 7, 1977, dedicated to the cultivars of Vekhov. Written by an employee of the Forest-Steppe Experimental Breeding Station, where this lilac was created.
Rubtzov et al. 1980. Vidy i sorta sireni, kul'tiviruemye v SSSR. Kiev; Naukova Dumka. – in Russian; Holetich, C.D. 1982. Lilac species and cultivars in cultivation in USSR. Lilacs 11(2):1-38. - translation of Rubtzov et al. 1982; Registered with the State Commission of the Russian Federation for Testing and Protection of Selection Achievements, No. 7508310, 1987; Photo on Jorgovani/Lilacs 2015 DVD.
Named for the wife of the originator.
Cultivar name established and accepted.

ELFE™ - see '**Dark Night**'.

ELFENKÖNIG™ - see '**Sunset**'.

'**Elihu Root**', *S. vulgaris*
Dunbar 1923; D VI
syn. - Dunbar no. 334
{'Gilbert' × ? }
McKelvey, The Lilac, 295-296 [1928]; Wister, Lilacs for America, 47 [1942], 29 [1953]
Named for Elihu Root, 1845-1937, American jurist and statesman, US secretary of war, 1899-1904, secretary of

state, 1905-1909, recipient of the Nobel prize for peace in 1912.
Cultivar name presumed registered 1953; name established and accepted.

'Elina Bystritskaya', *S. vulgaris*
'Элина Быстрицкая'
Dyagilev, B & Degtev, V. 2020; S VII/II
(Международная научная конференция "Syringa L.: коллекции, выращивание, использование")
"International Scientific Conference "Syringa L.: collections, cultivation, using" / Collection of Scientific Articles of Botanical Institute named after V.L. Komarov, Botanical Garden of Peter the Great BIN RAS. - St. Petersburg. -2020.- pp.23-27 (in Russian).
Named for the Russian actress.
Cultivar name established and accepted.

'Elinor', *S.* (Villosae Group), *S.* ×*prestoniae*
Preston 1928; S IV
syn. - 'Elinore', 'Leonora', 'Leonore', Preston No. 20-14-172
{*S. villosa* subsp. *villosa* × *S. komarowii* subsp. *reflexa*}
Macoun, Rep. Dom. Hort. 1928, 56 [1930]; Wister, Lilacs for America, 47, 64 [1942], 29, 48 [1953]; Pringle & Vrugtman, Lilacs - Quart. Jour. 20(4):112 [1991]; 'Elinor' has been distributed by Brand Peony Farm, Faribault, Minnesota, as 'Leonore', and by Select Plus Nursery as 'Leonora'; Photo on Jorgovani/Lilacs 2015 DVD.
Named for the Mother to King John in Shakespeare's *King John*.
Awards: RHS Award of Merit 1951; RHS Award of Garden Merit 1993.
Cultivar name presumed registered 1953; name established and accepted.

'Elinore Hill', *S. vulgaris*
Klager; S VII
Anon., ILS Newsletter 14(4):3-4 [1988]
Cultivar name not established.

Eliose - see '**Eloise**', *S.* (Villosae Group)
misspelled in Wister & Oppe, Arnoldia 31(3):122 [1971].

'Elisa', *S.* (Villosae Group)
Kasvi 1980s; S I
in litt. Kimmo Kolka to Vrugtman March 21, 2010
Cultivar name not established.

'Elizabeth', *S.* (Villosae Group), *S.* ×*prestoniae*
Preston date not known; ? ?
syn. - Preston ? 20-14-05
{*S. villosa* subsp. *villosa* × *S. komarowii* subsp. *reflexa*}
Preston, List of varieties of ornamental plants, originated in the Division of Horticulture, Central Experimental Farm, Ottawa, showing their respective parentage; undated typed list, p. 2 - name only.
Named for Elizabeth, queen to King Edward IV in Shakespeare's *King Richard III*.
Cultivar name not established and accepted; not now in cultivation.

Elizabeth Files - see '**Olive May Cummings**'
Wister & Oppe, Arnoldia 31(3):122 [1971] - name only, erroneous registration; see also Vrugtman, HortScience 26(5):477 [1991].
Cultivar name not established.
Nota bene: in: Fiala, Lilacs, 103, 217 [1988] - 'Elizabeth Files' should read: 'Olive May Cummings'.

'Elizabeth Mills', *S. vulgaris*
Klager 1930; S VII
Wister, Lilacs for America, 47 [1942], 29 [1953]
Named for Hulda Klager's daughter, Elizabeth Klager Mills (d. 1956).
Cultivar name presumed registered 1953; name established and accepted.

'Élizzz', *S.*
Moro, F. 2010; S III
{'Pixie' × ?}
Plant in cultivation at The Lilac Museum, Saint-Georges, QC - in lit. Fouquet to Vrugtman 4 Nov. 2016.
Named for Élise Dion, a lady socially involved in her community of Saint-Georges. Saint-Georges is located in the Beauce region of Quebec, Canada, where The Lilac Museum, Le Musée des Lilas, can be found.
Cultivar name established and accepted.

'Ella Emanuel', *S. vulgaris*
Margaretten; D V
{'Mme Lemoine' × ? }
Not reported in cultivation
Cultivar name not established.

'Ellen' - see 'Amigo', *S.* ×*chinensis*

Ellen Willmott - see **'Miss Ellen Willmott'**.

'Ellie-Marie', *S. vulgaris*
Havemeyer & Sears; S IV
syn. - 'Ellen Marie', 'Ellie Marie'
Wister, Lilacs for America, 29 [1953]; Eickhorst, ILS Lilac Newsletter 4(1):4-5 [1978]; Photo on Jorgovani/Lilacs 2015 DVD.
Cultivar name presumed registered 1953; name established and accepted.

'Elliott', *S. reticulata*
Origin not known; S I
marketed in the USA as Snowcap™
Carleton Plants, Cat. [2000]; Dirr, Manual of woody landscape plants, 6th ed., p. 1106 [2009].
Cultivar name established and accepted.

'**Eloise**', *S.* (Villosae Group)
Alexander Sr (not Lyden) 1969; S V
syn. - 'Eliose'
{*S.* ×*josiflexa* 'James Macfarlane' × *S.* ×*prestoniae* 'Ethel M. Webster'}
Alexander Sr, Cat. sheets [n.d.; rec'd March 1969]; Wister & Oppe, Arnoldia 31(3):122 [1971] - name only

and misspelled as 'Eliose'
Cultivar name registered 1970;
Cultivar not reported in cultivation.

'Eloise', *S. vulgaris*
Lyden (not Alexander Sr); S V
{parentage not known}
Cultivar name not established; probably no longer in cultivation.

'Elsa Maasik', *S. vulgaris*
Vaigla 1990; S VII
{'Andenken an Ludwig Späth' × ? }
Vrugtman, HortScience 26(5): 477 [1991]; Kivistik, Maakodu 1997(5):22-23 (ill.) [1997] - in Estonian; I. Semenov, Lilacs 48(2):65,63 (photo) [2019].
Named for Elsa Maasik, 1908-1991, Estonian opera singer.
Cultivar name registered 1990; name established and accepted.

'Elsdancer', *S. vulgaris*
Moore & Elsley probably 1980s; S II-VII
syn. - Ralph's Dwarf (cognomen); marketed as Tiny Dancer™
<www.plantsnouveau.com/plant/syringa-vulgaris-tiny-dancer>
Cultivar name established and accepted.

'Elsie Lenore', *S. vulgaris*
Fiala 1982; S V-VI
{'Sensation' × 'Sensation'}
Fiala, Lilacs, 100-101, 103, 107, 108, 188, 223, Pl. 22 [1988] - as colchicine induced tetraploid (?); Photo on Jorgovani/Lilacs 2015 DVD.
Named for Elsie Lenore Meile, 1921-2016, sister of the originator.
Cultivar name established and accepted.

'Eltigen', *S. vulgaris*
Klimenko Z., and Zykova V. 2013; S IV
in cultivation at Nikita Botanical Garden
Named in commemoration of the Kerch-Eltigen Operation of the Red Army, November 1943, at the Crimea's Eastern coast.
Cultivar name established and accepted.

'Ema Juuli', *S. vulgaris*
Mägi pre-2017; S VII
Photo by Aaron Mägi from Estonia seen on 2020 ILS Photo & Color Database.
Cultivar name not established.

'Emei Shan', *S. komarowii* subsp. *komarowii*
Ogisu and the Sir Harold Hillier Gardens, Ampfield House, UK; S VII
J. J. Cubey, Hanburyana 3:112-113 [2008].
Named for Éméi Shān or Mount Emei, Sichuan, China, where the seed was collected by Mikinori Ogisu on 18 October 1994 at an altitude of 2340m (Ogisu 94313). The seedling was selected and named by Roy Lancaster at the Sir Harold Hillier Gardens, United Kingdom (accession no. 1995.0291); flowering specimen [WSY0113676] and digital image [WSYD0001579] in the RHS Herbarium (WSY).
Awards: RHS Certificate of Preliminary Commendation as a flowering plant for exhibition; Hanburyana 3:112-113 [2008].
Note: The original plant died; it was not propagated.
Cultivar name established and accepted.

Emeljan Jarolsavskij - see 'Emel'yan Yaroslavskiĭ'.

'Emel'yan Yaroslavskiĭ', *S. vulgaris*
'Емельян Ярославский'
Kolesnikov; D V
syn. - 'Emeljan Jarolsavskij'
Rubtzov et al. 1980. Vidy i sorta sireni, kul'tiviruemye v SSSR. Kiev; Naukova Dumka. – in Russian; Holetich, C.D. 1982. Lilac species and cultivars in cultivation in USSR. Lilacs 11(2):1-38. - translation of Rubtzov et al. 1982.
Named for Emel'yan Mikhailovich Yaroslavskiĭ, born Minei Israilevich Gubelman, 1878-1943, Russian revolutionary, Soviet politician, communist party organizer and activist, journalist, and historian.
Cultivar name established and accepted.

'Emerald', *S. josikaea*
Schmidt; S VII
{*S. josikaea* × ? }
Vrugtman, HortScience 25(6):618 [1990]
Cultivar name registered 1989; name established and accepted.

'Emery Mae Norweb', *S. vulgaris*
Fiala 1980; D I
{'Gismonda' × 'Flora 1953'}
Knight, Lilacs-Proceedings 9:8 [1981] - a creamy double white; Fiala, Lilacs, 3, 91, 104, 135, 223 [1988].
Named for Emery Mae Holden-Norweb, 1896-1984, daughter of Albert F. Holden, who initiated the establishment of an institution for botanical education, known today as the Holden Arboretum, Kirtland, Ohio, USA; she was an important promoter and supporter of the Arboretum.
Cultivar name established and accepted.

'Émile Gentil', *S. vulgaris*
Lemoine 1915; D III
common name: Emile Gentil
Lemoine, Cat. No. 189, 22 [1915]; McKelvey, The Lilac, 296 [1928]; Stand. Pl. Names, 615 [1942] - as Emile Gentil; Wister, Lilacs for America, 47 [1942], 29 [1953]
Named for Émile Gentil, 1866-1914, French explorer and French Congo commissioner.
Cultivar name presumed registered 1953; name established and accepted.

'**Émile Lemoine**', *S. vulgaris*
    Lemoine 1889; D IV
    common name: Emil Lemoine
    Lemoine, Cat. No. 113, 19 [1889]; McKelvey, The Lilac, 296 [1928]; Stand. Pl. Names, 615 [1942] - as Emile Lemoine; Wister, Lilacs for America, 47 [1942], 29 [1953]
    Named for Paul Émile Prosper Lemoine 1862-1943, French horticulturist, son of Victor Lemoine.
    Cultivar name presumed registered 1953; name established and accepted.

'Emilia', *S.* (Villosae Group), *S.* ×*prestoniae*
    Preston; ? ?
    syn. - Preston No. 20-14-13
    {*S. villosa* subsp. *villosa* × *S. komarowii* subsp. *reflexa*}
    Macoun, Rep. Dom. Hort. 1828, [1930] - name only; Wister, Lilacs for America, 64 [1942], 48 [1953] - not in cultivation, no plants distributed
    Named for the Wife to Iago in Shakespeare's *Othello*.
    Cultivar name not established; probably extinct.

'**Emil Liebig**', *S. vulgaris*
    Späth 1887; D III
    syn. - Emile Leibig
    {chance seedling of unknown parentage}
    Späth, Cat. No. 69, 4 [1887]; McKelvey, The Lilac, 296-297 [1928]; Späth, Späth-Buch, 110 [1930]; Wister, Lilacs for America, 47 [1942], 29 [1953]
    Named for Emil Liebig, 1839-1887, horticulturist and nurseryman at Dresden, Germany, contemporary and colleague of Franz Ludwig Späth, 1839-1913.
    Cultivar name presumed registered 1953; name established and accepted.

emodi aurea, Emodi Aurea - see '**Aurea**' (*emodi*).

emodi aureo variegata - see '**Variegata**' (*emodi*).

emodi elegantissima - see '**Elegantissima**' (*emodi*).

emodi variegata - see '**Variegata**' (*emodi*).

'Engler Weisser Traum', *S. vulgaris*
    Engler pre-1985; S I
    syn. - 'Engler Weißer Traum', 'Engler's Weißer Traum', Engler Weissen Traum', 'Weisser Traum', 'White Dream'
    {mutation of 'Mme Florent Stepman'}
    reported in cultivation in Canada, Germany and The Netherlands; no lit. ref. located;
    Photo on Jorgovani/Lilacs 2015 DVD.
    Name: German for Engler white dream
    Cultivar name established and accepted.
    Forcing cultivar in the Netherlands.

'**Enid**', *S.* (Villosae Group), *S.* ×*josiflexa*
    Preston 1938; S V
    syn. - Preston No. 24-02-43
    {*S.* ×*josiflexa* 'Guinevere' × ? }
    Davis & Preston, RHS Conf. Ornamental flowering trees and shrubs. pp. 135-140 [1938]; Davis, Rep. Dom. Hort., Progress Report 1934-1948, 149 [1950]; Wister, Lilacs for America, 47, 64 [1942], 29, 48 [1953]
    Cultivar name presumed registered 1953; name established and accepted.

ENSKEDE, *S. reticulata*
    Origin not known; S I
    in litt Björn Aldén to F. Vrugtman, Nov. 10, 2007
    Not a cultivar name.

'Epaulettes', *S. pubescens* subsp. *microphylla*
    Fiala 1984; S VI
    syn. - 'Epaulette'
    {'Hers' × 'George Eastman'}
    Fiala, Lilacs, 51, 104, 108, 224, Pl. 32 [1988]
    Cultivar name established and accepted.

'Epifānija', *S. vulgaris*
    Upītis 1972; D I
    syn. - Eterna
    Kalniņš, Ceriņu jaunšķirnes Dobelē, Dārs un drava 1986 (12):13-15 - in Latvian; Strautiņa S. 1992. Ceriņi Dārzs un Drava. No. 6, pp.12-13; Strautiņa, S. 1996. Characteristics and propagation of lilacs obtained by P. Upītis. Problems of fruit plant breeding I. Jelgava. pp. 32-38; in litt. S. Strautiņa to F. Vrugtman [21 Dec. 2007] - 1972, D I
    Cultivar name established and accepted.

'Equinox Valley', *S. vulgaris* (?)
    Preuss ca 1980's; D VII
    {a re-named, un-identified older cultivar}
    Cultivar name not established and accepted.

'Ermita<u>zh</u>' (Hermitage), *S. vulgaris*
    'Эрмитаж'
    Aladin, S., Aladina, O., Polyakova, T., and Aladina, A. 2019; D II
    {'Président Poincaré' × OP}
    (Международная научная конференция "Syringa L.: коллекции, выращивание, использование")
    "International Scientific Conference "Syringa L.: collections, cultivation, using" / Collection of Scientific Articles of Botanical Institute named after V.L. Komarov, Botanical Garden of Peter the Great BIN RAS. - St. Petersburg. -2020.- pp.3-7 (in Russian); Photo exhibition of all varieties of the creative breeding group "Russian Lilac" at the Festival "Lilac February", St. Petersburg, Botanical Garden of Peter the Great BIN RAS, February 22-24, 2020.
    Named for the famous Hermitage Museum in St. Petersburg.
    Cultivar name established and accepted.

'**Erzherzog Johann**', *S. vulgaris*
    origin not known pre-1864; S IV
    syn. - 'Archduke John', 'Erherzog Johann', 'Erzerhog Johann'
    Petzold & Kirchner, Arb. Muscav., 495 [1864]; Moore,

Lilacs, 140 [1903] - as 'Archduke John'; McKelvey, The Lilac, 297 [1928]; Wister, Lilacs for America, 36, 48 [1942], 29 [1953]; Photo on Jorgovani/Lilacs 2015 DVD.
Named for Archduke Johann of Austria, 1782-1859, a well-respected mountaineer for whom also the orchid *Nigritella archiducis-joannis* was named.
Cultivar name presumed registered 1953; name established and accepted.

'Esības Prieks', *S. vulgaris*
Upītis 1950; S II-VII
syn. - 'Esibas Prieks', 'Ėsibas Prieks', 'Esiibas Prieks', 'Tikshanaas Prieks', Upītis No. 3130
{parentage not known}
Kalva, Ceriņi (Lilac), 165-166 [1980] - in Latvian; Rubtzov et al. 1980. Vidy i sorta sireni, kul'tiviruemye v SSSR. Kiev; Naukova Dumka. – in Russian; Holetich, C.D. 1982. Lilac species and cultivars in cultivation in USSR. Lilacs 11(2):1-38. - translation of Rubtzov et al. 1982; Kalniņš, Ceriņu jaunšķirnes Dobelē, Dārs un drava 1986 (12):13-15 - in Latvian; Strautiņa S. 1992. Ceriņi Dārzs un Drava. No. 6, pp.12-13; Vrugtman, HortScience 31(3):327 [1996]; Strautiņa, S. 2002. Ceriņu un jasmīnu avīze. LA, R., p. 62; in litt. S. Strautiņa to F. Vrugtman [21 Dec. 2007] - 1950, S II-VII; Semenov, Igor, Lilacs - Quart. Jour. 44(2):49, ill. 51 [2015] - as V-II; Photo on Jorgovani/Lilacs 2015 DVD.
Name: Latvian for joy of existence.
Cultivar name registered 1995; name established and accepted.

'Esmeralda', *S. vulgaris*
Kārkliņš 2003; D VII
photo from Dobele, Latvia by Natalia Savenko, seen in 2020 ILS Photo Database.
Cultivar name not established.

'Esperance', *S. vulgaris*
Lape; D VII
{'Kapriz' × ? }
Vrugtman, AABGA Bull. 17(3):68 [1984]
Named for the town of Esperance, New York, USA.
Cultivar name registered 1982;
Cultivar not reported in cultivation.

'Esta', *S. vulgaris*
Rankin; D IV
{parentage not known}
Wister, Arnoldia 23(4):81 [1963]
Cultivar name registered 1982;
Cultivar not reported in cultivation.

'Estelle Brugge', *S. vulgaris*
Rankin; S IV
{parentage not known}
Cultivar name not established; probably extinct.

'Esterka', *S.* (Villosae Group), *S.* ×*prestoniae*
Bugała pre-1970; S V
syn. - 'Estarka'
Bugała, Arboretum Kórnickie 15:61-70 [1970]; Wister & Oppe, Arnoldia 31(3):122 [1971]; Bugała, Lilacs - Quart. Jour. 24(4):90-91 [1995]; Photo on Jorgovani/Lilacs 2015 DVD.
Cultivar name registered 1970; name established and accepted.

'Esther Staley', *S.* ×*hyacinthiflora*
Clarke 1948; S VI
syn. - 'Ester Staley', 'Esther', 'Esther Stanley', 'Ester Stayley', 'Ester Stayli', ESTHER (trade designation used for cut flowers of this cultivar)
{'Mme F. Morel' × ? }
Clarke, US Plant Patent No. 768 [Dec. 16, 1947] - as S. vulgaris; Clarke, Cat. vol. 15, 9 [1948]; Woody Plant Register, AAN, No. 186 [1949]; Lilacs for America, 29 [1953]; Photo on Jorgovani/Lilacs 2015 DVD.
Named for Mrs Esther Staley [no dates], Riverbank, California, who pioneered the introduction of many garden plants in the San Joaquin Valley.
Awards: RHS Award of Merit 1961; RHS Award of Garden Merit 1993.
Cultivar name presumed registered 1953; name established and accepted.
Forcing cultivar in the Netherlands.

'Ethan Allen', *S. vulgaris*
Havemeyer & Eaton pre-1972
Niedz, ILS Newsletter 1(4):7-8 [1972]; Eickhorst, ILS Lilac Newsletter 4(1):4-5 [1978]
Named by Mark Eaton for his son-in-law Ethan Allen Owen.
Cultivar name not established; appears to be extinct.

'Ethel Child', *S. vulgaris*
Child pre-1978; S VII
syn. - 'Ethel Childs'
Vrugtman, Lilacs - Quart. Jour. 6(1):15 [1978]; Vrugtman, AABGA Bull. 13(4):106 [1979]; Fiala, Lilacs, 105, 261 [1988] - as 'Ethel Childs'
Named for Ethel Child, 1924-1968, daughter of the originator.
Cultivar name registered 1976; name established and accepted.

'Ethel Dupont', *S. vulgaris*
Havemeyer pre-1942; S VII
Stand. Pl. Names, 615 [1942] - as Ethel duPont; Wister, Lilacs for America, 48 [1942], 29 [1953]; Niedz, ILS Proceedings 1(4):8 [1972] - as blue, perhaps identical to 'True Blue', Havemeyer; Eickhorst, ILS Lilac Newsletter 4(1):4-5 [1978]
Named for Ethel du Pont Roosevelt Warren, 1916-1965, American heiress and socialite.
Cultivar name presumed registered in 1953; identity questionable; not reported in cultivation.

'Ethel M. Webster', *S.* (Villosae Group)
Preston 1948; S V
syn. -'Esthel M. Webster', 'Ethel Webster', Preston No. 30-07-01
{*S. komarowii* subsp. *reflexa* × ? ("*wolfii*" of Lemoine)}
see Lilacs of America [1953]
Preston, Gardening Illustrated [Dec. 1946] - indicating that the parent plant received as *S. wolfii* from Lemoine was misnamed; Davis, Rep. Dom. Hort., Progress Report 1934-1948, 151 [1950]; AAN reg'n card No. 471- as reg'd & int'd by E.A. Upton; Wister, Lilacs for America, 29 [1953]; Fiala, Lilacs, 79, 101, 108, 203, Pl. 55 [1988] - as 2nd generation ×*prestoniae*; Photo on Jorgovani/Lilacs 2015 DVD.
Cultivar name presumed registered 1953; name established and accepted.

'Ethiopia', *S. vulgaris*
origin not known pre-1929; S VII
Wister, Lilacs for America, 29 [1953]; Buckley, Greenhouse-Garden-Grass 8(3) [1969] - names Brand as originator (?); Photo on Jorgovani/Lilacs 2015 DVD.
Cultivar name presumed registered 1953; name established and accepted.

'Etna', *S. vulgaris*
Lemoine 1927; S VII
Lemoine, Cat. No. 200 bis, 7 [1917]; McKelvey, The Lilac, 297 [1928]; Wister, Lilacs for America, 48 [1942], 29 [1953]; Photo on Jorgovani/Lilacs 2015 DVD.
Named for the Sicilian (Italy) volcano.
Cultivar name presumed registered 1953; name established and accepted.

'Étoile de Mai', *S. vulgaris*
Lemoine 1905; D VII & I
Lemoine, Cat. No. 161, 29 [1905]; McKelvey, The Lilac, 297 [1928]; Wister, Lilacs for America, 48 [1942], 29 [1953] - as D VI; Photo on Jorgovani/Lilacs 2015 DVD.
Name: French for May star.
Cultivar name presumed registered 1953; name established and accepted.

'Étoile de Nancy', *S. vulgaris*
origin not known pre-1931; ? ?
B. O. Case & Son, Cat. [1931]; Wister, Lilacs for America, 36, 48 [1942], 29 [1953] - doubtful name, prob. 'Étoile de Mai' or 'Belle de Nancy'
Cultivar name not established.

'Evangeline', *S.* ×*hyacinthiflora*
Skinner (not Preston) 1934; D VI
syn. - 'Earliest Evangeline'
Skinner, Dropmore, Cat. 37 [1935]; Wister, Lilacs for America, 48 [1942], 29 [1953]; Skinner, Hort. Horizons, 49, 108 [1966]; Photo on Jorgovani/Lilacs 2015 DVD.
Cultivar name presumed registered 1953; name established and accepted.

'Evangeline', *S.* (Villosae Group), *S.* ×*prestoniae*
Preston (not Skinner) pre-1942; ? ?
Stand. Pl. Names, 615 [1942] - name only.
Cultivar name not established.

Evensong - see 'Eventide'
Clark, Lilacs - Proceedings 15(1):6 [1986] - should read 'Eventide'.

'Eventide', *S.* (Villosae Group)
Fiala 1980; S II
{(*S. komarowii* subsp. *komarowii* × *S. villosa* subsp. *wolfii*) × [(*S. tomentella* subsp. *sweginzowii* × *S. tomentella* subsp. *tomentella*) × *S. komarowii* subsp. *komarowii*], or 'Garden Peace' × 'Lark Song'}
Clark, Lilacs - Proceedings 15(1):6 [1986] - erroneously as 'Evensong'; Fiala, Lilacs 187, 224, Pl. 56 [1988] - as tetraploid
Cultivar name established and accepted.

'Evert de Gier', *S. vulgaris*
De Gier & Wezelenburg 2006; D III/II
Marketed in Europe as CARPE DIEM® and erroneously as 'Carpe Diem'
{'Krasavitsa Moskvy' × ? }
<http://www.newplants.nl/planten/s/syringa-vulgaris-carpe-diemr-pbr-evert-de-gier>
Named for Evert de Gier, father-in-law of Jan-Willem Wezelenburg jr.
Statutory registration: Plant Breeder's Rights: EU33550; USPP applied for (?).
Cultivar name established and accepted.

'Excel', *S.* ×*hyacinthiflora*
Skinner 1932; S IV
syn. - 'Excell', BLUE LAGOON (trade name used for cut flowers of this cultivar)
{*S. oblata* subsp. *dilatata* × *S. vulgaris*}
USDA Inventory No. 113, p. 14, No. 101379 [Sept. 1934]; Skinner, Dropmore, Cat. 37 [1935]; Woody Plant Register, AAN, No. 56 [1949]; Wister, Lilacs for America, 48 [1942], 29 [1953]; Skinner, Hort. Horizons, 49, 109 [1966] - as 'Excel' and 'Excell'; Condit, Lilacs - Quart. Jour.19(4):74, front cover color ill. [1990]; Photo on Jorgovani/Lilacs 2015 DVD.
Cultivar name presumed registered 1953; name established and accepted.
Forcing cultivar in the Netherlands.

'Excellens', *S. pubescens* subsp. *patula*
Lemoine ca 1936; S I
syn. - 'Excellans', 'Exellenc', *S. palibiniana excellens*, *S. velutina excellens*
Lemoine, Cat. 210, 26 [1936] - as *S. palibiniana excellens*; Wister, Lilacs for America, 48, 59 [1942], 29, 43 [1953]; Wyman, Arnoldia 8(7):34 [1948] - as pure white; Photo on Jorgovani/Lilacs 2015 DVD.
Cultivar name presumed registered 1953; name established and accepted.

'Excellent', *S. vulgaris*
    Eveleens Maarse 1938; S I
    {'Jan van Tol' × 'Mme Florent Stepman'}
    Dijkhuis, Gedenkboek Valck. Suringar, 128 [1942]; Lilacs for America, 29 [1953]; Eveleens Maarse, Dendron 9(1):11-12 [1954]; Photo on Jorgovani/Lilacs 2015 DVD.
    Awards: First Class Certificate 1938 (KMTP).
    Cultivar name presumed registered 1953; name established and accepted.

'Eximia', *S.* (Villosae Group)
    Olbrich 1899; S VI-V
    syn. - ×*henryi* 'Eximia', *josikaea eximia*, 'Rosea' (?)
    common name: Red Rose
    {*S. josikaea* × ? }
    Froebel, Cat. No. 124, 78 [1899]; Stand. Pl. Names, 264, 487 [1923] - as Red Rose; McKelvey, The Lilac, 57-59 [1928]; Wister, Lilacs for America, 48, 50 [1942], 29, 32 [1953] - as S V, see also 'Rosea' (*josikaea*); Photo on Jorgovani/Lilacs 2015 DVD.
    Cultivar name presumed registered 1953; name established and accepted.

'Extra White', *S. vulgaris*
    origin not known pre-1885; ? I
    486 [1923] - as Extra White; McKelvey, The Lilac, 297 [1928]
    Cultivar name not established.

Fairy Dust™ see **'Baildust'**.

'Falconskeape', *S. reticulata* subsp. *reticulata*
    Origin not known; S I
    syn. - 'Falconskeepe'
    Arbor Village Farm Nursery, Cat. 2000/2001 p. 64 - as 'Falconskeepe'
    Named for Falconskeape, the estate of Fr John Leopold Fiala, 1924-1990, priest, teacher, scientist and plantsman, Medina, Ohio, USA.
    Cultivar name not established.

'Fałe Bałtyku', *S. vulgaris*
    Karpow-Lipski 1961; S III
    syn. - 'Fale Baltyku', 'Fall Baltyku', 'Fall Bolteco'
    Wister & Oppe, Arnoldia 31(3):125 [1971] - erroneously as D III; Photo on Jorgovani/Lilacs 2015 DVD.
    Name: Polish for wave of the Baltic Sea.
    Cultivar name registered 1970; name established and accepted.

Fall Foliage, *S.* (species affiliation not known)
    origin not known ? ?
    Gilbert, Lilacs - Quart. Jour. 27(2):49-50 [1998]
    Cognomen; a plant designation, not a cultivar name.

'Fantasy', *S.* ×*hyacinthiflora*
    Clarke 1960; D VI
    Clarke, Cat., 42 [1960]; Wister, Arnoldia 23(4):81 [1963]; Photo on Jorgovani/Lilacs 2015 DVD.
    Cultivar name registered 1963; name established and accepted.

'Fantaziya', *S. vulgaris*
    'Фантазия'
    Vekhov 1952; D V
    syn. - 'Fantazia', 'Fantazija'
    Pikaleva, Lilacs - Quart. Jour. 23(4):85 [1994]; Photo on Jorgovani/Lilacs 2015 DVD.
    Cultivar name established and accepted.

'Farforovaya'
    'Фарфоровая'
    Kolesnikov pre-1953; S I
    {parentage not known}
    T. Polyakova, 2018, Мастер Сиреневой Кисти (Master of the Lilac Brush), p.109 - photo only.
    (to be completed)
    Name: Russian for porcelain.
    Cultivar name established and accepted.

'Far Horizon', *S. vulgaris*
    Polin; D III
    Wister & Oppe, Arnoldia 31(3):122 [1971]
    Cultivar name registered 1970;
    Cultivar not reported in cultivation.

Farmer Morel - see f. *morel*.

'Farrionensis', *S. vulgaris*
    origin not known pre-1905; S IV-V
    common name: Farrion
    Stand. Pl. Names, 486 [1923] - as Farrion; McKelvey, The Lilac, 297-298 [1928]; Wister, Lilacs for America, 36, 48 [1942], 29 [1953] - as S IV
    Cultivar name presumed registered 1953; name established and accepted.

'Father Fiala', *S.* (Ross, not Margaretten)
    Ross (?) pre-2014; S III *
    {origin & species affiliation not known}
    cultivated and described at Glasshouse Works <http://www.glasshouseworks.com/syringa-species-father-fiala&search=syringa>
    Name established and accepted.

Father Fiala (Margaretten, not Ross) - see **'Fiala Remembrance'**, *S. vulgaris*.

'Father John', *S. vulgaris*
    Brown 1993; S I
    syn. - Brown No. 7525-17
    {'Rochester' × 'Primrose'}
    Fiala, Lilacs, 220, Pl. 77 & rear page of dustcover [1988]; Vrugtman, HortScience 29(9):972 [1994]
    Named for Fr John Leopold Fiala, 1924-1990, priest, teacher, scientist and plantsman, Medina, Ohio, USA.
    Cultivar name registered 1993; name established and accepted.

Father John Fiala, Father John L. Fiala - see **'Fiala Remembrance'**.

'Father Patrick McCabe', *S. vulgaris*
  Berdeen 1998; ? ?
  King & Coggeshall, Lilacs - Quart. Jour. 27(2):49-50 [1998] - name only
  Cultivar name not established.

Favorite - see **'My Favorite'**.

FC 05, *S. vulgaris*
  Hoepfl 2007; S IV
  {'Flower City' × ?}
  Photos by Mary and Diane Meyer and T. Polyakova from Highland Park, Rochester NY seen in 2020 ILS Photo & Color Database.
  Breeder's designation only

FC 07 - see **'Tuesday'**.

FC 09, *S. vulgaris*
  Hoepfl (not yet introduced); S III
  {'Flower City'× ? }
  Hoepfl, Lilacs - Quart. Jour. 36(2):74-75 & back cover photo [2007]
  Breeder's designation only.

FC 10, *S. vulgaris*
  Hoepfl 2007; S VII/III
  {'Flower City' × ?}
  Photos by Savenko and DeBard from Highland Park, Rochester NY seen in 2020 ILS Photo & Color Database.
  Breeder's designation only.

FC 12, *S. vulgaris*
  Hoepfl (not yet introduced); S III
  {'Flower City'× ? }
  Hoepfl, Lilacs - Quart. Jour. 36(2):74-75 & back cover photo [2007]
  Breeder's designation only.

FC 15 - see 'Marcie Merlot'.

FC 20 see 'Highland Park'

'Federiko Garsia Lorka', *S. vulgaris*
  'Федерико Гарсиа Лорка'
  Aladin, S., Aladina, O., and Polyakova, T. 2011; D multicolored
  {'Olimpiada Kolesnikova' × OP}
  Registered with the State Commission of the Russian Federation for Testing and Protection of Selection Achievements, No. 8853109, 2011, and Patent No. 6883 (2012), valid until 31 December 2043; Vrugtman & Polyakova, Lilacs - Quart. Jour. 41(1): [2012]; Питомник-частный сад (Pitomnik i chastnyi sad; Nursery and private garden) 6/2014:14-20 (in Russian); Photo on Jorgovani; Вестник АППМ (Catalog in Vestnik APPM (Planting material association) magazine) 1/2018: 59-72 (in Russian); International scientific and practical conference (Международная и практическая конференция) "International Syringa 2018", Moscow, Moscow State University Botanical Garden, St. Petersburg, Botanical Garden of Peter the Great BIN RAS, Pavlovsk, May 21-27, 2018; pp. 43-47 (in Russian); Lilacs 2015 DVD;Lilacs-Quart.Jour. (49)3:2019
  Named for Federico del Sagrado Corazón de Jesús García Lorca, 1898-1936, Spanish dramatist, poet and theatre director.
  Cultivar name registered, established and accepted.

'Felice', *S.* ×*diversifolia*
  Origin not known; S IV
  {*S.* ×*diversifolia* × ?}
  <www.esveld.nl/wetenschappelijk.php?letter=s&group=syringa&ppagina=2> seen Nov. 23, 2011 - as pale lilac seedling of *S.* ×*diversifolia*.
  Cultivar name not established.

'Feliks Dzerzhinskiĭ', *S. vulgaris*
  'Феликс Дзержинский'
  Kolesnikov pre-1950; D IV
  Polyakova, 2018, "Master of the Lilac Inflorescence", p. 116; cultivar passport
  Polyakova, 2010, Istoriya Russkoĭ Sireni, p. 25; name only.
  Named for Feliks Edmundovich Dzerzhinskiĭ, 1877-1926; Russian revolutionary best known for organizing the Cheka, the Bolshevik secret police.
  Cultivar name established and accepted.

Fellemberg, Fellenburg - see 'Fellemburg' or 'Fellenberg'.

'Fellemburg', *S. vulgaris*
  origin not known pre-1942; S IV
  Wister, Lilacs for America, 36, 48 [1942] - perhaps misspellings of **'Charlemagne'**, reported in cultivation at Highland Park, Rochester, New York, pre-1942.
  Cultivar name not established.

'Fellenberg', *S.* ×*hyacinthiflora*
  origin not known pre-1952; S IV
  reported in cultivation pre-1952 at Elan Memorial Park, Berwick, Pennsylvania, as Syringa 'Fellemberg'; received (1952) and grown as such at Arnold Arboretum, Jamaica Plain, Massachusetts; received (1974) and grown as Syringa 'Fellenberg' at Royal Botanical Gardens, Hamilton, Ontario, Canada. Determined to belong in *Syringa* ×*hyacinthiflora* (1982); Photo on Jorgovani/Lilacs 2015 DVD.
  Cultivar name not established; confused name; identity uncertain.

'Fénelon', *S.* ×*hyacinthiflora*
  Lemoine 1936; S V
  syn. - 'Fenelon'
  Lemoine, Cat. No. 210, 25 [1936]; Wister, Lilacs for America, 48 [1942], 29 [1953];
  Photo on Jorgovani/Lilacs 2015 DVD.
  Named for François de Salignac de La Mothe-Fénelon, 1651-1715, French prelate and writer.
  Cultivar name presumed registered 1953; name established and accepted.

'Ferna Alexander', *S.* (Villosae Group)
Alexander Sr 1970; S V
{*S.* ×*josiflexa* 'James Macfarlane' × *S.* ×*prestoniae* 'Ethel M. Webster'}
Wister & Oppe, Arnoldia 31(3):122 [1971]; Fiala, ILS Newsletter 2(1):14 [1973]; Photo on Jorgovani/Lilacs 2015 DVD.
Cultivar name registered 1970; name established and accepted.

'Fernand L. Pegot', *S. vulgaris*
origin not known pre-1994; D VI
syn. - 'Fomand L. Pegot'
Microplant Nurseries, Wholesale pricelist, 6 [1994]
Cultivar name not established.

'Feya Sireni' (Lilac Fairy), *S. vulgaris*
'Фея Сирени'
Aladin, S., Aladina, O., Polyakova, T., and Aladina, A. 2019; D IV
{' Violetta' × OP}
(Международная научная конференция "Syringa L.: коллекции, выращивание, использование") "International Scientific Conference "Syringa L.: collections, cultivation, using" / Collection of Scientific Articles of Botanical Institute named after V.L. Komarov, Botanical Garden of Peter the Great BIN RAS. - St. Petersburg. -2020.- pp.3-7 (in Russian); Photo exhibition of all varieties of the creative breeding group "Russian Lilac" at the Festival "Lilac February", St. Petersburg, Botanical Garden of Peter the Great BIN RAS, February 22-24, 2020.
Named for the heroine of the fairy tale by S. Perrault and the ballet by P.I. Tchaikovsky "Sleeping Beauty."
Cultivar name established and accepted.

'Fiala Remembrance', *S. vulgaris*
Margaretten 1991; D I
syn. - 'Father Fiala' (not Ross), 'Father J. Fiala', 'Father John' (Margaretten, not Brown), 'Father John Fiala', 'Father John L. Fiala', 'Fiala Rememberance', 'Fr. John Fiala', 'John L. Fiala'
{'Mme Lemoine' × 'Edith Cavell'}
Clark, Lilacs - Quart. Jour. 20(3):69 [1991] - as 'Father John Fiala' and 'John L. Fiala' - erroneously listed as registered in 1989; Knight Hollow Nursery, 1996 Cultured cutting and liner descriptive list - as 'Fr. John Fiala'; McCown, Lilacs - Quart. Jour. 29(3):75 & back cover [2000] - on p.67 as 'Fiala Rememberance'; Vrugtman, Lilacs -Quart. Jour. 32(4):149 [2003]; Song Sparrow Nursery, Cat. 53 [2004] - erroneously as a Fiala creation; Photo on Jorgovani/Lilacs 2015 DVD.
Named for Fr John Leopold Fiala, 1924-1990, priest, teacher, scientist, writer and plantsman, Medina, Ohio, USA.
Cultivar name registered 2000; name established and accepted.

'Fialka Monmartra'
'Фиалка Монмартра'
Makedonskaya 2016 S II
{open pollinated seedling}
Statutory registration with the State Inspection for testing and protection of plant varieties of the Republic of Belarus; inventor's certificate No. 0005726 (Belarus) registered 2016. Makedonskaya N.V. Breeding Lilacs in Belarus Yesterday. TODAY: Materials of International scientific-practical conference "INTERNATIONAL SYRINGA 2018", Russia. Moscow: Moscow State University 2018.pp 36-40. Natalya Makedonskaya. Syringa Belarus. – Lilacs. Quarterly Journal of the International Lilac Society. 2019. VOL. 50· NUM. 1 PP.21-25.
Named for "The Violet of Montmartre", the famous operetta by the Hungarian composer Emmerich Kálmán.

'Finlandia', *S. josikaea*
origin not known pre-2016; ? ?
<http://www.esveld.nl/zoeken.php?zoekterm=syringa&product=planten&pagina=2> seen 8 Feb. 2017
Cultivar name not established and accepted.

Findling, *S. vulgaris*
origin not known pre-1974; ? ?
Cognomen, not a cultivar name.

'Fioletoviy Ghigant'; *S. vulgaris*
'Фиолетовый Гигант'
origin not known (possibly Luchnik)
Lyakh, Lilacs - Quart. Jour. 36(1):18 [2007] - name only
Cultivar name not established.

'Fioletovyĭ Sultan'; *S. vulgaris*
'Фиолетовый Султан'
Klimenko, V. & Z., & Grigor'ev 1955; S II
syn. - 'Fioletovyj Sultan'
{'Andenken an Ludwig Späth' × 'Jeanne d'Arc'}
Rubtzov et al. 1980. Vidy i sorta sireni, kul'tiviruemye v SSSR. Kiev; Naukova Dumka. – in Russian; Holetich, C.D. 1982. Lilac species and cultivars in cultivation in USSR. Lilacs 11(2):1-38. - translation of Rubtzov et al. 1982.
Name: Russian for purple sultan.
Cultivar name established and accepted.

'Firmament', *S. vulgaris*
Lemoine 1932; S III
syn. - 'Fairmament'
Lemoine, Cat. No. 227, 6 [1956]; Wister, Lilacs for America, 48 [1942], 29 [1953];
Photo on Jorgovani/Lilacs 2015 DVD.
Awards: RHS Award of Garden Merit 1993.
Cultivar name presumed registered 1953; name established and accepted.

F. K. Smith - see **'Forrest Kresser Smith'**.

Flamingo™ - see **'Edward J. Gardner'**.

'Flatograd', *S. vulgaris*
   origin not known pre-1989; ? ?
   {parentage not known}
   USDA-ARS GRIN database, PI No. 27815; from Bulgaria; historical record only.
   Cultivar name not established.

'Flirts', *S. vulgaris*
   Kārkliņš pre-2005; D V
   Strautiņa & Kaufmane, Dobeles ceriņi, pp. 14, 92 [2011]; Photo on Jorgovani/Lilacs 2015 DVD.
   Name: Latvian for flirt.
   Cultivar name established and accepted.

'Flora 1953', *S. vulgaris*
   Eveleens Maarse 1953; S I
   syn. - 'Flora', 'Flora White'
   {'G. J. Baardse' × 'Excellent'}
   Lilacs for America, 29 [1953] - as 'Flora'; Eveleens Maarse, Dendron 1(1):12 [1954]; Eveleens Maarse, Gartenwelt 54(23): ? [1954]; Tuinbouwgids 1954, 440 - as 'Flora'; Fiala, Lilacs, 91, 209 & Pl.72 [1988] - as 'Flora'; Photo on Jorgovani/Lilacs 2015 DVD.
   Named for the horticultural exposition "Flora 1953" in The Netherlands.
   Awards: Certificate of Merit 1953 (KMTP).
   Cultivar name presumed registered 1953; name established and accepted.

Flora × Pocahontas, *S. vulgaris*
   Waines pre-2017; S VII
   Photo by Savenko seen in 2020 ILS Photo & Color Database
   Breeder's designation, not a cultivar name

'Floréal', S. (Villosae Group), *S. ×nanceiana*
   Lemoine 1925; S V
   syn. - 'Floreal'
   {S. ×*henryi* 'Lutèce' × *S. tomentella* subsp. *sweginzowii* 'Superba'}
   Lemoine, Cat. No. 199, 20 [1925]; McKelvey, The Lilac, 107-108 [1928]; Wister, Lilacs for America, 48 [1942], 29 [1953]
   Named for the eighth month of the 1st Republic calendar, from Apr. 20 - May 19, which applies approximately to the date of flowering in France.
   Cultivar name presumed registered 1953; name established and accepted.

'Flore-albescente', *S. vulgaris*
   origin not known pre-1883; ? ?
   McKelvey, The Lilac, 298 [1928]
   Cultivar name not established.

flore bicolor, Flore Bicolor - see **'Bicolor'**.

flore duplo Liberti - see **'Azurea Plena'**.

'Florence', *S. vulgaris*
   Stone; S V
   Wister & Oppe, Arnoldia 31(3):122 [1971] - name only
   Cultivar name registered 1970;
   Cultivar not reported in cultivation.

'Florence Christine', *S. vulgaris*
   Stone; S IV
   Wister, Arnoldia 23(4):81 [1963] - name only; Photo on Jorgovani/Lilacs 2015 DVD.
   Cultivar name registered 1963; name established and accepted.

Florent Stepman - see **'Mme Florent Stepman'**.

'Flore plena', *S. vulgaris*
   origin not known pre-1892; D III
   syn. - 'Flore-Plena'
   Wister, Lilacs for America, 36, 48 [1942]
   Cultivar name not established.

Flore Pleno - see *S. vulgaris* 'Plena'.

'Flow Blue', *S. vulgaris*
   Fiala 1980; S III
   {'True Blue' × 'Mrs A. Belmont'}
   Fiala, Lilacs, 97, 223 [1988]
   Cultivar name established and accepted.

Flowerfesta®
   Flowerfesta® -- Trademark registration No. 1325355, published 25 January 2016; expiration date 22 January 2026; trademark holder: Plantipp B.V., Brunel 21, 3401 LJ IJsselstein, Netherlands.
   Nijnatten, pre-2017; a series of three selections, pink, white and purple.
   For cultivars see: 'Annys200817', 'Annys200810', and 'Annys200809', listed as selections of *S. pubescens* subsp. *pubescens*.

'Flower City', *S. vulgaris*
   Fenicchia 1983; S II-VII
   syn. - R92
   {'Rochester' × 'Madame Charles Souchet'}
   Vrugtman, AABGA Bull. 18(3):87 [1985]; Hoepfl & Rogers, Lilac Newsletter 14(7):6 [1988]; Fiala, Lilacs, 94, 108, 219, Pl. 10 [1988]; Lilacs - Proceedings 17(1): back cover ill. [1988]; K. Millham, Lilacs - Quart. Jour. 42(2):60 & ill. 65 [2013]; Photo on Jorgovani/Lilacs 2015 DVD.
   Named for the city of Rochester, New York, USA.
   Cultivar name registered 1983; name established and accepted.

'Fluffy Ruffles', *S. vulgaris*
   Klager; S IV
   Wister, Lilacs for America, 48 [1942], 29 [1953]; ILS Newsletter 14(4):3-4 [1988]
   Cultivar name presumed registered 1953; name established and accepted.

f. *morel*, *S. vulgaris*
   origin not known pre-1973; D III
   Chapman, Lilacs - Quart. Jour. 23(3):62 [1994] - misspelled forma *morel* as 'Farmer Morel'; plant received by Chapman 12/07/94 from RBG Kew Arboretum Nursery as *S. vulgaris* f. *morel*, accession no. 1993-685, propagated from 1973-19366; accession no longer in RBG Kew collection; original source not recorded by RBG Kew.
   (Perhaps identical to 'Francisque Morel' ?)

Fomand L. Pegot - see 'Fernand L. Pegot'.

'Forever and Always', *S. vulgaris*
   Moro, F. 2013; S to D V
   {'Belle de Nancy' × ?}
   Lilacs - Quart. Jour. 42(3):85 & 88 (photo) [2013]; in lit. Moro to Vrugtman July 13, 2013.
   Cultivar name established and accepted.

'Forrest Kresser Smith', *S.* ×*hyacinthiflora*
   Sobeck pre-1966; S IV
   syn. - 'F. K. Smith', 'Forest K. Smith', 'Mrs Forrest Kresser Smith', 'Mrs Forrest K. Smith'
   Wister, Arnoldia 26(3):13 [1966]
   Named for Mrs Forrest Kresser Smith, 1909-1999, first president, 1957-1967 of the Descanso Garden Guild (Descanso Gardens), La Cañada, California, USA; Photo on Jorgovani/Lilacs 2015 DVD.
   Cultivar name registered 1966; name established and accepted.
   Nota bene: Since this cultivar appears to be of 'Lavender Lady' ancestry see also: Pringle, Lilacs - Quart. Jour. 24(4):97-99 [1995]; and Vrugtman, HortScience 31(3):328 [1996].

'For Sharon', *S. vulgaris*
   Berdeen; ? ?
   King & Coggeshall, Lilacs - Quart. Jour. 27(2):49-50 [1998] - name only
   Named for Ken Berdeen's granddaughter-in-law.
   Cultivar name not established.

40 Let VLKSM, 40 Liet VLKSM - see 'Sorok Let Komsomola'.

'Foster Alexander'
   Fiala, Lilacs, 215 [1988] - erroneous name.

Foto 40 V.K. Gorb, *S.* (species affiliation not known)
   origin not known ? ?
   Reported in cultivation by Ole Heide
   Probably a breeder's designation, not a cultivar name.

'Fountain', *S.* (Villosae Group), *S.* ×*swegiflexa*
   Preston 1948; S V
   syn. - Preston No. 33-11-01
   {(*S. komarowii* subsp. *reflexa* × *S. tomentella* subsp. *sweginzowii*) × *S. komarowii* subsp. *reflexa*}
   Davis, Rep. Dom. Hort., Progress Report 1934-1948, 151 [1950]; AAN reg'n card No. 482; reg'd & int'd by E.A. Upton; Wister, Lilacs for America, 29 [1953]; Photo on Jorgovani/Lilacs 2015 DVD.
   Cultivar name presumed registered 1953; name established and accepted.

'Foxey Lady', *S.* (Series Pubescentes)
   Alexander III 2008; S V
   {*S. pubescens* subsp. *microphylla* × *S. pubescens* subsp. *pubescens*}
   Named in memory of a song by that name and the artist, Jimi Hendrix, 1942-1970.
   Vrugtman, Hanburyana 7:27-28 [2013]
   Cultivar name registered in 2012;
   Cultivar name established and accepted.

'Fraîcheur', *S. vulgaris*
   Lemoine 1946; S I
   Woody Plant Register, AAN, No. 68 [1949]; Lilacs for America, 29 [1953]; Photo on Jorgovani/Lilacs 2015 DVD.
   Name: French for freshness.
   Cultivar name presumed registered 1953; name established and accepted.

'Francine', *S. vulgaris*
   Klettenberg 1936; S VI
   Wister, Lilacs for America, 29 [1953]
   Cultivar name presumed registered 1953; name established and accepted.

'Francisca', *S.* (Villosae Group), *S.* ×*prestoniae*
   Preston 1928; S VII
   syn. - Preston No. 20-14-247
   {*S. villosa* subsp. *villosa* × *S. komarowii* subsp. *reflexa*}
   Macoun, Rep. Dom. Hort. 1928, 56 [1930] - name only; Wister Lilacs for America, 48, 64 [1942], 29, 48 [1953]; Alexander Sr, Cat. sheets [n.d.; received Feb. 1964]; Photo on Jorgovani/Lilacs 2015 DVD.
   Named for A Nun in Shakespeare's *Measure for Measure*.
   Cultivar name presumed registered 1953; name established and accepted.

'Francisque Morel', *S. vulgaris*
   Lemoine 1896; D IV
   syn. - 'Franziska Morell'
   Lemoine, Cat. No. 134, 9 [1896]; McKelvey, The Lilac, 298 [1928]; Wister, Lilacs for America, 48 [1942], 29 [1953]; Photo on Jorgovani/Lilacs 2015 DVD.
   Cultivar name presumed registered 1953; name established and accepted.

'Franco', *S.* (Villosae Group) ×*prestoniae*
   origin not known pre-2011; S ?
   appeared in 2011 inventory of Beaver Creek Nursery, Poplar Grove, Illinois, but was discontinued; no information on record at Beaver Creek Nursery.
   Cultivar name not established.

'François Delcor', *S. vulgaris*
   Delcor; ? ?

Wister, Lilacs for America, 29 [1953] - name only
Named for François (Franciscus) Delcor, 1879-1969,
proprietor of Pépinière Delcor, x - 1984, Lebbeke, Belgium.
Cultivar name not established.

'Frankfurter Frühling', *S. vulgaris*
Schweikart 1989; D V
also as - FRANKFURTER FRÜHLING™
denomination registered with the Bundessortenamt,
Germany, December 21, 1990, http://www.
bundessortenamt.de/internet20/ , holder/breeder: Hans
Schweikart - name only; Kyodo Trading Co. Ltd., Lilac
cat., 6 [April 1992]; Vrugtman, Lilacs - Quart. Jour.
25(2):40, 41 [1996]
Name: German for Frankfurt's spring.
Varietal denomination registered with the German
Bundessortenamt 1990;
Cultivar name established and accepted.

'Frank Klager', *S. vulgaris*
Klager 1928; S VII
Wister, Lilacs for America, 48 [1942], 29 [1953]; Fiala,
Lilacs, 105 [1988]; Photo on Jorgovani/Lilacs 2015 DVD.
Husband of Hulda Klager.
Cultivar name presumed registered 1953; name
established and accepted.

'Frank Meyer', *S. oblata*
Meyer & Fiala 1908/1988; S I
syn. - PI 23031, NA 37242, B-53673 (Bell, Glenn Dale);
Frank Meyer No. 693.
{collected by Frank N. Meyer at Fengtai, China, 1908 (PI 23031)}
Fiala, Lilacs, 59, 92, 123, 221 [1988] - as *S. oblata* var.
alba Rehder 'Frank Meyer', in cultivation at USNA and
used in breeding work by Donald Egolf; in litt. L.C.
Hatch to F. Vrugtman [April 2, 2003] - reported in
cultivation at Raulston Arboretum, Raleigh, NC, Acc.
No. 950000, rec'd 04 Jan. 1995; Fiala & Vrugtman, Lilacs:
A gardener's Encyclopedia, pp. 77-78 [2008]; Lura et al,
Hanburyana 7:37-40 [2013].
Named for Frank Nicholas Meyer (originally: Frans
Nicholaas Meijer), 1875-1918, Dutch-American botanist
and plant explorer.
Cultivar name established and accepted.

FRANK MORO – cognomen for an unknown cultivar obtained from Frank Moro and grown by J. Giles Waines at the University of California Riverside. It is a double form of IV-V color and probably a *S. ×hyacinthiflora*.

'Frank Paterson', *S. vulgaris*
Paterson 1960; S VII
syn. - 'Frank G. Paterson', 'Frank Patterson'
Schloen, US Plant Patent No. 2076 [Aug. 1, 1961];
Wister, Arnoldia 23(4):81 [1963] - erroneously as 'Frank
Patterson'; Sheridan Nurs., Cat., 83 [1971]; Photo on
Jorgovani/Lilacs 2015 DVD.
Cultivar name registered 1963; name established and
accepted.

'Frank's Fancy', *S. vulgaris*
Mezitt, E. 1970s; S VII
syn. - 'Franks Fancy'
{'Sensation' × OP}
Weston Nurseries, Cat. [1991]; Photo on Jorgovani/
Lilacs 2015 DVD.
Named by Ed Mezitt in honor of his friend, Frank
Goodwin. Dark purple.
Cultivar name established and accepted.

'Franktown', *S. vulgaris*
Speirs 2007; D I
{parentage not known}
original plant selected and collected 2007 by Speirs and
Lilac Team, Friends of the Central Experimental Farm,
Ottawa, on property of Claude and Cora Nolan (Park
Lot-1), Franktown, Ontario, Canada.
Speirs, J., Friends of the Central Experimental Farm,
Newsletter 28(2):6 [2016].
Named for the town of Franktown in the township of
Beckwith.
Cultivar name established and accepted.

'Fraser', *S. ×hyacinthiflora*
Skinner 1945; S V
Skinner, Dropmore Cat. 1945; Woody Plant Register,
AAN, No. 69 [1949]; Wister, Lilacs for America, 29
[1953]; Skinner, Hort. Horizons, 109 [1966]; Photo on
Jorgovani/Lilacs 2015 DVD.
Cultivar name presumed registered 1953; name
established and accepted.

'Fraseur', *S.* (species affiliation not known)
origin not known pre-1994; ? ?
listed in cultivation at Boskoop Research Station;
perhaps misspelling of 'Fraser'.
Cultivar name not established.

Frau Dammann - see **'Frau Bertha Dammann'**.

'Frau Bertha Dammann', *S. vulgaris*
Späth 1883; S I
syn. - 'Alba Bertha Dammann', 'Bertha Dammann', 'Frau
Berta Damman'
common name: Frau Dammann
{chance seedling of unknown parentage}
Späth, Cat., 3 [1883]; Kache, Gartenschönheit 5:81-82
[1924]; Späth, Späth-Buch, 110 [1930]; McKelvey, The
Lilac, 298, 563 [1928]; Stand. Pl. Names, 615 [1942] - as
Frau Dammann; Wister, Lilacs for America, 48 [1942],
29 [1953]
Name: Probably named for the wife of F.H. Dammann,
horticulturist and seedsman about the 1880s in Görlitz,
Saxony, Germany.
Cultivar name presumed registered 1953; name
established and accepted.

'Frau Hilda', *S. vulgaris*
Klager; D V

Anon., ILS Newsletter 14(4):3-4 [1988]; Stenlund, Lilacs-Quart. Jour. 20(2):41 [1991] - as pink
Cultivar name not established.

Frau Holle™ - see 'St Margaret'.

Frau Pfitzer - see 'Frau Wilhelm Pfitzer'.

'Frau Wilhelm Pfitzer', *S. vulgaris*
Pfitzer 1910; S V
syn. - 'Frau W. Pfitzer' (Wister, Lilacs for America, 30 [1953] erroneously lists 'Gen. Haig' as a synonym)
common name: Frau Pfitzer in Stand. Pl. Names, 615 [1942] - erroneously as identical to 'General Haig'
Kanzleiter, Gartenwelt 13:129 [1909]; Wilhelm Pfitzer, Cat., 178 [1911]; McKelvey, The Lilac, 299 [1928]; Wister, Lilacs for America, 48 [1942], 30 [1953]; Photo on Jorgovani/Lilacs 2015 DVD.
Cultivar name presumed registered 1953; name established and accepted.

'Fred C. Wilke', *S. vulgaris*
Klager 1934; S VII
syn. - 'Fred Wilke' (?)
Wister, Lilacs for America, 48 [1942], 30 [1953]
Cultivar name presumed registered 1953;
Cultivar not reported in cultivation.

'Frede Post', *S.* (species affiliation not known)
origin not known pre-1998; ? ?
Reported in cultivation by Ole Heide
Cultivar name not established.

'Frederick Douglass', *S. vulgaris*
Fenicchia 1972; S VI
syn. - 'Frederich Douglass', 'Frederick Douglas', R74
{'Rochester' × 'Edward J. Gardner'}
Clark, ILS Newsletter, Convention Issue, 7 [May 1972]; Clark, Arnoldia 32(3):133-135 [1972]; Hoepfl & Rogers, Lilac Newsletter 14(7):7 [1988] - as 'Madame Charles Souchet' × 'Rochester', and S III; Fiala, Lilacs, 103, 108, 219 [1988]; Vrugtman, HortScience 32(4):587-588 [1997]; K. Millham, Lilacs - Quart. Jour. 42(2):60 & ill. 65 [2013].
Named for Frederick Douglass, 1818-1895, American slave, abolitionist leader and author.
Cultivar name registered 1996; name established and accepted.

'Frederick Law Olmsted', *S. vulgaris*
Fenicchia 1988; S I
syn. - 'Channel 10', 'F. L. Olmsted', 'Frederick L. Olmsted', 'Frederick Law Olmstead', 'Frederick L. Olmstead', RAF538
{'Rochester' × 'Rochester'}
Hoepfl & Rogers, Lilac Newsletter 14(7):6 [1988]; Lilacs - Proceedings 17(1): back cover ill. [1988]; Vrugtman, HortScience 24(3):435 [1989] & 29(9):972 [1994]; K. Millham, Lilacs - Quart. Jour. 42(2):60-61 & ill. 66 [2013]; Photo on Jorgovani/Lilacs 2015 DVD.
Named for Frederick Law Olmsted, 1822-1903, American landscape architect.
Mature height 8-9'; lacks significant multipetaling of its parents.
Cultivar name registered 1988; name established and accepted.

'Fred L. Klager', *S. vulgaris*
Klager 1930; S VII
Wister, Lilacs for America, 48 [1942] - as S VI; Wister, Lilacs for America, 30 [1953]; Photo on Jorgovani/Lilacs 2015 DVD.
Cultivar name presumed registered 1953; name established and accepted.

'Fred Payne', *S. vulgaris*
Havemeyer 1943; S II
Stand. Pl. Names, 615 [1942] - as Fred. Payne; Wister, Lilacs for America, 48 [1942], 30 [1953]; Eickhorst, ILS Lilac Newsletter 4(1):4-5 [1978]; Photo on Jorgovani/Lilacs 2015 DVD.
Cultivar name presumed registered 1953; name established and accepted.

'Fred Wilke', *S. vulgaris*
Klager; D V
Anon., ILS Newsletter 14(4):3-4 [1988]; Stenlund, Lilacs-Quart. Jour. 20(2):41 [1991]
Cultivar name not established.

'Frede Post', *S.* (species affiliation not known)
origin not known, pre-1998; ? ?
Reported in cultivation by Ole Heide
Cultivar name not established.

'Freedom', *S.* (Villosae Group), *S.* ×*prestoniae*
Preston & Leslie 1936; S V
{parentage not known}
Wister, Lilacs for America, 30 [1953] - as a 1937 Isabella Preston introduction (information not confirmed); Cumming, Agric. Canada Public. 1628, 17 [1977] - as introduced in 1936; Photo on Jorgovani/Lilacs 2015 DVD.
Cultivar name presumed registered 1953; name established and accepted.

'French Giant', *S. vulgaris*
origin not known pre-1900; S IV
Stand. Pl. Names, 615 [1942] - name only; Wister, Lilacs for America, 36, 48 [1942].
see also **'Géant des Batailles'**.
Cultivar name not established.

French hybrids - *S. vulgaris*
Not a cultivar or group name
French Hybrids is a term frequently used for *S. vulgaris* cultivars
DataScape Botanical Index, p. 122 [1996].

Friesdorfer Stamm VI, *S. vulgaris*
Löbner
{rootstock selection} name only
Cultivar name not established; perhaps extinct.

'Fritz', *S. vulgaris*
   Klager 1928; D V
   syn. - 'Fritz Klager'
   Wister, Lilacs for America, 48 [1942] - as D V; Wister, Lilacs for America, 30 [1953] - as D VII; Northwest Rose Growers Inc. Lilac Liners [n.d.; 1999] - as 'Fritz Klager'; Photo on Jorgovani/Lilacs 2015 DVD.
   Cultivar name presumed registered 1953; name established and accepted.
   Nota bene: Plants reported in cultivation under this name which are single and purple are not true to name.

Fr. John Fiala - see **'Fiala Remembrance'**.

'Fructiferum', *S.* ×*chinensis*
   Gorb 2019; S VII
   Syn. – *S.* ×*chinensis* f. *fructiferum*
   Gorb, LILACS 49(3) :130-134 Summer 2019.
   Cultivar name not established.

'Fryderyk Chopin', *S. vulgaris*
   Karpow-Lipski 1958; S VI
   syn. - Siewka nr 154
   Karpow-Lipski, Arboretum Kórnickie, 3:104 [1958]
   Named for Frédéric Chopin, 1810-1849, Polish composer and pianist.
   Cultivar name established and accepted.

'Fuete' – A mistaken name

'Fürst Bülow', *S. vulgaris*
   Späth 1921; S VII-II
   syn. - 'Frst Blow', 'Fürst Blücher', 'Fuerst Buelow', etc.
   common name: Fuerst Bulow
   {'Andenken an Ludwig Späth' × 'Hyazinthenflieder'}
   Späth, Späth-Buch, 222 [1920]; Kache, Gartenschönheit 5:82 [1924]; McKelvey, The Lilac, 299 [1928]; Späth, Späth-Buch, 110, 304 [1930]; Stand. Pl. Names, 615 [1942] - as Fuerst Bulow; Wister, Lilacs for America, 48 [1942], 30 [1953]; Photo on Jorgovani/Lilacs 2015 DVD.
   Named for Prince Bernhard Heinrich von Bülow, 1849-1929, German statesman.
   Cultivar name presumed registered 1953; name established and accepted.

'Fürst Liechtenstein', *S. vulgaris*
   Späth 1887; S V
   syn. - 'Frst Lichtenstein', etc.
   common name: Fuerst Lichtenstein
   {chance seedling of unknown parentage}
   Späth, Cat. No. 69, 4 [1887]; Kache, Gartenschönheit 5:82 [1924]; McKelvey, The Lilac, 299 [1928]; Späth, Späth-Buch, 110, 304 [1930]; Stand. Pl. Names, 615 [1942] - as Fuerst Lichtenstein; Wister, Lilacs for America, 48 [1942], 30 [1953]; Photo on Jorgovani/Lilacs 2015 DVD.
   Named for Fürst Johannes II von und zu Liechtenstein, 1840-1929; remembered for the development of the gardens at the palace of Liechtenstein at Lednice (Eisgrub), southern Moravia, Czech Republic.
   Cultivar name presumed registered 1953; name established and accepted.

'Fyns Forår', *S.* ×*hyacinthiflora*
   Heide no date; S V
   Name: Danish for Funen spring
   <http://klerk.dk/wp-content/uploads/2014/08/Klerk_Russian_English_Exportcatalog_2010-2011.pdf> seen September 25, 2011
   Cultivar name established and accepted.

'G13099', *S. vulgaris*
   Grazzini R.A. 2020; S II
   {'Betsy Ross' × unnamed breeder seedling}
   Syn. – NEW AGE LAVENDER™
   Flower and bud color RHS84A.
   Seen on website for Star Roses and Plants May 15, 2020, available 2021.
   USPPAF #32,623, December 15, 2020.
   Cultivar name established and accepted.

'G13103', *S. vulgaris*
   Grazzini R.A. 2020; S I
   {'Frederick Law Olmstead' × unnamed breeder seedling}
   Syn. – NEW AGE WHITE™
   Bud color RHS 157D.
   Seen on website for Star Roses and Plants May 15, 2020, available 2021.
   USPP Dec. 22, 2020, # 32,670 P2.
   Cultivar name established and accepted.

'Gaby', *S. vulgaris*
   Bellion 2004; D II
   marketed in France as KINDY ROSE™
   <http://blemish.unimedia.fr/~minier/fichePlante.php?action=general&codePlante=4195&route=plantes-syringa-research> [seen Feb. 26, 2007]
   [breeder applied for CPVO variety denomination registration, December 2004]
   Cultivar name not established.

'Gaĭavata', *S.* (Villosae Group)
   'Гайавата' - see - **'Hiawatha'**

'Gaida', *S. vulgaris*
   Origin not known pre-2018; D V
   One unlabeled plant known to be in Dobele, Latvia per email of 2/1/2021 Ugis Pirs to Registrar.
   Cultivar name not established. Cultivar may be extinct.

'Gaistošais Sapnis', *S. vulgaris*
   Upītis 1972; S II & I
   syn. - 'Gaistosais Sapnis', 'Gaistoshais Sapnis', Upītis No. 2946
   {perhaps 'Sensation' × ? ; periclinal chimaera ?}
   Kalniņš, Ceriņu jaunšķirnes Dobelē, Dārs un drava 1986 (12):13-15 - in Latvian; Strautiņa, S. 1992. Ceriņi Dārzs un Drava. No. 6, pp.12-13; Strautiņa, S. 1996. Characteristics and propagation of lilacs obtained by P.

Upītis. Problems of fruit plant breeding I. Jelgava. pp. 32-38; Vrugtman, HortScience 31(3):327 [1996]; in litt. Gints Tenbergs to F. Vrugtman [May 25, 2000] - perhaps a seedling of 'Sensation'; Strautiņa, S. 2002. Ceriņu un jasmīnu avīze. LA, R., p. 62; in litt. S. Strautiņa to F. Vrugtman [21 Dec. 2007] - 1972, S II & I; Semenov, Igor, Lilacs - Quart. Jour. 44(2):50, ill. 55 [2015]; Photo on Jorgovani/Lilacs 2015 DVD.
Name: Latvian for eluding dream.
Cultivar name registered 1995; name established and accepted.

Gaizins - see **'Gaiziņkalns'**.

'Gaiziņkalns', *S. vulgaris*
Upītis 1958; D VII
syn. - 'Gaizinkalns', 'Gaĭzinkalns', 'Gaizin'kalns', 'Gaizinkalus', 'Gaizinjkalns', Upītis No. 3805
statutory epithet Gaizins
{parentage not known}
Kalva, Ceriņi (Lilac), 165-166 [1980] - in Latvian; Rubtzov et al. 1980. Vidy i sorta sireni, kul'tiviruemye v SSSR. Kiev; Naukova Dumka. – in Russian; Holetich, C.D. 1982. Lilac species and cultivars in cultivation in USSR. Lilacs 11(2):1-38. - translation of Rubtzov et al. 1982; Kalniņš, Ceriņu jaunšķirnes Dobelē, Dārs un drava 1986 (12):13-15 - in Latvian; Strautiņa, S. 1992. Ceriņi Dārzs un Drava. No. 6, pp.12-13; Strautiņa, S. 1996. Characteristics and propagation of lilacs obtained by P. Upītis. Problems of fruit plant breeding I. Jelgava. pp. 32-38; Vrugtman, HortScience 31(3):328 [1996]; Strautiņa, S. 2002. Ceriņu un jasmīnu avīze. LA, R., p. 62; in litt. S. Strautiņa to F. Vrugtman [21 Dec. 2007] - 1958, D VII; Semenov, Igor, Lilacs - Quart. Jour. 44(2):50, ill. 56 [2015]; Semenov, Igor, Lilacs - Quart. Jour. 44(2):50, ill. 56 [2015] - as VII/VI fading to II; Photo on Jorgovani/Lilacs 2015 DVD.
Statutory registration (breeder's rights) Nr. 298, CER-5, in Latvia [2004 - 2029] with the statutory epithet Gaizins. Named for Gaizinkalns which, at 312 m above sea level, constitutes the highest point in Latvia.
Cultivar name registered 1995; name established and accepted.

'Galina Ulanova', *S. vulgaris*
'Галина Уланова'
Kolesnikov 1953; S I
syn. - 'Galina Ulinova', 'Helen Ulanov', Kolesnikov No. 501
Howard, Arnoldia 19(6-7):31-35 [1959]; Gromov, Siren', 65, ill. 66 [1963]; Howard & Brizicky, AABGA Quart. Newsl. No. 64, 17-21 [1965]; Wister & Oppe, Arnoldia 31(3):125 [1971]; Gromov, Lilacs - Proceedings 2(4):10-18 [1974]; Rubtzov et al. 1980. Vidy i sorta sireni, kul'tiviruemye v SSSR. Kiev; Naukova Dumka. – in Russian; Holetich, C.D. 1982. Lilac species and cultivars in cultivation in USSR. Lilacs 11(2):1-38. - translation of Rubtzov et al. 1982; Photo on Jorgovani/Lilacs 2015 DVD.
Named for Galina Sergeyevna Ulanova, 1910-1998, first *prima ballerina assoluta* of the Soviet Union, and one of the greatest ballet dancers of the 20th century.
Note: there are three variants of this cultivar in Russia per Tatyana Polyakova.
Cultivar name registered 1970; name established and accepted.

Galpana - see **'Goplana'**.

'Gamma', *S. vulgaris*
Kārkliņš 2003; D VI ?
(no information; listed by T. Polyakova, 2014)
Name: Latvian for range.
Cultivar name not established.

'Garden Peace', *S.* (Villosae Group)
Fiala 1970; S V
{*S. komarowii* subsp. *komarowii* × *S. villosa* subsp. *wolfii*}
Fiala, Lilacs, 187, 188, 224 [1988] - as *S.* ×*clarkiana* J.L. Fiala (nothospecies epithet not validly published), and as induced tetraploid.
Cultivar name established and accepted.

'GARlisabzar', *S.* (Series Pubescentes)
Detrick S.A., Zary K.W. 2019; S V
{'MORjos060F' × 'Bailsugar'}
Syn. - Be Right Back™
Seen in Spring Hills Nursery online catalog 2-28-20 from Gardens Alive nursery. Reported to be a re-blooming dwarf variety growing to 3-4 feet in height.
Flower color RHS 73D, bud color RHS 37A.
USPP June 23, 2020, # 31,899.
Cultivar name established and accepted.

Gartendirektor Loebner - see **'Max Löbner'**.

'Garteninspector Gireoud', *S. vulgaris*
origin not known 1910; ? ?
Muskauer Baumschulen, Haupt-Katalog 1910, 37; McKelvey, The Lilac, 300 [1928] - perhaps identical with 'Hermann Gireoud'
Cultivar name not established.

'Garten Riva', *S. vulgaris*
Unknown; ? ?
Growing at Cherry Valley Lilacs, Cherry Valley NY USA
Seen September 14, 2019 on ILS Facebook page posted by Charle-Pan Dawson
Cultivar name not established.

Gaspard Callot - see **'Souvenir de Gaspard Callot'**.

'Gastello', *S. vulgaris*
'Тастелло'
Kolesnikov 1946; S III-IV
syn. - 'Capitan Gastello', 'Kapitan Gastello', 'Капитн Gastello'
Gromov, Siren', 110 [1963]; Bilov et al., Siren', 37 [1974]; Rubtzov et al. 1980. Vidy i sorta sireni, kul'tiviruemye v SSSR. Kiev; Naukova Dumka. – in Russian; Holetich, C.D. 1982. Lilac species and cultivars in cultivation in USSR. Lilacs 11(2):1-38. - translation of Rubtzov et al.

1982; Photo on Jorgovani/Lilacs 2015 DVD.
Named for Nikolaĭ Frantsevich Gastello, 1908-1941, World War II pilot and Hero of the Soviet Union.
Cultivar name established and accepted.

'Gaudichaud', *S. vulgaris*
Lemoine 1903; D III
Lemoine, Cat. No. 155, 30 [1903]; McKelvey, The Lilac, 300 [1928]; Wister, Lilacs for America, 48 [1942], 30 [1953]; Photo on Jorgovani/Lilacs 2015 DVD.
Named for Charles Gaudichaud-Beaupré, 1789-1854, French botanist.
Cultivar name presumed registered 1953; name established and accepted.

Gautois - see 'Le Gaulois'.

'Gavriil Derzhavin', *S. vulgaris*
'Гавриил Державин'
Aladin, S., Aladina, O., Polyakova, T., and Aladina, A. 2018; S IV
{sdlg 11-112* x 'Rus'}
* sdlg 11-112 was obtained from open pollinated seeds of 'Stefan Makowiecki'.
Международная и практическая конференция (International
scientific and practical conference) "International Syringa 2018", Moscow, Moscow State University Botanical Garden, St. Petersburg, Botanical Garden of Peter the Great BIN RAS, Pavlovsk, May 21-27, 2018; pp. 43-47.
Named for Gavriil Romanovich Derzhavin (Гавриил Романович Державин), 1743-1816, Russian poet and statesman.
Cultivar name established and accepted.

'Géant des Batailles', *S. vulgaris*
origin not known pre-1865; S IV
common name: Geant des Batailles; Giant of Battles
Koch, Wochenschr. Ver. Beförd. Gartenb. Preuss. 8:88 [1865]; Vaughan's Seed Store - Gardening Ill., Cat. 92 [1893]; McKelvey, The Lilac, 300 [1928]; Stand. Pl. Names, 615 [1942] - as Geant des Battailles; Wister, Lilacs for America, 48 [1942], 30 [1953]; Photo on Jorgovani/Lilacs 2015 DVD.
Cultivar name presumed registered 1953; name established and accepted.

'Geheimrat Heyder', *S. vulgaris*
Späth 1883; S IV
syn. - 'Conseiller Heyder'
{chance seedling of unknown parentage}
Späth, Cat., 3 [1883]; McKelvey, The Lilac, 300-301 [1928]; Späth, Späth-Buch, 110, [1930]; Wister, Lilacs for America, 48 [1942], 30 [1953]
Named for the 1882 president of the board of trustees of the Königliche Gärtnerlehranstalt at Potsdam, Germany.
Cultivar name presumed registered 1953; name established and accepted.

'Geheimrat Singelmann', *S. vulgaris*
Späth 1887; S VI
syn. - 'Conseiller Singelmann', 'Geheimrat Singelman', 'Geheimrat Singlemann', 'Geheymrat Singelman'
{chance seedling of unknown parentage}
Späth, Cat. No. 69, 4 [1887]; McKelvey, The Lilac, 301 [1928]; Späth, Späth-Buch, 110, [1930]; Wister, Lilacs for America, 48 [1942], 30 [1953]; Photo on Jorgovani/Lilacs 2015 DVD.
Named for Geheimer Oberregierungsrat Dr G. Singelmann, Berlin, the 1885-88 Director of the "Verein zur Beförderung des Gartenbaues in den königlich preußischen Staaten" (today's Deutsche Gartenbaugesellschaft).
Cultivar name presumed registered 1953; name established and accepted.

'Gehenworth', *S. vulgaris*
origin not known pre-1953; ? ?
Wister, Lilacs for America, 30 [1953] - name only
Cultivar name not established.

Geminal - see 'Germinal'.

'Gen. ..' - see 'General ..' or 'Général ..'.

'General Antonov', *S. vulgaris*
'Генерал Антонов'
Makedonskaya 2020; S IV
{open pollinated seedling}
Statutory registration with the State Inspection for testing and protection of plant varieties of the Republic of Belarus.
Named after the hero of the Second World War, General of the Soviet Army Alexei Antonov.
Cultivar name established and accepted.

'Général Drouot', *S. vulgaris*
Lemoine 1890; S IV
syn. - 'General Druot'
common name: General Drouot
Lemoine, Cat. No. 116, 9 [1890]; McKelvey, The Lilac, 301 [1928]; Stand. Pl. Names, 615 [1942] - as General Drouot; Wister, Lilacs for America, 48 [1942] - as S VII; Wister, Lilacs for America, 30 [1953]; Photo on Jorgovani/Lilacs 2015 DVD.
Named for Comte Antoine Drouot, 1774-1847, French soldier and general of artillery, "le Sage de la Grande Armée" according to Napoléon.
Cultivar name presumed registered 1953; name established and accepted.

'General Elwell S. Otis', *S. vulgaris*
Dunbar 1906; D IV
syn. - Dunbar no. 323
{'Gilbert' × ? }
McKelvey, The Lilac, 301-302 [1928]; Wister, Lilacs for America, 48 [1942], 30 [1953]; Photo on Jorgovani/Lilacs 2015 DVD.
Named in 1906 for Elwell S. Otis, 1838-1909, American

soldier and first US military governor of the Philippines, 1898-1900.
Cultivar name presumed registered 1953; name established and accepted.

'General Grant', *S. vulgaris*
Dunbar 1917; S VII
syn. - Dunbar no. 268
{parentage not known}
McKelvey, The Lilac, 302 [1928]; Wister, Lilacs for America, 48 [1942], 30 [1953]; Photo on Jorgovani/Lilacs 2015 DVD.
Named for Ulysses Simpson Grant, 1822-1885, American soldier and 18th president of the United States of America.
Cultivar name presumed registered 1953; name established and accepted.

'General Haig', *S. vulgaris*
Dunbar 1917; S V
{parentage not known}
McKelvey, The Lilac, 302 [1928]; Stand. Pl. Names, 615 [1942] - name only, erroneously listed as a synonym of 'Frau Wilhelm Pfitzer'; Wister, Stand. Pl. Names, 615 [1942] - Lilacs for America, 48 [1942], 30 [1953] - name only, erroneously listed as a synonym of 'Frau Wilhelm Pfitzer'
Named for Douglas Haig, 1st Earl Haig of Bemersyde, 1861-1928, Scottish soldier and field-marshal.
Cultivar name presumed registered 1953; name established and accepted.

'General John Pershing', *S. vulgaris*
Dunbar 1917 (not Lemoine); D III
syn. - Dunbar no. 240, 'General (John) Pershing', 'General Pershing'
{'Aline Mocqueris' × ? }
Dunbar, Florists Exch., 831 [Sept. 22, 1923] - as 'General Pershing'; McKelvey, The Lilac, 303 [1928] - as 'General John Pershing', new name; Wister, Lilacs for America, 48 [1942], 30 [1953] - as 'General (John) Pershing'; Photo on Jorgovani/Lilacs 2015 DVD.
Named for John Joseph Pershing, 1860-1948, American soldier, nicknamed "Black Jack".
Cultivar name presumed registered 1953; name established and accepted.

'General Kitchener', *S. vulgaris*
Dunbar 1917; D III
syn. - Dunbar no. 243, 'Gen. Kitchener'
{'Aline Mocqueris' × ? }
Dunbar, Florists Exch., 831 [Sept. 22, 1923]; McKelvey, The Lilac, 302-303 [1928]; Wister, Lilacs for America, 48 [1942], 30 [1953]
Named for Horatio Herbert Kitchener, 1st Earl Kitchener of Khartoum, 1850-1916, Irish soldier and statesman.
Cultivar name presumed registered 1953; name established and accepted.

'General Panfilov', *S. vulgaris*
'Генерал Панфилов'
Sagitova & Dzevitski 1990; D VII/II
Named for major general Ivan Vasilyevich Panfilov, 1892-1941, commander of the 316th Soviet Siberian infantry division defending Moscow in 1941, Hero of the Soviet Union.
Cultivar name not established.

'Général Pershing', *S. vulgaris*
Lemoine 1924 (not Dunbar); D V
syn. - 'Gen. Pershing' (Lemoine, not Dunbar)
common name: General Pershing
Lemoine, Cat. No. 198, 20 [1924]; McKelvey, The Lilac, 303-304 [1928]; Stand. Pl. Names, 615 [1942] - as General Pershing; Wister, Lilacs for America, 48 [1942], 30 [1953]; Photo on Jorgovani/Lilacs 2015 DVD.
Named for John Joseph Pershing, 1860-1948, American soldier, nicknamed "Black Jack".
Cultivar name presumed registered 1953; name established and accepted.

Général Poincaré, General Poincaré - see **'Président Poincaré'**.

'Général Schmidt', *S. vulgaris*
origin not known pre-1880; ? ?
McKelvey, The lilac, 304 [1928] - name only.
Cultivar name not established.

'General Sheridan', *S. vulgaris*
Dunbar 1917; D I
syn. - Dunbar no. 274
{'Princess Alexandra' × ? }
Dunbar, Florists Exch., 831 [Sept. 22, 1923]; McKelvey, The Lilac, 304 [1928]; Wister, Lilacs for America, 48 [1942], 30 [1953]; Photo on Jorgovani/Lilacs 2015 DVD.
Named for Philip Henry Sheridan, 1831-1888, American soldier.
Cultivar name presumed registered 1953; name established and accepted.

'General Sherman', *S. vulgaris*
Dunbar 1917; S V
syn. - Dunbar no. 225
{'Marlyensis Pallida' × ? }
Dunbar, Florists Exch., 831 [Sept. 22, 1923]; McKelvey, The Lilac, 304 [1928]; Wister, Lilacs for America, 48 [1942], 30 [1953]; Photo on Jorgovani/Lilacs 2015 DVD.
Named for William Tecumseh Sherman, 1820-1891, American soldier.
Cultivar name presumed registered 1953; name established and accepted.

'George Eastman', *S. pubescens* subsp. *microphylla*
Fenicchia 1978; S V-VI
syn. - 'Geo Eastman', 'Georg Eastmann'
{*S. pubescens* subsp. *microphylla* seedling}
Clark, ILS Newsletter 4(5):9 [1978]; Vrugtman, AABGA Bull. 13(4):109 [1979] & 15(3):72 [1981]; Hoepfl & Rogers, Lilac Newsletter 14(7):7 [1988]; Fiala, Lilacs, 50,

101, 104, 108 & Pl. 32 [1988]; Photo on Jorgovani/Lilacs 2015 DVD.
Named for George Eastman, 1854-1932, American inventor and philanthropist, founder of the Eastman Kodak Co and the Eastman School of Music in Rochester, New York, USA.
Cultivar name registered 1978; name established and accepted.

'George Ellwanger', *S. vulgaris*
Fenicchia 1972; S VII
syn. - 'George Ellwanger', RAF46
{'Rochester' × ?}
Clark, The Newsletter, ILS, Convention Issue, pp. 6-7 [May 1972]; Clark, Arnoldia 32(3):133-135 [1972]; Fiala, Lilacs, pp. 105, 219 [1988]; K. Millham, Lilacs - Quart. Jour. 42(2):62 [2013].
Named for George Ellwanger, 1816-1906, partner of Patrick Barry, Mount Hope Nurseries, Rochester, New York, USA.
Cultivar name established and accepted; probably extinct.

'George Emanuel', *S. vulgaris*
Margaretten; S II
{'Mme Lemoine' × ?}
reported in cultivation at University of Utah, USA
Cultivar name not established.

'George Landis', *S. vulgaris*
Lape; D VII
{'Kapriz' × ?}
Vrugtman, AABGA Bull. 17(3):68 [1984]; Photo on Jorgovani/Lilacs 2015 DVD.
Named for George E. Landis, 1911-1950, assistant professor of economics, Rensselaer Polytechnic Institute, Troy, New York, and benefactor of the George Landis Arboretum, Esperance, New York.
Cultivar name registered 1982; name established and accepted.

'Georges Battel', *S. vulgaris*
origin not known pre-1937; ? ?
B. O. Case & Son, Cat. [ca 1937], according to Upton Scrapbook 1:35 [1980]
Cultivar name not established.

'Georges Bellair', *S. vulgaris*
Lemoine 1900; D VI
syn. - 'Georg Bellair', 'Georges Bellaire'
Lemoine, Cat. No. 146, 12 [1900]; McKelvey, The lilac, 304-305 [1928]; Wister, Lilacs for America, 48 [1942], 30 [1953]; Photo on Jorgovani/Lilacs 2015 DVD.
Named for Georges Adolphe Bellair, 1860-1939, French horticulturist and writer, director of Parks at Versailles.
Cultivar name presumed registered 1953; name established and accepted.

'Georges Claude', *S. vulgaris*
Lemoine 1935; D III
Wister, Lilacs for America, 48 [1942], 30 [1953]; Photo on Jorgovani/Lilacs 2015 DVD.
Named for Georges Claude, 1870-1960, French industrial chemist, physicist, engineer and inventor.
Cultivar name presumed registered 1953; name established and accepted.

'George W. Aldridge', *S. vulgaris*
Dunbar 1923; S IV
syn. - Dunbar no. 218
{'Président Massart' × ?}
McKelvey, The Lilac, 305 [1928]; Wister, Lilacs for America, 48 [1942] - as S VI; Wister, Lilacs for America, 30 [1953]; Photo on Jorgovani/Lilacs 2015 DVD.
Named for George Washington Aldridge, 1856-1922, contractor, local politician nicknamed "Big Fellow", Rochester, New York, USA.
Cultivar name presumed registered 1953; name established and accepted.

'George W. Alexander', *S. vulgaris*
Dunbar pre-1927; ? IV
Wister, Nat. Hort. Mag. 6(1):1-16 [1927]
Questionable name; perhaps a misspelling of 'George W. Aldridge'.
Cultivar name not established; not reported in cultivation.

'Georgiĭ Sviridov', *S. vulgaris*
'Георгий Свиридов'
Aladin, S., Aladina, O. and Polyakova, T. 2015; D IV
{elite form 10-99-N × OP}
Садовник (Gardener) magazine 04 (140)/2017 :18-25; Вестник АППМ (Catalog in Vestnik APPM (Planting material association) magazine) 1/2018: 59-72 (in Russian).
Named for Georgii Vasilyevich Sviridov (Георгий Васильевич Свиридов), 1915-1998, Russian composer, pianist; People's Artist of the USSR (1970).
Cultivar name established and accepted.

'Geraint', *S.* (Villosae Group), *S.* ×*josiflexa*
Preston 1936; S IV
Wister, Lilacs for America, 30, 48 [1953]
Named for Sir Geraint, the eldest son of King Erbin of Dumnonia who was a Knight of Devon; Prince Geraint spent much time at King Arthur's Court in 5th century Britain.
Cultivar name presumed registered 1953; name established and accepted.

'Geraldine Smith', *S. vulgaris*
Rankin 1963; S I
syn. - VIRGIN WHITE (trade designation used for cut flowers of this cultivar)
{parentage not known}
Wister, Arnoldia 23(4):81 [1963]; Photo on Jorgovani/Lilacs 2015 DVD.
Cultivar name registered 1963; name established and accepted.
Forcing lilacs in the Netherlands.

'Germinal', *S.* (Villosae Group)
Lemoine 1939; S VI
syn. - 'Geminal'
{*S.* ×*henryi* × *S. tomentella* subsp. *tomentella*}
Wister, Lilacs for America, 49 [1942], 30 [1953]; Photo on Jorgovani/Lilacs 2015 DVD.
Named for the seventh month of the 1st Republic calendar (Mar. 21 - Apr. 19).
Cultivar name presumed registered 1953; name established and accepted.

'Gerrie Schoonenberg', *S. vulgaris*
Eveleens Maarse 1948; S I
syn. - 'Gerry Schoonenberg'
{'Maréchal Foch' × 'Excellent'}
Wister, Lilacs for America, 30 [1953]; Dendron 1(1):12 [1954]; Photo on Jorgovani/Lilacs 2015 DVD.
Awards: Certificate of Merit 1948 (KMTP).
Cultivar name presumed registered 1953; name established and accepted.

'Gertrude', *S.* (Villosae Group), *S.* ×*prestoniae*
Preston; ? ?
syn. - Preston No. 20-14-197
{*S. villosa* subsp. *villosa* × *S. komarowii* subsp. *reflexa*}
Macoun, Rep. Dom. Hort. 1928, 56 [1930]; Wister, Lilacs for America, 64 [1942], 48 [1953] - name only, not in cultivation, no plants distributed
Named for the queen of Denmark in Shakespeare's *Hamlet*.
Cultivar name not established; probably extinct.

'Gertrude Child', *S. vulgaris*
Child pre-1976; S VII
Vrugtman, Lilacs - Proceedings 6(1):15 [1978];
Vrugtman, AABGA Bull. 13(4):105 [1979]
Named for Gertrude Child, 1918-1955, daughter of the originator.
Cultivar name registered 1976; name established and accepted.

'Gertrude Clark', *S. vulgaris*
Fiala 1984; S I
{'Rochester' × 'Rochester' seedling}
Fiala, Lilacs, 91, 223, Pl.8 [1988]
Named for Mrs Gertrude Clark, Meredith, New Hampshire, USA, mother of Robert B. Clark.
Cultivar name established and accepted.

'Gertrude Leslie', *S.* ×*hyacinthiflora*
Skinner 1954; D I
Wister, Lilacs for America, 30 [1953]; Skinner, Hort. Horizons, 108 [1966]; Photo on Jorgovani/Lilacs 2015 DVD.
Named for Mrs W. R. Leslie (née Bruce), wife to the superintendent, Dominion Agricultural Experiment Station, Morden, Manitoba, Canada.
Cultivar name presumed registered 1953; name established and accepted.

'Ghizo' – A misspelling of 'Guizot'

Giant - see **'Gigantea'** (*S. vulgaris*).

Giant of Battles - see **'Géant des Batailles'**.

'Gigantea', *S. villosa* subsp. *villosa*
pre-1798; ? ?
Enum. Plts. Hort. Kew, 172 [1798] - name only; McKelvey, The Lilac, 467 [1928] - name only; RHS Plant Finder database, Plant Finder Reference Library CD-ROM 1998/99 - name only.
Cultivar name not established.

'Gigantea', *S. vulgaris*
Ellwanger & Barry 1867; S V
common name: Giant
Ellwanger & Barry Cat. No. 2, 43 [1867]; Stand. Pl. Names, 486 [1923] - as Giant; McKelvey, The Lilac, 305 [1928]; Wister, Lilacs for America, 49 [1942], 30 [1953]; Photo on Jorgovani/Lilacs 2015 DVD.
Cultivar name presumed registered 1953; name established and accepted.

'Gigantea de Marly', *S. vulgaris*
origin not known pre-1879; ? ?
Baumann, Cat. No. 159, 38 [1879]; McKelvey, The Lilac, 305 [1928] - name only
Cultivar name not established.

'Gilbert', *S. vulgaris*
Lemoine 1911; S IV
Lemoine, Cat. No. 179, 37 [1911]; McKelvey, The Lilac, 305 [1928]; Wister, Lilacs for America, 49 [1942], 30 [1953]; Photo on Jorgovani/Lilacs 2015 DVD.
Named for Nicolas Joseph Laurent Gilbert, 1751-1780, French satyric poet.
Cultivar name presumed registered 1953; name established and accepted.

'Gimborn's China Pearl', *S. pekinensis*
[de Jong] 2005; S I
de Jong, Dendroflora 41:74 [2005]
Cultivar name established and accepted.

'Giraldii', *S. oblata* subsp. *oblata*
Sprenger 1903; S VII-V
syn. - *S. giraldi*, *S. oblata* var. *giraldii*
Lemoine, Cat. No. 179, p. 2, [1911] - "Lilas hybrides de *Syringa vulgaris* et de *S.* Giraldii", resulting in EH-G or "Early Hybrid of giraldii" cultivars of *S.* ×*hyacinthiflora*; McKelvey, The Lilac, pp. 182-186 [1928]; P. S. Green & Mei-Chen Chang in Flora of China 15:285 [1996]; Vrugtman, Lilacs - Quart. Jour. 38(2):60-63[2009] - as 'Giraldii'; Photo on Jorgovani/Lilacs 2015 DVD.
Named for the Rev. Giuseppe Giraldi, x -1901, Italian missionary and plant collector, who's collections are in the Biondi-Giraldi Herbarium at the Botanical Museum, Florence, Italy.
Cultivar name established and accepted.

'**Gisela**', *S.* (*S.* ×*hyacinthiflora*)
  Kopp 1999; D V
  varietal denomination registered with the Bundessortenamt, Germany, June 22, 1999 <www.bundessortenamt.de/internet30> holder/breeder: Emil Kopp - name only;
  Cultivar name established and accepted.

'**Gismonda**', *S. vulgaris*
  Lemoine 1939; D VI
  syn. - 'Grismonda'
  Lemoine, Cat. No. 225, 5 [1954]; Wister, Lilacs for America, 49 [1942], 30 [1953];
  Photo on Jorgovani/Lilacs 2015 DVD.
  Named, perhaps, for a heroine in French literature.
  Cultivar name presumed registered 1953; name established and accepted.

'**G. J. Baardse**', *S. vulgaris*
  Eveleens Maarse 1943; S VI
  syn. - 'Bardsee', 'Baardsee', 'G. J. Baardsee', 'G. J. Bardse', Baardse (trade designation used for cut flowers of this cultivar)
  {'Ambassadeur' × 'Hugo de Vries'}
  Wister, Lilacs for America, 30 [1953]; Eveleens Maarse, Dendron 1(1):12 [1954];
  Photo on Jorgovani/Lilacs 2015 DVD.
  Forcing cultivar in the Netherlands.
  Awards: Certificate of Merit 1943 (KMTP), First Class Certificate 1953 (KMTP).
  Cultivar name presumed registered 1953; name established and accepted.

'**Glacier**', *S. vulgaris*
  Fiala 1981; D I
  {('Gismonda' × 'Flora 1953') × 'Rochester'}
  Fiala, Lilacs, 91, 223 [1988]
  Cultivar name established and accepted.

'**Gladwyne**', *S. vulgaris*
  Henry, M.G.; S VII
  Wister, Lilacs for America, 49 [1942], 30 [1953]
  Cultivar name presumed registered 1953; name established and accepted.

Gloire . . . - see also Glory . . .

'**Gloire d'Aalsmeer**', *S. vulgaris*
  Maarse, J.D. 1938; S I
  syn. - 'Glory of Aalsmeer'
  {mutation of 'Marie Legraye'}
  Dijkhuis, in Gedenkboek J. Valckenier Suringar, p. 128 [1942]; Wister, Lilacs for America, 30 [1953]; Photo on Jorgovani/Lilacs 2015 DVD.
  Awards: Certificate of Merit 1934; First Class Certificate 1936 (KMTP).
  Cultivar name presumed registered 1953; name established and accepted.

'**Gloire de Bordeaux**', *S. vulgaris*
  origin not known pre-1865; ? ?
  McKelvey, The Lilac, 306 [1928] - name only; Wister, Lilacs for America, 36, 49 [1942] - name only
  Cultivar name not established.

'**Gloire de Cass**', *S. vulgaris*
  origin not known pre-1915; S III
  Blossom, Landscape Arch., April 1915, p. 140, & Oct. 1923, p. 33; McKelvey, The Lilac, 306 [1928].
  Cultivar name not established.

Gloire de Croncels - see '**De Croncels**'.

'**Gloire de la Rochelle**', *S. vulgaris*
  origin not known pre-1865; S IV
  syn. - 'Gloria Rupellae'
  Baudriller, Cat. No. 43, 142 [1800]; McKelvey, The Lilac, 306 [1928]; Wister, Lilacs for America, 49 [1942], 30 [1953]; Photo on Jorgovani/Lilacs 2015 DVD.
  Cultivar name presumed registered 1953; name established and accepted.

'**Gloire de Lorraine**', *S. vulgaris*
  Lemoine 1876; S VI
  Lemoine, Cat. No. 74, 9 [1876]; McKelvey, The Lilac, 306 [1928]; Wister, Lilacs for America, 49 [1942], 30 [1953]; Photo on Jorgovani/Lilacs 2015 DVD.
  Cultivar name presumed registered 1953; name established and accepted.

'**Gloire de Moulins**', *S. vulgaris*
  origin not known pre-1867; S V
  syn. - 'Gloria de Moulins', 'Gloria Molinae'
  Baudriller, Cat. No. 43, 142 [1880]; McKelvey, The Lilac, 307 [1928]; Wister, Lilacs for America, 49 [1942] - as S IV; Wister, Lilacs for America, 30 [1953]; Photo on Jorgovani/Lilacs 2015 DVD.
  Cultivar name presumed registered 1953; name established and accepted.

'**Gloire de Versailles**', *S. vulgaris*
  origin not known pre-1925; S ?
  possibly identical to 'Versaliensis'
  McKelvey, The Lilac, 307-308 [1928] - as confused name
  Cultivar name not established.

Gloria Rupellae - see '**Gloire de la Rochelle**'.

'**Glorija**', *S. vulgaris*
  Kārkliņš 2003; D II
  Strautiņa & Kaufmane, Dobeles ceriņi, p. 92 [2011]
  Name: Latvian for glory.
  Cultivar name established and accepted.

Glory . . . - see also Gloire . . .

'**Glory**', *S. vulgaris*
  Havemeyer 1943; S VI
  Wister, Lilacs for America, 45 [1943], 30 [1953];
  Kammerer, Morton Arb. Bull. Pop. Info. 36(6):27-29

[1961]; Eickhorst, ILS Lilac Newsletter 4(1):4-5 [1978]; Lilacs - Quart. Jour. 21(2): front cover ill. [1992]; Photo on Jorgovani/Lilacs 2015 DVD.
Cultivar name presumed registered 1953; name established and accepted.

Glory of Aalsmeer - see **'Gloire d'Aalsmeer'**.

Glory of Horstenstein - see **'Ruhm von Horstenstein'**.

'Glory of Mt. Hope', *S. vulgaris*
Ellwanger & Barry 1868; S VI
Ellwanger & Barry, Cat. No. 2, 43 [1867]; McKelvey, The Lilac, 308 [1928]; Wister, Lilacs for America, 49 [1942], 30 [1953]
Named for Mount Hope Nurseries, Rochester, New York, USA.
Cultivar name presumed registered 1953; name established and accepted.

'Godfrey', *S. vulgaris*
origin not known pre-1942; D IV
Wister, Lilacs for America, 36 & 49 [1942].
Cultivar name not established, not reported in cultivation in 1953.

'Godron', *S. vulgaris*
Lemoine 1908; D III
syn. - 'Godroy', 'Gordon', 'Gudron', 'Gudrun'
Lemoine, Cat. No. 170, 30 [1908]; McKelvey, The Lilac, 308 [1928]; Wister, Lilacs for America, 49 [1942], 30 [1953]; Photo on Jorgovani/Lilacs 2015 DVD.
Named for Dominique Alexandre Godron, 1807-1880, French botanist.
Cultivar name presumed registered 1953; name established and accepted.

Godroy - see **'Godron'**.

Goizet - see **'Guizot'**

'Golden Eclipse', *S. reticulata* subsp. *reticulata*
Bakker 2000; S I *
J.C. Bakker & Sons, Reference Guide 2000-2001, pp.12 & 27 (ill.); Vrugtman, HortScience 38(6):1301 [2003]; Photo on Jorgovani/Lilacs 2015 DVD.
United States Plant Patent No. 15,990 [September 20, 2005]; Canadian Plant Breeders' Rights registration No. 1505, effective 2003-09-05 to 2021-09-05.
Cultivar name registered 2002; name established and accepted.

golden garden - see **'Jin Yuan'**.

'Goliath', *S. vulgaris*
origin not known pre-1870; S VI
L. van Houtte, Cat. No. 130, 252 [1869] - name only; McKelvey, The Lilac, 308-309 [1928]; Wister, Lilacs for America, 49 [1942], 30 [1953]; Photo on Jorgovani/Lilacs 2015 DVD.
Cultivar name presumed registered 1953; name established and accepted.

'Golubaya', *S. vulgaris*
'Голубая'
Kolesnikov pre-1963; S III
syn. - 'Azure', 'Golubaia', 'Golubaja', 'Golubava', 'Golubaya', Kolesnikov No. 241
{(Kolesnikov No. 11 × 'Mechta') × 'Decaisne'}
Gromov, A., Siren', 82 [1963]; Howard & Brizicky, AABGA Quart. Newsl. No. 64, 17-21 [1965]; Lilacs - Proceedings 2(4):16 [1974]; Rubtzov et al. 1980. Vidy i sorta sireni, kul'tiviruemye v SSSR. Kiev; Naukova Dumka. – in Russian; Holetich, C.D. 1982. Lilac species and cultivars in cultivation in USSR. Lilacs 11(2):1-38. - translation of Rubtzov et al. 1982; Photo on Jorgovani/Lilacs 2015 DVD.
Name: Russian for blue.
Cultivar name established and accepted.

'Golubka Tesly', *S. vulgaris*
'Голубка Теслы'
Aladin, S., Aladina, O., Polyakova, T., and Aladina, A. 2015; S IV/III
{'Flora 1953' × 'Madame Charles Suchet'}
Садовник (Gardener) magazine 04 (140)/2017 :18-25; Вестник АППМ (Catalog in Vestnik APPM (Planting material association) magazine) 1/2018: 59-72 (in Russian); International scientific and practical conference (Международная и практическая конференция) «International Syringa 2018», Moscow, Moscow State University Botanical Garden, St. Petersburg, Botanical Garden of Peter the Great BIN RAS, Pavlovsk, May 21-27, 2018; pp. 43-47 (in Russian).
Russian for dove or pigeon of Tesla, referring to Tesla's friendship with the tame pigeon he rescued in New York City; Nicolet Tesla, 1856-1943, Serbian inventor in electrical and radio engineering.
Cultivar name established and accepted.

'Goneril', *S.* (Villosae Group), *S.* ×*prestoniae*
Preston date not known; ? ?
syn. - Preston ? 20-14-01
{*S. villosa* subsp. *villosa* × *S. komarowii* subsp. *reflexa*}
Preston, List of varieties of ornamental plants, originated in the Division of Horticulture, Central Experimental Farm, Ottawa, showing their respective parentage; undated typed list, p. 2 - name only.
Named for Goneril, Daughter to Lear, King of Britain in Shakespeare's *King Lear*.
Cultivar name not established and accepted; not know in cultivation.

'Goplana', *S.* (Villosae Group), *S.* ×*prestoniae*
Bugała pre-1970; S V
syn. - 'Galpana'
Bugała, Arboretum Kórnickie 15:61-70 [1970]; Wister & Oppe, Arnoldia 23(3): 122 [1971]; Bugała, Lilacs - Quart. Jour. 24(4):90-91 [1995]; Photo on Jorgovani/Lilacs 2015 DVD.
Cultivar name registered 1970; name established and accepted.

'Gordon' - see **'Godron'**.

'Gornyĭ Potok', S. vulgaris
'горный поток'
Sagitova & Dzevitski pre-2014; S VII
Photo by Oleg Dzevitskiy in Almaty, Kazakhstan seen in 2020 ILS Photo & Color Database.
Russian for mountain stream.
Cultivar name not established.

'Gortenziya', *S. vulgaris*
'Тортензия'
Kolesnikov 1930; S IV-V
syn. - 'Gotensiia', 'Gortensia', 'Gortensiia', 'Gortenzija', 'Hortensia'
{'Congo' × ?}
Howard, Arnoldia 19(6-7):31-35 [1959]; Gromov, A., Siren', 87-88 [1963]; Howard & Brizicky, AABGA Quart. Newsl. No. 64, 17-21 [1965]; Wister & Oppe, Arnoldia 31(3):125 [1971] - erroneously as 'Gotensiia'; Gromov, Lilacs - Proceedings 2(4):16 [1974] - erronously as 'Gortensia'; Rubtzov et al. 1980. Vidy i sorta sireni, kul'tiviruemye v SSSR. Kiev; Naukova Dumka. – in Russian; Holetich, C.D. 1982. Lilac species and cultivars in cultivation in USSR. Lilacs 11(2):1-38. - translation of Rubtzov et al. 1982; Photo on Jorgovani/Lilacs 2015 DVD.
Name: Russian for hydrangea.
Cultivar name registered 1970; name established and accepted.

'Goscote Purity', *S. pubescens* subsp. *patula*
Goscote; S I
{mutation of 'Miss Kim'}
van der Werf, Plants 5(2):71 [2000]; withdrawn from the trade (in litt. D. Cox, Jun.13/00); http://www.goscote.co.uk/ [April 18, 2002]
Cultivar name not established.

'Governor Wentworth', *S. vulgaris*
Origin not known lilacs planted ca 1750 at the Governor Wentworth Estate, Newcastle, New Hampshire; S V/VII
syn. - WENWORTH (Wenworth)
Anon. (Probably J. L. Fiala), ILS Proceedings 2(4):10 [1974] - as "all of the same clone" and "pinkish-lavender in bloom and a deeper pink in bud."
Named for Benning Wentworth [1696-1770]; colonial governor of New Hampshire [1741-1766]. See also <http://wentworthcoolidge.org/?page_id=236>
Cultivar name established and accepted.

'Govorit Leningrad', *S. vulgaris*
'Говорит Ленинград'
Aladin, S., Aladina, O., Polyakova, T., and, Aladina, A. 2017; S II/IV
{'Gilbert' × OP}
IX International Scientific Conference (IX Международная научная конференция "Цветоводство: история, теория, практика") " Floriculture: history, theory, practice" , St. Petersburg, Botanical Garden of Peter the Great BIN RAS, September 7-13, 2019 (in Russian).
Named for the radio of the besieged Leningrad ("Leningrad Speaks"). During World War II, it was the only connection with the outside world.
Cultivar name established and accepted

'Grace', *S.* ×*hyacinthiflora*
Preston pre-1942; S VII
syn. - Preston No. 22-01-08
{*S. vulgaris* 'Negro' × *S.* ×*hyacinthiflora* 'Lamartine'}
Davis, Rep. Dom. Hort., Progress Report 1934-1948, 150 [1950]; Wister, Lilacs of America, 49, 64 [1942], 30, 48 [1953]; Photo on Jorgovani/Lilacs 2015 DVD.
Cultivar name presumed registered 1953; name established and accepted.

'Grace Mackenzie', *S.*
Skinner 1942; S IV
syn. - 'Grace MacKenzie'
{*S. oblata* subsp. *dilatata* × *S.* ×*persica* var. *alba*}
Dropmore Cat. [1942]; Woody Plant Register, AAN, No. 57 [1949]; Wister, Lilacs for America, 49 [1942], 30 [1953]; Skinner, Hort. Horizons, 109-110 [1966]; Vrugtman, ILS Newsletter 8(8):9 [1982]; Photo on Jorgovani/Lilacs 2015 DVD.
Cultivar name presumed registered 1953; name established and accepted.

'Grace Orthwaite', *S. vulgaris*
Brand 1937; S V
Brand Peony Farms, Cat., 11 [1941]; Wister, Lilacs for America, 49 [1942], 30 [1953]; Photo on Jorgovani/Lilacs 2015 DVD.
Cultivar name presumed registered 1953; name established and accepted.

'Grace Wyman', *S. vulgaris*
Berdeen; D VI
{'Paul Thirion' × 'Edmund Boissier'}
Vrugtman, AABGA Bulletin 16(4):132 [1982]; King & Coggeshall, Lilacs - Quart. Jour. 27(2):49-50 [1998] - name only; Photo on Jorgovani/Lilacs 2015 DVD.
Named for Ken Berdeen's neighbor.
Cultivar name not established.

'Gradimir', *S. vulgaris*
origin not known pre-1930; S IV
syn. - 'Gradimi', 'Gradimii'
Späth, Späth-Buch, 303, 304 [1930]; Wister, Lilacs for America, 36 & 49 [1942] - name only, as 'Gradimi'.
Cultivar name not established.

Graf von Humboldt - see **'De Humboldt'**.

'Grand-Duc Constantin', *S. vulgaris*
Lemoine 1895; D III
syn. - 'Grand duc Constantin'
Lemoine, Cat. No. 131, 10 [1895]; Kache,

Gartenschönheit 5:82 [1924]; McKelvey, The Lilac, 309 [1928]; Wister, Lilacs for America, 49 [1942], 30 [1953]; Photo on Jorgovani/Lilacs 2015 DVD.
Named, perhaps, for Constantin I, king of Greece, 1861-1923.
Cultivar name presumed registered 1953; name established and accepted.

'Grandiflora', *S. vulgaris*
origin not known pre-1831; ? ?
McKelvey, The Lilac, 309-310 [1928] - as confused name
Cultivar name not established.

Grandiflora Alba - see **'Alba Grandiflora'**.

'Grandma's Purple', *S. vulgaris*
origin not known 2014; S VII
<www.girardnurseries.com/product-p/llgrapurc3.5.htm>

GREAT WALL™ - see **'WFH2'**.

Great White - see **'Alba Grandiflora'**.

'Grecrimdoll', *S.* [Pubescentes Series]
Greenleaf 2016; S VI-V
{parentage not recorded}
marketed in the USA as CRIMSON DOLL™
Garden Debut 2016 Cat. p.28.
Cultivar name established and accepted.

'Gregor', *S. vulgaris*
Mägi pre-2017; S VII
Photo by Mägi in Estonia seen in 2020 ILS Photo & Color Database.
Cultivar name not established.

'Greswt', *S. pubescens* subsp. *patula*
Greenleaf 2011; S VI-III
marketed in the USA as MISS KIM SWEET TREAT™ or SWEET TREAT™
{"selection out of 'Miss Kim'"}
<www.greenleafnursery.com/index.cfm/fuseaction/plants.plantDetail/plant_id/2937/genus/Syringa/index.htm> seen July 4, 2011; Garden Debut 2016 Cat. p. 28.
Cultivar name established and accepted.

'Grete Wormdal', *S. josikaea*
origin not known pre-1978; S VI
syn. - 'Grete', klon 313
Lønø, Norsk Hagetident, 7-8/85, pp. 395-397 [1985]; Kjær, Gartneryrket (G.Y.) 1987:274; Bjerkestrand & Sandved, Grøntanleggsplanter utvalgt for norske forhold 1986-1987-1988 [1989] pp. 25-26 & ill. p. 16; Vrugtman, Lilacs - Quart. Jour. 25(2):41-42 [1996]
Cultivar name established and accepted.

Gudron - see **'Godron'**.

'Guild's Pride', *S.* ×*hyacinthiflora*
Sobeck; S IV
syn. - 'Pride of the Guild'

Wister, Arnoldia 26(3):13 [1966]
Cultivar name registered 1966; name established and accepted.
Nota bene: Since this cultivar appears to be of 'Lavender Lady' ancestry, see also: Pringle, Lilacs - Quart. Jour. 24(4):97-99 [1995]; and Vrugtman, HortScience 31(3):328 [1996].

'Guinevere', *S.* (Villosae Group), *S.* ×*josiflexa*
Preston 1925; S VI
syn. - Preston No. 20-06-01
{*S. josikaea* × *S. komarowii* subsp. *reflexa*}
Davis, Rep. Dom. Hort., Progress Report 1934-1948, 149 [1950]; Wister, Lilacs for America, 49, 50, 64 [1942], 31, 32, 48 [1953]; Buckley, Arboretum Notes 16:22 [1961] - as planted in 1925; Photo on Jorgovani/Lilacs 2015 DVD.
Named for Queen Guinevere, character from Guinevere, poem by Alfred, Lord Tennyson, 1809-1892.
Cultivar name presumed registered 1953; name established and accepted.

'Guizot', *S. vulgaris*
Lemoine 1897; D IV
syn. - Goizet
Lemoine, Cat. No. 137, 23 [1897]; McKelvey, The Lilac, 310 [1928]; Wister, Lilacs for America, 49 [1942], 30 [1953]; Photo on Jorgovani/Lilacs 2015 DVD.
Named for François Pierre Guillaume Guizot, 1787-1874, French historian and statesman.
Cultivar name presumed registered 1953; name established and accepted.

'Gul'der', *S. vulgaris*
'Тульдер'
Sagitova & Dzevitskaya 1994; D VI
varietal denomination registered 1994, No. 16, State Register of Selected Achievements in Republic of Kazakhstan
Cultivar name not established.

'Gul'nar', *S. vulgaris*
'Тульнар'
Sagitova; D I
{parentage not known}
Kazakh magazine "Tsvetochnui Dom", 2008, #1 'Iz otechestvennoi sekllektsii, Rodom iz Kazakhstana', page 8 – Цветочный Дом, 2008, No.1, "Из отечественной селекции. Родом из Казахстана", стр.8.
Name: Kazakh for "like a flower".
Cultivar name not established.

'Gul'nazira', *S. vulgaris*
'Тульназира'
Sakharova 1973; S V
syn. - 'Gulnazira', Sakharova No. 1391
{'Congo' × ? }
Sakharova, Introduktsiya i selektsiya dekorativnykh rastenii v Bashkirii, 30 [1978] - in Russian; Rubtzov et al. 1980. Vidy i sorta sireni, kul'tiviruemye v SSSR. Kiev;

Naukova Dumka. – in Russian; Holetich, C.D. 1982. Lilac species and cultivars in cultivation in USSR. Lilacs 11(2):1-38. - translation of Rubtzov et al. 1982; Photo on Jorgovani/Lilacs 2015 DVD.
Name: In Arabic and Farsi meaning "beautiful flower"; also a Bashkir female name.
Cultivar name established and accepted.

'Gvardeĭskaya', *S. vulgaris*
'Твардейская'
Aladin, S., Aladina, O., and Polyakova, T. 2015; S VI
{'Indya' × OP}
Садовник (Gardener) magazine, 05 (141)/2017 :16-22; Вестник АППМ (Catalog in Vestnik APPM (Planting material association) magazine) 1/2018: 59-72 (in Russian); named for The Guards.
Cultivar name established and accepted.

'Gwendolyn', *S. vulgaris*
Alverson A. pre-2014; S IV
Grown from OP seed by Alice Mae Alverson in Cherry Valley, NY USA.
Seen by the Registrar at Cherry Valley Lilacs, Cherry Valley NY USA June 2019.
Information provided by Charle-Pan Dawson in email to Registrar 6/9/2019.
Named for a family member.

'Gwen Marie', *S. vulgaris*
Berdeen; D ? *
{'Paul Thirion × ? }
Vrugtman, AABGA Bulletin 16(4):132 [1982]; King & Coggeshall, Lilacs - Quart. Jour. 27(2):49-50 [1998] - name only
Named for Ken Berdeen's daughter-in-law.
cultivar not established; not reported in cultivation.

'Gwynne', *S.* (Villosae Group)
Preston (?); S V
{*S. komarowii* subsp. *reflexa* × *S. tomentella* subsp. *sweginzowii*}
Wister, Lilacs for America, 31 [1953] - listed as being in the collection in Ottawa, but could not be traced in 2005, probably extinct
Cultivar name presumed registered 1953; name established and accepted.

'Gzhel', *S. vulgaris*
'Гжель'
Aladin, S., Aladina, O., Polyakova, T., and Aladina, A. 2016; S III
{'Firmament' × OP}
IX International Scientific Conference (IX Международная научная конференция "Цветоводство: история, теория, практика") "and Floriculture side by side Floriculture: history, theory, practice", St. Petersburg, Botanical Garden of Peter the Great BIN RAS, September 7-13, 2019 (in Russian)
Named for one of the centers for Russian folkcraft for the production of ceramics with hand-made pale blue painting.
Cultivar name established and accepted.

'Hagny', *S.* (Villosae Group)
Olsen & Gram 1935; S VI & V
syn. - 'Hyacintsyren', A.O. No. 1
{*S. villosa* subsp. *wolfii* × *S. komarowii* subsp. *reflexa*}
Aksel Olsen, Cat. No. 140, 36 [1935] & No. 250, 22 [1952]; Wister & Oppe, Arnoldia 31(3):122 [1971] - name only; Photo on Jorgovani/Lilacs 2015 DVD.
Cultivar name registered 1970; name established and accepted.

hairy lilac - see *S. pubescens*.

'Halfrid', *S.* (Villosae Group)
Olsen & Gram 1952; S V
syn. - A.O. No. 3
{*S. villosa* subsp. *wolfii* × *S. komarowii* subsp. *reflexa*}
Aksel Olsen, Cat. No. 250, 22 [1952].
Cultivar name established and accepted.

Halia mocqueris - see **'Alina Mocqueris'**.

'Halina Gołąbska', *S. vulgaris*
Karpow-Lipski; ? I
syn. - KL 18
Anon., Lista odmian roślin ozdobnych 1971, 17; Lista . . . 1973, 25 - in Polish
Named (probably) for the daughter of the originator.
Varietal denomination registered COBORU 1971; Cultivar name established and accepted.

'Hallelujah', *S. vulgaris*
Havemeyer & Eaton 1954; S VI
Wister, Lilacs for America, 31 [1953] - as S VII; Lilac Land, Cat. [1954]; Niedz, ILS Newsletter (4):7-8 [1972]; Eickhorst, ILS Lilac Newsletter 4(1):4-5 [1978]; Photo on Jorgovani/Lilacs 2015 DVD.
Cultivar name presumed registered 1953; name established and accepted.

'Hanafubuki', *S. pubescens* subsp. *pubescens*
'花ふぶき'
Ihara 2018; S VI
{*S. pubescens* subsp. *pubescens* 'Smile Kaho' × *S. pubescens* subsp. *pubescens* 'Smile Kaho', seedling 2011S1128008#6}
registered 17 November 2018 by Hideo Ihara Tokiwa 450-1, Minamiku, Sapporo, Hokkaido, 005 - 0863 Japan,
Named for the blizzard of falling cherry-blossom flowers.
Cultivar name registered 2018; name established and accepted.

'Hanataba', *S. pubescens* subsp. *microphylla*
'花束'
Ihara 2004; S VII
syn. - seedling no. 20040520002#2.
{*S. pubescens* subsp. *microphylla* 'Superba' × *S. pub.* subsp. *micr.* 'Superba'}

(Vrugtman, Cultivated Plant Diversity ... 2017)
Name: Japanese for bouquet.
Cultivar name registered 2017; name established and accepted.

'Handel', S. (Villosae Group), S. ×prestoniae
Skinner 1932; S V
USDA Plant Inventory No. 97679 [Feb.26, 1932]; Wister, Lilacs for America, 49 [1942], 31 [1953]; Skinner, Hort. Horizons, 109 [1966]; Photo on Jorgovani/Lilacs 2015 DVD.
Cultivar name presumed registered 1953; name established and accepted.

'Hantengri' - see **'Khan-Tengri'**

Harlin - see **'Käthe Härlin'**.

'Harmonija', S. vulgaris
Kārkliņš pre-2005; D I
under evaluation at Latvia State Institute of Fruit Growing, Dobele
Name: Latvian for harmony.
Cultivar name not established.

'Harukaze', S. pubescens subsp. pubescens
'春風'
Ihara 2012; S VII
syn. - seedling no. 2011S1128008#4.
{S. pubescens subsp. pubescens 'Smile Kaho' × S. pubescens subsp. pubescens 'Smile Kaho'}
(Vrugtman, Cultivated Plant Diversity ... 2017)
Name: Japanese for spring breeze.
Cultivar name registered 2017; name established and accepted.

'Hathaway', S. ×chinensis
Hathaway; ? ?
Wister, Lilacs for America, 31 [1953] - name only
Cultivar name not established;
Cultivar not reported in cultivation.

'Hausener Gold', S.
no information; 1988; ? ?
Statutory registration? UPOV list

'Hazel', S. vulgaris
Lyden; ? ?
Wister & Oppe, Arnoldia, 31(3):122 [1971] - name only
Cultivar name registered 1970 without description;
Cultivar not reported in cultivation.

'Hazel Opper', S. ×hyacinthiflora
Rankin; S IV
{parentage not known}
Wister, Lilacs for America, 31 [1953]
Cultivar name presumed registered 1953; name established and accepted.

'Heather', S. vulgaris
Havemeyer pre-1942; S I
Wister, Lilacs for America, 49 [1942], 31 [1953]; Lilac Land, Cat. [1954]; Niedz, ILS Newsletter 1(4):7-8 [1972]; Eickhorst, ILS Lilac Newsletter 4(1):4-5 [1978]; Photo on Jorgovani/Lilacs 2015 DVD.
Cultivar name presumed registered 1953; name established and accepted.

'Heather Haze', S. ×hyacinthiflora
Lammerts 1953; S V
{(Lammerts C112 × Lammerts 42-108-4) × (Lammerts 42-109-4 × ?)}
Lammerts, US Plant Patent No. 3885 [May 11, 1976]; Vrugtman, Lilacs - Proceedings 6(1):16 [1978] & 7(1):37 [1979]; Vrugtman, AABGA Bull. 13(4):107 [1979]
Cultivar name registered 1976; name established and accepted.
Nota bene: Since this cultivar appears to be of 'Lavender Lady' ancestry see also: Pringle, Lilacs - Quart. Jour. 24(4):97-99 [1995]; and Vrugtman, HortScience 31(3):328 [1996].

'Heavenly Blue', S. vulgaris
Blacklock ca 1943; S III
Rowancroft Gardens, Cat. No. 9, 95 [n.d.; 1943?] - erroneously as D; Cat. No. 10, 50 [n.d.; 1944?] as single; Wister, Lilacs for America, 49 [1942], 31 [1953] - erroneously as D III; Photo on Jorgovani/Lilacs 2015 DVD.
Cultivar name presumed registered 1953; name established and accepted.

'Hecla', S. (Villosae Group), S. ×prestoniae
Skinner 1936; S V-I
Wister, Lilacs for America, 49 [1942], 31 [1953] - as S I; Skinner, Hort. Horizons, 50, 109 [1966] - as rose-colored, and first listed in 1936; Photo on Jorgovani/Lilacs 2015 DVD.
Named for Hecla Provincial Park, Manitoba, Canada.
Cultivar name presumed registered 1953; name established and accepted.

'Hedin', S. (Villosae Group)
Skinner 1935; S V
{S. villosa subsp. villosa × S. tomentella subsp. sweginzowii}
Wister, Lilacs for America, 49 [1942]; Wyman, Arnoldia 8(7):32 [1948]; Woody Plant Register, AAN, No. 53 [1949]; Wister, Lilacs for America, 31 [1953]; Skinner, Hort. Horizons, 49, 109 [1966] - introduced in 1935; Photo on Jorgovani/Lilacs 2015 DVD.
Named, perhaps, for Sven Anders Hedin [1865-1952], Swedish explorer and geographer.
Cultivar name presumed registered 1953; name established and accepted.

'Heiki Tamm', S. vulgaris
Mägi pre-2018; S VII

Semenov, I., Lilacs 48(2):71 [2019].
Cultivar name not established.

'Heimdal', *S. pubescens* subsp. *pubescens*
Origin not known; S VII
<http://www.internationalplantnames.com/searchpages/webform1.aspx> - name only (seen Nov. 7, 2006); <http://www.havenet.dk/?menupunkt=butikken&pkt=1&grp=8&id=2947> (seen Nov. 7, 2006)
Name: Heimdal is the southernmost borough in Trondheim, Norway.
Cultivar name not established.

Heinrich Martin - see **'Henri Martin'**.

'Helen', *S.* (Villosae Group), *S.* ×*prestoniae*
Skinner 1935 (not Vaigla); S V-I
Wister, Lilacs for America, 31 [1953]; Skinner, Hort. Horizons, 109, 84, Pl.33 [1966]; Skinner's Nursery Ltd., Cat. 1975, item No. 105; Photo on Jorgovani/Lilacs 2015 DVD.
Named for Helen Bell Cumming, 1915-1009, teacher and registered nurse, from 1947 wife of the originator.
Cultivar name presumed registered 1953; name established and accepted.

Helen, Vaigla (not Skinner) - see **'Leenu'**.

'Helena', *S.* (Villosae Group), *S.* ×*prestoniae*
Preston; S IV
syn. - 'Helen', 'Helene', Preston No. 20-14-06
{*S. villosa* subsp. *villosa* × *S. komarowii* subsp. *reflexa*}
Macoun, Rep. Dom. Hort. 1928, 56 [1930]; Wister, Lilacs for America, 64 [1942], 31, 48 [1953] - not in cultivation, no plants distributed
Named for A Gentlewoman in Shakespeare's *All's Well that End Well*.
Cultivar name not established, probably extinct.

'Helena Agathe Keessen', *S. vulgaris*
Keessen, W. 1936; S I
syn. - 'Helena Keessen', 'Helene Agathe Keesen', 'Helene Keesen'
{mutation of 'Mme Florent Stepman'}
Wister, Lilacs for America, 31 [1953] - erroneously as 'Helene Agathe Keessen'; van Dale 2:427 [1963] - as 'Helena Keessen'; Bilov, V. D. et al., Siren', 78 [1974] - as 'Helene Keesen', in Russian; Photo on Jorgovani/Lilacs 2015 DVD.
Named for Helena Agathe, born August 28, 1936, daughter of Gerardus Albertus Keessen, co-owner of Terra Nova nursery, Aalsmeer, The Netherlands.
Cultivar name presumed registered 1953; name established and accepted.

'Helen Blasberg', *S. vulgaris*
Monroe County Parks, Rochester, NY pre-1999, S V
{F2 seedling of 'Rochester'}
Vrugtman, *Lilacs-Quarterly Journal* 40(1):17-18 [2011]

Named for the wife of professor Charles Blasberg, Dept of Horticulture, and first director of the Horticulture Farm, University of Vermont, USA.
Cultivar name not established and accepted; the name was given to a single plant not worthy to be propagated and distributed.

'Helen Champlin', *S. vulgaris*
University of New Hampshire pre-1985
{parentage not known}
Haskell et al., Lilacs. Proceedings of the International Lilac Society 15(1):45 [1986] - name only; Rogers, in litt. Owen Rogers to Vrugtman, Feb.28/05 - the original plant died of *Armillaria melea* and was never propagated and never described.
Named for Helen Hussey Champlin [1887-1976], one of the founders of the University of New Hampshire Lilac Arboretum.
Cultivar name not established; extinct.

Helene Grunewald - see **'Perle von Teltow'**.

Helene Keesen - see **'Helene Agathe Keesen'**.

'Helen Palagge', *S. vulgaris*
Rankin; S I
syn. - 'Helen Pellage'
Wister, Arnoldia 23(4):81 [1963]; Fiala, Lilacs, p. 208 [1988] - as 'Helen Pellage', S VII; Clark, Lilacs-Quart. Jour. 20(2):34 [1991]
Cultivar name registered 1963; name established and accepted.

'Helen Schloen', *S. vulgaris*
Schloen 1962; S VII
Wister, Arnoldia 23(4):81 [1963] - erroneously as originated by Paterson, undated personal communication Schloen to Holetich; Photo on Jorgovani/Lilacs 2015 DVD.
Cultivar name registered 1963; name established and accepted.

Helen Ulanov - see **'Galina Ulanova'**.

'Helgi', *S. vulgaris*
Vaigla; D II/V (IV/I per Semenov)
{'Mrs Edward Harding' × ?}
Kivistik, Maakodu 1997(5):22-23 (ill.) [1997] - in Estonian; I. Semenov, Lilacs 48(2):65 (front cover photo) [2019].
Cultivar name established and accepted.

'Heliotrope', *S. vulgaris*
Brahy-Ekenholm 1860; S IV
Wister, Lilacs for America, 31 [1953]
Cultivar name presumed registered 1953; name established and accepted.

'Heloise', *S.* (Villosae Group), *S.* ×*prestoniae*
Skinner 1932; S V-I
USDA Plant Inventory No. 97680 [Feb.26, 1932]
Cultivar name not established.

'Henriette Ernst', *S. vulgaris*
   origin not known pre-1939; S VI
   Fr. Grunewald, Cat., 14 [1939].
   Cultivar name established and accepted.

'Henri Martin', *S. vulgaris*
   Lemoine 1912; D IV
   syn. - 'Heinrich Martin', 'Henry Martin'
   Lemoine, Cat. No. 182, 37 [1912]; McKelvey, The Lilac, 310 [1928]; Wister, Lilacs for America, 49 [1942], 31 [1953]; Photo on Jorgovani/Lilacs 2015 DVD.
   Named for Bon Louis Henri Martin, 1810-1883, French historian, author of the 15-volume "Histoire de France".
   Cultivar name presumed registered 1953; name established and accepted.

'Henri Robert', *S. vulgaris*
   Lemoine 1936; D II
   Lemoine, Cat. No. 212, 21 [1938]; Wister, Lilacs for America, 49 [1942], 31 [1953];
   Photo on Jorgovani/Lilacs 2015 DVD.
   Named for Henri-Robert, 1863-1936, French lawyer, historian and member of the Académie Française.
   Cultivar name presumed registered 1953; name established and accepted.

'Henri Vandendriessche', *S. vulgaris*
   Vandendriessche 1922; S VI
   Wister, Lilacs for America, 31 [1953]
   Named for the elder son of the originator.
   Cultivar name presumed registered 1953; name established and accepted.

'Henry Clay', *S. vulgaris*
   Dunbar 1923; S I
   syn. - Dunbar no. 329, 'Henri Clay'
   {'A. B. Lamberton' × ? }
   McKelvey, The Lilac, 319 [1928]; Wister, Lilacs for America, 49 [1942], 31 [1953];
   Photo on Jorgovani/Lilacs 2015 DVD.
   Named for Henry Clay, 1777-1852, American statesman and orator.
   Cultivar name presumed registered 1953; name established and accepted.

henryi alba - see **'Alba'** (× *henryi*).

henryi eximia - see **'Eximia'** (*josikaea*).

'Henry Wadsworth Longfellow', *S. vulgaris*
   Dunbar 1920; D VI
   syn. - Dunbar no. 245, 'Henry W. Longfellow'
   common name: Henry Longfellow
   {'Aline Mocqueris' × ? }
   Dunbar, Florist Exch., 831 [Sept. 22, 1923]; Wister, Nat. Hort. Mag. 6(1):1-16 [1927] - as D III; McKelvey, The Lilac, 310-311 [1928]; Stand. Pl. Names, 615 [1942] - as Henry Longfellow; Wister, Lilacs for America, 49 [1942], 31 [1953]; Photo on Jorgovani/Lilacs 2015 DVD.
   Named for Henry Wadsworth Longfellow, 1807-1882, American poet.
   Cultivar name presumed registered 1953; name established and accepted.

'Henry Ward Beecher', *S. vulgaris*
   Dunbar 1923; D IV
   syn. - Dunbar no. 345
   common name: Henry Beecher
   {'Princesse Clémentine' × ? }
   McKelvey, The lilac, 311 [1928]; Stand. Pl. Names, 615 [1942] - as Henry Beecher; Wister, Lilacs for America, 49 [1942], 31 [1953]
   Named for Henry Ward Beecher, 1813-1887, American congregationalist clergyman and writer.
   Cultivar name presumed registered 1953; name established and accepted.

Henry W. Longfellow - see **'Henry Wadsworth Longfellow'**.

Hericarthiana, Hericartiana, Hercorthiana - see 'Herycorthiana'.

'Hermann Eilers', *S. vulgaris*
   probably Sinai pre-1913; S V
   syn. - 'Herman Eilers';
   trade designations: SCHÖNER VON FRANKFURT, SINAI HELL LILA, SINAI LILA;
   and probably: BEAUTY OF FRANKFURT, PINK BEAUTY OF FRANKFORT, and FRANKFURTER FLIEDER
   Schetelig, Cat. [1913]; McKelvey, The Lilac, 311, 358 [1928]; Wister, Lilacs for America, 49, 56 [1942], 31, 38 [1953]; Meyer, Flieder 53-54 [1952] - as identical with 'Sinai Lila'; Photo on Jorgovani/Lilacs 2015 DVD.
   Named for Hermann F. Eilers [no dates], florist (Handelsgärtner) in St Petersburg, Russia, until 1918, who imported forced lilac branches from Großgärtnerei Friedrich Sinai, Frankfurt, Germany (in litt. Wilhelm Sinai Sr to F. Vrugtman, Aug.18/80).
   Cultivar name presumed registered 1953; name established and accepted.
   Forcing cultivar in the Netherlands and Germany from the late 1800s; also known as SINAI LILA.

'Hermann Gireoud', *S. vulgaris*
   Gireoud pre-1924; S IV-V
   McKelvey, The Lilac, 300 [1928]; Späth, Späth-Buch, 304 [1930]
   Named for Friedrich August Hermann Gireoud, 1821-1896, Horticulturist, Sagan, Silesia (now Zagan, Poland), and Berlin, Germany.
   Cultivar name established and accepted.

'Hermia', *S.* (Villosae Group), *S. ×prestoniae*
   Preston 1928; S V
   syn. - Preston No. 20-15-20
   {*S. villosa* subsp. *villosa* × *S. komarowii* subsp. *reflexa*}
   Macoun, Rep. Dom. Hort. 1928, 56 [1930] - name only; Wister, Lilacs for America, 49, 64 [1942], 31, 48 [1953]
   Named for the Daughter to Egeus in Shakespeare's

Midsummer Night's Dream.
Cultivar name presumed registered 1953; name established and accepted.

'Hermione', *S.* (Villosae Group), *S.* ×*prestoniae*
Preston (not Skinner) 1937; S V
Wister, Lilacs for America, 49, 64 [1942], 31, 48 [1953]; Davidson et al., Landscape Plants at the Morden Arboretum [1994] - received at Morden Research Station, Morden, Manitoba, Canada, in 1937
Named for the queen to Sicilia in Shakespeare's *Winter's Tale.*
Cultivar name presumed registered 1953; name established and accepted.

'Hermione', *S.* (Villosae Group)
Skinner (not Preston) 1932; ? ?
{*S. villosa* subsp. *villosa* × *S. tomentella* subsp. *sweginzowii*)
USDA Plant Inventory No. 101380 [Nov.16, 1932]
Cultivar name not established.

'Hero', *S.* (Villosae Group), *S.* ×*prestoniae*
Preston; ? ?
syn. - 'Hera', Preston No. 20-14-204
{*S. villosa* subsp. *villosa* × *S. komarowii* subsp. *reflexa*}
Macoun, Rep. Dom. Hort. 1928, 56 [1930]; Wister, Lilacs for America, 64 [1942], 48 [1953] - as 'Hera'; not in cultivation, no plants distributed
Named for the Daughter to Leonato in Shakespeare's *Much Ado About Nothing.*
Cultivar name not established, probably extinct.

'Hers', *S. pubescens* subsp. *microphylla*
Hers & ? pre-1953; S V
syn. - *julianae* 'Hers Variety', 'Hers Form'
{presumably grown from seed collected by J. Hers in China}
Wister, Lilacs for America, 49, 50 [1942], 31, 32 [1953]; Fiala, Lilacs, 39, 50, 101, 107, Pl. 32 [1988]; Vrugtman, Lilacs-Quart. Journ. 28(4):100-102 [1999]; Photo on Jorgovani/Lilacs 2015 DVD.
Named for Joseph Hers, 1884-1965, Belgian railroad official, who collected botanical specimens while working in northern China, 1900-1930.
Cultivar name presumed registered 1953; name established and accepted.
Nota bene: No reference has been found as to who grew the plants from the seed collected by J. Hers, and who introduced the cultivar.

'Herycorthiana', *S. vulgaris*
origin not known pre-1865; S VII/II
syn. - 'Hericarthiana', 'Hericorthina'
Alnarps Trädgards Sortimentskatalog, p. 68 [1902] - as 'Hericarthiana'; McKelvey, The Lilac, 311, 563 [1928] - confused name
Named for the town of Héricourt, Haute-Saône, France.
Cultivar name not established, probably extinct.

'Heterophylla', *S.*
Skinner; ? ?
syn. - *S. heterophylla*
{(*S. oblata* subsp. *dilatata* × *S. vulgaris*) × *S. pinnatifolia*}
Wister, Lilacs for America, 31 [1953] - name only; Pringle, Baileya 21(3):103 [1981]
Cultivar name not established; probably extinct.

'Heterophylla', *S. vulgaris*
Zhuo Lihuan; S VII
Zhuo, L.H., Bull. Bot. Research (Harbin) 9(4):131-134, pl.: f. 3-4 [1989] - in Chinese, Latin description.
Cultivar name not established; rejected epithet (Latin form).

'Hiawatha', *S.* (Villosae Group), *S.* ×*prestoniae*
Skinner 1932; S VI
{*S. villosa* subsp. *villosa* × *S. komarowii* subsp. *reflexa*}
USDA Plant Inventory No. 97681 [Feb.26, 1932]; Wister, Lilacs for America, 49 [1942], 31 [1953]; Woody Plant Register, AAN, No. 55[1949] Skinner, Hort. Horizons, 109 [1966]; Registered with the State Commission of the Russian Federation for Testing and Protection of Selection Achievements, No. 9810216, 2001, as 'Тайавата'; Photo on Jorgovani/Lilacs 2015 DVD.
Named for the Indian hero of Longfellow's poem "The Song of Hiawatha".
Cultivar name presumed registered 1953; name established and accepted.

'Hien', *S. pubescens* subsp. *pubescens*
'飛燕'
Ihara 2018; S VII/II
{*S. pubescens* subsp. *pubescens* 'Palibin' seedling 200405200001#8 × *S. pubescens* subsp. *pubescens* 'Hoshikuzu' seedling 2011S1128007#8}
registered 17 November 2018 by Hideo Ihara Tokiwa 450-1, Minamiku, Sapporo, Hokkaido, 005-0863 Japan.
The name in Japanese means "swallow in flight."
Cultivar name registered 2018; name established and accepted.

'High Lama', *S.* (Villosae Group)
Fiala; S IV
{*S.* ×*josiflexa* 'Royalty' × *S. komarowii* subsp. *komarowii*}
Fiala, Lilacs, 224 [1988]
Cultivar name established and accepted.

'Highland Park', *S. vulgaris*
Hoepfl 2007: S III
syn. - FC 20
{'Flower City' × ? }
Hoepfl, Lilacs - Quart. Jour. 36(2):74-75 and front & back cover photos [2007] - background information only; Millham, Lilacs - Quart. Jour. 42(4):130 & photo 132 [2013] - reference to FC 20; Millham, Lilacs - Quart. Jour.43(2):52 [2014] - as S III; Hoepfl, Lilacs - Quart. Jour. 43(3):90 & photo 91 [2014] - "with many radially double florets".

Named for Highland Park, Rochester, New York, site of the lilac collection.
Cultivar name established and accepted.

'High Noon', *S. vulgaris*
Havemeyer & Eaton 1953; D I
Wister, Lilacs for America, 31 [1953]; Eickhorst, ILS Lilac Newsletter 4(1):4-5 [1978]
Cultivar name presumed registered 1953;
Cultivar not reported in cultivation.

'Hina-arare', *S. pubescens* subsp. *pubescens*
'雛あられ'
Ihara 2004; S VII
syn. - seedling no. 20040520001#2.
{*S. pubescens* subsp. *pubescens* 'Palibin' × *S. pubescens* subsp. *pubescens* 'Palibin'}
(Vrugtman, Cultivated Plant Diversity ... 2017)
Named for the colorful Japanese sweet rice crackers for Girl's Day (March 3).
Cultivar name registered 2017; name established and accepted.

'Hippolyte Maringer', *S. vulgaris*
Lemoine 1909; D IV
syn. - 'Hippolyt Maringer'
Lemoine, Cat. No. 173, 8 [1909]; McKelvey, The Lilac, 312 [1928]; Wister, Lilacs for America, 49 [1942], 31 [1953]; Photo on Jorgovani/Lilacs 2015 DVD.
Named for Hippolyte Maringer, mayor of the city of Nancy, France, 1892-1904.
Cultivar name presumed registered 1953; name established and accepted.

'Hiram H. Edgerton', *S. vulgaris*
Dunbar 1919; S VII
syn. - Dunbar no. 216
{'Lilarosa' × ? }
Dunbar, Florists Exch., 831 [Sept. 22, 1923]; McKelvey, The Lilac, 312 [1928]; Wister, Lilacs for America, 49 [1942], 31 [1953]; Photo on Jorgovani/Lilacs 2015 DVD.
Named for Hiram Haskell Edgerton, 1847-1922, contractor, politician, promoter of public parks, mayor 1908-1922 of Rochester, New York, USA.
Cultivar name presumed registered 1953; name established and accepted.

Hirsuta - see *S. villosa* subsp. *wolfii* var. *hirsuta*.

'Hirvas', *S. villosa* subsp. *villosa*
origin not known pre-2005; S V-I
Pihlajaniemi, J. Appl. Bot. and Food Quality 79:107-116 [2005]
Cultivar name not established.

'H. J. Moore', *S. vulgaris*
Paterson; S II
Anon., The Evening Telegram, June 6 [1939].
Cultivar name registered 1963; name established and accepted.

'Hoffnung', *S. vulgaris*
origin not known pre-1959; S VII
Vrugtman, AABGA Bull. 16(4):132 [1982]
Name: German for hope.
Cultivar name not established.

'Holger', *S.* (Villosae Group)
Tolppola 1975; S I
{*S. josikaea* × ? }
syn. - 'Alba'
Wickman, Lilacs - Quart. Jour. 28(2):42 [1999]; Haggren, Allt om Trädgård 3-01, p.39 [2001] - syn.: *S. josikaea* 'Alba'; MTT (Agrifood Research Finland) cat. Varmennetun taimituotannon emokasvihinnasto vuonna 2010, p. 53
Named for Holger Tolppola, 1926-1995, founder of Tolppolas Plantskola, Finland.
Cultivar name established and accepted.

'Holly Ann', *S. vulgaris*
Klager; S VII
Wister, Lilacs for America, 49 [1942], 31 [1953]
Cultivar name presumed registered 1953; not reported in cultivation.

'Holte', *S. josikaea*
Horntvedt; S VI
syn. - klon 312
Lønø, Norsk Hagetident, 7-8/85, pp. 395-397 [1985]; Kjær, Gartneryrket (G.Y.) 1987:274; Bjerkestrand & Sandved, Grøntanleggsplanter utvalgt for norske forhold 1986-1987-1988 [1989] pp. 25-26 & ill. p. 16; Vrugtman, Lilacs - Quart. Jour. 26(2):41-42 [1996]
Cultivar name established and accepted.

'Holy Maid', *S. vulgaris*
Fiala 1984; S V
{'Macrostachya' × 'Rochester'}
Fiala, Lilacs, 100, Pl. 82 [1988]
Cultivar thought to be extinct per ILS Preservation Committee 2019
Cultivar name established and accepted.

Hope - see 'Nadezhda'.

'Hope Heller', *S. vulgaris*
Margaretten; S III
{'Mme Lemoine' × ? }
Not reported in cultivation
Cultivar name not established.

'Horace', *S.* (Villosae Group), *S.* ×*prestoniae*
Skinner 1932; S VI
Wister, Lilacs for America, 49 [1942], 31 [1953]
Cultivar name presumed registered 1953; name established and accepted.

HORN OF PLENTY - see 'Rog Izobiliia'.

Hortensia - see **'Gortenziya'**.

'Hortulanus Witte', *S. vulgaris*
   origin not known pre-1897; ? ?
   common name: Witte
   Stand. Pl. Names, 486, 488 [1923] - as Witte; Wister, Nat. Hort. Mag. 6(1):15 [1927] - name only; McKelvey, The Lilac, 312 [1928] - name only
   Named for Heinrich Witte, 1825-1917, horticulturist, horticultural author, conservator at the Leiden University Botanical Garden 1855-1898, The Netherlands.
   Cultivar name not established; probably extinct.

'Hosanna', *S. vulgaris*
   Fiala 1970; D II
   {'Gismonda' × 'Rustica'; seedling treated with colchicine; mixoploid}
   Vrugtman, Lilacs - Proceedings 7(1):35 [1979]; Vrugtman, AABGA Bull. 13(4):107-108 [1979]; Fiala, Lilacs, 94, 223, Pl.11 [1988]; Photo on Jorgovani/Lilacs 2015 DVD.
   Cultivar name registered 1977; name established and accepted.

'Hoshikuzu', *S. pubescens* subsp. *pubescens*
   '星屑'
   Ihara 2004; S VII
   syn. - seedling no. 20040520001#1.
   {*S. pubescens* subsp. *pubescens* 'Palibin' × *S. pubescens* subsp. *pubescens* 'Palibin'}
   (Vrugtman, Cultivated Plant Diversity ... 2017)
   Name: Japanese for stardust.
   Cultivar name registered 2017; name established and accepted.

'Hoshi-no-suna', *S. pubescens* subsp. *pubescens*
   '星の砂'
   Ihara 2004; S VII
   syn. - seedling no. 20040520001#3.
   {*S. pubescens* subsp. *pubescens* 'Palibin' × *S. pubescens* subsp. *pubescens* 'Palibin'}
   (Vrugtman, Cultivated Plant Diversity ... 2017)
   Named for star sand, the exoskeletons of foraminifera, in Japanese.
   Cultivar name registered 2017; name established and accepted.

'Huan Zi', *S.* ×*hyacinthiflora*
   no information yet pre-1999; S VII
   Reported in cultivation by (Ms) Mingxia Bai, Harbin Landscape Research Institute, Harbin, Heilongjiang Province; Photo on Jorgovani/Lilacs 2015 DVD.
   Awards: Bronze Award in International Horticultural Exhibitions, Kunming, 1999.
   Cultivar name not established.

'Hua Cai', *S.* (Vulgaris Series)
   Cui, Hongxia 1999;
   {*S. protolaciniata* × *S. oblata*}
   (not yet published; Variety Rights applied for in 2014) in cultivation and under observation at Beijing Institute of Botany in 2015.
   Name: Chinese for cadenza.
   Cultivar name not established.

Huffan - misspelling of 'Buffon'
   from plant inventory, De Planten Tuin, Oirschot, NL
   http://www.esveld.nl/collecties/collsyringa.htm [February 9, 2004]

'Hugo de Vries', *S. vulgaris*
   Keessen, K. 1927; S VII
   syn. - 'Hugo de Vrier', 'Professor Hugo de Vries'
   Nat. Nurseryman 35:258 [1927]; McKelvey, The Lilac, 560 [1928]; Wister, Lilacs for America, 49 [1942] - as S VI; Wister, Lilacs for America, 31 [1953]; Photo on Jorgovani/Lilacs 2015 DVD.
   Named for Hugo Marie de Vries, 1848-1935, Dutch botanist and geneticist.
   Cultivar name presumed registered 1953; name established and accepted.

'Hugo Koster', *S. vulgaris*
   Koster (or van Tol) 1914; S IV
   syn. - 'Hugh Koster'
   Anon., Jour. Hort. Home Farmer, ser. 3, 66:260 [March 13, 1913]; KcKelvey, The Lilac, 312-313 [1928]; Wister, Lilacs for America, 49 [1942], 31 [1953]; Jongkind, Seringensortiment voor de trek, p.4 [1997] - lists J. van Tol Hzn as originator; Photo on Jorgovani/Lilacs 2015 DVD.
   Cultivar name presumed registered 1953; name established and accepted.
   Forcing cultivar in the Netherlands.

'Hugo Mayer', *S. vulgaris*
   Eveleens Maarse 1950; S III
   {'Decaisne' × 'Ambassadeur'}
   Wister, Lilacs for America, 31 [1953]; Eveleens Maarse, Dendron 1(1):12 [1954]
   Awards: Certificate of Merit 1950 (KMTP).
   Cultivar name presumed registered 1953; name established and accepted.

'Hulda', *S. vulgaris*
   Klager 1929; S VII
   syn. - 'Dark Purple'
   Cooley Nursery, Cat., 8 [1929]; McKelvey, The Lilac, 559 [1928]; Photo on Jorgovani/Lilacs 2015 DVD.
   Cultivar name established and accepted.

'Hulda Klager', *S. vulgaris*
   Klager; D V
   ILS Newsletter 14(4):3-4 [1988]
   Cultivar name not established.

Humboldt - see 'De Humboldt'.

'Humility', *S. vulgaris*
   origin not known possibly Fiala; S I
   Chapman, Lilacs - Quart. Jour. 26(2):48 [1997] - name

only; Chapman, in litt. Aug. 26, 1997 - as S, pale lilac; according to other sources S pale blue or dirty blue; Anon., Lilacs - Quart. Jour. 33(1):11 [2004] - as S I
Cultivar name not established.

'Humphrey', *S. vulgaris*
origin not known pre-1975; S IV
In cultivation at Scott Arboretum, Swarthmore, PA, in 1975 (S146065), but not listed by Wister 1953; in cultivation at Arnold Arboretum in 2017 (AA281-79); Peterson, Lilacs - Proceedings 16(1):19 [1987] - name only; no lit. ref. located (fv 18 May, 2017).
Cultivar name not established.

Hungarian lilac - see *S. josikaea* J. Jacq. ex Rchb.

Hungarian lilac - see **'Lutèce'**.

'Hunting Tower', *S.* (Villosae Group)
Skinner 1942; S I
{*S. villosa* subsp. *villosa* × *S. tomentella* subsp. *sweginzowii*}
Wister, Lilacs for America, 50 [1942], 31 [1953]; Registered with the State Commission of the Russian Federation for Testing and Protection of Selection Achievements, No. 9810214, 2001, as 'Хантинг Тауер'; Photo on Jorgovani/Lilacs 2015 DVD.
Cultivar name presumed registered 1953; name established and accepted.

'H. W. Sargent', *S. vulgaris*
origin not known pre-1903; ? II
Parsons, Cat., 40 [1903]; McKelvey, The Lilac, 313 [1928]
Cultivar name not established.

'Hyacinth', *S. vulgaris*
Klager; ? VII
Anon., ILS Newsletter 14(4):3-4 [1988]; Stenlund, Lilacs - Quart. Jour. 20(2): [1991] - as pink.
Cultivar name not established.

HYACINTHFLOWER - see **'Hyazinthenflieder'**.

Hyacinthiflora - see *S. ×hyacinthiflora*.

'Hyacinthiflora Plena', *S. ×hyacinthiflora*
Lemoine 1878; D III
syn. - 'Hyacinthiflora' (if D III); *S. ×hyacinthiflora* 'Plena' (Hortus Third, p. 1090 [1976])
common name: Double Hyacinth lilac
{*S. vulgaris* 'Azurea Plena' × *S. oblata*}
Lemoine, Cat. No. 78:6 [1878]; Ellwanger & Barry, Cat., [1892]; McKelvey, The Lilac, 193- 195 [1928]; Stand. Pl. Names, 615 [1942]; Wister, Lilacs for America, 50 [1942], 31 [1953] - as 'Liberti' × *oblata*, this is in error, the female parent is *S. vulgaris flore duplo Liberti* or 'Azurea Plena'; Photo on Jorgovani/Lilacs 2015 DVD.
Cultivar name presumed registered 1953; name established and accepted.
Nota bene: This cultivar name must be maintained to distinguish it, the nominate cultivar, from all subsequent cultivars of *S. ×hyacinthiflora* Rehder.

Hyacintsyren - see **'Hagny'**.

'Hyazinthenflieder', *S. vulgaris*
Späth 1906; S IV
syn. - 'Hyacinthenfleider'
{'Mons. Maxime Cornu' × 'Andenken an Ludwig Späth'} – Not to be confused with *Syringa ×hyacinthiflora* Rehder – Späth, Cat. No. 121, 132 [1906]; Kache, Gartenschönheit 5:82 [1924]; McKelvey, The Lilac, 313 [1928]; Späth, Späth-Buch, 110, 304 [1930]; Wister, Lilacs for America, 50 [1942], 31 [1953]; Photo on Jorgovani/Lilacs 2015 DVD.
Name: German for hyacinth-lilac.
Cultivar name presumed registered 1953; name established and accepted.

'Hybrida', *S. vulgaris*
origin not known pre-1841; S VII/IV
McKelvey, The Lilac, 313 [1928] - as confused name; Wister, Lilacs for America, 50 [1942], 31 [1953] - no affiliation given.
Cultivar name not established.

'Hyperion', *S. vulgaris*
Sass (H.E., H.P. or J.) pre-1982; D V-VI
Peterson, Lilacs - Proceedings 16(1):19 [1987] - name only; Peterson in litt. to Vrugtman [Sep. 02, 2007] - named and introduced by Caroline (last name not known), proprietress of Nick's Nursery (no information); Photo on Jorgovani/Lilacs 2015 DVD.
Named, perhaps, for Hyperion, one of the smaller moons of Saturn, which has a reddish tint.
Cultivar name not established.

'H. Zabel', *S. josikaea*
Froebel 1899; S IV/II
syn. - *josikaea zabel*, 'Zabel', 'Zabeli'
Froebel, Cat. No. 124, 79 [1899]; McKelvey, The Lilac, 59-60 [1928]; Wister, Lilacs for America, 49, 50, 60 [1942], 31, 32, 44 [1953]; Photo on Jorgovani/Lilacs 2015 DVD.
Named for Hermann Zabel, 1832-1912, German botanist.
Cultivar name presumed registered 1953; name established and accepted.

Iaimes Ausma - see 'Jaunaa Ausma'.

'Ib Jensen', *S.* (species affiliation not known)
origin not known ? ?
reported in cultivation by Ole Heide, Thisted, Denmark [1998]
Cultivar name not established.

'Idyllwild', *S. vulgaris*
Ballreich 1999; S III
syn. - 8-208
Ballreich, Lilacs - Quart. Jour. 28(4):91 [1999] - name

only; Vrugtman, Lilacs -Quart. Jour. 32(4):150 [2003] - as S III
Named for the town of Idyllwild, California, USA.
Cultivar name established and accepted.

'Igor', *S. vulgaris*
Mägi pre-2018; S II
Semenov, I., Lilacs 48(2):68,64 (photo) [2019].
Cultivar name not established.

'Igor' Severyanin', *S. vulgaris*
'Игорь Северянин'
Aladin, S., Aladina, O., Polyakova, T., and Aladina, A. 2019; D IV
{'Katherine Havemeyer' × OP}
(Международная научная конференция "Syringa L.: коллекции, выращивание, использование")
"International Scientific Conference "Syringa L.: collections, cultivation, using" / Collection of Scientific Articles of Botanical Institute named after V.L. Komarov, Botanical Garden of Peter the Great BIN RAS. - St. Petersburg. -2020.- pp.3-7 (in Russian);
Photo exhibition of all varieties of the creative breeding group "Russian Lilac" at the Festival "Lilac February", St. Petersburg, Botanical Garden of Peter the Great BIN RAS, February 22-24, 2020.
The cultivar is dedicated to the famous Russian poet Igor Severyanin (Igor Vasilyevich Lopyrev, 1887-1941), a Petersburger, an outstanding representative of the poetry of the Silver Age, in love with the northern spring and blooming lilacs.
Cultivar name established and accepted.

'Igra v biser', *S. vulgaris*
'Игра в Бисер'
Aladin, S., Aladina, O., Polyakova, T., and, Aladina, A. 2017; S I
{'Avalanche' × OP}
IX International Scientific Conference (IX Международная научная конференция "Цветоводство: история, теория, практика") " Floriculture: history, theory, practice" , St. Petersburg, Botanical Garden of Peter the Great BIN RAS, September 7-13, 2019 (in Russian).
Named for "The game of beads" by G. Hesse - a search for a deep connection between objects that belong to completely different fields of science and art.
Cultivar name established and accepted.

'Ikars', *S. vulgaris*
Kārkliņš 2003; D II
Strautiņa & Kaufmane, Dobeles ceriņi, p. 92 [2011]; Photo on Jorgovani/Lilacs 2015 DVD.
Name: A man's name.
Cultivar name established and accepted.

'Ilona', *S. vulgaris*
Rankin; S IV/VI
{parentage not known}
perhaps in cultivation under the name 'Helen Palagge' - See: Vrugtman, Lilacs - Quart. Jour. 27(1):21-22 [1998]
Cultivar name not established; probably not in cultivation.

'Ilse Grunewald', *S. vulgaris*
Grunewald pre-1939; S V
Fr. Grunewald, Cat., 14 [1939].
Named for the daughter of the originator, Ilse, born 20 July 1903.
Cultivar name established and accepted.

'Il'ya Muromets', *S. vulgaris*
'Илья Муромец'
Aladin, S., Aladina, O., Polyakova, T., and Aladina, A. 2014; S IV
{'Mechta' × OP}
Садовник (Gardener) magazine 04 (140)/2017 :18-25; Вестник АППМ (Catalog in Vestnik APPM (Planting material association) magazine) 1/2018: 59-72 (in Russian)
Named for an ancient fictional Russian folk hero of the 16th century.
Cultivar name established and accepted.

'Ilūzija', *S. vulgaris*
Kārkliņš 2003; D V
Strautiņa & Kaufmane, Dobeles ceriņi, p. 92 [2011]; Photo on Jorgovani/Lilacs 2015 DVD.
Name: Latvian for illusion.
Cultivar name established and accepted.

'Imants Ziedonis', *S. vulgaris*
Upītis 1975; S II
syn. - 'Imants Siedonis', 'Nerimtiigais Ziedonis', 'Ziedonis', Upītis No. 2802
Kalniņš, L., Ceriņu jaunšķirnes Dobelē, Dārs un drava 1986 (12):13-15 - in Latvian; Strautiņa, S. 2002. Ceriņu un jasmīnu avīze. LA, R., p. 62; in litt. S. Strautiņa to F. Vrugtman [21 Dec. 2007] - 1975, S II; Semenov, Igor, Lilacs - Quart. Jour. 44(2):49, ill. 53 [2015] - as 'Nerimtīgais Ziedonis', II&III; Photo on Jorgovani/Lilacs 2015 DVD.
Named for Imants Ziedonis, 1933-2013, the famous Latvian poet who, as a young man was a close associate of the originator.
Cultivar name established and accepted.

'Imogen', *S.* (Villosae Group), *S. ×prestoniae*
Preston 1928; ? ?
syn. - Preston No. 20-14-205
{*S. villosa* subsp. *villosa* × *S. komarowii* subsp. *reflexa*}
Macoun, Rep. Dom. Hort. 1928, 56 [1930] - name only; Wister, Lilacs for America, 64 [1942], 48 [1953] - not in cultivation, no plants distributed
Named for the Daughter to Cymbeline in Shakespeare's *Cymbeline*.
Cultivar name not established.

'**Independence**', *S. vulgaris*
   Fenicchia 1988; S I
   syn. - RF1, 'Independent', INDEPENDENT (trade designation used for cut flowers of this cultivar)
   {'Rochester' × ?}
   Hoepfl & Rogers, Lilac Newsletter 14(7):6 [1988]; Fiala, Lilacs, Pl.8 [1988]; Vrugtman, HortScience 32(4):588 [1997]; K. Millham, Lilacs - Quart. Jour. 42(2):61 & ill. 68 [2013]; Photo on Jorgovani/Lilacs 2015 DVD.
   Cultivar name registered 1996; name established and accepted.
   Forcing cultivar in the Netherlands.

'Indes', *S. vulgaris*
   Mezitt, R.W. 1991; S VI-VII
   {'Sensation' × ?}
   Weston Nurseries, Cat. [1991]; Ornamental Plants plus Version 2.0, 01/01/98, Mich. State Univ. www.msue.msu.edu/msue/imp/modop/00001423.html
   Cultivar name not established.

'**Indiya**', *S. vulgaris*
   'Индия'
   Kolesnikov 1955; S IV
   syn. - 'India', 'Indija', 'Indya', Kolesnikov No. 124
   {'Zarya Kommunizma' × 'Kolesnikov No. 105'}
   Howard, Arnoldia 19(6-7):31-35 [1959]; Gromov, Siren', 97 [1963]; Howard & Brizicky, AABGA Quart. Newsl. No. 64, 17-21 [1965]; Wister & Oppe, Arnoldia 31(3):125 [1971] - as S VI and 'India'; Gromov, Lilacs - Proceed. 2(4):17[1974]; Rub<u>tz</u>ov et al. 1980. Vidy i sorta sireni, kul'tiviruemye v SSSR. Kiev; Naukova Dumka. – in Russian; Holetich, C.D. 1982. Lilac species and cultivars in cultivation in USSR. Lilacs 11(2):1-38. - translation of Rub<u>tz</u>ov et al. 1982; Photo on Jorgovani/Lilacs 2015 DVD.
   Cultivar name registered 1970; name established and accepted.

'Inez', *S.* ×*diversifolia*
   Origin not known; S I-IV
   {*S.* ×*diversifolia* × ?}
   <www.esveld.nl/wetenschappelijk.php?letter=s&group=syringa&ppagina=2> seen Nov. 23, 2011 - as pale lilac, almost white seedling of *S.* ×*diversifolia*.
   Cultivar name not established.

'**Inez**', *S. vulgaris*
   Rankin; S I
   {parentage not known}
   Wister, Arnoldia 23(4):81 [1963]
   Cultivar name registered 1963; not reported in cultivation.

INGWERSEN'S DWARF - see '**Palibin**'
   Wister, Arnoldia 23(4):77-83 [1963]
   Not a cultivar name; erroneous registration.

'Insignis', *S. vulgaris*
   International Exhibition, 1876, US Centennial Commission, Volume 11, p. 310 - name only.
   Cultivar name not established.

Insignis Rubra - see '**Rubra Insignis**'
   Harzer Baumschulen, Cat. 1917-18, p. 83 [1917] - as 'isignis rubra', dunkelrot; Notcutt, Cat. [1934].

'Interlude', *S. vulgaris*
   origin not known 1975; D VII
   Wayside Gardens, Cat., 34 [1975]; Vrugtman, AABGA Bull. 16(4):131 [1982].

'Intermedia', *S. vulgaris*
   origin not known pre-1880; ? ?
   Froebel, Cat. No. 90, 78 [1880]; McKelvey, The Lilac, 314 [1928] - confused name
   Cultivar name not established.

'**Iolanta**', *S. vulgaris*
   'Иоланта'
   D<u>y</u>agilev; pre 1992, D V-IV
   {'Obman<u>shch</u>itsa' × OP}
   D<u>y</u>agilev, Lilacs - Quart. Jour. 22(1):19 [1993]; Pikaleva, Lilacs - Quart. Jour. 23(4):85 [1994].
   (Международная научная конференция "Syringa L.: коллекции, выращивание, использование")
   "International Scientific Conference "Syringa L.: collections, cultivation, using" / Collection of Scientific Articles of Botanical Institute named after V.L. Komarov, Botanical Garden of Peter the Great BIN RAS. - St. Petersburg. -2020.- pp.23-27 (in Russian).
   A woman's name in Russian, translates as Yolanda.
   Cultivar name established and accepted.

'Iona', *S. vulgaris*
   Orchard, between 1912 & 1940s, ? ?
   Named for the daughter of the originator.
   No report of being in cultivation
   http://www.mhs.mb.ca/docs/people/orchard_h.shtml
   http://www.manitobaaghalloffame.com/ahofmember/orchard-harold/

'**Iran**', *S. vulgaris*
   'Иран'
   Origin not known; D III-IV
   Rub<u>tz</u>ov et al. 1980. Vidy i sorta sireni, kul'tiviruemye v SSSR. Kiev; Naukova Dumka. – in Russian; Holetich, C.D. 1982. Lilac species and cultivars in cultivation in USSR. Lilacs 11(2):1-38. - translation of Rub<u>tz</u>ov et al. 1982.
   Cultivar name established and accepted.

'Iras', *S.* (Villosae Group), *S.* ×*prestoniae*
   Preston; ? ?
   Wister, Lilacs for America, 64 [1942], 48 [1953] - name only, not in cultivation, no plants distributed.
   Named for the Attendant to Cleopatra in Shakespeare's *Antony and Cleopatra*.
   Cultivar name not established, probably extinct.

Ir. A. W. van de Plassche - see **'Director General van de Plassche'**.

Irdinia - see **'Irvina'**.

'Irena Karpow-Lipska', *S. vulgaris*
Karpow-Lipski 1958; D IV
syn. - 'Irene Karpow-Lipska', KL 24, Siewka nr 11
{'Michel Buchner' × ? }
Karpow-Lipski, Arboretum Kórnickie 3:104-105 [1958]; varietal denomination registered COBORU 1971; Wister & Oppe, Arnoldia 31(3):125 [1971] - as 'Irene Karpow-Lipska'; Anon., Lista odmian roślin ozdobnych 1973, p. 25 - in Polish; Anon., Lilak Pospolity - COBO Informator 8/78 [1976]; statutory registration.
Named for the second wife of the originator.
Cultivar name established and accepted; name registered.

'Irene', *S.* (species affiliation not known)
Berdeen 1982; S III
Vrugtman, AABGA Bulletin 16(4):132 [1982]; King & Coggeshall, Lilacs - Quart. Jour. 27(2):49-50 [1998] - name only
Named for a friend of Ken Berdeen.
Cultivar name not established.

Irene - see **'Mrs Irene Slater'**.

'Irvina', *S. vulgaris*
Klager 1920; S VII
syn. - 'Irdina', 'Irvinia'
Wister, Lilacs for America, 50 [1942], 31 [1953]; Anon., ILS Newsletter 14(4):3 [1988] - as S V
Cultivar name presumed registered 1953; name established and accepted.

'Irving', *S.* (Villosae Group), *S.* ×*swegiflexa*
Preston pre-1953; S V
{*S. komarowii* subsp. *reflexa* × *S. tomentella* subsp. *sweginzowii*}
Wister, Lilacs for America, 31 [1953]
Cultivar name presumed registered 1953; name established and accepted.

'Isabella', *S.* (Villosae Group), *S.* ×*prestoniae*
Preston 1927; S IV
syn. - Preston No. 20-14-114, likely CANADA GEM™
{*S. villosa* subsp. *villosa* × *S. komarowii* subsp. *reflexa*}
McKelvey, The Lilac, 111-112, t. 38 [1928]; Macoun, Rep. Dom. Hort. 1928, 53-54 [1930]; Anon., Jour. RHS 66:339 [1941]; Wister, Lilacs for America, 50, 64 [1942], 31, 48 [1953]; Photo on Jorgovani/Lilacs 2015 DVD.
[One of the original two *S.* ×*prestoniae* McKelvey cultivars selected, named and described by McKelvey; see also 'W. T. Macoun'.]
Named for the originator, Isabella Preston 1881-1965, Canadian plant breeder.
Awards: RHS Award of Merit 1941.
Cultivar name presumed registered 1953; name established and accepted.

'Isa Villu', *S. vulgaris*
Mägi pre-2018; S VII
Semenov, I., Lilacs 48(2):68 [2019].
Cultivar name not established.

'Itegarde de Rothschild', *S. vulgaris*
origin not known pre-1942; D IV
Wister, Lilacs for America, 36, 50 [1942] - probably misspelled name
Cultivar name not established, not reported in cultivation in 1953.

Ivan Michurin - see **'I. V. Michurin'**.

'I. V. Michurin', *S. vulgaris*
'И. В. Мичурин'
Kolesnikov 1941; D IV-V
syn. - 'Ivan Michurin', Kolesnikov No. 212
{'Michel Buchner' × 'Grand-Duc Constantin'}
Kolesnikov, Lilac, 24 [1955]; Howard, Arnoldia 19(6-7):31-35 [1959]; Gromov, Siren', 76 [1963]; Howard & Brizicky, AABGA Quart. Newsl. No. 64, 17-21 [1965]; Wister & Oppe, 31(3):125 [1971] - as D I and 'Ivan Michurin'; Gromov, Lilacs - Proceedings 2(4):10-18 [1974]; Rubtzov et al. 1980. Vidy i sorta sireni, kul'tiviruemye v SSSR. Kiev; Naukova Dumka. – in Russian; Holetich, C.D. 1982. Lilac species and cultivars in cultivation in USSR. Lilacs 11(2):1-38. - translation of Rubtzov et al.
1982; Photo on Jorgovani/Lilacs 2015 DVD.
Named for Ivan Vladimirovich Michurin, 1855-1935, Russian horticulturist who postulated the theory that acquired characteristics were heritable ("Michurinism").
Cultivar name registered 1970; name established and accepted.

'Ivory', *S.* (species affiliation not known)
origin not known ? ?
Arboreta & Garden Guide, Plant Finder Reference Library 1998/99 CD-ROM

IVORY BOULEVARD™ - see 'Mathies'

IVORY PILLAR™ - see 'Willamette'

'Ivory Silk', *S. reticulata* subsp. *reticulata*
Pokluda 1973; S I
{*S. reticulata* subsp. *reticulata* seedling}
Sheridan Nurseries, Cat., 46 [1973]; American Nurseryman 168(1):14 [1988]; Gressley, Lilacs - Quart. Jour. 29(3):84-85 [2000]; Photo on Jorgovani/Lilacs 2015 DVD.
Awards: Pennsylvania Horticultural Society's Gold Medal in 1996; 2000 Theodore Klein Plant Award Winner of the University of Kentucky Nursery & Landscape Program.
Cultivar name established and accepted.

'Izobilie', *S. vulgaris*
'Изобилие'
Kolesnikov pre-1953; D IV
syn. - 'Izobiliie', 'Izobilije', Kolesnikov No. 394

{'Kolesnikov No. 50' × ('Käthe Härlin' × 'Réaumur')}
Howard, Arnoldia 19(6-7):31-35 [1959]; Gromov, Siren',
81-82 [1963] - in Russian; Howard & Brizicky, AABGA
Quart. Newsl. No. 64, 17-21 [1965] - as ABUNDANCE;
Wister & Oppe, Arnoldia 31(3):125 [1971] - as D V
and 'Izobiliie'; Lilacs - Proceedings 2(4):10-18 [1974];
Rubtzov et al. 1980. Vidy i sorta sireni, kul'tiviruemye
v SSSR. Kiev; Naukova Dumka. – in Russian; Holetich,
C.D. 1982. Lilac species and cultivars in cultivation in
USSR. Lilacs 11(2):1-38. - translation of Rubtzov et al.
1982; Photo on Jorgovani/Lilacs 2015 DVD.
Name: Russian for abundance.
Cultivar name registered 1970; name established and
accepted.

'Jaan', S. ×hyacinthiflora
Vaigla 1990; S VI (IV/V per Semenov)
{'Clarke's Giant' × ? }
Kivistik, Maakodu 1997(5):22-23 (ill.) [1997] - in
Estonian; I. Semenov, Lilacs 48(2):65,60 (photo) [2019].
Cultivar name established.

'Jaanika', S. vulgaris
Vaigla pre-2001; D IV/II (D II per Semenov)
listed on http://aed.rapina.ee/sirelid.htm [seen 5 Nov.
2005]; I. Semenov, Lilacs 48(2):65,58 (photo) [2019].
Cultivar name not established.

'Jaanus', S. vulgaris
Mägi before 2018; S III
{no information}
picture seen 16 Sep. 2018; Semenov, I., Lilacs 48(2):68,66
(photo) [2019].
Cultivar name not established.

'Jack Alexander', S. (species affiliation not known)
Alexander Sr; ? ?
syn. - 'Alexander's Rose Red'
Wister & Oppe, Arnoldia 31{3}:122 [1971] - name only
Cultivar name registered 1970 without description;
Cultivar not reported in cultivation.

'Jack Smith', S. vulgaris
Rankin; S IV
{parentage not known}
Wister, Arnoldia, 23(4):81 [1963]
Cultivar name registered 1963;
Cultivar not reported in cultivation.

Jacquenetta, Jacquinette - see 'Jaquenetta'.

'Jacques Callot', S. vulgaris
Lemoine 1876; S IV
Lemoine, Cat. No. 74, 10 [1876]; McKelvey, The Lilac,
314 [1928]; Wister, Lilacs for America, 50 [1942], 32
[1953]; Photo on Jorgovani/Lilacs 2015 DVD.
Named for Jaques Callot, 1592-1650, French designer
and engraver.
Cultivar name presumed registered 1953; name
established and accepted.

JACQUES ELLIOT, S. vulgaris
origin not known
photo by Z. Borzan on Lilacs/Jorgovani 2014 DVD;
one plant by that name presumed to have been in the
collection at County of Monroe Department of Parks,
Rochester, New York, USA.; in litt. Millham to Vrugtman
18 August 2014 - plant not located and not in records.
Not a cultivar name.

Jacquet - see 'Anna Elisabeth Jaquet'.

Jacquinette - see 'Jaquenetta'.

'Jaga', S. (Villosae Group), S. ×prestoniae
Bugała pre-1970; S II
Bugała, Arboretum Kórnickie 15:61-70 [1970]; Wister &
Oppe, Arnoldia 31(3):122 [1971]; Bugała, Lilacs - Quart. Jour.
24(4):90-91 [1995]; Photo on Jorgovani/Lilacs 2015 DVD.
Cultivar name registered 1970; name established and
accepted.

'Jagienka', S. (Villosae Group), S. ×prestoniae
Bugała pre-1970; S IV
Bugała, Arboretum Kórnickie 15:61-70 [1970]; Wister &
Oppe, Arnoldia 31(3):122 [1971]; Bugała, Lilacs - Quart.
Jour. 24(4):90-91 [1995]; Photo on Jorgovani/Lilacs 2015
DVD.
Cultivar name registered 1970; name established and
accepted.

'Jake Thomas', S. vulgaris
Klager; D VII
Anon., ILS Newsletter 14(4):3-4 [1988]; Photo on
Jorgovani/Lilacs 2015 DVD.
Cultivar name established and accepted.

'Jako', S. vulgaris
Mägi pre-2017; S VII
Photo from Estonia by Semenov, seen in 2020 ILS Photo
Database.
Cultivar name not established.

'Jakobsen's Delight', S. villosa subsp. wolfii
Olsen & Jakobsen 1960; S V*
{seedling selection}
syn. - 'Jakobsen's Pink Delight' at Sir Harold Hillier
Gardens, UK
Propagated and introduced by Arne Vagn Jakobsen,
Syringa villosa subsp. wolfii 'Jakobsen's Delight' is a
chance seedling with variegated foliage found by his
father in 1960 in the nursery and Geographic Garden of
the late Aksel Olsen (1887-1982) at Kolding, Denmark -
in litt. Jakobsen to Vrugtman [2012].
Cultivar name not established.

Jaltinskaja Prelest - see 'Yaltinskaya Prelest"

Jambul - see 'Dzhambul'.

'James Berdeen', S. vulgaris
Berdeen 1998; S IV
Berdeen, in litt. to Nieds [Nov.16/1970] - as S V, orig. ca
1960; Vrugtman, AABGA Bulletin 16(4):132 [1982]; King

& Coggeshall, Lilacs - Quart. Jour. 27(2):49-50 [1998] - name only; Vrugtman, Encyclopedia, 312 [2008]; Photo on Jorgovani/Lilacs 2015 DVD.
Named for the originator's grandson.
Cultivar name established and accepted.

'James Booth', *S. vulgaris*
Eichler 1862; S VI
Anon., Hamburger Garten- und Blumenzeitung 392-393 [1862]; McKelvey, The Lilac, 314, 560 [1928]; Wister, Lilacs for America, 50 [1942] - as S III; Wister, Lilacs for America, 32 [1953]; Photo on Jorgovani/Lilacs 2015 DVD.
Named for James Booth, 1770-1814, Scottish landscape gardener and nurseryman (James Booth und Söhne), co-designer of Jenischpark, Hamburg-Flottbek, Germany, ca 1800.
Cultivar name presumed registered 1953; name established and accepted.

'James Macfarlane', *S.* (Villosae Group)
Yeager 1959; S V
syn. - a variety of misspellings
{*S.* ×*josiflexa* 'Royalty' × ? }
Wister, Lilacs for America, 32 [1953]; Yeager, New Hampshire Agri. Exp. Sta. Bull. 461, 11 [1959]; Rogers, Lilacs - Quart. Jour. 23(3):53 [1994] - misspellings of cultivar name and true-to-name; Photo on Jorgovani/Lilacs 2015 DVD.
Named for James Macfarlane, 1864-1950, Horticulturist at the University of New Hampshire, USA, 1915-1949.
Cultivar name presumed registered 1953; name established and accepted.

'James Maddox', *S. vulgaris*
Rankin; D V
{parentage not known}
Clark, Lilacs - Quart. Jour. 20(2):34 [1991]
Cultivar name not established.

James Munroe - see **'President Monroe'**.

'James Stuart', *S. vulgaris*
Havemeyer pre-1942; S VI
syn. - 'James Steward'
Wister, Lilacs for America, 50 [1942], 32 [1953]; Lilac Land, Cat. [1954]; Eickhorst, ILS Lilac Newsletter 4(1):4-5 [1978]; Photo on Jorgovani/Lilacs 2015 DVD.
Cultivar name presumed registered 1953; name established and accepted.

'Jane', *S. vulgaris*
Rankin; D IV
{parentage not known}
Wister, Arnoldia 23(4):81 [1963]
Cultivar name registered 1963;
Cultivar not reported in cultivation.

'Jane Day', *S. vulgaris*
Havemeyer pre-1942; S VII

Wister, Lilacs for America, 50 [1942], 32 [1953]; Eickhorst, ILS Lilac Newsletter 4(1):4-5 [1978]; Photo on Jorgovani/Lilacs 2015 DVD.
Cultivar name presumed registered 1953; name established and accepted.

'Jane Ellen', *S. vulgaris*
Wiles; S V
Wister, Lilacs for America, 32 [1953] - as S III; Siebenthaler, Cat. No. 168, 21 [1954]
Cultivar name presumed registered 1953; name established and accepted.

'Jane Smith', *S. vulgaris*
Rankin; D II
{parentage not known}
Wister, Lilacs for America, 32 [1953]
Cultivar name presumed registered 1953; name established and accepted.

'Jan van Tol', *S. vulgaris*
van Tol ca 1916; S I
syn. - 'J.C. Van Tol'
Anon., Maandschr. Ned. Maatsch. Tuinb. [Maart 22, 1916]; McKelvey, The Lilac, 314-315 [1928]; Wister, Lilacs for America, 50 [1942], 32 [1953]; Photo on Jorgovani/Lilacs 2015 DVD.
Awards: Certificates of Merit 1916 (KMTP).
Cultivar name presumed registered 1953; name established and accepted.

japonica, *S.* - *S. reticulata* subsp. *reticulata*
Ellwanger & Barry, Cat., [1892] - as new species from Japan, becoming a good-sized tree.

japonica var. *argentea* - see 'Argentea' (*reticulata* subsp. *reticulata*).

'Jaquenetta', *S.* (Villosae Group), *S.* ×*prestoniae*
Preston; S ?
{*S. villosa* subsp. *villosa* × *S. komarowii* subsp. *reflexa*}
syn. - 'Jacquenetta', 'Jacquinette', Preston No. 20-14-18
Macoun, Rep. Dom. Hort. 1928, 56 [1930] - name only; USDA Plant Inventory No. 101, 20 (PI 81991) [Apr. 1931] - name only; Wister, Lilacs for America, 64 [1942], 48 [1953] - name only, not in cultivation, no plants distributed; anon., Lilacs - Proceedings 11(1):19 [1982] - name only
Named for A Country Wench in Shakespeare's *Love's Labour's Lost*.
Cultivar name not established, probably extinct.

Jaquet - see **'Anna Elisabeth Jaquet'**.

'Jass', *S.*
Mägi pre-2018 ; ? ?
Semenov, I., Lilacs 48(2) :71 [2019].
Cultivar name not established.

'Jaunā Ausma', *S. vulgaris*
Upītis ca 1970; S II

syn. - 'Iaimes Ausma'
Kaliņš, Dārz un drava 1986, No. 12, 13-15 - in Latvian; in litt. S. Strautiņa to F. Vrugtman [22 Jan. 2008] - ca 1970, S II
Name: Latvian for new dawn
Cultivar name established and accepted.

'Jaunkalsnavas Nakts', *S. vulgaris*
Upītis 1958; S III/II
syn. - Upītis No. 0080301. Some nurseries in Russia sell this cultivar under the name of Иоанская Ночь (Ioanskaya Noch').
Kaliņš, Dārs un drava 1986, No. 12, 13-15 - in Latvian; Strautiņa, S. 1992. Ceriņi Dārzs un Drava. No. 6, pp.12-13; Strautiņa, S. 1996. Characteristics and propagation of lilacs obtained by P. Upītis. Problems of fruit plant breeding I. Jelgava. pp. 32-38; Strautiņa, S. 2002. Ceriņu un jasmīnu avīze. LA, R., p. 62; in litt. S. Strautiņa to F. Vrugtman [21 Dec. 2007] - 1958, S III/II; Photo on Jorgovani/Lilacs 2015 DVD.
Name: Latvian for nights of the village of Jaunkalsnava.
Cultivar name established and accepted.

J. C. van Tol - see **'Jan van Tol'**.

J. de Messemaeker, J. de Messemaker - see **'Mons. J. Demessemaeker'**.

'JDB123 whitehouse', *S. pubescens* subsp. *pubescens*
Bakale Jr. 2020; S I/V
{'Palibin' × OP}
USPP PP 31664, April 14, 2020.
Flower color RHS 76D-NN155C , bud color RHS 76D.
Cultivar name established and accepted.

'Jean Bart', *S. vulgaris*
Lemoine 1889; D V
Lemoine, Cat. No. 113, 19 [1889]; McKelvey, The Lilac, 315 [1928]; Wister, Lilacs for America, 50 [1942], 32 [1953]; Photo on Jorgovani/Lilacs 2015 DVD.
Named for Jean Barth (or Bart), 1651-1702, French privateer and naval hero.
Cultivar name presumed registered 1953; name established and accepted.

'Jean Brendjens', *S. vulgaris*
Klettenberg 1939; S II
Wister, Lilacs for America, 32 [1953]
Cultivar name presumed registered 1953; name established and accepted.

'Jean Desrailles', *S. vulgaris*
origin not known pre-1926; ? ?
Wister, Lilacs for America, 36, 50 [1942]
Cultivar name not established, not reported in cultivation in 1953.

'Jean Macé', *S. vulgaris*
Lemoine 1915; D V
syn. - 'Jean Mace'
Lemoine, Cat. No. 189, 21 [1915]; McKelvey, The Lilac, 315-316 [1928]; Wister, Lilacs for America, 50 [1942], 32 [1953]; Photo on Jorgovani/Lilacs 2015 DVD.
Named for the French educator Jean Macé, 1915-1894.
Cultivar name presumed registered 1953; name established and accepted.

'Jeanne d'Arc', *S. vulgaris*
Lemoine 1902; D I
Lemoine, Cat. No. 152, 8 [1902]; Kache, Gartenschönheit 5:82 [1924]; McKelvey, The Lilac, 316 [1928]; Wister, Lilacs for America, 50 [1942], 32 [1953]; Photo on Jorgovani/Lilacs 2015 DVD.
Named for Jeanne d'Arc, 1412-1431, the "Maid of Orleans", France.
Cultivar name presumed registered 1953; name established and accepted.

'Jeanne Morie', *S. vulgaris*
origin not known ? ?
McKelvey, The Lilac, 316 [1928]
Cultivar name not established.

'Jeanne Saint-Didier', *S. vulgaris*
origin not known pre-1906; S V
McKelvey, The Lilac, 316 [1928]; Wister, Lilacs for America, 50 [1942]
Cultivar name not established, not reported in cultivation in 1953.

'Jean Saint-Didier' *S. vulgaris*,
origin not known pre-1907; S I
Wister, Lilacs for America, 36 [1942]
Cultivar name not established, not reported in cultivation in 1953.

'Jef Aelbrecht', *S.* Villosae Group
Aelbrecht 2009; S VI
in cultivation at Zilverspar nursery; no additional information available.
Cultivar name not established.

'Jefferson Berdeen', *S. vulgaris*
Berdeen 2005; D VI
Vrugtman, AABGA Bulletin 16(4):132 [1982]; Peterson, Lilacs - Proceedings 16(1):19 [1987] - name only; King & Coggeshall, Lilacs - Quart. Jour. 27(2):49-50 [1998] - name only; Vrugtman, Encyclopedia, 312 [2008]; Photo on Jorgovani/Lilacs 2015 DVD.
Named for the originator's grandson.
Cultivar name established and accepted.

'Jeffrey', *S. vulgaris*
Peterson; D VI
Peterson, Lilacs - Proceedings 16(1):19 [1987] - name only; Lambert & Fricke, Lilacs - Quart. Jour. 26(2):57 [1997] - name only
Cultivar name not established.

'Jeflady', *S.* (Pubescentes Series)
Durand & Ronald, 2016; S II
syn - Little Lady™, 'Little Lady'

{*S. pubescens* subsp. *patula* 'Miss Kim' × *S. pubescens* subsp. *pubescens* 'Palibin'}
Flower color RHS NN155D, bud color RHS 77A.
New Plants for 2017, Jeffries Nurseries, pp. 2, 335 & 36, 2017.
U.S. PP 30331 April 2, 2019, filed June 1, 2017
Cultivar name established and accepted.

'**Jeftini**', *S.* (Villosae Group)
Durand J.R, 2020; S V
Syn – Pinktini™
Dwarf cultivar resulting from a cross between 'Charisma' (known to be affected by phytoplasma) and 'Miss Canada'
Seen in the online catalog from Jeffries Nurseries Ltd (CA) March 12, 2020. USPP 32,724, January 5, 2021
Cultivar name established and accepted.

Jelena Vekhova - see 'Elena Vekhova'.

'**Jenja**', *S. vulgaris*
Upītis pre-1970; S V-VII
photo on Lilacs/Jorgovani DVD, 2nd ed. 2015; in cultivation at the Latvian State Institute of Fruit-Growing, Dobele; in litt. Igor Semenov to C. Holetich 16 March 2015; Photo on Jorgovani/Lilacs 2015 DVD.
Name: short form of Eugeni; named for a secretary of the originator.
Cultivar name not established

'**Jennie C. Jones**', *S. vulgaris*
Rankin; D I
{parentage not known}
Wister, Arnoldia 23(4):81 [1963]
Cultivar name registered 1963;
Cultivar not reported in cultivation.

'**Jennifer Morrison**', *S. vulgaris*
Berdeen; S VII
Peterson, Lilacs - Proceedings 16(1):19 [1987] - name only; King & Coggeshall, Lilacs - Quart. Jour. 27(2):49-50 [1998] - name only
Named for the granddaughter of the local doctor in Kennebunk, Maine.
Cultivar name not established.

Jenny - see '**Josée**'.

'**Jēra Maigums**', *S. vulgaris*
Upītis ca 1970; D II
syn - 'Jeera Maigums'
Kaliņš, Dārs un drava 1986, No. 12, 13-15 - in Latvian; in litt. S. Strautiņa to F. Vrugtman [22 Jan. 2008] - ca 1970, D II
Name: Latvian for tenderness of yeanling.
Cultivar name established and accepted.

'**Jesse Hepler**', *S.* (Villosae Group), *S.* ×*josiflexa*
Rogers 1978; S VII
syn. - 'Jessie Hepler'
{'Royalty' × 'Maybelle Farnum'}
Anon., New Hampshire Sunday News [May 15, 1977]; Vrugtman, Lilacs – Proceedings 7(1):36 [1979]; Vrugtman, AABGA Bull. 13 (4):108 [1979]; Lilacs – Quart. Jour. 24(3): front cover ill. [1995]; J. Bentley, Lilacs 42(2):57-58, ill. Inside front cover [2013]; Photo on Jorgovani/Lilacs 2015 DVD.
Named for Jesse Raymond Hepler, 1883(?)-1962; professor of horticulture and plantbreeder, 1917-1956, Univ. of New Hampshire; garden writer for The Portsmouth Herald, radio and TV personality.
Cultivar name registered 1977; name established and accepted.

'**Jessica**', *S.* (Villosae Group), *S.* ×*prestoniae*
Preston 1928; S II
syn. - Preston No. 20-14-22
{*S. villosa* subsp. *villosa* × *S. komarowii* subsp. *reflexa*}
Macoun, Rep. Dom. Hort. 1928, 56 [1930] - name only; USDA Plant Inventory No. 101, 20 (PI 81992) [Apr. 1931] - name only; Davis, Rep. Dom. Hort., Progress Report 1934-1948, 148 [1950]; Wister, Lilacs for America, 50, 64 [1942], 32, 48 [1953]; Photo on Jorgovani/Lilacs 2015 DVD.
Named for the Daughter to Shylock in Shakespeare's *Merchant of Venice*.
Cultivar name presumed registered 1953; name established and accepted.

'**Jessie Gardner**', *S. vulgaris*
Gardner 1956; S II
syn. - Gardner No. 472
Wister, Lilacs for America, 32 [1953]; Gardner, US Plant Patent No. 1444 [Jan. 3, 1956]; Edw. J. Gardner Nursery, Price list, 6 [1956]; Photo on Jorgovani/Lilacs 2015 DVD.
Cultivar name presumed registered 1953; name established and accepted.

'**Jewel**', *S.* ×*hyacinthiflora*
Becker; D V
{*S. oblata* × ? }
Wister, Lilacs for America, 32 [1953] - erroneously as S V; Wister, Lilac Registrations (mimeogr. list), 4 [n.d.; ca 1968] - as D V; Photo on Jorgovani/Lilacs 2015 DVD.
Cultivar name presumed registered 1953; name established and accepted.

'**J. Herbert Alexander**', *S.* (Villosae Group), *S.* ×*josiflexa*
Lyden; D V
{*S.* ×*josiflexa* 'James Macfarlane' × ? }
Wister, Arnoldia 23(4):81 [1963] - as a *S.* ×*prestoniae*
Named for John Herbert Alexander Sr, 1893-1977, nurseryman of Middleboro, Massachusetts, USA.
Cultivar name registered 1963.
Cultivar not reported in cultivation.

'**Jill Alexander**', *S.* (Villosae Group)
Alexander Sr; S V
{*S.* ×*josiflexa* 'James Macfarlane' × *S.* ×*prestoniae* 'Ethel M. Webster'}

Alexander Sr, Cat. sheets [n.d., rec'd January 1970]; Wister & Oppe, Arnoldia 31(3):122 [1971] - name only
Cultivar name registered 1970;
Cultivar not reported in cultivation.

'Jimmy Howarth', *S. vulgaris*,
Paterson; S I
Anon., The Evening Telegram [June 6, 1939]; Wister, Arnoldia 23(4):81 [1963]
Cultivar name registered 1963; name established and accepted.

'Jin Yuan', *S. pekinensis*
Dong Baohua & Chen Junyu 2003; S I
syn. - 'Bei Jing Huang', 'Beijing Huang', 'Jinyuan'
{mutation of *S. pekinensis* with yellow flowers; selected at the Botanical Garden of the Municipality of Beijing, from seedlings grown from seed collected in the Beijing mountains by [Mr] Dong Baohua}
Cui Hongxia, The Lilac, p. 50 & illustration (in Chinese) [2000] - as 'Bei Jing Huang'; Guo Ling, Scienta Silvae Sinicae 44(1):170 [2008]; Vrugtman, Lilacs Quart. Jour. 34(1):12-13 [2005].
Zhang, Donglin, and Michael Dirr. 2004. Potential New Ornamental Plants from China. SNA Research Conference Volume 49, plant Breeding & Evaluation Section 601. Text posted on http://www.umaine.edu/maineplants/MyPub/SNA04China.pdf,
Photos posted on http://www.umaine.edu/maineplants/sna04dz.pdf, November 24, 2004 - 'Jin Yuan' is listed as 'Beijing Huang'.
Name: Chinese for golden garden.
Cultivar name registered in 2003, plant variety right No. 20040010, with the Office for the Protection of New Varieties of Ornamental Plants of the State Forestry Administration in Beijing, People's Republic of China as 'Jinyuan'; statutory registration.
Cultivar name established and accepted.

'JN Upright Select', *S. pubescens* subsp. *patula*
Yanny 2005; S VII
{*S. pubescens* subsp. *patula* 'Miss Kim' × ? }
syn. - BLUE YANNY (cognomen used at first release to ILS members in May 2017); VIOLET UPRISING™
<http://patft.uspto.gov/netacgi/nph-Parser?-Sect1=PTO2&Sect2=HITOFF&p=1&u=%2F-netahtml%2FPTO%2Fsearch-bool.tml&r=11&f=G&l=50&co1=AND&d=PTXT&s2=Syringa&OS=Syringa&RS=Syringa>
US Plant Patent No. 28959, 13 February 2018; statutory registration.
Cultivar name established.

'Joan', *S.* (Villosae Group), *S.* ×*prestoniae*
Preston 1928; ? ?
{*S. villosa* subsp. *villosa* × *S. komarowii* subsp. *reflexa*}
Wister, Lilacs for America, 64 [1942], 48 [1953] - name only, not in cultivation, no plants distributed
Named for Joan of Arc in Shakespeare's *King Henry VI*, Part I.
Cultivar name not established.

'Joan Dunbar', *S. vulgaris*
Dunbar 1923; D I
syn. - Dunbar no. 343
{'Thunberg' × ? }
McKelvey, The Lilac, 316 [1928]; Wister, Lilacs for America, 50 [1942], 32 [1953];
Photo on Jorgovani/Lilacs 2015 DVD.
Cultivar name presumed registered 1953; name established and accepted.

JO BIG PURPLE - see **'SMSJBP7'**
also: JO BIG PUR
listed by Rångedala Plantskola, Sweden; listed by Willy De Nolf, Belgium, 2011-2018 as *S. microphylla* JO BIG PURPLE®;
Cognomen, not a cultivar name.

JO CASCADE, *S.*
Spring Meadow Nursery, selection by Tim Wood
listed by Willy De Nolf, Belgium, 2011-2018 as *S. microphylla* JO CASCADE®; listed by Pflanzmich, Germany, as 'Jo Cascade' and still in cultivation, in litt. Pflanzmich to Vrugtman 12 January 2018; listed by Kordes Jungpflanzen, Germany, January 2018.
Cognomen for a selection that was never introduced commercially (in litt. T. Wood to F. Vrugtman July 17, 2016), but some plants did enter the trade, and 'Jo Cascade' is in use as a cultivar epithet.

'Joel', *S. vulgaris*
Fiala 1981; S V
{'General Sherman' × 'Flora 1953'}
Fiala, Lilacs, 223 [1988]; Photo on Jorgovani/Lilacs 2015 DVD.
Name: Probably named for Joel Margaretten, 1910-1998, dentist and lilac grower (Margaretten Park), Leona Valley, California, USA.
Cultivar name established and accepted.

'Johan Mensing', *S. vulgaris*
Eveleens Maarse 1938; S II
syn. - 'Johann Mensing'
{'Marie Legraye' × 'Mme Florent Stepman'}
Dijkhuis, in Gedenkboek Valckenier Suringar, 128 [1942]; Wister, Lilacs for America, 32 [1953]; Eveleens Maarse, Dendron 1(1):12 [1954]; Photo on Jorgovani/Lilacs 2015 DVD.
Plant patent registration in the Netherlands, Centraal Rassenregister No. S 116, 1951-1968.
Awards: First Class Certificate 1938 (KMTP).
Cultivar name presumed registered 1953; name established and accepted.

'Johanna', *S. vulgaris*
Mägi pre-2017; S VII
Photo from Estonia by Mägi, seen in 2020 ILS Photo

Database.
Cultivar name not established.

John Adams - see **'President John Adams'**.

'John Dunbar', *S. vulgaris*
Fenicchia; S II
syn. - R101RAF164
{'Rochester' × ?}
Clark, The Newsletter, ILS, Convention Issue, pp. 6-7 [May 1972]; K. Millham, Lilacs -Quart. Jour. 42(2):61 & ill. 68 [2013]; Photo on Jorgovani/Lilacs 2015 DVD.
Named for John Dunbar 1859-1927, American horticulturist and lilac hybridizer.
Cultivar name established and accepted.

'John Kennedy', *S. vulgaris*
Berdeen 1982; D I
syn. - 'President John F. Kennedy'; see also 'President Kennedy'
{'Mme Lemoine' × ?}
Vrugtman, AABGA Bulletin 16(4):132 [1982]; Fiala, Lilacs, 217 [1988] - as 'President John F. Kennedy'; King & Coggeshall, Lilacs - Quart. Jour. 27(2):49-50 [1998] - name only; Vrugtman, Encyclopedia, 312 [2008]; Photo on Jorgovani/Lilacs 2015 DVD.
Named for John Fitzgerald Kennedy, 1917-1963, 35th president of the USA.
Cultivar name established and accepted.

John L. Fiala - see **'Fiala Remembrance'**.

'John Margaretten', *S. vulgaris*
Margaretten; D III
{'Mme Lemoine' × ?}
Cultivar name not established; not reported in cultivation.

John of Monmouth - see **'John's Favorite'**
Wister, Arnoldia 23(4):77-83 [1963] - name only
Cultivar name not established; erroneous cultivar name registration in 1963.

'John's Favorite', *S. vulgaris*
Lyden; S VII
syn. - 'John of Monmouth'
{mutation of 'Charles X'}
Wister, Arnoldia 23(4):81 [1963]
Cultivar name registered 1963; name established and accepted.

'John Wister', *S. vulgaris*
Margaretten; ? ?
Reported in cultivation, Royal Botanical Gardens, Hamilton, Ontario, Canada
Named for John Caspar Wister, 1887-1982, horticulturist, Swarthmore, Pennsylvania.
Cultivar name not established.

'Jonkheer G. F. van Tets', *S. vulgaris*
Eveleens Maarse 1940; S IV
syn. - 'Jonkheer van Tets', 'Jonkheer G. P. Van Tets'
{mutation of 'Hugo de Vries'}
Wister, Lilacs for America, 32 [1953] - erroneously as 'Jonkheer G. P. van Tets'; Eveleens Maarse, Dendron 1(1):11 [1954]; Photo on Jorgovani/Lilacs 2015 DVD.
Named for Jonkheer Gerard Frederik van Tets, Heer van Goidschalxoord en Neder-Slingerland, 1875-1968, chairman of the Koninklijke Maatschappij Tuinbouw en Plantkunde 1917-1947.
Awards: Certificate of Merit 1940 (KMTP).
Cultivar name presumed registered 1953; name established and accepted.

'Jordan', *S. vulgaris*
origin not known pre-1926; D IV
Wister, Lilacs for America, 32 [1953]
Cultivar name presumed registered 1953; name established and accepted.

'Josée' - see also 'MORjos 060F'
Cultivar name registered 1978; name established and accepted.

Josée™ - see also 'MORjos 060F', **'Josée'**.

Joséé Marti — see 'Khose Marti'

×*josiflexa* rubra - see **'Rubra'**, *S.* (Villosae Group) (×*josiflexa*).

josikaea eximia - see **'Eximia'** (*josikaea*).

josikaea flore rubra - see **'Rubra'** (*josikaea*).

josikaea monstrosa - see 'Monstrosa' (*josikaea*).

josikaea pallida - see **'Pallida'** (*josikaea*).

josikaea rosea - see 'Rosea' (*josikaea*).

josikaea var. *rubra* - see **'Rubra'** (*josikaea*).

josikaea zabeli - see **'H. Zabel'**.

JosReBloom, *S.*
Wood; no information
{parentage not available, but probably a 'Josée' seedling}
in lit Wood to Vrugtman 3 January 2018 - unreleased selection at Spring Meadow Nursery used for hybridization; seed parent of '**SMNJRPI**' and '**SMNJRPU**'.
Cognomen, not a cultivar name.

'Joyce', *S. vulgaris*
Klager; S V
Wister, Lilacs for America, 50 [1942], 32 [1953]
Cultivar name presumed registered 1953;
Cultivar not reported in cultivation.

'Joyce Burke', *S. vulgaris*
Berdeen; ? ?
King & Coggeshall, Lilacs - Quart. Jour. 27(2):49-50 [1998] - name only
Named for a family friend from Ipswich, Massachusetts.
Cultivar not established.

'**J. R. Koning**', *S. vulgaris*
  Eveleens Maarse 1955; S IV
  Wister, Arnoldia 23(4):81 [1963]; Photo on Jorgovani/Lilacs 2015 DVD.
  Awards: Certificate of Merit 1955 (KMTP).
  Named for the director of parks of the municipality of Amsterdam, 1920s and 1940s.
  Cultivar name registered 1963; name established and accepted.

'**Juan Ban Fen**', *S. vulgaris*
  Zang & Fan; D ?
  Zang & Fan, Pl. Introd. Acclimatization 3:117-121 [1983] - in Chinese
  Cultivar name not established.

'**Jubilee**', *S. vulgaris*
  Moro, F. 2007; S VI
  {'Excellent' × ?}
  <http://www.spi.8m.com/vulgariscdncat.html>seen July 28, 2014.
  Named in celebration of Queen Elizabeth's 50 years as queen of England.
  Cultivar name established and accepted.

Jubileinaja, Jubileinaya, Jubilejnaja - see '<u>Yubileinaya</u>'.

Judd - see '**William H. Judd**'.

'**Judy's Pink**', *S.* ×*hyacinthiflora*
  de Wilde; S V
  Wister & Oppe, Arnoldia 31(3):122 [1971]
  Cultivar name registered 1970;
  Cultivar not reported in cultivation.

'**Jugendtraum**', *S. vulgaris*
  Löbner pre-1947; S II
  syn. - 'Jugundtraum'
  Meyer, Flieder, 72 [1952]; Wister, Lilacs for America, 32 [1953]; Vrugtman, Lilacs - Quart. Jour. 22(3):90-92 [1993]
  Name: German for childhood dream.
  Cultivar name presumed registered 1953; name established and accepted.

'**Jules Ferry**', *S. vulgaris*
  Lemoine 1907; D V
  syn. - 'Julius Ferry'
  Lemoine, Cat. No. 167, 8 [1907]; McKelvey, The Lilac, 316-317 [1928]; Wister, Lilacs for America, 50 [1942], 32 [1953]; Photo on Jorgovani/Lilacs 2015 DVD.
  Named for Jules François Camille Ferry, 1832-1893, French statesman.
  Cultivar name presumed registered 1953; name established and accepted.

'**Jules Simon**', *S. vulgaris*
  Lemoine 1908; D III
  syn. - 'Mme Jules Simon'
  Lemoine, Cat. No. 170, 8 [1908]; McKelvey, The Lilac, 317 [1928]; Wister, Lilacs for America, 50, 53 [1942], 32, 36 [1953]; Photo on Jorgovani/Lilacs 2015 DVD.
  Named for Jules François Simon, 1814-1896, French statesman, philosopher and biographer.
  Cultivar name presumed registered 1953; name established and accepted.

'**Julia**', *S.* (Villosae Group), *S.* ×*henryi*
  Wickman 1993 (not Preston); S V
  {chance seedling; *S. josikaea* × *S. villosa* subsp. *villosa* (?)}
  Wickman, K., Lilacs - Quart. Jour. 28(2):41-42, back cover (top) [1999]; Photo on Jorgovani/Lilacs 2015 DVD.
  Cultivar name established and accepted.

'**Julia**', *S.* (Villosae Group), *S.* ×*prestoniae*
  Preston (not Wickman); S ?
  syn. - Preston No. 20-14-11
  {*S. villosa* subsp. *villosa* × *S. komarowii* subsp. *reflexa*}
  Macoun, Rep. Dom. Hort. 1928, 56 [1930] - name only; USDA Plant Inventory No. 101, 20 (PI 81993) [Apr. 1931] - name only; Wister, Lilacs for America, 64 [1942], 48 [1953] - name only, not in cultivation, no plants distributed
  Named for A Lady of Verona in Shakespeare's *Two Gentlemen of Verona*.
  Cultivar name not established, probably extinct.

'**Julia Hiers**', *S. vulgaris*
  origin not known pre-2000; ? ?
  at one time in cultivation at Monrovia Nursery Co. http://www.monrovia.com/PlantInf.nsf/269905a1f-b059eb48825683c0080938a/$searchForm!Search-View&Seq=1[Dec.10/2000], and in litt. Proud to Vrugtman [Jan.02/2001]
  Cultivar name not established.

julianae alba (Upton) - see 'Alba', Upton (*pubescens* subsp. *microphylla*).

'**Julie Ann Berdeen**', *S. vulgaris*
  Berdeen; D III
  Vrugtman, AABGA Bulletin 16(4):132 [1982]; King & Coggeshall, Lilacs - Quart. Jour. 27(2):49-50 [1998] - name only
  Named for granddaughter of Ken Berdeen.
  Cultivar not established.

'**Julien Gérardin**', *S. vulgaris*
  Lemoine 1916; D IV
  syn. - 'Julien Gerardin'
  common name: Julien Gerardin
  Lemoine, Cat. No. 190, 24 [1916]; Havemeyer, Garden Mag. 25:233 [1917]; McKelvey, The Lilac, 317 [1928]; Stand. Pl. Names, 616 [1942] - as Julien Gerardin; Wister, Lilacs for America, 50 [1942], 32 [1953]; Photo on Jorgovani/Lilacs 2015 DVD.
  Cultivar name presumed registered 1953; name established and accepted.

'Juliet', *S.* (Villosae Group), *S.* ×*prestoniae*
Preston 1928; S VI
syn. - 'Juliette', Preston No. 20-14-141
{*S. villosa* subsp. *villosa* × *S. komarowii* subsp. *reflexa*}
Macoun, Rep. Dom. Hort. 1928, 56 [1930]; Wister, Lilacs for America, 50, 64 [1942], 32, 48 [1953]; Photo on Jorgovani/Lilacs 2015 DVD.
Named for the Daughter of Capulet in Shakespeare's *Romeo and Juliet*.
Cultivar name presumed registered 1953; name established and accepted.

Junost - see 'Yunost'.

Jurij Gargarin - see 'Yuriĭ Gagarin'.

'Justii', *S. vulgaris*
origin not known pre-1865; S III
syn. - 'Josti', 'Just', 'Justi'
McKelvey, The Lilac, 317-318 [1928] - descriptions vary (S and D); Wister, Lilacs for America, 50 [1942], 32 [1953] - as 'Justi', S III; Photo on Jorgovani/Lilacs 2015 DVD.
Cultivar name presumed registered 1953; name established and accepted.

'Jutrzenka', *S.* (species affiliation not known)
origin not known ? ?
reported in cultivation by Ole Heide, Thisted, Denmark [1998]
Name: Polish for morning star.

'Jutrzenka Pomorza', *S. vulgaris*
Karpow-Lipski 1961; S V
syn. - 'Jutrezenka Parmorza'
Wister & Oppe, Arnoldia 31(3):125 [1971]; Photo on Jorgovani/Lilacs 2015 DVD.
Name: Polish for morning star of Pomerania.
Cultivar name registered 1970; name established and accepted.

Juzhanka - see 'Yuzhnaya'.

Juzhnaja Noch - see 'Yuzhnaya Noch".

J. Von Tol - see 'Jan van Tol'.

'J. Wołowicki', *S. vulgaris*
Karpow-Lipski 1958; D V
syn. - Siewka nr 3
Karpow-Lipski, Arboretum Kórnickie 3:104 [1958]
Cultivar name established and accepted.

'Kabuki', *S. pubescens* subsp. *pubescens*
Ihara 2020; S VII
Florets RHS 70B, Buds RHS 72A
{*S. pubescens* subsp. *pubescens* 'Hoshikuzu' × *S. pubescens* subsp. *pubescens* (seedling no. 20040520001#8)}
Syn. – seedling no. 2011S1128006#5, 'Kanoko'
Named for one of the traditional Japanese arts, a play unique to Japan.
Registration completed 2/7/21.
Cultivar name registered, established and accepted.

'Kabul', *S. protolaciniata*
Origin not known; S II
syn. - *afghanica* Hort., *afghanica* 'Kabul', (not *afghanica* C.K. Schneider)
{presumably a selection of *S. protolaciniata* P.S.Green & M.C.Chang}
Green, Kew Magazine 6(3):116-124, Pl. 132 [1989]; Lilacs - Quart. Jour. 18(4): back cover, right: 'Kabul', left *S. laciniata* (reprinted from Kew Magazine loc. cit.) [1989]; Vrugtman, HortScience 25(6):618 [1990]; Photo on Jorgovani/Lilacs 2015 DVD.
Named by Peter S. Green for the city of Kabul, Afghanistan.
Cultivar name registered 1989; name established and accepted.

Kaethe Haerlin - see **'Käthe Härlin'**.

'Kaisma', *S. vulgaris*
Upītis ca 1970; S II
Reported in cultivation at Dobele Hort. Exp. Stn., in litt. S. Strautiņa to F. Vrugtman [Nov. 13, 2002]; in litt. S. Strautiņa to F. Vrugtman [22 Jan. 2008] - ca 1970, S II
Name: Kaisma is a Latvian girl's name.
Cultivar name established and accepted. Cultivar may be extinct.

Kalama - see **'City of Kalama'**.

'Kallen Cole', *S.vulgaris*
Peterson 2003; D V
{'Beth' × OP}
In private collection (KA) in USA per email to Registrar 10-4-19.
Named for the developer's niece.
Cultivar name not established.

'Kaminari-kozo', *S.*
'雷小僧'
Ihara 2018; S VI
{*S.* 'MORjos 060F' × *S.* 'MORjos 060F', seedling 2011S#1128004#1}
registered 17 November 2018 by Hideo Ihara Tokiwa 450-1, Minamiku, Sapporo, Hokkaido, 005 - 0863 Japan.
Name in Japanese means "child of lightning."
Cultivar name registered 2018; name established and accepted.

'Kannika', *S. vulgaris*
Vaigla pre-2001; S IV/V (IV-VI per Semenov)
Syn. – 'Kannike'
listed on http://aed.rapina.ee/sirelid.htm [seen 5 Nov. 2005]; I. Semenov, Lilacs 48(2):65 [2019].
Cultivar name not established.

'Kanoko', *S.* (Pubescentes Series)
鹿の子

Ihara 2019; S VII
Private communication from Ihara to Registrar December 20, 2019, photo seen.
Cultivar name not established.

'Kaoridama', *S. pubescens* subsp. *pubescens*
'香り玉'
Ihara 2004; S VII
syn. - seedling no. 20040520001#4.
{*S. pubescens* subsp. *pubescens* 'Palibin' × *S. pubescens* subsp. *pubescens* 'Palibin'}
(Vrugtman, Cultivated Plant Diversity ... 2017)
Name: Japanese for pomander.
Cultivar name registered 2017; name established and accepted.

Kapitan Gastello - see 'Gastello'.

'Kapitan Teliga', *S. vulgaris*
Karpow-Lipski 1973; S VII-II
syn. - KL 28, 'Mikołaj Kopernik'
{'Masséna' × ?}
Anon., Lista odmian roślin ozdobnych 1971, 17; Lista . . . 1973, 25; Lista . . . 1980, 152 - in Polish; Anon., Lilak Pospolity - COBO Informator 8/78 [1976]; Photo on Jorgovani/Lilacs 2015 DVD.
Named for Leonid Teliga, 1917-1970, Poland, who singlehandedly circumnavigated the earth in 1967-69 on his 34-foot yawl Opty.
varietal denomination registered COBORU 1971; Cultivar name established and accepted.

'Kapriz', *S. vulgaris*
'Каприз'
Kolesnikov 1952; D IV-V
syn. - 'Caprice'
Miel'nik, Trudy Alma-Atinsk. Bot. Sada Akad. Nauk Kazakh. SSR 6:60-86 [1961]; Brizicky, AABGA Quart. Newsl. No. 64, 22 [1965] - as Whim; Wister & Oppe, Arnoldia 31(3):125 [1971] - as D IV; Rubtzov et al. 1980. Vidy i sorta sireni, kul'tiviruemye v SSSR. Kiev; Naukova Dumka. – in Russian; Holetich, C.D. 1982. Lilac species and cultivars in cultivation in USSR. Lilacs 11(2):1-38. - translation of Rubtzov et al. 1982; Photo on Jorgovani/Lilacs 2015 DVD.
Name: Russian for caprice.
Cultivar name registered 1970; established and accepted.

'Karbunkul', *S. vulgaris*
'Карбункул'
Dyagilev pre-1994, ? ?
Pikaleva, Lilacs - Quart. Jour. 23(4):84 [1994].
Named for the carbuncle gemstone, the red garnet.
Cultivar name not established.

'Kardynał', *S. vulgaris*
Karpow-Lipski 1986; S VII-II
syn. - 'Cardinal', 'Kardinal', 'Kardynal'
Anon., Lista odmian roślin ozdobnych 1986, 59 - as 'Cardinal'; Lista . . . 1987, 57 - as S I; Fiala, Lilacs, 214 - erroneously as D VI [1988]; Vrugtman, HortScience 24(3):435 [1989]; Photo on Jorgovani/Lilacs 2015 DVD.
Cultivar name registered 1988; name established and accepted.

'Karen', *S. pubescens* subsp. *microphylla*
Fiala 1993; S V-I
Arbor Village Nursery, Cat. [Fall 2003]; Beaver Creek Nursery, Liner Notes, 3 [2003] - name only; Dirr, Manual of woody landscape plants, 6th ed., p. 1104 [2009].
Named for Karen T. Murray, executive director [1983-1993] of Falconskeape Gardens and Ameri-Hort Research, Medina, Ohio.
Cultivar name established and accepted.

'Karin', *S.* ×*hyacinthiflora*
Vaigla pre-2001; S VI-V (II-VI per Semenov)
Semenov, Lilacs 48(2):65, 46 (photo) [2019].
Cultivar name established and accepted.

'Karla', *S. pubescens* subsp. *microphylla*
Ballreich pre-2004; S II
Anon., Tentative list of lilacs for auction. Lilacs - Quart. Jour. 33(1):10 [2004] - in cult. Max Peterson
Named for Karla Davis, daughter of the originator.
Cultivar name not established.

'Karl Hoffman', *S. vulgaris*
origin not known perhaps Hulda Klager (doubtful); D VII
reported in cultivation in New Zealand, in litt. Beryl Lee to Vrugtman 30 August 2015; Beryl Lee, Lilacs - Quart. Jour. 46(2):63 [2017] - name only; listed by Blue Mountain Nurseries, Tapanui, New Zealand, as having "double purple flowers with a paler reverse. Ht 2m."
<http://www.bmn.co.nz/product/syringa-karl-hoffman-2/>
Cultivar name established and accepted.

Karlsruhensis - see 'Carlsruhensis'.

Karl X - see **'Charles X'**.

'Karszubiana', *S. vulgaris*
origin not known pre-1928; S II
Starcs, Mitt. Deutsch. Dendr. Ges. 40:42 [1928].

'Karukaze', *S.* (Pubescentes Series)
Ihara 2019; S VII
Private communication from Ihara to Registrar December 20, 2019, photo seen.
Cultivar name not established.

'Kate Bergen', *S. vulgaris*
Berdeen; D V
Vrugtman, AABGA Bulletin 16(4):132 [1982]; Peterson, Lilacs - Proceedings 16(1):20 [1987] - name only; King & Coggeshall, Lilacs - Quart. Jour. 27(2):49-50 [1998] - name only.
Named for the daughter of originator's friend and neighbor.
Cultivar name established and accepted.

Kate Harlin - see **'Käthe Härlin'**.

'Käte Härlin', *S. vulgaris*
Pfitzer, W. Sr. 1910; S I
syn. - 'Ekaterina Herling', 'Harlin', 'Kaethe Haerlin', 'Kate Hardin', 'Kathe', 'Käthe Härlin'
common name: Kate Harlin
Kanzleiter, Gartenwelt 13:129, t. fig. 3 [1909]; Wilhelm Pfitzer, Cat., 178 [1911]; Kache, Gartenschönheit 5:82 [1924]; McKelvey, The Lilac, 318 [1928]; Stand. Pl. Names, 616 [1942] - as Kate Harlin; Wister, Lilacs for America, 51 [1942], 32 [1953] - erroneously as 'Kate Harlin'; Photo on Jorgovani/Lilacs 2015 DVD.
Named for Katharina Maria (Käte) Schaller-Härlin, 1877-1973; portrait painter; Stuttgart, Germany.
Cultivar name presumed registered 1953; name established and accepted.

'Kate Sessions', *S.* ×*hyacinthiflora*
Clarke 1942; S V
Wister, Lilacs for America, 51 [1942] - as S VI; Clarke, Cat. 16:8 [1949]; Woody Plant Register, AAN. No. 185 [1949]; Wister, Lilacs for America, 32 [1953]; Kammerer, Morton Arb. Bull. Pop. Info. 36(6):27-29 [1961]; Photo on Jorgovani/Lilacs 2015 DVD.
Named for Miss Katherine Olivia Sessions, 1857-1940, nurserywoman and San Diego's first "City Gardener", USA.
Cultivar name presumed registered 1953; name established and accepted.

Kathe - see **'Käthe Härlin'**.

'Katharina', *S.* (Villosae Group), *S.* ×*prestoniae*
Preston 1928; S V
syn. - 'Katherina', Preston No. 20-14-34, etc.; corrected to 'Katharina' because of the derivation of the name.
{*S. villosa* subsp. *villosa* × *S. komarowii* subsp. *reflexa*}
Macoun, Rep. Dom. Hort. 1928, 56 [1930] - name only; Macoun, Rep. Dom. Hort. 1930, 67 [1931]; Wister, Lilacs for America, 51, 64 [1942], 32, 48 [1953]; Photo on Jorgovani/Lilacs 2015 DVD.
Named for The Shrew (Katharina) in Shakespeare's *Taming of the Shrew*.
Cultivar name presumed registered 1953; name established and accepted.

'Katherine', *S. vulgaris*
Klager 1939; S VII
Wister, Lilac for America, 51 [1942], 32 [1953]
Cultivar name presumed registered 1953;
Cultivar not reported in cultivation.

'Katherine Havemeyer', *S. vulgaris*
Lemoine 1922; D V
syn. - 'Katharine Havemeyer', 'Katharina Havemeyer', 'Katherina Havemeyer' 'Katharine Havemeyere', 'Katherine Havermeyer', 'Katharine Mavemeyer'
Lemoine, Cat. No. 196, 19 [1922]; McKelvey, The Lilac, 318 [1928]; Wister, Lilacs for America, 51 [1942], 32 [1953]; Photo on Jorgovani/Lilacs 2015 DVD.
Awards: RHS Award of Merit 1933; Award of Garden Merit 1969.
Named for Katherine Aymer Sands, 1873-1951, wife to T. A. Havemeyer.
Awards: RHS Award of Garden Merit 1993.
Cultivar name presumed registered 1953; name established and accepted.

'Katherine Jones', *S.* ×*hyacinthiflora*
Clarke pre-1953; S VI
Wister, Lilacs for America, 32 [1953]
Cultivar name presumed registered 1953; name established and accepted.

'Kathleen Cowan', *S. vulgaris*
Berdeen; D III
Vrugtman, AABGA Bulletin 16(4):132 [1982]; King & Coggeshall, Lilacs - Quart. Jour. 27(2):49-50 [1998] - name only
Named for a friend of Ken Berdeen, flower show judge, Brewer, Maine.
Cultivar not established.

'Kathy McGuire', *S. vulgaris*
Berdeen; pre-1983; S VII/IV
syn. - 'Kathy Mcquire', 'Kathy McQuire'
Peterson, Lilacs - Proceedings 16(1):20 [1987] - as 'Kathy Mcquire', name only; King & Coggeshall, Lilacs - Quart. Jour. 27(2):49-50 [1998] - name only; Photo on Jorgovani/Lilacs 2015 DVD.
Cultivar name established and accepted.

KATHY TURNER, *S. vulgaris*
Fenicchia no dates; S I
The selection was never propagated; not established as a cultivar.
Cognomen; proposed to be named for Cathy Ann Turner [1962 -] from Rochester, New York, the 1992 and 1994 Olympic gold medalist in short track speed skating.

'K. A. Timiryazev', *S. vulgaris*
'К. А. Тимирязев'
Kolesnikov 1955; S IV
syn. - 'K. A. Timeryazen', 'K. A. Timiriazev', 'K. A. Timirjazev', Kolesnikov No. 119
Howard, Arnoldia 19(6-7):31-35 [1959]; Gromov, Siren', 111 [1963]; Howard & Brizicky, AABGA Quart. Newsl. No. 64, 17-21 [1965]; Wister & Oppe, Arnoldia 31(3):125 [1971] - as S VII and 'K. A. Timiriazev'; Gromov, Lilacs - Proceedings 2(4):17 [1974]; Rubtzov et al. 1980. Vidy i sorta sireni, kul'tiviruemye v SSSR. Kiev; Naukova Dumka. – in Russian; Holetich, C.D. 1982. Lilac species and cultivars in cultivation in USSR. Lilacs 11(2):1-38. - translation of Rubtzov et al. 1982; Photo on Jorgovani/Lilacs 2015 DVD.
Named for Kliment Arkad'evich Timiryazev, 1843-1920, Russian botanist and physiologist.
Cultivar name registered 1970; name established and accepted.

Katinka (*microphylla*) - see **'Miss Kim'** (*pubescens* subsp. *patula*).

'Katya', *S. vulgaris*
'Катя'
Sagitova; D IV
{parentage not known}
Cultivar name not established.

'Katyusha', *S. vulgaris*
'Катюша'
Aladin, S., Aladina, O., and Polyakova, T. 2014; D II/IV
{elite form 8-926 × 'Lavoisier'}
Приусадебное хозяйство (Annex to the magazine Homestead farming: "Flowers in the garden and at home. Brushes and paints") 08/2015: 5-14; Питомник-частный сад (Pitomnik i chastnyi sad; Nursery and private garden) 3/2015:14-22; Садовник (Gardener) magazine, 05 (141)/2017 :16-22; Вестник АППМ (Catalog in Vestnik APPM (Planting material association) magazine) 1/2018: 59-72 (in Russian).
Name: Katyusha is the diminutive of Катя (Kátja or Katya). Named for famous and beloved song in Russia.
Cultivar name established and accepted.

'Kazakhstanskaya', *S. vulgaris*
'Казахстанская'
Mel'nik; 1971,S II
syn. - 'Kazachstanskaja'
{'Volcan' × OP }
Syn. – seedling 13
Rubanik, V. G. et al., Siren' - Syringa L., publishing house "Kaĭnar", Alma-Ata [1977] pp 53-54 - in Russian; Rubtzov et al. 1980. Vidy i sorta sireni, kul'tiviruemye v SSSR. Kiev; Naukova Dumka. – in Russian; Holetich, C.D. 1982. Lilac species and cultivars in cultivation in USSR. Lilacs 11(2):1-38. - translation of Rubtzov et al. 1982.
Named for Kazakhstan.
Cultivar name established and accepted.

'Kazakhstanskiĭ Suvenir', *S. ×hyacinthiflora*
'Казахстанский Сувенир'
Mel'nik; 1971, S II
syn. - 'Sabit Mukanov', 'Kazachstanskij Suvenir', seedling No. 56
{'Buffon' × ? }
Rubanik, V. G. et al., Siren' - Syringa L., publishing house "Kaĭnar", Alma-Ata [1977] p 56- in Russian; Rubtzov et al. 1980. Vidy i sorta sireni, kul'tiviruemye v SSSR. Kiev; Naukova Dumka. – in Russian; Holetich, C.D. 1982. Lilac species and cultivars in cultivation in USSR. Lilacs 11(2):1-38. - translation of Rubtzov et al. 1982.
Name: Russian for Kazakhstan souvenir.
Cultivar name established and accepted.

'Kazino', *S. vulgaris*
Kārkliņš 2003; D III/IV
Photo on Jorgovani/Lilacs 2015 DVD; photo by Semenov on ILS 2019 photo database.
Name: Latvian for casino.
Cultivar name not established.

'Keito', *S. ×hyacinthiflora*
Kawahara 2000; S V
{'Esther Staley' × ? }
Named for the daughter of a friend of the originator.
(Vrugtman, Cultivated Plant Diversity ... 2017)
Cultivar name registered 2016; name established and accepted.

'Ken Berdeen', *S. vulgaris*
Berdeen (not Lyden); S VII
Peterson, Lilacs - Proceedings 16(1):20 [1987] - name only
Cultivar name not established.

'Ken Berdeen', *S. vulgaris*
Lyden (not Berdeen); D I
Wister, Arnoldia 23(4):81 [1963]; King & Coggeshall, Lilacs - Quart. Jour. 27(2):49-50 [1998]
Named for Kenneth Berdeen, 1907-1986, amateur lilac breeder, Kennebunk, Maine, USA.
Cultivar name registered 1963; name established and accepted.

'Kenneth W. Berdeen II', *S. vulgaris*
Berdeen; D IV
syn. - 'Kenneth W. Berdeen 2nd'
Vrugtman, AABGA Bulletin 16(4):132 [1982]; Peterson, Lilacs - Proceedings 16(1):20 [1987] - name only; King & Coggeshall, Lilacs - Quart. Jour. 27(2):49-50 [1998] - name only
Named for the originator's grandson.
Cultivar name established and accepted.

'KFBX 15', *S. pubescens* subsp. *patula*
origin not known ? ?
reported in cultivation at NCCPG Collection, Suffolk, UK
Cultivar name not established.

'Khan-Tengri'; *S. vulgaris*
'Хан-Тенгри'
Dyagilev; 1989, D III - IV
Syn. – 'Khantengri'
Dyagilev, Lilacs - Quart. Jour. 22(1):20 [1993]
(Международная научная конференция "Syringa L.: коллекции, выращивание, использование")
"International Scientific Conference "Syringa L.: collections, cultivation, using" / Collection of Scientific Articles of Botanical Institute named after V.L. Komarov, Botanical Garden of Peter the Great BIN RAS. - St. Petersburg. -2020.- pp.23-27 (in Russian).
Named for Khan Tengri or Hantengri Peak, the highest mountain of the Tian Shan mountain range, located on the China—Kyrgyzstan—Kazakhstan border.
Cultivar name established and accepted.

'Khoroshee Nastroenie', *S. vulgaris*
'Хорошиее Настроение'

Smol'skiĭ & Bibikova 1964; S I
{'Mme Abel Chatenay' × 'Réaumur'}
Pikaleva, Lilacs - Quart. Jour. 23(4):85 [1994];
Tereshchenko, Lilacs in the South-East of Ukraine, p. 65 [2002] - as 'Khoroshee Nastroenie'; Semenov, Igor, Lilacs - Quart. Jour. 43(3):85-87 [2014].
Name: Russian for good mood.
Cultivar name established and accepted.

'Khose Marti', *S. vulgaris*
'Хосе Марти'
Aladin, S., Aladina, O., and Polyakova, T. 2016; S VII
{'elite form STK-56' × OP}
Syn. – 'José Marti'
Садовник (Gardener) magazine 04 (140)/2017 :18-25; Вестник АППМ (Catalog in Vestnik APPM (Planting material association) magazine) 1/2018: 59-72 (in Russian).
Named for José Julián Martí y Pérez, 1853-1895, Cuban poet, writer, publicist, translator, philosopher and revolutionary, leader of the liberation movement of Cuba from Spain.
Cultivar name established and accepted.

'Kievlyanka', *S. vulgaris*
'Киевлянка'
Rubtzov & Zhogoleva 1956; S IV
syn. - 'Kievljanka'
{'Katherine Havemeyer' × ? }
Rubtzov et al. 1980. Vidy i sorta sireni, kul'tiviruemye v SSSR. Kiev; Naukova Dumka. – in Russian; Holetich, C.D. 1982. Lilac species and cultivars in cultivation in USSR. Lilacs 11(2):1-38. - translation of Rubtzov et al. 1982.
Name: Russian for a woman living in Kiev.
Cultivar name established and accepted.

'Killu', *S.*
Mägi pre-2018; ? ?
Semenov, I., Lilacs 48(2):68 [2019].
Cultivar name not established.

'Kim', *S.* (Villosae Group)
Preston 1942; S II
{probably *S. josikaea* × ? }
Davis, Rep. Dom. Hort., Progress Report 1934-1948, 150 [1950]; Wister, Lilacs for America, 51, 63 [1942], 32, 48 [1953]; Laar, Dendroflora 27:82 [1990] - erroneously presumes that 'Miss Kim' (*S. pubescens* subsp. *patula*) is identical to 'Kim' (*S.* ×*prestoniae*); Photo on Jorgovani/Lilacs 2015 DVD.
Awards: RHS Award of Merit 1958.
Cultivar name presumed registered 1953; name established and accepted.

'Kimmy Marie', *S. vulgaris*
Klager; S V
Anon., ILS Newsletter 14(4):3-4 [1988]
Cultivar name not established.

King Albert - see **'Roi Albert'**.

'Kingsville', *S. vulgaris*
Hohman 1947; S VII
{parentage not known}
Woody Plant Register, AAN, No. 70 [1949]; Wister, Lilacs for America, 32 [1953]
Named for the town of Kingsville, Maryland, USA; Photo on Jorgovani/Lilacs 2015 DVD.
Cultivar name presumed registered 1953; name established and accepted.

'Kitchen Blue', *S. vulgaris*
Fiala; S III
Anon., Lilacs - Quart. Jour. 18(3):73 {1989] - name only; in cultivation at Holden Arboretun, buds dark purple (in lit. DeBard to Vrugtman, 3 Sep. 2018). Verified by Registrar a S III on visit May 2020; provenance was a gift from Fiala on a grafted rootstock of *S.* ×*persica* on 17 October 1978 after propagation at Forsythe Nurseries in Dansville NY.
Double forms known to exist are not true to name.
Cultivar name not established.

'Kivi Ats', *S.* ×*hyacinthiflora*
Vaigla 1956; S VI (VI/II per Semenov)
syn. - 'Kiva Ats', 'Adolf Vaigla'
{'Esther Staley' × ? }
Kivistik, Maakodu 1997(5):22-23 (ill.) [1997] - in Estonian; Chapman, Lilacs - Quart. Jour. 30(1):4 [2001] - as 'Kiva Ats'; I. Semenov, Lilacs 48(2):65 [2019].
Cultivar name established and accepted.

'Kjell', *S. josikaea*
origin not known 1998; S VII
Wickmans Plantskola
<https://www.tawi.fi/~wiplant/hackar_2014_sortimentslista.pdf>
Cultivar name established and accepted.

'Klager', *S. vulgaris*
origin not known ? ?
Wister, Lilacs for America, 51 [1942]
Cultivar name not established.

'Klager Dark Dense Truss', *S. vulgaris*
Klager 1915; S VII
syn. - 'Dark Dense Truss'
Wister, Lilacs for America, 51 [1942], 32 [1953]
Cultivar name presumed registered 1953;
Cultivar not reported in cultivation.

'Klager Dark Navy Blue', *S. vulgaris*
Klager 1915; S VI
Wister, Lilacs for America, 51 [1942] - as S III; Wister, Lilacs for America, 32, [1953]
Cultivar name presumed registered 1953; name established and accepted.

Klager Dark Purple - see **'City of Gresham'**.

'Klager Dark Red', *S. vulgaris*
Klager 1915; S VI

Wister, Lilacs for America, 51 [1942], 33 [1953]
Cultivar name presumed registered 1953;
Cultivar not reported in cultivation.

'**Klager Dark Rose**', *S. vulgaris*
Klager 1915; S VII
Wister, Lilacs for America, 51 [1942] - as S V; Wister, Lilacs for America 33 [1953]
Cultivar name presumed registered 1953; name established and accepted.

'**Klager Large Dark Double Very Fine**', *S. vulgaris*
Klager 1915; D VII
Wister, Lilacs for America, 51 [1942], 33 [1953]
Cultivar name presumed registered 1953;
Cultivar not reported in cultivation.

'**Klager Large Dense Truss**', *S. vulgaris*
Klager 1915; D VII
Wister, Lilacs for America, 51 [1942], 33 [1953]
Cultivar name presumed registered 1953;
Cultivar not reported in cultivation.

'**Klager Late Bloomer**', *S. vulgaris*
Klager 1915; S IV
Wister, Lilacs for America, 51 [1942], 33 [1953]
Cultivar name presumed registered 1953; name established and accepted.

'**Klager Light Pink Abundant Bloomer**', *S. vulgaris*
Klager 1915; S V
syn. - 'Klager Light Pink'
Wister, Lilacs for America, 51 [1942], 33 [1953]
Cultivar name presumed registered 1953;
Cultivar not reported in cultivation.

'**Klager Loose Panicle**', *S. vulgaris*
Klager 1915; S IV
Wister, Lilacs for America, 51 [1942], 33 [1953]
Cultivar name presumed registered 1953;
Cultivar not reported in cultivation.

'Klager's Double Blue', *S. vulgaris*
Klager; D III
Ballreich, Lilacs - Quart. Jour. 22(2):32 [1993] - name only; Kilcoyne, Lilacs - Quart. Jour.36(2):83 [2007] - name only
Cultivar name not established.

'Klage's Double Purple', *S. vulgaris*
Origin not known; D VII
syn. - 'Klager's Double'
Northwest Rose Growers Inc. listing [seen Apr.28/99]; Hulda Klager Lilac Garden http://www.lilacgardens.com/purple.html [June 5, 2002] - as 'Klager's Double'
Cultivar name not established.

'Klager's Dwarf Blue', *S. vulgaris*
origin not known ? III
Wister, Lilacs for America, 51 [1942]; Vrugtman, Quart. Jour. 28(3):76 [1999] - name only
Cultivar name not established.

'Klager's Large Double Purple, *S. vulgaris*'
Origin not known; D VII
Wister, Lilacs for America, 51 [1942]
Cultivar name not established.

'Klager's Magenta', *S. vulgaris*
origin not known ? VI
Wister, Lilacs for America, 51 [1942]
Cultivar name not established.

'**Klmone**', *S. pubescens* subsp. *patula*
Klehm 2000; S V
{parentage not known}
marketed in North America as Miss Susie™
Bachman's Nursery, Cat. p. 248 [2001] - as 'Miss Susie', name only; Beaver Creek Nursery, BCN Plant Line™ Current Nursery Stock list p.18 [Summer 2001] - Miss Susie™, trademark only; http://www.klehm.com/includes/plantlistsub.cfm?type=Woodies&subtype=Lilacs&startrow=1 [April 18, 2002]; Vrugtman, HortScience 38(6):1301 [2003]
Cultivar name registered; name established and accepted.

'Knipper-Chekhova'; *S. vulgaris*
'Книппер-Чехова'
Klimenko, V.& Z., & Grigor'ev 1955; S VII
Rubtzov et al. 1980. Vidy i sorta sireni, kul'tiviruemye v SSSR. Kiev; Naukova Dumka. – in Russian; Holetich, C.D. 1982. Lilac species and cultivars in cultivation in USSR. Lilacs 11(2):1-38. - translation of Rubtzov et al. 1982.
Named for Olga Leonardovna Knipper-Chekhova, 1868-1959, Russian actress and the wife to playwright Anton Chekhov.
Cultivar name established and accepted.

'**Knyaginya Irina**', *S. vulgaris*
'Княгиня Ирина'
Makedonskaya 2017, S/D V
{open pollinated seedling}
Statutory registration with the State Inspection for testing and protection of plant varieties of the Republic of Belarus. Makedonskaya N.V. Breeding Lilacs in Belarus Yesterday TODAY: Materials of International scientific-practical conference "INTERNATIONAL SYRINGA 2018", Russia. Moscow: Moscow State University 2018.pp 36-40. Natalya Makedonskaya. Syringa Belarus. – Lilacs. Quarterly Journal of the International Lilac Society. 2019. VOL. 50· NUM. 1 PP.21-25.
Named for Irina Paskevich-Erivanskaya, 1835-1925, also know as the fairest princess of Warsaw, benefactor to the town of Gomel, Belarus, translator of Leo Tolstoy's novel "War and Peace" to French, English, Hungarian, Dutch, Polish, and Turkish; deprived of her wealth following the

1917 Bolshewik revolution she spent the remaining years of her life in oblivion.

'Knyaz' Serebryan'yĭ, *S. vulgaris*
'Князь Серебряный'
Aladin, S., Aladina, O., Polyakova, T., and Aladina, A. 2018; S V-IV
{sdlg 11-112* x ? }
*sdlg 11-112 was obtained from open pollinated seeds of 'Stefan Makowiecki'.
Международная научно-практическая конференция (International
scientific and practical conference) "International Syringa 2018", Moscow, Moscow State University Botanical Garden, St. Petersburg, Botanical Garden of Peter the Great BIN RAS, Pavlovsk, May 21-27, 2018; pp. 43-47.
Named for Knyaz' Serebryan'yĭ, Prince Silver, character from The Tale of the Times of Ivan the Terrible, a historical novel by A. K. Tolstoy published in 1863.
Cultivar name established and accepted.

'Kobierski', *S. vulgaris*
Karpow-Lipski; D IV
Wister & Oppe, Arnoldia 13(3):125 [1971]
Name: Perhaps named for Stanislaus Kobierski, 1910-1972, German soccer player.
Cultivar name registered 1970; name established and accepted.

Kochaloyski - see 'P. P. Konchalovskiĭ'
Beaver Creek Nursery, Liner Notes, 3 [2003] - name only, misspelling.

Koenigin Luise - see **'Königin Luise'**.

'Koenig Johann', *S. vulgaris*
origin not known pre-1880; ? ?
syn. - 'Roi Jean'
McKelvey, The Lilac, 318 [1928] - as confused name
Named for Prince Johann von Wettin, 1801-1873, king of Saxony, 1854-1873.
Cultivar name not established.

'Kogi', *S. vulgaris*
Kopp; S V
{'Mirabeau' × ? }
Cultivar name not established.

'Koki-no-iro', *S.* (Pubescentes Series)
'古希の色'
Ihara 2018; S VII
{*S.* 'MORjos 060F' × *S.* 'MORjos 060F', seedling 2011S#1128004#6} registered 17 November 2018 by Hideo Ihara Tokiwa 450-1, Minamiku, Sapporo, Hokkaido, 005 - 0863 Japan.
The name in Japanese means the noble color purple symbolizing and celebrating the (in past times rar) longevity of people of 70 years of age.
registered 17 November 2018 by Hideo Ihara Tokiwa 450-1, Minamiku, Sapporo, Hokkaido, 005 - 0863 Japan.
Cultivar name registered 2018; name established and accepted.

KOLESNIKOV'S SEEDLING 328, probably *S. vulgaris*
Kolesnikov 1968; S VII
T. Polyakova , 2018, Мастер Сиреневой Кисти (Master of the Lilac Brush), p.107, photo with description in Russian - yet unnamed selection.

Kolesnikov
{For information on Kolesnikov's work and methods see: Kolesnikov, L. 1955. Lilac. Foreign Languages Publishing House, Moscow.
Howard, R. A. 1959. A booklet on lilacs from Russia. Arnoldia 19(6-7):31-35. Gromov, A. 1974. Leonid Alekseevich Kolesnikov...creator of Russian lilacs. Lilacs - Proceedings 2(4):11-18 [1974].
T. Polyakova, 2010, Istoriya Russkoĭ Sireni. Памяти Колесникова. (history of Russian lilac. Memory of Kolesnikov).}
Kolesnikov
No. 014 - see 'Nevesta'.
No. 032 - see 'Tamara Kolesnikova'.
No. 039 - see 'Znamya Lenina'.
No. 050 - not named; ? ?
No. 061 - see 'Sholokhov'.
No. 077 - see 'Utro Moskvy'.
No. 086 - see 'Olimpiada Kolesnikova'.
No. 088 - see 'Privet Otchizne'.
No. 104 - see 'Sumerki'.
No. 105 - not named; S II/VII.
No. 110 - not named; S II/VII.
No. 119 - see 'K. A. Timiryazev'.
No. 124 - see 'Indiya'.
No. 153 - see 'Zarya Kommuniszma'.
No. 176 - see 'Sorok Let Komsomola'.
No. 201/103 - see 'Leonid Leonov'.
No. 202 - see 'Priznanie'.
No. 205 - see 'Druzhba Narodov'.
No. 208 - not named; ? ?
No. 210 - see 'M. I. Kalinin'.
No. 212 - see 'I. V. Michurin'.
No. 230 - see 'Mechta'.
No. 237 - see 'Krasavitsa Moskvy'.
No. 241 - see 'Golubaya'.
No. 247 - see 'Laureat'.
No. 267 - see 'Mariya Nagibina'.
No. 282 - see 'Marshall Vasilevskiĭ'.
No. 300 - see 'Sovietskaya Arktika'.
No. 302 - see 'Nikolaĭ Ostrovskiĭ'.
No. 321 - see 'Pioner'.
No. 328 - see Kolesnikov Seedling No 328.
No. 335 - see 'Krasnaya Moskva'.
No. 384 - see 'Pamyat' o S. M. Kirove'.
No. 388 - see 'P. P. Konchalovskiĭ'.
No. 394 - see 'Izobilie'.
No. 427 - see 'Obmanshchitsa'.

No. 443 - see 'Alekeĭ Mares'ev'.
No. 462 - see 'Rog Izobiliya' (cultivar name not established).
No. 501 - see 'Galina Ulanova'.
No. 508 - see 'Nebo Moskvy'.
No. 520 - see 'Marshal Zhukov'.
No. 525 - see 'Ogni Moskvy'.
No. 724 - see 'Dzhavakharlal Neru'.
No. 728 - see 'Nadezhda'.
No. 739 - see 'Kremlëvskie Kuranty'.
No. 745 - see 'Radzh Kapur'.

Kolkhoznica - see 'Kolkhoznitsa'.

'Kolkhoznitsa', S. vulgaris
  'Колхозница'
  Kolesnikov 1932; D VI
  syn. - 'Kolkhoznica'
  Rubtzov et al. 1980. Vidy i sorta sireni, kul'tiviruemye v SSSR. Kiev; Naukova Dumka. – in Russian; Holetich, C.D. 1982. Lilac species and cultivars in cultivation in USSR. Lilacs 11(2):1-38. - translation of Rubtzov et al. 1982.
  Named for the Russian collective farmers.
  Cultivar name established and accepted.

Komarof lilac - see *S. komarowii* subsp. *komarowii* C.K. Schneider.

'Kompliments', S. vulgaris
  Kārkliņš pre-2005; D V
  Strautiņa & Kaufmane, Dobeles ceriņi, p. 92 [2011]
  Name: Latvian for compliment.
  Cultivar name established and accepted.

'Komsomolka', S. vulgaris
  'Комсомолка'
  Kolesnikov 1950; D IV
  syn. - 'Comsomolka'
  Bilov et al., Siren', 49 [1974] - in Russian; Rubtzov et al. 1980. Vidy i sorta sireni, kul'tiviruemye v SSSR. Kiev; Naukova Dumka. – in Russian; Holetich, C.D. 1982. Lilac species and cultivars in cultivation in USSR. Lilacs 11(2):1-38. - translation of Rubtzov et al. 1982; Photo on Jorgovani/Lilacs 2015 DVD.
  Named for the female Young Communist League Member.
  Cultivar name established and accepted.

'Komsomol'tsy Dvadtsatykh Godov', S. vulgaris
  'Комсомольцы Двадцатых Годов'
  Stashkevich pre-1990; S VI
  syn. - 'Komsomoletz 20 godov'
  Gromov, Lilacs 2(4):16 [1974]; Fiala, Lilacs, 215 & 261 [1988]; Photo on Jorgovani/Lilacs 2015 DVD.
  Named for the Young Communist League Members of the Twenties.
  Cultivar name established and accepted.

Konchaloskii - see 'P. P. Konchalovskiĭ'
  Peterson, Lilacs - Proceedings 16(1):20 [1987] - name only, misspelling.

'Konfetti', S. vulgaris
  'Конфетти'
  Kravchenko 1970; D IV-VI
  {'Congo' × 'Belle de Nancy'}
  Kravchenko L. Culture of lilacs in Uzbekistan. Publishing house "Uzbekistan", Tashkent, 1970 p. 12.
  Rubtzov et al. 1980. Vidy i sorta sireni, kul'tiviruemye v SSSR. Kiev; Naukova Dumka. – in Russian; Holetich, C.D. 1982. Lilac species and cultivars in cultivation in USSR. Lilacs 11(2):1-38. - translation of Rubtzov et al. 1982.
  Cultivar name established and accepted.

Kongo - see **'Congo'**.

'Königin Luise', S. vulgaris
  Pfitzer 1921; S I
  syn. - 'Koenigin Luise', 'Konigin Luise'
  Pfitzer, Cat. [1921]; McKelvey, The Lilac, 318-319 [1928]; Wister, Lilacs for America, 51 [1942], 33 [1953]; Photo on Jorgovani/Lilacs 2015 DVD.
  Named for Princess Luise Augusta Wilhelmina Amelia von Mecklenburg-Strelitz, 1776-1810, wife to King Friedrich Wilhelm III of Prussia.
  Cultivar name presumed registered 1953; name established and accepted.

'Koningsloo', S. vulgaris
  Draps 1938; S II
  Wister, Lilacs for America, 33 [1953]
  Named for the municipality of Koningsloo, Belgium.
  Cultivar name presumed registered 1953; name established and accepted.

'Konstantin Zaslonov', S. vulgaris
  'Константин Заслонов'
  Smol'skiĭ & Bibikova 1964; S V
  {'Hyazinthenflieder' × 'Réaumur'}
  Rubtzov et al. 1980. Vidy i sorta sireni, kul'tiviruemye v SSSR. Kiev; Naukova Dumka. – in Russian; Holetich, C.D. 1982. Lilac species and cultivars in cultivation in USSR. Lilacs 11(2):1-38. - translation of Rubtzov et al. 1982; Semenov, Igor, Lilacs - Quart. Jour. 43(3):85-87 & photo89 [2014]; Photo on Jorgovani/Lilacs 2015 DVD.
  Named for Konstantin Sergeevich Zaslonov, 1909-1942, a leader of partisan movement in Belorussia; (partisan pseudonym Diadia Kostia; born Dec. 25, 1909 [Jan. 7, 1910]); Hero of the Soviet Union.
  Cultivar name established and accepted.

'Konstanty Karpow', S. vulgaris
  Karpow-Lipski 1953; S V
  syn. - Siewka nr 95
  Karpow-Lipski, Arboretum Kórnickie 3:102 [1958]; Wister & Oppe, Arnoldia 31(3):126 [1971] - erroneously as D V; Fiala, Lilacs, 101, 214 [1988] - as D; Vrugtman, HortScience 24(3):435-436 [1989]
  Named for the father (or grandfather?) of the originator.
  Cultivar name registered 1970; name established and accepted.

Korea, *S.* (species affiliation not known)
    origin not known pre-1973; ? ?
    reported in cultivation at Morden Research Centre
    Cultivar name not established.

Kórnik 1 to 13, *S. vulgaris*
    Yet unnamed selections made prior to 2008 by
    Władysław Bugała of seedlings of 'Maréchal Foch' at the
    Kórnik Arboretum, Poland.
    Konopinska, Lilacs 37(3):94-95 [2008]; Chapman, Lilacs
    37(4):110 [2008].
    Breeder's codes, not cultivar names.

Kórnik 2, *S. vulgaris*
    Bugala pre-2008; S V
    Photo seen on 2020 ILS Photo Database.
    Breeder's code, not a cultivar name.

Kórnik 3, *S. vulgaris*
    Bugala pre-2008; S V
    Photo seen on 2020 ILS Photo Database.
    Breeder's code, not a cultivar name.

Kórnik 4, *S. vulgaris*
    Bugala pre-2008; S VII
    Photo seen on 2020 ILS Photo Database.
    Breeder's code, not a cultivar name.

Kórnik 6, *S. vulgaris*
    Bugala pre-2008; S V
    Photo seen on 2020 ILS Photo Database.
    Breeder's code, not a cultivar name.

Kórnik 7, *S. vulgaris*
    Bugala pre-2008; S V
    Photo seen on 2020 ILS Photo Database.
    Breeder's code, not a cultivar name.

Kórnik 8, *S. vulgaris*
    Bugala pre-2008; S VII
    Photo seen on 2020 ILS Photo Database.
    Breeder's code, not a cultivar name.

Kórnik 9, *S. vulgaris*
    Bugala pre-2008; S V
    Photo seen on 2020 ILS Photo Database.
    Breeder's code, not a cultivar name.

Kórnik 10, *S. vulgaris*
    Bugala pre-2008; S VII
    Photo by Vasily Gorb taken at Kornik Arboretum seen
    6/19 on ILS 2020 Photo Database.
    Breeder's code, not a cultivar name.

Kórnik 11, *S. vulgaris*
    Bugala pre-2008; S V
    Photo seen on 2020 ILS Photo Database.
    Breeder's code, not a cultivar name.

Kórnik 12, *S. vulgaris*
    Bugala pre-2008; S V
    Photo seen on 2020 ILS Photo Database.
    Breeder's code, not a cultivar name.

'Kosmonavt', *S. vulgaris*
    'Космонавт'
    Vekhov 1952; D V-II
    Rubtzov et al. 1980. Vidy i sorta sireni, kul'tiviruemye
    v SSSR. Kiev; Naukova Dumka. – in Russian; Holetich,
    C.D. 1982. Lilac species and cultivars in cultivation in
    USSR. Lilacs 11(2):1-38. - translation of Rubtzov et al.
    1982; Photo on Jorgovani/Lilacs 2015 DVD.
    Name: Russian for cosmonaut.
    Cultivar name not established; may not have been
    introduced.

'Kosmos', *S. vulgaris*
    'Космос'
    Shtan'ko & Mikhaïlov 1956; S II
    syn. - 'Kosmo', 'Kosmas'
    {'Mrs Edward Harding' × ?}
    Bilov et al., Siren', 50 [1974] - in Russian; Rubtzov et al.
    1980. Vidy i sorta sireni, kul'tiviruemye v SSSR. Kiev;
    Naukova Dumka. – in Russian; Holetich, C.D. 1982.
    Lilac species and cultivars in cultivation in USSR. Lilacs
    11(2):1-38. - translation of Rubtzov et al. 1982; Photo on
    Jorgovani/Lilacs 2015 DVD.
    Name: Russian for space; it characterizes the color of this
    cultivar.
    Cultivar name established and accepted.

'Kōun', *S.* (Pubescentes Series)
    '香雲'
    Ihara 2012; S VII
    syn. - seedling no. 2011S1128004#8.
    {*S.* 'MORjos 060F' × *S.* 'MORjos 060F'}
    (Vrugtman, Cultivated Plant Diversity ... 2017)
    Named for the smoke of incense that rises and looks like
    a cloud.
    Cultivar name registered 2017; name established and
    accepted.

'Kraft', *S. vulgaris*
    'Крафт'
    Origin not known; S VII
    Tereshchenko, Lilacs in the South-East of Ukraine, p. 75
    [2003];
    Cultivar name established and accepted.

'Krasavitsa Bashkirii', *S. vulgaris*
    'Красавица Башкирий'
    Sakharova 1973; D IV-V
    syn. - Sakharova No. 2549
    {'Mme Lemoine' × 'Ruhm von Horstenstein'}
    Sakharova, Introduktsiya i selektsiya dekorativnykh
    rastenii v Bashkirii, 32-33 [1978] - in Russian; Photo on
    Jorgovani/Lilacs 2015 DVD.
    Name: Russian for "beauty of Bashkiria".
    Cultivar name established and accepted.

'**Krasavitsa Moskvy**', *S. vulgaris*
  'Красавица Москвы'
  Kolesnikov 1947; D I
  syn. - 'Krasavica Moskvy', 'Krasavita Moskvy', 'Krasavitsa Moskvi', 'Krasavitsa Muskovy', 'Krasavitza Moskvy', Kolesnikov No. 237, Moskvas pärla, Schöne Von Moskau, Moskavy (trade designation used for cut flowers of this cultivar); trade designations: Beauty Of Moscow, Belle De Moscou, Mädchen Aus Moskau, and in Germany as Schöne Von Moskau™ (#305349864; G. & J. Rosskamp)
  {'Belle de Nancy' × 'I. V. Michurin'}
  Howard, Arnoldia 19(6-7):31-35 [1959]; Gromov, A., Siren', 72-73 [1963]; Howard & Brizicky, AABGA Quart. Newsl. No. 64, 17-21 [1965]; Wister & Oppe, Arnoldia 31(3):125 [1971] - misspelled 'Krasavita Moskvy'; Gromov, Lilacs - Proceedings 2(4):18 [1974]; Rubtzov et al. 1980. Vidy i sorta sireni, kul'tiviruemye v SSSR. Kiev; Naukova Dumka. – in Russian; Holetich, C.D. 1982. Lilac species and cultivars in cultivation in USSR. Lilacs 11(2):1-38. - translation of Rubtzov et al. 1982; Lilacs - Proceedings 17(1): back cover ill. [1988]; Vrugtman, HortScience 31(3):328 [1996]; Photo on Jorgovani/Lilacs 2015 DVD.
  Name: Russian for beauty of Moscow.
  Cultivar name registered 1970; name established and accepted.
  Forcing lilacs in the Netherlands.

'**Krasavitsa Peterburga**', *S. vulgaris*
  'Красавица Петербурга'
  Reinvald 2018; D VII/IV
  {bud mutation of 'Krasavitsa Moskvy'}—discovered in 2003
  Name: Russian for Beauty of Petersburg.
  Information in email from Tatyana Polyakova to Mark DeBard December 2019.
  Cultivar name not yet established, but descriptive article submitted for publication.

'**Krasnaya Moskva**', *S. vulgaris*
  'Красная Москва'
  Kolesnikov 1952; S VII
  syn. - Kolesnikov No. 335, 'Krasnaja Moskva', prob. also 'Krasnaya'
  marketed in the USA as Pride Of Moscow
  {('Pasteur' × 'Congo') × 'Kolesnikov No. 110'}
  Gromov, Lilacs - Proceedings 2(4):17 [1974]; Rubtzov et al. 1980. Vidy i sorta sireni, kul'tiviruemye v SSSR. Kiev; Naukova Dumka. – in Russian; Holetich, C.D. 1982. Lilac species and cultivars in cultivation in USSR. Lilacs 11(2):1-38. - translation of Rubtzov et al. 1982.
  Name: Russian for red Moscow.
  Cultivar name established and accepted.

'**Krasotka**', *S. villosa* subsp. *wolfii*
  'Красотка'
  Pshennikova 2006; S IV & I
  Registered with the State Commission of the Russian Federation for Testing and Protection of Selection Achievements, No. 9358790, 2006; Certificate of authorship No. 45065. Pshennikova, L.M. 2007. Lilacs, cultivated in the Botanical Garden-Institute FEB RAS, p. 18; Photo on Jorgovani/Lilacs 2015 DVD.
  Name: Russian for beautiful girl.
  Cultivar name established and accepted.

'**Krasunya Kyeva**', *S. vulgaris*
  'Красуня Києва'
  Heide & Gorb 1988; S V
  Syn. – 'Krasavitsa Kyeva'
  Email from V. Gorb 10-30-19 to Mark DeBard; Photo by Ole Heide from Denmark seen in ILS 2020 Photo DVD.
  Name: Ukrainian for "Beauty of Kyiv"
  Cultivar name not established.

'**Kremlëvskie Kuranty**', *S. vulgaris*
  'Кремлёвские Куранты'
  Kolesnikov 1960; S IV
  syn. - Kolesnikov No. 739
  {'Congo' × ('Monge' × Kolesnikov No. 105)}
  Gromov, Lilacs - Proceedings 2(4):17 [1974]; Rubtzov et al. 1980. Vidy i sorta sireni, kul'tiviruemye v SSSR. Kiev; Naukova Dumka. – in Russian; Holetich, C.D. 1982. Lilac species and cultivars in cultivation in USSR. Lilacs 11(2):1-38. - translation of Rubtzov et al. 1982; Photo on Jorgovani/Lilacs 2015 DVD.
  Named for the Kremlin Chimes.
  Award of Garden Merit RHS 2012.
  Cultivar name established and accepted.

Kreuteriana - see '**Mme Kreuter**'.

'**Kristīne Baltpurviņa**', *S. vulgaris*
  Upītis 1970; S I
  syn. - 'Kristiine Baltpurvinja', 'Upiisha Velte', Upītis No. 64-4
  Kalva, V., Ceriņi (Lilac), 165-166 [1980] - in Latvian; Kalniņš, Ceriņu jaunšķirnes Dobelē, Dārs un drava 1986 (12):13-15 - in Latvian; Strautiņa, S. 2002. Ceriņu un jasmīnu avīze. LA, R., p. 62; in litt. S. Strautiņa to F. Vrugtman [22 Jan. 2008] - synonym 'Upiisha Velte'
  Named for Kristīne Baltpurviņa, Latvian author, the great love of the originator.
  Cultivar name established and accepted.

'**Kristjan**', *S. vulgaris*
  Vaigla pre-2001; S II-III
  listed on /www.ak.rapina.ee/?cab=58&tekst=10035 [seen 2 Dec. 2007]; I. Semenov, Lilacs 48(2):65 [2019].
  Cultivar name not established.

'**Kristjan Paluteder**', *S. vulgaris*
  Mägi pre-2017; S VII
  Photo from Estonia by Mägi, seen in 2020 ILS Photo Database.
  Cultivar name not established.

'**Kruzhevnitsa**', *S. vulgaris*
  'Кружевница'
  Luchnik pre-1994; D IV/V

Pikaleva, Lilacs - Quart. Jour. 23(4):85 [1994]; in litt. Demidov to Vrugtman [Jan.5/01] - as double lilac-pink and originated by Luchnik; Photo on Jorgovani/Lilacs 2015 DVD.
Name: Russian for lace maker.
Cultivar name established and accepted.

'Kryl'ya Nadezhdy', S, vulgaris
'Крылья Надежды'
Aladin, S., Aladina, O., Polyakova, T., and Aladina, A. 2018; S IV-III
{'Nadezhda' x OP}
Международная и практическая конференция (International scientific and practical conference) "International Syringa 2018", Moscow, Moscow State University Botanical Garden, St. Petersburg, Botanical Garden of Peter the Great BIN RAS, Pavlovsk, May 21-27, 2018; in oral presentation only; IX International Scientific Conference (IX Международная научная конференция "Цветоводство: история, теория, практика") " Floriculture: history, theory, practice" , St. Petersburg, Botanical Garden of Peter the Great BIN RAS, September 7-13, 2019 (in Russian).
Name: Russian for Wings of hope.
Cultivar name established and accepted.

'Krymskaya Krasavitsa', S. vulgaris
'Крымская Красавица'
Klimenko, V. 1955; S III-IV
syn. - 'Krymskaja Krasavica'
Rubtzov et al. 1980. Vidy i sorta sireni, kul'tiviruemye v SSSR. Kiev; Naukova Dumka. – in Russian; Holetich, C.D. 1982. Lilac species and cultivars in cultivation in USSR. Lilacs 11(2):1-38. - translation of Rubtzov et al. 1982.
Name: Russian for Crimean beauty.
Cultivar name established and accepted.

'Krymskaya Lazur'', S. vulgaris
"Крымская Лазурь'
Klimenko, V.& Z. & Grigor'ev 1955; S II-III
syn. - 'Krymskaja Lazur'
Rubtzov et al. 1980. Vidy i sorta sireni, kul'tiviruemye v SSSR. Kiev; Naukova Dumka. – in Russian; Holetich, C.D. 1982. Lilac species and cultivars in cultivation in USSR. Lilacs 11(2):1-38. - translation of Rubtzov et al. 1982.
Name: Russian for Crimean azure.
Cultivar name established and accepted.

'Ks. Bonifacy Jundziłł', S. vulgaris
Karpow-Lipski; S IV
syn. - Siewka nr 161
Karpow-Lipski, Arboretum Kórnickie, 3:104 [1958]
Named for Father Bonifacy Jundziłł, 1761-1847, Polish priest and botanist at the University of Wilno (now Vilnius, Lithuania).
Cultivar name established and accepted.

'Kum-Bum', S. (Villosae Group)
Fiala 1969; S II *
syn. - 'Aurea Tomentella', 'Kum Bum', tomentella aurea ; there is a variant in the trade with white florets that is not true to the original name.
marketed in Australia as Phillip Adams since Kum-Bum appears to be not an acceptable name in Australia
{S. tomentella subsp. tomentella ×?}
Wister & Oppe, Arnoldia 31(3):122 [1971] - name only; Fiala, Lilacs 76, 109, 224, Pl.2 [1988] - as chemically induced tetraploid; Vrugtman, HortScience 24(3):436 [1989]; Photo on Jorgovani/Lilacs 2015 DVD.
Named for the Kum-Bum Monastery, the largest and most important monastic college in Eastern Tibet.
Cultivar name registered 1970; name established and accepted.

'Kumpu', S. pubescens subsp. pubescens
'薫風'
Ihara 2004; S VII
syn. - seedling no. 20040520001#14.
{S. pubescens subsp. pubescens 'Palibin' × S. pubescens subsp. pubescens 'Palibin'}
(Vrugtman, Cultivated Plant Diversity ... 2017)
Name: Japanese for balmy breeze.
Cultivar name registered 2017; name established and accepted.

'Kurbads', S. vulgaris
Kārkliņš 2003; D III/II
Strautiņa & Kaufmane, Dobeles ceriņi, pp. 14, 92 [2011]; Photo on Jorgovani/Lilacs 2015 DVD.
Kurbads is the name of a legendary hero from Latvian fairytales; born magically from a white mare, he grew up very fast and was unimaginably strong.
Cultivar name established and accepted.

'Kurchavaya', S. vulgaris
'Курчавая'
Kravchenko 1970; D II
{'Congo' × 'Belle de Nancy'}
Kravchenko L. Culture of lilacs in Uzbekistan. Publishing house "Uzbekistan", Tashkent, 1970 p. 11-12.
Name: Russian for curly.
Cultivar name established and accepted.

'Kurskaya Duga', S. vulgaris
'Курская Дуга'
Aladin, S., Aladina, O., Polyakova, T., and, Aladina, A. 2018; S VII/ II
{elite form 8-236*× OP}
(*elite form 8-236 was obtained from open pollination of the cultivar 'Monge')
IX International Scientific Conference (IX Международная научная конференция "Цветоводство: история, теория, практика") " Floriculture: history, theory, practice" , St. Petersburg, Botanical Garden of Peter the Great BIN RAS, September 7-13, 2019 (in Russian); IInd All-Russian

scientific-practical conference with international participation (II Всероссийская научно-практическая конференция с международным участием) " Botanical Gardens in the XXI Century: Biodiversity Conservation, Development Strategy and Innovative Solutions Belgorod, Botanical Garden of NRU "BelSU", September 23-26, 2019; pp.141-145 (in Russian).
Named for one of the key battles of World War II. The Kursk Bulge (Курская дуга) became the site of fierce battles between the Soviet army and the German Wehrmacht during the Battle of Kursk (July 5 - August 23, 1943).
Cultivar name established and accepted.

'K'yanti', *S. vulgaris*
　'Кьянти'
　Aladin, S., Aladina, O., Polyakova, T., and Aladina, A. 2017; S VI
　{' Monge' × OP}
　(Международная научная конференция "Syringa L.: коллекции, выращивание, использование") "International Scientific Conference "Syringa L.: collections, cultivation, using" / Collection of Scientific Articles of Botanical Institute named after V.L. Komarov, Botanical Garden of Peter the Great BIN RAS. - St. Petersburg. -2020.- pp.3-7 (in Russian); Photo exhibition of all varieties of the creative breeding group "Russian Lilac" at the Festival "Lilac February", St. Petersburg, Botanical Garden of Peter the Great BIN RAS, February 22-24, 2020.
　Russian name for Chianti. This cultivar resembles a bright ruby colored, noble wine from Tuscany, the pride of Italian winemakers.
　Cultivar name established and accepted.

K17 (*S. vulgaris*)
　Origin not known; S V
　Hauta-aho, Lilacs - Quart. Jour. 35(4):119 [2006] - unidentified old selection growing in the Helsinki region, Finland.
　Cognomen, not a cultivar name.

'La Cañada', *S.* ×*hyacinthiflora*
　Sobeck; S V
　syn. - 'La Canada'
　Wister, Arnoldia 26(3):13 [1966] as 'La Canada'.
　Named for the town of La Cañada (now City of La Cañada-Flintridge), California, USA.
　Cultivar name registered 1966; name established and accepted.
　Nota bene: Since this cultivar appears to be of 'Lavender Lady' ancestry see also: Pringle, Lilacs - Quart. Jour. 24(4):97-99 [1995]; and Vrugtman, HortScience 31(3):328 [1996].

'Lacera', *S. oblata* subsp. *dilatata*
　Zhuo Lihuan; S VII
　Zhuo, L.H., Bull. Bot. Research (Harbin) 9(4):131-134, pl.: f. 3-4 [1989] - in Chinese, Latin description.
　Cultivar name not established; rejected epithet (Latin form).

Laciniata - see *S.* ×*laciniata* Mill.

'Ladoga', *S. vulgaris*
　'Ладога'
　Aladin, S., Aladina, O., and Polyakova, T. 2015; S IV-III
　{'Flora 1953' × OP}
　Питомник-частный сад (Pitomnik i chastnyi sad; Nursery and private garden) 3/2015:14-22 (in Russian); Приусадебное хозяйство (Annex to the magazine Homestead farming: "Flowers in the garden and at home. Brushes and paints") 08/2015: 5-14; Садовник (Gardener) magazine, 05 (141)/2017 :16-22; Вестник АППМ (Catalog in Vestnik APPM (Planting material association) magazine) 1/2018: 59-72 (in Russian).
　Named for Lake Ladoga in northwestern Russia, part of the Volga-Baltic Waterway, connecting the Volga River with the Baltic Sea. See also 'Doroga Zhizni'.
　Cultivar name established and accepted.

'Lady Lindsay', *S. vulgaris*
　Havemeyer pre-1942; S VI
　Wister, Lilacs for America, 51 [1942], 33 [1953]; Lilac Land, Cat., [1954]; Eickhorst, ILS Lilac Newsletter 4(1):4-5 [1978]; Anon., ILS Lilac Newsletter 11(1):6-8 [1985]; Photo on Jorgovani/Lilacs 2015 DVD.
　Cultivar name presumed registered 1953; name established and accepted.

'Lady Lucille', *S. vulgaris*
　Klager; S V
　Anon., ILS Newsletter 14(4):3-4 [1988]; Macore Co. Inc. photo library [Nov.28, 1999] http://www.macore.com/photolib.htm; Anon., Lilacs - Quart. Jour. 33(1):11 [2004]; Photo on Jorgovani/Lilacs 2015 DVD.
　Cultivar name not established.

'Lady Stanley', *S. vulgaris*
　origin not known pre-1969; ? ?
　in litt. - name only
　Cultivar name not established.

'Lady Uarda', *S. vulgaris*
　Larsen; S VI
　syn. - 'Lady Urada'
　{parentage not known}
　Anon., American Nurseryman 145(10):103 [1977] - as 'Lady Urada'; Vrugtman, AABGA Bull. 18(3):87 [1984]; Vrugtman, Lilac Newsletter 11(5):10 [1985]
　United States Plant Patent No. 4,009 [Jan. 11, 1977].
　Cultivar name registered 1983; name established and accepted.

'La France', *S. vulgaris*
　Klettenberg 1935; S V
　Klettenberg, Cat., 25 [1935]; Wister, Lilacs for America, 33 [1953]
　Cultivar name presumed registered 1953; name established and accepted.

'Laine', *S.* ×*hyacinthiflora*
Vaigla 1985; S V (IV-V per Semenov)
{'Esther Staley' × ? }
Kivistik, Maakodu 1997(5):22-23 [1997] - in Estonian; I. Semenov, Lilacs 48(2):65,58 (photo) [2019].
Cultivar name established and accepted.

'Lake Bled', *S. vulgaris*
Lumley; S VI
syn. - 'Marley' (not 'Marleyensis')
{from native collected seed; Lake Bled Mountain, Slovenia}
Lumley, Lilac Land list [n.d., pre-1974] - as 'Marly'; Vrugtman, AABGA Bull. 13(4):109 [1979]
Named for Lake Bled Mountain, Slovenia.
Cultivar name registered 1978; name established and accepted.

'Lalique', *S. vulgaris*
Fiala 1983; S III
{'True Blue' × 'Rochester'}
Fiala, Lilacs, 223 [1988].
Cultivar name established and accepted.

'La Lorraine', *S.* ×*chinensis*
Lemoine 1899; S VI
syn. - varina 'La Lorraine'
Lemoine Cat. No. 143, 10 [1899]; McKelvey, The Lilac, 425 [1928]; Wister, Lilacs for America, 51 [1942], 33 [1953]
Named for the former province of northeastern France.
Cultivar name presumed registered 1953; name established and accepted.

'Lamarck', *S. vulgaris*
Lemoine 1886; D III
syn. - 'La March', 'La Marck', 'Le Marke'
Lemoine, Cat. No. 104, 16 [1886]; McKelvey, The Lilac, 319 [1928]; Wister, Lilacs for America, 51 [1942], 33 [1953]; Photo on Jorgovani/Lilacs 2015 DVD.
Named for Jean Baptiste Pierre Antoine de Monet, Chevalier de Lamarck, 1744-1829, French naturalist and pre-Darwinian evolutionist.
Cultivar name presumed registered 1953; name established and accepted.

'Lamartine', *S.* ×*hyacinthiflora*
Lemoine 1911; S V
{*S. vulgaris* × *S. oblata* Giraldii; see Lemoine Cat. no. 179}
syn. - 'Lambert', *praecox* 'Lamartine'
Lemoine, Cat. No. 179, 6 [1911] - as "Lilas hybrides de *Syringa vulgaris* et de *S.Giraldii*"; McKelvey, The Lilac, 198 [1928]; Späth, Späth Buch, 302 [1930]; Wister, Lilacs for America, 51 [1942], 33 [1953]; Photo on Jorgovani/Lilacs 2015 DVD.
Named for Alphonse Marie Louis de Lamartine, 1790-1869, French poet, statesman and historian.
Awards: RHS Award of Merit 1927.
Cultivar name presumed registered 1953; name established and accepted.
Nota bene: Harold N. Moldenke proposed the nothospecies *S.* ×*lamartina* for the progeny of *S. vulgaris* × *S. oblata* var. *giraldii*; however, *S.* ×*hyacinthiflora* applies to all progeny of *S. vulgaris* × *S. oblata*. (Moldenke; Phytologia 5:341 [1956]).

'La Mauve', *S. vulgaris*
Lemoine 1893; D V
Lemoine, Cat. No. 125, 16 [1893]; McKelvey, The Lilac, 319 [1928]; Wister, Lilacs for America, 51 [1942], 33 [1953]; Photo on Jorgovani/Lilacs 2015 DVD.
Named for the Mauve Decade (1890's), the decade which took its color from the widespread and enthusiastic application during that time of (later Sir) William Perkin's Mauveine, the first of the aniline dyes which have made microscopy what it is today.
Cultivar name presumed registered 1953; name established and accepted.

Lambert - see **'Lamartine'**.

'Lambertine', *S. vulgaris*
Klager; S VII
Anon., ILS Newsletter 14(4):304 [1988]
Cultivar name not established.

'Lambouline' or 'Lambanline', *S. vulgaris*
origin not known pre-1926; S VI
Stand. Pl. Names, 616 [1942] - as Lambouline, doubtful name; Wister, Lilacs for America, 37 & 51 [1942] - doubtful name
Cultivar name not established, not reported in cultivation in 1953.

'Languis', *S. vulgaris*
origin not known pre-1872; S V
syn. - 'Langius', 'Longuis'
Dauvesse, Cat. No. 36, 47 [1872] - name only; Klettenberg, Cat. [1923] - as 'Langius', fleur simple, pâle; McKelvey, The Lilac, 319-320, 563 [1928] - descriptions vary (S and D), origin uncertain; Wister, Lilacs for America, 51 [1942] - as S III; Wister, Lilacs for America, 33 [1953] - as S V; Photo on Jorgovani/Lilacs 2015 DVD.
Cultivar name presumed registered 1953; name established and accepted.

'Lan Meng', *S.* ×*hyacinthiflora*
Zang Shuying 1962; D III
{*S. oblata* Lindl. × *S. vulgaris* L. 'Alba-plena'}
selection in cultivation at Beijing Botanical Garden in 2015; Photo on Jorgovani/Lilacs 2015 DVD.
Name: Chinese for blue dream.
Cultivar name established and accepted.

'Laplace', *S. vulgaris*
Lemoine 1913; S VII
syn. - 'La Place'
Lemoine, Cat. No. 185, 40 [1913]; McKelvey, The Lilac, 320 [1928]; Wister, Lilacs for America, 51 [1942], 33

[1953]; Photo on Jorgovani/Lilacs 2015 DVD.
Named for Pierre Simon, Marquis de Laplace, 1749-1827, French mathematician and astronomer.
Cultivar name presumed registered 1953; name established and accepted.

Large White - see 'Alba Major'.

'Larissa', S.
Mägi pre-2018; ? ?
Semenov, I., Lilacs 48(2):71 [2019].
Cultivar name not established.

'Lark Song', S. (Villosae Group)
Fiala 1968; S V
{(S. tomentella subsp. sweginzowii × S. tomentella subsp. tomentella) × S. komarowii subsp. komarowii}
Fiala, Lilacs, 102, 108, 124, 187, 224, Pl. 56 [1988] - as colchicine induced tetraploid,
information not consistent; Photo on Jorgovani/Lilacs 2015 DVD.
Cultivar name established and accepted.

'Late Bloomer', S. vulgaris
origin not known ? ?
perhaps identical to 'Klager Late Bloomer'
B. O. Case and Son, Cat. [ca 1937] in Upton Scrapbook 1:35 [1980]

late lilac - see S. villosa subsp. villosa Vahl.

'La Tour d'Auvergne', S. vulgaris
Lemoine 1888; D VI
syn. - 'Tour d'Avergne'
Lemoine, Cat. No. 110, 10 [1888]; McKelvey, The Lilac, 320 [1928]; Wister, Lilacs for America, 51 [1942], 33 [1953]; Photo on Jorgovani/Lilacs 2015 DVD.
Named for Théophile Malo Corret de la Tour d'Auvergne, 1743-1800, French soldier, known as "The First Grenadier of France".
Cultivar name presumed registered 1953; name established and accepted.

'Lauma', S. vulgaris
Kārkliņš 2003; ? VII
Photo on Jorgovani/Lilacs 2015 DVD.
Name: A woman's name.
Cultivar name not established.

'Laura', S. vulgaris
Orchard, between 1912 & 1940s, ? ?
Named for the daughter of the originator.
No report of being in cultivation
http://www.mhs.mb.ca/docs/people/orchard_h.shtml
http://www.manitobaaghalloffame.com/ahofmember/orchard-harold/

'Laura', S.
Mägi pre-2019; S V
Photo seen in 2020 ILS Photo & Color Database
Cultivar name not established.

'Laura Cox', S. vulgaris
Pfitzer, W. 1907; S IV
{parentage not known}
Pfitzer, Hauptkatalog [1907]; McKelvey, The Lilac, 320-321 [1928]; Wister, Lilacs for America, 51 [1942], 33 [1953]
Cultivar name presumed registered 1953; name established and accepted.

'Laura L. Barnes', S. vulgaris
Barnes, L.L.; D III
Wister, Lilacs for America, 51 [1942], 33 [1953]; Photo on Jorgovani/Lilacs 2015 DVD.
Named for Laura Leggett Barnes (Mrs Albert C.), 1873-1966, American horticulturist.
Cultivar name presumed registered 1953; name established and accepted.

'Laureat', S. vulgaris
'Лауреат'
Kolesnikov 1953; D III
Syn. - Sdl No 247, was named in honor of the receipt of the Stalin Prize by Kolesnikov in 1952.
Polyakova, 2018, "Master of the Lilac Inflorescence", p. 112; cultivar passport
Name: Russian for laureate
Cultivar name established and accepted.

'Laurentian', S. ×hyacinthiflora
Skinner 1945; S III
Woody Plant Register, AAN, No. 59 [1949]; Wister, Lilacs for America, 33 [1953]; Skinner, Hort. Horizons, 109 [1966]; Photo on Jorgovani/Lilacs 2015 DVD.
Named for the Laurentian Plateau, also known as the Canadian Shield or the Precambrian Shield.
Cultivar name presumed registered 1953; name established and accepted.

'Lauri', S. vulgaris
Mägi pre-2017 ; S VII
Photo from Estonia by Mägi, seen in 2020 ILS Photo Database.
Cultivar name not established.

'Lavaliensis', S. vulgaris
origin not known pre-1865; S V
syn. - 'de Laurel', 'Laval', lavaliensis
McKelvey, The Lilac, 321 [1928]; Wister, Lilacs for America, 51 [1942], 33 [1953]; Photo on Jorgovani/Lilacs 2015 DVD.
Named for the city of Laval, Mayenne, France.
Cultivar name presumed registered 1953; name established and accepted.
Forcing cultivar in the Netherlands.

'Lavandovii', S. vulgaris
'Лавандовый'
Dyagilev 1993, S IV
Pikaleva, Lilacs - Quart. Jour. 23(4):85 [1994]
Name: Russian for lavender color
Cultivar name not established.

Lavanensis - see **'De Louvain'**.

'LaVee', *S. vulgaris*
Klager; S VII
syn. - 'Lavee'
Anon., ILS Newsletter 14(4):3-4 [1988]
Cultivar name not established.

'Lavender Lace', *S. vulgaris*
origin not known ? ?
Anon., Lilacs - Proceedings 13(1):22 [1984] - name only
Cultivar name not established.

'Lavender Lady', *S.* ×*hyacinthiflora*
Lammerts 1953; S VII
syn. - 'Monis'
Lammerts, US Plant Patent No. 1,238 [Jan. 5, 1954] - parentage information incomplete; Wister, Arnoldia 23(4):81 [1963] - as *S. vulgaris* L. × *S. laciniata* Mill.; Monrovia Nur., Cat., 81, 83 [1968] - as *S. vulgaris*; Monrovia Nur., Cat., 107 [1988] - erroneously as Lavender Lady™ 'Monis'; Pringle, Lilacs - Quart. Jour. 24(4):97-99 [1995] - as *S.* ×*hyacinthiflora*; Vrugtman, HortScience 31(3):328 [1996] - registration correction to *S.* ×*hyacinthiflora*; Photo on Jorgovani/Lilacs 2015 DVD.
Cultivar name registered 1963; name established and accepted.

'Lavender Lassie', *S.* ×*hyacinthiflora*
Morey 1967; S VII
{'Lavender Lady' × ? }
Wister, Lilac Registrations (mimeogr. list), 5 [n.d.; ca 1967].
Cultivar name registered 1967; name established and accepted.
Nota bene: Since this cultivar appears to be of 'Lavender Lady' ancestry; see also: Pringle, Lilacs - Quart. Jour. 24(4):97-99 [1995]; and Vrugtman, HortScience 31(3):328 [1996].

'Lavender Pearl', *S. vulgaris*
Klager 1915; D IV
Wister, Lilacs for America, 51 [1942], 33 [1953]
Cultivar name presumed registered in 1953;
Cultivar not reported in cultivation.

La Vestale - see **'Vestale'**.

'La Vierge', *S. vulgaris*
Bertin pre-1890; S I
syn. - 'La Vièrge'
Carrière, Rev. Hort., 425 [1890]; du Parc, Tijdschr. Boomteelt., 314-317 [1901]; McKelvey, The Lilac, 321, 563 [1928].
Named for the Virgin Mary.
Cultivar name established and accepted.

'Lavinia', *S.* (Villosae Group), *S.* ×*prestoniae*
Preston 1928; S IV
{*S. villosa* subsp. *villosa* × *S. komarowii* subsp. *reflexa*}
syn. - Preston No. 20-14-26
Maccoun, Rep. Dom. Hort. 1928, 56 [1930] - name only; Wister, Lilacs for America, 51, 64 [1942]; 33, 48 [1953]; Photo on Jorgovani/Lilacs 2015 DVD.
Named for the Daughter to Titus in Shakespeare's *Titus Andronicus*.
Cultivar name presumed registered 1953; name established and accepted.

'Lavoisier', *S. vulgaris*
Lemoine 1913; S V
syn. - 'Voci', 'Volcie', 'La Voicie'
Lemoine, Cat. No. 185, 40 [1913]; McKelvey, The lilac, 321 [1928]; Wister, Lilacs for America, 51, 60 [1942], 33, 43 [1953]; Photo on Jorgovani/Lilacs 2015 DVD.
Named for Antoine Laurent Lavoisier, 1743-1794, French chemist, founder of modern chemistry.
Cultivar name presumed registered 1953; name established and accepted.

Lavrov - see 'S. V. Lavrov'.

'Lawrence Wheeler', *S. vulgaris*
Gardner 1968; S III
syn.: Gardner No. 509, 'S. L. Wheeler'
Fiala, Lilacs, 97 [1988]
Cultivar name established and accepted.

'Lebedushka', *S. vulgaris*
'Лебёдушка'
Smol'skiĭ & Bibikova 1964; S I
{'Mme Abel Chatenay' × 'Réaumur'}
syn. - 'Lebyoduschka'
Bilov et al., Siren', 51 [1974] - in Russian; Rubtzov et al. 1980. Vidy i sorta sireni, kul'tiviruemye v SSSR. Kiev; Naukova Dumka. – in Russian; Holetich, C.D. 1982. Lilac species and cultivars in cultivation in USSR. Lilacs 11(2):1-38. - translation of Rubtzov et al. 1982; Semenov, Igor, Lilacs -Quart. Jour. 43(3):85-87 & photo 88 [2014]; Photo on Jorgovani/Lilacs 2015 DVD.
Name: Russian for swan beauty or cygnet.
Cultivar name established and accepted.

Le Caulois - see **'Le Gaulois'**.

'LECburg', *S. vulgaris*
Daniels & Ludekens 1989; S VII
marketed in the USA as Burgundy Queen®
{presumably a mutation of 'Monge'}
L. E. Cooke Cat. 12 [1993] - as Burgundy Queen®; Rogers, Lilacs - Quart. Jour. 27(1):2 [1998] - erroneously as 'Burgundy Queen'; Photo on Jorgovani/Lilacs 2015 DVD.
Cultivar name established and accepted.

'Ledokhod', *S. vulgaris*
'Ледоход'
Aladin, S., Aladina, O., Polyakova, T., and Aladina A. 2015; S V-IV
{'Condorcet' × OP}
Statutory registration, Russia, State Register and Plant

Patent No. 80052/ 8058582 (2019)
Садовник (Gardener) magazine 04 (140)/2017
:18-25; Вестник АППМ (Catalog in Vestnik APPM
(Planting material association) magazine) 1/2018:
59-72 (in Russian); II All-Russian scientific-practical
conference with international participation (II
Всероссийская научно-практическая конференция с
международным участием) « Botanical Gardens in the
XXI Century: Biodiversity Conservation, Development
Strategy and Innovative Solutions Belgorod, Botanical
Garden of NRU «BelSU», September 23-26, 2019;
pp.141-145(in Russian)
Name: Russian for ice drift.
Cultivar name established and accepted.

'Lee Jewett Walker', *S. vulgaris*
Berdeen 1981; S V
{'Lucie Baltet' × 'Cora Lyden'}
syn. - 'Lee Jewett', 'Mrs Lee Jewett Walker', Berdeen No. 7-22
Vrugtman, AABGA Bull. 13(4):110 [1979] - erroneously as a double (D V); Fiala, Lilacs, 100, 107, Pl. 19 [1988]; Rogers, in litt. to Vrugtman [Jul.11/1995] - as S V; Vrugtman, Lilacs - Quart. Jour. 24(1):23 [1995]; King & Coggeshall, Lilacs - Quart. Jour. 27(2):49-50 [1998] - name only; Vrugtman, Lilacs - Quart. Jour. 32(4):149 [2003]; Peterson in litt. to Vrugtman, undated, postmark Nov. 13, 2003; Vrugtman, Lilacs - Quart. Jour. 33(1):20 [2004] - S V confirmed; Vrugtman, HortScience 39(6):1524 [2004]; Photo on Jorgovani/Lilacs 2015 DVD.
Named for a friend of the originator from Kennebunk, Maine.
Cultivar name registered 1978; name established and accepted.

'Leenu', *S. vulgaris*
Vaigla; D VII/V (VI-IV per Semenov)
{'Mrs Edward Harding' × ? }
syn. - 'Helen' (Vaigla, not Skinner)
Kivistik, Maakodu 1997(5):22-23 (ill.) [1997] - as 'Helen', in Estonian; I. Semenov, Lilacs 48(2):65 (inside front cover photo) [2019].
Cultivar name established and accepted.

'Legacy', *S. villosa* subsp. *villosa*
USDA-NRCS Bismarck 1999; S V
syn. - ND-83, USDA P.I. 540443
{plants under this name are grown from Breeder's Seed or Certified Seed}
Vrugtman, Lilacs-Quart. Jour. 36(2):75-77 [2007]; Photo on Jorgovani/Lilacs 2015 DVD.
Cultivar name established and accepted.

'Le Gaulois', *S. vulgaris*
Lemoine 1884; D IV
syn. - 'Le Caulois', 'Le Gautois'
Lemoine, Cat. No. 98, 12 [1884]; McKelvey, The Lilac, 321 [1928]; Wister, Lilacs for America, 48, 51 [1942], 33 [1953]
Name: French for the Gallic.
Cultivar name presumed registered 1953; name established and accepted.

'Leila Romer', *S. vulgaris*
Margaretten; S III
{'Mme Lemoine' × ? }
reported in cultivation at Royal Botanical Gardens, Ontario, Canada; Photo on Jorgovani/Lilacs 2015 DVD.
Cultivar name not established.

Le Marke - see **'Lamarck'**.

'Lemoinei', *S. vulgaris*
Lemoine 1878; D IV
syn. - flore duplo Lemoinei, flore pleno Lemoinei, S. Lemoinei, Lemoinei flore pleno
common name: Double Lemoine
Lemoine, Cat. No. 80, 8 [1878]; Stand. Pl. Names, 486 [1923] - as Double Lemoine; McKelvey, The Lilac, 321-322 [1928]; Wister, Lilacs for America, 51 [1942], 33 [1953]; Photo on Jorgovani/Lilacs 2015 DVD.
Awards: RHS First Class Certificate 1884.
Cultivar name presumed registered 1953; name established and accepted.

'Lemonade', *S. vulgaris*
origin not known pre-1997; ? ?
Van Vloten Nurs., cat. p.90 [1997] - name only; in litt., no longer in production (Casey van Vloten to Vrugtman, Sep.19/2000).
Cultivar name not established.

'Lena', *S. vulgaris*
origin not known ? ?
anon., Lilacs - Quart. Jour. 17(1):26 [1988] - name only
Cultivar name not established.

'Leningradskaya Simfoniya', *S. vulgaris*
'Ленинградская Симфония'
Aladin, S., Aladina, O.N., and Polyakova, T. 2015; S II
{'Mechta' × OP}
Питомник-частный сад (Pitomnik i chastnyi sad; Nursery and private garden) 3/2015:14-22 (in Russian); Приусадебное хозяйство (Annex to the magazine Homestead farming: "Flowers in the garden and at home. Brushes and paints") 08/2015: 5-14; Садовник (Gardener) magazine, 05 (141)/2017 :16-22; Вестник АППМ (Catalog in Vestnik APPM (Planting material association) magazine) 1/2018: 59-72 (in Russian).
Named for Symphony No. 7 Op. 60, "Leningrad", composed by Dimitri Shostakovich (Дмитрий Дмитриевич Шестакович) in 1942, in the days of the Leningrad blockade.
Cultivar name established and accepted.

'Le Nôtre', *S. vulgaris*
Lemoine 1922; D II
common name: Le Notre
Lemoine, Cat. No. 196, 18 [1922]; McKelvey, The Lilac,

322 [1928]; Stand. Pl. Names, 616 [1942] - as Le Notre; Wister, Lilacs for America, 51 [1942], 33 [1953]; Photo on Jorgovani/Lilacs 2015 DVD.
Named for André Le Nôtre, 1613-1700, French landscape architect and creator of French landscape-gardening.
Cultivar name presumed registered 1953; name established and accepted.

'Leona Valley', *S. vulgaris*
Margaretten; S III
{'Mme Lemoine' × ? }
Named for the town of Leona Valley, California, USA.
Cultivar name not established; not reported in cultivation.

'Leone Gardner', *S. vulgaris*
Gardner 1956; S VII
syn.: Gardner No. 451, 'Leone Hanratty'
Edw. J. Gardner Nursery, Price list, 6 [1956]; Wister & Oppe, Arnoldia 31(3):122 [1971] - name only; Photo on Jorgovani/Lilacs 2015 DVD.
Cultivar name registered 1970; name established and accepted.

'Léon Gambetta', *S. vulgaris*
Lemoine 1907; D IV
syn. - 'Leo Gambetta', 'Leon Gambetta'
Lemoine, Cat. No. 169, 8 [1907]; McKelvey, The Lilac, 323 [1928]; Wister, Lilacs for America, 51 [1942], 33 [1953] - as 'Leon Gambetta'; Lilacs - Quart. Jour. 21(3):front & back cover ill. [1992]; Photo on Jorgovani/Lilacs 2015 DVD.
Named for Léon Michel Gambetta, 1832-1882, French lawyer and statesman.
Cultivar name presumed registered 1953; name established and accepted.

'Leonid Kolesnikov', *S. vulgaris*
'Леонид Колесников'
Kolesnikov 1924; D II
Rubtzov et al. 1980. Vidy i sorta sireni, kul'tiviruemye v SSSR. Kiev; Naukova Dumka. – in Russian; Holetich, C.D. 1982. Lilac species and cultivars in cultivation in USSR. Lilacs 11(2):1-38. - translation of Rubtzov et al. 1982; Photo on Jorgovani/Lilacs 2015 DVD.
Named for Leonid Alekseevitch Kolesnikov, 1893-1968, Russian amateur plant breeder.
Cultivar name established and accepted.

'Leonid Leonov', *S. vulgaris*
'Леонид Леонов'
Kolesnikov 1941; S IV & II
syn. - 'Leonid Leonow', Kolesnikov No. 201/103
{Kolesnikov No. 110 × 'Andenken an Ludwig Späth'}
Kolesnikov, Lilac, 26,27 [1955]; Howard, Arnoldia 19(6-7):31-35 [1959]; Gromov, A., Siren', 107, ill. [1963]; Howard & Brizicky, AABGA Quart. Newsl. No. 64, 17-21 [1965]; Wister & Oppe, Arnoldia 31(3):126 [1971] - as 'Leonid Leonow', S II; Gromov, Lilacs - Proceedings 2(4):11-18 [1974]; Rubtzov et all. 1980. Vidy i sorta sireni, kul'tiviruemye v SSSR. Kiev; Naukova Dumka. – in Russian; Holetich, C.D. 1982. Lilac species and cultivars in cultivation in USSR. Lilacs 11(2):1-38. - translation of Rubtzov et al. 1982; Photo on Jorgovani/Lilacs 2015 DVD.
Named for Leonid Maksimovich Leonov, 1899-1994, Russian novelist and playwright.
Cultivar name registered 1970; name established and accepted.

'Leonie Lambert', *S. vulgaris*
Lambert 1909; S VII
Peter Lambert, Cat., 102 [1912]; McKelvey, The Lilac, 323 [1928]; Wister, Lilacs for America, 51 [1942], 33 [1953]; Photo on Jorgovani/Lilacs 2015 DVD.
Cultivar name presumed registered 1953; name established and accepted.

'Léon Liberton', *S. vulgaris*
Stepman-Demessemaeker; S IV
syn. - 'Leon Liberton'
Wister, Lilacs for America, 33 [1953] as 'Leon Liberton'
Named for Léon Liberton, 1865- x, Belgian horticulturist.
Cultivar name presumed registered 1953; name established and accepted.

Léon Mathieu - see **'Mons. Léon Mathieu'**.

Leonora, Leonore - see **'Elinor'**
Pringle & Vrugtman, Lilacs - Quart. Jour. 20(4):112 [1991].

'Leonov', *S. vulgaris*
'Леонов'
Kravchenko 1970; S II-V
{'Lamartine' x OP}
Kravchenko L. Culture of lilacs in Uzbekistan. Publishing house "Uzbekistan", Tashkent, 1970 p. 13.
Name after cosmonaut Alexei Leonov.
Cultivar name established and accepted.

'Léon Portier', *S. vulgaris*
Bruchet; S VI
syn. - 'Leon Portier'
McKelvey, The lilac, 323 [1928]; Wister, Lilacs for America, 51 [1942], 33 [1953]
Cultivar name presumed registered; not reported in cultivation in 1953.

'Léon Simon', *S. vulgaris*
Lemoine 1888; D IV
syn. - 'Leon Simon', 'Leo Simon'
Lemoine, Cat. No. 110, 10 [1888]; McKelvey, The Lilac, 323 [1928]; Wister, Lilacs for America, 51 [1942] - as D VI; Wister, Lilacs for America, 33 [1953] - as 'Leon Simon'; Photo on Jorgovani/Lilacs 2015 DVD.
Named for Dr Léon Simon, 1798-1867, Hahnemann's pupil in Paris, cofounder of the first Medical Homeopathical Magazine of Paris.
Cultivar name presumed registered 1953; name established and accepted.

'Leon Wyczółkowski', *S. vulgaris*
Karpow-Lipski 1958; S VI
syn. - 'Leon Wyczolkowski', Siewka nr 35
Karpow-Lipski, Arboretum Kórnickie, 3:102 [1958]; Wister & Oppe, Arnoldia 31(3):126 [1971] - as 'Leon Wyczolkowski'
Named for Leon Wyczółkowski, 1852-1936, Polish painter and graphic artist.
Cultivar name registered 1970; name established and accepted.

'Léopold II', *S. vulgaris*
Stepman-Demessemaeker pre-1906; S IV
syn. - 'Leopold II'
{'Dr Lindley' × 'Marie Legraye'}
Fl. Stepman-Demessemaeker, Cat. [1908]; McKelvey, The Lilac, 324 [1928]; Wister, Lilacs for America, 51 [1942], 33 [1953]
Named for Léopold II, 1835-1909, king of Belgium 1865-1909.
Cultivar name presumed registered 1953; name established and accepted.

'Léopold III', *S. vulgaris*
Klettenberg 1935; S VII
syn. - 'Leopold III'
Klettenberg, Cat., 25 [1935]; Wister, Lilacs for America, 33 [1953]
Named for Léopold III, 1901-1983, king of Belgium.
Cultivar name presumed registered 1953; name established and accepted.

'Leprechaun', *S. vulgaris*
origin not known ? ?
Fiala, Lilacs, p. 112, 107 [1988] - name only
Cultivar name not established.

'Le Printemps', *S. vulgaris*
Lemoine 1901; D V
Syn. - 'Printemps'
Lemoine, Cat. No. 149, 29 [1901]; McKelvey, The Lilac, 324 [1928]; Wister, Lilacs for America, 51 [1942], 33 [1953]; Photo on Jorgovani/Lilacs 2015 DVD.
Name: French for springtime.
Cultivar name presumed registered 1953; name established and accepted.

'Le Progrès', *S. ×chinensis*
Lemoine 1903; S IV
syn. - 'Le Progress', Varina le progrès
common name: Le Progres and Progress
Lemoine, Cat. No. 155, 29 [1903]; Stand. Pl. Names, 487 [1923] - as Progress; McKelvey, The Lilac, 425 [1928]; Wister, Stand. Pl. Names, 616 [1942] - as Le Progres; Lilacs for America, 51 [1942], 33 [1953]
Cultivar name presumed registered 1953; name established and accepted.

'Lesnaya Pesnya', *S. vulgaris*
'Лесная Песня'
Rubtzov, Zhogoleva & Lyapunova; S III-IV
{'Charles X' × ? }
Rubtzov et al., Siringarii (lilac garden), 42 [1961].
Name: Russian for forest song.
Cultivar name established and accepted.

'Lesnoï Landysh', *S. vulgaris*
'Лесной Ландыш'
Aladin, S., Aladina, O., Polyakova, T., and Aladina, A. 2019; S I
{'Flora 1953' × OP}
(Международная научная конференция "Syringa L.: коллекции, выращивание, использование") "International Scientific Conference "Syringa L.: collections, cultivation, using" / Collection of Scientific Articles of Botanical Institute named after V.L. Komarov, Botanical Garden of Peter the Great BIN RAS. - St. Petersburg. -2020.- pp.3-7 (in Russian); Photo exhibition of all varieties of the creative breeding group "Russian Lilac" at the Festival "Lilac February", St. Petersburg, Botanical Garden of Peter the Great BIN RAS, February 22-24, 2020.
Russian for Forest Lily of the Valley. The shape and size of the flowers are very similar to the flowers of fragrant forest lily of the valley.
Cultivar name established and accepted.

'Lesostepnaya', *S. vulgaris*
'Лесостепная'
Vekhov 1952; D II
syn. - 'Lesostepnaja', 'Lesostepnoaya'
{'Comte de Kerchove' × ? }
Rubtzov et al. 1980. Vidy i sorta sireni, kul'tiviruemye v SSSR. Kiev; Naukova Dumka. – in Russian; Holetich, C.D. 1982. Lilac species and cultivars in cultivation in USSR. Lilacs 11(2):1-38. - translation of Rubtzov et al. 1982; Anon., Lilacs - Quart. Jour. 33(1):11 [2004] - as D V-VI; Photo on Jorgovani/Lilacs 2015 DVD.
Named for the Lesostepnaya Experimental Breeding Station (LOSS), Meshchersk, Lipetzk Region, Russia.
Cultivar name established and accepted.

'Lesya Ukrainka', *S. vulgaris*
'Леся Украинка'
Klimenko, V. & Z., & Grigor'ev 1955 (not Gorb); S VII
syn. - 'Lesja Ukrainka'
{'Mme Lemoine' × S. vulgaris}
Rubtzov et al. 1980. Vidy i sorta sireni, kul'tiviruemye v SSSR. Kiev; Naukova Dumka. – in Russian; Holetich, C.D. 1982. Lilac species and cultivars in cultivation in USSR. Lilacs 11(2):1-38. - translation of Rubtzov et al. 1982; Photo on Jorgovani/Lilacs 2015 DVD.
Named for Ukrainian author Larysa Petrivna Kosach-Kvitka whose pen name was Lesya Ukrainka, 1871-1913, poet, writer and critic.
Cultivar name established and accepted.

'Lesya Ukrainka', *S. vulgaris*
'Леся Українка'
Gorb 1996; D I
{'Princesse Clémentine' × ?}
in litt. (Gorb to Vrugtman Jan. 22, 1997) - as 'Lesya Ukraynka'.
Named for Ukrainian author Larysa Petrivna Kosach-Kvitka whose pen name was Lesya Ukrainka, 1871-1913, poet, writer and critic.
Cultivar name not established.

'Letha E. House', *S. vulgaris*
Fiala 1990; S IV
syn. - 'Letha House'
{'Flora 1953' × ('General Sherman' × 'Maréchal Foch')}
Ameri-Hort Research, descriptive list [n.d.; ca 1990]; Knight Hollow Nursery, 1996 Cultured cutting and liner descriptive list
Named for Letha E. House, 1880-1968, American philanthropist and founder of the Letha E. House Foundation.
Cultivar name not established.

'Letniĭ Dozhd" (Summer Rain), *S. vulgaris*
'Летний Дождь'
Aladin, S., Polyakova, T., Aladina, O., and Aladina, A. 2012; S V
{'Gortyenziya' × OP}
(Международная научная конференция "Syringa L.: коллекции, выращивание, использование") "International Scientific Conference "Syringa L.: collections, cultivation, using" / Collection of Scientific Articles of Botanical Institute named after V.L. Komarov, Botanical Garden of Peter the Great BIN RAS. - St. Petersburg. -2020.- pp.3-7 (in Russian); Photo exhibition of all varieties of the creative breeding group "Russian Lilac" at the Festival "Lilac February", St. Petersburg, Botanical Garden of Peter the Great BIN RAS, February 22-24, 2020.
The abundant, heavy inflorescences look like warm, generous, summer rain.
Cultivar name established and accepted.

'Letniĭ Sad', *S. vulgaris*
'Летний сад'
Aladin, S., Aladina, O., Polyakova, T., and Aladina, A. 2016; S IV
{'Christophe Colomb' × OP}
Садовник (Gardener) magazine 04 (140)/2017 :18-25; Вестник АППМ (Catalog in Vestnik APPM (Planting material association) magazine) 1/2018: 59-72 (in Russian).
Name: Russian for Summer Garden, in honor of the ancient park in the center of St. Petersburg, laid down by Peter the First.
Cultivar name established and accepted.

Létourneau, *S.*
Moro, F. 201x; S I
{??}
plant in cultivation at The Lilac Museum, Saint-Georges, QC - in lit. Fouquet to Vrugtman 6 Nov. 2016.
Cultivar name not established.

'Le Troyes', *S.* ×*chinensis*
Origin not known; S IV
Stand. Pl. Names, 616 [1942] - as Le Troyes; Wister, Lilacs for America, 51 [1942], 33 [1953]; probably misspelling of 'Le Progrès' - see Vrugtman, Lilacs - Quart. Jour 22(4):123-125 [1993], or a misspelling of Les Troyens, in which case it may have been named for the opera *Les Troyens*, 1856-1859 by the French romantic composer Hector Berlioz, 1803-1869.
Cultivar name not established.

'Le'veille', *S. reticulata*
Origin not known; S ?
Lambert & Fricke, Lilacs - Quart. Jour. 26(2):57 [1997] - name only
Cultivar name not established.

'Lewis Maddock', *S.* ×*hyacinthiflora*
Rankin 1963; S IV-V
syn. - 'Lewis Maddon', 'Lewis Maddox'
{parentage not known}
Wister, Arnoldia 23(4):81 [1963] - as *S. vulgaris*, S IV; Fiala, Lilacs, pp. 58, 101, 107 (as 'Lewis Maddox'), 207, 208 & Pl. 41 [1988] - as *S.* ×*hyacinthiflora*, S V; Clark, Lilacs - Quart. Jour. 20(2):34 [1991] - as S V; Chapman, Lilacs - Quart. Jour. 25(4):98[1996] - 'Louis Maddock'; Photo on Jorgovani/Lilacs 2015 DVD.
Named for Lewis Maddock, a garden keeper who worked for the originator.
Cultivar name registered 1963; name established and accepted.

'Libby Erickson', *S.* ×*hyacinthiflora*
Waines, no date; S V/IV
{'Cheyenne' × ?}
Lilacs - Quart. Jour. 47(1):11 [2018] - name only; in lit. Waines to Vrugtman 27 March 2018 - as S V/IV, female parent either 'Cheyenne' or a ×*hyacinthiflora* cultivar.
Cultivar name not established and accepted.

'Liberti', *S. vulgaris*
Libert-Darimont pre-1847; S III
syn. - 'Libert', 'Liberty' (not flore duplo liberti)
C. Lemaire, Fl. Serres 3:252b [1847]; McKelvey, The Lilac 324-325, 563 [1928]; Wister, Lilacs for America, 51 [1942], 33 [1953] - as D III
Cultivar name presumed registered 1953; name established and accepted.

'Līderis', *S. vulgaris*
Kārkliņš 2003; D VII/II
Strautiņa & Kaufmane, Dobeles ceriņi, p. 92 [2011]; Photo on Jorgovani/Lilacs 2015 DVD.
Name: Latvian for leader.
Cultivar name established and accepted.

Liega - see '**Liega**'.

'**Liega**', *S. vulgaris*
Upītis 1970; D I
syn. - Upītis No. 62-42
statutory epithet Liega
Kalva, V., Ceriņi (Lilac), 165-166 [1980] - in Latvian; Kalniņš, Ceriņu jaunšķirnes Dobelē, Dārs un drava 1986 (12):13-15 - in Latvian; Strautiņa, S. 1996. Characteristics and propagation of lilacs obtained by P. Upītis. Problems of fruit plant breeding I. Jelgava. pp. 32-38; Strautiņa, S. 2002. Ceriņu un jasmīnu avīze. LA, R., p. 62; in litt. S. Strautiņa to F. Vrugtman [21 Dec. 2007] - 1970, D I; Photo on Jorgovani/Lilacs 2015 DVD.
statutory registration (breeder's rights) Nr. 291, CER-1, in Latvia [2004 - 2029] with the statutory epithet Liega.
Name: Liega is a Latvian girl's name.
Cultivar name established and accepted; name registered.

'**Liegas Kaiminiene**', *S. vulgaris*
Upītis 1970; S IV
Photo from Dobele, Latvia by Natalia Savenko, seen in 2020 ILS Photo Database.
Cultivar name not established.

Lights of Dombas - see '**Ogni Donbassa**'.

'**Liina**', *S. vulgaris*
Vaigla 1946; D V (V-I per Semenov)
{parentage not known}
Kivistik, Maakodu 1997(5):22-23 (ill.) [1997] - in Estonian; I. Semenov, Lilacs 48(2):65 [2019].
Cultivar name established and accepted.

'**Liisa**', *S. vulgaris*
originator not known, 2009; S III/II
original plant discoverd on Vanha-Markkula's farm at Lievestuore parish, near Jyväskylä, Finland.
MTT (Agrifood Research Finland) cat. Varmennetun taimituotannon emokasvihinnasto vuonna 2010, p. 52.
Cultivar name established and accepted.

'**Liksme**', *S. vulgaris*
Upītis 1970; S VII
Photo from Dobele, Latvia by Natalia Savenko, seen in 2020 ILS Photo Database.
Cultivar name not established.

'**Lilac Hill**', *S. vulgaris*
Wiles; S V
Wister, Lilacs for America, 33 [1953]
Cultivar name presumed registered 1953; name established and accepted.

'**Lilac Lady**', *S. vulgaris*
Margaretten (not Peterson); D I
 syn. - 'Reva Ballreich', name given by Margaretten but not accepted and established
{'Mme Lemoine' × ?}
Vrugtman, Hanburyana 7:29 [2013]; Photo on Jorgovani/Lilacs 2015 DVD.
Named for Reva Ballreich, 1925-2009, president of the International Lilac Society, 1992-1997.
Cultivar name registered 2012 by Frank Moro; name established and accepted.

Lilac Princess - see '**Syrenprinsessen**'.

'**Lilac Sunday**', *S.* ×*chinensis*
Alexander III 1997; S VII
{parentage not known}
Alexander III, Arnoldia 57(1):12-13, back cover ill. [1997]; Alexander III, Taunton's fine Gardening No. 66:32 & 37 ill. [Apr. 1999]; Vrugtman, HortScience 34(4):600 [1999]; Lilacs - Quart. Jour. 28(4):112-113 & front cover ill. [1999]; Photo on Jorgovani/Lilacs 2015 DVD.
Known for its lateral buds and massive 2 ft. panicles.
Cultivar name registered 1998; name established and accepted.

'**Lilarosa**', *S. vulgaris*
origin not known pre-1887; S V
syn. - 'Lila Rosa'
Späth, Cat. No. 69, 115 [1887]; Moore, Lilacs, 154 [1903]; McKelvey, The Lilac, 325 [1928]; Wister, Lilacs for America, 51 [1942], 33 [1953]; Photo on Jorgovani/Lilacs 2015 DVD.
Cultivar name presumed registered 1953; name established and accepted.

Lilas Charlemagne - see '**Charlemagne**'.

'Lilas d'Azur à fleurs doubles', *S. vulgaris*
Brahy-Ekenholm 1854; D III
Belgische Dendrologie 1994, p. 191
Cultivar name not established.

'Lila Wonder', *S. vulgaris*
Bunnik 2005; S IV & I
{mutation of 'Dark Koster', 1997}
Patricia Boon, Een wonder van een sering. De Telegraaf, T25, 17 April 2005
[breeder applied for CPVO variety denomination registration, April 2006]
Cultivar name established and accepted.

'**Liliana**', *S. vulgaris*
Bojarczuk & Zieliński 1992; S I
{mutation of 'Miss Ellen Willmott'}
Bojarczuk & Zieliński, Rocznik Polskiego Towarzystwa Dendrologicznego 61:9-12, ill. [2013]; Photo on Jorgovani/Lilacs 2015 DVD; (Vrugtman, Cultivated Plant Diversity ... 2017)
Named for the granddaughter of Thomasz Bojarczuk.
Cultivar name registered 2014; name established and accepted.

'**Lillian Davis**', *S. vulgaris*
Stone; S I
Wister & Oppe, Arnoldia 31(3):122 [1971] - name only

Cultivar name registered 1970;
Cultivar not reported in cultivation.

'Lillian Lee', *S. vulgaris*
Klager 1935; S V
Wister, Lilacs for America, 51 [1942], 33 [1953]; Photo on Jorgovani/Lilacs 2015 DVD.
Cultivar name presumed registered 1953; name established and accepted.

'Lilovaya Piramida', *S. vulgaris*
'Лиловая Пирамида'
Mel'nik 1977 D IV-III
syn. - 'Lilovaja Piramida', seedling No. 154
{'Henri Martin' × OP }
Rubanik, V. G. et al., Siren' - Syringa L., publishing house "Kaĭnar", Alma-Ata [1977] p 58- in Russian; Rubtzov et al. 1980. Vidy i sorta sireni, kul'tiviruemye v SSSR. Kiev; Naukova Dumka. – in Russian; Holetich, C.D. 1982. Lilac species and cultivars in cultivation in USSR. Lilacs 11(2):1-38. - translation of Rubtzov et al. 1982.
Name: Russian for lilac pyramid.
Cultivar name established and accepted.

'Lilovaya Purga', *S. vulgaris*
'Лиловая Пурга'
Klimenko, V.& Z., & Grigor'ev 1955; S V
syn. - 'Lilovaja Purga'
{'Mme Casimir Périer' × 'Andenken an Ludwig Späth'}
Rubtzov et al. 1980. Vidy i sorta sireni, kul'tiviruemye v SSSR. Kiev; Naukova Dumka. – in Russian; Holetich, C.D. 1982. Lilac species and cultivars in cultivation in USSR. Lilacs 11(2):1-38. - translation of Rubtzov et al. 1982.
Name: Russian for purple snowstorm.
Cultivar name established and accepted.

'Lilovaya Raketa', *S. vulgaris*
'Лиловая Ракета'
Klimenko, V. 1955; S IV-V
syn. - 'Lilovaja Raketa'
{*S. vulgaris* × 'Andenken an Ludwig Späth'}
Rubtzov et al. 1980. Vidy i sorta sireni, kul'tiviruemye v SSSR. Kiev; Naukova Dumka. – in Russian; Holetich, C.D. 1982. Lilac species and cultivars in cultivation in USSR. Lilacs 11(2):1-38. - translation of Rubtzov et al. 1982.
Name: Russian for purple rocket.
Cultivar name established and accepted.

Lindley, Lindleyana, Lindleyi - see **'Dr Lindley'**.

'Ling Tong', *S.* (Villosae Group)
Fiala 1987; S II
{*S. tomentella* subsp. *sweginzowii* × (*S. tomentella* subsp. *yunnanensis* × *S.* ×*prestoniae* 'Isabella')}
Fiala, Lilacs, 224 [1988]
Named for Ling Tong (Gongji), 189-237, imperial corps commander, Yuhang, Zhe Jiang Province, China.
Cultivar name established and accepted.

Linnaeus - see **'Linné'**.

'Linné', *S. vulgaris*
Lemoine 1890; D VI
syn. - 'Linnaeus'
common name: Linne
Lemoine, Cat. No. 116, 13 [1890]; McKelvey, The Lilac, 325-326 [1928]; Stand. Pl. Names, 616 [1942] - as Linne; Wister, Lilacs for America, 51 [1942], 33 [1953]; Photo on Jorgovani/Lilacs 2015 DVD.
Named for Carl von Linné (Carolus Linnaeus), 1707-1778, Swedish naturalist and physician.
Cultivar name presumed registered 1953; name established and accepted.

'Lipchanka', *S. vulgaris*
'Липчанка'
Vekhov 1952; S II
Журнал "Цветоводство" №7, 1977 год, стр. 11.
Magazine "Tsvetovodstvo" ("Floriculture") No. 7, 1977, p. 11
Rubtzov et al. 1980. Vidy i sorta sireni, kul'tiviruemye v SSSR. Kiev; Naukova Dumka. – in Russian; Holetich, C.D. 1982. Lilac species and cultivars in cultivation in USSR. Lilacs 11(2):1-38. - translation of Rubtzov et al. 1982; Photo on Jorgovani/Lilacs 2015 DVD.
The name means a woman who lives in the city of Lipetsk.
Cultivar name not established.

'Lita Emanuel', *S. vulgaris*
Margaretten; D IV
{'Mme Lemoine' × ? }
Cultivar name not established; not reported in cultivation.

'Little Bit', *S. vulgaris*
Berdeen 1985; S V
Maurice Lockwood, in litt. to Vrugtman [Apr.17/1985] - semi-dwarf selection, name only; Peterson, Lilacs - Proceedings 16(1):20 [1987] - name only; Vrugtman, Lilacs -Quart. Jour. 32(4):149 [2003] - S V
Cultivar name established and accepted.

Little Boy Blue - see **'Wonderblue'**.
Clark, Lilacs - Quart. Jour. 18(2):42 [1989]; Vrugtman, HortScience 29(9):972 [1994].

LITTLE DARLING™ - see **'SMSDTL'**.

LITTLE LADY™ - see **'Jeflady'**.

'Little Miss Muffet', *S. vulgaris*
Fiala 1965; S V-VI
syn. - 'Miss Muffet'
{'Mrs Edward Harding' × 'Macrostachya'}
Vrugtman, Lilacs - Proceedings 7(1):35 [1979]; Vrugtman, AABGA Bull. 13(4):108 [1979]; Fiala, Lilacs, 101, 223, Pl.84 [1988] - as seedling colchicine treated; presumably mostly tetraploid; Photo on Jorgovani/Lilacs 2015 DVD.
Named for a nursery rhyme character.
Cultivar name registered 1977; name accepted and established.

'Little Pinkie', *S. vulgaris*
    origin not known ? ?
    Lewis, Pacific Hort. 49(4):40-41 [1988]
    Cultivar name not established.

Little Star of Kiev - see 'Zviozdochka Kieva'.

'Liza Chaikina', *S. vulgaris*
    'Лиза Чайкина'
    Kolesnikov 1946, S I
    {parentage not known}
    Polyakova, 2010, Istoriya Russkoĭ Sireni, p. 34 - name only; T. Polyakova , 2018, Мастер Сиреневой Кисти (Master of the Lilac Brush), p. 108 - photo only. Seen on a Facebook post 5/27/20 by the Lomonosov Botanical Garden of the Moscow State University. Named for Liza Chaikina (Елизаве́та Ива́новна Ча́йкина), 1918-1941, partisan and Hero of the Soviet Union.
    Cultivar name established and accepted.

'Lobelia', *S. villosa* subsp. *villosa*
    origin not known ? ?
    Wister, Lilacs for America, 51 [1942] - name only
    Cultivar name not established.

Lockwood Unknown, *S. vulgaris*
    Origin not known; S II
    Peterson, Lilacs - Proceedings 16(1):20 [1987]
    Cognomen, not a cultivar name.

'Logo', *S. vulgaris*
    Origin not known; D VI
    Caprice Farm Nursery Inventory system, A. Rogers, 05/07/84; Photo on Jorgovani/Lilacs 2015 DVD.
    Cultivar name not established.

'Lois Amee Utley', *S. vulgaris*
    Fiala 1986; D V
    {'Rochester' × 'Mme Antoine Buchner'}
    syn. - 'Lois Utley'
    Fiala, Lilacs, 100, 107, 223, Pl.18 [1988]; Photo on Jorgovani/Lilacs 2015 DVD.
    Named for Lois Amee Utley (no dates) wife of William Ultey (no dates) of Clyde New York proprietors of the Grape Hill Farm lilac collection, now defunct.
    Cultivar name established and accepted.

'L'Oncle Tom', *S. vulgaris*
    Lemoine 1903; S VII
    common name: Uncle Tom
    Lemoine, Cat. No. 155, 31 [1903]; Stand. Pl. Names, 486, 488 [1923] - as Uncle Tom; McKelvey, The lilac, 326 [1928]; Wister, Lilacs for America, 52 [1942], 34 [1953]; Photo on Jorgovani/Lilacs 2015 DVD.
    Named for the hero of Harriet Elizabeth Stowe's 1852 novel "Uncle Tom's Cabin".
    Cultivar name presumed registered 1953; name established and accepted.

Longcluster - see **'Macrostachya'**.

Long Fellow - see 'White Long Fellow'.

'Longifolia', *S. pekinensis*
    origin not known pre-1910; ? ?
    syn. - *pekinensis longifolia* Koehne (?)
    Späth, Cat. No. 143, 130 [1910]; McKelvey, The Lilac, 506 [1928]
    Cultivar name not established.

Longview - see **'City of Longview'**.

'Lorenz Booth', *S. vulgaris*
    origin not known pre-1876; ? ?
    McKelvey, The Lilac, 326 [1928]
    Named for Lorenz Booth, son of James Booth (see **'James Booth'**).
    Cultivar name not established.

'Lori Z', *S. vulgaris*
    Klager; S V/VII
    Anon., ILS Newsletter 14(4):3-4 [1988]
    Cultivar name not established.

'Los Angelès', *S. vulgaris*
    Klettenberg 1934; S VI
    syn. - 'Los Angeles'
    Klettenberg, Cat., 20 [1934]: Wister, Lilacs for America, 34 [1953] - as 'Los Angeles'
    Cultivar name presumed registered 1953; name established and accepted.

Lotta - see 'MORjos 060F'.

'Louis Bonaparte', *S. vulgaris*
    origin not known pre-1851; S ?
    syn. - 'Louis Buonaparte'
    Lawson's List of Seed Plants [1851]; International Exhibition, 1876, US Centennial Commission, Volume 11, p. 310 - name only.
    Cultivar name not established.

'Louise', *S. vulgaris*
    Klager; D IV
    Wister, Lilacs for America, 52 [1942], 34 [1953]
    Cultivar name presumed registered 1953;
    Cultivar not reported in cultivation.

Louise Baltet - see **'Lucie Baltet'**.

'Louise-Marie', *S. vulgaris*
    Brahy-Ekenholm 1861; S I
    {'Charles X' × 'Noisette'}
    Duvivier, Jour. Hort. Pratique Belgique, sér. 2, 5:241 [1861]; McKelvey, The Lilac, 326-327 [1928]; Wister, Lilacs for America, 52 [1942], 34 [1953] - as 'Louise Marie'
    Named for queen Louise-Marie, 1812-1850, wife to King Léopold I of Belgium.
    Cultivar name presumed registered 1953;
    Cultivar not reported in cultivation.

'Louise Souchard', *S. vulgaris*
　Origin not known; S I
　Caprice Farm Nursery Inventory system, A. Rogers, 05/07/84
　Cultivar name not established.

Louis Gilles - see 'Souvenir de Mme Louis Gielis'.

'Louis Henry', *S. vulgaris*
　Lemoine 1894; D VI
　Lemoine, Cat. No. 128, 10 [1894]; McKelvey, The Lilac, 327 [1928]; Wister, Lilacs for America, 52 [1942], 34 [1953]; Photo on Jorgovani/Lilacs 2015 DVD.
　Named for Louis Henry, 1853-1903, French botanist and horticulturist.
　Cultivar name presumed registered 1953; name established and accepted.

'Louis Pasteur', *S. vulgaris*
　origin not known pre-1953; S VII
　(perhaps identical to 'Pasteur')
　Krüssmann, Index Tremoniensis, 154 [1970]. Seen in "Syringa Cultivar Catalog" (2019) by Natalia Savenko, photo from Main Botanical Garden of Moscow State University.
　Named for Louis Pasteur, 1822-1895, French chemist and bacteriologist.
　Cultivar name not established.

'Louis van Houtte', *S. vulgaris*
　origin not known pre-1877; S VI
　syn. - 'Van Houtte'
　L. van Houtte, Cat. No. 175-vv, 54 [1877]; McKelvey, The Lilac, 327-328 [1928]; Wister, Lilacs for America, 52 [1942], 34 [1953] - as synonym of 'Dr Lindley' (?)
　Named for Louis Benoît van Houtte, 1810-1876, Belgian florist, botanist, educator.
　Cultivar name presumed registered 1953; name established and accepted.

'Lourene Wishart', *S. vulgaris*
　Fiala (not Margaretten) 1980; D V
　syn. - 'Laurene Wishart'
　{'Rochester' × 'Edward J. Gardner'}
　Fiala, Lilacs, 100, 107, 223 [1988]; Photo on Jorgovani/Lilacs 2015 DVD.
　Named for Lourene Bratts Wishart, 1892-1989, of Lincoln, Nebraska; Regional Vice President, Plains Region of the International Lilac Society. See also ILS Journal 13(1):4; 19(1):2.
　Cultivar name established and accepted.

'Lourene Wishart', *S. vulgaris*
　Margaretten (not Fiala); S III & I
　{'Mme Lemoine' × ? }
　Cultivar name not established.

'Louvain', *S.* ×*hyacinthiflora* (not **'De Louvain'**, *S. vulgaris*)
　Skinner 1962; S II
　Dropmore, Cat. [1962]; Wister, Arnoldia 23(4):81 [1963]
　Named for the town of Louvain, capital of the province of Flemish Brabant, Belgium (French: Louvain; Flemish: Leuven; German: Löwen).
　Cultivar name registered 1963; name established and accepted.

Louvain, *S. vulgaris* - see **'De Louvain'** (*S. vulgaris*) (not *S.* ×*hyacinthiflora* **'Louvain'**).
　Note: Louvain is used as a common name for 'De Louvain' in Stand. Pl. Names, 486 [1923].

Louvainiensis - see **'De Louvain'**.

'Louvois', *S.* ×*hyacinthiflora*
　Lemoine 1921; S II
　Lemoine, Cat. No. 195, 19 [1921]; McKelvey, The Lilac, 198 [1928]; Wister, Lilacs for America, 52 [1942], 34 [1953]; Photo on Jorgovani/Lilacs 2015 DVD.
　Named for François Michel le Tellier, Marquis de Louvois, 1641-1691, French statesman, war minister of Louis XIV.
　Cultivar name presumed registered 1953; name established and accepted.

Lovanensis - see **'De Louvain'**.

Lovaniensis - see **'De Louvain'**.

'Lover's Spell', *S.* ×*hyacinthiflora*
　Moro, F. 2009; S VII
　{'Forrest Kresser Smith' × ? }
　<http://www.spi.8m.com/hyacinthifloracdncat.html>
　Cultivar name established and accepted.

'Lovrov' – synonym for 'S. V. Lavrov'

'Lucelle', *S. vulgaris*
　Robinson, Edward 1945; S VI
　{'Lucie Baltet' × ? }
　Wister, Arbor. Bot. Gard. Bull. 1(2):19 [1967]; Robinson, Cat. [1968]; Photo on Jorgovani/Lilacs 2015 DVD.
　Cultivar name registered 1967; name established and accepted.

'Lucetta', *S.* (Villosae Group), *S.* ×*prestoniae*
　Preston 1928; S VI
　syn. - Preston No. 20-14-54
　{*S. villosa* subsp. *villosa* × *S. komarowii* subsp. *reflexa*}
　Macoun, Rep. Dom. Hort. 1928, 56 [1930]; Wister, Lilacs for America, 52, 64 [1942], 34, 48 [1953]; Photo on Jorgovani/Lilacs 2015 DVD.
　Named for the Waiting-woman to Julia in Shakespeare's *Two Gentlemen of Verona*.
　Cultivar name presumed registered 1953; name established and accepted.

'Luch Vostoka'; *S. vulgaris*
　'Луч Востока'
　Mel'nik pre-1977; D V
　{'Katherine Havemeyer' × OP}
　Syn. – seedling No. 6
　Rubanik, V. G. et al., Siren' - Syringa L., publishing house

"Kaĭnar", Alma-Ata [1977] p 53- in Russian; Rubtzov et al. 1980. Vidy i sorta sireni, kul'tiviruemye v SSSR. Kiev; Naukova Dumka. – in Russian; Holetich, C.D. 1982. Lilac species and cultivars in cultivation in USSR. Lilacs 11(2):1-38. - translation of Rubtzov et al. 1982; Dyagilev, Lilacs - Quart. Jour. 22(1):20 [1993]; Pikaleva, Lilacs - Quart. Jour. 23(4):86 [1994].
Name: Russian for Ray of the East.
Cultivar name established and accepted.

'Luciana', *S.* (Villosae Group), *S.* ×*prestoniae*
Preston pre-1930; ? ?
syn. - 'Lucinia', Preston No. 20-14-66
Macoun, Rep. Dom. Hort. 1928, 56 [1930] - name only, as 'Lucinia'; Wister, Lilacs for America, 64 [1942], 48 [1953] - not in cultivation, no plants distributed
Named for the Sister to Adriana in Shakespeare's *Comedy of Errors*.
Cultivar name not established, probably extinct.

'Lucie Baltet', *S. vulgaris*
Baltet pre-1888; S V
syn. - 'Louise Baltet', 'Lucy Baltet', 'Lusi Balte', 'Lusie', 'Luzie Baltet'; see also 'Clyde Lucie', LUSIE (trade designation used for cut flowers of this cultivar)
Carrière, Rev. Hort. 21 [1888]; McKelvey, The Lilac, 328 [1928]; Wister, Lilacs for America, 52 [1942], 34 [1953]; Lilacs - Quart. Jour. 20(4):back cover ill. [1991]; see also: Vrugtman, Lilacs - Quart. Jour. 23(3):75-76 [1994]; Photo on Jorgovani/Lilacs 2015 DVD.
Named for Lucie Baltet Dumont [no dates], daughter of Charles Baltet, France.
Cultivar name presumed registered 1953; name established and accepted.
Forcing cultivar in the Netherlands.

'Lucienne Bruchet', *S. vulgaris*
Bruchet 1924; S I
McKelvey, The Lilac, 328 [1928]; Wister, Lilacs for America, 52 [1942], 34 [1953]
Cultivar name presumed registered 1953; name established and accepted.

'Lucienne Guillaud', *S. vulgaris*
origin not known pre-1908; D I
syn. - 'Lucienne Guillaume'
Fl. Stepman-De Messemaeker, Suppl. to Gen. Cat., 2 [1908]; McKelvey, The Lilac, 328 [1928] - as confused name; Wister, Lilacs for America, 34 [1953]
Cultivar name presume registered 1953; name established and accepted.

Lucienne Guillaume - see **'Lucienne Guillaud'**.

Lucinia - see 'Luciana'.

'Lucy Bergen', *S. vulgaris*
Berdeen 2005; S III
King & Coggeshall, Lilacs - Quart. Jour. 27(2):49-50 [1998] - name only; Vrugtman, Encyclopedia, 312 [2008]
Named for the daughter of the originator's friend and neighbor.
Cultivar name established and accepted.

LUDWIG SPAETH - see **'Andenken an Ludwig Späth'** (*S. vulgaris*)
Nota bene: LUDWIG SPAETH has been recorded under Art. 13, ex. 2, ICNCP-2009, as a trade designation for North America for **'Andenken an Ludwig Späth'**.

'Lullaby', *S. vulgaris*
Fiala 1984; D II-IV
{'Rochester' × 'Gismonda'}
Fiala, Lilacs, 94, 107, 223, Pl.11 [1988]
Cultivar name established and accepted.

'Lumina', *S.* (Villosae Group), *S.* ×*josiflexa* (?)
VanderZalm pre-2001; S V
Van's Inc. Nurs. [June 12, 2001] http://www.lilac-King.com - very similar to 'James Macfarlane', but flowering one week earlier, marketed for 1 or 2 seasons only
Cultivar name not established.

'Luminifera', *S.* (species affiliation not known)
origin not known ? ?
in litt. C. Chapman to F. Vrugtman [Jul. 2/91]; at one time grown by Hillier Nursery, but no records located; Chapman, Lilacs - Quart. Jour. 26(2):45 [1997] - as *S. luminifera*.
Cultivar name not established.

'Lumley Yellow', *S. vulgaris*
Lumley; S I
{mutation of 'Primrose'}
reported in cultivation at US National Arboretum [1979], name only
Cultivar name not established.

'Lundenes', *S.* (Villosae Group)
origin not known 1989; S VII
{*S. josikaea* seedling or, possibly: *S. komarowii* subsp. *reflexa* × *S. josikaea*; Molberg [1998]}
L. Molberg, Gartneryrket 12/1998:23; Sortsliste for Nord-Norge 1989; in litt. O.B. Hansen to F. Vrugtman, March 15, 2000
Cultivar name established and accepted.

'Lunnaya Sonata', *S. vulgaris*
'Лунная соната'
Aladin, S., Aladina, O., Polyakova, T., and Aladina, A. 2019; S I
{' Flora 1953' × OP}
(Международная научная конференция "Syringa L.: коллекции, выращивание, использование")
"International Scientific Conference "Syringa L.: collections, cultivation, using" / Collection of Scientific Articles of Botanical Institute named after V.L. Komarov, Botanical Garden of Peter the Great BIN RAS. - St. Petersburg. -2020.- pp.3-7 (in Russian); Photo exhibition

of all varieties of the creative breeding group "Russian Lilac" at the Festival "Lilac February", St. Petersburg, Botanical Garden of Peter the Great BIN RAS, February 22-24, 2020.
Russian for Moonlight Sonata. The cultivar is dedicated to the great composer L. V. Beethoven and his masterpiece - *Moonlight Sonata*.
Cultivar name established and accepted.

'Lunnyĭ Svet', *S. vulgaris*
'Лунный Свет'
Smol'skiĭ & Bibikova 1964; D I
syn. - 'Lunnyi Svet'
{'Mme Abel Chatenay' × 'Réaumur'}
Rubtzov et al. 1980. Vidy i sorta sireni, kul'tiviruemye v SSSR. Kiev; Naukova Dumka. – in Russian; Holetich, C.D. 1982. Lilac species and cultivars in cultivation in USSR. Lilacs 11(2):1-38. - translation of Rubtzov et al. 1982; Semenov, Igor, Lilacs - Quart. Jour. 43(3):85-87 & photo 89 [2014]; Photo on Jorgovani/Lilacs 2015 DVD.
Name: Russian for moonlight.
Cultivar name established and accepted.

'Luo Lan Zi', *S. ×hyacinthiflora*
Zang & Fan 1962; D II
syn. - 'Luo lan zi', 'Luo Lan-Zi', 'Luolan Zi', 'Luolanzi'
{*S. oblata* Lindl. × *S. vulgaris* L. 'Alba-plena'}
Zang & Fan, Pl. Introd. Acclimatization 3:117-121 [1983] - in Chinese; Zang, Fan & Li, Acta Horticulturae 404:63-67 [1995]; Yoshikawa, Kyoto Engei (Kyoto Horticulture), 84:21-23 [?] - in Japanese; Vrugtman, HortScience 32 (4):588 [1997]; Anon., Beijing Bot. Garden 2006:24, ill. - as 'Luo Lan Zi'; Cui, Hongxia, et al. 2009. Scientia Horticulturae 121:186–191; Photo on Jorgovani/Lilacs 2015 DVD.
Cultivar name registered 1996; name established and accepted.

'Lustrous', *S. vulgaris*
Franklin, M.L. 1970; S V
syn. - 'Arbutus Pink'
{parentage not known}
Wister & Oppe, Arnoldia 31(3):123 [1971]; Vrugtman, Lilacs - Quart. Jour. 23(3):75 [1994]; (Perhaps in the collection at the Minnesota Landscape Arboretum; Tim McCauley)
Cultivar name registered 1970, name established and accepted.

'Lutèce', *S.* (Villosae Group), *S. ×henryi*
Henry, L pre-1901; S II
syn. - 'Lutece'
common - hybrid Hungarian lilac
{*S. josikaea* × *S. villosa* subsp. *villosa*}
Simon-Louis, Cat., 67 [1900]; McKelvey, The Lilac, 102-105 [1928]; Wister, Lilacs for America, 49, 52 [1942], 31, 34 [1953]; Photo on Jorgovani/Lilacs 2015 DVD.
Named for the city of Paris, France; Lutèce is derived from *Lutetia parisiorum, Parisii*.
Cultivar name presumed registered 1953; name established and accepted.

'Lutens', *S. vulgaris*
Barankiewicz; S V-VII *
{induced mutation of 'Maréchal Foch'}
Anon., Lista odmian roślin ozdobnych 1994; Anon., Lilacs - Quart. Jour. 25(2):33, front & back cover ill., 2 February 1998 [1996]; W. Bugała to Vrugtman, in litt. 6 May 1996; Photo on Jorgovani/Lilacs 2015 DVD.
Cultivar name established and accepted.

'Lychorida', *S.* (Villosae Group), *S. ×prestoniae*
Preston 1937; S V
Wister, Lilacs for America, 52 [1942], 34 [1953]; Davidson et al, Landscape Plants at the Morden Arboretum [1994] - received at Morden Research Station in 1937
Named for the Nurse to Marina in Shakespeare's *Pericles*.
Cultivar name presumed registered 1953; name established and accepted.

'Lynette', *S.* (Villosae Group), *S. ×josiflexa*
Preston 1938; S VII
syn. - Preston No. 24.02.25
{*S. ×josiflexa* 'Guinevere' × ? }
Davis, Rep. Dom. Hort., Progress Report 1934-1948, 149 [1950]; Wister, Lilacs for America, 52, 64 [1942], 34, 48 [1953]; Davidson et al, Landscape Plants at the Morden Arboretum [1994] - received at Morden Research Station in 1938; Photo on Jorgovani/Lilacs 2015 DVD.
Cultivar name presumed registered 1953; name established and accepted.

'Lynette Sirois', *S. vulgaris*
Berdeen 1968; D III
{'General John Pershing' × ? }
Berdeen, in litt. to J. C. Wister [May 1/1968]; Wister & Oppe, Arnoldia 31(3):122 [1971]; King & Coggeshall, Lilacs - Quart. Jour. 27(2):49-50 [1998] - name only
Named for the granddaughter of the originator.
Cultivar name registered 1970; name established and accepted.

Lynn - see **'Penda'**.

'Lynne', *S. vulgaris*
Slater 1975; VII/V
{'Dr Brethour' × ? }
 Lilacs - Quarterly Journal 21(1):back cover, upper right, photograph with Mrs Irene Slater, but mislabeled as "Irene"; Anon., "Lilacs added to Tower Hill Garden", Parry Sound North Star Newspaper, 2016, Issue 28, page 2, - as 'Lynne', double pink flowers.
Cultivar name established and accepted;
Cultivar name registered 2017 (publication pending).

L 1623, *S. pekinensis*
origin not known pre-1997; ? ?
reported in cultivation at NCCPG, Suffolk, UK
Probably not a cultivar name.

'Ma Bennett', *S. vulgaris*
Klager; S IV

Wister, Lilacs for America, 52 [1942], 34 [1953]
Cultivar name presumed registered 1953;
Cultivar not reported in cultivation.

Mackinac Island Lilac™, *S. vulgaris*
Christie; S IV
original cultivar name, if any, not known
a selection of common lilac sold on Mackinac Island, Michigan, ca 2003/2004 by Mackinac Island Florist, at that time operated by Steve & Terri Christie. About 1,000 plants were produced. It appears that the trademark is no longer maintained.
Photo on Jorgovani/Lilacs 2015 DVD.
No cultivar name was proposed.

'Macrostachya', *S. vulgaris*
Renaud 1874; S V
common name: Longcluster
Froebel, Cat. No. 116, 16 [1892]; Stand. Pl. Names, 486 [1923] - as Longcluster; McKelvey, The Lilac, 328-329 [1928]; Wister, Lilacs for America, 52 [1942], 34 [1953]; Sprenger, Cat., "3rd List of Plants," 2 [1903]; Photo on Jorgovani/Lilacs 2015 DVD.
Cultivar name presumed registered 1953; name established and accepted.

'Macrothursus', *S. vulgaris*
origin not known pre-1841; ? ?
Oudin, Cat., 22 [1841]; McKelvey, The Lilac, 330 [1928]
- confused name
Cultivar name not established.

'Macrothyrsa', *S. pekinensis*
origin not known pre-1903; S I
syn. - *pekinensis macrothyrsa*
Sprenger, Cat., "3rd List of Plants", 2 [1903]; McKelvey, The Lilac, 505 [1928].
Cultivar name established and accepted.

Mad. . . . - see: Madame . . ., Mme . . ., Mademoiselle . . ., Mlle . . .

Madame . . . - see also: Mme . . .

'Madame A. J. Klettenberg', *S. vulgaris*
Klettenberg 1930; D I
syn. - 'Mme A. J. Klettenberg'
common name: A. J. Klettenberg in Stand. Pl. Names, 614 [1942]
Klettenberg, Cat., 18 [1930]; Wister, Lilacs for America, 36, 43 [1942], 35 [1953] - as 'Mme A. J. Klettenberg'
Named for either the first or the second wife of Antoine Joseph Klettenberg.
Cultivar name presumed registered 1953; name established and accepted.

'Madame Charles Souchet', *S. vulgaris*
Lemoine 1949; S III
syn. - 'Mme Charles Souchet', 'Mme Chas. Couchet', 'Mme Chas. Souchet'
Wister, Lilacs for America, 36 [1953]; Lemoine, Cat. No. 225, 6 [1954]
Awards: Certificate of Merit 1952 (KMTP); Photo on Jorgovani/Lilacs 2015 DVD.
Named for Julienne Jeanne Catherine Boullet, 1897-1977, the wife of Charles Eugène Souchet, 1894-1977, producers of forced lilacs at Vitry-sur-Seine, Paris, France. Madame Souchet was a *Chevalier de l'ordre du Mérite agricole*, Charles Souchet a *Commandeur de l'ordre du Mérite agricole*.
Cultivar name presumed registered 1953; name established and accepted.

Madame C. Perriere - see **'Mme Casimir Périer'**.

'Madame Delaruelle-Klettenberg', *S. vulgaris*
Klettenberg 1935; S IV
syn. - 'Mme Delaruelle-Klettenberg'
Klettenberg, Cat., 25 [1935]; Wister, Lilacs for America, 36 [1953]
Cultivar name presumed registered 1953; name established and accepted.

Madame Edward Harding - see **'Mrs Edward Harding'**.

'Madame Hankar-Solvay', *S. vulgaris*
Klettenberg 1935; S III
syn. - 'Mme Hankar-Solvay'
Klettenberg, Cat., 26 [1935]; Wister, Lilacs for America, 36 [1953]
Cultivar name presumed registered 1953; not reported in cultivation.

'Madame la Comtesse Oswald de Kerchove de Denterghem', *S. vulgaris*
Klettenberg 1930; D I
syn. - 'Madame la Comtesse Osw. de Kerkhove de Dentergem'
Klettenberg, Cat., 18 [1930] & 20 [1934]; Wister, Lilacs for America, 36 [1953]
Named for Marie-Wilhelmine Lippens, 1850-1918, wife to Oswald Charles Eugene, Comte de Kerchove de Denterghem, 1844-1906, Belgian politician and amateur botanist.
Cultivar name presumed registered 1953; name established and accepted.

Madame Mosier - see **'Mme Moser'**.

'Madame Rosel', *S. vulgaris*
Eveleens Maarse 1953; S IV
syn. - 'Mme Rosel'
{'Maréchal Foch' × 'Hugo de Vries'}
Wister, Lilacs for America, 36 [1953]; Dendron 1(1):12 [July 1954]; Wister, Arnoldia 23(4):81 [1963]; Photo on Jorgovani/Lilacs 2015 DVD.
Awards: First Class Certificate 1953 (KMTP).
Cultivar name registered 1953 & 1963; name established and accepted.

Madame Stepman - see **'Mme Florent Stepman'**.

MÄDCHEN AUS MOSKAU - see '**Krasavi<u>ts</u>a Moskvy**'.

'**Madeleine Lemaire**', *S. vulgaris*
Lemoine 1928; D I
Wister, Lilacs for America, 52 [1942], 34 [1953]; Photo on Jorgovani/Lilacs 2015 DVD.
Named for Madeleine Lemaire, 1845-1928, French painter.
Cultivar name presumed registered 1953; name established and accepted.

Mad. Emile Lemoine - see '**Mme Lemoine**'.

Mademoiselle . . . - see also: Mlle . . .

'**Mademoiselle Fernande Viger**', *S. vulgaris*
Lecointe 1894; S I
syn. - 'Mlle Fernande Viger'
Fossey, in Jardin 10:210, fig. 101 [1896]; McKelvey, The Lilac, 337 [1928]; Wister, Lilacs for America, 53 [1942], 35 [1953] - as 'Mlle Fernande Viger'; Photo on Jorgovani/Lilacs 2015 DVD.
Cultivar name presumed registered 1953; name established and accepted.

Mademoiselle Marie Legraye - see '**Marie Legraye**'.

'**Maestro Jānis Zirnis**', *S. vulgaris*
Upītis 1992; S IV
Syn. - Spēta Bērns'
Photo from Dobele, Latvia by Natalia Savenko seen in 2020 ILS Photo Database.
Cultivar name not established.

'**Magellan**', *S. vulgaris*
Lemoine 1915; D VI
Lemoine, Cat. No. 188, 14 [1915]; McKelvey, The Lilac, 338 [1928]; Wister, Lilacs for America, 52 [1942], 34 [1953]; Photo on Jorgovani/Lilacs 2015 DVD.
Named for Ferdinand Magellan, ca 1480-1521, Portuguese circum-navigator.
Cultivar name presumed registered 1953; name established and accepted.

'**Maggie Brooks**', *S. vulgaris*
Fenicchia & Millham 2011; S II
Millham, Lilacs - Quart. Jour. 41(2):54 [2012]; Vrugtman, Hanburyana 7:26 [2013]; K. Millham, Lilacs - Quart. Jour. 42(2):61, ill. 71 [2013].
Named Ms Maggie A. Brooks (b. 1955), broadcasting personality and politician, County Executive of Monroe County, New York.
Cultivar name registered 2011; name established and accepted.

'**Maģija**', *S. vulgaris*
Kārkliņš 2003; D VII
Strautiņa & Kaufmane, Dobeles ceriņi, p. 92 [2011]; Photo on Jorgovani/Lilacs 2015 DVD.
Name: Latvian for magic.
Cultivar name established and accepted.

'**Maiden's Blush**', *S.* ×*hyacinthiflora*
Skinner 1966; S V
syn. - 'Maiden Blush', 'Maidens Blush'
marketed in Germany as ROSENROT, in Denmark as ROSARÖD; marketed in Europe also as ROSENROT.
Skinner, Horticultural Horizons, p. 50, 110 [1966] - as *S. microphylla* var. *superba* × (*S. oblata* var. *dilatata* × *S. vulgaris*); Wister, Arnoldia 26(3):14 [1966]; Pringle, Baileya 21(3):105-108, 113 [1981] - as *S.* ×*hyacinthiflora*; Photo on Jorgovani/Lilacs 2015 DVD.
Cultivar name registered 1966; name established and accepted.
Forcing cultivar in the Netherlands.

'**Maiennacht**', *S. vulgaris*
Löbner pre-1947; S V
Meyer, Flieder, 72 [1952]; Wister, Lilacs for America, 34 [1953]; Vrugtman, Lilacs - Quart. Jour. 22(3):90-95 [1993].
Cultivar name presumed registered 1953; name established and accepted.

'**Maĭgul**', *S. vulgaris*
'Майгуль'
Sagitova 1994; S VII & V
varietal denomination registered 1994, No. 15, State Register of Selected Achievements in Republic of Kazakhstan;
Cultivar name established and accepted.

'**Maiia**', *S. vulgaris*
'Майя'
Sagitova, ?; D III
Photo by Milada Dzevitskaya seen on 2020 ILS Photo & Color Database.
Cultivar name not established.

MAIJA - see '**Maija Vieshņja**'.

'**Maija Viešņja**', *S. vulgaris*
Upītis 1991; S VII/V
syn. - Upītis No. 4797, 'Maija Vieshņja'
statutory epithet Maija Viesna
Strautiņa, S., Ceriņu un jasmīnu avīze. LA, R., p. 62 [2002] - in Latvian; in litt. S. Strautiņa to F. Vrugtman [Dec. 12, 2007] - 1991, S VII/V
statutory registration (breeder's rights) Nr. 296, CER-3, in Latvia [2004 - 2029] with the statutory epithet.
Name: Latvian for guest of May.
Cultivar name established and accepted; name registered.

'**Mainzer Rad**', *S. vulgaris*
Schweikhart; D V-II
Maethe, in Deutsche Baumschule 7/1993, 301 - in German
Named for the Mainzer Rad, or the Mainzer Wheel, in the coat of arms of the city of Mainz, Germany.
Cultivar name established and accepted.

'**Maĭskoe Utro**', *S. vulgaris*
'Майское Утро'

Mel'nik; 1971, S VII/V
syn. - 'Majskoe Utro', seedling No. 21
{'Congo' × OP}
Rubanik, V. G. et al., Siren' - Syringa L., publishing house "Kaĭnar", Alma-Ata [1977] p 53- in Russian; Rubtzov et al. 1980. Vidy i sorta sireni, kul'tiviruemye v SSSR. Kiev; Naukova Dumka. – in Russian; Holetich, C.D. 1982. Lilac species and cultivars in cultivation in USSR. Lilacs 11(2):1-38. - translation of Rubtzov et al. 1982.
Name: Russian for May morning.
Cultivar name established and accepted.

'Maître Georges Hermans', *S. vulgaris*
Lambrechts 1952; D VI
syn. - 'Maitre Georges Hermans'
Wister, Lilacs for America, 34 [1953]
Cultivar name presumed registered 1953; name established and accepted.

'Maiu', *S.*
Mägi pre-2018; S III/IV
Semenov, I., Lilacs 48(2):68,66 (photo) [2019].
Cultivar name not established.

Maiwunder', *S. vulgaris*
Origin not known; D? IV?
<www.piccoplant.de/htm/english/produkte.htm> seen July 19, 2019
Name: means May Wonder
Cultivar name not established.

'Majeskie', *S.* (species affiliation not known)
origin not known ? III
Stenlund, Lilacs - Quart. Jour. 20(2):41 [1991]
Cultivar name not established.

'Major', *S.* ×*chinensis*
origin not known pre-1887; S ?
Späth, Cat. No. 69, 114 [1887]; McKelvey, The Lilac, 426 [1928]
Cultivar name not established.

'Major', *S. reticulata*
origin not known ? ?
Reported in cultivation at Morden Research Centre.
Cultivar name not established.

'Major', *S. vulgaris*
origin not known pre-1872; ? ?
common name: Major
Stand. Pl. Names, 487 [1923] - as Major; McKelvey, The Lilac, 338 [1928] - confused name; Wister, Nat. Hort. Mag. 6(1):1-16 [1927]; Wister, Lilacs for America, 37, 52 [1942]
Cultivar name not established, not reported in cultivation in 1953.

'Maksim Gor'kiĭ', *S. vulgaris*
'Максим Горький'
Kolesnikov 1939; S II
syn. - 'Maxim Gor'kiy' 'Maxim Gorky'
Pikaleva, Lilacs - Quart. Jour. 23(4):86 [1994]; Photo on Jorgovani/Lilacs 2015 DVD.
Named for Maksim Gorky, pen name of Alekseĭ Maksimovich Peshkov, 1868-1936, famous Russian novelist.
Cultivar name established and accepted.

'Malakhov', *S. vulgaris*
'Малахов'
Kolesnikov 1955; S II
Wister & Oppe, Arnoldia 31(3):126 [1971]
Named for Malakhov Hill, Crimea, Ukraine, site of the Sebastopol fortress and battles of the Crimean War 1853/56.
Cultivar name registered 1970; name established and accepted.

'Malduguns', *S. vulgaris*
Kārkliņš 2003; D V
Strautiņa & Kaufmane, Dobeles ceriņi, pp. 14, 92 [2011]
Name: Latvian for will-o'-the-wisp.
Cultivar name established and accepted.

Manchurian lilac - see *S. pubescens* subsp. *patula* or *S. reticulata* var. *amurensis*.

'Manshuk', *S. vulgaris*
'Маншук'
Sagitova; ? ?
{'Tadeush' × ? }
syn. - S-19(3)Named for staff sergeant Manshuk Zhiengalievne Mametova, 1922-1943, Hero of the Soviet Union, whose monument stands in Uralsk, Kazakhstan.
Cultivar name not established.

'Marat Kazeĭ', *S. vulgaris*
'Марат Казей'
Smol'skiĭ & Bibikova 1964; S III
syn. - 'Marat Kazai', 'Marat Kazei', 'Marat Kazej'
{'Hyazinthenflieder' × 'Réaumur'}
Rubtzov et al. 1980. Vidy i sorta sireni, kul'tiviruemye v SSSR. Kiev; Naukova Dumka. – in Russian; Holetich, C.D. 1982. Lilac species and cultivars in cultivation in USSR. Lilacs 11(2):1-38. - translation of Rubtzov et al. 1982; Semenov, Igor, Lilacs -Quart. Jour. 43(3):85-87 [2014].
Named for Marat Kazeĭ, 1929-1944, World War II teenage partisan and Hero of the Soviet Union, whose monument stands in Minsk, Belarus.
Cultivar name established and accepted.

'Marceau', *S. vulgaris*
Lemoine 1913; S VI
Lemoine, Cat. No. 185, 6 [1913]; McKelvey, The Lilac, 339 [1928]; Wister, Lilacs for America, 52 [1942], 34 [1953]; Photo on Jorgovani/Lilacs 2015 DVD.
Named for François Séverin Marceau-Desgraviers, 1769-1796, French soldier and general.
Cultivar name presumed registered 1953; name established and accepted.

'Marchall Vasilesky' - see 'Mar<u>sh</u>al Vasilevskiĭ'.

'Marchioness of Lorne', *S. vulgaris*
Dougall; ? III
Dougall., Canadian Horticulturist 2(1):8 [1879]
Named for Louise Caroline Alberta, Lady John Campbell, Marchioness of Lorne, Duchess of Argyll, 1848-1939, née Princess of Great Britain and Ireland, daughter of Queen Victoria; the Canadian province of Alberta and Lake Louise were also named for her (see also 'Marquis of Lorne').
Cultivar name not established; not reported in cultivation, probably extinct.

'Marcie Merlot', *S. vulgaris*
Hoepfl 2007: S VII
syn. - FC 15
{'Flower City' × ? }
Hoepfl, Lilacs - Quart. Jour. 36(2):74-75 [2007] - background information only; Millham, Lilacs - Quart. Jour. 42(4):130 & photo inside cover [2013] - reference to FC 15; Millham, Lilacs - Quart. Jour. 43(2):52 [2014] - as S VII; photo on Lilacs/Jorgovani 2014 DVD; Hoepfl, Lilacs - Quart. Jour. 43(3):90 & photo 91 [2014] - as S VII, "unfolding foliage reddish".
Named for the wine by that name, hinting at the similarity in color of florets and foliage.
Cultivar name established and accepted.

'Marc Micheli', *S. vulgaris*
Lemoine 1898; D V
syn. - 'Marc Hicheli', 'Marc Michel', 'Marc Michelli', 'Markus Micheli', 'Marc Mitchell'
Lemoine, Cat. No. 140, 10 [1898]; McKelvey, The Lilac, 339 [1928]; Wister, Lilacs for America, 52 [1942], 34 [1953]; Photo on Jorgovani/Lilacs 2015 DVD.
Named for Marc Micheli, 1844-1902, French horticulturist.
Cultivar name presumed registered 1953; name established and accepted.

'Mare', *S. vulgaris*
Mägi 2017 ; S VII
Photo from Estonia by Mägi, seen in 2020 ILS Photo Database.
Cultivar name not established.

'Maréchal de Bassompierre', *S. vulgaris*
Lemoine 1897; D VI
syn. - 'Marechal de Bassompierre', 'Marschall von Bassompierre'
Lemoine, Cat. No. 137, 10 [1897]; McKelvey, The Lilac, 339-340 [1928]; Wister, Lilacs for America, 52 [1942], 34 [1953]; Photo on Jorgovani/Lilacs 2015 DVD.
Named for Baron François de Bassompierre, 1579-1646, Marshal of France, courtier, author.
Cultivar name presumed registered 1953; name established and accepted.

'Maréchal Foch', *S. vulgaris*
Lemoine 1924; S VI
syn. - 'Foch', 'Marechal de Foch', 'Marechal Foch', 'Marshal Foche', FOCH (trade designation used for cut flowers of this cultivar)
Lemoine, Cat. No. 198, 20 [1924]; McKelvey, The Lilac, 340 [1928]; Wister, Lilacs for America, 52 [1942], 34 [1953]; Photo on Jorgovani/Lilacs 2015 DVD.
Named for Ferdinand Foch, 1851-1929, French soldier, author and professor of Strategy at the École Supérieure de Guerre.
Awards: RHS Award of Merit 1935.
Cultivar name presumed registered 1953; name established and accepted.
Forcing cultivar in the Netherlands.

'Maréchal Lannes', *S. vulgaris*
Lemoine 1910; D III
syn. - 'Marechal Lannes', 'Marschall Lannes'
Lemoine, Cat. No. 176, 7 [1910]; McKelvey, The Lilac, 340 [1928]; Wister, Lilacs for America, 52 [1942] - as D II; Wister, Lilacs for America, 34 [1953]; Photo on Jorgovani/Lilacs 2015 DVD.
Named for Jean Lannes, Duc de Montebello, 1769-1809, French soldier and marshal of Napoléon.
Cultivar name presumed registered 1953; name established and accepted.

'Marengo', *S. vulgaris*
Lemoine 1923; S IV
syn. - 'Margengo'
Lemoine, Cat. No. 197, 20 [1923]; McKelvey, The Lilac, 340-341 [1928]; Wister, Lilacs for America, 52 [1942], 34 [1953]; Photo on Jorgovani/Lilacs 2015 DVD.
Named for Marengo, where Napoleon defeated Austria, June 14, 1800.
Cultivar name presumed registered 1953; name established and accepted.

'Marat Kazeĭ' *S. vulgaris*
Smol'skiĭ & Bibikova pre-1966; ?
Per Makedonska<u>ya</u> and Okuneva in Lilacs 46(1):23, Bibikova labeled as unpromising, excluded from collection, last flowered 1989, now extinct.
Cultivar name not established.

'Margaret', S. (Villosae Group), *S. ×prestoniae*
Preston 1928; S V
{*S. villosa* subsp. *villosa* × *S. komarowii* subsp. *reflexa*}
syn. - Preston No. 20-14-221
Macoun, Rep. Dom. Hort. 1928, 56 [1930]; Wister, Lilacs for America, 64 [1942], 48 [1953] - not in cultivation, no plants distributed
Named for the Wife to King Henry VI in Shakespeare's *King Henry VI*, Part II.
Cultivar name not established, probably extinct.

'Margaret Fenicchia', *S. vulgaris*
Fenicchia 1997; S VII/II

{'Rochester' × ? }
syn. - RAF No. 1825
Vrugtman, HortScience 33(4):588-589 [1998]; in litt., Hoepfl to Vrugtman [Nov.29/2003] - Fiala, Lilacs, Pl. 78, lilac No. 1825 [1988]; K. Millham, Lilacs - Quart.Jour. 42(2):61 & ill. 69 [2013]; Photo on Jorgovani/Lilacs 2015 DVD.
Cultivar name registered 1997; name established and accepted.

'Margaretha', *S. vulgaris*
Buis 1952; S I
{mutation of 'Mme Florent Stepman'}
Wister, Lilacs for America, 34 [1953]; Bunnik/Stapel, in litt. January 3, 2000; Cornelis van Dam, in lit January 11, 2000 - no longer in cultivation, but sports very similar or identical to 'Margaretha' turn up regularly, recognizable by their wrinkled flower buds.
Named for Margaretha Annie Buis, born in 1935, daughter to the originator.
Cultivar name established and accepted.
Formerly a forcing cultivar in the Netherlands.

'**Margaret Opper**', *S. vulgaris*
Rankin; S IV
{parentage not known}
Wister, Arnoldia 23(4):82 [1963]
Cultivar name registered 1963;
Cultivar not reported in cultivation.

'**Margaret Rice Gould**', *S. vulgaris*
Brand pre-1953; S VII
AAN reg'n card No. 471; Wister, Lilacs for America, 34 [1953]; Photo on Jorgovani/Lilacs 2015 DVD.
Cultivar name presumed registered 1953; name established and accepted.

'**Margot Grunewald**', *S. vulgaris*
Grunewald 1913; D III
Fr. Grunewald, Cat., 14 [1939]; Wister, Lilacs for America, 34 [1953] - name only; Fiala, Lilacs, 97, Pl. 14 [1988]; Photo on Jorgovani/Lilacs 2015 DVD.
Cultivar name presumed registered 1953; name established and accepted.

'**Marguerite**', *S. vulgaris*
Klager 1928; S VII
Wister, Lilacs for America, 52 [1942], 34 [1953]
Cultivar name presumed registered 1953;
Cultivar not reported in cultivation.

'Maria', *S.* (Villosae Group), *S.* ×*henryi*
Kolkka 1979; S I
{open pollinated seedling of unknown origin}
Kolkka, SORBIFOLIA 37(1)27-36, ill. p. 32 (2006) (in Finnish)
Cultivar name established and accepted.

'Maria', *S. vulgaris*
Sagitova & Dzevitski pre-2014; D I
Photo by Oleg Dzevitskiy seen in 2020 ILS Photo & Color Database
Cultivar name not established.

'Mariam Cooley' - see '**Miriam Cooley**'.

'Mariana', *S.* (Villosae Group), *S.* ×*prestoniae*
Preston; ? ?
{*S. villosa* subsp. *villosa* × *S. komarowii* subsp. *reflexa*}
syn. - Preston No. 20-14-78
Macoun, Rep. Dom. Hort. 1928, 56 [1930]; Wister, Lilacs for America, 64 [1942]; 48 [1953] - not in cultivation, no plants distributed
Named for The Betrothed of Angelo in Shakespeare's *Measure for Measure.*
Cultivar name not established, probably extinct.

Marie Chaykowski - see 'Marie Frances'.

'**Marie Finon**', *S. vulgaris*
Lemoine 1923; S I
Lemoine, Cat. No. 197, 20 [1923]; McKelvey, The Lilac, 341 [1928]; Wister, Lilacs for America, 52 [1942], 34 [1953]; Photo on Jorgovani/Lilacs 2015 DVD.
Cultivar name presumed registered 1953; name established and accepted.

'Marie Frances', *S. vulgaris*
Fiala 1983; S V
syn. - 'Marie Chaykowski', 'Marie Graykowski'
{'Edward J. Gardner' × 'Rochester'}
Fiala, Lilacs, 100, 223 [1988] - on pp. 99, 100 & 107 as 'Marie Chaykowski' but indexed on p. 262 as 'Marie Frances', the name intended; Knight Hollow Nursery, 1998 Cultured cutting and liner descriptive list; Photo on Jorgovani/Lilacs 2015 DVD.
Named for Marie Frances Chaykowski, sister of the originator.
Cultivar name established and accepted.

'**Marie Guille**', *S. vulgaris*
Bruchet pre-1924; S I
McKelvey, The Lilac, 341 [1928]; Wister, Lilacs for America, 52 [1942], 34 [1953]
Named (probably) for Marie Guille, who married Mauger, Archbishop of Rouen, the banished uncle of William Duc of Normandy (The Conqueror), in 1055, on the Channel Island of Guernsey.
Cultivar name presumed registered 1953; name established and accepted.

'**Marie Legraye**', *S. vulgaris*
Legraye pre-1879; S I
{parentage not known}
syn. - 'Mademoiselle Marie Legraye', 'Marie LeGraye', 'Marie Legray', 'Mlle Marie Legraye', 'Marie Leguay'
C.J.E. Morren, Belg. Hort. 29:135, pl. 8 [1879] - as 'Mademoiselle Marie Legraye'; McKelvey, The Lilac, 341-342 [1928]; Wister, Lilacs for America, 52 [1942], 34 [1953]; Photo on Jorgovani/Lilacs 2015 DVD.
Named for Marie Anne Victoire Legraye, 1833-1903,

florist, Établissement Marie Legraye, Liège, Belgium.
Cultivar name presumed registered 1953; name established and accepted.
Forcing cultivar in the Netherlands (only at Fa Heeren).

'Marie Legraye Folii Aureis', *S. vulgaris*
origin not known pre-1900; S I *
syn. - 'Marie Legraye Foliis Aureis', 'Maie Legraye à feuilles dorées'
{mutation of 'Marie Legraye'}
Martinet, Arbres, Arbust., 93 [1900]; McKelvey, The Lilac, 342 [1928]; Wister, Nat. Hort. Mag. 6(1):1-16 [1927]; Wister, Lilacs for America, 52 [1942], 34 [1953]
Cultivar name presumed registered 1953; name established and accepted.

Marie Leguay - see **'Marie Legraye'**.

'Marie Lemoine', *S. vulgaris*
Origin not known; S I
Tingle, Wholesale Price List, 18 [1947].
Questionable name.

'Marie Marcelin', *S. vulgaris*
origin not known pre-1953; D V
Wister, Lilacs for America, 34 [1953] - name only; Vrugtman, Lilacs -Quart. Jour. 32(4):149 [2003] - as D V; Photo on Jorgovani/Lilacs 2015 DVD.
Cultivar name established and accepted.

'Marie Rogers', *S.* (Villosae Group)
Rogers and Oakes; S II (multipetaled)
{Rogers 86-1 × OP }
Rogers, Lilacs Quart. J. 23(4):107 [1994] - parentage of 86-1; Vrugtman, HortScience 40(6):1597 [2005] & 42(1):5 [2006]; J. Bentley, Lilacs 42(2):58 [2013].
Selected and named by Oakes for Marie Rose (Alberti) Rogers 1931- 2017, wife to Owen M. Rogers, originator.
Cultivar name registered 2003; name established and accepted.

'Mariette Vermorel', *S. vulgaris*
origin not known pre-1908; D I
Fl. Stepman-De Messemaeker, Suppl. to Gen. Cat., 2 [1908]; McKelvey, The Lilac, 342 [1928]; Wister, Lilacs for America, 34 [1953]
Cultivar name presumed registered 1953; name established and accepted.

'Marilyn Sue', *S. reticulata*
Arborvillage ca 1976; S I
Arborvillage Farm Nursery Cat. [2006]; Klehm's Song Sparrow Farm and Nursery, 2017 - as new foliage with slight burgundy-bronze tint http://www.songsparrow.com/catalog/plantdetails.cfm?ID=5112&type=WOODY,&pagetype=plantdetails&plant_name=Syringa%20reticulata%20%27Marilyn%20Sue%27 [seen May 9, 2017]
Cultivar name established and accepted.

'Marina Raskova', *S. vulgaris*
'Марина Раскова'
Kolesnikov pre-1954; D
Rubtzov et al. 1980. Vidy i sorta sireni, kul'tiviruemye v SSSR. Kiev; Naukova Dumka. – in Russian; Holetich, C.D. 1982. Lilac species and cultivars in cultivation in USSR. Lilacs 11(2):1-38. - translation of Rubtzov et al. 1982.
Named for major Marina Raskova, 1912-1943, aviatress, Hero of the Soviet Union, who formed three women's aviation regiments during World War II. (See also 'Polina Osipenko'.)
Cultivar name not established.

'Mariya Nagibina', *S. vulgaris*
'Мария Нагибина'
Kolesnikov pre 1950; D III-IV
Syn. - Sdl No 267
Polyakova, 2018, "Master of the Lilac Inflorescence", p. 116; cultivar passport
Polyakova , 2010, Istoriya Russkoĭ Sireni, p. 25; name only.
Named after biologist Maria Nagibina (botanical garden of Moscow State University) mentor of Kolesnikov
Cultivar name established and accepted.

'Mark Drie', *S.*
origin not known pre-2007; ? ?
Kilcoyne, Lilacs-Quart. Jour. 36(2):82 [2007] - name only
Cultivar name established and accepted.

Markus Micheli - see **'Marc Micheli'**.

Marley - see **'Lake Bled'**
Lumley, Lilac Land list [n.d., pre-1974].

Marliensis . . . . - see **'Marlyensis'**.

Marly - see **'Marlyensis'**.

'Marlyensis', *S. vulgaris*
origin not known pre-1733; S IV
syn. - 'Marleyensis', 'Marliensis', 'Marlyensis Rubra', *purpurea*, 'Rouge de Marly', 'Rubra de Marley', 'Violaceae', *S. vulgaris* var. *purpurea* Weston
common names: Marly, Red Marley
Stand. Pl. Names, 487, 488 [1923] - as Marly and Red Marly; McKelvey, The Lilac, 239-241 [1928]; Wister, Lilacs for America, 52 [1942], 35 [1953]; Photo on Jorgovani/Lilacs 2015 DVD.
Cultivar name presumed registered 1953; name established and accepted.

'Marlyensis Bicolor', *S. vulgaris*
origin not known pre-1885; ? ?
Dieck, Haupt-Cat. Zöschen, 78 [1885]; McKelvey, The Lilac, 342 [1928]
Cultivar name not established.

Marlyensis Florealba, Marleyensis flora alba - see **'Marlyensis Pallida'**.

'Marlyensis Flore Pleno', *S. vulgaris*
origin not known pre-1885; ? ?
McKelvey, The Lilac, 342 [1928].

'Marlyensis Pallida', *S. vulgaris*
origin not known pre-1864; S IV
syn. - 'Marleyensis Pallida', 'Marliensis pallida', 'Marlyensis florealba'
common names: Pale Marly, White Marly
Stand. Pl. Names, 487 [1923] - as Pale Marly and White Marly; McKelvey, The Lilac, 342-343 [1928]; Wister, Lilacs for America, 52 [1942], 35 [1953]; Photo on Jorgovani/Lilacs 2015 DVD.
Cultivar name presumed registered 1953; name established and accepted.

Marlyensis Rubra - see **'Marlyensis'**.

Marly Rouge - see **'Marlyensis'**.

'Marquis of Lorne', *S. vulgaris*
Dougall 1880; ? ?
Dougall, Canadian Horticulturist 3(7):103 [1880]
Named for Ian Campbell, 1845-1914, Marquis of Lorne, eldest son and heir of the Duke of Argyle, Governor General of Canada 1878-1883.
Cultivar name not established; probably no longer in cultivation.

'Marshal Bagramyan', *S. vulgaris*
'Маршал Баграмян"
Aladin, S., Aladina, O., and Polyakova, T. 2015; D V
{'Emile Lemoine' × 'Elena Rosse'}
Питомник-частный сад (Pitomnik i chastnyi sad; Nursery and private garden) 2/2015: 32-38 (in Russian); Приусадебное хозяйство (Annex to the magazine Homestead farming: "Flowers in the garden and at home. Brushes and paints") 08/2015: 5-14; Вестник АППМ (Catalog in Vestnik APPM (Planting material association) magazine) 1/2018: 59-72 (in Russian);
Named for Ivan Khristoforovich Bagramyan (Иван Христофорович Баграмян), 1897–1982, Marshal of the Soviet Union and Hero of the Soviet Union.
Cultivar name established and accepted.

'Marshal Biryuzov', *S. vulgaris*
'Маршал Бирюзов'
Aladin, S., Arkhangel'skii, V., Aladina, O., Akimova, S., and Okuneva I. 2011; S IV-V
{'Stefan Makovetskii' × OP}
Registered with the State Commission of the Russian Federation for Testing and
Protection of Selection Achievements, No. 8853110, 2011; Питомник-частный сад
(Pitomnik i chastnyi sad; Nursery and private garden) 2/2015:32-40 (in Russian); Photo on Jorgovani/Lilacs 2015 DVD; Приусадебное хозяйство (Annex to the magazine Homestead farming: "Flowers in the garden and at home. Brushes and paints") 08/2015: 5-14; Вестник АППМ (Catalog in Vestnik APPM (Planting material association) magazine) 1/2018: 59-72 (in Russian).
Named for Sergey Semyonovich Biryuzov (Сергей Семенович Бирюзов), 1904-1964, Marshal of the Soviet Union and Hero of the Soviet Union.
Cultivar name registered, established and accepted.

'Marshal Chuĭkov', *S. vulgaris*
'Маршал Чуйков'
Aladin, S., Aladina, O., Polyakova, T., and Aladina, A. 2019; S VII
{'Monge' × OP?}
(Международная научная конференция "Syringa L.: коллекции, выращивание, использование") "International Scientific Conference "Syringa L.: collections, cultivation, using" / Collection of Scientific Articles of Botanical Institute named after V.L. Komarov, Botanical Garden of Peter the Great BIN RAS. - St. Petersburg. -2020.- pp.3-7 (in Russian); Photo exhibition of all varieties of the creative breeding group "Russian Lilac" at the Festival "Lilac February", St. Petersburg, Botanical Garden of Peter the Great BIN RAS, February 22-24, 2020.
Named for the outstanding commander, twice Hero of the Soviet Union, the hero of Stalingrad Vasily Ivanovich Chuykov (1900-1982).
Cultivar name established and accepted.

'Marshal Govorov', *S. vulgaris*
'Маршал Говоров'
Aladin, S., Aladina, O., and Polyakova, T. pre-2017; D VII/II
{elite form 09-307 × OP}
Садовник (Gardener) magazine, 05 (141)/2017 :16-22; Вестник АППМ (Catalog in Vestnik APPM (Planting material association) magazine) 1/2018: 59-72 (in Russian).
Named for Leonid Alseksandrovich Govorov (Леонид Александрович Говоров), 1897-1955, Marshal of the Soviet Army and defender of Leneingrad during World War II.
Cultivar name established and accepted.

'Marshal Konev', *S. vulgaris*
'Маршал Конев'
Aladin, S., Arkhangel'skii, V., Polyakova, T., Aladina, O., and Okuneva, I. 2011; D III-IV
{'Président Grévy' × OP}
Registered with the State Commission of the Russian Federation for Testing and Protection of Selection Achievements, No. 8853119, 2011; Питомник-частный сад (Pitomnik i chastnyi sad; Nursery and private garden) 2/2015:32-40; Садовник (Gardener) magazine, 05 (141)/2017 :16-22; Вестник АППМ (Catalog in Vestnik APPM (Planting material association) magazine) 1/2018: 59-72 (in Russian); Photo on Jorgovani/Lilacs 2015 DVD.
Named for Ivan Stepanovich Konev (Иван Степанович

Конев), 1897-1973, Marshal of the Soviet Union and Hero of the Soviet Union.
Cultivar name registered, established and accepted.

'Mar**sh**al Malinovskiĭ', *S. vulgaris*
'Маршал Малиновский'
Aladin, S., Arkhangel'skii, V., Okuneva, I., Aladina, O., and Akimova, S. 2011; D VII-IV
{'Condorcet' × OP}
Registered with the State Commission of the Russian Federation for Testing and Protection of Selection Achievements, No. 8853111, 2011; Питомник-частный сад (Pitomnik i chastnyi sad; Nursery and private garden) 2/2015: 32-38 (in Russian); Садовник (Gardener) magazine, 05 (141)/2017 :16-22; Вестник АППМ (Catalog in Vestnik APPM (Planting material association) magazine) 1/2018: 59-72 (in Russian); Photo on Jorgovani/Lilacs 2015 DVD.
Named for Rodion Iakovlevich Malinovskii (Родион Яковлевич Малиновский), 1898-1967, Marshal of the Soviet Union and Hero of the Soviet Union.
Cultivar name registered, established and accepted.

'Mar**sh**al Rokossovskiĭ', *S. vulgaris*
'Маршал Рокоссовский'
Aladin, S., Aladina, O., and Polyakova, T. 2013; D VII-IV
{'Maximowicz' × 'Cavour'}
Приусадебное хозяйство (Annex to the magazine Homestead farming: "Flowers in the garden and at home. Brushes and paints") 08/2015: 5-14; Садовник (Gardener) magazine, 05 (141)/2017 :16-22; Вестник АППМ (Catalog in Vestnik APPM (Planting material association) magazine) 1/2018: 59-72 (in Russian);
Named for Konstantin Konstantinovich Rokossovskii (Константин Константинович Рокоссовский), 1896-1968, Soviet officer of Polish origin who became Marshal of the Soviet Union, Marshal of Poland and served as Poland's Defense Minister and Hero of the Soviet Union.
Cultivar name established and accepted.

'Mar**sh**al Sokolovskiĭ', *S. vulgaris*
'Маршал Соколовский'
Aladin, S., Arkhangel'skii, V., Polyakova, T., and Okuneva, I. 2011; S VII
{'Monge' × OP}
Registered with the State Commission of the Russian Federation for Testing and Protection of Selection Achievements, No. 8853114, 2011; Питомник-частный сад (Pitomnik i chastnyi sad; Nursery and private garden) 2/2015:32-40 (in Russian); Приусадебное хозяйство (Annex to the magazine Homestead farming: "Flowers in the garden and at home. Brushes and paints") 08/2015: 5-14; Вестник АППМ (Catalog in Vestnik APPM (Planting material association) magazine) 1/2018: 59-72 (in Russian); Photo on Jorgovani/Lilacs 2015 DVD.
Named for Vasily Danilovich Sokolovsky (Василий Данилович Соколовский), 1897-1968, Marshal of the Soviet Union and Hero of the Soviet Union.
Cultivar name registered, established and accepted.

'**Mar**shal Vasilevskiĭ', *S. vulgaris*
'Маршал Василевский'*
Kolesnikov 1963; D IV-V
syn. - 'Marchal Vasilesky', 'Marshal Vasilevskii', 'Marshal Vasilevskij', 'Marshal Vasilevskiy', Kolesnikov No. 282
Howard, Arnoldia 19(6-7):31-35 [1959]; Gromov, A., Siren', 80 [1963]; Howard & Brizicky, AABGA Quart. Newsl. No. 64, 17-21 [1965]; Wister & Oppe, Arnoldia 31(3):125 [1971] - as 'Marshal Vasilevskii'; Rubtzov et al. 1980. Vidy i sorta sireni, kul'tiviruemye v SSSR. Kiev; Naukova Dumka. – in Russian; Holetich, C.D. 1982. Lilac species and cultivars in cultivation in USSR. Lilacs 11(2):1-38. - translation of Rubtzov et al. 1982; Photo on Jorgovani/Lilacs 2015 DVD.
Named for Aleksandr Mikhaĭlovich Vasilevskiĭ, 1895-1977, Chief of the Soviet General Staff in World War II.
Cultivar name registered 1970; name established and accepted.

'Marshal **Zh**ukov', *S. vulgaris*
'Маршал Жуков'
Kolesnikov 1948; S IV-VI
syn. - Kolesnikov No. 520, 'Marschal Zhukov', 'Marshal Zhukov'
{'M. I. Kalinin' × Kolesnikov No. 105}
Bilov, V. D., et al., Siren' [1974]; Gromov, Lilacs - Proceedings 2(4):17 [1974]; Rubtzov et al. 1980. Vidy i sorta sireni, kul'tiviruemye v SSSR. Kiev; Naukova Dumka. – in Russian; Holetich, C.D. 1982. Lilac species and cultivars in cultivation in USSR. Lilacs 11(2):1-38. - translation of Rubtzov et al. 1982; Photo on Jorgovani/Lilacs 2015 DVD.
Named for Georgĭ Konstantinovich Zhukov, 1896-1974, Soviet Marshal and defender of Stalingrad in World War II.
Cultivar name established and accepted.

'Marsianka', *S. vulgaris*
'Марсианка'
Klimenko, V. 1955; S II
{'Andenken an Ludwig Späth' × 'Jeanne d'Arc'}
Rubtzov et al. 1980. Vidy i sorta sireni, kul'tiviruemye v SSSR. Kiev; Naukova Dumka. – in Russian; Holetich, C.D. 1982. Lilac species and cultivars in cultivation in USSR. Lilacs 11(2):1-38. - translation of Rubtzov et al. 1982.
Cultivar name established and accepted.

'Martha', *S. vulgaris*
Klager 1930; S I
Wister, Lilacs for America, 52 [1942], 35 [1953]; ILS Newsletter 14(4):3-4 [1988]; Photo on Jorgovani/Lilacs 2015 DVD.
Cultivar name presumed registered 1953; name established and accepted.

'**Martha Kounze**', *S. vulgaris*
Havemeyer pre-1953; D V
Wister, Lilacs for America, 35 [1953]; Eickhorst, ILS Lilac Newsletter 4(1):4-5 [1978]; Photo on Jorgovani/Lilacs 2015 DVD.
Cultivar name presumed registered 1953; name established and accepted.

'**Martha Stewart**', *S. vulgaris*
Fenicchia; S II/III
{'Rochester' × ? }
Vrugtman, HortScience 31(3):327 [1996]; Roach, Martha Stewart Living, 92, 93 ill. [May 1996]; K. Millham, Lilacs - Quart. Jour. 42(2):61 & ill. 69 [2013]; Photo on Jorgovani/Lilacs 2015 DVD.
Named for Martha Helen Stewart (née Kostyra), born 1941; American business magnate, television host, author, and magazine publisher.
Cultivar name registered 1995; name established and accepted.

'**Martin**', *S. ×hyacinthiflora*
Vaigla pre-2001; S VI/IV (VI-III per Semenov) listed on http://aed.rapina.ee/sirelid.htm [seen 5 Nov. 2005]; I. Semenov, Lilacs 48(2):65 (back cover photo) [2019].
Cultivar name not established.

'**Martine**', *S. vulgaris*
Spaargaren 1954; S I
Marchal, Jaarverslag Proefstation Aalsmeer, 120 [1954]; Wister, Arnoldia 23(4):82 [1963]; Photo on Jorgovani/Lilacs 2015 DVD.
Named for Martine Spaargaren, 1916-1991, plant breeder (Proeftuin, Rijks Tuinbouw Winterschool; 1936-1940), Aalsmeer, The Netherlands.
Awards: Certificate of Merit 1954 (KMTP).
Cultivar name registered 1963; name established and accepted.

'**Mar'ushka**', *S. vulgaris*
'Марьюшка'
Sagitova & Dzevitski pre-2014; S IV
Photo by Sergei Dzevitskiy in Almaty, Kazakhstan seen in 2020 ILS Photo & Color Database.
Cultivar name not established.

'**Mar'yam**', *S. vulgaris*
'Марьям'
Sagitova 1994; S VII & V
varietal denomination registered 1994, No. 14, State Register of Selected Achievements in Republic of Kazakhstan; statutory registration.
Cultivar name established and accepted.

'**Mary Blanchard**', *S. vulgaris*
Yeager 1958; S II
{'Congo' × ? }
Yeager, New Hampshire Agric. Exp. Sta. Bull. 461, 13 [1959]; Wister, Arnoldia 23(4):82 [1963]; J. Bentley, Lilacs 42(2):58 [2013].
Named for Mary Fisher Blanchard, 1894-1953, amateur gardener and lilac grower, active member of the Milford Garden Club, New Hampshire, USA.
Cultivar name registered 1963; name established and accepted
Nota bene: Plants in cultivation may not be true to name.

'**Mary C. Bingham**', *S.* (Villosae Group)
Alexander Sr 1976; S V
{*S. ×josiflexa* 'James Macfarlane' × *S. ×prestoniae* 'Ethel M. Webster'}
Alexander Sr, Cat. sheets [Spring 1976] - as S V
Cultivar name established and accepted.
Nota bene: Susequently to the introduction of the above cultivar other selections may have been substituted under the same name; plants growing at the Arnold Arboretum, lineage 784-85 and 745-80, are authenticated, and propagules documented to that lineage are true to name (in litt. J. H. Alexander III to Vrugtman Feb.1/01).

'**Mary Ellen**', *S. vulgaris*
Hughes; D I
{parentage not known}
Seen in 2019 in Freek Vrugtman personal archives from photo in 2005 by Hughes.
Cultivar name not established.

'**Mary Evelyn White**', *S.* (Villosae Group)
Alexander Sr; S V
{*S. ×josiflexa* 'James Macfarlane' × *S. ×prestoniae* 'Ethel M. Webster'}
Wister & Oppe, Arnoldia 31(3):123 [1971]
Cultivar name registered 1970;
Cultivar not reported in cultivation.

'**Mary Gardner**', *S. ×hyacinthiflora*
Gardner 1956; S III
syn.: 'Gardner No. 444', 'Mary Ann Gardner'
Edw. J. Gardner Nursery, Price list, 6 [1956]; Wister & Oppe, Arnoldia 31(3):123 [1971] - as 'Mary Ann Gardner'; Photo on Jorgovani/Lilacs 2015 DVD.
Cultivar name registered 1970; name established and accepted.

'**Mary K. Houts**', *S.*
(species affiliation not known)
Alexander Sr pre-1974; S V
{parentage not known}
AABGA Bull. 17(3):69 [1983] - name only; Photo on Jorgovani/Lilacs 2015 DVD.
Nota bene: This appears to be not a single clone! No original description available.
Cultivar name not established.

'**Mary Short**', *S. ×hyacinthiflora*
Fiala 1979; D V
syn. - 'Mary A. Short'
{'Pocahontas' × 'Esther Staley'}

Fiala, Lilacs, 224, Pl. 45 [1988]; Photo on Jorgovani/ Lilacs 2015 DVD.
Named for Mary Short, sister of Clare Short of Elyria, Ohio, USA, friend and travelling companion of the originator.
Cultivar name established and accepted.

'Masséna', *S. vulgaris*
Lemoine 1923; S VI
syn. - 'Massena', 'Messena'
Lemoine, Cat. No. 197, 20 [1923]; McKelvey, The Lilac, 343 [1928]; Wister, Lilacs for America, 52 [1942], 35 [1953]; Photo on Jorgovani/Lilacs 2015 DVD.
Named for André Masséna, 1758-1817, French soldier, the greatest of Napoleon's marshals
Awards: RHS Award of Merit 1928, Award of Garden Merit 1930.
Cultivar name presumed registered 1953; name established and accepted.

'Mathies', *S. reticulata*
Mathies; S I (?)
distributed in Canada as Ivory Boulevard™ <http://www.copf.org/plants_list.asp?Assignee=Cannor%20Nurseries%20Ltd.> - name only [seen 01/02/2007]
Named for the originator, John Mathies, nurseryman, Cannor Nurseries, Chilliwack, BC, Canada.
Cultivar name not established.

'Mathieu de Dombasle', *S. vulgaris*
Lemoine 1882; D IV
syn. - 'Mathieu de Dombasie'
Lemoine, Cat. No. 92, 7 [1882]; McKelvey, The Lilac, 343-344 [1928]; Wister, Lilacs for America, 52 [1942], 35 [1953]; Photo on Jorgovani/Lilacs 2015 DVD.
Named for Christophe Joseph Mathieu de Dombasle, 1777-1843, agronomist and founder of the agricultural college [1819], Nancy, France.
Cultivar name presumed registered 1953; name established and accepted.

'Matthew's Purple', *S.*
(species affiliation not known)
Origin not known; S VII
Macore Co. Inc. photo library [Nov.28, 1999] http://www.macore.com/photolib.htm
Cultivar name not established; not detected in cultivation.

'Måttsund', *S. josikaea*
Arboretum Norr 1980s; S II
Bengtsson, http://student.jmg.gu.se/itv99/hemsidor2/mans/texter/garden/garden.html [Mar.26/99] - name only; http://www.komplett-tradgard.se/syren-ungersk-syren-syringa-josikaea-mattsund/ [Mar.10/16] - florets violet
Named (perhaps) for the village of Måttsund, ca 20 km from Luleå, Norrbotten county, northern Sweden
Cultivar name established and accepted.

'Maude A. Bushnell', *S.*
(species affiliation not known)
McLean; ? ?
Cultivar name not established.

'Maud Notcutt', *S. vulgaris*
Eveleens Maarse 1956; S I
syn. - 'Maud Norcott', 'Maude Notcutt', 'White Superior' (?)
{'Excellent' × 'G. J. Baardse'}
Anon., Jour. RHS 82:449 [1957] & Extracts Proc. RHS 82(2):23 [1957]; Gartenwelt 58(2): [Jan.18, 1958]; Wister, Arnoldia 23(4):82 [1963]; R.C. Notcutt Ltd., Book Cat. of Nursery Stock 2:84 [1964]; Photo on Jorgovani/Lilacs 2015 DVD.
Named for Maud Hetty Smith Fielding, ca 1864-1955, wife of Roger Crompton Notcutt, 1869-1938 and chairman of Notcutts Garden Centre, 1946-1955, Woodbridge, Suffolk, United Kingdom.
Awards: RHS Award of Merit 1957.
Cultivar name registered 1963; name established and accepted.

'Maureen', *S. ×hyacinthiflora*
Preston pre-1936; S IV
syn. - Preston No. 22.01.03
{(*S. vulgaris* 'Negro' × *S. ×hyacinthiflora* 'Lamartine') × ? }
Davis, Rep. Dom. Hort. 1931, 1932 and 1933, 143 [1936], & Progress Report 1934-1948, 150 [1950]; Wister, Lilacs for America, 52, [1942] - as S VII; Wister, Lilacs for America, 35 [1953]; Photo on Jorgovani/Lilacs 2015 DVD.
Awards: RHS Award of Merit 1942.
Cultivar name presumed registered 1953; name established and accepted.

'Maurice Barrès', *S. vulgaris*
Lemoine 1917; S III
syn. - 'Maurice Barres'
Lemoine, Cat. No. 191, 24 [1917]; McKelvey, The Lilac, 344 [1928]; Wister, Lilacs for America, 52 [1942], 35 [1953] - as 'Maurice Barres'; Photo on Jorgovani/Lilacs 2015 DVD.
Named for August Maurice Barrès, 1862-1923, French statesman and novelist.
Cultivar name presumed registered 1953; name established and accepted.

'Maurice de Vilmorin', *S. vulgaris*
Lemoine 1900; D IV
syn. - 'Maurice De Vilmorin', possibly: 'Mme de Vilmorin'
Lemoine, Cat No. 146, 12 [1900]; McKelvey, the Lilac, 344 [1928]; Wister, Lilacs for America, 53, 54 [1942], 35, 36 [1953]; Photo on Jorgovani/Lilacs 2015 DVD.
Named for Auguste Louis Maurice Lévêque de Vilmorin, 1849-1918, French horticulturist.
Cultivar name presumed registered 1953; name established and accepted.

'Maurice Lockwood', *S. vulgaris*
Berdeen pre-1987; D IV & I

syn. - 'M. L.'
Peterson, Lilacs - Proceedings 16(1):20 [1987] - as "M. L. (Maurice Longwood)" - name only; King & Coggeshall, Lilacs - Quart. Jour. 27(2):49-50 [1998] - name only; Vrugtman, Lilacs -Quart. Jour. 32(4):149 [2003] - as D IV & I
Named for a friend of the originator.
Cultivar name established and accepted.

Mauritz Eichler - see **'Moritz Eichler'**.

'Mauve Mist', *S. vulgaris*
Havemeyer & Eaton; S VI
Wister, Arnoldia 23(4):82 [1963] - name only; Eickhorst, ILS Lilac Newsletter 4(1):4-5 [1978] - name only; Vrugtman, Lilacs - Quart. Jour. 32(4):149 [2003] - as S VI; Anon., Lilacs - Quart. Jour. 33(1):11 [2004] - as S II-VI; Photo on Jorgovani/Lilacs 2015 DVD.
Cultivar name registered 1963; name established and accepted.

Maxie - see **'Maximowicz'**.

Maxima Colbert - see **'Colbert'**
Wister, Lilacs for America, 53 [1942], 35 [1953] - descriptions as D VI and D IV, respectively.

Maxime Cornu, Maxine Cornu - see **'Mons. Maxime Cornu'**.

'Maximowicz', *S. vulgaris*
Lemoine 1906; D II
syn. - 'Maxie'
Lemoine, Cat. No. 164, 29 [1906]; McKelvey, The Lilac, 344 [1928]; Wister, Lilacs for America, 53 [1942], 35 [1953]; Photo on Jorgovani/Lilacs 2015 DVD.
Named for Carl Johann (Ivanovic) Maximowicz, 1827-1891, Russian botanist.
Cultivar name presumed registered 1953; name established and accepted.

'Maximus', *S. vulgaris*
Sagitova, ?, ? ?
Chapman, 36(3):100(2007), and 38(3):83(2009) - name only
Cultivar name not established.

'Max Löbner', *S.* ×*hyacinthiflora*
Löbner ca 1947; S VII
syn. - 'Gartendirektor Löbner', 'Max Loebner'
{'Andenken an Ludwig Späth' × 'Mirabeau'}
Meyer, Flieder, 72 [1952]; Wister, Lilacs for America, 35 [1953]; Vrugtman, Lilacs - Quart. Jour. 22(3):90-92 [1993]; Photo on Jorgovani/Lilacs 2015 DVD.
Named for Max Löbner, 1869-1947, Königlicher Gartenbauinspektor, Gartenbauschule Dresden-Pillnitz; German horticulturist and educator.
Cultivar name presumed registered 1953; name established and accepted.

'Max Peterson', *S. vulgaris*
Berdeen 1983; D VI-IV
Berdeen, invoice to Max Peterson [Apr.13/1983]; M. Peterson, in litt. to C. D. Holetich [Jan.24/1992]; reported in cultivation at Meadowlark Hill Gardens [1993] - name only; King & Coggeshall, Lilacs - Quart. Jour. 27(2):49-50 [1998] - name only; Anon., Lilacs - Quart. Jour. 33(1):11 [2004] - erroneously as S VI; Vrugtman, Encyclopedia, 312 [2008]; Photo on Jorgovani/Lilacs 2015 DVD.
Named for a friend of the originator from Ogallala, Nebraska.
Cultivar name established and accepted.

'Maya', *S. vulgaris*
Sagitova & Dzevitski pre-2014; D II
Photos by Oleg Dzevitskiy in Almaty, Kazakhstan seen in 2020 ILS Photo & Color Database.
Cultivar name not established.

'Maybelle Farnum', *S.* (Villosae Group), *S.* ×*josiflexa*
Yeager 1961; S VII
syn. - 'Mabel Farnum'
{'James Macfarlane' × ('Royalty' × ?)}
Yeager, New Hampshire Agric. Exp. Sta. Bull. 461, 13 [1959]; Wister, Arnoldia 23(4):82 [1963]; J. Bentley, Lilacs 42(2):58 [2013].
Named for Ms Maybelle W. Farnum, 1879-1953, active member of Garden Clubs and promoter of lilacs, Rhode Island and New Hampshire, USA.
Cultivar name registered 1963; name established and accepted.

'May Day', *S. vulgaris*
Clarke 1966; S V
syn. - 'Mayday'
Clarke, Wholesale Price List, 8 [1968]; Wister & Oppe, Arnoldia 31(3):123 [1971]; Photo on Jorgovani/Lilacs 2015 DVD.
Cultivar name registered 1970; name established and accepted.

Mazais Princis - see **'Mazais Princis'**.

'Mazais Princis', *S. vulgaris*
Upītis 1989; S I
Syn. - Upītis No. 5577
statutory epithet Mazais Princis
Strautiņa, S. 2002. Ceriņu un jasmīnu avīze. LA, R., p. 62; in litt. S. Strautiņa to F. Vrugtman [21 Dec. 2007] - 1989, S I
Statutory registration (breeder's rights) Nr. 292, CER-2, in Latvia [2004 - 2029] with the statutory epithet Mazais Princis
Name: Latvian for little prince.
Cultivar name established and accepted.

'McMaster Centennial', *S. vulgaris*
Brown 1987; D I
syn. - Brown No. 7524-107
{'Primrose' × 'St Joan'}
Vrugtman, HortScience 23(3):458 [1988] & 24(3):436 [1989]; Graham, Pappus 18(1):26-27 [1999]; Photo on Jorgovani/Lilacs 2015 DVD.

Named for McMaster University, Hamilton, Ontario, Canada, founded in 1887.
Cultivar name registered 1987; name established and accepted.

'Me<u>ch</u>ta', *S. vulgaris*
'Мечта'
Kolesnikov 1941; S III-IV
syn. - 'Mechta', 'Meczta', 'Mieczta', 'Metchta', Metschta', Kolesnikov No. 230
{'Sholokhov' × ?}
Kolesnikov, Lilac, 26, 35 [1955]; Howard, Arnoldia 19(6-7):31-35 [1959] - as Dream, & 31(3):126 [1971] - as 'Mieczta', S II; Gromov, A., Siren', 89 [1963]; Howard & Brizicky, AABGA Quart. Newsl. No. 64, 17-21 [1965]; Wister & Oppe, Arnoldia 31(3):126 [1971] - as S II and 'Mieczta'; Gromov, Lilacs - Proceedings 2(4):16 [1974]; Rub<u>tz</u>ov et al. 1980. Vidy i sorta sireni, kul'tiviruemye v SSSR. Kiev; Naukova Dumka. – in Russian; Holetich, C.D. 1982. Lilac species and cultivars in cultivation in USSR. Lilacs 11(2):1-38. - translation of Rub<u>tz</u>ov et al. 1982; Photo on Jorgovani/Lilacs 2015 DVD.
Name: Russian for dream.
Cultivar name registered 1970; name established and accepted.

'Me<u>ch</u>ta', *S. vulgaris*
'Мечта'
Krav<u>ch</u>enko (not Kolesnikov) 1970; S II
{'Marie Legraye' × OP}
Krav<u>ch</u>enko L. Culture of lilacs in Uzbekistan. Publishing house "Uzbekistan", Tashkent, 1970 p. 17,18.
Name: Russian for dream.
Cultivar name established and accepted.

'Me<u>ch</u>ta Materi', *S. vulgaris*
'Мечта Матери'
Klimenko, V.& Z., & Grigor'ev 1955; S VII
Rub<u>tz</u>ov et al. 1980. Vidy i sorta sireni, kul'tiviruemye v SSSR. Kiev; Naukova Dumka. – in Russian; Holetich, C.D. 1982. Lilac species and cultivars in cultivation in USSR. Lilacs 11(2):1-38. - translation of Rub<u>tz</u>ov et al. 1982.
Name: Russian for mother's dream.
Cultivar name established and accepted.

'Medeo'; *S. vulgaris*
'Медео'
Mel'nik, Rubanik & D<u>y</u>agilev 1989, S V
D<u>y</u>agilev, Lilacs - Quart. Jour. 22(1): 20 [1993]; Pikaleva, Lilacs - Quart. Jour. 23(4):86 [1994]
Named for Kompleks Medeo, the high-altitude (1691 m) natural ice speed-skating stadium in Kazakhstan, first built in 1951.
Cultivar name established and accepted.

'Media', *S. vulgaris*
origin not known pre-1864; S III
Petzold & Kirchner, Arb. Muscav., 495 [1864]; McKelvey, The Lilac, 345 [1928].

'Medovyï Spas', *S. vulgaris*
'Медовый Спас'
Aladin, S., Aladina, O., and Polyakova, T. 2016; S V {'Skromnitsa' × ?} = {Obtained from open pollinated 'Skromnitsa' variety}.
Садовник (Gardener) magazine 04 (140)/2017 :18-25; Вестник АППМ (Catalog in Vestnik APPM (Planting material association) magazine) 1/2018: 59-72 (in Russian).
Named for Honey Spas (Honey Savior), an Orthodox holiday among the Slavs, celebrated on August 1 when an intensive collection of honey and its consecration begins.
Name: Russian for "views of honey"; the eye stops at this unusual lilac, reminiscent of the color of buckwheat honey.
Cultivar name established and accepted.

'Meitenes Maigums', *S. vulgaris*
Upītis 1972; S IV
Photo from Dobele, Latvia in 2018 taken by Natalia Savenko, seen in 2020 ILS Photo Database.
Cultivar name not established.

'Mélanie Grégoire', *S.*
Moro, F. 2016; S I
{seedling of unknown parentage}
https://www.facebook.com/SelectPlusLilacs (1 June 2016).
Named for Mélanie Grégoire, horticultural columnist for radio and television and speaker.
Cultivar name not established; probably never cloned.

'Mélide La Marck', *S. vulgaris*
origin not known pre-1941; S V
Lilac Time in Lombard, 10 [1941].

Mélide Laurent - see **'Mlle Mélide Laurent'**.

'Melissa', *S.*
Vaigla no date; S V
https://translate.google.ca/translate?hl=en&sl=et&u=http://ak.rapina.ee/jaan/puuv/art/11,05,07vaigla_sireliaretajana.html&prev=search - name & color pink.
Named for the elder daughter of the originator.
Cultivar name established and accepted.

'Melissa Oakes', *S.* ×*hyacinthiflora*
Oakes 1977; S V
{parentage not known}
syn. - 'Melissa', 'Milissa Oakes'
Vrugtman, AAGBA Bulletin 14(3):95 [1980] - as cultivar of *S. oblata*; Fiala, Lilacs, Pl. 45 [1988]; Vrugtman, HortScience 23(3):458 [1988] & 24(3):436 [1989]
Cultivar name registered 1979; name established and accepted.

'**Mefisto**', *S. vulgaris*
  origin not known ? ?
  listed by Pieter Zwijnenburg Jr, Boskoop, NL, <www.kwekerijen.net/planten/index.cfm?fuseaction=detail&plt_id=43160&omschr=Syringa%20vulgaris%20%27Mefisto%27>
  Cultivar name not established; questionable name.

'**Merlann**', *S. vulgaris*
  Keaffaber; S VII
  {'Sensation' × ? }
  Vrugtman, AABGA Bull. 17(3):67 [1984]
  Name formed by combining the first names of the originators, Merle and Anna Keaffaber.
  Cultivar name registered 1982; name established and accepted.

'**Merville de Poitre**', *S. vulgaris*
  Origin not known; D II-V
  in cultivation at Lottah Nursery, Tasmania, Australia.
  Photo on Jorgovani/Lilacs 2015 DVD.
  Cultivar name not established.

'**Mervin**', *S. vulgaris*
  Mägi pre-2017; S VII
  Photo from Estonia by Mägi, seen in 2020 ILS Photo Database.
  Cultivar name not established.

'**Meshcherochka**', *S. vulgaris*
  'Мещерочка'
  Vekhov 1952; S IV-V
  {'Charles X' × ? }
  Журнал "Цветоводство" №3, 1988 год, стр. 13.
  Magazine "Tsvetovodstvo" ("Floriculture") No. 3, 1988, p. 13. Also Pikaleva, Lilacs - Quart. Jour. 23(4):86 [1994]
  Meshcherochka is the affectionate name for the Meshchera region, where the Forest-Steppe Experimental Breeding Station (LOSS) is located.
  Cultivar name established and accepted.

'**Metel'-Zavirukha**', *S. vulgaris*
  Метель-Завируха
  Makedonskaya 2017, S I
  {open pollinated seedling}
  Statutory registration with the State Inspection for testing and protection of plant varieties of the Republic of Belarus. Makedonskaya N.V. Breeding Lilacs in Belarus Yesterday TODAY: Materials of International scientific-practical conference "INTERNATIONAL SYRINGA 2018", Russia. Moscow: Moscow State University 2018.pp 36-40. Natalya Makedonskaya. Syringa Belarus. – Lilacs. Quarterly Journal of the International Lilac Society. 2019. VOL. 50 - NUM. 1 PP.21-25.
  Name: Russian (Metel') and Belorussian (Zavirukha) for Snowstorm

'**Metensis**', *S.* ×*chinensis*
  origin not known ca 1860; S I-V
  syn. - many; see McKelvey, The Lilac, 420 [1928]
  common name: Pale Chinese
  {mutation of 'Saugeana'}
  Stand. Pl. Names, 264, 487 [1923] - as Pale Chinese; McKelvey, The Lilac, 420-421 [1928]; Wister, Lilacs for America, 53 [1942], 35 [1953]; Photo on Jorgovani/Lilacs 2015 DVD.
  Cultivar name presumed registered 1953; name established and accepted.

Metschta - see '**Mechta**'.

'Mevr. Annie Ouwerkerk' - see 'Annie Ouwerkerk'

Mevrouw Dr Kenis - see '**Souvenir de Mevrouw Dr Kenis**'.

'**Mevrouw Lombarts**', *S. vulgaris*
  Lombarts 1932; S I
  Wister, Lilacs for America, 35 [1953]
  Cultivar name presumed registered 1953; name established and accepted.

meyeri var. *spontanea* Mei-Chen Chang (included in *S. pubescens* subsp. *microphylla*)
  Chang & Chen. 1990. Invest. Stud. Nat. 10:32-40.

meyeri Hort. non C.K. Schneider - see '**Palibin**'.

'Michael Brestiner' - probably misspelling of '**Michel Buchner**'
  Wister, Lilacs for America, 37, 53 [1942].

'**Michel Buchner**', *S. vulgaris*
  Lemoine 1885; D IV
  syn. - 'Buchner', 'Michael Bchner', 'Michael Buchner', 'Michael Büchner', 'Michel Butcher', 'Michele Buchner'
  Lemoine, Cat. No. 101, 8 [1885]; McKelvey, The Lilac, 345 [1928]; Wister, Lilacs for America, 53 [1942], 35 [1953]; Photo on Jorgovani/Lilacs 2015 DVD.
  Awards: RHS Award of Merit 1891.
  Cultivar name presumed registered 1953; name established and accepted.

'**Michelle**', *S.*
  Joren? no date; S VII
  name, description and picture at http://www.seringen.nl/range-lilacs/michelle-7
  Cultivar name not yet estalished or accepted.
  Forcing lilacs in the Netherlands.

micropetala, *S. komarowii* subsp. *reflexa*, f. (forma)
  Gorb date not known; S ?
  selected as a cultivar from seed of unknown origin
  Gorb 1989 Сирени на Украина, p. 57
  Cultivar name not established; after 1958 cultivar names in Latin form are not established.

microphylla var. *minor* - see '**Palibin**'
  Pringle, Lilacs - Quart. Jour. 19(4):79 [1990].

microphylla superba - see '**Superba**'.

'Midnight', *S. vulgaris*
Fiala 1984; S VII
{'Agincourt Beauty' × 'Violet Glory'}
Fiala, Lilacs, 223 [1988]
Cultivar name established and accepted.

'Midnight Sun', *S. vulgaris*
Hoepfl 1994: S II
syn. - FC 22
{'Flower City' × ? }
Hoepfl, Lilacs - Quart. Jour. 36(2):74-75 and front & back cover photos [2007] - background information only; (Vrugtman, Cultivated Plant Diversity ... 2017)
Name: The color of the flowers reflects the changing tones in the sky during the longer days in the far North.
Cultivar name registered 2016; name established and accepted.

'Midwest Gem', *S. vulgaris*
Sass, H.P. ca 1942; D V
Wister, Lilacs for America, 35 [1953]; Fiala, Lilacs, 101 [1988]; Photo on Jorgovani/Lilacs 2015 DVD.
Cultivar name presumed registered 1953; name established and accepted.

Mieczta - see **'Mechta'**.

'M. I. Kalinin', *S. vulgaris*
'М. И. Калинин'
Kolesnikov 1941; S II-IV
syn. - Kolesnikov No. 210, 'M. L. Kalinin'
{Kolesnikov No. 105 × 'Réaumur'}
Gromov, Lilacs - Proceedings 2(4):17 [1974]; Rubtzov et al. 1980. Vidy i sorta sireni, kul'tiviruemye v SSSR. Kiev; Naukova Dumka. – in Russian; Holetich, C.D. 1982. Lilac species and cultivars in cultivation in USSR. Lilacs 11(2):1-38. - translation of Rubtzov et al. 1982.
Named for Mikhaïl Ivanovich Kalinin, 1875-1946, Soviet politician.
Cultivar name established and accepted.

'Mikhaïlo Lomonosov', *S. vulgaris*
'Михайло Ломоносов'
Aladin, S., Aladina, O., and Polyakova, T. 2011; D IV-V
{'Montaigne' × OP}
Registered with the State Commission of the Russian Federation for Testing and Protection of Selection Achievements, No. 8853113, 2011, and Patent No. 6882 (2012), valid until 31 December 2043; Питомник-частный сад (Pitomnik i chastnyi sad; Nursery and private garden) 2/2013:24-34 (in Russian); Вестник АППМ (Catalog in Vestnik APPM (Planting material association) magazine) 1/2018: 59-72 (in Russian); Photo on Jorgovani/Lilacs 2015 DVD.
Named for Mikhail Vasil'evich Lomonosov (Михаил Васильевич Ломоносов), 1711-1765, great Russian scientist, polymath and poet, who founded Moscow State Univeristy.
Cultivar name registered, established and accepted.

'Mikhail Vrubel", *S. vulgaris*
'Михаил Врубель'
Aladin, S., Aladina, O., Polyakova, T., and Aladina, A. 2019; D VI-II
{'Président Poincaré' × OP}
(Международная научная конференция "Syringa L.: коллекции, выращивание, использование") "International Scientific Conference "Syringa L.: collections, cultivation, using" / Collection of Scientific Articles of Botanical Institute named after V.L. Komarov, Botanical Garden of Peter the Great BIN RAS. - St. Petersburg. -2020.- pp.3-7 (in Russian); Photo exhibition of all varieties of the creative breeding group "Russian Lilac" at the Festival "Lilac February", St. Petersburg, Botanical Garden of Peter the Great BIN RAS, February 22-24, 2020.
This cultivar got its name in honor of the great Russian artist of the Art Nouveau era, Mikhail Alexandrovich Vrubel (1856-1910). The purple color of lilac is typical of the color of his paintings.
Cultivar name established and accepted.

'Mikołaj Karpow-Lipski', *S. vulgaris*
Karpow-Lipski 1958; S III
{'Masséna' × ? }
syn. - 'Siewka nr 16'
Karpow-Lipski, Arboretum Kórnickie 3:102 [1958]; Anon., Lista odmian roślin ozdobnych 1973, 25
Named for Mikołaj Karpow-Lipski 1896-1981, Polish horticulturist and plant breeder.
Varietal denomination registered COBORU 1973; Cultivar name established and accepted.

'Mikołaj Kopernik' - see **'Kapitan Teliga'**
Anon., Lista odmian roślin ozdobnych 1973, 25.

'Milada', *S. vulgaris*
'Милада'
Sagitova 1994; S V/VII
varietal denomination registered 1994, No. 9, State Register of Selected Achievements in Republic of Kazakhstan; statutory registration
Named for the daughter of the originator.
Cultivar name established and accepted.

'Milda', *S. vulgaris*
Kārkliņš 2003; S VII/II
under evaluation at Latvia State Institute of Fruit Growing, Dobele; Photo on Jorgovani/Lilacs 2015 DVD.
Name: A women's name.
Cultivar name not established.

'Mildred Luetta', *S. vulgaris*
Hetz 1950; D VII
Hetz (Fairview Evergreen Nurseries), Cat., 24 [Sept. 10, 1950]; Wister, Lilacs for America, 35 [1953] - erroneously as S VII; Wister, Lilac Registrations (mimeogr. list), 4 [n.d.; ca 1968] - as D VII; Photo on Jorgovani/Lilacs 2015 DVD.

Cultivar name presumed registered 1953; name established and accepted.

'Miloserdie', *S. vulgaris*
'Милосердие'
Aladin, S., Aladina, O., Polyakova, T., and Aladina A. pre-2017; D V
{'Christophe Colomb' × OP}
Садовник (Gardener) magazine 04 (140)/2017 :18-25; Вестник АППМ (Catalog in Vestnik APPM (Planting material association) magazine) 1/2018: 59-72 (in Russian).
Name: Russian for mercy.
Cultiver name established and accepted.

'Milton', *S. vulgaris*
Lemoine 1910; S VII
Lemoine, Cat. No. 176, 31 [1910]; McKelvey, The Lilac, 345 [1928]; Wister, Lilacs for America, 53 [1942], 35 [1953]; Photo on Jorgovani/Lilacs 2015 DVD.
Named for John Milton, 1608-1674, English poet.
Cultivar name presumed registered 1953; name established and accepted.

'Milui', *S. vulgaris*
Mägi pre-2017; S VII
Photo from Estonia by Mägi, seen in 2020 ILS Photo Database.
Cultivar name not established.

'Minaret', *S. vulgaris (previously rhodopea)*
origin not known pre-2011; ? ?
<www.esveld.nl/wetenschappelijk.php?letter=s&group=syringa&ppagina=4> seen Nov. 23, 2011 - no descriptive information.
Cultivar name not established.

'Minchanka', *S. vulgaris*
'Минчанка'
Smol'skiĭ & Bibikova 1964; S II
syn. - 'Minchanka', 'Minschanka', 'Mintschanka'
{'Mme Abel Chatenay' × 'Réaumur'}
Bilov et al., Siren', 60 [1974] - in Russian; Rubtzov et al. 1980. Vidy i sorta sireni, kul'tiviruemye v SSSR. Kiev; Naukova Dumka. – in Russian; Holetich, C.D. 1982. Lilac species and cultivars in cultivation in USSR. Lilacs 11(2):1-38. - translation of Rubtzov et al. 1982; Semenov, Igor, Lilacs -Quart. Jour. 43(3):85-89 & photo on front cover [2014]; Photo on Jorgovani/Lilacs 2015 DVD.
Name: Russian for lady of Minsk.
Cultivar name established and accepted.

'Mindent', *S. vulgaris*
Bellion 2007; D I
{improved Mme Lemoine (sport?)}
marketed in France as Dentelle d'Anjou®, 'Dentelle d'Anjou'
Cultivar name established and accepted.

'Minister Dąb-Kocioł', *S. vulgaris*
Karpow-Lipski 1961; S III
syn. - 'Minister Dab Kociol'
Wister & Oppe, Arnoldia 31(3):126 [1971]; Fiala, Lilacs, 97, 214 [1988]
Named for Stanisław Dąb-Kocioł, Polish minister of agriculture in the 1950s.
Cultivar name registered 1970; name established and accepted.

'Minkarl', *S. vulgaris*
Minier (B. Fourrier, USA) 2006; D V
{bud mutation of 'Krasavitsa Moskvy'}
marketed in France by Minier nursery as Rose De Moscou®
Plant breeders' rights registered by Pépinières Minier.
Cultivar name established and accepted.

'Minnehaha', *S.* ×*hyacinthiflora*
Skinner 1932; S V
{mutation of }
Wister, Lilacs for America, 53 [1942], 35 [1953]; Skinner, Hort. Horizons, 109 [1966]
Named for Minnehaha, Saskatchewan, Canada.
Cultivar name presumed registered 1953; name established and accepted.

Minor (*microphylla*) - see **'Palibin'**.

'Minor', *S. reticulata*
origin not known pre-1962; ? ?
Reported at Morden Research Station, Manitoba, Canada
name not established.

'Minskaya Krasavitsa', *S.*
'Минская Красавица'
Makedonskaya 2013, S V
{open pollinated seedling}
Statutory registration with the State Inspection for testing and protection of plant varieties of the Republic of Belarus; registered 2016, no. 2013910. (Vrugtman, Journal of Cultivated Plant Diversity ... 2018)
Makedonskaya N.V. Breeding Lilacs in Belarus Yesterday. TODAY: Materials of International scientific-practical conference "INTERNATIONAL SYRINGA 2018", Russia. Moscow: Moscow State University 2018. pp 36-40. Natalya Makedonskaya. Syringa Belarus. – Lilacs. Quarterly Journal of the International Lilac Society. 2019. VOL. 50 · NUM. 1 PP.21-25.
Named for the women living in Minsk.
Cultivar name registered 2014; name established and accepted.

'Minuet', *S.* (Villosae Group)
Cumming 1972; S VII
{*S.* ×*josiflexa* 'Redwine' × *S.* ×*prestoniae* 'Donald Wyman'}
Cumming, Can. Hort. Council, Rep. Comm. Hort. Res. 1971, 182 [1972]; Cumming, Agric. Canada Public. 1628,

17, fig. 20 [1977]; Photo on Jorgovani/Lilacs 2015 DVD.
Awards: Award of Merit [Feb.17, 1981], Western Canadian Soc. for Horticulture.
Cultivar name established and accepted.

'Mirabeau', *S.* ×*hyacinthiflora*
Lemoine 1911; S IV
syn. - *praecox* 'Mirabeau'
Lemoine, Cat. No. 179, 6 [1911]; McKelvey, The Lilac, 198 [1928]; Wister, Lilacs for America, 53 [1942] - as D IV; Wister, Lilacs for America, 35 [1953]; Photo on Jorgovani/Lilacs 2015 DVD.
Named for Honoré Gabriel Riqueti, Comte de Mirabeau, 1749-1791, French revolutionary politician and orator.
Cultivar name presumed registered 1953; name established and accepted.

'Miranda', *S.* (Villosae Group), *S.* ×*prestoniae*
Preston 1928; S V
syn. - Preston No. 20-14-38
{*S. villosa* subsp. *villosa* × *S. komarowii* subsp. *reflexa*}
Macoun, Rep. Dom. Hort. 1928, 56 [1930]; Wister, Lilacs for America, 53, 64 [1942], 35, 48 [1953]
Named for the Daughter to Prospero in Shakespeare's *The Tempest*.
Cultivar name presumed registered 1953; name established and accepted.

'Mirāža', *S. vulgaris*
Kārkliņš 2003; D VII
Strautiņa & Kaufmane, Dobeles ceriņi, pp. 14, 92 [2011]; Photo on Jorgovani/Lilacs 2015 DVD.
Name: Latvian for the mirage.
Cultivar name established and accepted.

'Mirdza', *S.*
Upītis 1972; S II
Seen in "Syringa Cultivar Catalog" (2019) p. 330 by Natalia Savenko, growing in Dobele, Latvia.
Cultivar name established and accepted.

'Mireille', *S. vulgaris*
Lemoine 1904; D I
Lemoine, Cat. No. 158, 31 [1904]; McKelvey, The Lilac, 346 [1928]; Wister, Lilacs for America, 53 [1942], 35 [1953]; Photo on Jorgovani/Lilacs 2015 DVD.
Cultivar name presumed registered 1953; name established and accepted.

'Mirell', *S. vulgaris*
Mägi pre-2017; S VII
Photos from Estonia by Mägi and Semenov, seen in 2020 ILS Photo Database.
Cultivar name not established.

'Miriam Cooley', *S. vulgaris*
Klager 1931; S V
Cooley, Cat., 7 [1930]; Wister, Lilacs for America, 53 [1942], 35 [1953]; Fiala, Lilacs, 101 [1988]; Vrugtman, Lilacs - Quart. Jour. 28(3):77 [1999] - erroneously as 'Mariam Cooley'.
Cultivar name presumed registered 1953; name established and accepted.

'Mirklja Vara', *S. vulgaris*
Upītis ca 1970; S V/II
Kalniņš, Dārs un drava 1986, No. 12, 13-15 - in Latvian; in litt. S. Strautiņa to F. Vrugtman [22 Jan. 2008] - ca 1970, S V/II
Name: Latvian for blink power.
Cultivar name established and accepted. May no longer be in cultivation.

'Mirnoe Nebo', *S. vulgaris*
'Мирное Небо'
Rubanik & Dyagilev 1989; D III/IV
Dyagilev, Lilacs - Quart. Jour. 22(1):19 [1993]; Pikaleva, Lilacs - Quart. Jour. 23(4):86 [1994].
(Международная научная конференция "Syringa L.: коллекции, выращивание, использование")
"International Scientific Conference "Syringa L.: collections, cultivation, using" / Collection of Scientific Articles of Botanical Institute named after V.L. Komarov, Botanical Garden of Peter the Great BIN RAS. - St. Petersburg. -2020.- pp.23-27 (in Russian).
The Russian name means Peaceful Sky.
Cultivar name established and accepted.

'Mirza Galib', *S. vulgaris*
'Мирза Галиб'
Kolesnikov; S VII/VI-II
Gromov, Lilacs - Proceedings 2(4):17 [1974]
Named for Mirza Assad-Ullah Khan (Ghalib), ca 1797-1869, writer of Urdu poetry.

'Miss Aalsmeer', *S. vulgaris*
Maarse, H. pre-1943; S II
Wister, Lilacs for America, 35 [1953] - as ? VII; Fiala, Lilacs, 106, 209 [1988] - erroneously as a D. Eveleens Maarse origination
Awards: Certificate of Merit 1943 (KMTP).
Cultivar name presumed registered 1953; name established and accepted.

Miss America - see 'Agnes Smith'.

'Miss Canada', *S.* (Villosae Group)
Cumming 1967; S V
{*S.* ×*josiflexa* 'Redwine' × *S.* ×*prestoniae* 'Hiawatha'}
Wister, Arbor. Bot. Gard. Bull 1(2):19 [1967]; Cumming, Ann. Rep. Ornam. Pl. Breeders 1973, 8 [1973]; Cumming, Agric. Canada Public. 1628, 17, fig. 21 [1977]; Photo on Jorgovani/Lilacs 2015 DVD.
"Named in honour of the Canada Centennial Year and in commemoration of the breeding work of the late Ms Isabel Preston of Ottawa and Dr F. L. Skinner of Dropmore, Manitoba." (Wister, Arbor. Bot. Gard. Bull 1(2):19 [1967]).
Cultivar name registered 1967; name established and accepted.

'Miss Ellen Willmott', *S. vulgaris*
　Lemoine 1903; D I
　syn. - 'Ellen Willmott', 'Miss Ellen Willmont', 'Miss Willmot', 'Miss Willmott'
　common name: Ellen Willmott
　Lemoine, Cat. No. 155, 8 [1903]; Stand. Pl. Names, 486 [1923] - as Ellen Willmott; McKelvey, The Lilac, 346 [1928]; Wister, Lilacs for America, 47, 53 [1942], 29, 35 [1953] - as 'Ellen Willmott'; Photo on Jorgovani/Lilacs 2015 DVD.
　Named for Ellen Ann Willmott, 1860-1934, British rosarian.
　Cultivar name presumed registered 1953; name established and accepted.

'Miss Elly', *S.* Villosae Group
　Minier pre-2007; S V
　in cultivation at Zilverspar nursery; no other information available
　Cultivar name not established.

'Missimo', *S.* ×*hyacinthiflora*
　Clarke 1944; S VI
　{seedling of unknown double lilac}
　Clarke, Cat. 11:10 [1944]; Woody Plant Register, AAN, No. 71 [1949]; Wister, Lilacs for America, 35 [1953]; Dvorak, Lilac study, ILS, 50 [1978]
　Cultivar name presumed registered 1953; name established and accepted.

Miss Japan, *S.* (Villosae Group)
　Noordam ca 2004; S IV or V (?)
　this an unregistered trade designation used by Piet Noordam for an older, registered cultivar, the name of which has not been disclosed <www.twest.nl> <http://www.havlis.cz/karta_en.php?kytkaid=959> as S V (probably identical to 'Bellicent')
　Not a cultivar name.

'Miss Kim', *S. pubescens* subsp. *patula*
　Meader & Yeager 1954; S II
　syn. - 'Katinka', 'Miss Kin'
　{One of seven seedlings raised from seed collected by E. M. Meader in the Pouk Han Mountains, Korea, in 1947}
　Yeager, New Hampshire Agric. Exp. Sta. Bull. 461, 12-13 [1959]; Wister, Arnoldia 23(4):82 [1963] - name only; Laar, Dendroflora 27:82 [1990] - erroneously presumes that 'Miss Kim' (*S. pubescens* subsp. *patula*) is identical to 'Kim' (*S.* ×*prestoniae*); Praskac, Cat., [1995] - as *S. microphylla* 'Katinka'; J. Bentley, Lilacs 42(2):58, ill. Inside back cover [2013]; Photo on Jorgovani/Lilacs 2015 DVD.
　Named by Elwyn M. Meader for "any or all beautiful Misses Kim of Korea".
　Awards: RHS Award of Garden Merit 1993.
　Cultivar name registered 1963; name established and accepted.

Miss Kim Sweet Treat™ - see 'Greswt'.

'Miss Millie', *S. vulgaris*
　Hughes 1994; D V
　{parentage not known}
　Grown at the Lilac Farm (defunct) in Cambridge Springs, PA, USA 1975-2005 from seeds obtained in Vienna, Lichtenstein, France, Germany, Denmark, and Jefferson's home in Virginia.
　Named for Millie Hughes, wife of the originator.
　Cultivar name not established.

Miss Muffet - see 'Little Miss Muffet'
　Fiala, Lilacs, 101, 112, 115, 262 [1988] - erroneously as 'Miss Muffet'.

Miss Poland, *S.* (Villosae Group)
　Noordam ca 2004; S V (?)
　this an unregistered trade designation used by Piet Noordam for an older, registered cultivar, the name of which has not been disclosed <www.twest.nl>. <http://boomkwekerijmarcelvannijnatten.nl/index.php?option=com_content&task=view&id=585&Itemid=46> as S V (probably identical to 'Lynette')
　Not a cultivar name.

Miss Susie™ - see 'Klmone'.

Miss USA™ - see **Agnes Smith**.

Miss Willmott - see **'Miss Ellen Willmott'**.

Mister . . . - see also: Mr . . .

'Mister Big', *S. vulgaris*
　Havemeyer & Eaton 1954; D VI
　syn. - 'Mr Big'
　Wister, Lilacs for America, 35 [1953]; Lilac Land, Cat. [1954]; Niedz, ILS Newsletter 1(4):7-8 [1972]; Eickhorst, ILS Lilac Newsletter 4(1):4-5 [1978]; Fiala, Lilacs, 103, 216 [1988].
　Cultivar name presumed registered 1953;
　Cultivar not reported in cultivation.

Mister X – a cognomen for an unknown Vaigla hybrid in Estonia. Seen in Lilacs 48(2):64.

'Miyabi', *S.* (Pubescentes Series)
　'雅'
　Ihara 2012; S VII
　syn. - seedling no. 2011S1128004#11.
　{*S.* 'MORjos 060F' × *S.* 'MORjos 060F'}
　(Vrugtman, Cultivated Plant Diversity ... 2017)
　Name: Japanese for graceful.
　Cultivar name registered 2017; name established and accepted.

M. J. De Messemaeker - see **Mons. J. De Messemaeker**.

M. L. (Maurice Lockwood) - see 'Maurice Lockwood'.

M. Léon Mathieu - see **Mons. Léon Mathieu**.

Mlle . . . - see also: Mademoiselle . . .

Mlle Amelia Duprat - see '**Mme Amélie Duprat**'.

Mlle Fernande Viger - see '**Mademoiselle Fernande Viger**'.

'**Mlle Lepage**', *S. vulgaris*
   origin not known pre-1915; D III
   syn. - 'Mlle Le Page'
   Blossom, Landscape Arch., 141 [April 1915]; McKelvey, The Lilac, 338 [1928]
   perhaps identical to 'Mons. Lepage', syn. - 'M. Le Page'.

'**Mlle Mélide Laurent**', *S. vulgaris*
   origin not known 1898; S V/IV
   syn. - 'Mademoiselle Melide Laurent', 'Mélide Laurent', 'Melide Laurent', 'Mlle Melide Laurent', 'Mme Melide Laurent'
   Barbier, Cat., 129 [1898]; McKelvey, The Lilac, 338 [1928]; Wister, Lilacs for America, 53 [1942], 35 [1953]; Photo on Jorgovani/Lilacs 2015 DVD.
   Cultivar name presumed registered 1953; name established and accepted.

Mme . . . - see also: Madame . . . or Mad. . . .

'**Mme Abel Chatenay**', *S. vulgaris*
   Lemoine 1892; D I
   {'Marie Legraye' × ? double}
   syn. - 'Abel Chatney', 'Mad. Abel Chatenay'
   Lemoine, Cat. No. 122, 10 [1892]; Kache, Gartenschönheit 5:82 [1924]; McKelvey, The Lilac, 330 [1928]; Wister, Lilacs for America, 53 [1942], 35 [1953]; Photo on Jorgovani/Lilacs 2015 DVD.
   Named for Augustine-Delphine Chatenay, 1857-1928, wife of Abel Chatenay, nurseryman and grower of lilacs at Vitry-sur-Seine near Paris, France.
   Cultivar name presumed registered 1953; name established and accepted.

Mme A. J. Klettenberg - see '**Madame A. J. Klettenberg**'.

'**Mme Amélie Duprat**', *S. vulgaris*
   origin not known pre-1900; D VI
   syn. - 'Mme A. Duprat', 'Mme Amelie Duprat'
   Barbier, Cat., 132 [1900]; McKelvey, The Lilac, 330 [1928]; Wister, Lilacs for America, 53 [1942], 35 [1953]; Photo on Jorgovani/Lilacs 2015 DVD.
   Cultivar name presumed registered 1953; name established and accepted.

'**Mme Antoine Buchner**', *S. vulgaris*
   Lemoine 1909; D V
   syn. - 'A. Buckner', 'Antoine Buchner', 'Mme Antione Buchner', 'Mme Antoine Büchner', 'Mme P. Buckner', BUCHNER (trade designation used for cut flowers of this cultivar)
   Lemoine, Cat. No. 173, 7 [1909]; McKelvey, The Lilac, 330-331 [1928]; Wister, Lilacs for America, 53 [1942], 35 [1953]; Photo on Jorgovani/Lilacs 2015 DVD.
   Awards: RHS Award of Merit 1982.
   Cultivar name presumed registered 1953; name established and accepted.
   Forcing cultivar in the Netherlands.

'**Mme Auguste Gouchault**', *S. vulgaris*
   Gouchault 1916; D I
   syn. - Mme August Gouchault'
   McKelvey, The Lilac, 331 [1928]; Wister, Lilacs for America, 53 [1942], 35 [1953]; Photo on Jorgovani/Lilacs 2015 DVD.
   Cultivar name presumed registered 1953; name established and accepted.

'**Mme Briot**', *S. vulgaris*
   Briot 1877; S VI
   syn. - 'Madame Briot'
   Carrière, Rev. Hort., 227 [1877]; McKelvey, The Lilac, 331 [1928]; Wister, Lilacs for America, 53 [1942] - as D I; Wister, Lilacs for America, 35 [1953]; Photo on Jorgovani/Lilacs 2015 DVD.
   Cultivar name presumed registered 1953; name established and accepted.

Mme Bruchet - see '**Mme Catherine Bruchet**'.

'**Mme Casimir Périer**', *S. vulgaris*
   Lemoine 1894; D I
   syn. - 'Casimir Perrier', 'Casimir Périer', 'C. Perier', 'Madame Casimir Perriere', 'Madame C. Perriere', 'Mad. Cas. Perier', 'Mme Casimer Perier', 'Mme Casimir Perier'
   Lemoine, Cat. No. 128, 10 [1894]; Kache, Gartenschönheit 5:82 [1924]; McKelvey, The Lilac, 331-332 [1928]; Wister, Lilacs for America, 53 [1942], 36 [1953]; Photo on Jorgovani/Lilacs 2015 DVD.
   Named, probably, for the wife to Jean Pierre Paul Casimir-Périer, 1847-1907, French statesman.
   Cultivar name presumed registered 1953; name established and accepted.

'**Mme Catherine Bruchet**', *S. vulgaris*
   Bruchet pre-1908; D I
   syn. - 'Catherine Bruchet', 'Madame Bruchet', 'Mme Catherine Buchner'
   McKelvey, The Lilac, 332 [1928]; Wister, Lilacs for America, 53 [1942], 36 [1953]; Photo on Jorgovani/Lilacs 2015 DVD.
   Cultivar name presumed registered 1953; name established and accepted.

Mme Charles Souchet - see '**Madame Charles Souchet**'.

'**Mme Delaruelle-Klettenberg**', *S. vulgaris*
   Klettenberg 1935; S IV
   Wister, Lilacs for America, 36 [1953]
   Cultivar name presumed registered 1953; not reported in cultivation.

'**Mme Delcor**', *S. vulgaris*
   Delcor ca 1950; S I
   Wister, Lilacs for America, 36 [1953]

Named for Agnes Melanie Van Weyenbergh, 1894-1979, wife of François Delcor, proprietor of Pépinière Delcor, x -1984, Lebbeke, Belgium.
Cultivar name presumed registered 1953; name established and accepted.

'Mme de Miller', *S. vulgaris*
Lemoine 1901; D I
syn. - 'Mme De Miller'
Lemoine, Cat. No. 149, 8 [1901]; McKelvey, The Lilac, 332 [1928]; Wister, Lilacs for America, 53 [1942], 36 [1953]
Cultivar name presumed registered 1953; name established and accepted.

Mme de Vilmorin - see '**Maurice de Vilmorin**'.

'Mme Dupont', *S. vulgaris*
origin not known ca 1922; ? ?
McKelvey, The Lilac, 332 [1928]
Cultivar name not established.

'Mme Emil Dupont', *S. vulgaris*
Origin not known; D IV
van Gemeren, Lilacs - Proceedings 11(1):25 [1982] - name only.
Photo by Mark DeBard taken at Montreal Botanic Gardens seen in ILS 2020 Photo DVD.

'Mme Fallières', *S. vulgaris*
Bruchet pre-1908; S IV
syn. - 'Mme Failiere', 'Mme Fallieres'
McKelvey, The Lilac, 332 [1928]; Wister, Lilacs for America, 53 [1942], 36 [1953]; Photo on Jorgovani/Lilacs 2015 DVD.
Named for Mme Fallières, wife to Armand Fallières, 1841-1931, French president, 1906-1913.
Cultivar name presumed registered 1953; name established and accepted.

'Mme Felix', *S. vulgaris*
Felix & Dykhuis 1924; S I
{'Marie Legraye' × ? }
syn. - 'Mme Felix Dykhuis', 'Mrs Felix'
Felix & Dijkhuis, Trade Letter [July 25, 1924]; McKelvey, The Lilac, 333 [1928]; Wister, Lilacs for America, 53 [1942], 36 [1953]; Photo on Jorgovani/Lilacs 2015 DVD.
Named for the wife of the originator.
Awards: Silver Gilt Medal, Haarlem, 1925; Certificate First Class, Boskoop, 1925 (KMTP).
Cultivar name presumed registered 1953; name established and accepted.
Formerly a forcing cultivar in the Netherlands.

'Mme Florent Stepman', *S. vulgaris*
Stepman-Demessemaeker 1908; S I
syn. - 'Mme Florence Stepman', 'Mme Florens Stepman', 'Mme Florentine Stepman', 'Mme Fl. Stepman', 'Madame Stepman', 'Florent Stepman', 'Mrs Stepman', 'Stepman', STEPMAN (trade designation used for cut flowers of this cultivar)
{'Dr Lindley' × 'Marie Legraye'}
Fl. Stepman-Demessemaeker, Cat., 1 [1908]; McKelvey, The Lilac, 333 [1928]; Wister, Lilacs for America, 53 [1942], 36 [1953]; Photo on Jorgovani/Lilacs 2015 DVD.
Awards: First Class Certificate 1910 (KMTP).
Named for Marie Josèphe De Messemaeker, 1864-1935, wife to Florent Stepman.
Cultivar name presumed registered 1953; name established and accepted.
Forcing cultivar in the Netherlands.

'Mme F. Morel', *S. vulgaris*
Morel, F. 1892; S VI
syn. - 'Madame F. Morel', 'Mme Françisque Morel'
{'Rubra Insignis' × ? }
Morel, Rev. Hort., 108 [1892]; McKelvey, The Lilac, 333-334 [1928]; Wister, Lilacs for America, 53 [1942], 36 [1953]; Lilacs - Quart. Jour. 20(4): back cover ill. [1991]; Photo on Jorgovani/Lilacs 2015 DVD.
Awards: Certificate of Merit 1915 (KMTP).
Named for the wife of Françisque Morel at the suggestion of the friend in whose garden the lilac grew (loc. cit. p. 334).
Cultivar name presumed registered 1953; name established and accepted.

Mme Francisque Morel - see '**Mme F. Morel**'.

'Mme François Peeters', *S. vulgaris*
Stepman-Demessemaeker pre-1917; S V
syn. - 'Mme Francois Peeters'
Klettenberg, Cat., 23 [1923]; Wister, Lilacs for America, 36 [1953]
Named for the wife of François Peeters [no dates], Belgian orchid specialist.
Cultivar name presumed registered 1953; not reported in cultivation.

'Mme Georges Hermans', *S. vulgaris*
Lambrechts 1952; D VII
syn. - 'Maître Georges Hermans'
Wister, Lilacs for America, 36 [1953]
Cultivar name presumed registered 1953; not reported in cultivation.

'Mme Henri Guillaud', *S. vulgaris*
Bruchet pre-1908; D VI
McKelvey, The Lilac, 334 [1928]; Wister, Lilacs for America, 53 [1942] - as D IV; Wister, Lilacs for America, 36 [1953]; Photo on Jorgovani/Lilacs 2015 DVD.
Cultivar name presumed registered 1953; name established and accepted.

'Mme Jeanne Cornu', *S.* ×*chinensis*
Henry, L. 1901; S V
syn. - *dubia rosea*
Henry, Jour. Soc. Hort. France, Ser. 4, 2:748 [1901]; McKelvey, The Lilac, 426 [1928]; Wister, Lilacs for America, 53 [1942], 36 [1953]

Cultivar name presumed registered 1953; name established and accepted.

'Mme Jules Finger', *S. vulgaris*
Lemoine 1887; D IV
Lemoine, Cat. No. 107, 8 [1887]; McKelvey, The Lilac, 334 [1928]; Wister, Lilacs for America, 53 [1942], 36 [1953]; Photo on Jorgovani/Lilacs 2015 DVD.
Cultivar name presumed registered 1953; name established and accepted.

Mme Jules Simon - see **'Jules Simon'**.

'Mme Kneyer', *S. vulgaris*
van Houtte (?) pre-1893; D ?
syn. - 'Mad. Kneyer'
L. van Houtte, Cat. No. 255-G, 36 [1893] - "with double flowers"; McKelvey, The Lilac, 335 [1928]
Cultivar name not established.

'Mme Kreuter', *S. vulgaris*
origin not known pre-1880; S VI
syn. - 'Kreuteriana', 'Madame Kreuter'
Baudriller, Cat. No. 43, 142 [1880] - as 'Kreuteriana'; McKelvey, The Lilac, 335 [1928]; Wister, Lilacs for America, 53 [1942] - as S V; Wister, Lilacs for America, 36 [1953]; Photo on Jorgovani/Lilacs 2015 DVD.
Cultivar name presumed registered 1953; name established and accepted.

'Mme Lemoine', *S. vulgaris*
Lemoine 1890; D I
{'Marie Legraye' × ? double}
syn. - 'Madame Lemoine', 'Mad. Emile Lemoine', 'Mad. Lemoine'
Lemoine, Cat No. 116, 13 [1890]; Kache, Gartenschönheit 5:82 [1924]; McKelvey, The Lilac, 335-336 [1928]; Wister, Lilacs for America, 53 [1942], 36 [1953]; Photo on Jorgovani/Lilacs 2015 DVD.
Awards: RHS Award of Merit 1891, Award of Garden Merit 1937, First Class Certificate 1897; Award of Garden Merit 1993.
Cultivar name presumed registered 1953; name established and accepted.
Formerly a forcing cultivar in the Netherlands.

'Mme Léon Mathieu', *S. vulgaris*
Stepman-De Messemaeker 1905; S I
syn. - 'Mme Leon Mathieu'
Wister, Lilacs for America, 36 [1953]
Named for Marie Elisabeth Adeline Hensmans, 1825-1905, wife to Léon Jean Amand Ghislain Mattieu, Belgium. (Spelling varies: Mathieu and Matthieu.)
Cultivar name presumed registered 1953; name established and accepted.

'Mme Léon Simon', *S. vulgaris*
Lemoine 1897; D IV
syn. - Mme Leon Simon'
Lemoine, Cat. No. 137, 10 [1897]; McKelvey, The Lilac, 336 [1928]; Wister, Lilacs for America, 54 [1942], 36 [1953]; Photo on Jorgovani/Lilacs 2015 DVD.
Named for the wife to Dr Léon Simon; see 'Léon Simon'.
Cultivar name presumed registered 1953; name established and accepted.

'Mme Léopold Draps', *S. vulgaris*
Draps 1945; S I
syn. - 'Mme Leopold Draps'
Wister, Lilacs for America, 36 [1953]
Named for Jeanne Charlotte Thomaes, wife to J.B. Léopold Draps.
Cultivar name presumed registered 1953; name established and accepted.

Mme LePage or Madame Lepage - see **'Mons. Lepage'**.

Mme Louis Gialis - see 'Souvenir de Mme Louis Gielis'
Fox Hill Nursery, Cat. 1997/98, p. 27.

'Mme Louis Henry', *S. ×chinensis*
Chenault 1912; S IV
Chenault, Cat., 19 [1912]; McKelvey, The Lilac, 426 [1928]; Wister, Lilacs for America, 54 [1942], 36 [1953]
Cultivar name presumed registered 1953; not reported in cultivation.

'Mme Moser', *S. vulgaris*
Briot 1877; S I
syn. - 'Madame Moser', 'Madame Mosier'
Carrière, Rev. Hort., 227 [1877]; McKelvey, The Lilac, 336-337 [1928]; Wister, Lilacs for America, 54 [1942], 36 [1953]; Photo on Jorgovani/Lilacs 2015 DVD.
Cultivar name presumed registered 1953; name established and accepted.

Mme Nadja N.®, *S ×hyacinthiflora*
Kopp 1999; D VII
in cultivation at Piccoplant, Germany.
<http://www.piccoplant.de/en/assortment/lilacs>
Cultivar name not known.

Mme P. Buckner - see **'Mme Antoine Buchner'**.

'Mme Pierre Verhoeven', *S. vulgaris*
Verhoeven 1936; S VII
Wister, Lilacs for America, 36 [1953]
Cultivar name presumed registered 1953; not reported in cultivation.

'Mme Plantier', *S. vulgaris*
origin not known pre-1890; ? ?
Froebel, Cat. No. 122, 22 [ca 1890]; McKelvey, The Lilac, 337 [1928]
Cultivar name not established.

'Mme René Pechere', *S. vulgaris*
Klettenberg 1938; S IV
syn. - 'Mme Rene Pechere'
Wister, Lilacs for America, 36 [1953]
Named for the wife of René Pechère, 1908-2002, Belgian

landscape architect, author and educator.
Cultivar name presumed registered 1953; not reported in cultivation.

'Mme R. Foyer', *S. vulgaris*
origin not known pre-1923; S II
syn. - 'Mme R. Goyer'
Smits, Cat., 24 [1923]; McKelvey, The Lilac, 337 [1928]; Wister, Lilacs for America, 37, 54 [1942] - as 'Mme R. Goyer', S IV; Wister, Lilacs for America, 36 [1953]; Photo on Jorgovani/Lilacs 2015 DVD.
Cultivar name presumed registered 1953; name established and accepted.

Mme R. Goyer - see **'Mme R. Foyer'**.

'Mme Th. Liberton', *S. vulgaris*
Liberton pre-1915; S VI
Wister, Lilas for America, 36 [1953]
Cultivar name presumed registered 1953; not reported in cultivation.

'Mme Victor Bottemanne', *S. vulgaris*
Klettenberg 1938; S III
Wister, Lilacs for America, 36 [1953]
Named for the wife of Belgian landscape architect Victor Bottemanne, 1887–1947.
Cultivar name presumed registered 1953; not reported in cultivation.

Mme Victor Lemoine - perhaps **'Victor Lemoine'** or **'Mme Lemoine'**.

Mme Viger - see 'Mademoiselle Fernande Viger'
McKelvey, The Lilac, 337 [1928].
Mme Vilmorin - possibly **'Maurice de Vilmorin'**
Farr, Cat. "Better Plants", 59 [1922]; McKelvey, The Lilac, 337 [1928] - possibly a misnomer; Wister, Lilacs for America, 54 [1942], 36 [1953] - 'Mme de Vilmorin'.

'Moe', *S. josikaea*
Horntvedt; S VI
syn. - klon 316
Lønø, Norsk Hagetident, 7-8/85, pp. 395-397 [1985]; Kjær, Gartneryrket (G.Y.) 1987:274; Bjerkestrand & Sandved, Grøntanleggsplanter utvalgt for norske forhold 1986-1987-1988 [1989] pp. 25-26 & ill. p. 16; Vrugtman, Lilacs - Quart. Jour. 25(2):41-42 [1996].
Cultivar name established and accepted.

'Mohawk', *S. vulgaris*
Lape; S VII
{'Kapriz' × ? }
Vrugtman, AABGA Bull. 17(3):67 [1984]
Named for the Mohawk people or the Mohawk river valley, New York, USA.
Cultivar name registered 1982;
Cultivar not reported in cultivation.

'Mollie Ann', *S. vulgaris*
Fiala 1983; S IV
{'Rochester' × 'Violet Glory'}
Fiala, Lilacs, 95, 107, 223, Pl.23 [1988]; Photo on Jorgovani/Lilacs 2015 DVD.
Named for Mollie Ann Pesata, sister of the originator.
Cultivar name established and accepted.

'Molodogvardeĭtsy', *S. vulgaris*
'Молодогвардейцы'
Kolesnikov
Polyakova, 2010, Istoriya Russkoĭ Sireni, p. 43; name only.
Named for the members of Molodaya gvardiya, the Communist Youth underground resistance fighters.
Cultivar name not established.

'Monastyrskaya', *S. vulgaris*
'Монастырская'
Aladin, S., Aladina, O., Polyakova, T., and Aladina, A. 2017; S I
{'Flora 1953' × OP}
(Международная научная конференция "Syringa L.: коллекции, выращивание, использование")
"International Scientific Conference "Syringa L.: collections, cultivation, using" / Collection of Scientific Articles of Botanical Institute named after V.L. Komarov, Botanical Garden of Peter the Great BIN RAS. - St. Petersburg. -2020.- pp.3-7 (in Russian); Photo exhibition of all varieties of the creative breeding group "Russian Lilac" at the Festival "Lilac February", St. Petersburg, Botanical Garden of Peter the Great BIN RAS, February 22-24, 2020.
This cultivar creates a feeling of cleanliness and lightness and echoes the white lime of the monastery walls on an early sunny morning.
Cultivar name established and accepted.

'Monge', *S. vulgaris*
Lemoine 1913; S VII
Lemoine, Cat. No. 185, 40 [1913]; McKelvey, The Lilac, 347 [1928]; Wister, Lilacs for America, 54 [1942], 36 [1953]; Photo on Jorgovani/Lilacs 2015 DVD.
Named for Gaspard Monge, 1746-1818, French mathematician and physicist.
Cultivar name presumed registered 1953; name established and accepted.

'Monika', *S. vulgaris*
Mägi pre-2018 ; S VII
Semenov, I., Lilacs 48(2) :68; photo from Estonia by Mägi seen on 2020 ILS Photo Database.
Cultivar name not established.

'Monique Lemoine', *S. vulgaris*
Lemoine 1939; D I
Wister, Lilacs for America, 54 [1942]; Lemoine, Cat. No. 225, 5 [1954]; Wister, Lilacs for America, 36 [1953]; Photo on Jorgovani/Lilacs 2015 DVD.
Awards: Certificate of Merit 1953 (KMTP); RHS Award of Merit 1958.

Cultivar name presumed registered 1953; name established and accepted.

Monis - see '**Lavender Lady**'.

'**Monore**', *S. vulgaris*
Moore 1987; S III/VII
marketed in the USA as BLUE SKIES®, US Trademark No. 1,435,871 [April 7, 1987]
marketed in Germany as BLUE SKIES
{'Esther Staley' × ? }
Monrovia Nursery, Wholesale Cat., 107, 108 (ill.) [1987]; Vrugtman, HortScience 24(3):435 [1989]; Photo on Jorgovani/Lilacs 2015 DVD.
United States Plant Patent No. 6,877 [June 27, 1989].
Cultivar name registered 1988; name established and accepted.

Monroe Centennial - see '**Bicentennial**'
AABGA Bulletin 17(3):69 [1983].

Monsieur . . . - see also: Mons. . . .

'**Monsieur Eugène Resteau**', *S. vulgaris*
Klettenberg 1934; S VI
syn. - 'Mons. Eugene Resteau'
Klettenberg, Cat., 21 [1934]; Wister, Lilacs for America, 36 [1953]
Cultivar name presumed registered 1953; not reported in cultivation.

'**Monsieur Georges Boël**', *S. vulgaris*
Klettenberg 1934; S VI
syn. - 'Mons. Georges Boel'
Klettenberg, Cat., 21 [1934]; Wister, Lilacs for America, 36 [1953]
Named for Georges Boël, x-1939, proprietor of Le château Boël de Falaën, Belgium.
Cultivar name presumed registered 1953; not reported in cultivation.

'Monsieur Raymond Poincaré', *S. vulgaris*
Origin not known; D II
possibly identical with 'Président Poincaré'
Hemeray-Aubert, Cat., item No. 136 [1972].

Mons. . . . - see also: Monsieur . . .

'Mons. Gorriel', *S.* ×*hyacinthiflora*
origin not known pre-1939; ? ?
Wister, Lilacs for America, 36 [1953]
Cultivar name not established.

'**Mons. J. De Messemaeker**', *S. vulgaris*
Stepman-Demessemaeker 1909; S VII
syn. - 'J. de Messemaeker', 'Monsieur J. De Messemaeker', 'Monsieur J. Demessemaeker', 'Mons. J. de Messemaeker'
{'Andenken an Ludwig Späth' × 'Dr Lindley'}
Fl. Stepman-Demessemaeker, Suppl. Gen. Cat., 1 [1909]; McKelvey, The Lilac, 347 [1928]; Wister, Lilacs for America, 50 [1942], 31 [1953]
Named for Pierre Jean Demessemaeker [no dates], nurseryman and florist at Sint-Jans-Molenbeek, Belgium, and father-in-law of Grégoire Florent Stepman. Jean Demessemaeker founded his nursery in 1860; after Florent Stepman married Marie Josèphe Demessemaeker in 1889 the firm became known as Stepman-De Messemaeker.
Award: "Diplôme d'honneur au Meeting horticole de Bruxelles, 16 mai 1909".
Cultivar name presumed registered 1953; name established and accepted.
Nota bene: Although the name of the cultivar appears originally as 'M. J. De Messemaeker', the version 'Mons. J. De Messemaeker' has been adopted since "M." can be mistaken for an abbreviated first name.
Nota bene: Although in the literature consulted the name of the originator is mostly spelled "Stepman-De Messemaeker", the 1889 marriage document shows the name as "Demessemaeker". Additional evidence is the name of a street in Sint-Jans-Molenbeek: "Pierre Jean Demessemaekerstraat".

'**Mons. Léon Mathieu**', *S. vulgaris*
Stepman-Demessemaeker 1906; S VI
syn. - 'Leon Mathieu', 'Léon Mathieu', 'Mons. Leon Mathieu'
{'Dr Lindley' × 'Marie Legraye'}
Fl. Stepman-Demessemaeker, Cat., [1908], 2; McKelvey, The Lilac, 347-348 [1928]; Wister, Lilacs for America, 51 [1942] - as S VII; Wister, Lilacs for America, 33 [1953] - as 'Leon Mathieu'; Photo on Jorgovani/Lilacs 2015 DVD.
Named for Léon Jean Amand Ghislain Mathieu, amateur horticulturist of Louvain, Belgium. (Spelling varies: Mathieu and Matthieu.)
Nota bene: Although the name of the cultivar appears originally as 'M. Léon Mathieu', the version 'Mons. Léon Mathieu' has been adopted since "M." can be mistaken for an abbreviated first name.
Cultivar name presumed registered 1953; name established and accepted.

'**Mons. Lepage**', *S. vulgaris*
Lemoine 1889; S III
syn. - 'M. le Page', 'M. Lepage', 'Mons. LePage', 'Mons. Le Page'; probably also: 'Mlle Lepage', 'Mme Lepage', 'Monsieur Lepage'
Lemoine, Cat. No. 113, 9 [1889]; Havemeyer, Gard. Mag. 25:233 [1917]; McKelvey, The Lilac, 348 [1928]; Wister, Lilacs for America, 54 [1942], 36 [1953] - as 'Mons. Le Page'; Photo on Jorgovani/Lilacs 2015 DVD.
Cultivar name presumed registered 1953; name established and accepted.

'**Mons. Maxime Cornu**', *S. vulgaris*
Lemoine 1886; D V
syn. - 'Maxime Cornu', 'Maxine Cornu', 'M. Maxime Cornu, 'Mons. Maxime', 'Mons. Maxim Cornu', 'Mons. Maxine Cornu'
Lemoine, Cat. No. 104, 7 [1886]; McKelvey, The Lilac, 264, 348-349 [1928]; Wister, Lilacs for America, 53

[1942], 35 [1953] - as 'Maxime Cornu'; Photo on Jorgovani/Lilacs 2015 DVD.
Named for Marie Maxime Cornu, 1843-1901, French horticulturist and academic.
Cultivar name presumed registered 1953; name established and accepted.

'Monstrosa', *S. josikaea*
origin not known pre-1865; S I
Jäger, Ziergehölze, 529 [1865]; McKelvey, The Lilac, 60 [1928]; reported in cultivation at Ole Heide, DK [1988]
Cultivar name established and accepted.

'Mons. Van Aerschot', *S. vulgaris*
Stepman-Demessemaeker pre-1908; S IV
syn. - 'Mons. Van Aerschot', 'M. van Aerschot', 'Van Aerschoft', 'Van Aerschot', 'Van Aerschott', 'Von Oberschott'
Fl. Stepman-Demessemaeker, Cat., 11 [1908]; Turbat, Cat., 75 [1923]; McKelvey, The Lilac, 349 [1928]; Wister, Lilacs for America, 59 [1942], 42 [1953] - as 'Van Aerschot'; Photo on Jorgovani/Lilacs 2015 DVD.
Cultivar name presumed registered 1953; name established and accepted.
Nota bene: Although the name of the cultivar appears originally as 'M. Van Aerschot', the version 'Mons. Van Aerschot' has been adopted since "M." can be mistaken for an abbreviated first name.

'Montaigne', *S. vulgaris*
Lemoine 1907; D V
Lemoine, Cat. No. 167, 31 [1907]; McKelvey, The lilac, 349 [1928]; Wister, Lilacs for America, 54 [1942], 36 [1953]; Photo on Jorgovani/Lilacs 2015 DVD.
Named for Michel Eyquem de Montaigne, 1533-1592, French essayist.
Cultivar name presumed registered 1953; name established and accepted.

'Mont Blanc', *S. vulgaris*
Lemoine 1915; S I
syn. - 'Mount Blanc', 'Mt. Blanc'
Lemoine, Cat. No. 189, 22 [1915]; McKelvey, The Lilac, 349 [1928]; Wister, Lilacs for America, 54 [1942], 36 [1953]; Photo on Jorgovani/Lilacs 2015 DVD.
Named for the highest peak in the French-Italian Alps.
Cultivar name presumed registered 1953; name established and accepted.

Montebello - see **'Comte Adrien de Montebello'**.

'Monténégro', *S. vulgaris*
origin not known ca 1930; S VII-II
Klettenberg Cat., 18 [1930].
Named for Montenegro, republic in the Balkans.
Cultivar name established and accepted.

'Montesquieu', *S. ×hyacinthiflora*
Lemoine 1926; S VI
syn. - *praecox* 'Montesquieu'
Lemoine, Cat. No. 199 bis, 8 [July 1926]; McKelvey, The Lilac, 199 [1928]; Wister, Lilacs for America, 54 [1942], 36 [1953]; Photo on Jorgovani/Lilacs 2015 DVD.
Named for Charles de Secundat, Baron de la Brèda et Montesquieu, 1689-1755, French philosopher, jurist and writer.
Cultivar name presumed registered 1953; name established and accepted.

'Montgolfier', *S. vulgaris*
Lemoine 1905; S VI
Lemoine, Cat. No. 161, 8 [1905]; McKelvey, The Lilac, 349-350 [1928]; Wister, Lilacs for America, 54 [1942], 36 [1953]
Named for brothers Joseph Michel, 1740-1810, and Jacques Étienne Montgolfier 1745-1799, French aeronautical inventors.
Cultivar name presumed registered 1953; name established and accepted.

'Monument', *S. vulgaris*
Lemoine 1934; S I
Wister, Lilacs for America, 54 [1942], 36 [1953]; Photo on Jorgovani/Lilacs 2015 DVD.
Cultivar name presumed registered 1953; name established and accepted.
Forcing cultivar in the Netherlands.

'Monument Carnot', *S. vulgaris*
Lemoine 1895; D V
syn. - 'Mons. Carnot'
Lemoine, Cat. No. 131, 10 [1895]; McKelvey, The Lilac, 350 [1928]; Wister, Lilacs for America, 54 [1942], 36 [1953]; Photo on Jorgovani/Lilacs 2015 DVD.
Named in commemoration of Marie François Sadi Carnot, 1837-1894, president of the French Republic.
Cultivar name presumed registered 1953; name established and accepted.

'Mood Indigo', *S. vulgaris*
Clarke 1946; S II
syn. - 'Munindigo'
Clarke, Wholesale Price List, 23 [1948]; Woody Plant Register, AAN, No. 72 [1949]; Wister, Lilacs for America, 36 [1953]; Photo on Jorgovani/Lilacs 2015 DVD.
Named for Mood Indigo, the classical jazz composition by Duke Ellington, 1899-1974, USA.
Cultivar name presumed registered 1953; name established and accepted.

'Moonbeam', *S.* (species affiliation not known)
origin not known 2004; S II
Anon., Lilacs - Quart. Jour. 33(1):11 [2004]
Cultivar name not established.

'Moondust', *S. vulgaris*
Moro, F. 2008; D I & VII
{bud mutation of 'Nadezhda'}
F. Moro, Lilacs - Quart. Jour. 41(2):55, ill. back cover [2012]; Vrugtman, Hanburyana 7:29 [2013].

Cultivar name registered 2012; name established and accepted.

'Moonglow', *S. vulgaris*
Scott; S III & V
Wister, Lilacs for America, 54 [1942] - as S V; Wayside, Cat., 54 [Spring 1971]; Lake County Nursery Exchange, Cat., 72 [1974] - as S III
Cultivar name established and accepted.

'Moonlight', *S. vulgaris*
Havemeyer 1943; S III
Wister, Lilacs for America, 54 [1942], 37 [1953]; Eickhorst, ILS Lilac Newsletter 4(1):4-5 [1978]; Anon., ILS Lilac Newsletter 11(1):6-8 [1985]
Cultivar name presumed registered 1953; name established and accepted.

'Moritz Eichler', *S. vulgaris*
Eichler 1862; S III
syn. - 'Mauritz Eichler'
Eichler, Garten-Nachr. 7:27 [1862] in Wochenschr. Ver. Beförd. Gartenb. Preuss. [1862]; Anon., Hamburger Garten- und Blumenzeitung 392-393 [1862]; McKelvey, The Lilac, 350, 560, 563 [1928]; Wister, Lilacs for America, 54 [1942], 37 [1953]
Named for Friedrich Moritz Eichler (? - 1861), horticulturist, Chemnitz, Saxony, Germany.
Cultivar name presumed registered 1953; name established and accepted.

MORjos 060F, *S.*
Morel, G. 1974; S IV-V
syn. - 'Jenny', **'Josée'**, Josee, 'Lotta', tribida
'Josee' marketed in France as JOSÉE™, trademark No. 3769 [July 19, 1971]
marketed in Australia as LOTTA
{(*S. pubescens* subsp. *microphylla* × *S. pubescens* subsp. *patula*) × *S. pubescens* subsp. *pubescens*}
Pépinières Minier, Cat., 62 [Automne 1974]; Vrugtman, AABGA Bull. 13(4):109 [1979] - as 'JOSÉE'®; Lottah Nursery online Cat., Nov. 11, 2003 - as 'Lotta' <http://www.lottah.com/catalog.htm>; Song Sparrow Nursery, Cat. 52 [2004] - as *tribrida* 'Josee'; Photo on Jorgovani/Lilacs 2015 DVD.
Cultivar name established and accepted; name (**'Josée'**) registered 1978.

MORNING IN MOSCOW - see 'Utro Moskvy'.

'Morton', *S. pekinensis*
Rock & Bachtell 1993; S I
syn.: 'Chicago Tower', CG88-005, MA No. 172-26sd, 'Watertown'
marketed in the USA as CHINA SNOW™ Peking lilac (formerly WATER TOWER®)
{selection grown from seed collected by Joseph F. C. Rock at an elevation of 2700 m in Central Gansu, China [No. 13506], and distributed by the Arnold Arboretum pre. 1920; original tree as MA No. 172-26sd planted 1922 in Morton Arboretum}
McKelvey, The Lilac, 487 [1928] - ref. to J.F.C. Rock's collections; Anon., Woody Plts. of the Morton Arb., 369 [1990] - as MA No. 172-26, loc. CC - 67/84-69; CHICAGOLAND GROWS® Inc., 1992 Annual Report, 9 [1993 ?] - as 'Morton'; Doc. CLG/ACCESSIONS, 1 [05/16/94]; Bachtell, Comb. Proc. Internat. Pl. Propag. Soc. 44:568-572 [1994]; Chicagoland Grows, Inc., Plant Accessions List [2/27/96]; Chicago Botanic Garden, March 20, 1999, Illinois' Best Plants, http://doug.nslsilus.org/cgi-bin/illinoisBest/plantindex.pl; Anon., Lilacs-Quart. Jour. 29(1):19 [2000] - as WATERTOWER®; Select Plus Nurs., Cat. [2000] - erroneously as 'Watertown'; Anon., Seasons, Newsletter The Morton Arboretum, Jan/Feb 2000, pp. 8-9, ill.; Vrugtman, HortScience 38(6):1301 [2003]; Photo on Jorgovani/Lilacs 2015 DVD.
Named for the Morton Arboretum, Lisle, Illinois, USA.
Cultivar name registered 2002; name established and accepted.

MOSCOW SKY - see **'Nebo Moskvy'**.

MOSKAVY - see **Krasavi<u>ts</u>a Moskvy**.

'Moskovskiĭ Universitet', *S. vulgaris*
'Московский Университет'
Kolesnikov & Mironovi<u>ch</u> 1986; D IV
syn. - 'Moskovskij Universitet', 'Moskovskiy Universitet'
Pikaleva, Lilacs - Quart. Jour. 23(4):86, 91 [1994]; Registered with the State Commission of the Russian Federation for Testing and Protection of Selection Achievements, No. 8803536, 1998; Polyakova, 2010, Istoriya Russkoĭ Sireni, p. 105; Photo on Jorgovani/Lilacs 2015 DVD.
Named for Moscow University, Moscow, Russian Federation.
Cultivar name registered, established and accepted.

'Moskvi<u>ch</u>ka', *S. vulgaris*
'Москвичка'
Aladin, S., Aladina, O., and Polyakova, T. 2016; S IV/V
{'Me<u>ch</u>ta' × OP}
Садовник (Gardener) magazine 04 (140)/2017 :18-25; Вестник АППМ (Catalog in Vestnik APPM (Planting material association) magazine) 1/2018: 59-72 (in Russian); II All-Russian scientific-practical conference with international participation (II Всероссийская научно-практическая конференция с международным участием) « Botanical Gardens in the XXI Century: Biodiversity Conservation, Development Strategy and Innovative Solutions Belgorod, Botanical Garden of NRU «BelSU», September 23-26, 2019; pp.141-145 (in Russian).
Name: Russian for a woman who lives in Moscow.
Cultivar name established and accepted.

'Mother Louise', *S. vulgaris*
Fiala 1969; D I

{'Carley' × 'Flora 1953'}
Fiala, Lilacs, 91, 223 [1988] - as tetraploid F1
Named for the French nun and author Mother Louise Margaret Claret de la Touche, 1868-1915.
Cultivar established and accepted; not reported in cultivation.

Mount... - see also Mt...

'Mountain Haze', *S. vulgaris*
Clarke (not Lammerts) 1946; S VI
{'Mme F. Morel' × ?}
Clarke, Cat. 16:8 [1949]; Woody Plant Register, AAN, No. 73 [1949]; Wister, Lilacs for America, 37 [1953]
Cultivar name presumed registered 1953; name established and accepted.

'Mountain Haze',
Lammerts, not Clarke
Wister, Lilac Registrations (mimeogr. list), 4 [n.d.; ca 1968] - cultivar of *Ceanothus* L or California lilac, not a *Syringa*.

'Mount Baker', *S.* ×*hyacinthiflora*
Skinner 1961; S I
syn. - 'Schneeweißchen'
marketed in Germany as SCHNEEWEISSCHEN™ (No. 307071502; G. & J. Rosskamp) - in USA misspelled SCHNEEWEIBSCHEN
Wister, Arnoldia 23(4):82 [1963]; Skinner, Hort. Horizons, 108 [1966]; Lilacs - Quart. Jour. 22(3): back cover ill. [1993]; Photo on Jorgovani/Lilacs 2015 DVD.
Named for Mount Baker in Washington State, USA.
Cultivar name registered 1963; name established and accepted.

'Mount Domogled', *S. vulgaris* Anderson; S IV
syn. - 'Anderson nana', *nana*, *S. vulgaris nana*
{collected on Muntele Domugled (Mount Domogled), Romania}
USDA Plant Inventory No. 122, p. 34-35, PI No. 108774 [Oct. 1939]; Wister, Lilacs for America, 54, 60 [1942], 37, 43 [1953] - as S. vulgaris nana, S V; Wister & Oppe, Arnoldia 31(3):123 [1971] - name only; Hyypio, Lilacs - Proceedings 8(1):61-64 [1980]; Photo on Jorgovani/Lilacs 2015 DVD.
Named for Mount Domogled (Muntele Domugled), Romania.
Cultivar name registered 1953 & 1970; name established and accepted.

Mr... - see also: Mister...

'Mramornaya', *S. vulgaris*
'Мраморная'
Sagitova; ? ?
no information
Name: Russian for marble.
Cultivar name not established.

'Mrs A. Belmont', *S. vulgaris*
Havemeyer pre-1942; S III
syn. - 'Mrs August Belmont'
Wister, Lilacs for America, 54 [1942], 37 [1953]; Eickhorst, ILS Lilac Newsletter 4(1):4-5 [1978]
Named for Eleanor Robson Belmont, 1879-1979, English-American actress, writer, nurse, founder of the Metropolitan Opera Guild, New York City.
Cultivar name presumed registered 1953; name established and accepted.

'Mrs Berneasha', *S. vulgaris*
Klager; D VII & I
Anon., ILS Newsletter 14(4):3-4 [1988]; Stenlund, Lilacs - Quart. Jour. 20(2):41 [1991]
Cultivar name established and accepted.

'Mrs B. S. Williams', *S. vulgaris*
Havemeyer pre-1942; S IV
Wister, Lilacs for America, 54 [1942]
Cultivar name not established; probably extinct.

'Mrs Calvin Coolidge', *S. vulgaris*
Franklin, A.B. ca 1935; S VI
syn. - 'Mrs Calvin Cooledge', 'Mrs Coolidge'
Wister, Lilacs for America, 54 [1942], 37 [1953]; Franklin, Cat., 2 [1972]; Photo on Jorgovani/Lilacs 2015 DVD.
Named for the wife of the 30th president of the USA.
Cultivar name presumed registered 1953; name established and accepted.

'Mrs Charles Davis', *S. vulgaris*
Stone; ? ?
Wister & Oppe, Arnoldia 31(3):123 [1971] - name only
Cultivar name registered 1970, but without description; not reported in cultivation.

'Mrs Cleveland', *S. vulgaris*
Theidel ca 1915; S VII
{new name for an older cultivar; original name not known}
Wister, Lilacs for America, 37 [1953] - as renamed by R. P. Theidel
Named for the wife of Stephen Grover Cleveland, 22nd and 24th president of the USA.
Cultivar name not established.

Mrs Coolidge - see **'Mrs Calvin Coolidge'**.

'Mrs Edward Harding', *S. vulgaris*
Lemoine 1922; D VI
syn. - 'Edward Harding', 'Madame Edward Harding', 'Mrs Ed Harding'
Lemoine, Cat. No. 196, 19 [1922]; McKelvey, The Lilac, 346 [1928]; Wister, Lilacs for America, 54 [1942], 37 [1953]; Photo on Jorgovani/Lilacs 2015 DVD.
Named for Alice Harding (née Howard), ca 1846-1938, American writer (The book of the peony, 1917, and other horticultural books).

Awards: RHS Award of Garden Merit 1969 & 1993.
Cultivar name presumed registered 1953; name established and accepted.

'Mrs Eleanor Roosevelt', *S. vulgaris*
Margaretten; S VI
syn. - 'Mrs E. Roosevelt'
{'Mme Lemoine' × ? }
reported in NCCPG Coll., UK [1997]; Gilbert, Lilacs - Quart. Jour. 27(2):55 [1998] - name only; Photo on Jorgovani/Lilacs 2015 DVD.
Named for Eleanor Roosevelt, 1884-1962, American humanitarian, wife of Franklin Delano Roosevelt, 32nd president of the USA.
Cultivar name established and accepted.

'Mrs Elizabeth Peterson', *S. vulgaris*
Havemeyer; S III
Wister, Lilacs for America, 37 [1953]; Lilac Land, Cat. [1954]; Eickhorst, ILS Lilac Newsletter 4(1):4-5 [1978]
Cultivar name presumed registered 1953; name established and accepted.

Mrs E. van Nes - see **'C. B. van Nes'**.

'Mrs Fannie W. Heath', *S. vulgaris*
Nelson, Caspar; D VII
syn. - 'Mrs Fannie Heath'
Wister, Arnoldia 23(4):82 [1963] - name only; color update by C. Holetich in lit. 10 April 2015 as D III & IV. All picture on ILS Photo Database show D IV.
Cultivar name registered 1963, but without description; name established and accepted.

Mrs Felix - see **'Mme Felix'**.

'Mrs Flanders', *S. vulgaris*
Havemeyer pre-1942; S VII
Wister, Lilacs for America, 54 [1942], 37 [1953]; Eickhorst, ILS Lilac Newsletter 4(1):4-5 [1978]; Anon, Lilacs - Quart. Jour. 17(1):26 [1988]
Cultivar name presumed registered 1953; name established and accepted.

Mrs Forrest Kresser Smith, Mrs Forrest K. Smith - see **'Forrest Kresser Smith'**.

'Mrs Harry Bickle', *S. vulgaris*
Rolph 1956; S V
Rowancroft Garden, Cat. No. 15, 30 [n.d.; prob. spring 1957]; Wister, Arnoldia 23(4):82 [1963] - with ref. to Rowancroft, Cat. No. 17, 30 [n.d.; prob. 1963]; Photo on Jorgovani/Lilacs 2015 DVD.
Cultivar name registered 1963; name established and accepted.

'Mrs H. J. Cran', *S. vulgaris*
origin not known; S VI
Wister, lilacs for America, 37 [1953] - name only; Peterson, Lilacs - Proceedings 16(1):21 [1987] - name only; Photo on Jorgovani/Lilacs 2015 DVD.
Cultivar name presumed registered 1953; name established and accepted.

'Mrs Irene Slater', *S. vulgaris*
Slater 1980; S II-II/III
syn. - Irene, Slater's Irene
{'Dr Brethour' × ? }
Note: Anon., Lilacs - Quart. Jour. 21(1): back cover, upper right [1992] - the lilac shown is not 'Mrs Irene Slater', Irene, or Slater's Irene.
RHS Color Chart [1966]: Newly opened florets: Violet Group 84B; older florets fading to Violet-Blue Group 92C.
Named for Mrs Irene Slater née Dart, 1920-2003, wife of the originator.
Cultivar name established and accepted;
Cultivar name registered in 2002 (publication pending).

'Mrs J. Herbert Alexander', *S.* (Villosae Group)
Alexander Sr 1970; S V
syn. - 'Mrs J. H. Alexander'
{*S.* ×*josiflexa* 'James Macfarlane' × *S.* ×*prestoniae* 'Ethel M. Webster'}
Wister, Arbor. Bot. Gard. Bull. 1(2):20 [1967] - name only; Alexander Sr, Cat. sheets [n.d.; rec'd January 1970]; Anon., Lilacs - Quart. Jour. 17(1):27 [1988] - name only; Photo on Jorgovani/Lilacs 2015 DVD.
Cultivar name registered 1967; name established and accepted.

'Mrs John S. Williams', *S. vulgaris*
Havemeyer pre-1953; S IV
Wister, Lilacs for America, 37 [1953]; Eickhorst, ILS Lilac Newsletter 4(1):4-5 [1978]
Cultivar thought to be extinct per ILS Preservation Committee 2019
Cultivar name presumed registered 1953; name established and accepted.

'Mrs John W. Davis', *S. vulgaris*
Havemeyer pre-1942; D VI
Wister, Lilacs for America, 54 [1942], 37 [1953]; Eickhorst, ILS Lilac Newsletter 4(1):4-5 [1978]
Cultivar name presumed registered 1953;
Cultivar not reported in cultivation.

'Mrs Katherine Margaretten', *S. vulgaris*
Margaretten; D III
syn. - 'Mrs K. Margaretten'
{'Mme Lemoine' × ? }
reported in cultivation at Royal Botanical Gardens, Ontario, Canada; and NCCPG collection, Suffolk, UK; Photo on Jorgovani/Lilacs 2015 DVD.
Cultivar name established and accepted.

Mrs Klager, *S. vulgaris*
origin not known pre-2000; ? ?
Van Vloten Nurs., cat. p.90 [1997] - name only; in litt., erroneous name (Casey van Vloten to Vrugtman, Sep.19/2000).

'Mrs Liang', *S. vulgaris*
origin not known ? ?
B. O. Case & Sons, Cat. [1912]; Wister, Lilacs for America, 37, 54 [1942]
Cultivar name not established.

'Mrs McKelvey', *S. vulgaris*
origin not known pre-1935; D IV
Wister, Lilac for America, 37 [1953]; Univ. of Wisconsin, Arb. News 23(2):13 [1974]; Photo on Jorgovani/Lilacs 2015 DVD.
Named for Susan Delano (Mrs Charles Wylie McKelvey), 1883-1964, American botanist and author of the 1928 monograph on the genus *Syringa*.
Cultivar name presumed registered 1953; name established and accepted.

'Mrs Morgan', *S. vulgaris*
Klager 1928; D V
syn. - 'Mrs Morgan Cooley'
Cooley, Cat., 7 [1928]; McKelvey, The Lilac, 560 [1928]; Wister, Lilacs for America, 54 [1942], 37 [1953]; Anon., ILS Newsletter 14(4):3-4 [1988]; Fiala, Lilacs, 200 [1988] - as 'Mrs Morgan Cooley'
Cultivar name presumed registered 1953; name established and accepted.

'Mrs Nadeau', *S. vulgaris*
Berdeen pre-1983; D V & III
King & Coggeshall, Lilacs - Quart. Jour. 27(2):49-50 [1998] - name only
Named for a friend of the originator from Kennebunk, Maine.
Cultivar not established.

'Mrs Nancy Reagan', *S. vulgaris*
Margaretten; D II
{'Mme Lemoine' × ? }
Macore Co. Inc. photo library [Nov.28, 1999] http://www.macore.com/photolib.htm - as 'Nancy Regan'; reported in cultivation at Royal Botanical Gardens, Ontario, Canada; and NCCPG collection, Suffolk, UK; Photo on Jorgovani/Lilacs 2015 DVD.
Named for Nancy Davis Reagan, 1921-2016, wife of Ronald Wilson Reagan, 40th president of the USA.
Cultivar name established and accepted.

'Mrs Regina Margaretten', *S. vulgaris*
Margaretten; S IV &
{'Mme Lemoine' × ? }
Not reported in cultivation
Cultivar name not established.

'Mrs R. L. Gardner', *S. vulgaris*
Gardner 1956; S VII
syn.: Gardner No. 441, 'Mrs Robert M. Gardner'
Gardner, US Plant Patent No. 1443 [Jan. 3, 1956]; Edw. J. Gardner Nursery, Price list, 6 [1956]; Wister, Arnoldia 23(4):82 [1963] - as 'Mrs Robert M. Gardner', name only

Cultivar name registered 1963; name established and accepted.

Mrs R. W. Mills - see '**Carmine**'.

Mrs Stepman - see '**Mme Florent Stepman**'.

'Mrs Trapman', *S. vulgaris*
Havemeyer 1943; S VII
Wister, Lilacs for America, 53 [1942], 37 [1953]; Eickhorst, ILS Lilac Newsletter 4(1):4-5 [1978]
Cultivar name presumed registered 1953; name established and accepted.

'Mrs Warren Harding', *S. vulgaris*
Klager; ? V
Stenlund, Lilacs - Quart. Jour, 20(2):41 [1991] - as red
Named for the wife of Warren Gamaliel Harding, 1865-1923, 29th president of the USA.
Cultivar name not established.

'Mrs Watson Webb', *S. vulgaris*
Havemeyer pre-1942; S VI
Wister, Lilacs for America, 54 [1942] - as S V; Wister, Lilacs for America, 37 [1953]; Eickhorst, ILS Lilac Newsletter 4(1):4-5 [1978]; Photo on Jorgovani/Lilacs 2015 DVD.
Named for Electra Havemeyer Webb, 1888-1960, a collector of American antiques and founder of Shelburne Museum, wife of James Watson Webb.
Cultivar name presumed registered 1953; name established and accepted.

'Mrs W. E. Marshall', *S. vulgaris*
Havemeyer 1924; S VII
syn. - 'W. E. Marshall', 'William Marshall'
{'L'Oncle Tom' × 'Negro'}
McKelvey, The Lilac, 346-347 [1928]; Wister, Lilacs for America, 54 [1942], 37 [1953]; Niedz, ILS Newsletter 1(4):7-8 [1972]; Eickhorst, ILS Lilac Newsletter 4(1):4-5 [1978]; Photo on Jorgovani/Lilacs 2015 DVD.
Named for Mrs W. E. Marshall, wife of the originator's friend, New York lily specialist and author William Emerson Marshall, 1872-1937.
Cultivar name presumed registered 1953; name established and accepted.

'Mr Wayne', *S. vulgaris*
Hughes; S VII
{parentage not known}
Named for Wayne Hughes, the originator.
Cultivar name not established.

M. Scholochov - see '<u>Sholokhov</u>'.

'Mt Hood', *S. vulgaris*
Klager; D I
syn. - 'Mount Hood'
Anon., ILS Newsletter 14(4):3-4 [1988]
Named for Mount Hood, Oregon, USA.
Cultivar name established and accepted.

'Mulatka', *S. vulgaris*
'Мулатка'
Mikhaĭlov & Rybakina 1980; S VI
Pikaleva, Lilacs - Quart. Jour. 23(4):86 [1994]; Chapman, Lilacs - Quart. Jour. 27(2):45 [1998]; Photo on Jorgovani/Lilacs 2015 DVD.
Name: Russian for Mulatto woman.
Cultivar name established and accepted.

Mulatka mutant – see 'Tatyanin Den'

'Munchkin', *S. vulgaris*
Fiala 1981; S III
{'True Blue' × 'Rochester'}
Fiala, Lilacs, 115, 223 [1988]
Named for the squeaky-voiced little people in L. Frank Baum's "The Wizard of Oz".
Cultivar name established and accepted.

Murasaki-shikibu – see 'Shishi'

'Muriel', *S.* ×*hyacinthiflora*
Preston pre-1936; S VII
syn. - Preston No. 22.04.09
{*S. vulgaris* 'Negro' × *S.* ×*hyacinthiflora* 'Lamartine'}
Davis, Rep. Dom. Hort. 1931, 1932 and 1933, 143 [1936] & Progress Report 1934-1948, 150 [1950]; Wister, Lilacs for America, 54 [1942], 37 [1953]; Photo on Jorgovani/Lilacs 2015 DVD.
Cultivar name presumed registered 1953; name established and accepted.

'Murillo', *S. vulgaris*
Lemoine 1901; D VII & IV
Lemoine, Cat. No. 149 [1901]; McKelvey, The Lilac, 350 [1928]; Wister, Lilacs for America, 54 [1942], 37 [1953]
Named for Bartholomé Esteban Murillo, 1618-1682, Spanish painter, founder of the Academy of Seville.
Cultivar name presumed registered 1953; name established and accepted.

M. Van Aerschot - see 'Mons. Van Aerschot'.

'My Blue Heaven', *S. vulgaris*
Sass (?) 2004; S III
Anon., Lilacs - Quart. Jour. 33(1):11 [2004]
Cultivar name established and accepted.

'My Favorite', *S. vulgaris*
Klager 1928; D VI
syn. - 'Favorite'
Cooley, Cat., 7 [1928]; McKelvey, The Lilac, 561 [1928]; Wister, Lilacs for America, 54 [1942], 37 [1953]; ILS Newsletter 14(4):3-4 [1988]; Fiala, Lilacs, 200 [1988]; Photo on Jorgovani/Lilacs 2015 DVD.
Cultivar name presumed registered 1953; name established and accepted.

'Myshkin', *S. vulgaris*
'Мышкин'
Aladin, S., Aladina, O., and, Polyakova, T. 2016; S II
{'Cavour' × OP}
Вестник АППМ (Catalog in Vestnik APPM (Planting material association) magazine) 1/2018: 59-72 (in Russian).
Named for Myshkin, small Russian town in Yaroslavl Oblast, located on the left bank of the Volga; original settlement dating back to the 15th century.
Cultivar name established and accepted.

Mystery, *S.*
ca 1993
Beaver Creek Nursery, Wholesale Cat., 39 [1994] - as S III; Anon., DataScape Botanical Index, 107 [1994], 122 [1996], 658 [2001]; Vrugtman, Lilacs - Quart. Jour. 24(3):69-70 [1995]
Cognomen for an unknown, named cultivar.

M36 (*S. vulgaris*)
Origin not known; S III
Hauta-aho, Lilacs - Quart. Jour. 35(4):119 [2006] - unidentified old selection growing in the Helsinki region, Finland.
Cognomen, not a cultivar name.

M56 (*S. vulgaris*)
Origin not known; S VI
Hauta-aho, Lilacs - Quart. Jour. 35(4):119 [2006] - unidentified old selection growing in the Helsinki region, Finland.
Cognomen, not a cultivar name.

'Nadezhda', *S. vulgaris*
'Надежда'
Kolesnikov pre-1960; D III-IV
syn. - HOPE, 'Nadesha', 'Nadezda', 'Nadjezhda', Kolesnikov No. 728, WILD RIVER DOUBLE LILAC (trade designation)
Bilov et al., Siren', 64 [1974] - in Russian; Gromov, Lilacs - Proceedings 2(4):18 [1974]; Rubtzov et al. 1980. Vidy i sorta sireni, kul'tiviruemye v SSSR. Kiev; Naukova Dumka. – in Russian; Holetich, C.D. 1982. Lilac species and cultivars in cultivation in USSR. Lilacs 11(2):1-38. - translation of Rubtzov et al. 1982; Lilacs - Quart. Jour. 25(3): front cover ill. [1996]; Photo on Jorgovani/Lilacs 2015 DVD.
N.B. This cultivar has become confused with 'P. P. Konchalovski' in collections all over the world. While they are clearly two different cultivars, they appear identical to most examiners.
Name: Russian for hope.
Cultivar name established and accepted.
Forcing cultivar in the Netherlands.

'Nadezhda Krupskaya', *S. vulgaris*
'Надежда Крупская'
Kolesnikov pre-1960; D I
T. Polyakova, 2018, Мастер Сиреневой Кисти (Master of the Lilac Brush), p.108 - photo only.
in cultivation at Smolny Garden, St Petersburg (in litt.

Polyakova to Vrugtman March 2016); no lit. ref. Seen on Facebook post 5/27/20 from Lomonosov Botanical Garden of the Moscow State University. T. Polyakova, 2018, Мастер Сиреневой Кисти (Master of the Lilac Brush), p.108 - photo only.
Named for Nadezhda Konstantinovna "Nadya" Krupskaya (Наде́жда Константи́новна Кру́пская), 1869-1939; Russian Bolshevik revolutionary and politician; wife of Lenin (Vladimir Ilyich Ulyanov), 1898 until his death in 1924.
Cultivar name not established.

'Nafisa', *S. vulgaris*
'Нафиса'
Sakharova 1973; S V & I
syn. - Sakharova No. 1705
{'Jules Simon' × 'Congo'}
Sakharova, Introduktsiya i selektsiya dekorativnykh rastenii v Bashkirii, 31-32 [1978] - in Russian; Photo on Jorgovani/Lilacs 2015 DVD.
Name: In Arabic graceful or charming; also a Bashkir female name.
Cultivar name established and accepted.

'**Nagareboshi**', *S. pubescens* subsp. *pubescens*
'流れ星'
Ihara 2012; S VII
syn. - seedling no. 2011S1128007#5
{*S. pubescens* subsp. *pubescens* seedling no. 20040520001#8 × *S. pubescens* subsp. *pubescens* 'Hoshikuzu'}
(Vrugtman, Cultivated Plant Diversity ... 2017)
Name: Japanese for shooting star.
Cultivar name registered 2017; name established and accepted.

'Nakai', *S. oblata* subsp. *dilatata*
Wilson & Fiala 1988; S V
{raised from seed sample No. 9232 collected by E. H. Wilson in 1917 in Korea}
Fiala, Lilacs, 59-61 [1988]; Vrugtman, Lilacs - Quart. Jour. 25(2):37-38 [1996]; Vrugtman, Lilacs -Quart. Jour. 32(4):151-152 [2003] - reported to be in cultivation; see also McKelvey, The Lilac, 186-188 [1928], and Wilson, Jour. Arnold Arb. 1:41 [1919].
Named by J. L. Fiala in 1988 for Takenoshin Nakai, 1882-1952, Japanese botanist.
Cultivar name established and accepted.

'Namejs', *S. vulgaris*
Kārkliņš, 2003; S VII
Photo from Dobele, Latvia taken by Natalia Savenko, seen in 2020 ILS Photo Database.
Cultivar name not established.

'Nana', *S.* ×*chinensis*
origin not known ? ?
Hortus III., 1090 [1976]
Cultivar name not established.

'Nana', *S. oblata* subsp. *dilatata*
Origin not known; S III
syn. - *S. oblata dilatata nana*
Fiala, Lilacs, 115 [1988]
Cultivar name not established; doubtful name.

'**Nana**', *S. oblata* subsp. *oblata*
Upton 1941; S V-VI
syn. - *S. oblata* var. *giraldii nana*
Horticultural News 9(10):3-4 [1943]; Upton Nursery Co., Cat. [n.d.]; Wister, Lilacs for America, 54, 55 [1942], 37 [1953]; Upton Scrapbook 1:69 [1986]
Cultivar name presumed registered 1953; name established and accepted.

'Nana', *S. vulgaris*
origin not known pre-1884; S VI
common name: Nana
Miller, Dict. Engl. Names Plants, 77 [1884]; Ellwanger & Barry, Cat., [1892]; Stand. Pl. Names, 487 [1923] - as Nana; McKelvey, The Lilac, 350 [1928]; Photo on Jorgovani/Lilacs 2015 DVD.
Cultivar name established and accepted.

nana (*S. vulgaris*), Anderson - see '**Mount Domogled**'.

'Nanclin', *S. vulgaris*
origin not known pre-1930; D ?
Klettenberg, Cat. [1930] - probably misspelling of '**Naudin**', Lemoine.

'Nancy Alexander', *S.* (species affiliation not known)
Alexander Sr; ? ?
in litt. J. H. Alexander Sr to Vrugtman, Feb. 9, 1973, and N. Alexander to Vrugtman, Oct. 6, 1976
original plant existed, but was renamed
Cultivar name not established; not reported in cultivation.

'**Nancy Frick**', *S. vulgaris*
Havemeyer pre-1942; S V
Wister, Lilacs for America, 54 [1942], 37 [1953]; Eickhorst, ILS Lilac Newsletter 4(1):4-5 [1978]; Photo on Jorgovani/Lilacs 2015 DVD.
Cultivar name presumed registered 1953; name established and accepted.

Nancy Regan - see 'Mrs Nancy Regan'.

'**Nanook**', *S. vulgaris*
Eveleens Maarse 1951; S I
Wister, Lilacs for America, 37 [1953]
Named for Nanook, Inuit (Eskimo) hero in the 1922/23 Canadian movie production "Nanook of the North", directed and photographed by Robert J. Flaherty.
Awards: Certificate of Merit 1951 (KMTP).
Cultivar name presumed registered 1953; name established and accepted.

'**Naomi**', *S. vulgaris*
Klager 1934; S VII

Wister, Lilacs for America, 54 [1942], 37 [1953]
Cultivar name presumed registered 1953; name established and accepted.

'Narragansett', *S. vulgaris*
Origin unknown ca 1985; S IV
Seen at http://www.combinedroselist.com/freedom-gardens.html and in personal email of September 28, 2019 from Peter Schneider to Mark DeBard
Found on Narragensett Avenue in Lakewood, OH USA by Peter Schneider
Cultivar name not established; possibly a cognomen for an older cultivar.

'**Naudin**', *S. vulgaris*
Lemoine 1913; D IV
Lemoine, Cat. No. 185, 40 [1913]; McKelvey, The Lilac, 350-351 [1928]; Wister, Lilacs for America, 54 [1942], 37 [1953]; Photo on Jorgovani/Lilacs 2015 DVD.
Named for Charles Victor Naudin, 1815-1899, French botanist.
Cultivar name presumed registered 1953; name established and accepted.

'Nazgyul'', *S. vulgaris*
'Назгюль'
Sagitova; ? ?
no information
Cultivar name not established.

'Nebbia d'un Bacio', *S. vulgaris*
Moro, F. 2013; S V
{'Krasavitsa Moskvy' × ?}
Lilacs - Quart. Jour. 42(3):85 & 87 (photo) [2013]; in lit. Moro to Vrugtman July 13, 2013
Name: Italian for mist of a kiss.
Cultivar name established and accepted.

'Nebesnaia Sin'', *S. vulgaris*
'Небесная синь'
Sagitova & Dzevitski pre-2014; S II
Photo by Oleg Dzevitskiy in Almati, Kazakhstan seen in 2020 ILS Photo & Color Database.
Russian for Heavenly Blue.
Cultivar name not established.

'**Nebo Moskvy**', *S. vulgaris*
'Небо Москвы'
Kolesnikov 1963; D III-IV-VI
syn. - Kolesnikov No. 508, 'Nebo Moskovy', 'Niebo Moskvy'
marketed in the USA as Moscow Sky
{'Mme Casimir Périer' × 'Snowflake'}
Howard, Arnoldia 19(6-7):31-35 [1959]; Gromov, A., Siren', 85 [1963]; Howard & Brizicky, AABGA Quart. Newsl. No. 64, 17-21 [1965]; Wister & Oppe, Arnoldia 31(3):125 [1971] - as 'Niebo Moskvy'; Gromov, Lilacs - Proceedings 2(4):18 [1974]; Rubtzov et al. 1980. Vidy i sorta sireni, kul'tiviruemye v SSSR. Kiev; Naukova Dumka. – in Russian; Holetich, C.D. 1982. Lilac species and cultivars in cultivation in USSR. Lilacs 11(2):1-38. - translation of Rubtzov et al. 1982; Photo on Jorgovani/Lilacs 2015 DVD.
Name: Russian for Moscow sky.
Cultivar name registered 1970; name established and accepted.

'Nebraska Dawn', *S. vulgaris*
Peterson pre-2004; D VI
{'Red Giant' × ?}
Anon., Lilacs - Quart. Jour. 33(1):11 [2004]; in litt. Peterson to Vrugtman Mar.3/06
Cultivar name not established.

'Necker', *S. ×hyacinthiflora*
Lemoine 1920; S V
syn.: 'Praecox Necker'
Lemoine, Cat. No. 194, 18 [1920]; McKelvey, The Lilac, 199 [1928]; Wister, Lilacs for America, 54 [1942], 37 [1953]; Photo on Jorgovani/Lilacs 2015 DVD.
Named for Noël-Joseph de Necker, 1730-1793, French botanist.
Cultivar name presumed registered 1953; name established and accepted.
Forcing cultivar in the Netherlands.

'Negro', *S. vulgaris*
Lemoine 1899; S VII
Lemoine, Cat. No. 143, 24 [1899]; Kache, Gartenschönheit 5:82 [1924]; McKelvey, The Lilac, 351 [1928]; Wister, Lilacs for America, 54 [1942], 37 [1953]; Photo on Jorgovani/Lilacs 2015 DVD.
Cultivar name presumed registered 1953; name established and accepted.

'**Neizvestn'iï Soldat**', *S. ×hyacinthiflora*
'Неизвестный солдат'
Pshennikova, L. 2016; S IV
{'Bogdan Khmel'nitskyi' × *S. oblata* subsp. *dilatata*}
Polyakova T., Dvoryak N. "Pobednaya siren' " ("Victory Lilac") Belgorod, 2020, page 43.
Patent No. 10045, dated 2019-02-18 to 2049-12-31 by Botanical Garden Institute FEB RAS (Vladivostok, Russia); https://botsad.ru/
Name: Russian for Unknown Soldier, referencing the unknown dead soldiers of World War II.
Cultivar name established and accepted.

'**Nellie Bean**', *S.* (Villosae Group), *S. ×josiflexa*
Yeager 1959; S VII
syn. - 'Nelly Beam'
{'Royalty' × ?}
Yeager, New Hampshire Agric. Exp. Sta. Bull. 461, 11 [1959]; Wister, Arnoldia 23(4):82 [1963] - as *S. ×prestoniae* 'Nellie Bean'; Alexander Sr, Cat. sheets [n.d.; rec'd Feb. 1964]; Fiala, Lilacs, 106, 108 220, 259, Pl. 80 [1988] - as *S. ×prestoniae*; Bentley, Lilacs 42(2):59, ill. Front cover [2013]; Photo on Jorgovani/Lilacs 2015 DVD.

Named for Mrs Nellie Eva Cunningham Bean [1869-1945], active member and flower show judge of the Franklin Garden Club, New Hampshire, USA; see also: J. Bentley, Lilacs - Quart. Jour. 41(4):121-123 [2012].
Cultivar name registered 1963; name established and accepted.

'**Nellie Maria**', *S. vulgaris*
Lyden; S VI
syn. - 'Nellie Marie'
Wister, Arnoldia 23(4):82 [1963] - misspelled 'Nellie Marie'; Photo on Jorgovani/Lilacs 2015 DVD.
Cultivar name registered 1963; name established and accepted.

'**Nepovtorimaya**', *S. vulgaris*
'Неповторимая'
Ve<u>kh</u>ov 1952; S IV-V
syn. - 'Nepovtorimaja'
{'Comte de Kerchove' × ? }
Журнал "Цветоводство" № 7, 1977 год, стр. 11.
Magazine "<u>Ts</u>vetovodstvo" ("Floriculture") No. 7, 1977, p. 11 Rub<u>tz</u>ov et al. 1980. Vidy i sorta sireni, kul'tiviruemye v SSSR the same date -1952, page 76) Rub<u>tz</u>ov et al. 1980. Vidy i sorta sireni, kul'tiviruemye v SSSR. Kiev; Naukova Dumka. – in Russian; Holetich, C.D. 1982. Lilac species and cultivars in cultivation in USSR. Lilacs 11(2):1-38. - translation of Rub<u>tz</u>ov et al. 1982.
Name: Russian for uniquely.
Cultivar name established and accepted.

Nerimtiigais Ziedonis - see 'Imants Ziedonis'.

'**Nerissa**', *S.* (Villosae Group), *S.* ×*prestoniae*
Preston 1928; S VI
syn. - Preston No. 20-14-49
{*S. villosa* subsp. *villosa* × *S. komarowii* subsp. *reflexa*}
Macoun, Rep. Dom. Hort. 1928, 57 [1930]; Wister, Lilacs for America, 54, 64 [1942], 37, 48 [1953]; Photo on Jorgovani/Lilacs 2015 DVD.
Named for the Waiting-maid to Portia in Shakespeare's *Merchant of Venice*.
Cultivar name presumed registered 1953; name established and accepted.

'**Nesterka**', *S. vulgaris*
'Нестерка'
Smol'skiĭ & Bibikova 1964; S IV
{'Hyazinthenflieder' × 'Reaumur'}
Pikaleva, Lilacs - Quart. Jour. 23(4):86 [1994]; in litt. Garanovi<u>ch</u> & Makedonsk<u>ay</u>a to Vrugtman, Feb.19/01; in litt. Igor Semenov to Vrugtman 13 August 2014; Photo on Jorgovani/Lilacs 2015 DVD.
Named for Nesterka, a character of the Belarusian folklore.
Cultivar name established and accepted.

'**Nevesta**', *S.* ×*hyacinthiflora*
'Невеста'
Kolesnikov 1956 (not Rub<u>tz</u>ov et al.); S V
syn. - Kolesnikov No. 14
{*S.* ×*hyacinthiflora* 'Buffon' × (Kolesnikov No. 411 × 'Mme Antoine Buchner')}
Gromov, Lilacs - Proceedings 2(4):16 [1974] - as *S. vulgaris*; Photo on Jorgovani/Lilacs 2015 DVD.
Name: Russian for bride.
Cultivar name established and accepted.

'**Nevesta**', *S. vulgaris*
'Невеста'
Rub<u>tz</u>ov, <u>Zh</u>ogoleva & L<u>ya</u>punova (not Kolesnikov); S I
{'Marie Legraye' × ? }
Rub<u>tz</u>ov, L.I., et al., Siringariĭ (lilac garden), 42 [1961] - in Russian.
Name: Russian for bride.
Cultivar name established and accepted.

'**Nevskaya Volna**', *S. vulgaris*
'Невская Волна'
Grigorieva, V. & Grichachina, T.; D III 1971
{'Alphonse Lavallée' × 'Michel Buchner'}
sdlg No. 511
Registered by the USSR State Committee for Inventions and Discoveries in the State Register of Breeding Achievements of the USSR No. 8507821, 1985.
Certificate No. 4565
Magazine "<u>Ts</u>vetovodstvo" No. 10, 1977 p.18.
"<u>Ts</u>vetovodstvo" No. 3, 1988, p. 13
Information provided by Elena Olegovna Kuzmina, chief agronomist of the Control and Seed Experimental Station (KCOC) in 1978 - 1993.
Name: Russian for Neva wave, St Petersburg.
Cultivar name established and accepted; name registered.

NEW HAMPSHIRE, *S.* (Villosae Group)
Origin not known; S IAnon., Lilacs - Quart. Jour. 19(3):63 [1990]
Probably a cognomen and identical to *S.* (Villosae Group) 'Agnes Smith' (*S.* ×*josiflexa*).

NEW HAMPSHIRE DARK GREEN, *S.* (Villosae Group)
Rogers pre-1990; S V
{probably a *S.* ×*josiflexa* seedling × ? }
syn. - N. H. Dark Green
Anon., Lilacs - Quart. Jour 21(4):93 [1992] - name only; Anon., Lilacs - Quart. Jour. 28(2):37-39 [1999] - name only; in litt. O.M. Rogers to F. Vrugtman September 6 and October 3, 2000
Cognomen; not a cultivar name.

'**New Patriot**', *S. vulgaris* (?)
Krsnak 1985; D II/III *
{sport of unidentified plant, probably an old cultivar}
United States Plant Patent No. 17,110 [September 19, 2006] - statutory registration; F. Vrugtman & J. Krsnak.

Lilacs - Quart. Jour. 35(2):54-55 [2006].
Cultivar name established and accepted.

New Pink, *S. vulgaris*
origin not known pre-1938; ? V
Wister, Lilacs for America 37, 54 [1942] - doubtful name, or no name at all
Cultivar name not established, not reported in cultivation in 1953.

NEW YORK, *S.* (Villosae Group), *S.* ×*prestoniae*
Chapman 2001; S I *
syn. - NF62(a)/91; 'New York!'
{variegated sport of a seedling of 'Elinor' × ? }
Chapman, Lilacs - Quart. Jour. 30(4):112 [2001] - name only; 31(4):80-81 & front cover [2002] - assignment of this cultivar epithet is not yet final; F. Moro at http://lilacs.freeservers.com/varigatedlilacs.html [Jan.13/06] - as 'New York'; http://www.spi.8m.com/Specialtylilacs.html [Jan. 15/09]; Chapman, 38(3):83(2009) - as 'New York!'.
Per Tatyana Polyakova, the originator named this lilac after the city of New York, NY, USA after the 2001 terrorist attacks, a city that he loved and an event that shocked him.
Cognomen;
Cultivar name not established.

'Nezhnost', *S. vulgaris*
'Нежность'
Sagitova; S V
photo seen on 2020 ILS Photo & Color Database
name is Russian for tenderness or delicacy.
Cultivar name not established, cultivar may have been lost.

'Nezhnost', *S. vulgaris*
'Нежность'
Vekhov 1952; D V
syn. - 'Nezhnostj'
Журнал "Цветоводство" № 7, 1977 год, стр. 11.
Magazine "Tsvetovodstvo" ("Floriculture") No. 7, 1977, p. 11
Rubtzov et al. 1980. Vidy i sorta sireni, kul'tiviruemye v SSSR the same date -1952, page 76
Naukova Dumka. – in Russian; Holetich, C.D. 1982. Lilac species and cultivars in cultivation in USSR. Lilacs 11(2):1-38. - translation of Rubtzov et al. 1982; Photo on Jorgovani/Lilacs 2015 DVD.
Name: Russian for tenderness.
Cultivar name established and accepted. Cultivar may have been lost.

'Neznakomka', *S.* ×*hyacinthiflora*
'Незнакомка'
Pshennikova 2007; S IV & III
Pshennikova, L.M. 2007. Lilacs, cultivated in the Botanical Garden-Institute FEB RAS, p. 54; Registered with the State Commission of the Russian Federation for Testing and Protection of Selection Achievements, No. 9253062, 2008; Photo on Jorgovani/Lilacs 2015 DVD.
Name: Russian for stranger.
Cultivar name registered, established and accepted.

N. H. Dark Green - see NEW HAMPSHIRE DARK GREEN.
Parentage still under question [Sept 15, 2000, per Owen Rogers correspondence]

'Niance', *S. vulgaris*
Kārkliņš date not known; D VII
(no information; listed by T. Polyakova, 2014); Photo on Jorgovani/Lilacs 2015 DVD.
Name: Latvian for the nuance.
Cultivar name not established.

Niebo Moskvy - see '**Nebo Moskvy**'.

'Niewinność', *S. vulgaris*
Karpow-Lipski 1960; D V
Wister & Oppe, Arnoldia 31(3):126 [1971]
Name: Polish for innocence.
Cultivar name registered 1970; name established and accepted.

'Night', *S. vulgaris*
Havemeyer pre-1941; S VII
Wister, Lilacs for America, 54 [1942], 37 [1953]; Kammerer, Morton Arb. Bull. Pop. Info. 36(6):27-29 [1961]; USDA Plant Inventory No. 173, 108 (PI 306311) [May 1965]; Eickhorst, ILS Lilac Newsletter 4(1):4-5 [1978]; Photo on Jorgovani/Lilacs 2015 DVD.
Cultivar name presumed registered 1953; name established and accepted.

'Night Song', *S. vulgaris*
origin not known pre-1982; D II
{parentage not known}
in litt. Peterson Mar.4/06 - plant received from Donald Egolf ca 1982, semi-double.
Cultivar name not established.

'Nigra', *S. vulgaris*
origin not known pre-1864; S VII
possibly the same as '**Nigricans**'
McKelvey, The Lilac, 351 [1928]
Cultivar name not established.

'Nigricans', *S. vulgaris*
origin not known pre-1869; S VII
syn. - *S. vulgaris nigricans*; possibly same as 'Nigra'
Wochenschr. Ver. Beförd. Gartenb, Preuß. 12:49 [1869]; McKelvey, The Lilac, 351-352 [1928]; Wister, Lilacs for America, 55 [1942], 37 [1953]
Cultivar name presumed registered 1953; name established and accepted.

'Nike', *S.* (Villosae Group), *S.* ×*prestoniae*
Bugała pre-1970; S II
Bugała, Arboretum Kórnickie 15:61-70 [1970]; Wister & Oppe, Arnoldia 31(3):123 [1971]; Bugała, Lilacs - Quart.

Jour. 24(4):90-91 [1995]; Photo on Jorgovani/Lilacs 2015 DVD.
Cultivar name registered 1970; name established and accepted.

'Nikitskaya', *S. vulgaris*
'Никитская'
Kostetskiĭ 1954; S IV
'Lilacs', volume 45(4) Fall 2016 "Breeding in the Crimea" by Vera Zykova
Pikaleva, Lilacs - Quart. Jour. 23(4):87 [1994]; in lit. Tatyana Polyakova to Vrugtman (23 June 2015) - originator Kostecki
Cultivar name established and accepted.

'Nikolaĭ Gumilev', *S. vulgaris*
'Николай Гумилев'
Aladin, S., Aladina, O., Polyakova, T., and, Aladina, A. 2017; S IV
{'Prokhorovka'× OP}
IX International Scientific Conference (IX Международная научная конференция "Цветоводство: история, теория, практика") " Floriculture: history, theory, practice" , St. Petersburg, Botanical Garden of Peter the Great BIN RAS, September 7-13, 2019 (in Russian).
Named for Gumilev Nikolaii Stepanovich, 1886-1921, the outstanding Russian poet of the Silver Age, prose writer, translator, literary critic and traveler.
Cultivar name established and accepted.

'Nikolai Kostecki' - see 'Nikolaĭ Kostetskiĭ'

'Nikolaĭ Kostetskiĭ'
'Николай Костецкий'
Kostetskiĭ 1954; S IV
{parentage not known}
syn. - 'Nikolai Kostecki', 'Nikolay Kostetsky'
Pikaleva, Lilacs - Quart. Jour. 23(4):87 [1994]; in lit. Tatyana Polyakova to Vrugtman (23 June 2015) - as 'Nikolaĭ Kostetski', originator Kostetskiĭ. 'Lilacs', 45(4):Fall 2016, "Breeding in the Crimea" by Vera Zykova.
Named for the originator, Nikolaĭ Danilovich Kostetskiĭ (probably after his death in 1948); 1873-1948, Soviet breeder, biologist, teacher, gardener, agronomist and theorist of Agriculture.
Cultivar name established and accepted.

'Nikolaĭ Mikhaĭlov', *S. vulgaris*
'Николай Михайлов'
Mikhaĭlov & Fyodorova 2002; S VII
{'Flora 1953' × 'Lady Lindsay'}
'Lilac. Collection of lilacs of MBG RAS' Okuneva, I., Mikhailov, N., Demidov, A. 2008, page 68
Chapman, Lilacs - Quart. Jour. 32(1):17-18 [2003] - translated from N. L. Mikhaĭlov in Tsvetovodstvo, May-June issue (in Russian); Photo on Jorgovani/Lilacs 2015 DVD.
Named for the originator, Nikolaĭ Leonidovich Mikhaĭlov, Russian horticulturist and plant breeder [1923-2019].
Cultivar name established and accepted.

'Nikolaĭ Ostrovskiĭ', *S. vulgaris*
'Николай Островский'
Kolesnikov; D V
syn. - Kolesnikov No. 302
Gromov, A., Siren', 77 [1963]; Howard & Brizicky, AABGA Quart. Newsl. No. 64, 17-21 [1965]; Polyakova, 2010, Istoriya Russkoĭ Sireni, p. 128.
Named for Nikolai Alexeevich Ostrovsky, 1904-1936, Soviet socialist writer during the Stalin era; author of "How the Steel Was Tempered", 1936.
Cultivar name established and accepted.

'Nina', *S. ×hyacinthiflora*
'Нина'
Mikhaĭlov & Rybakina 2002; D V
{'Esther Staley' × 'Krasavitsa Moskvy'}
Chapman, Lilacs - Quart. Jour. 32(1):17-18 [2003] - translated from N. L. Mikhaĭlov in Tsvetovodstvo, May-June issue (in Russian); http://home.onego.ru/~otsoppe/enciclop/kustar/syring_s.html (July 26, 2003); Photo on Jorgovani/Lilacs 2015 DVD.
Named for Nina Andreyevna [contemporary], wife of Nikolaĭ Leonidovich Mikhaĭlov.
Cultivar name established and accepted.

'Nina Baker', *S. vulgaris*
Rankin; S IV
{parentage not known}
Wister, Arnoldia 23(4):82 [1963]
Cultivar name registered 1963; name established and accepted; not reported in cultivation.

'Niobe', *S. vulgaris*
Spaargaren 1958; S I
Wister, Arnoldia 23(4):82 [1963]
Awards: Certificate of Merit 1958 (KMTP).
Cultivar name registered 1963; name established and accepted.

'Nivelles', *S. vulgaris*
Mahaux; ? VII
Wister, Lilacs for America, 37 [1953] - description incomplete
Cultivar name not established.

No. 26, S.
Mägi pre-2018; ? ?
Semenov, I., Lilacs 48(2):71 [2019].
Not a cultivar name.

No. 71, *S. vulgaris*
Lemke; D III/IV
syn. - 'Dr Lemke'
Wister, Lilacs for America, 28 [1953] - as 'Dr Lemke', name only; Vrugtman, Lilacs - Proceedings 12(1):21 [1984]; Photo on Jorgovani/Lilacs 2015 DVD.
Not a cultivar name.

No. 123, *S.*
  Mägi pre-2018; ? ?
  Semenov, I., Lilacs 48(2):71 [2019].
  Not a cultivar name.

No. 125, *S. vulgaris*
  Lemke; D IV&V
  Photo on Jorgovani/Lilacs 2015 DVD.
  Not a cultivar name.

No. 131, *S. vulgaris*
  Mägi pre-2018; S II
  syn. – '#131-12E'
  Semenov, I., Lilacs 48(2): 68, 69 (photo) [2019].
  Not a cultivar name.

No. 307, *S. vulgaris*
  Fenicchia; ? VI
  {'Rochester' × ? }
  Fiala, Lilacs, pl. 1 [1988] - as 'Rochester Hybrid # 307;
  not reported in cultivation.
  Not a cultivar name.
  No 2903 Upītis after No 307

No. 2903, *S. Vulgaris*
  Upitis pre-2019; S VII
  Reported in cultivation at Nat'l Bot G, Salalpils, and in
  Dobele, Latvia.
  Not a cultivar name.

No. 8027, *S.*
  Upītis no date; S VII
  Semenov, Igor, Lilacs - Quart. Jour. 44(2): ill. inside back
  cover [2015] - in cultivation at Latvian State Institute
  of Fruit-Growing (formerly Auglkopîbas Laboratoija),
  Dobele, Latvia.
  Breeder's designation, not a cultivar name.

No. 62(a)/91, *S.* (Villosae Group), *S.* ×*prestoniae*
  Chapman; S VII *
  {'Elinor' × ? }
  Chapman, Lilacs - Quart. Jour. 30(4):112 [2001] -
  reference only
  Breeder's designation, not a cultivar name.

No. 75116-16, *S. vulgaris*
  Brown; S VII
  Fiala, Lilacs, p. 106 & pl. 77 [1988]; in litt. D. Eveleigh
  to F. Vrugtman [January 13, 2004] - plant has not been
  propagated and is no longer extant.
  Breeder's designation, not a cultivar name.

No. 86-1, *S.* (Villosae Group), *S.* ×*josiflexa*
  Rogers 1994; D ?
  {Rogers 74-4 × Rogers 70-5}
  Note bene: R74-4 parentage {R69-1 (James Macfarlane ×
  OP) × 'Agnes Smith'}
  Also, R 70-5 parentage {'Royalty' × 'Agnes Smith'}
  Rogers, Lilacs - Quart. Jour. 23(4):107 [1994] - seedling
  with radial double florets and compact thyrses; seed
  parent to 'Marie Rogers'; Presumed lost after the
  destruction of the lilac collection at University of New
  Hampshire in 2011.
  Most multipetaling of all Villosae Group. Distributed at
  1994 ILS convention.
  Breeder's designation (cognomen), not a cultivar name.

'**Nocturne**', *S.* (Villosae Group), *S.* ×*prestoniae*
  Preston & Leslie 1936; S III
  {parentage not known}
  Stand. Pl. Names, 616 [1942] - name only; Wister, Lilacs
  for America, 55 [1942], 37 [1953]; Buckley, Greenh. -
  Garden - Grass, 8(3):4 [1969]; Cumming, Agric. Canada
  Public. 1628, 17 [1977] - as introduced in 1936; Photo on
  Jorgovani/Lilacs 2015 DVD.
  Cultivar name presumed registered 1953; name
  established and accepted.

Noisette - see '**Noisettiana Alba**'; see also 'Pallida' (*S. vulgaris*).

'Noisettiana', *S. vulgaris*
  International Exhibition, 1876, US Centennial
  Commission, Volume 11, p. 310 - name only.
  Cultivar name not established.

'**Noisettiana Alba**', *S. vulgaris*
  origin not known pre-1892; S I
  syn. - *S. noisettiana*
  common name - Noisette
  Ellwanger & Barry, Cat., [1892]; Parsons, Cat., 49 [1889];
  Stand. Pl. Names, 487 [1923] - as Noisette; McKelvey,
  The Lilac, 352-353 [1928]; Wister, Lilacs for America, 55
  [1942], 37 [1953]
  Cultivar name presumed registered 1953; name
  established and accepted.

Nokomis, *S.* (Villosae Group), *S.* ×*prestoniae*
  Preston pre-1942; ? ?
  Stand. Pl. Names, 616 [1942] - name only
  Cultivar name not established; information appears to be
  incorrect.

'**Nokomis**', *S.* ×*hyacinthiflora*
  Skinner 1934; S IV
  Wister, Lilacs for America, 55 [1942], 37 [1953]; Skinner,
  Hort. Horizons, 50, 83, Pl 30, 109 [1966]; Photo on
  Jorgovani/Lilacs 2015 DVD.
  Named for Nokomis Lake, Manitoba, Canada.
  Cultivar name presumed registered 1953; name
  established and accepted.

'Nokt**yu**rn', *S. vulgaris*
  'Ноктюрн'
  Potutova; S VII
  syn. - 'Noctjurn' (not *S.* ×*prestoniae* 'Nocturne')
  Rub**t**zov et al. 1980. Vidy i sorta sireni, kul'tiviruemye v
  SSSR. Kiev; Naukova Dumka. – in Russian; Holetich, C.D.
  1982. Lilac species and cultivars in cultivation in USSR.
  Lilacs 11(2):1-38. - translation of Rub**t**zov et al. 1982.
  Name: Russian for nocturne.
  Cultivar name established and accepted.

'Norah', *S.* ×*hyacinthiflora*
Preston pre-1931; S IV
syn. - Preston No. 22.04.16
{*S. vulgaris* 'Negro' × *S.* ×*hyacinthiflora* 'Lamartine'}
Davis, Rep. Dom. Hort. 1931, 1932 and 1933, 143 [1936]; & Progress Report 1934-1948, 150 [1950]; Wister, Lilacs for America, 55 [1942], 37 [1953]; Photo on Jorgovani/Lilacs 2015 DVD.
Cultivar name presumed registered 1953; name established and accepted.

'Normandiya-Neman', *S. vulgaris*
'Нормандия-Неман'
Aladin, S., Polyakova, T., and Aladina, O. 2014; S IV
{'Flora 1953' × OP}
Питомник-частный сад (Pitomnik i chastnyi sad; Nursery and private garden) 3/2015:14-22; Приусадебное хозяйство (Annex to the magazine Homestead farming: "Flowers in the garden and at home. Brushes and paints") 08/2015: 5-14; Садовник (Gardener) magazine, 05 (141)/2017 :16-22; Вестник АППМ (Catalog in Vestnik APPM (Planting material association) magazine) 1/2018: 59-72 (in Russian).
Named for the Normandie-Niemen regiment composed of 99 pilots which was sent by General de Gaulle in 1943 to aid the Soviet Union during the Second World War.
Cultivar name established and accepted.

Norrby, *S. josikaea*
origin not known ? ?
local selection from the village of Norrby, Sweden, sold by one nursery in northern Sweden (in litt Björn Aldén to F. Vrugtman, Nov. 10, 2007).
Not a cultivar name.

'Norrfjärden', *S. vulgaris*
origin not known pre-1996; D III
syn. - 'Norrfjrden'
first seen: Carlson-Nilsson, www.hvf.slu.se/trad/pryd/norrfjardeng.html, Apr. 21, 1999; more recently in cultivation at Wickmans Plantskola and Piccoplant Mikrovermehrungen GmbH
Named for town of Norrfjärden in northern Sweden. Possibly a renamed older cultivar.
Cultivar name established and accepted.

'Nostalgia', *S.* ×*hyacinthiflora*
Moro, F. 2009; S I
{'Forrest Kresser Smith' × ? }
<http://www.spi.8m.com/hyacinthifloracdncat.html>
Named to honour the International Lilac Society for 40 years of development work.
Cultivar name established and accepted.

Notgeriana - see **'Prince Notger'**.

'Nouveau', *S.* ×*diversifolia*
Sax & Upton 1944; S V
{*S. pinnatifolia* × *S. oblata* subsp. *oblata*; grown from seed received from the Arnold Arboretum, resulting from the cross made by Dr Karl Sax in 1929}
Anderson and Rehder, J. Arnold Arb. 16:362-363 [1935]; Woody Plant Register, AAN, No. 27 [1949]; Wister, Lilacs for America, 37 [1953]
Cultivar name presumed registered 1953; name established and accepted.

'Noziedēt Kopā', *S. vulgaris*
Upītis 1970; S II
Photo from Dobele, Latvia by Natalia Savenko, seen in 2020 ILS Photo Database.
Cultivar name not established.

'Oakes Double White', *S. vulgaris*
Origin not known; D I
syn. - 'Oake's Double White', 'Oakes' Double White', Oakes Homestead
{cognomen for a renamed unknown older cultivar}
Wister, Arnoldia 23(4);82 [1963] - erroneously as 'Oake's Double White'; Meader, ILS Pipeline 3(2):3 [1977]; Vrugtman, HortScience 31(3):328 [1996]; Photo on Jorgovani/Lilacs 2015 DVD.
Cultivar name registered 1963; name established and accepted.

Oakes Homestead, *S. vulgaris*
see - **'Oakes Double White'**
Anon., Lilacs - Quart. Jour. 33(1):11 [2004] - in cultivation at Max Peterson, Meadowlark Hill Gardens, Ogallala, Nebraska, USA; Kent Milham, Lilacs - Quart. Jour. 42(3):97, ill. p. 99 - seen at John Thurlow's nursery, West Newbury, MA, probably 'Oakes Double White'.

'Obélisque', *S. vulgaris*
Lemoine 1894; D I
{'Marie Legraye' × ? double}
syn. - 'Obélessque', 'Obelisk', 'Obelisque'
common name: Obelisk
Lemoine, Cat. No. 128, 15 [1894]; Stand. Pl. Names, 487 [1923] - as Obelisk; McKelvey, The Lilac, 353 [1928]; Wister, Lilacs for America, 55 [1942], 37 [1953]; Photo on Jorgovani/Lilacs 2015 DVD.
Cultivar name presumed registered 1953; name established and accepted.

'Oberon', *S.* (Villosae Group), *S.* ×*prestoniae*
Preston 1937; S V
syn. - Preston No. 24.05.82
{*S.* ×*prestoniae* seedling No. S.20.14.82 × ? }
Davis & Preston, RHS Conf. Ornamental flowering trees and shrubs. pp. 135-140 [1938]; Davis, Rep. Dom. Hort., Progress Report 1934-1948, 148 [1950]; Wister, Lilacs for America, 55, 64 [1942], 37, 48 [1953]; Buckley, Arboretum Notes 16:22 [1961] - as planted in 1937; Photo on Jorgovani/Lilacs 2015 DVD.
Named for the king of the Fairies in Shakespeare's *Midsummer Night's Dream*.
Cultivar name presumed registered 1953; name established and accepted.

Oblata - see *S. oblata*.

Oblata Dilatata - see *S. oblata* subsp. *dilatata*.

oblata dilatata superba - see 'Superba' (*oblata* subsp. *dilatata*).

Oblata Giraldi - see *S. oblata* subsp. *oblata*.

oblata var. *giraldii nana* - see '**Nana**' (*oblata* subsp. *oblata*).

oblata var. *typica* f. *rubro-coerulea* - see 'Rubro-coerulea'.

'Obman<u>shchits</u>a', *S. vulgaris*
    'Обманщица'
    Kolesnikov pre-1940; D III-IV-V
    syn. - Kolesnikov No. 427, 'Obmanshchica'
    Gromov, A., Siren', 94 [1963]; Howard & Brizicky, AABGA Quart. Newsl. No. 64, 17-21 [1965]; Rub<u>tz</u>ov et al. 1980. Vidy i sorta sireni, kul'tiviruemye v SSSR. Kiev; Naukova Dumka. – in Russian; Holetich, C.D. 1982. Lilac species and cultivars in cultivation in USSR. Lilacs 11(2):1-38. - translation of Rub<u>tz</u>ov et al. 1982; Polyakova, 2010, Istori<u>y</u>a Russkoï Sireni, p. 130; Photo on Jorgovani/Lilacs 2015 DVD.
    Name: Russian for deceiver.
    Cultivar name established and accepted.

'Octavia', *S.* (Villosae Group), *S.* ×*prestoniae*
    Preston 1928; S V
    syn. - Preston No. 20-14-93
    {*S. villosa* subsp. *villosa* × *S. komarowii* subsp. *reflexa*}
    Macoun, Rep. Dom. Hort. 1928, 57 [1930]; Wister, Lilacs for America, 55, 64 [1942], 37, 48 [1953]
    Named for the Wife to Antony in Shakespeare's *Antony and Cleopatra*.
    Cultivar name presumed registered 1953; name established and accepted.

'Oden', *S. josikaea*
    Valtinat pre-1999; S II
    syn. - ODENSALA KLON 1 (pre1999)
    {sport of *S. josikaea* 'Odensala'}
    Eplantor 1999, p. 5; Haggren, Allt om Trädgård 3-01, p.40 [2001];
    Named for Oden one of the Aesir gods.
    Cultivar name established and accepted.

'Odensala', *S. josikaea*
    Edvardsson (?) 1940s (?), S IV
    Said to be a selection from plants naturalized in the Odensala area.
    <http://www.esveld.nl/htmldiaen/s/syjode.htm> with photo (seen 14 May 2017)
    Named for Odensala, Jäämtland, Sweden.
    Cultivar name established and accepted.

'Oeil de Paupre', *S. vulgaris*
    origin not known pre-1941; S I
    Lilac Time in Lombard, 7 [1940 or 1941]; Stand. Pl. Names, 616 [1942] - name only; Wister, Lilacs for America, 37, 55 [1942]
    Cultivar name not established, not reported in cultivation in 1953.

'Ogni Donbassa', *S. vulgaris*
    'Огни Донбасса'
    Rub<u>tz</u>ov, <u>Zh</u>ogoleva, L<u>ya</u>punova 1956; D IV
    syn. - 'Ogni Dombassa', 'Ongi Dombassa'
    {'Charles Joly' × ? }
    Gromov, A., 121 Siren', [1963]; Howard & Brizicky, AABGA Quart. Newsl. No. 64, 17-21 [1965]; Bilov et al., Siren', 64 [1974] - in Russian; Rub<u>tz</u>ov et al. 1980. Vidy i sorta sireni, kul'tiviruemye v SSSR. Kiev; Naukova Dumka. – in Russian; Holetich, C.D. 1982. Lilac species and cultivars in cultivation in USSR. Lilacs 11(2):1-38. - translation of Rub<u>tz</u>ov et al. 1982; Photo on Jorgovani/Lilacs 2015 DVD.
    Name: Russian for lights of Donbass (the Donbass Oblast of Ukraine). The tips of the purple petals have white spots, resembling the coal miners' helmet lanterns working in deep mines; Donbassa is an abbreviation of the Donetsk Coal Basin where the mines are located.
    Cultivar name established and accepted.

'Ogni Donetska', *S. vulgaris*
    'Огни Донецка'
    Tere<u>shch</u>enko 2002; S IV
    {'Hyazinthenflieder' × ? }
    Tere<u>shch</u>enko, Lilacs in the South-East of Ukraine, p. 115-116 [2002]; Chapman & Semyonova, Lilacs - Quart. Jour. 33(1):14-15 [2003] - translated from Tere<u>shch</u>enko, 2002.
    Name: Russian for lights of Donetsk, the city where this lilac was originated.
    Statutary registration UANA 2002;
    Cultivar name established and accepted.

'Ogni Moskvy', *S. vulgaris*
    'Огни Москвы'
    Kolesnikov 1942; S VII
    syn. - Kolesnikov No. 525, 'Obni Moskvy', 'Ongi Moskvy'
    {(Kolesnikov No. 105 × 'Pasteur') × (Kolesnikov No. 110 × 'Zar<u>ya</u> Kommunizma')}
    Gromov, Lilacs - Proceedings 2(4):17 [1974]; Rub<u>tz</u>ov et al. 1980. Vidy i sorta sireni, kul'tiviruemye v SSSR. Kiev; Naukova Dumka. – in Russian; Holetich, C.D. 1982. Lilac species and cultivars in cultivation in USSR. Lilacs 11(2):1-38. - translation of Rub<u>tz</u>ov et al. 1982; Photo on Jorgovani/Lilacs 2015 DVD.
    Name: Russian for lights of Moscow.
    Cultivar name established and accepted.

'**Old Fashioned**', *S. vulgaris*
    Clarke, J. 1967; S III
    Clarke, Wholesale Price List, 8 [1968]; Wister & Oppe, Arnoldia 31(3):123 [1971] - name only; Photo on Jorgovani/Lilacs 2015 DVD.
    Cultivar name registered 1970; name established and accepted.

'**Old Glory**', *S.* ×*hyacinthiflora*
Egolf & Pooler 2006; S III-VII
syn. - NA62974; PI 641803
{*S.* ×*hyacinthiflora* 'Sweet Charity' × *S.* ×*hyacinthiflora* 'Pocahontas'}
USDA-ARS Notice of Release [March 24, 2006]; Pooler, HortScience 43(2):544–545 [2008]; nomenclatural standard deposited at United States National Arboretum Herbarium (NA); NA-0041455; Hanburyana 4:56 [2009]; Photo on Jorgovani/Lilacs 2015 DVD.
Old Glory is a common nickname for the Flag of the United States, bestowed by William Driver, an early nineteenth century American sea captain.
Cultivar name registered 2007; name established and accepted.

'**Old Lace**', *S.* ×*hyacinthiflora*
Lammerts; S V
{(Lammerts C112 × Lammerts 42-108-3) × (Lammerts 42-109-4 × ?)}
Lammerts, US Plant Patent No. 3893 [May 25, 1976]; Vrugtman, Lilacs - Proceedings 6(1):17 [1978]; Vrugtman, AABGA Bull. 13(4):107 [1979].
Cultivar name registered 1976; name established and accepted.
Nota bene: Since this cultivar appears to be of 'Lavender Lady' ancestry see also: Pringle, Lilacs - Quart. Jour. 24(4):97-99 [1995]; and Vrugtman, HortScience 31(3):328 [1996].

'**Old Rose**', *S. vulgaris*
Klager 1928; S V
Wister, Lilacs for America, 55 [1942], 38 [1953]; Photo on Jorgovani/Lilacs 2015 DVD.
Cultivar name presumed registered 1953; name established and accepted.

'**Oleg**', *S. vulgaris*
'Олег'
Sagitova 1994; D V/VII
varietal denomination registered 1994, No. 13, State Register of Selected Achievements in Republic of Kazakhstan; statutory registration.
Named for the son of the originator.
Cultivar name established and accepted.

'**Ol'ga**', *S. vulgaris*
'Ольга'
Sagitova 1981; S I
syn. - S-12
{'Vestalka'(?) × ? }
Cultivar name not established.

'**Ol'ga Berghol'z**', *S. vulgaris*
'Ольга Берггольц'
Aladin, S., Aladina, O., Polyakova, T., and Aladina, A. 2018; D V
{sdlg 09-119*× OP}
*sdlg 09-119 was obtained from open pollinated seeds of 'Zhemchuzhina'.
Международная и практическая конференция (International scientific and practical conference) «International Syringa 2018», Moscow, Moscow State University Botanical Garden, St. Petersburg, Botanical Garden of Peter the Great BIN RAS, Pavlovsk, May 21-27, 2018; pp. 43-47.
Named for Ol'ga Fëdorovna Berghol'z (Ольга Фёдоровна Берггольц), 1910-1975, Soviet poet, writer, playwright and journalist; most famous for her work on the Leningrad radio during the city's blockade, when she became the symbol of city's strength and determination. (Wikipedia).
Cultivar name established and accepted.

'**Olimpiada Kolesnikova**', *S. vulgaris*
'Олимпиада Колесникова'
Kolesnikov 1941; D IV-V
{'Tamara Kolesnikova' × 'Berryer'}
syn. - Kolesnikov No. 86, 'Olumpiada Kolesnikova', 'Olympiada Kolesnikova'
Kolesnikov, Lilac, 29, 32 [1955]; Howard, Arnoldia 19(6-7):31-35 [1959]; Gromov, Siren', 74-75 (1963) - in Russian; Howard & Brizicky, AABGA Quart. Newsl. No. 64, 17-21 [1965]; Wister & Oppe, Arnoldia 31(3):125 [1971] - as D I?; Gromov, Lilacs - Proceedings 2(4):18 [1974] - as violet purple; Rubtzov et al. 1980. Vidy i sorta sireni, kul'tiviruemye v SSSR. Kiev; Naukova Dumka. – in Russian; Holetich, C.D. 1982. Lilac species and cultivars in cultivation in USSR. Lilacs 11(2):1-38. - translation of Rubtzov et al. 1982 - as lilac-pink; Photo on Jorgovani/Lilacs 2015 DVD.
Named for Olympiada Nikolaevna Kolesnikova, x - 1965, wife to Leonid Alekseevich Kolesnikov.
Award of Garden Merit RHS 2012.
Cultivar name registered 1970; name established and accepted.

'**Olive May Cummings**', *S. vulgaris*
Berdeen 1979; D V-II
syn. - 'Elizabeth Files', 'Olive Mae Cummings'
Vrugtman, AABGA Bull. 13(4):110 [1979]; Fiala, Lilacs, 94, Pl. 76 [1988] - erroneously as 'Elizabeth Files'; Vrugtman, HortScience 26(5):477 [1991]; King & Coggeshall, Lilacs - Quart. Jour. 27(2):49-50 [1998] - name only; Photo on Jorgovani/Lilacs 2015 DVD.
Named for a friend of the originator from Portland, Maine.
Cultivar name registered 1978; name established and accepted.

'**Olivia**', *S.* (Villosae Group), *S.* ×*prestoniae*
Preston 1928; S VI
{*S. villosa* subsp. *villosa* × *S. komarowii* subsp. *reflexa*}
syn. - Preston No. 20-14-64
Macoun, Rep. Dom. Hort. 1928, 57 [1930]; Wister, Lilacs for America, 55, 64 [1942], 38, 48 [1953]; Photo on Jorgovani/Lilacs 2015 DVD.
Named for A Rich Countess in Shakespeare's *Twelfth Night*.
Cultivar name presumed registered 1953; name established and accepted.

'Olivier de Serres', *S. vulgaris*
Lemoine 1909; D III
syn. - 'Oliver de Serres'
Lemoine, Cat. No. 173, 8 [1909]; McKelvey, The Lilac, 353-354 [1928]; Wister, Lilacs for America, 55 [1942], 38 [1953]; Photo on Jorgovani/Lilacs 2015 DVD.
Named for Olivier de Serres, 1539-1619, French agronomist.
Cultivar name presumed registered 1953; name established and accepted.

'Olya', *S. vulgaris*
'Оля'
Aladin, S., Arkhangelskii, V., Polyakova, T., and Akimova, S. 2011; S IV
{'Mechta' × OP}
Registered with the State Commission of the Russian Federation for Testing and Protection of Selection Achievements, No. 8853116, 2011; Вестник АППМ (Catalog in Vestnik APPM (Planting material association) magazine) 1/2018: 59-72 (in Russian);
Named for Olga Aladina (Ольга Николаевна Аладина), Doctor of Agricultural Sciences, professor of the Russian State Agrarian University - Moscow Timiryazev Agricultural Academy, journalist, contemporary Russian lilac breeder, member of the creative breeding group "Russian Lilac", Moscow. ("Olya" is a diminutive nickname for "Olga").
Cultivar name registered, established and accepted.

Olympia - see **'City of Olympia'**.

'Onarga', *S. villosa* subsp. *villosa*
origin not known pre-1951; S II
Melrose, Lilacs - Proceedings 7(1):23 [1978] - name only; Photo on Jorgovani/Lilacs 2015 DVD.
Named, possibly, for the legendary figure Onarga, daughter of the great chief of the Iroquois.
Cultivar name established and accepted.

ONDERSTAM 104, *S.*
Kromwijk 2006.
{parentage?}
Rootstock for lilacs to be forced under glass; a selection less susceptible but not resistant to *Verticillium dahliae*, the soil borne pathogen causing Verticillium wilt.
Arca Kromwijk, Nieuwe onderstam minder vatbaar voor verticillium. Vakblad voor de Bloemisterij 05-2014:40-41 <https://issuu.com/hortipoint/docs/vbb_05-2014>
Cognomen; not a cultivar name.

'Ophelia', *S.* (Villosae Group), *S.* ×*prestoniae*
Preston 1928; S V
{*S. villosa* subsp. *villosa* × *S. komarowii* subsp. *reflexa*}
syn. - Preston No. 20-14-72
Macoun, Rep. Dom. Hort. 1928, 57 [1930] - name only; Wister, Lilacs for America, 55, 64 [1942], 38, 48 [1953]
Named for the Daughter to Polonius in Shakespeare's *Hamlet*.
Cultivar name presumed registered 1953; name established and accepted.

ORANGUTANG®, *S.* ×*laughalot*
Cultivar name unknown.
Syn.- Orangetan, Monkey Business
Hatch 2019; S VIII
Photo seen on ILS Lilac Photo database and in email from Freek Vrugtman to Registrar 7-16-2019.
Cognomen, not a cultivar name. To be shared with and noticed only by lilac aficionados.

'Orchid Beauty', *S.* ×*chinensis*
Hilborn pre-1945; S VI
Wister, Lilacs for America, 38 [1953]; Photo on Jorgovani/Lilacs 2015 DVD.
Cultivar name presumed registered 1953; name established and accepted.

'Orchid Chiffon', *S.* ×*hyacinthiflora*
Sass, H.E. pre-1953; S V
Wister, Lilacs for America, 38 [1953]
Cultivar name presumed registered 1953; name established and accepted.

'Origami', *S. vulgaris*
Bugała ca 1986; S V
{'Maréchal Foch' × ? }
Zieliński, J., P. Kosiński, and T. Bojarczuk 2016. 'Origami'–a new cultivar of common lilac (*Syringa vulgaris*). Rocznik Polskiego Towarzystwa Dendrologicznego 64:67-70, Fig. 1-7; (Vrugtman, Cultivated Plant Diversity ... 2017).
Named for the characteristically strongly reflexed corolla lobes.
Cultivar name registered 2016; name established and accepted.

'Oskar Villem', *S. vulgaris*
Mägi pre-2017; S I
Photo taken in Estonia by Mägi, seen in 2020 ILS Photo Database.
Cultivar name not established.

'Ostankino', *S. vulgaris*
'Останкино'
Shtan'ko & Mikhaĭlov 1956; S III
{'Maximowicz' × ? }
Bilov et al., Siren', 65 [1974] - in Russian; Rubtzov et al. 1980. Vidy i sorta sireni, kul'tiviruemye v SSSR. Kiev; Naukova Dumka. – in Russian; Holetich, C.D. 1982. Lilac species and cultivars in cultivation in USSR. Lilacs 11(2):1-38. - translation of Rubtzov et al. 1982; Photo on Jorgovani/Lilacs 2015 DVD.
Named for the Ostankino district of Moscow where the Main Botanical Garden is located, and famous for the Ostankinsky Palace, summer residence of count Nikolaĭ Sheremetyev, built in the 1790s, north of Moscow, Russia.
Cultivar name established and accepted.

'Ostrander', *S. vulgaris*
Klager 1928; D VII
syn. - 'Ostrander Cooley'
Cooley, Cat., 7 [1928]; McKelvey, The Lilac, 561 [1928]; Wister, Lilacs for America, 55 [1942], 38 [1953]; Fiala, Lilacs, 106, 108, 200, Pl.25 [1988] - as 'Ostrander' and 'Ostrander Cooley'; Photo on Jorgovani/Lilacs 2015 DVD.
Cultivar name presumed registered 1953; name established and accepted.

'Othello', *S. vulgaris*
Lemoine 1900; S VI
Lemoine, Cat. No. 146, 24 [1900]; Kache, Gartenschönheit 5:82 [1924]; McKelvey, The Lilac, 354 [1928]; Wister, Lilacs for America, 55 [1942], 38 [1953]
Named for the Moor in Shakespeare's tragedy and Verdi's opera.
Cultivar name presumed registered 1953; name established and accepted.

'Ottawa', *S.* (Villosae Group), *S.* ×*swegiflexa*
Preston pre-1953; S V
{*S. komarowii* subsp. *reflexa* × *S. tomentella* subsp. *sweginzowii*}
Wister, Lilacs for America, 36 [1953]; Photo on Jorgovani/Lilacs 2015 DVD.
Named for Ottawa, Ontario, the capital city of Canada.
Cultivar name presumed registered 1953; name established and accepted.

Our Candy Queen, *S.*
origin not known pre-2007; ? ?
Kilcoyne, Lilacs-Quart. Jour. 36(2):82 [2007] - name only
Cultivar name not established.

OWEN ROGERS – synonym for UNH DWARF

'Ozhidanie', *S. vulgaris*
'Ожидание'
Mel'nik 1977; D V
{'Katherine Havemeyer' × OP}
Rubanik, V. G. et al., Siren' - Syringa L., publishing house "Kaïnar", Alma-Ata [1977] p 56, - in Russian.
Name: Russian for expectation
Cultivar name established and accepted.

Pale Chinese - see **'Metensis'** (*S.* ×*chinensis*).

Pale Hungarian - see **'Pallida'** (*S. josikaea*).

Pale Marly - see **'Marlyensis Pallida'**.

'Palibin', *S. pubescens* subsp. *pubescens*
origin not known pre-1920; S V
syn. - *microphylla minor* (dwarf littleleaf lilac); *meyeri* sensu Hort. non C.K. Schneid. (Meyer lilac), non Nakai; *palibiniana* Hort. *non* Nakai (dwarf Korean lilac); *palibininana* 'Meyeri'; *velutina* sensu Hort. non Komarov (dwarf lilac); 'Ingwersen's Dwarf' (*velutina*); Shau Ting Hsien (?)
common - see above under synonyms
McKelvey, The Lilac, 169-172 [1928] - as *S. meyeri*, Meyer No. 694, PI No. 23032; Wister, Arnoldia 23(4):81 [1963] - as 'Ingwerson's Dwarf'; Alexander III, Arnoldia 38(3):56-81 [1978] - name only; Krüssmann, Handbuch der Laubgehölze ed.2, 3:399 [1978]; Green, Curtis Bot. Mag. 182(3):117-120, t.778 [1979]; Pringle, Lilacs - Proceedings 7(1):50-70 [1979]; Vrugtman, AABGA Bull. 15(3):71-72 [1981]
on variability of 'Palibin': J. Cross, in litt. [1985]; Pirc, Deutsche Baumschule 9/1996:533; Peter Green to Vrugtman, in litt. 17 July 1998; Photo on Jorgovani/Lilacs 2015 DVD.
Named for Ivan Vladimirovich Palibin, 1872-1949, Russian botanist.
Awards: RHS Award of Merit 1984; RHS Award of Garden Merit 1993.
Cultivar name registered 1980; name established and accepted.

'Palibin Pearl', *S. pubescens* subsp. *pubescens*
origin not known pre-1988; S I
Anon., Lilacs - Quart. Jour. 21(4):105 [1992] - in cultivation at Arnold Arboretum (AA number 266-88-A) - as *s. meyeri* 'Alba', name only. (Vrugtman, Cultivated Plant Diversity ... 2017)
Cultivar name registered 2012; name established and accepted.

palibiniana Hort. non Nakai - see **'Palibin'**.

palibiniana excellens - see **'Excellens'** (*S. pubescens* subsp. *patula*).

palibiniana 'Meyeri' - see **'Palibin'** (*S. pubescens* subsp. *pubescens*).

'Pallens', *S.* (Villosae Group)
Lemoine 1931; S V
syn. - *reflexa pallens*, *reflexa pallida*
{*S. komarowii* subsp. *reflexa* × *S. tomentella* subsp. *tomentella* (?)}
Lemoine, Cat. No. 210, 26 [1936]; Wister, Lilacs for America, 55, 57 [1942], 38, 40 [1953]
Cultivar name presumed registered 1953; name established and accepted.

'Pallida', *S. josikaea*
origin not known pre-1865; S II
syn. - *josikaea pallida*
common name: Pale Hungarian
Jäger, Ziergehölze, 529 [1865]; Stand. Pl. Names, 264, 487 [1923] - as Pale Hungarian; McKelvey, The Lilac, 60-61 [1928]; Wister, Lilacs for America, 50, 55 [1942], 32, 38 [1953] - as S IV
Cultivar name presumed registered 1953; name established and accepted.

'Pallida', *S. vulgaris*
origin not known pre-1826; ? ?

Noisette, Man. Gen. Pl. 3:410 [1826]; McKelvey, The lilac, 354 [1928]
Cultivar name not established.

'Palluau', *S. vulgaris*
origin not known pre-1853; ? ?
Leroy, Cat. [1853]; McKelvey, the Lilac, 354 [1928]
Named (perhaps) for the municipality of Palluau, Département de la Vendée, France; or for Count Louis de Buade de Palluau de Frontenac, 1622-1698, ninth governor of New-France, 1672-1682.
Cultivar name not established.

'Pamyat' o . . .' - Память о (or Russian for commemoration of . . .)

'Pamyati Akademika K. I. Satpaeva', *S. vulgaris*
'Памяти Академика К. И. Сатпаева'
Mel'nik 1971, S III/II
{'Henri Martin' × OP}
Syn. – seedling No. 51
Rubanik, V. G. et al., Siren' - Syringa L., publishing house "Kaĭnar", Alma-Ata [1977] p 55, - in Russian; Rubtzov et al. 1980. Vidy i sorta sireni, kul'tiviruemye v SSSR. Kiev; Naukova Dumka. – in Russian; Holetich, C.D. 1982. Lilac species and cultivars in cultivation in USSR. Lilacs 11(2):1-38. - translation of Rubtzov et al. 1982.
Named in commemoration of Academician Kanysh Imantaevich Satpaev, 1899-1964, prominent Kazakh geologist and first president of Kazakhstani Academy of Sciences (1946), Almaty, Kazakhstan.
Cultivar name established and accepted.

'Pamyati A. T. Smol'skoĭ', *S. vulgaris*
'Памяти А. Т. Смольской'
Smol'skiĭ & Bibikova 1964; S IV
syn. - 'Pamjati A. T. Smol'skoj', 'Pamyati A. T. Smolskii'
{'Andenken an Ludwig Späth' × 'Hyazinthenflieder'}
Rubtzov et al. 1980. Vidy i sorta sireni, kul'tiviruemye v SSSR. Kiev; Naukova Dumka. – in Russian; Holetich, C.D. 1982. Lilac species and cultivars in cultivation in USSR. Lilacs 11(2):1-38. - translation of Rubtzov et al. 1982; Semenov, Igor, Lilacs - Quart. Jour. 43(3):85-87 & photo 88 [2014]; Photo on Jorgovani/Lilacs 2015 DVD.
Named in commemoration of the mother of Nikolaĭ Vladislavovich Smol'skiĭ, one of the originators.
Cultivar name established and accepted.

'Pamyati B. K. Dyagileva', *S. vulgaris*
'Памяти Б.К. Дягилева'
Dyagilev & Degtev 2020; D IV
{'Nebo Moskvy' × OP}
(Международная научная конференция "Syringa L.: коллекции, выращивание, использование")
"International Scientific Conference "Syringa L.: collections, cultivation, using" / Collection of Scientific Articles of Botanical Institute named after V.L. Komarov, Botanical Garden of Peter the Great BIN RAS. - St. Petersburg. -2020.- pp.23-27 (in Russian).
Russian for "In memory of BK Dyagilev", senior Kazakh agronomist and breeder (1937-2012).
Cultivar name established and accepted.

'Pamyatnik Zhertvam Fashizma', *S. vulgaris*
'Памятник Жертвам Фашизма'
Kolesnikov pre-1960; S VII/II
Name: Russian for "Monument to the victims of fascism".
in cultivation at Smolny Garden, St Petersburg (in litt. Polyakova to Vrugtman March 2016)

'Pamyat' o Chekhove', *S. vulgaris*
'Память о Чехове'
Klimenko, V.&Z. & Grigor'ev 1955; S VII
syn. - 'Pamjat' o Chekhove'
Rubtzov et al. 1980. Vidy i sorta sireni, kul'tiviruemye v SSSR. Kiev; Naukova Dumka. – in Russian; Holetich, C.D. 1982. Lilac species and cultivars in cultivation in USSR. Lilacs 11(2):1-38. - translation of Rubtzov et al. 1982.
Named in commemoration of Anton Pavlovich Chekhov, 1860-1904, Russian author.
Cultivar name established and accepted.

'Pamyat' o Geroyakh-Panfilovtsakh', *S. vulgaris*
'Память о Героях-Панфиловцах'
Kolesnikov pre-1968
Polyakova, 2010, Istoriya Russkoĭ Sireni, p. 34; name only.
Named for major general Ivan Vasilyevich Panfilov, 1892-1941, commander of the 316th Soviet Siberian infantry division defending Moscow in 1941; Hero of the Soviet Union.
Cultivar name not established.

'Pamyat' o Kolesnikove', *S. vulgaris*
'Память о Колесникове'
Kolesnikov & Mikhaĭlov 1974; D I
{selected by Mikhaĭlov from seedlings originally raised by Kolesnikov; parentage not known}
syn. - 'Pamyati Kolesnikova', 'Pamiat o Kolesnikove', 'Pamyat' o Kolesnikove'
Luneva, Z. S., et al., Siren', 109 [1989] - as 'Pamyat' o Kolesnikove'; Photo on Jorgovani/Lilacs 2015 DVD - as 'Pamyat' o Kolesnikove'; T. Polyakova, 2018, Мастер Сиреневой Кисти (Master of the Lilac Brush).
Name: According to Nikolaĭ Leonidovich Mikhaĭlov this lilac commemorates Leonid Alekseevich Kolesnikov, 1893-1968, Russian amateur plant breeder, and was intended to be named 'Pamyati Kolesnikova' (in litt. Tatyana Polyakova to Vrugtman 19 August 2014). The accepted name means "Memory about Kolesnikov".
Cultivar name established and accepted.

'Pamyat' o S. M. Kirove', *S. vulgaris*
'Память о С. М. Кирове'
Kolesnikov 1943; D IV
syn. - Kolesnikov No. 384, 'Pamiat o S. M. Kirove', 'Pamjat' o S. M. Kirove', 'Pamjatj o S. M. Kirove'; Blue Moon, trade name used for cut flowers of this cultivar, also listed by Green Shop, Japan, 2017 Cat. p.6

{'Belle de Nancy' × 'I. V. Michurin'}
Kolesnikov, Lilac, 24 [1955]; Howard, Arnoldia 19(6-7):31-35 [1959] & 31(3):125, 126 [1971] - as D II; Gromov, Siren', 120 (1963); Howard & Brizicky, AABGA Quart. Newsl. No. 64, 17-21 [1965]; Wister & Oppe, Arnoldia 31(3):125 [1971] - as D II; Gromov, Lilacs - Proceedings 2(4):18 [1974]; Rubtzov et al. 1980. Vidy i sorta sireni, kul'tiviruemye v SSSR. Kiev; Naukova Dumka. – in Russian; Holetich, C.D. 1982. Lilac species and cultivars in cultivation in USSR. Lilacs 11(2):1-38. - translation of Rubtzov et al. 1982; Photo on Jorgovani/Lilacs 2015 DVD.
Named in commemoration of Sergeĭ Mironovich Kirov, 1886-1934, Communist Party Secretary, Leningrad (now St Petersburg), Russia.
Cultivar name registered 1970; name established and accepted.
Forcing cultivar in the Netherlands.

'Pamyat' o Tripol'skoy Tragediĭ', S. vulgaris
'Память о Трипольской Трагедии'
Kolesnikov pre-1950; D II
{parentage not known}
T. Polyakova, 2018, Мастер Сиреневой Кисти (Master of the Lilac Brush), p.109 - photos only.
(to be completed)
Named for the Trypillia Tragedy, in memory of the 1919 Incident in Trypillia village, in which nationalist forces under Danylo Terpylo massacred a squad of young people of the Komsomol league from Kyev. (Wikipedia).
Cultivar name established and accepted.

'Pamyat' o Vavilove', S. vulgaris
'Память о Вавилове'
Vekhov 1952; D V
syn. - 'Pamjat' o Vavilove'
Журнал "Цветоводство" № 7, 1977 год, стр. 11.
Magazine "Tsvetovodstvo" ("Floriculture") No. 7, 1977, p. 11
Rubtzov et al. 1980. Vidy i sorta sireni, kul'tiviruemye v SSSR. Kiev; Naukova Dumka. – in Russian; Holetich, C.D. 1982. Lilac species and cultivars in cultivation in USSR. Lilacs 11(2):1-38. - translation of Rubtzov et al. 1982; Photo on Jorgovani/Lilacs 2015 DVD.
Named in commemoration of Nikolaĭ Ivanovich Vavilov, 1887-1943, Russian botanist and plant geneticist, author of Origin and geography of cultivated plants, 1987.
Cultivar name established and accepted.

'Pamyat' o Vekhove', S. vulgaris
'Память о Вехове'
Vekhov 1952; D II
syn. - 'Pamyat o Vekhove'
(Name given in 1972) Журнал "Цветоводство" № 7, 1977 год, стр. 11. Magazine "Tsvetovodstvo" ("Floriculture") No. 7, 1977, p. 11
Rubtzov et al. 1980. Vidy i sorta sireni, kul'tiviruemye v SSSR. Kiev; Naukova Dumka. – in Russian; Holetich, C.D. 1982. Lilac species and cultivars in cultivation in USSR. Lilacs 11(2):1-38. - translation of Rubtzov et al. 1982.
Named in commemoration of Nikolaĭ Kuz'mich Vekhov, 1887-1956, horticulturist, Lesostepnaya Experimental Breeding Station (LOSS), Meshchersk, Lipetzk Region, Russia.
Cultivar name established and accepted.

'Pamyaty Galima & Vicentia', S.
Sagitova 1975; D II ?
{'Mechta' × mix of pollen of 'Mariam' & Nos 17(4) & 5}
Cultivar name not established.

'Panna Dorota Gołąbecka', S. vulgaris
Karpow-Lipski 1952; D I
Wister & Oppe, Arnoldia 31(3):126 [1971]
Cultivar name registered 1970; name established and accepted.

'Panteons', S. vulgaris
Kārkliņš 2003; S VII
Photo on Jorgovani/Lilacs 2015 DVD.
Name: Latvian for the Pantheon.
Cultivar name not established.

'Papa Lambert', S. vulgaris
origin not known pre-1967; D VI
Sheridan Nurseries, Cat., 45 [1967].
Cultivar name not established.

'Papa Sass', S.vulgaris
Sass & Peterson pre-2019; D III*
Parentage unknown.
Developed from a sucker of a plant on the Sass farm in Omaha, NE, USA.
In private collection (KA) in USA per email to Registrar 10-4-19.
Cultivar name not established.

'Paradise', S. vulgaris
Kettler 1941; S VII
Wister, Lilacs for America, 55 [1942], 38 [1953]
Cultivar name presumed registered 1953; name established and accepted.

'Pārsteigums', S. vulgaris
Upītis 1950; S II & I
{'Sensation' × ? ; periclinal chimaera ?}
syn. - 'Paarsteigums', 'Parsteigums', 'Sensaacija', 'Sensācija', 'Upītis No. 3833'
Kalniņš, L., Ceriņu jaunšķirnes Dobelē, Dārs un drava 1986 (12):13-15 - in Latvian; Strautiņa, S. 1992. Ceriņi Dārzs un Drava. No. 6, pp.12-13; in litt. G. Tenbergs to F. Vrugtman [May 25, 2000] - seedling of 'Sensation'; Strautiņa, S. 2002. Ceriņu un jasmīnu avīze. LA, R., p. 62; in litt. S. Strautiņa to F. Vrugtman [21 Dec. 2007] - 1950, S II & I; Photo on Jorgovani/Lilacs 2015 DVD.
Name: Latvian for surprise.
Cultivar name established and accepted.

'Partizan', *S. vulgaris*
    'Партизан'
    Kolesnikov pre-1950; D IV
    Polyakova, 2018, "Master of the Lilac Inflorescence", p. 114; cultivar passport
    Polyakova, 2010, Istoriya Russkoï Sireni, p. 34; name only.
    Named for the World War II partisans,
    Cultivar name not established.

'Partizanka', *S. vulgaris*
    'Партизанка'
    Smol'skiĭ & Bibikova 1964; S IV
    {'Andenken an Ludwig Späth' × 'Hyazinthenflieder'}
    Bilov et al, Siren', 66 [1974] - in Russian; Rubtzov et al. 1980. Vidy i sorta sireni, kul'tiviruemye v SSSR. Kiev; Naukova Dumka. – in Russian; Holetich, C.D. 1982. Lilac species and cultivars in cultivation in USSR. Lilacs 11(2):1-38. - translation of Rubtzov et al. 1982; Photo on Jorgovani/Lilacs 2015 DVD; Semenov, Igor, Lilacs -Quart. Jour. 43(3):85-89 & photo 88 [2014].
    Named for the World War II female partisans.
    Cultivar name established and accepted.

'Pascal', *S. ×hyacinthiflora*
    Lemoine 1916; S IV
    Lemoine, Cat. No. 190, 25 [1916]; McKelvey, The Lilac, 199 [1928]; Wister, Lilacs for America, 55 [1942], 38 [1953]; Photo on Jorgovani/Lilacs 2015 DVD.
    Named for Blaise Pascal, 1623-1662, French mathematician, physicist, theologian and man-of-letters.
    Cultivar name presumed registered 1953; name established and accepted.

'Pasteur', *S. vulgaris*
    Lemoine 1903; S VII
    Lemoine, Cat. No. 155, 8 [1903]; Kache, Gartenschönheit 5:82 [1924]; McKelvey, The Lilac, 354 [1928]; Wister, Lilacs for America, 55 [1942], 38 [1953]; Photo on Jorgovani/Lilacs 2015 DVD.
    Named for Louis Pasteur, 1822-1895, French chemist and bacteriologist.
    Cultivar name presumed registered 1953; name established and accepted.

'Patience', *S.* (Villosae Group), *S. ×prestoniae*
    Preston 1928; S IV
    syn. - Preston No. 20-14-236
    {*S. villosa* subsp. *villosa* × *S. komarowii* subsp. *reflexa*}
    Macoun, Rep. Dom. Hort. 1928, 57 [1930]; Wister, Lilacs for America, 55, 64 [1942], 38, 48 [1953]; Photo on Jorgovani/Lilacs 2015 DVD.
    Named for the Woman to Queen Katharine in Shakespeare's *King Henry VIII*.
    Cultivar name presumed registered 1953; name established and accepted.

'Pat Pesata', *S. vulgaris*
    Fiala 1981; S III
    syn. - 'Patrick Peseta'
    {'Rochester' × 'True Blue'}
    Fiala, Lilacs, 96, 98, 108, Pl. 82 [1988]; Photo on Jorgovani/Lilacs 2015 DVD.
    Named for brother-in-law of the originator.
    Cultivar name established and accepted.

'Patricia', *S. ×hyacinthiflora*
    Preston pre-1931; D VI
    syn. - Preston No. 22.17.13
    {*S. ×hyacinthiflora* 'Lamartine' × ? }
    Davis, Rep. Dom. Hort. 1931, 1931 and 1933, 143 [1936] & Progress Report 1934-1948, 150 [1950]; Wister, Lilacs for America, 55 [1942] - as D III; Wister, Lilacs for America, 38 [1953]; Photo on Jorgovani/Lilacs 2015 DVD.
    Cultivar name presumed registered 1953; name established and accepted.

'Patrick Henry', *S. vulgaris*
    Dunbar 1923; D IV
    {'Vestale' × ? }
    syn. - Dunbar no. 300
    Wister, Nat. Hort. Mag. 6(1):1-16 [1927] - as D III; McKelvey, The Lilac, 354 [1928]; Wister, Lilacs for America, 55 [1942], 38 [1953]; Photo on Jorgovani/Lilacs 2015 DVD.
    Named for Patrick Henry, 1736-1799, American lawyer, statesman and orator, first governor of the State of Virginia.
    Cultivar name presumed registered 1953; name established and accepted.

Patrick Peseta - see 'Pat Pesata'.

'Patriot', *S.* (Villosae Group)
    Moro, F. 2002; S VII
    {mutation of 'Minuet'}
    Select Plus, <www.spi.8m.com/products.htm> [June 1, 2002]
    Cultivar name established and accepted.

'Patriot', *S. vulgaris*
    'Патриот'
    Aladin, S., Aladina, O., Polyakova, T., and Aladina, A. 2018; S II
    {sdlg 09-217* × 'Violetta')
    *sdlg 09-217 was obtained from open pollinated seeds of 'Cavour'.
    Международная и практическая конференция (International scientific and practical conference) «International Syringa 2018», Moscow, Moscow State University Botanical Garden, St. Petersburg, Botanical Garden of Peter the Great BIN RAS, Pavlovsk, May 21-27, 2018; pp. 43-47.
    Cultivar name established and accepted.

'Paul Cocardeau', *S.* (species affiliation not known)
    origin not known pre-1953; ? ?
    Wister, Lilacs for America, 38 [1953] - name only
    Cultivar name not established.

'Paul Deschanel', *S. vulgaris*
  Lemoine 1924; D VI
  syn. - 'Deschanel'
  Lemoine, Cat. No. 198, 20 [1924]; McKelvey, The Lilac, 355 [1928]; Wister, Lilacs for America, 55 [1942], 38 [1953]; Photo on Jorgovani/Lilacs 2015 DVD.
  Named for Paul Eugène Louis Deschanel, 1856-1922, president of France, 1899-1902.
  Cultivar name presumed registered 1953; name established and accepted.

'Paul Hariot', *S. vulgaris*
  Lemoine 1902; D VII
  syn. - 'Paul Heriott'
  Lemoine, Cat. No. 152, 8 [1902]; Kache, Gartenschönheit 5:82 [1924]; McKelvey, The Lilac, 355 [1928]; Wister, Lilacs for America, 55 [1942], 38 [1953]; Photo on Jorgovani/Lilacs 2015 DVD.
  Named for Paul Auguste Hariot, 1854-1917, French botanist.
  Cultivar name presumed registered 1953; name established and accepted.

'Paul Henry Lang', *S. vulgaris*
  Rankin; S VI
  {parentage not known}
  Cultivar name not established; probably not introduced.

'Paulina', *S.* (Villosae Group), *S.* ×*prestoniae*
  Preston 1927; S VII
  syn. - Preston No. 20-14-83
  {*S. villosa* subsp. *villosa* × *S. komarowii* subsp. *reflexa*}
  Macoun, Rep. Dom. Hort. 1928, 57 [1930]; Wister, Lilacs for America, 38, 48 [1953]; Wister, Lilacs for America, 55, 64 [1942], 38, 48 [1953]; received at Morden Research Station in 1937
  Named for the Wife to Antigonus in Shakespeare's *Winter's Tale*.
  Cultivar name presumed registered 1953; name established and accepted.

'Pauline Beck', *S. vulgaris*
  Rankin; S IV
  {parentage not known}
  Wister, Arnoldia 23(4):82 [1963]
  Cultivar name registered 1963;
  Cultivar not reported in cultivation.

'Pauline Fiala', *S. vulgaris*
  Fiala 1983; S II & I
  {'Sensation' × 'Flora 1953'}
  Fiala, Lilacs, 94, 223 [1988]; Photo on Jorgovani/Lilacs 2015 DVD.
  Named for the sister-in-law of the originator.
  Cultivar name established and accepted.

'Pauline Holcomb', *S. vulgaris*
  Rankin; S VII
  {parentage not known}
  Cultivar name not established; probably extinct.

Paul Lebrun - see **'Président Lebrun'**.

Paul Robsen, Paul Robson, Paul Robeson - see **'Pol' Robson'**.

'Paul Thirion', *S. vulgaris*
  Lemoine 1915; D VI
  syn. - 'Paul Therion'
  Lemoine, Cat. No. 189, 22 [1915]; McKelvey, The Lilac, 355 [1928]; Wister, Lilacs for America, 55 [1942], 38 [1953]; Photo on Jorgovani/Lilacs 2015 DVD.
  Named for Paul Thirion, 1873-1925, horticulturist at Nancy Parks, France.
  Awards: RHS Award of Merit 1927, Award of Garden Merit 1969.
  Cultivar name presumed registered 1953; name established and accepted.

'Paulus', *S.* (Villosae Group), *S.* ×*henryi*
  origin not known pre-2005; S V
  Pihlajaniemi, J. Appl. Bot. and Food Quality 79:107-116 [2005] - name only
  Cultivar name not established.

'Pavlinka', *S. vulgaris*
  'Павлинка'
  Smol'skiĭ & Bibikova 1964; D VII
  syn. - 'Pavlynka'
  {'Mme Abel Chatenay' × 'Réaumur'}
  Bilov et al., Siren', 65 [1974] - in Russian; Rubtzov et al. 1980. Vidy i sorta sireni, kul'tiviruemye v SSSR. Kiev; Naukova Dumka. – in Russian; Holetich, C.D. 1982. Lilac species and cultivars in cultivation in USSR. Lilacs 11(2):1-38. - translation of Rubtzov et al. 1982; Semenov, Igor, Lilacs -Quart. Jour. 43(3):85-87 [2014]; Photo on Jorgovani/Lilacs 2015 DVD.
  Name: Girl's name in Belorussia, like Paulina.
  Cultivar name established and accepted.

'Paysagiste Gabriel Roger', *S. vulgaris*
  Klettenberg 1934; D V
  Klettenberg, Cat., 20 [1934]; Wister, Lilacs for America, 38 [1953]
  Cultivar name presumed registered 1953; name established and accepted.

'Peacock', *S. vulgaris*
  Klager; S V
  Anon., ILS Newsletter 14(4):3-4 [1988]; Stenlund, Lilacs - Quart. Jour. 20(2):41 [1991]; Macore Co. Inc. photo library [Nov.28, 1999] http://www.macore.com/photolib.htm
  Cultivar name not established.

'Pearl', *S. vulgaris*
  origin not known pre-1930; S I
  {probably a French cultivar, or a Dunbar cultivar, renamed by Clarke 1930}
  Clarke, Garden Aristocrats (cat.) 7:12 [1940]; Wister, Lilacs for America, 55 [1942], & 38 [1953]; Clarke, loc. cit. 16:11 [1949] - "Real name unknown"; Photo on

Jorgovani/Lilacs 2015 DVD.
Although this is a cognomen, cultivar name presumed registered 1953; name established and accepted.

'Pearl Martin', *S. vulgaris*
Klager; S VII
Northwest Rose Growers Inc. listing [seen Apr.28/99]
Cultivar name established and accepted.

'Pearl Seeker', *S. vulgaris*
Upītis 1968; S I
syn. - 'Peerlju Zvejnieks', Pērļu Zvejnieks Upītis No. 66-36, 'Pērļu Zvejnieks'
{parentage not known}
Kalniņš, L., Ceriņu jaunšķirnes Dobelē, Dārs un drava 1986 (12):13-15 - in Latvian; Strautiņa, S. 1992. Ceriņi Dārzs un Drava. No. 6, pp.12-13; Strautiņa, S. 1996. Characteristics and propagation of lilacs obtained by P. Upītis. Problems of fruit plant breeding I. Jelgava. pp. 32-38; Vrugtman, HortScience 31(3):327-328 [1996]; Strautiņa, S. 2002. Ceriņu un jasmīnu avīze. LA, R., p. 62; in litt. S. Strautiņa to F. Vrugtman [21 Dec. 2007] - 1968, S I; Photo on Jorgovani/Lilacs 2015 DVD.
Statutory registration (breeder's rights) Nr. 297, CER-4, in Latvia [2004 - 2029] with the statutory epithet 'Pearl Seeker'
Named for the book Pērļu Zvejnieks (Pearl Seeker or Pearl Fisher), 1895, by Jānis Poruks, 1871-1911, Latvian author.
Cultivar name statutorily registered 1995; name established and accepted.

'Pearl White', *S. vulgaris*
origin not known pre-1977; S I
Peterson, Lilacs - Proceedings 16(1):21 [1987] - name only, obtained from Kelly Brothers Nurs., New York State, not identical to 'Pearl'
Cultivar name not established.

'Peau de Chamois', *S. vulgaris*
Clarke 1936; S VI
Clarke, Cat. 6:16 [1939]; Wister, Lilacs for America, 55 [1942], 38 [1953]
Cultivar name presumed registered 1953; name established and accepted.

'Pēdējais Sveiciens', *S. vulgaris*
Kārkliņš 2003; D VII
Photo from Dobele, Latvia by Natalia Savenko, seen in 2020 ILS Photo Database.
Cultivar name not established.

'Peerless Pink', *S. vulgaris*
Eveleens Maarse 1953; S V
syn. - 'Perles Pink', Perlis Pink'
{'Excellent' × 'Johan Mensing'}
Wister, Lilacs for America, 38 [1953]; Tuinbouwgids 1954, 440 - in Dutch; Photo on Jorgovani/Lilacs 2015 DVD.
Awards: Certificate of Merit 1953 (KMTP).
Cultivar name presumed registered 1953; name established and accepted.

Peerlju Zvejnieks - see: **'Pērļu Zvejnieks'.**

'Peggy', *S.* ×*hyacinthiflora*
Preston 1931; S III
syn. - Preston No. 22.17.07
{*S.* ×*hyacinthiflora* 'Lamartine' × ?}
Davis, Rep. Dom. Hort. 1931, 1931 and 1933, 143 [1936] & Progress Report 1934-1948, 150 [1950]; Wister, Lilacs for America, 55 [1942], 38 [1953]; Photo on Jorgovani/Lilacs 2015 DVD.
Cultivar name presumed registered 1953; name established and accepted.

pekinensis longifolia - see 'Longifolia' (*S. pekinensis*).

pekinensis macrothyrsa - see 'Macrothyrsa' (*S. pekinensis*).

pekinensis pendula - see 'Pendula' (*S. pekinensis*).

'Pelican', *S. vulgaris*
Origin not known; S V
Wister, Lilacs for America, 38 [1953]
Cultivar name presumed registered 1953; reported in cultivation.

'Penda', *S.*
Wood 2008; S VII
syn. - 'Lynn'; marketed in the USA as BLOOMERANG®, Registered US trademark No. 3655456, July 14, 2009.
{*S.* 'Josée' × ?}
Wayside Gardens as 'Lynn' [August 5, 2008]; United States Plant Patent No. 20,575, 15 December 2009, statutory registration; Canadian Plant Breeders' Rights No. 4071, effective 2011-05-31 to 2029-05-31; D:\Documents\Lilacs\Lilac Register\ILS Register 2019\Vrugtman\Register\<http:\www.whiteflowerfarm.com\67561-product.html>Wood, Lilacs Quart. Journ. 38(4):129-131 [2009], photos on centrefold and back cover; Vrugtman, Hanburyana 5:6-7 [2011]; Photo on Jorgovani/Lilacs 2015 DVD.
Cultivar name established and accepted.

'Pendula', *S. oblata*
origin not known pre-1942; S V
syn. - *S. oblata pendula*
Wister, Lilacs for America, 55 [1942], 37, 38 [1953] - identity not established
Cultivar name not established.

'Pendula', *S. oblata* subsp. *dilatata*
Wilson & Kelsy 1917; S V
{from seed collected by E. H. Wilson in China in 1917}
Meyer, Flieder, p.19 [1952] - as *S. oblata* var. *dilatata* f. Pendula; in litt. J. H. Alexander III to F. Vrugtman [March 20, 2006] - 2 plants (AA 291-40) received from Mrs Daniel C. Hunt, May 23, 1940, obtained by Mrs

Hunt ca 1926 from Kelsey Highland Nursery, Boxford, Massachusetts, where it was grown from seed collected by E. H. Wilson in China in 1917, plants no longer in existence.
Cultivar name established and accepted.

'Pendula', *S. pekinensis*
Temple 1887; S I
syn. - *S. ligustrina pekinensis pendula*; *S. pekinensis* var. *pendula* Dipp.common name: Weeping Peking
Shady Hill Nurs. (Temple), Cat., 9 [1886 ?]; Temple, Gard. Monthly 29:35[1887]; Ellwanger &Barry, Cat., [1892] - as *S. ligustrina pekinensis pendula*; Dippel, Handb. Laubholzk. 1:119 (1889); Stand. Pl. Names, 264, 488 [1923] - as Weeping Peking; McKelvey, The Lilac, 504-505 [1928]; Wister, Lilacs for America, 56 [1942], 38 [1953]
Cultivar name presumed registered 1953; name established and accepted.

pendulous lilac - see *S. komarowii* subsp. *reflexa*.

'Pépin de Herstal', *S. vulgaris*
Brahy-Ekenholm; S VI
Wister, Lilacs for America, 38 [1953]
Named for Pépin II de Herstal, also known as Pépin the Younger, 645-714, politician, mayor of the palace of Austrasie, France.
Cultivar name presumed registered 1953; name established and accepted.

'Pepper Salt', *S. vulgaris*
Margaretten; S VII/I
{'Mme Lemoine' × ? }
Cultivar name not established; not reported in cultivation.

'Perdita', *S.* (Villosae Group), *S.* ×*prestoniae*
Preston; ? ?
syn. - Preston No. 20-14-50
Macoun, Rep. Dom. Hort. 1928, 57 [1930] - name only; Wister, Lilacs for America, 64 [1942]; 48 [1953] - not in cultivation, no plants distributed
Named for the Daughter to Hermione in Shakespeare's *Winter's Tale*.
Cultivar name not established, probably extinct.

'Perky Artie', *S. vulgaris*
Klager; S VII
Anon., ILS Newsletter 14(4):3-4 [1988]; Stenlund, Lilacs - Quart. Jour. 20(2):41 [1991]
Cultivar name not established.

'Perlamutrovaya', *S. vulgaris*
'Перламутровая'
Sagitova 1981; ? ?
{'Milada' × ? }
Name: Russian for pearl.
Cultivar name not established.

'Pērle', *S. vulgaris*
Kārkliņš 2003; D V
Strautiņa & Kaufmane, Dobeles ceriņi, pp. 14, 92 [2011]; Photo on Jorgovani/Lilacs 2015 DVD.
Name: Latvian for pearl.
Cultivar name established and accepted.

'Perle von Stuttgart', *S. vulgaris*
Pfitzer 1910; D IV
syn. - 'Pere an Stuttgart', 'Perle Von Stuttgart'
Kanzleiter, Gartenwelt 13:129 [1909]; Wilhelm Pfitzer, Cat., 178 [1911]; McKelvey, The Lilac, 356 [1928]; Wister, Lilacs for America, 56 [1942] - as D VI; Wister, Lilacs for America, 38 [1953]; Photo on Jorgovani/Lilacs 2015 DVD.
Name: German for pearl of Stuttgart.
Cultivar name presumed registered 1953; name established and accepted.

'Perle von Teltow', *S. vulgaris*
Grunewald 1913; S VI
syn. - 'Helene Grunewald', 'Perle von Telton'; No. 01
Teschendorff, Möller's Deutsch. Gärtn.-Zeit. 28:440 [1913]; McKelvey, The Lilac, 356-357 [1928]; Wister, Lilacs for America, 56 [1942], 38 [1953]; Photo on Jorgovani/Lilacs 2015 DVD.
Name: German for pearl of Teltow.
Cultivar name presumed registered 1953; name established and accepted.

'Pērļu Zvejnieks' - see **'Pearl Seeker'**.

Persian - see *S.* ×*persica*.

Persian Red - see **'Saugeana'** (*S.* ×*chinensis*).

×*persica* var. *gigantea* - see **'Gigantea'** (*S. vulgaris*).

×*persica* var. *rubra* - see **'Rubra'** (*S.* ×*persica*).

'Pervyĭ Sneg', *S. villosa* subsp. *wolfii*
'Первый Снег'
Pshennikova 2006; S I
Registered with the State Commission of the Russian Federation for Testing and Protection of Selection Achievements, No. 9358789, 2006; Certificate of authorship № 45064 Pshennikova, L.M. 2007. Lilacs, cultivated in the Botanical Garden-Institute FEB RAS, p. 18.
Name: Russian for first snow.
Cultivar name registered, established and accepted.

'Peterburzhenka', *S. vulgaris*
'Петербурженка'
Aladin, S., Aladina, O., and Polyakova, T., and Aladina, A. 2016; S I
{'Tat'yana Polyakova' × 'Vechernii Zvon'}
Садовник (Gardener) magazine 04 (140)/2017 :18-25; Вестник АППМ (Catalog in Vestnik APPM (Planting material association) magazine) 1/2018: 59-72 (in Russian).
Named for the women of St. Petersburg, Russia.
Cultivar name established and accepted.

Peterson's, *S. vulgaris*
  origin not known pre-1931; S IV
  Wister, Lilacs for America, 38 [1953]
  Cognomen, not a cultivar name.

Peterson's Unknown, *S. vulgaris*
  Origin not known; S IV
  Anon., Lilac - Proceedings 17(1):22 [1988] - in cultivation at Rochester Parks, NY.
  Cognomen, not a cultivar name.

Peterson Unknown, *S.* (species affiliation not known)
  Origin not known; S IV
  Peterson, Lilacs - Proceedings 16(1):21 [1987]
  Cognomen, not a cultivar name.

'Petit Chou-hei', *S. pubescens* subsp. *pubescens*
  Ihara 2012; S VII
  syn. - seedling no. 2011S1128007#1
  {*S. pubescens* subsp. *pubescens* seedling no. 20040520001#8 × *S. pubescens* subsp. *pubescens* 'Hoshikuzu'}
  (Vrugtman, Cultivated Plant Diversity ... 2017)
  Named for Chou-hei Ihara [2013 -], son of Rimi and Hideo Ihara.
  Cultivar name registered 2017; name established and accepted.

'Petite Illene', *S. vulgaris*
  Klager; S V
  Anon., ILS Newsletter 14(4):3-4 [1988]
  Cultivar name not established.

'Ph. de Vilmorin', *S. vulgaris*
  origin not known ? ?
  Minier, Les arbres ont des idées [n.d., prob 1994] - lists 'Ph. de Vilmorin' as staminate parent of 'Princesse Sturdza'
  Named for Joseph Marie Philippe Lévêque de Vilmorin, 1872-1917, French horticulturist.
  Cultivar name not established.

'Phebe', *S.* (Villosae Group), *S.* ×*prestoniae*
  Preston 1928; S V
  syn. - Preston No. 20-14-240
  {*S. villosa* subsp. *villosa* × *S. komarowii* subsp. *reflexa*}
  Macoun, Rep. Dom. Hort. 1928, 57 [1930] - name only; Wister, Lilacs for America, 64 [1942], 38, 48 [1953] - not in cultivation, no plants distributed; reported as planted at Morden Research Station in 1937, but no longer in the collection, probably extinct
  Named for A Shepherdess in Shakespeare's *As You Like It*.
  Cultivar name presumed registered 1953; name established and accepted.

'Philémon', *S. vulgaris*
  Cochet ca 1840; S VII
  syn. - 'Philemon', 'Pilémon Cochet'
  {seedling of un-known parentage}
  Lescuyer, Hort. Français, 248 [1855]; McKelvey, The Lilac, 357-358 [1928]; Wister, Lilacs for America, 56 [1942], 38 [1953] - as 'Philemon'; Photo on Jorgovani/Lilacs 2015 DVD.
  Named for the Philémon Cochet, 1823-1898, elder son of the originator.
  Awards: First Class, 1855.
  Cultivar name presumed registered 1953; name established and accepted.

'Philippi', *S. vulgaris*
  origin not known pre-1938; ? ?
  Wister, Lilacs for America, 37, 56 [1942]
  Cultivar name not established, not recorded in cultivation in 1953.

PHILLIP ADAMS - see **'Kum-Bum'**
  Lottah Nursery, Tasmania, Australia, http://www.lottah.com/mini3/padams.htm [June 10, 2004].
  (Phillip Andrew Hedley Adams (1939- x), contemporary Australian radio personality, writer and film-maker, Officer of the Order of Australia, Australian Humanist of the Year (1987), Senior ANZAC Fellow).

'Phillis Alexander', *S.* (Villosae Group), *S.* ×*prestoniae*
  Alexander Sr; S V
  {parentage not known}
  Wister & Oppe, Arnoldia 31(3):123 [1971] - epithet misspelled 'Phyliss Alexander'
  Named for daughter-in-law Phillis Alexander.
  Cultivar name registered 1970;
  Cultivar not reported in cultivation.

'Phrynia', *S.* (Villosae Group), *S.* ×*prestoniae*
  Preston; ? ?
  {*S. villosa* subsp. *villosa* × *S. komarowii* subsp. *reflexa*}
  Wister, Lilacs for America, 64 [1942], 48 [1953] - not in cultivation, no plants distributed
  Named for the Mistress to Alcibiades in Shakespeare's *Timon of Athens*.
  Cultivar name not established, probably extinct.

'Pierre Joigneaux', *S. vulgaris*
  Lemoine 1892; D IV
  syn. - 'Pierre Coigneaux', 'Pierre Joigneauz'
  Lemoine, Cat. No. 122, 10 [1892]; McKelvey, The Lilac, 358 [1928]; Wister, Lilacs for America, 56 [1942], 38 [1953]; Photo on Jorgovani/Lilacs 2015 DVD.
  Named for Pierre Joigneaux, 1815-1892, French horticulturist and journalist.
  Cultivar name presumed registered 1953; name established and accepted.

'Pilli', *S. vulgaris*
  Mägi pre-2017; S VII
  Photo taken in Estonia by Igor Semenov and seen in 2020 ILS Photo Database.
  Cultivar name not established.

'Pilvi', *S. vulgaris*
  Origin not known pre-2017; S V

Photo taken in Hongiston Nursery taken by Mari Ranki and timo Saarimaa, and seen in 2020 ILS Photo Database.
Cultivar name not established.

Pink Beauty of Frankford, Pink Beauty of Frankfort - see '**Hermann Eilers**'.

'**Pink Bluet**', *S. vulgaris*
Rankin; S V
{parentage not known}
Wister, Arnoldia 23(4):82 [1963]
Cultivar name registered 1963;
Cultivar not reported in cultivation.

'**Pink Candy**', *S.* (Pubescentes Series, primarily *S. pubescens* subsp. *pubescens*)
Ihara 2020; S V
{'Kaoridama' × {'Palibin' × 'Superba'}
Syn. – seedling no. 2014S120114#2
Registration submitted 2/7/21 with photo.
Cultivar name registered, established and accepted.

'**Pink Cloud**', *S.* ×*hyacinthiflora*
Clarke 1947 (not Klager); S VI
{parentage not known}
Clarke, Cat. 16:8 [1949]; Woody Plant Register, AAN, No. 74 [1949]; Wister, Lilacs for America, 39 [1953]; Photo on Jorgovani/Lilacs 2015 DVD.
Cultivar name presumed registered 1953; name established and accepted.

'Pink Cloud', *S.* (species affiliation not known)
Klager (not Clarke); S V
Hulda Klager Lilac Garden, http://www.lilacgardens.com/pink.html#Pink%20Cloud [June 5, 2002]
Cultivar name not established.

'Pink Dan', *S. vulgaris*
Origin not known; D V
Anon., Lilacs - Proceedings 11(1):20 [1982] - name only; reported in cultivation at Central Experimental Farm, Ottawa, Ontario [2003]; Photo on Jorgovani/Lilacs 2015 DVD.
Cultivar name not established.

'Pink Dawn', *S.* (Villosae Group), *S.* ×*prestoniae*
Origin not known; S V
{parentage not known}
Peterson, Lilacs - Proceedings 16(1):24 [1987] - name only
Cultivar name not established.

Pink Delight, *S.* (*pubescens* subsp. *patula* ?)
Origin not known; S V
{parentage not known}
Peterson, Lilacs - Proceedings 16(1):25 [1987] - cognomen for unidentified plant purchased from Hillier's and Sons, Winchester, UK, in 1976.
Probably a cognomen for named cultivar that lost its label.

'Pink Diamond', *S. vulgaris*
Peterson pre-2004; D V
{'Carolyn Mae' × ? ; sibling seedling to 'Reva Ballreich'}
Anon., Tentative list of lilacs for auction. Lilacs - Quart. Jour. 33(1):11 [2004] - name only; in litt. Peterson to Vrugtman, 23 March 2010, this selection is indistinguishable from 'Reva Ballreich'.
Cultivar name not established.

'Pink Elizabeth', *S. vulgaris*
Klager; S V
Anon., ILS Newsletter 14(4):3-4 [1988]; Microplant Nurseries, Wholesale price list, 6 [1994]; Johnson, photographer, Lilacs 35(3): back cover [2006] - photograph; Photo on Jorgovani/Lilacs 2015 DVD.
Cultivar name not established.

'Pink Fawn', *S. vulgaris*
origin not known pre-1984; ? V
Anon., Lilacs - Proceedings 13(1):23 [1984] - reported at Vale of Aherlow, Chieppo collection
Cultivar name not established.

'**Pink Flower Select**', *S. pubescens* subsp. *patula*
Yanny 2016; S V
{'Miss Kim' × ? }
marketed in the US as Dream Cloud™
<http://plantsnouveau.com/plant/syringa-patula-dream-cloud/> seen 19 Aug. 2018
USPP 29477, 10 July 2018.
Cultivar name established.

'Pink Havemeyer', *S.* (species affiliation not known)
origin not known pre-1977; ? V
reported in Brighton Parks, UK, collection
Cultivar name not established.

'Pink Hyacinth', *S. oblata*
origin not known ? ?
Peterson, Lilacs - Proceedings 16(1):24 [1987].
Cultivar name not established.

'Pink Hyacinth', *S. vulgaris*
origin not known pre-1944; D V
Cole Nursery Co., Cat., 22 [1944].
Cultivar name not established.

'**Pink Ice**', *S. pubescens* subsp. *pubescens*
Ihara 2018; S VI
{*S. pubescens* subsp. *pubescens* 'Smile Kaho' × *S. pubescens* subsp. *pubescens* 'Smile Kaho', seedling 2011S1128008#2}
registered 17 November 2018 by Hideo Ihara Tokiwa 450-1, Minamiku, Sapporo, Hokkaido, 005 - 0863 Japan.
Cultivar name registered 2018; name established and accepted.

'Pinkie', *S. vulgaris*
Mahaux (not 'Pinkie', Rankin); S V
{cognomen for an unknown older cultivar}

Wister, Lilacs for America, 38 [1953]
Cognomen;
Cultivar name not established.

'Pinkie', *S. vulgaris*
Rankin (not 'Pinkie', Mahaux); S V
{parentage not known}
Wister, Arnoldia 23(4):82 [1963]; Photo on Jorgovani/Lilacs 2015 DVD.
Cultivar name registered 1963; name established and accepted.

'Pinkinsun', *S. vulgaris*
Rankin; S V
syn. - 'Pink-in-sun'
{parentage not known}
Wister, Arnoldia 23(4):82 [1963]
Cultivar name registered 1963;
Cultivar not reported in cultivation.

Pink Lace, Lammerts (not Sass) - see 'Heather Haze'.

'Pink Lace', *S. vulgaris*
Sass, J. (not Lammerts) 1953; S V
Wister, Lilacs for America, 39 [1953]; Photo on Jorgovani/Lilacs 2015 DVD.
Cultivar name presumed registered 1953; name established and accepted.

PINK LIZY, *S.* (species affiliation not known)
origin not known ? V
Macore Co. Inc. photo library [Nov.28, 1999] http://www.macore.com/photolib.htm

'Pink Mist', *S. vulgaris*
Havemeyer & Eaton 1953; S V
syn. - 'Pine Mist'
Wister, Lilacs for America, 39 [1953]; Lilac Land Cat. [1954]; Niedz, ILS Newsletter 1(4):7-8 [1972] - as 'Pine Mist'; Eickhorst, ILS Lilac Newsletter 4(1):4-5 [1978]; Photo on Jorgovani/Lilacs 2015 DVD.
Cultivar name presumed registered 1953; name established and accepted.

'Pink Parasol', *S. pubescens* subsp. *microphylla*
Fiala 1983; S V
{'Hers' × 'George Eastman'}
Fiala, Lilacs, 51, 101, 224, Pl. 32 [1988]; Photo on Jorgovani/Lilacs 2015 DVD.
Cultivar name established and accepted.

Pink Pearl - see 'Albida'.

'Pink Perfection', *S. vulgaris*
Castle; D V
Fiala, Lilacs, 207 [1988] - name only; Vrugtman, Lilacs -Quart. Jour. 32(4):149 [2003] - as D V; Photo on Jorgovani/Lilacs 2015 DVD.
Cultivar name established and accepted.

'Pink Perfume', *S.*
Nijnatten 2000, S V
{*S. pubescens* subsp. *pubescens* 'Palibin' × *S. pubescens* subsp. *microphylla* 'Superba'}
BLOOMERANG® Registered US trademark No. 3655456, July 14, 2009; USPP 24,252.
Plant Breeder's Rights registered, EU.28262, by Nijnatten & Valkplant BV, 2011; Plant Breeder's Rights registered, Canada, certificate No. 5054, as '**Pink Perfume**', by Nijnatten & BioFlora Inc., effective 2015-06-30.
Cultivar name established and accepted.
NOTE: No longer in production by Spring Meadow Nursery; replaced by *S.* '**SMNJRPI**'.

Pink Princess - see '**Princess Pink**'.

'Pink Ruth', *S. vulgaris*
Klager; S V
Anon., ILS Newsletter 14(4):3-4 [1988]
Cultivar name not established.

'Pink Spray', *S.* ×*hyacinthiflora*
Clarke 1948; S V
{cross between unnamed seedlings}
Clarke, Cat. 16:8 [1949]; Clarke, US Plant Patent No. 831 [Apr. 12, 1949] - as *S. vulgaris*; Woody Plant Register, AAN, No. 75 [1949]; Wister, Lilacs for America, 39 [1953]; Photo on Jorgovani/Lilacs 2015 DVD.
Cultivar name presumed registered 1953; name established and accepted.

PINK SURPRISE, *S.* ×*chinensis*
origin not known ? V
Peterson, Lilacs - Proceedings 16(1):25 [1987]; erroneous listing, Peterson in litt., Peterson to Vrugtman [May 26, 2006].
Not a cultivar name.

pinnate lilac - see *S. pinnatifolia* Hemsl.

Pinnatifolia - see *S. pinnatifolia* Hemsl.

'Pioner', *S. vulgaris*
'Пионер'
Kolesnikov 1951; S IV-V-VII
syn. - Kolesnikov No. 321, 'Pioneer', 'Pionier'
{Kolesnikov No. 105 × 'Zarya Kommunizma'}
Howard, Arnoldia 19(6-7):31-35 [1959]; Gromov, A., Siren', 98 [1963]; Howard & Brizicky, AABGA Quart. Newsl. No. 64, 17-21 [1965]; Wister & Oppe, Arnoldia 31(3):125 [1971] - as S VII and 'Pioneer'; Gromov, Lilacs - Proceedings 2(4):17 [1974]; Rubtzov et al. 1980. Vidy i sorta sireni, kul'tiviruemye v SSSR. Kiev; Naukova Dumka. – in Russian; Holetich, C.D. 1982. Lilac species and cultivars in cultivation in USSR. Lilacs 11(2):1-38. - translation of Rubtzov et al. 1982; Photo on Jorgovani/Lilacs 2015 DVD.
Named for the members of the largest children's public organization in Russia, the pioneer youth or Pionerii.
Cultivar name registered 1970; name established and accepted.

'Piotr Chosiński', *S. vulgaris*
   Karpow-Lipski 1960; D VI
   Wister & Oppe, Arnoldia 31(3):126 [1971]
   Cultivar name registered 1970; name established and accepted.

'Pixie', *S. vulgaris*
   Fiala 1981; S I
   {'Rochester' × 'Rochester'}
   Fiala, Lilacs, 223 [1988]; Photo on Jorgovani/Lilacs 2015 DVD.
   Nota bene: Probably not related to either 'Blue Pixie' or 'Red Pixie'.
   Cultivar name established and accepted.

Pjatidesjatiletije Oktjabrja - see 'Pyatidesyatiletie Oktyabrya'.

'P. K. Ozolin', *S. vulgaris*
   'П. К. Озолин'
   Kravchenko 1970; D V
   {'Marie Legraye' × 'Émile Gentil'}
   Kravchenko L. Culture of lilacs in Uzbekistan. Publishing house "Uzbekistan", Tashkent, 1970 p. 11.
   Rubtzov et al. 1980. Vidy i sorta sireni, kul'tiviruemye v SSSR. Kiev; Naukova Dumka. – in Russian; Holetich, C.D. 1982. Lilac species and cultivars in cultivation in USSR. Lilacs 11(2):1-38. - translation of Rubtzov et al. 1982.
   Named for P. K. Ozolin, horticultural author.
   Cultivar name established and accepted.

'Planchon', *S. vulgaris*
   Lemoine 1908; D VI
   Lemoine, Cat. No. 170, 30 [1908]; McKelvey, The Lilac, 358-359 [1928]; Wister, Lilacs for America, 56 [1942], 39 [1953]; Photo on Jorgovani/Lilacs 2015 DVD.
   Named for Jules Émile Planchon, 1823-1888, French botanist, professor at Montpellier.
   Cultivar name presumed registered 1953; name established and accepted.

Plena (*S. ×hyacinthiflora*) - see **'Hyacinthiflora Plena'**.

'Plena', *S. vulgaris*
   origin not known pre-1841; D III
   syn. - *flore pleno, flore-pleno, fl. pleno, pleno*
   Oudin, Cat., 22 [1841]; Ellwanger & Barry, Cat., [1892] - as flore pleno; McKelvey, The Lilac, 359 [1928]; Stand. Pl. Names, 615 [1942].
   Cultivar name established and accepted.

'PNI 7523', *S. reticulata* subsp. *reticulata*
   Flemer 1988; S I
   {plants under this name are grown from seed; probably a topovariant}
   marketed in the USA as REGENT™ and REGENT BRAND Japanese tree lilac; marketed in Europe as 'Regent'
   Princeton Nurseries, Wholesale Price List, 87 [1988]; Princeton Nurseries ceased operations in 2010.
   Cultivar name established and accepted.

'Pobednyĭ Put", *S. vulgaris*
   'Победный Путь'
   Grigorieva, V. & Grichachina, T; S IV-V 1971
   {'Charles X' × 'Lamarck'}
   Sdlg No. 512
   Registered by the USSR State Committee for Inventions and Discoveries in the State Register of Breeding Achievements of the USSR № 8507830, 1985. Certificate No. 4566
   Magazine "Tsvetovodstvo" ("Floriculture") No. 3, 1988, p. 13
   Information provided by Elena Olegovna Kuzmina, chief agronomist of the Control and Seed Experimental Station (КСОС) in 1978 - 1993.
   Name: Russian for winning way.
   Cultivar name established and accepted; name registered.

'Pocahontas', *S. ×hyacinthiflora*
   Skinner 1935; S II
   syn. - 'Pokahontas', ПОКАХОНТАС (trade designation used for cut flowers of this cultivar)
   Wister, Lilacs for America, 56 [1942]; Woody Plant Register, AAN, No. 14 [1949]; Wister, Lilacs for America, 56 [1942], 39 [1953]; Skinner, Hort. Horizons, 50, 109 [1966]; Fiala, Lilacs, 94 [1988] - as II; Lilacs - Quart. Jour. 22(4):back cover ill. [1993]; Photo on Jorgovani/Lilacs 2015 DVD.
   Named for Pocahontas, ca 1595-1617, an Indian princess, daughter of Powhatan, chief of the Algonquian Indians in the Tidewater region of Virginia, USA.
   Cultivar name presumed registered 1953; name established and accepted.
   Forcing cultivar in the Netherlands.

'Podarok Mame', *S. vulgaris*
   'Подарок Маме'
   Sagitova 1991; S VII & V
   Varietal denomination registered 1991, No. 5519, State Register of Selected Achievements in USSR; Chapman, photo, Lilacs - Quart. Jour. 38(4): inside front cover ill. [1993] - misspelled 'Podorak Mame'
   Name: Russian for present for mum.
   Cultivar name established and accepted.

'Podmoskovnye Vechera', *S. vulgaris*
   'Подмосковные Вечера'
   Aladin, S., Aladina, O., Polyakova, T. and Aladina, A. 2016; D II
   Statutory registration, Russia, State Register and Plant Patent No. 80049/8058579 (2019)
   {elite form 8-88-7H × elite form 10-117}
   Садовник (Gardener) magazine 04 (140)/2017 :18-25; Вестник АППМ (Catalog in Vestnik APPM (Planting material association) magazine) 1/2018: 59-72 (in Russian); II All-Russian scientific-practical conference with international participation (II Всероссийская научно-практическая конференция с международным участием) « Botanical Gardens in the XXI Century: Biodiversity Conservation, Development Strategy and Innovative Solutions Belgorod, Botanical

Garden of NRU «BelSU», September 23-26, 2019; pp.141-145 (in Russian).
Name: Russian for Moscow region evenings.
Cultivar name established and accepted.

'Polesskaya Legenda', *S. vulgaris*
'Полесская Легенда'
Smol'skiï & Bibikova 1964; S VII
syn. - 'Polesskaja Legenda'
{'Andenken an Ludwig Späth' × 'Hyazinthenflieder'}
Rubtzov et al. 1980. Vidy i sorta sireni, kul'tiviruemye v SSSR. Kiev; Naukova Dumka. – in Russian; Holetich, C.D. 1982. Lilac species and cultivars in cultivation in USSR. Lilacs 11(2):1-38. - translation of Rubtzov et al. 1982; Semenov, Igor, Lilacs - Quart. Jour. 43(3):85-87 [2014]; Photo on Jorgovani/Lilacs 2015 DVD.
Name: Russian for Legend of Poleskie, a part of Belarus.
Cultivar name established and accepted.

'Polina Osipenko', *S. vulgaris*
'Полина Осипенко'
Kolesnikov 1941; D I
Kolesnikov, Lilac, 26 [1955]; Rubtzov et al. 1980. Vidy i sorta sireni, kul'tiviruemye v SSSR. Kiev; Naukova Dumka. – in Russian; Holetich, C.D. 1982. Lilac species and cultivars in cultivation in USSR. Lilacs 11(2):1-38. - translation of Rubtzov et al. 1982; Photo on Jorgovani/Lilacs 2015 DVD.
Named for Polina Denisovna Osipenko (nee Dudnik), 1907-1939, Soviet aviatress, Hero of the Soviet Union. (See also 'Marina Raskova').
Cultivar name established and accepted.

Polin seedling, *S. vulgaris*
prob. Polin pre-1971; ? ?
Anon., Lilacs - Proceedings 17(1):27 [1988] - name only.
Cognomen; not a cultivar name.

Polin White, *S. vulgaris*
prob. Polin pre-1971; ? I
Anon., Lilacs - Proceedings 17(1):27 [1988] - name only.
Cognomen; not a cultivar name.

'Polly Hagaman', *S. vulgaris*
Margaretten; S III&I-III
{'Mme Lemoine' × ? }
reported in cultivation at Royal Botanical Gardens, Ontario, Canada
Named for Mrs C. B. Hagaman, Arvada, Colorado, see Lilacs - Proceedings 16(1):13, 32 [1987].
Cultivar name established and accepted.

'Polly Hill', *S.*
Fiala?; no information
Lilacs -Quart. Jour. 47(1):11 [2018] - name ony
Cultivar name not established and accepted.

'**Polly Stone**', *S. vulgaris*
Gardner; D VI
Wister & Oppe, Arnoldia 31(3):123 [1971]
Cultivar name registered 1971;
Cultivar not reported in cultivation.

'Pol' Robson', *S. vulgaris*
'Поль Робсон'
Kolesnikov 1965; S IV-III
syn. - 'Paul Robeson', 'Paul Robson', 'Pol Robson'
Wister & Oppe, Arnoldia 31(3):126 [1971] - as S III; Rubtzov et al. 1980. Vidy i sorta sireni, kul'tiviruemye v SSSR. Kiev; Naukova Dumka. – in Russian; Holetich, C.D. 1982. Lilac species and cultivars in cultivation in USSR. Lilacs 11(2):1-38. - translation of Rubtzov et al. 1982 - Quart. Jour. 26(2):front cover ill. [1997]; Photo on Jorgovani/Lilacs 2015 DVD.
Named for Paul Leroy Bustill Robeson, 1898-1976, American lawyer, actor, singer and civil rights activist.
Cultivar name registered 1970; name established and accepted.

'Poltava', *S. vulgaris*
'Полтава'
Rubtzov & Zhogoleva 1956; S II-IV
{'Ruhm von Horstenstein' × ? }
Rubtzov et al. 1980. Vidy i sorta sireni, kul'tiviruemye v SSSR. Kiev; Naukova Dumka. – in Russian; Holetich, C.D. 1982. Lilac species and cultivars in cultivation in USSR. Lilacs 11(2):1-38. - translation of Rubtzov et al. 1982; Photo on Jorgovani/Lilacs 2015 DVD.
Named for the city of Poltava, an important cultural center and a major transportation hub in the Ukraine.
Cultivar name established and accepted.

Pom - see '**Pom Pom**'.

'Pomerain', *S. vulgaris*
origin not known pre-1936; ? ?
Wister, Lilacs for America, 37, 56 [1942] - probably misspelling of 'Philemon'
Cultivar name not established, not recorded in cultivation in 1953.

'**Pomorzanka**', *S. vulgaris*
Karpow-Lipski 1962; S V
Wister & Oppe, Arnoldia 31(3):126 [1971]
Name: Polish for Pomeranian young lady.
Cultivar name registered 1970; name established and accepted.

'**Pom Pom**', *S. vulgaris*
Robinson 1937; S IV
syn. - 'Pom'
{parentage not known}
Gaybird Nursery Cat., 7 [196.(?)] - as 'Pom Pom' (*S. villosa* subsp. *villosa* × *S. vulgaris*); Wister, Arb. Bot. G. Bull. 1(2):19 [1967] - as S VI and 'Pom'; Vrugtman, Lilacs - Proceedings 7(1):37 [1979]; Vrugtman, AABGA Bull. 13(4):108-109 [1979]; Pringle, Baileya 21(3):110-113 [1981] - as *S. vulgaris*; Photo on Jorgovani/Lilacs 2015 DVD.

Cultivar name registered 1966; name established and accepted.

'Porcelain Blue', *S. vulgaris*
Fiala 1981; S III
syn. - 'Blue Porcelain', 'Porcelaine Blue'
{'Rochester' × 'Mrs A. Belmont'}
Fiala, Lilacs, 96, 98, 223 [1988]; Photo on Jorgovani/Lilacs 2015 DVD.
Cultivar name established and accepted.

'Portia', *S.* (Villosae Group), *S.* ×*prestoniae*
Preston 1928; S V
syn. - Preston No. 20-14-56
{*S. villosa* subsp. *villosa* × *S. komarowii* subsp. *reflexa*}
Macoun, Rep. Dom. Hort. 1928, 57 [1930]; USDA Plant Inventory No. 101, 20 (PI 81994) [Apr. 1931]; Wister, Lilacs for America, 56, 64 [1942]; 39, 48 [1953]; Photo on Jorgovani/Lilacs 2015 DVD.
Named for the Wife to Brutus in Shakespeare's *Cæsar*.
Cultivar name presumed registered 1953; name established and accepted.

'Pozdnyaya Vishnyovaya', *S. vulgaris*
'Поздняя Вишнёвая'
Kravchenko 1970; D VI
syn. - 'Pozdnjaja Vishnevaja'
{'Andenken an Ludwig Späth' × 'Émile Gentil'}
Kravchenko L. Culture of lilacs in Uzbekistan. Publishing house "Uzbekistan", Tashkent, 1970 p. 16
Rubtzov et al. 1980. Vidy i sorta sireni, kul'tiviruemye v SSSR. Kiev; Naukova Dumka. – in Russian; Holetich, C.D. 1982. Lilac species and cultivars in cultivation in USSR.
Lilacs 11(2):1-38. - translation of Rubtzov et al. 1982.
Name: Russian for late cherry.
Cultivar name established and accepted.

'P. P. Konchalovskiĭ', *S. vulgaris*
'П. П. Кончаловский'
Kolesnikov 1956; D III-IV
syn. - Kolesnikov No. 388, 'Konchaloskii', 'P. P. Konchalovskii', P. P. Konchalovskii', 'P. P. Konchalovskij'
{('Victor Lemoine' × 'Jules Simon') × 'Président Poincaré'}
Gromov, A., Siren', 84[1963]; Howard & Brizicky, AABGA Quart. Newsl. No. 64, 17-21 [1965]; Lilacs - Proceedings 2(4):18 [1974]; Rubtzov et al. 1980. Vidy i sorta sireni, kul'tiviruemye v SSSR. Kiev; Naukova Dumka. – in Russian; Holetich, C.D. 1982. Lilac species and cultivars in cultivation in USSR. Lilacs 11(2):1-38. - translation of Rubtzov et al. 1982; Photo on Jorgovani/Lilacs 2015 DVD.
(N.B. This cultivar has become confused with 'Nadezhda' in collections all over the world. While they are clearly two different cultivars, they appear identical to most examiners.)
Named for Pyotr Petrovich Konchalovskiĭ, 1876-1956, Ukrainian born Russian painter, one of the founders of "The Jack of Diamonds" group.
Cultivar name established and accepted.

praecox 'Catinat' - see '**Catinat**' (*S.* ×*hyacinthiflora*).
'Lamartine' - see '**Lamartine**' (*S.* ×*hyacinthiflora*).
'Mirabeau' - see '**Mirabeau**' (*S.* ×*hyacinthiflora*).
'Montesquieu' - see '**Montesquieu**' (*S.* ×*hyacinthiflora*).
'Vauban' - see '**Vauban**' (*S.* ×*hyacinthiflora*).

praecox pl. 'Vauban' - see '**Vauban**' (*S.* ×*hyacinthiflora*).

'Prairial', *S.* (Villosae Group)
Lemoine 1936; S V
{*S.* ×*henryi* × *S. tomentella* subsp. *tomentella*}
Lemoine, Cat. No. 210, 25 [1936] - as *S.* ×*henryi*; Wyman, Arnoldia 8(7):32 [1948] - as *S.* ×*henryi* × *S. tomentella*; Wister, Lilacs for America, 56 [1942], 39 [1953]; Hillier's manual of trees & shrubs, 389 [1971] - as *S.* ×*henryi* × *S. tomentella*; Photo on Jorgovani/Lilacs 2015 DVD.
Named for the 9th month of the 1st Republic calendar (May 20 - June 19).
Cultivar name presumed registered 1953; name established and accepted.

'Prairie Gem', *S.* (species affiliation not known)
origin not known ? ?
in cultivation at Herman Geers, Boskoop; no lit. ref.
Cultivar name not established.

'Prairie Petite', *S. vulgaris*
Viehmeyer 1996; S VII
syn. - lilac NP 103
{from neutron irradiated seed of unknown parentage}
Lindgren, Viehmeyer & Ublinger, HortScience 31(1):166 [1996]; Vrugtman, HortScience 32(4):587 [1997]; Briggs Nursery, Cat., 33 [1998]; Photo on Jorgovani/Lilacs 2015 DVD.
Cultivar name registered 1994; name established and accepted.

'Preludija', *S. vulgaris*
Kārkliņš 2003; S III ?
(no information; listed by T. Poliakova, 2014)
Name: Latvian for prelude.
Cultivar name not established.

'Pres. Alexander', *S. vulgaris*
Dunbar; ? ?
Wister, Nat. Hort. Mag. 6(1):1-16 [1927]
doubtful name
Cultivar name not established; not reported in cultivation.

'Pres. Franklin D. Roosevelt', *S.* (species affiliation not known)
Margaretten; ? ?
Gilbert, Lilacs - Quart. Jour. 27(2):55 [1998] - name only, identity uncertain (see 'President Roosevelt' and 'President F. D. Roosevelt')
Cultivar name not established.

'President Alix', *S. vulgaris*
   origin not known pre-1925; S VII
   Stand. Pl. Names, 617 [1942] - name only; Wister, Lilacs for America, 37, 56 [1942] - as 'Pres. Alix'
   Cultivar name not established, not reported in cultivation in 1953.

'Président Carnot', *S. vulgaris*
   Lemoine 1890; D IV
   common name: President Carnot
   Lemoine, Cat. No. 116, 14 [1890]; McKelvey, The Lilac, 359-360 [1928]; Stand. Pl. Names, 617 [1942] - as President Carnot; Wister, Lilacs for America, 56 [1942], 39 [1953]; Photo on Jorgovani/Lilacs 2015 DVD.
   Named for Marie François Sadi Carnot, 1837-1894, president of the French Republic.
   Cultivar name presumed registered 1953; name established and accepted.

'Président Chauvet', *S. vulgaris*
   Bruchet 1924; D II
   common name: President Chauvet
   McKelvey, The Lilac, 360 [1928] - no longer in cultivation; Stand. Pl. Names, 617 [1942] - as Presidnet Chauvet; Wister, Lilacs for America, 56 [1942], 39 [1953]
   Named for Gustave Chauvet, 1840-1933, president, Association française pour l'avancement des sciences.
   Cultivar name presumed registered 1953;
   Cultivar not reported in cultivation.

'President Eisenhower', *S. vulgaris*
   Lyden 1966; D V
   Wister, Arnoldia 23(4):82 [1963]
   Named for Dwight David Eisenhower, 1890-1969; general, 34th president of the USA.
   Cultivar name registered 1963;
   Cultivar not reported in cultivation.

'Président Fallières', *S. vulgaris*
   Lemoine 1911; D IV
   syn. - 'Präsident Sallières', Pres. Fallieres'
   common name: President Fallieres
   Lemoine, Cat. No. 179, 5 [1911]; McKelvey, The Lilac, 360-361 [1928]; Stand. Pl. Names, 617 [1942] - as President Fallieres; Wister, Lilacs for America, 56 [1942], 39 [1953]; Photo on Jorgovani/Lilacs 2015 DVD.
   Named for Armand Fallières, 1841-1931, president of France 1906-1913.
   Cultivar name presumed registered 1953; name established and accepted.

President F. D. Roosevelt - see '**Victorie**'.

'Président Grévy', *S. vulgaris*
   Lemoine 1886; D III
   syn. - 'Pres. Grevy'
   common name: President Grevy
   Lemoine, Cat. No. 104, 7 [1886]; Kache, Gartenschönheit 5: opp. 82 - color ill. [1924]; McKelvey, The Lilac, 361 [1928]; Stand. Pl. Names, 617 [1942] - as President Grevy; Wister, Lilacs for America, 56 [1942], 39 [1953]; Photo on Jorgovani/Lilacs 2015 DVD.
   Named for François Paul Jules Grévy, 1807-1891, French statesman, president of France 1879-1887.
   Awards: RHS Award of Merit 1892.
   Cultivar name presumed registered 1953; name established and accepted.

'President Harding', *S. vulgaris*
   Dunbar 1922; S VII
   syn. - Dunbar no. 235
   {'Aline Mocqueris' × ? }
   Dunbar, Florists Exch., 831 [Sept. 22, 1923]; McKelvey, The Lilac, 361-362 [1928]; Wister, Lilacs for America, 56 [1942], 39 [1953]
   Named for Warren Gamaliel Harding, 1865-1923, 29th president of the USA.
   Cultivar name presumed registered 1953; name established and accepted.

'Président Hayes', *S. ×chinensis*
   Lemoine 1889; S VI
   syn. - *dubia* 'Président Hayes', 'Pres. Heyes', 'President Harjes'
   common name: President Hayes
   Lemoine, Cat. No. 113, 9 [1889]; McKelvey, The Lilac, 426-427 [1928]; Stand. Pl. Names, 617 [1942] - as President Hayes; Wister, Lilacs for America, 56 [1942], 39 [1953]; Photo on Jorgovani/Lilacs 2015 DVD.
   Named for Rutherford Birchard Hayes, 1822-1893, lawyer and general, 19th president of the USA, 1877-1881.
   Cultivar name presumed registered 1953; name established and accepted.

'President John Adams', *S. vulgaris*
   Dunbar 1923; D I
   syn. - Dunbar no. 321, 'John Adams'
   {'Thunberg' × ? }
   Wister, Nat. Hort. Mag. 6(1):1-16 [1927]; McKelvey, The Lilac, 362 [1928]; Wister, Lilacs for America, 56 [1942], 39 [1953]; Photo on Jorgovani/Lilacs 2015 DVD.
   Named for John Adams, 1735-1826, 2nd president of the USA.
   Cultivar name presumed registered 1953; name established and accepted.

President John F. Kennedy - see 'John Kennedy'.

'President Kennedy', *S. vulgaris*
   origin not known ? ?
   Anon., Lilacs - Proceedings 17(1):27 [1988] - name only, perhaps identical to 'John Kennedy'.
   Cultivar name not established.

'Président Lambeau', *S. vulgaris*
   Klettenberg 1936 (not Stepman-Demessemaeker); S IV
   Wister, Lilacs for America, 39 [1953]; Photo on Jorgovani/Lilacs 2015 DVD.

Cultivar name presumed registered 1953;
Cultivar not reported in cultivation.

'Président Lambeau', *S. vulgaris*
Stepman-Demessemaeker pre-1906 (not Klettenberg); S V
common name: President Lambeau
syn. - 'President Lambeau'
{'Dr Lindley' × 'Marie Legraye'}
Fl. Stepman-Demessemaeker, Cat., 2 [1908]; McKelvey, The Lilac, 362 [1928]; Stand. Pl. Names, 617 [1942] - as President Lambeau; Wister, Lilacs for America, 56 [1942], 39 [1953]; Photo on Jorgovani/Lilacs 2015 DVD.
Named for Firmin Joseph Lambeau, 1866-1939, president of the "Tribunal de commerce", Brussels, Belgium; lover of orchids and promoter of ornamental plants.
Cultivar name presumed registered 1953; name established and accepted.

'Président Lebrun', *S. vulgaris*
Cassegrain 1933; S V
syn. - 'Paul Lebrun'
common name: President Lebrun
Stand. Pl. Names, 617 [1942] - as President Lebrun; Wister, Lilacs for America, 56 [1942], 39 [1953]; Photo on Jorgovani/Lilacs 2015 DVD.
Named for Albert Lebrun, 1871-1950, president of France.
Cultivar name presumed registered 1953; name established and accepted.

'President Lincoln', *S. vulgaris*
Dunbar 1916; S III
syn. - Dunbar no. 202, 'Pres. Lincoln'
{'Alba Virginalis' × ? }
Anon., Horticulture 26:35 [1917], 27:534 [1918], 27:625, , 1923]; McKelvey, The Lilac, 362-363 [1928]; Wister, Lilacs for America, 56 [1942]; Wister, Lilacs for America, 39 [1953] - as S II; Anon., ILS Lilac Newsletter 11(1):6-8 [1985]; Johnson, photographer, Lilacs 35(3):back cover [1987] - photograph; Photo on Jorgovani/Lilacs 2015 DVD. frontispiece [1918]; Dunbar, Florists Exch., 831 [Sept. 22
Named for Abraham Lincoln, 1809-1865, 16th president of the USA.
Cultivar name presumed registered 1953; name established and accepted.

'Président Loubet', *S. vulgaris*
Lemoine 1901; D VI
syn. - 'President Loubert'
common name: President Loubet
Lemoine, Cat. No. 149, 8 [1901]; McKelvey, The Lilac, 363 [1928]; Stand. Pl. Names, 617 [1942] - as President Loubet; Wister, Lilacs for America, 56 [1942], 39 [1953]; Photo on Jorgovani/Lilacs 2015 DVD.
Named for Émile Loubet, 1837-1929, French statesman and 7th president of the Republic.
Cultivar name presumed registered 1953; name established and accepted.

'Président Massart', *S. vulgaris*
Brahy-Ekenholm 1861; S VII
common name: President Massart
Duvivier, Jour. Hort. Pratique Belg. ser. 2, 5:265 [1861]; McKelvey, The Lilac, 363-364 [1928]; Stand. Pl. Names, 617 [1942] - as President Massart; Wister, Lilacs for America, 56 [1942], 39 [1953]; Photo on Jorgovani/Lilacs 2015 DVD.
Named for the one-time president of the royal horticultural society of Liège, Belgium.
Cultivar name presumed registered 1953; name established and accepted.

'President Monroe', *S. vulgaris*
Dunbar 1923; D II
syn. - Dunbar no. 340 'James Munroe'
{'Thunberg' × ? }
Wister, Nat. Hort. Mag. 6(1):1-16 [1927] - as D III; McKelvey, The Lilac, 364 [1928]; Wister, Lilacs for America, 56 [1942] - as D V; Wister, Lilacs for America, 39 [1953] - as D IV; Photo on Jorgovani/Lilacs 2015 DVD.
Named for James Monroe, 1758-1831, 5th president of the USA.
Cultivar name presumed registered 1953; name established and accepted.

'Président Poincaré', *S. vulgaris*
Lemoine 1913; D VI
syn. - 'General Poincaré', 'President Poincaire'
common name: President Poincare
Lemoine, Cat. No. 185, 6 [1913]; McKelvey, The Lilac, 364 [1928]; Stand. Pl. Names, 617 [1942] - as President Poincare; Wister, Lilacs for America, 56 [1942], 39 [1953]
Named for Raymond Nicolas Landry Poincaré, 1860-1934, French statesman, author, and president of France 1913-1920; Photo on Jorgovani/Lilacs 2015 DVD.
Cultivar name presumed registered 1953; name established and accepted.

President Reva Ballreich - see **'Reva Ballreich'**.

'President Ronald Reagan', *S. vulgaris*
Margaretten pre-2015; D III
{'Mme Lemoine' × ? }
reported in cultivation at Royal Botanical Gardens, Ontario, Canada.
In cultivation at Highland Park, Rochester NY USA.
Photo on Jorgovani/Lilacs 2015 DVD.
Named for Ronald Wilson Reagan, 1911-2004, 40th president of the USA 1981-1989.
Cultivar name established and accepted.

President Ronsard - see **'Ronsard'**.

'President Roosevelt', *S. vulgaris*
Dunbar 1919; S VII
syn. - Dunbar no. 229, 'Pres. Roosevelt'
{'Aline Mocqueris' × ? }

Dunbar, Florists Exch., 831 [Sept. 22, 1923]; McKelvey, The Lilac, 364 [1928]; Wister, Lilacs for America, 56 [1942], 39 [1953]; Photo on Jorgovani/Lilacs 2015 DVD.
Named for Theodore Roosevelt, 1858-1919, 26th president of the USA.
Cultivar name presumed registered 1953; name established and accepted.

'President Theodore Roosevelt', S. (species affiliation not known)
origin not known ? ?
see also 'Theodore Roosevelt' and 'President Roosevelt'
Reported in cultivation in Prairie Regional Trials, pre-1993.
Cultivar name not established.

'Président Viger', *S. vulgaris*
Lemoine 1900; D III
syn. - 'Pres. Viger', 'Viger'
common name: President Viger
Lemoine, Cat. No. 146, 12 [1900]; McKelvey, The Lilac, 364-365 [1928]; Stand. Pl. Names, 617 [1942] - as President Viger; Wister, Lilacs for America, 57 [1942], 39 [1953]; Photo on Jorgovani/Lilacs 2015 DVD.
Named for Albert Viger, 1843-1926, French minister of agriculture 1893-1899.
Cultivar name presumed registered 1953; name established and accepted.

Preston, Isabella, breeder's designations and cultivar names
No. 20-03-01 see 'Diana'.
No. 20-06-01 see 'Guinevere'.
No. 20-11-241 see 'Juliet'.
No. 20-14-02 see 'Adriana'.
No. 20-14-08 see 'Bianca'.
No. 20-14-11 see 'Julia'.
No. 20-14-13 see 'Emilia'.
No. 20-14-18 see 'Jaquenetta'.
No. 20-14-19 see 'Dorcas'.
No. 20-14-20 see 'Hermia'.
No. 20-14-22 see 'Jessica'.
No. 20-14-26 see 'Lavinia'.
No. 20-14-34 see 'Katharina'.
No. 20-14-38 see 'Miranda'.
No. 20-14-49 see 'Nerissa'.
No. 20-14-50 see 'Perdita'.
No. 20-14-51 see 'W. T. Macoun'.
No. 20-14-54 see 'Lucetta'.
No. 20-14-56 see 'Portia'.
No. 20-14-64 see 'Olivia'.
No. 20-14-66 see 'Luciana'.
No. 20-14-72 see 'Ophelia'.
No. 20-14-78 see 'Mariana'.
No. 20-14-83 see 'Paulina'.
No. 20-14-93 see 'Octavia'.
No. 20-14-99 see 'Silvia'.
No. 20-14-111 see 'Timandra'.
No. 20-14-114 see 'Isabella'.
No. 20-14-115 see 'Titania'.
No. 20-14-124 see 'Tamora'.
No. 20-14-135 see 'Cassandra'.
No. 20-14-140 see 'Alice'.
No. 20-14-149 see 'Valeria'.
No. 20-14-150 see 'Beatrice'.
No. 20-14-156 see 'Blanch'.
No. 20-14-157 see 'Cordelia'.
No. 20-14-162 see 'Charmian'.
No. 20-14-164 see 'Cressida'.
No. 20-14-168 see 'Constance'.
No. 20-14-172 see 'Elinor'.
No. 20-14-176 see 'Celia'.
No. 20-14 179 see 'Desdemona'.
No. 20-14-180 see 'Viola'.
No. 20-14-195 see 'Audrey'.
No. 20-14-197 see 'Gertrude'.
No. 20-14-204 see 'Hero'.
No. 20-14-205 see 'Imogen'.
No. 20-14-211 see 'Virgilia'.
No. 20-14-214 see 'Ursula'.
No. 20-14-221 see 'Margaret'.
No. 20-14-233 see 'Rosalind'.
No. 20-14-236 see 'Patience'.
No. 20-14-240 see 'Phebe'.
No. 20-14-247 see 'Francisca'.
No. 20-14-251 see 'Regan'.
No. 20.15.18 see 'Calphurnia'.
No. 22.01.03 see 'Maureen'.
No. 22.01.08 see 'Grace'.
No. 22.04.09 see 'Muriel'.
No. 22.04.16 see 'Norah'.
No. 22.17.07 see 'Peggy'.
No. 22.17.13 see 'Patricia'.
No. 24.02.05 see 'Bellicent'.
No. 24.02.25 see 'Lynette'.
No. 24.02.43 see 'Enid'.
No. 24.05.82 see 'Oberon'.
No. 26.01.09 see 'Kim'.
No. 26.05.23 see 'Romeo'.
No. 30.01.47 see 'Elaine'.
No. 30.07.01 see 'Ethel M. Webster'.
No. 33.11.01 see 'Fountain'.

'Pride of Descanso', *S. ×hyacinthiflora*
origin not known pre-1974; ? I
Select Nurseries, Cat., 58 [1975]
Cultivar name not established.

'Pride of Rochester', *S. vulgaris*
origin not known pre-1892; ? ?
Parsons, Cat., 9 [1892]; McKelvey, The Lilac, 365 [1928]
Cultivar name not established.

Pride of the Guild - see **'Guilds Pride'**.

'Primrose', *S. vulgaris*
Maarse Jbzn, G. 1949; S I
syn. - 'Primerose', 'Yellow Wonder'; probably includes

'Primrose' (Holden)
{mutation of 'Marie Legraye'; perhaps a periclinal chimera}
Gardener's Chron., Jul. 2, 1949, p. 1 - as 'Yellow Wonder';
Anon., Jour. R.H.S. 75(9):413 [1950]; G. Maarse, US Pl.
Pat. No. 1108 [June 1952]; Wister, Lilacs for America,
39 [1953]; Eveleens Maarse, Dendron 1(1):13 [1954];
Vrugtman & Eickhorst, Lilacs - Proceedings 9:28-30
[1981]; Photo on Jorgovani/Lilacs 2015 DVD.
Introducer: J. Spek, Boskoop, Netherlands [1949];
Wayside Gardens, Mentor, Ohio, USA [1953]
Awards: RHS Award of Merit 1950; First Class
Certificate 1953 (KMTP).
First foreign produced cultivar patented in the USA.
USPP 01108 June 24, 1952.
Cultivar name presumed registered 1953; name
established and accepted.
Forcing cultivar in the Netherlands.

Primrose (Canada clone), *S. vulgaris*
Origin not known; S I
Reported in cultivation NCCPG Coll., Suffolk, UK.
Cognomen, not a cultivar name.

Primrose (Holden), *S. vulgaris*
(Holden Arb. No. 63-78); S I
syn. - 'Sterntaler'
marketed in Germany as STERNTALER™ (No. 305349872;
G. & J. Rosskamp)
{presumably a mutation of 'Primrose'}
Fiala, Lilacs, [1988], p. 92 - as "Holden Arboretum
selection" or "Primrose H", and p. 209 - as "Holden
Arboretum strain"; Kircher Baumschulen, Cat.
2002/2003, p.2 - as pink (V)
Cultivar name not established; not recognized as a
distinct cultivar.

Primrose (Holden Arb. PP 1108), *S. vulgaris*
Origin not known; S I
Anon., Lilacs - Quart. Jour. 18(3):73 [1989] - name only.
Cognomen, not a cultivar name.

'Prince Albert de Liège', *S. vulgaris*
Klettenberg 1935; S III
Klettenberg, Cat., 26 [1935]; Wister, Lilacs for America,
39 [1953]
Named for Albert Félix Humbert Théodore Christian
Eugène Marie, 1934- , (Albert II, king of Belgium 1993-
2013), son of Léopold III.
Cultivar name presumed registered 1953; name
established and accepted.

'Prince Baudouin', *S. vulgaris*
Klettenberg 1935; S VI
Klettenberg, Cat., 6 [1935]; Wister, Lilacs for America,
39 [1953]
Named for Boudewijn Albert Charles Léopold Axel
Marie Gustave, Prince of Belgium, 1930-1993, king of
Belgium 1951-1993.
Cultivar name presumed registered 1953; name
established and accepted.

PRINCE CHARMING™ - see 'Bailming'.

'Prince de Beauvau', *S. vulgaris*
Lemoine 1897; D IV
Lemoine, Cat. No. 137, 10 [1897]; McKelvey, The Lilac,
365 [1928]; Wister, Lilacs for America, 57 [1942] - as
D III; Wister, Lilacs for America, 39 [1953]; Photo on
Jorgovani/Lilacs 2015 DVD.
Named (probably) for Charles Juste François Victurnien,
Prince de Beauvau-Craon, 1793-1864, France.
Cultivar name presumed registered 1953; name
established and accepted.

'Princei', *S. vulgaris*
origin not known pre-1844; ? II
syn. - 'Prinzei'
Prince, Cat., 70 [1844]; McKelvey, The Lilac, 365 [1928].

'Prince Impérial', *S. vulgaris*
Dubois 1861; S VI
syn. - 'Prince Imperia'
common name: Prince Imperial
Larché, Hort. Français, 143 [1861]; McKelvey, The
Lilac, 365-366 [1928]; Stand. Pl. Names, 617 [1942] - as
Prince Imperial; Wister, Lilacs for America, 57 [1942], 39
[1953]; Photo on Jorgovani/Lilacs 2015 DVD.
Named for Eugène Louis Napoléon, Prince Impérial,
1856-1879, son of Emperor Napoléon III and his wife
Empress Eugénie (de Montijo).
Cultivar name presumed registered 1953; name
established and accepted.

'Prince Léopold', *S. vulgaris*
Klettenberg 1930; S VI
Klettenberg, Cat., 18 [1930]; Wister, Lilacs for America,
37, 56 [1942], 39 [1953] - as "probably 'Léopold II' "
Named for Léopold Phillippe Charles Albert Meinard
Hubertus Marie Miguel, prince of Belgium, 1901-1983,
king of Belgium (Léopold III) 1934-1951.
Cultivar name presumed registered 1953; name
established and accepted.

'Prince Marie', *S. vulgaris*
origin not known pre-1910; ? ?
syn. - 'Prince Marie aus Sichrow'; possibly misspelling of
'Princesse Marie'
McKelvey, The Lilac, 366 [1928]
Cultivar name not established.

'Prince Notger', *S. vulgaris*
origin not known pre-1841; S III
syn. - 'Prince Nottger', 'Prince Nutger', 'Prinz Notger', *S.
vulgaris* var. *notgeriana*
Oudin, Cat., 22 [1841]; McKelvey, The Lilac, 366-367
[1928]; Wister, Lilacs for America, 57 [1942], 39 [1953];
Photo on Jorgovani/Lilacs 2015 DVD.
Named for Notger, prince-bishop of Lotharingia at
Liège, Belgium, 930-1008.
Cultivar name presumed registered 1953; name
established and accepted.

'Prince of Wales', *S. vulgaris*
>Dougall 1874; S IV
>Windsor Nurseries, Cat. [1874]; Dougall, Canadian Horticulturist 2(1):8 [1879]; Ellwanger & Barry, Cat. No. 2, 89 [1886]; McKelvey, The Lilac, 367 [1928]; Wister, Lilacs for America, 57 [1942], 39 [1953]; Photo on Jorgovani/Lilacs 2015 DVD.
>Named for Edward, Prince of Wales, 1841-1910, King Edward VII of Great Britain.
>Cultivar name presumed registered 1953; name established and accepted.

Princess . . . - see also: Princesse . . . , Prinses . . . , Prinzessin . . .

'Princess Alexandra', *S. vulgaris*
>Dougall 1874; S I
>syn. - 'Princess Alexandria'
>Windsor Nurseries, Cat. [1874]; Dougall, Canadian Horticulturist 2(1):8 [1879]; Ellwanger & Barry, Cat., [1892]; McKelvey, The Lilac, 367-368 [1928]; Wister, Lilacs for America, 57 [1942], 39 [1953]; Anon., ILS Lilac Newsletter 11(1):6-8 [1985]; Photo on Jorgovani/Lilacs 2015 DVD.
>Named for Alexandra, 1844-1925, queen-consort of King Edward VII of Great Britain.
>Cultivar name presumed registered 1953; name established and accepted.

'Princess Beatrice', *S. vulgaris*
>Dougall 1880; S I
>Dougall, Canadian Horticulturist 3(7):103 [1880]
>Photo by Ole Heide seen on 2020 ILS DVD
>Named for Princess Beatrice, 1857-1944, youngest daughter of Queen Victoria of Great Britain.
>Cultivar name not established.

'Princess Clementine' - see **'Princesse Clémentine'**.

'Princesse Camille de Rohan', *S. vulgaris*
>Brahy-Ekenholm pre-1856; S V
>syn. - 'Camille de Rohan', 'Princess Camille de Rohan'
>C.F.A. Morren, Belg. Hort. 6:97 [1856]; McKelvey, The Lilac, 368 [1928]; Wister, Lilacs for America, 57 [1942], 39 [1953]; Photo on Jorgovani/Lilacs 2015 DVD.
>Named, probably, for the wife [no dates] of Camille, prince de Rohan [no dates], a botanist and dendrologist, proprietor of Sychrov castle, Bohemia.
>Cultivar name presumed registered 1953; name established and accepted.

'Princesse Clémentine', *S. vulgaris*
>Mathieu pre-1906; D I
>{'Mme Lemoine' × 'Marie Legraye'}
>syn. - 'Princess Clementine'
>common name: Princesse Clementine
>parentage information seen on Pl. 33 in La Tribune Horticulture (Supplement) 4 Mai 1907, (Pl. 33 in collection of Tatyana Polyakova); Fl. Stepman-Demessemaeker, Suppl. Gen. Cat., 2 [1908]; McKelvey, The Lilac, 368-369 [1928]; Stand. Pl. Names, 617 [1942] - as Princesse Clementine; Wister, Lilacs for America, 57 [1942], 40 [1953]; Photo on Jorgovani/Lilacs 2015 DVD.
>Named for Princesse Clémentine of Belgium, 1872-1955; 1910 she married the Prince Victor Napoleon, 1862-1926, and became Princesse Napoleon.
>Awards: ". . . un diplôme d'honneur au Meeting horticole de Bruxelles, 20 mai 1906".
>Cultivar name presumed registered 1953; name established and accepted.

Princesse Clotilde - see **'Prinzessin Klotilde'**.

'Princesse Elisabeth d'Angleterre', *S. vulgaris*
>Klettenberg 1937; S V
>Wister, Lilacs for America, 40 [1953]
>Named for Princess Elisabeth, since 1952 Queen Elisabeth II of the United Kingdom.
>Cultivar name presumed registered 1953; name established and accepted.

'Princesse Joséphine-Charlotte', *S. vulgaris*
>Klettenberg 1934; S I
>Klettenberg, Cat., 21 [1934]; Wister, Lilacs for America, 40 [1953]
>Named for her Royal Highness the Grand-Duchess Joséphine-Charlotte Ingeborg Elisabeth Marie José Marguerite Astrid, princesse of Belgium, 1927- x].
>Cultivar name presumed registered 1953; name established and accepted.

'Princesse Maria', *S. vulgaris*
>International Exhibition, 1876, US Centennial Commission, Volume 11, p. 310 - name only - probably 'Princesse Marie'.

'Princesse Marianne', *S. vulgaris*
>origin not known pre-1875; ? ?
>possibly syn. of 'Princesse Marie'
>L. van Houtte, Cat. No. 165, 18 [1875] - name only; McKelvey, The Lilac, 369 [1928]
>Named for the Dutch princess Marianne, 1810-1883, daughter of King William I and Wilhelmina of Prussia.
>Cultivar name not established.

'Princesse Marie', *S. vulgaris*
>Bertin pre-1846; S V
>syn. - 'Princess Marie'; see also 'Prince Marie'
>Oudin, Cat., 11 [1846]; McKelvey, The Lilac, 369 [1928]; Wister, Lilacs for America, 57 [1942], 39 [1953]; Wister, Lilacs for America, 57 [1942], 39 [1953] - as 'Princess Marie'; Photo on Jorgovani/Lilacs 2015 DVD.
>Cultivar name presumed registered 1953; name established and accepted.

'Princesse Marie-José', *S. vulgaris*
>Stepman-Demessemaeker (?) 1913; S ?
>Klettenberg, Cat., 23 [1923]; Wister, Lilacs for America, 40 [1953]
>Named for Marie-José Charlotte Sophie Amélie Henriette Gabrielle, princes of Belgium, 1906-2001, queen of Italy, 1946, wife to HRH Umberto Nicola

Tomasso Giovanni Maria, prince of Piedmont, king of Italy, 1946.
Cultivar name presumed registered;
Cultivar not reported in cultivation.

'Princesse Murat', *S. vulgaris*
origin not known pre-1889; S I
Parsons, Cat., 50 [1889]; McKelvey, The Lilac, 370 [1928].

'**Princesse Sturdza**', *S. vulgaris*
Bellion 1995; S V/IV
{'Sensation' × 'Ph. de Vilmorin'}
Minier, Les arbres ont des idées [ca 1994]; Vrugtman, HortScience 31(3):327 [1996].
Named for the Norwegian-born Princess Greta Sturdza (née Kvaal), 1915-2009, amateur horticulturist, Varengeville-sur-mer, Normandy, France; president International Dendrology Union, 2002.
Cultivar name registered 1995; name established and accepted.

'Princess Louise', *S. vulgaris*
Dougall 1880; ? ?
Dougall, Canadian Horticulturist 3(7):103 [1880]
Named for Louise Caroline Alberta, Lady John Campbell, Marchioness of Lorne, Duchess of Argyll, 1848-1939, née Princess of Great Britain and Ireland, daughter of Queen Victoria; the Canadian province of Alberta and Lake Louise were also named for her (see also 'Marchioness of Lorne').
Cultivar name not established; probably extinct.

'**Princess Pink**', *S. vulgaris*
Klager 1938; S V
syn. - 'Pink Princess'
Wister, Lilacs for America, 59 [1942]; 39 [1953]; Caprice Farm Nursery Inventory system, A. Rogers, 05/07/84 - as 'Pink Princess'; ILS Newsletter 14(4):3-4 [1988]
Cultivar name presumed registered 1953; name established and accepted.

'**Prince Wolkonsky**', *S. vulgaris*
Bellion 1995; D V/IV
syn. - 'Prince Wolkousky'
{'Charles Joly' × 'Sensation'}
Minier, Les arbres on des idées [ca 1994]; Vrugtman, HortScience31(3):327 [1996]; Ahlers, Lilacs - Quart. Jour. 30(2): Back Cover ill. [2001]
Named for Prince Peter Wolkonsky, 1900(?)-1997, painter and horticulturist, creator of "Les Jardins de Kerdalo" in Trédarzec, northern Brittany, France.
Cultivar name registered 1995; name established and accepted.

'**Prinses Beatrix**', *S. vulgaris*
Maarsen, P. & G. 1938; S I
syn. - 'Princess Batrix'
Dijkhuis, Gedenkboek Valckenier Suringar, 128 [1942]; Wister, Lilacs for America, 40 [1953]; Photo on Jorgovani/Lilacs 2015 DVD.
Named for Princess Beatrix, 1938- x, daughter of Queen Juliana of The Netherlands.
Cultivar name presumed registered 1953; name established and accepted.

'Prinsessa Mathilde' *S. vulgaris*
origin not known pre-1902; S ?
Alnarps Trädgards Sortimentskatalog, p. 68 [1902]
Named (perhaps) for Mathilde Laetitia Wilhelmine Bonaparte, Princesse Française, 1820-1904
Cultivar name not established.

Printemps - see '**Le Printemps**'.

'**Prinzessin Klotilde**', *S. vulgaris*
origin not known pre-1923; S I
syn. - 'Princesse Clotilde'
Klettenberg, Cat. [1923] - as 'Princesse Clotilde'; Wister, Lilacs for America, 40 [1953] - as 'Prinzessin Klotilde'; Photo on Jorgovani/Lilacs 2015 DVD.
Cultivar name presumed registered 1953; name established and accepted.

Prinz Notger - see '**Prince Notger**'.

'**Priscilla**', *S. vulgaris*
Havemeyer 1944; S VI
syn. - 'Priscella'
Wister, Lilacs for America, 57 [1942], 40 [1953]; Kammerer, Morton Arb. Bull. Pop. Info. 36(6):27-29 [1961]; Eickhorst, ILS Lilac Newsletter 4(1):4-5 [1978]; Photo on Jorgovani/Lilacs 2015 DVD.
Named for Priscilla, grand-niece of T. A. & K. Havemeyer, sister of Carley (see 'Carley').
Cultivar name presumed registered 1953; name established and accepted.

'Privet Ot*chizne*', *S. vulgaris*
'Привет Отчизне'
Kolesnikov pre-1950; D II
Syn. - No 88
Polyakova, 2018, "Master of the Lilac Inflorescence", p. 116; cultivar passport
Polyakova, 2010, Istoriya Russkoĭ Sireni, p. 25; name only.
Name: Russian for Greetings to the Fatherland
Cultivar name not established.

'Priznanie', *S. vulgaris*
'признание'
Kolesnikov pre-1968; D III-IV
Syn. - No. 202
Polyakova, 2018, "Master of the Lilac Inflorescence", p. 114; cultivar passport
Name: Russian for Confession.
Cultivar name not established.

'**Prodige**', *S. vulgaris*
Lemoine 1928; S VII
syn. - 'Protege' or 'Protégé' (a misspelling)
Lemoine, Cat. No. 201 bis, 8 [1928]; McKelvey, The

Lilac, 561 [1928]; Wister, Lilacs for America, 57 [1942], 40 [1953]; Photo on Jorgovani/Lilacs 2015 DVD. Cultivar name presumed registered 1953; name established and accepted.

Prof. . . . - see also: Professor . . .

'Prof. Białobok', *S. vulgaris*
Karpow-Lipski 1961; D V
syn. - 'Prof. Bialobok'
Wister & Oppe, Arnoldia 31(3):126 [1971] - as 'Prof Bialobok'; Photo on Jorgovani/Lilacs 2015 DVD.
Named for Stefan Białobok, 1909-1992, director, 1945-1980, of the Institute for Dendrology, Kórnik, Poland.
Cultivar name registered 1970; name established and accepted.

'Prof. Burvenich', *S. vulgaris*
origin not known pre-1953; S V
Wister, Lilacs for America, 40 [1953]
Named for Lucas Frédéric Burvenich, 1857-1917, Belgian horticulturist, botanical author.
Cultivar name presumed registered 1953; Cultivar not reported in cultivation.

'Prof. Edmund Jankowski', *S. vulgaris*
Karpow-Lipski 1958; S III
syn. - 'Professor Edmund Jankowski', Siewka nr 6
Karpow-Lipski, Arboretum Kórnickie 3:102 [1958]; Wister & Oppe, Arnoldia 31(3):126 [1971]; Photo on Jorgovani/Lilacs 2015 DVD.
Named for Edmund Jankowski, 1849-1938, professor of horticulture at the Agricultural College of Warsaw, Poland.
Cultivar name registered 1970; name established and accepted.

'Prof. E. H. Wilson', *S. vulgaris*
Havemeyer 1943; D I
syn. - 'Professor E. H. Wilson'
Wister, Lilacs for America, 57 [1942], 40 [1953]; Eickhorst, ILS Lilac Newsletter 4(1):4-5 [1978]; Photo on Jorgovani/Lilacs 2015 DVD.
Named for Ernest Henry Wilson, 1876-1930, American botanist and plant explorer.
Cultivar name presumed registered 1953; name established and accepted.

'Profesor Dr Jos. Thomayer', *S. vulgaris*
Thomayer 1922; D VII
{parentage not known}
Thomayerovy Stromové Školky, Cat. p.38 [n.d.]
Named for Josef Thomayer, 1853-1927, physician and author, brother of the originator, Prague, Czechoslovakia.
Cultivar name not established; not reported in cultivation.

Professor . . . - see also: Prof. . . .

'Professor A. L. Lypa', *S. vulgaris*
'Профессор А. Л. Лыпа'
Tereshchenko 2002; D IV-V
{'Lavoisier' × ?}
Tereshchenko, Lilacs in the South-East of Ukraine, p. 112 [2002]; Chapman & Semyonova, Lilacs - Quart. Jour. 33(1):15 [2003] - translated from Tereshchenko, 2002
Named for Alexeï Lavrentievich Lypa, 1908-1991, botanist, plant breeder, professor at Kiev National University, Ukraine.
Statutory registration UANA [2002]; Cultivar name established and accepted.

'Professor E. Stöckhardt', *S. vulgaris*
Eichler 1862; S IV
syn. - 'Prof. B. Stockhart', 'Professor E. Stoekhardt', 'Professor Stockhard', 'Professeur Stoeckhardt'
Eichler, Garten-Nachr. 7:27 [1862] in Wochenschr. Ver. Beförd. Gartenb. Preuss. [1862]; Anon., Hamburger Garten- und Blumenzeitung 392-393 [1862]; Ellwanger & Barry, Cat., [1892] - as 'Prof. E. Stockhardt'; McKelvey, The Lilac, 370, 561 [1928]; Stand. Pl. Names, 617 [1942] - as Professor E. Stoekhardt (sic); Wister, Lilacs for America, 57 [1942] - as D II; Wister, Lilacs for America, 40 [1953]
Named for Julius Adolph Stöckhardt (Stoeckhardt), 1809-1886; chemist, agronomist, founder of smoke-pollution research; Forstakademie Tharandt, Saxony, Germany.
Cultivar name presumed registered 1953; name established and accepted.

Professor Hugo de Vries - see **'Hugo de Vries'**.

'Professor M. L. Reva', *S. vulgaris*
'Профессор М. Л. Рева'
Tereshchenko 2002; D IV-V
{'Lavoisier' × ?}
Tereshchenko, Lilacs in the South-East of Ukraine, p. 114-115, ill. back cover upper right [2002]; Chapman & Semyonova, Lilacs - Quart. Jour. 33(1):16 [2003] - translated from Tereshchenko, 2002
Named for Mikhaïl Lukich Reva, 1922-1997, botanist, ecologist, professor at Donetsk National University, Ukraine.
Varietal denomination registered UANA [2002]; Cultivar name established and accepted.

Professor R. B. Clark - see 'Professor Robert B. Clark'.

'Professor Robert B. Clark', *S. vulgaris*
Fiala 1983; S I-V
syn. - 'Professor R. B. Clark', 'Professor Robert Clark', 'Prof. Robert B. Clark'
{('Rochester' × 'Edward J. Gardner') × 'Rochester'}
Fiala, Lilacs, 92, 99, 100, 108, Pl. 81 [1988]
Named for Robert Brown Clark, 1914-2005, American botanist; founding member of the International Lilac Society.
Cultivar name established and accepted.

'Professor Sargent', *S. vulgaris*
Späth 1889; S VI
syn. - 'Prof. Sargent'
{chance seedling of unknown parentage}
Späth, Cat. No. 76, 3 [1889]; McKelvey, The Lilac, 370 [1928]; Späth, Späth-Buch, 110, 305 [1930]; Wister, Lilacs for America, 57 [1942], 40 [1953]; Photo on Jorgovani/Lilacs 2015 DVD.
Named for Charles Sprague Sargent, 1841-1927, American botanist and author, founder of the Arnold Arboretum of Harvard University.
Cultivar name presumed registered 1953; name established and accepted.

'Professor V. I. Chopik', *S.*
Tereshchenko pre-2007; S IV
{'Bogdan Khmel'nitskii' × ?}
Tereshchenko S. "A souvenir from Donetsk", article in the magazine "Vestnik Tsvetovoda" №10 (78), 2007
Named after a Professor of Botany at Kiev National University.
Cultivar name established and accepted.

'Prof. Hoser', *S. vulgaris*
Hoser pre-1930; D III
syn. - 'Hoser', 'Professor Hoser', 'Prof. P. Hoser'
{'Dame Blanche' (D I) + 'Président Poincaré' (D VI); claimed to be a graft chimera}
Hoser, Gartenbauwissenschaft 8:451-454 [1934] - in German; Wister & Oppe, Arnoldia 31(3):126 [1971]; Bugała, Drzewa i Krzewy, 518 [1979] - in Polish; Photo on Jorgovani/Lilacs 2015 DVD - plant incorrectly labelled.
Named for Peter Hoser, 1857-1939, Polish horticulturist and nurseryman.
Note: Plants seen and reported all have double, blue florets; so far no evidence reported of a graft chimera with double, white and double, magenta florets.
Cultivar name registered 1970; name established and accepted.

'Prof. Jósef Brzeziński', *S. vulgaris*
Karpow-Lipski 1938; D V
syn. - 'Professor Jósef Brzeziński', 'Professor Josef Brzezinski', 'Prof. Josef Brzezinski', Prof. Joseph Brzezinski', Siewka nr 146
Karpow-Lipski, Arboretum Kórnickie 3:105, 108 [1958]; Wister & Oppe, Arnoldia 31(3):126 [1971] - as 'Prof. Josef Brzezinski'; Photo on Jorgovani/Lilacs 2015 DVD.
Named for Jósef Brzeziński, 1862-1939, professor of horticulture and botany, Jagiellone University, Cracow, Poland.
Cultivar name registered 1970; name established and accepted.

Prof. P. Hoser - see **'Prof. Hoser'**.

'Prof. Roman Kobendza', *S. vulgaris*
Karpow-Lipski 1958; D IV
syn. - Siewka nr 18
Karpow-Lipski, Arboretum Kórnickie 3:108 [1958]; Wister & Oppe, Arnoldia 31(3):126 [1971]
Named for Roman Kobendza, 1886-1955, professor of dendrology, Agricultural College, Warsaw, Poland.
Cultivar name registered 1970; name established and accepted.

Progress - see **'Le Progrès'**.

'Prokhorovka', *S. vulgaris*
'Прохоровка'
Aladin, S., Aladina, O., Polyakova, T., and, Aladina, A. 2018; S II
{'Gilbert' × OP}
IX International Scientific Conference (IX Международная научная конференция "Цветоводство: история, теория, практика") " Floriculture: history, theory, practice" , St. Petersburg, Botanical Garden of Peter the Great BIN RAS, September 7-13, 2019 :... (in Russian); II All-Russian scientific-practical conference with international participation (II Всероссийская научно-практическая конференция с международным участием) " Botanical Gardens in the XXI Century: Biodiversity Conservation, Development Strategy and Innovative Solutions, Belgorod, Botanical Garden of NRU "BelSU", September 23-26, 2019; pp.141-145 (in Russian).
Named for the Prokhorovsky field (Прохоровское поле) in the Belgorod region, where during the World War II one of the largest tank battles in military history took place.
Cultivar name established and accepted.

'Prophecy', *S. tomentella* subsp. *yunnanensis*
Fiala 1969; S II
{*S. tomentella* subsp. *yunnanensis* × *S. tomentella* subsp. *yunnanensis*}
Fiala, Lilacs, 81, 224, Pl. 57 [1988] - as induced tetraploid; Photo on Jorgovani/Lilacs 2015 DVD.
Cultivar name established and accepted.

'Proshchanie Slavyanki', *S. vulgaris*
'Прощание славянки'
Aladin, S., Aladina, O., and Polyakova, T. 2016; S IV
{'Mechta' × OP}
Садовник (Gardener) magazine, 05 (141)/2017 :16-22; Вестник АППМ (Catalog in Vestnik APPM (Planting material association) magazine) 1/2018: 59-72 (in Russian).
Named for the Russian march "Farewell to the Slavs"; dedicated to all Slavic women.
Cultivar name established and accepted.

Protege - a misspelling; see entries under 'Yankee Doodle'.

Pubescens - see *S. pubescens* Turcz.

'Puck', *S.* (Villosae Group), *S.* ×*prestoniae*
Preston 1942; S VI
{parentage not known}
Wister, Lilacs for America, 57, 64 [1942], 40, 48 [1953]

Named for A Fairy in Shakespeare's *Midsummer Night's Dream*.
Cultivar name presumed registered 1953; name established and accepted.

'Pulverulenta tricolor', *S. vulgaris*
Baudriller pre-1889; ? ?
Späth, Cat. No. 76, 123 [1889]; McKelvey, The Lilac, 370 [1928]; Wister, Lilacs for America, 37, 57 [1942], 40 [1953].
Cultivar name not established.

'Puritan', *S. vulgaris*
origin not known pre-1963; ? ?
Reported at Jermyns Lane Arb. of Hillier Nurs. Ltd and at the Arnold Arboretum
Cultivar name not established.

'Purple Balloon', *S. pubescens*
Ihara 2020; S VII
Floret RHS 70B, Bud RHS 72A
{*S. pubescens* subsp. *pubescens* 'Kaoridama' × seedling no. 20100615#1 (*S. pubescens* subsp. *pubescens* 'Palibin' × *S. pubescens* subsp. *microphylla* 'Superba')}
Syn. – seedling no. 2014S120114#4, 'Shigyoku'
Registration submitted 2/7/21.
Cultivar name registered, established and accepted.

'Purple Gem', *S.* ×*hyacinthiflora*
Clarke 1960; S VII
Clarke, Cat., 43 [1960]; Wister, Arnoldia 23(4):82 [1963]
Cultivar name registered 1963; name established and accepted.

'Purple Glory', *S.* ×*hyacinthiflora*
Clarke 1948; S VII
{unknown double lilac × ? }
Clarke, Cat. 16:8 [1949]; Woody Plant Register, AAN, No. 143 [1949]; Clarke, US Pl. Pat. No. 946 [June 13, 1950] - as S. vulgaris; Wister, Lilacs for America, 40 [1953] - as "Early Hybrid of giraldi"; Photo on Jorgovani/Lilacs 2015 DVD.
Cultivar name presumed registered 1953; name established and accepted.

'Purple Haze', *S.*
Alexander III 2005; S VII
{*S. protolaciniata* × *S. oblata* subsp. *dilatata*}
Vrugtman, HortScience 40(6):1597 [2005]; Photo on Jorgovani/Lilacs 2015 DVD.
Named in memory of a song by that name and the artist, Jimi Hendrix, 1942-1970.
Cultivar name registered 2003; name established and accepted.

'Purple Heart', *S.* ×*hyacinthiflora*
Clarke 1948; S VII
{cross between unnamed seedlings}
AAN reg'n card No. 517; Clarke, Cat. 16:9 [1949]; Clarke, US Pl. Pat. No. 832 [April 12, 1949] - as S. vulgaris; Wister, Lilacs for America, 40 [1953]
Cultivar name presumed registered 1953; name established and accepted.

Purple Mystery, *S. vulgaris*
origin not known; D VII
Peterson, Lilacs - Proceedings 16(1):22 [1987]; Vrugtman, Lilacs - Quart. Jour. 32(4):149 [2003] - as D VII; most likely a named cultivar that lost its label.
Cognomen; not a cultivar name.

Purple Splendour - see **'Splendor'**.

purpurea (*S. vulgaris*), Purpurea - see **'Marlyensis'**.

'Purpurea duplex', *S.* ×*chinensis*
Henry, L.; D VII
{*S. persica* var. *laciniata* × ? }
Henry, Jour. Soc. Hort. France, ser. 4, 2:748 [1901]; McKelvey, The Lilac, 427 [1928]
Cultivar name not established; probably never introduced.

'Purpurea Grandiflora', *S. vulgaris*
origin not known pre-1841; ? ?
Oudin, Cat., 22 [1841]; McKelvey, The Lilac, 371 [1928]
Cultivar name not established.

'Purpurea Plena', *S. vulgaris*
origin not known pre-1846; D VII
Oudin, Cat. 11 [1846]; McKelvey, The Lilac, 371 [1928].

'Purpurea Rubra', *S. vulgaris*
origin not known pre-1885; ? ?
Dieck, Haupt-Cat. Zöschen, 78 [1885]; McKelvey, The Lilac, 371 [1928]
Cultivar name not established.

'P<u>ya</u>tides<u>ya</u>tiletie Okt<u>ya</u>br<u>ya</u>', *S. vulgaris*
'Пятидесятилетие Октября'
Kolesnikov & Mironovi<u>ch</u> 1986; S II/V
syn. - 'Pjatidesjatiletije Oktjabrja', 'Pyatidesyatiletij Oktjabrya', 'Pyatidesyatiletije Oktjabrya', 50-LETIE OKT<u>YA</u>BR<u>YA</u>
Pikaleva, Lilacs - Quart. Jour. 23(4):87; Novikov & Pikaleva, Lilacs - Quart. Jour.23(4):91 [1994]; Registered with the State Commission of the Russian Federation for Testing and Protection of Selection Achievements, No. 8803552, 1998; Polyakova, 2010, Istoriya Russkoĭ Sireni, p. 117; Photo on Jorgovani/Lilacs 2015 DVD.
Named for the fiftieth anniversary of the Red October Revolution 1917.
Cultivar name established and accepted.

'Pyramidal', *S. vulgaris*
Lemoine 1886; D IV
syn. - *pyramidalis*, 'Pyramidalis'
common name: Pyramidal
Lemoine, Cat. No. 104, 8 [1886]; Stand. Pl. Names, 487 [1923] - as Pyramidal; McKelvey, The Lilac, 371 [1928]; Wister, Lilacs for America, 57 [1942], 40 [1953]; Photo

on Jorgovani/Lilacs 2015 DVD.
Cultivar name presumed registered 1953; name established and accepted.

'Pyramidalis Alba', *S. vulgaris*
origin not known pre-1845; S I
syn. - 'Blanc Pyramidal', 'Alba Pyramidalis', *pyramidalis alba*
Oudin, Cat., 6 [1845]; McKelvey, The Lilac, 372 [1928]; Wister, Lilacs for America, 57 [1942], 40 [1953]; Photo on Jorgovani/Lilacs 2015 DVD.
Cultivar name presumed registered 1953; name established and accepted.

'Quadricolor', *S. vulgaris*
Behnsch pre-1890; S IV *
Späth, Cat. No. 76, 123 [1889]; McKelvey, The Lilac, 372 [1928]; Wister, Lilacs for America, 57 [1942], 40 [1953]; Photo on Jorgovani/Lilacs 2015 DVD.
Cultivar name presumed registered 1953; name established and accepted.

'Quartet', *S.* (Villosae Group)
Fiala 1984; S V
{(*S. tomentella* subsp. *sweginzowii* × *S. tomentella* subsp. *tomentella*) × (*S. komarowii* subsp. *komarowii* × *S. villosa* subsp. *wolfii*)}
Fiala, Lilacs, 102, 224, Pl. 56 [1988]
Cultivar name established and accepted.

'Queen Anne', *S. vulgaris*
Pillow 1926; S I
Wister, Lilacs for America, 57 [1942], 40 [1953]
Named for Anne, 1665-1714, daughter of James II and Anne Hyde, queen of England 1702-1714.
Cultivar name presumed registered 1953; name established and accepted.

'Queen Elizabeth', *S. vulgaris*
Paterson 1939; S III
The Evening Telegram [June 6, 1939]
Named for The Honourable Elizabeth Angela Marguerite Bowes-Lyon, 1900-2002, Duchess of York, 1922, Queen Elizabeth 1936, The Queen Mother 1952.
Cultivar name established and accepted.

Queen of the Netherlands - see 'Reine des Pays-Bas'.

'Queen Victoria', *S. vulgaris*
Dougall, 1874; ? III-VII & I
Windsor Nurseries, Cat. [1874]; Dougall, Canadian Horticulturist 2(1):8 [1879]
Named for Alexandrina Victoria, 1819-1901, queen of the United Kingdom of Great Britain and Ireland, and empress of India.
Cultivar name not established; not reported in cultivation; probably extinct.

'Rå', *S. josikaea*
Horntvedt; S II/III
syn. - klon 318
Lønø, Norsk Hagetident, 7-8/85, pp. 395-397 [1985]; Kjær, Gartneryrket (G.Y.) 1987:274; Bjerkestrand & Sandved, Grøntanleggsplanter utvalgt for norske forhold 1986-1987-1988 [1989] pp. 25-26 & ill. p. 16; Vrugtman, Lilacs - Quart. Jour 25(2):41-42 [1996].
Cultivar name established and accepted.

'Rabbit's Eyes', *S. pubescens* subsp. *microphylla*
Ihara 2003; S VII
{*S. pubescens* subsp. *microphylla* 'Superba' × *S. pubescens* subsp. *microphylla* 'Superba'} Seedling number 20040520002#3.
(Vrugtman, Cultivated Plant Diversity ... 2017)
Cultivar name registered, name established and accepted.

'Rabelais', *S. vulgaris*
Lemoine 1896; D I
Lemoine, Cat. No. 134, 15 [1896]; McKelvey, The Lilac, 372 [1928]; Wister, Lilacs for America, 57 [1942], 40 [1953]
Named for François Rabelais, ca 1494-1553, French satirist-humorist.
Cultivar name presumed registered 1953; name established and accepted.

'Radiance', *S. vulgaris*
Fiala 1985; D V
{'Rochester' × 'Elsie Lenore'}
Fiala, Lilacs, 100, 223 [1988]
Cultivar name established and accepted.

'Radmila', *S. vulgaris*
'Радмила'
Aladin, S., Aladina, O., Polyakova, T., and Aladina A. 2016; D V
{elite form 09-119 × OP}
Садовник (Gardener) magazine 04 (140)/2017 :18-25; Вестник АППМ (Catalog in Vestnik APPM (Planting material association) magazine) 1/2018: 59-72 (in Russian).
Named for Radmila Tonkovic (1957-), Serbian military pilot, aviation journalist, editor, writer and publicist, Doctor of philology, professor.
Cultivar name established and accepted.

'Radost", *S. vulgaris*
'Радость'
Sagitova; ? ?
{'Miriam' × ? }
Name: Russian for joy.
Cultivar name not established.

'Radostnaya', *S. vulgaris*
'Радостная'
Kravchenko; S V
{'Andenken an Ludwig Späth' × OP}
Kravchenko L. Culture of lilacs in Uzbekistan. Publishing house "Uzbekistan", Tashkent, 1970 p. 11

Rubtzov et al. 1980. Vidy i sorta sireni, kul'tiviruemye v SSSR. Kiev; Naukova Dumka. – in Russian; Holetich, C.D. 1982. Lilac species and cultivars in cultivation in USSR. Lilacs 11(2):1-38. - translation of Rubtzov et al. 1982.
Name means Joyful in Russian.
Cultivar name established and accepted.

'Radost' Pobedy', *S. vulgaris*
'Радость Победы'
Klimenko, V.&Z., & Grigor'ev 1955; S V/VII
Rubtzov et al. 1980. Vidy i sorta sireni, kul'tiviruemye v SSSR. Kiev; Naukova Dumka. – in Russian; Holetich, C.D. 1982. Lilac species and cultivars in cultivation in USSR. Lilacs 11(2):1-38. - translation of Rubtzov et al. 1982.
Name: Russian for the joy of victory.
Cultivar name established and accepted.

'Radzh Kapur', *S. vulgaris*
'Радж Капур'
Kolesnikov 1955; S IV-VI
{'Indiya' × 'Pioner'}
syn. - 'Brodyaga', Kolesnikov No. 745, 'Radzh Kapur', 'Rag Kapoor', 'Raj Kapur', 'Raj Kapoor'
Bilov, V. D., et al, Siren', 73 [1974] - in Russian; Gromov, Lilacs - Proceedings 2(4):17 [1974]; Rubtzov et al. 1980. Vidy i sorta sireni, kul'tiviruemye v SSSR. Kiev; Naukova Dumka. – in Russian; Holetich, C.D. 1982. Lilac species and cultivars in cultivation in USSR. Lilacs 11(2):1-38. - translation of Rubtzov et al. 1982; Pikaleva, Lilacs - Quart. Jour. 23(4):84 [1994] - as 'Brodyaga' (Russian for vagrant); Photo on Jorgovani/Lilacs 2015 DVD.
Named for Raj Kapoor, 1924-1988, legendary Indian actor, producer and director of Bollywood movies, which also became popular in Russia.
Cultivar name established and accepted.

RAF 162, *S.*
Fenicchia 1970; S VII
Photo by Mary and Diane Meyer at Highland Park, Rochester NY seen in 2020 ILS Photo & Color Database.
Breeder's designation, not a cultivar name.

RAF 219 (R83), *S.*
Fenicchia 1970; D II
Photo by Mary and Diane Meyer at Highland Park, Rochester NY seen in 2020 ILS Photo & Color Database.
Breeder's designation, not a cultivar name.

Rag Kapoor - see 'Radzh Kapur'.

'Raimonds Bočs', *S. vulgaris*
Upītis 1972; S VII
Photo seen from Dobele, Latvia by Natalia Savenko in 2020 ILS Lilac Photo Database.
Cultivar name not established.

'Rajah', *S. vulgaris*
Mezitt, R.W. 1991; S VI
{'Sensation' × ? }
Ornamental Plants plus Version 2.0, 01/01/98, Mich. State Univ. www.msue.msu.edu/msue/imp/modop/00001423.html; Weston Nurseries, Cat., 135 [1998]
Cultivar name established and accepted.

Raj Kapur - see 'Radzh Kapur'.

'Ralph', *S. vulgaris*
Rankin pre-1988; S IV
{parentage not known}
Fiala, Lilacs, 208 [1988]
Cultivar name established and accepted.

Ralph's Dwarf - see 'Elsdancer'
Cognomen used at Beaver Creek Nursery <http://www.beavercreeknursery.com/plantdetails.cfm?ID=824>

'Ralph W. Stone', *S. vulgaris*
Stone 1971; S VII
Wister & Oppe, Arnoldia 31(3):123 [1971]
Cultivar name registered 1970; name established and accepted; probably extinct.

'Ramona', *S.* ×*hyacinthiflora*
Erickson & Waines; S VII
syn: 'Ramone', 'Romona'
{'Pocahontas' × ?}
Waines, Lilacs - Quart. Jour. 26(3):80 [1997] - name only as 'Romona'; Waines, Lilacs - Quart. Jour. 34(2):49 [2005] - a tentatively named selection; Ann Platzer, UCRBG 32(3):3 [Fall 2012]; 2016 ILS lilac auction record - as 'Ramone'.
Named for Helen Hunt Jackson's novel *Ramona*, and the community of Ramona in San Diego County, California, USA.
Nota bene: Not to be confused with Ramona lilac or wooly-leaf mountain lilac, common names for *Ceanothus tomentosus* native to California)
Cultivar name established and accepted.

'R. and B. Mills', *S. vulgaris*
Klager; S VII
Anon., ILS Newsletter 14(4):3-4 [1988]
Named for Roland Robert Mills (b. 1911, son of RW Mills and Elizabeth Klager) and either Betty Mills, grandchildren of Hulda Klager, or William Klager Mills (b. 1909, son of RW Mills and Elizabeth Klager).
Cultivar name established and accepted.

'Rapsodija', *S. vulgaris*
Kārkliņš 2003; D VII/II
under evaluation at Latvia State Institute of Fruit Growing, Dobele
Photo on Jorgovani/Lilacs 2015 DVD.
Name: Latvian for rhapsody.
Cultivar name not established.

'Rassvet', *S. vulgaris*
　'Рассвет'
　Mel'nik, Rubanik & Dyagilev pre-1994; S II
　Pikaleva, Lilacs - Quart. Jour. 23(4):87 [1994]
　Name: Russian for dawn or daybreak.
　Cultivar name established and accepted.

'Rauno', *S.* ×*hyacinthiflora*
　Vaigla pre-2001; S V/IV (V-III per Semenov)
　listed on http://aed.rapina.ee/sirelid.htm [seen 5 Nov. 2005]; I. Semenov, Lilacs 48(2):65 [2019].
　Cultivar name not established.

'Ray Baker', *S. vulgaris*
　Baker pre-1988; ? ?
　Reported in R. B. Clark's collection in 1988 (D VII ?)
　Cultivar name not established.

'Ray Halward', *S. vulgaris*
　Margaretten; S IV
　{'Mme Lemoine' × ? }
　Named for Ray Halward, 1917-1989, plant propagator at Royal Botanical Gardens, Ontario, Canada. Reported in cultivation at University of Utah, USA
　Cultivar name established and accepted.

'R. B. Mylls', *S. vulgaris*
　Origin not known; S V
　Reported in the Hulda Klager Lilac Garden Society collection in 1999
　(probably identical to 'R and B. Mills')
　Cultivar name not established.

'**Réaumur**', *S. vulgaris*
　Lemoine 1904; S VI
　syn. - 'Reamur', 'Reaumur'
　Lemoine, Cat. No. 158, 8 [1904]; McKelvey, The Lilac, 372-373 [1928]; Wister, Lilacs for America, 57 [1942], 40 [1953]; Photo on Jorgovani/Lilacs 2015 DVD.
　Named for René Antoine Fercault de Réaumur, 1683-1757, French physicist.
　Cultivar name presumed registered 1953; name established and accepted.

Redbird or Red Bird - see '**Redbud**'.

'**Redbud**', *S. vulgaris*
　Robinson 1959; S VI
　syn. - 'Redbird', 'Red Bird', Red Bud'
　{'Mme F. Morel' × ? }
　Wister, Arbor. Bot. Gard. Bull. 1(2):20 [1967]; Photo on Jorgovani/Lilacs 2015 DVD.
　Cultivar name registered 1967; name established and accepted.

'**Red Feather**', *S. vulgaris*
　Ruliffson 1953; D VI
　{mutation of 'Léon Simon'}
　Wister, Lilacs for America, 40 [1953]
　Cultivar name presumed registered 1953; name established and accepted.

'Red Giant', *S. vulgaris*
　Sass, H. E. & Peterson; S VI
　Peterson, Lilacs - proceedings 16(1):22 [1987] - name only; Photo on Jorgovani/Lilacs 2015 DVD.
　Cultivar name established and accepted.

Red Guide - see '**Rubra Insignis**'.

'Red Holger', *S. josikaea*
　origin not known pre-2016, S VI?
　{sport of 'Holger' ?}
　<http://www.esveld.nl/zoeken.php?zoekterm=syringa&product=planten&pagina=2>
　seen 8 Feb. 2917
　Cultivar name not established and accepted.

red Hungarian lilac - see '**Rubra**' (*S. josikaea*).

'Red Lavender', *S.* ×*hyacinthiflora*
　Wallace 1971; S VI
　　Beaverlodge Nursery, Cat., 22 [1971]
　Cultivar name established and accepted.

red Persian lilac - see '**Rubra**' (*S.* ×*persica*).

'Red Pixie', S.
　Peterson ca 1987; S VI-V
　{parentage uncertain; perhaps open pollinated S. pubescens subsp. microphylla 'Hers'; ♂ perhaps S. pubescens subsp. Pubescens; 1 of 8 seedlings of 'Hers' } (not related to S. vulgaris 'Pixie', Fiala 1981)
　Peterson, Lilacs - Proceedings 16(1):25 [1987] - name only; Select Plus International, Cat. Spring 2002 <http://spi.8m.com/products.htm> [April 2002] - as S. julianae 'Red Pixie', dark reddish-purple fading to pale pink; Song Sparrow Nursery, Cat. 52 [2004]; Anon., Lilacs - Quart. Jour. 33(1):11 [2004]; Photo on Jorgovani/Lilacs 2015 DVD.
　Cultivar name established and accepted.

red rose lilac - see '**Eximia**' (Villosae Group).

'Red Rothomagensis', *S.* ×*chinensis*
　Baldwin pre-1934; S VII
　Hopp & Blair, Vermont Agric. Exp. Stn. Bull. No. 677 [1973]; Photo on Jorgovani/Lilacs 2015 DVD.
　Cultivar name established and accepted.
　Nota bene: 'Red Rothomagensis' is a clone propagated and distributed in North America exclusively for use at phenological observation stations; it is not identical to 'Saugeana'. Anon. (Clark), ILS Pipeline 3(5):4-5 [May 1977]; Vrugtman, ILS Pipeline 3(5):6-7 [May 1977]; Marsolais, Pringle & White, Taxon 42:531-537 [1993] - as genetically distinguishable from *S.* ×*chinensis* 'Saugeana'.

'**Redwine**', *S.* (Villosae Group)
　Preston & Leslie 1936; S VI
　{parentage not known}
　syn. - 'Red Wine'

Wister, Lilacs for America, 57 [1942], 40 [1953] - as ×prestoniae; Buckley, Greenhouse-Garden-Grass 8(3):4 [1969] - as ×prestoniae; Cumming, ASHS Ann. Rep. Ornam. Pl. Breeders, 7[1973] - as ×josiflexa; Cumming, Agric. Canada Public. 1628, 17 [1977] - as introduced in 1936; Fiala, Lilacs, 79, 203 & 217 [1988] - on pp. 79 & 203 as ×prestoniae; Photo on Jorgovani/Lilacs 2015 DVD.
Cultivar name presumed registered 1953; name established and accepted.

reflexa pallens - see '**Pallens**' (Villosae Group).

'**Regan**', *S.* (Villosae Group), *S.* ×*prestoniae*
Preston 1928; S V
syn. - Preston No. 20-14-251
{*S. villosa* subsp. *villosa* × *S. komarowii* subsp. *reflexa*}
Macoun, Rep. Dom. Hort. 1928, 57 [1930]; Wister, Lilacs for America, 57, 64 [1942], 40, 48 [1953]; Photo on Jorgovani/Lilacs 2015 DVD.
Named for the Daughter to King Lear in Shakespeare's *King Lear*.
Cultivar name presumed registered 1953; name established and accepted.

REGENT® - see 'PNI 7523'

'**Regia**', *S. vulgaris*
origin not known pre-1885; ? ?
Dieck, Haupt-Cat. Zöschen, 78 [1885]; McKelvey, The Lilac, 373 [1928] - confused name
Cultivar name not established.

'**Reine Astrid**', *S. vulgaris*
Klettenberg 1935; S V
Klettenberg, Cat., 26 [1935]; Wister, Lilacs for America, 40 [1953]
Named for Astrid Sophie Louise Thyra, 1905-1935, daughter of prince Charles of Sweden, wife to Crown Prince Léopold, 1926, queen of Belgium, 1930-1935.
Cultivar name presumed registered 1953; name established and accepted.

'Reine des Pays-Bas', *S. vulgaris*
Legraye (?) pre-1874; S I
C.J.E. Morren, Belg. Hort. 24:176 [1874]; McKelvey, The Lilac, 373 [1928] - perhaps identical with and an earlier name for 'Marie Legraye'.
Named for Queen Sophie (von Würtemberg), 1818-1877, wife to King Willem III of The Netherlands.
Cultivar name not established; not reported in cultivation.

'**Reine Elisabeth**', *S. vulgaris*
Stepman-Demessemaeker 1909; S I
syn. - 'Reine Elizabeth'
Fl. Stepman-Demessemaeker, Suppl. Gen. Cat., 1 [1909]; McKelvey, The Lilac, 373 [1928]; Wister, Lilacs for America, 57 [1942], 40 [1953]; Photo on Jorgovani/Lilacs 2015 DVD.
Named for Duchess Elisabeth Gabrielle Valérie Marie, 1876-1965, wife of Albert I, king of Belgium.
Cultivar name presumed registered 1953; name established and accepted.

'**Reine Marguerite**', *S. vulgaris*
origin not known pre-1897; D V
McKelvey, The Lilac, 373 [1928]; Wister, Lilacs for America, 57 [1942], 40 [1953]; Photo on Jorgovani/Lilacs 2015 DVD.
Named, perhaps, for Reine Marguerite de Bourgogne de Navarre, 1293-1315.
Cultivar name presumed registered 1953; name established and accepted.

'**Reine Marie-Henriette**', *S. vulgaris*
origin not known pre-1923; S ?
Klettenberg, Cat. [1923].
Named for Marie Henriette Anne, 1836-1902, Archduchess of Austria, wife to Léopold II, king of Belgium.
Cultivar name not established; not reported in cultivation.

Remarquable - see 'Spectabilis'.

'Renee', *S. vulgaris*
Mezitt, R.W. 1991; S V-VII
{'Sensation' × ? }
Weston Nurseries, Cat. [1991]
Cultivar name established and accepted.

'**René Jarry-Desloges**', *S. vulgaris*
Lemoine 1905; D III
syn. - 'Renatus Jarry-Desloges', 'Rene Jarry Desloges'
Lemoine, Cat. No. 161, 8 [1905]; McKelvey, The Lilac, 373-374 [1028]; Wister, Lilacs for America, 57 [1942], 40 [1953]; Photo on Jorgovani/Lilacs 2015 DVD.
Named for René Jarry-Desloges, 1868-1951, astronomer and amateur horticulturist of Menton-Garavan, France.
Cultivar name presumed registered 1953; name established and accepted.

'**Renoncule**', *S. vulgaris*
Lemoine 1881; D IV
syn. - 'Ranunculiflora'
Lemoine, Cat. No. 89, 6 [1881]; McKelvey, The Lilac, 374 [1928]; Wister, Lilacs for America, 57 [1942], 40 [1953]; Photo on Jorgovani/Lilacs 2015 DVD.
Name: French for *Ranunculus* or buttercup.
Cultivar name presumed registered 1953; name established and accepted.

'**Renovation**', *S. vulgaris*
Klettenberg 1934; S VI
Klettenberg, Cat., 21 [1934]; Wister, Lilacs for America, 40 [1953]
Cultivar name presumed registered 1953; name established and accepted.

'Reva Ballreich' (Margaretten, not Peterson) - see **'Lilac Lady'**.

'Reva Ballreich', *S. vulgaris*
  Peterson 1988 (not Margaretten); D V
  {'Carolyn Mae' × ? ; sibling seedling to 'Pink Diamond'}
  Ballreich, Lilacs - Quart. Jour. 28(4):91 & ill. back cover [1999]; Vrugtman, HortScience 35(4):549 [2000]
  Named for Reva Ballreich, 1925-2009, president of the International Lilac Society 1992-1997.
  Cultivar name registered 1999; name established and accepted.

RÊVE BLEU™ - see 'Delreb'.

'Rhapsody', *S. vulgaris*
  Fiala 1983; S III
  {'Rochester' × 'Mrs A. Belmont'}
  Fiala, Lilacs, 98, 223 [1988]
  Cultivar name established and accepted.

'Rhodopea', *S. vulgaris* - see *S. rhodopea*
  Velen., included in *S. vulgaris* L.; S IV
  McKelvey, The Lilac, 217 [1928] - as collected by Stŕbrný in the Rhodope Mountains in 1900 and cultivated at the botanical garden at Prague; Wister, Lilacs for America, 57 [1942], 40 [1953]; Pringle, Lilacs - Quart. Jour. 19(4):75-80 [1990] - sometimes recognized as a *S. vulgaris* cultivar, but not a uniform clone
  Cultivar name not established.

'Richard A. Fenicchia', *S. vulgaris*
  Fenicchia 1997; D VII
  syn. - 'Richard Fenicchia', R-83
  {parentage not known}
  Vrugtman, HortScience 33(4):588-589 [1998]; Hoepfl, Lilacs - Quart. Jour. 30(2): Front Cover ill. [2001]; K. Millham, Lilacs - Quart. Jour. 42(2):61 & ill. 71 [2013].
  Named for Richard Americo Fenicchia, 1908-1997, American horticulturist.
  Cultivar name registered 1997; name established and accepted.

'Riet Bruidegom', *S. vulgaris*
  Eveleens Maarse 1950; S I
  {'Reine Elisabeth' × 'Mme Florent Stepman'}
  Wister, Lilacs for America, 40 [1953]; Eveleens Maarse, Dendron 1(1):12 [1954]; Photo on Jorgovani/Lilacs 2015 DVD.
  Awards: Certificate of Merit 1950 (KMTP).
  Cultivar name presumed registered 1953; name established and accepted.

'Rio-Rita', *S. vulgaris*
  'Рио-Рита'
  Aladin, S., Aladina, O., Polyakova, T.,and Aladina, A. 2015; S IV
  {'elite form 10-401' × OP}
  Садовник (Gardener) magazine, 05 (141)/2017 :16-22; Вестник АППМ (Catalog in Vestnik АРРМ (Planting material association) magazine) 1/2018:

59-72 (in Russian); International scientific and practical conference (Международная и практическая конференция) «International Syringa 2018», Moscow, Moscow State University Botanical Garden, St. Petersburg, Botanical Garden of Peter the Great BIN RAS, Pavlovsk, May 21-27, 2018; pp. 43-47 (in Russian)
  Named for the 1930's pop paso doble "For You, Rio-Rita".
  Cultivar name established and accepted.

'Rising Sun', *S. pekinensis*
  Skogerboe; S I
  {seedling; original tree at Valley Nursery, Helena, Montana}
  reported at Fort Collins Wholesale Nursery <www.ftcollinswholesalenursery.com>
  Cultivar name not established.

'Ritoniemi', *S. vulgaris*
  origin not known ca 2001; S VI
  distributed by Wickmans Plantskola http://www.tawi.fi/~wiplant/uddamod.html [Apr.3/01] - name only
  Cultivar name not established.

Reka Bordeaux – a working seedling name later changed, fate unknown.

'R. M. Mills', *S. vulgaris*
  Klager; D V
  Fiala, Lilacs, 200 [1988] - listed erroneously as identical to 'Roland Mills', which has been described as S VII
  Cultivar name not established.

'Robert Dunham', *S. vulgaris*
  Rankin; S IV
  {parentage not known}
  Wister, Arnoldia 23(4):82 [1963]
  Cultivar name registered 1963;
  Cultivar not reported in cultivation.

'Robert Hagie', *S. vulgaris*
  origin not known ? ?
  listed by Pieter Zwijnenburg Jr, Boskoop, NL, <www.kwekerijen.net/planten/index.cfm?fuseaction=detail&plt_id=43192&omschr=Syringa vulgaris 'Robert Hagie'>
  Cultivar name not established.

Robusta - see **'Robuste Albert'**.

'Robuste Albert', *S. vulgaris*
  Maarse Hzn & Keessen.
  syn. - A1, 'Robusta'
  {a rootstock selection made in the 1930s at the Fa Eveleens & Maarse}
  Sytsema, Proefbschrijving [1990]; Rijsewijk, Boomkwekerij 45/1994:24-25; Deutsche Baumschule 7/1995, 321 - clonal rootstock selected for ease of propagation by tissue culture; varietal denomination registered with Raad voor het Kwekersrecht, The Netherlands, NRR No. 17652, 04-12-1997 (PBR by Eveleesns en Maarse, but terminated 01-07-2003, and

company deregistered).
Cultivar name established and accepted; probably no longer in cultivation (2016).

'**Rochambeau**', *S. vulgaris*
Lemoine 1919; S VII
Lemoine, Cat. No. 193, 22 [1919]; McKelvey, The Lilac, 374-375 [1928]; Wister, Lilacs for America, 57 [1942], 40 [1953]; Photo on Jorgovani/Lilacs 2015 DVD.
Named for Jean Baptiste Donatien de Vimeur, Comte de Rochambeau, 1715-1807, French soldier and marshal of France.
Cultivar name presumed registered 1953; name established and accepted.

'**Rochester**', *S. vulgaris*
Grant 1971; S I
{'Edith Cavell' × ? }
Wister, Lilac Registration (mimeogr. suppl.), p. 4 [ca 1967] - as "registered 1965"; Wister & Oppe, Arnoldia 31(3):123 [1971] - correction; Clark, Arnoldia 32(3):133-135 [1971]; Fiala, Lilacs, 92, Pl. 6 [1988]; Grant, Lilacs - Quart. Jour. 22(2):front cover ill. & 29 [1993]; Millham, Lilacs - Quart. Jour. 42(4):130 [2013]; Photo on Jorgovani/Lilacs 2015 DVD.
Named 1963 for the city of Rochester, New York, USA.
Cultivar name registered 1965; name established and accepted.
Nota bene: One report of plants not true to name, florets blue with white margins, marketed in the USA; 09 August 2015. Also, tested for tetraploidy and found to be diploid by Ryan Contreras at Oregon State University 2019.

ROCHESTER 99, *S. vulgaris*
de Belder; ? ?
{seedling of 'Rochester'}
Belgische Dendrologie 1994, p. 191 - name only, listed as seed-parent of 'Slava'; in litt. X. Misonne to D. De Meyere, [January 12, 2004].
Breeder's designation, not a cultivar name.

ROCHESTER STRAIN; *S. vulgaris*
Anon. (Clark, R. B.), American Nurseryman 134(7):60-61 [Oct. 1, 1971]; Clark, Garden Center Bull. (Garden Center of Rochester, NY) 28(8):2 [1972]; Clark, Arnoldia 32(3):133-135 [1972]; Fiala, Lilacs, 216, 219 [1988]
Not an established and accepted Group name.
Nota bene: Robert B. Clark created this apparent grouping to include the progeny of the heavy textured, multi-petaled *S. vulgaris* 'Rochester'; however, no recognizable attributes or characters are described. There is no known definitive list of cultivars belonging to the so-called ROCHESTER STRAIN.

'**Rodi**', *S. komarowii* subsp. *reflexa*
'Roði'
Origin not known; S V
https://sites.google.com/site/treogrunnar/Home/flowering-shrubs/syringa-reflexa-rodi
Name: Icelandic for red; so named for its burgundy foliage.
Nota bene: ICNCP Recommendation 21G (21G.1.) states: "A cultivar name should not be published if its epithet consists solely of a word or words that may be descriptive (adjectival) and that could refer to some character or characters common or with the potential to become common in cultivars of the denomination class concerned."

ROGERS 86-1 - see 86-1

'**Rog Izobiliya**', *S. vulgaris*
'Рог Изобилия'
Kolesnikov pre-1960; S IV
syn. - Kolesnikov No. 462
Gromov, A., Siren', 88 [1963]; Howard & Brizicky, AABGA Quart. Newsl. No. 64, 17-21 [1965]
Name: Russian for horn of plenty.
Cultivar name established and accepted.

'**Roi Albert**', *S. vulgaris*
Stepman-Demessemaeker 1909; S VI
syn. - 'King Albert'
{'Dr Lindley' × ?}
Stepman-Demessemaeker Suppl. Gen. Cat., 1 [1909]; McKelvey, The Lilac, 375 [1928]; Wister, Lilacs for America, 57 [1942] - as S V; Wister, Lilacs for America, 40 [1953]; Photo on Jorgovani/Lilacs 2015 DVD.
Named for Albert I, 1875-1934, third king of Belgium, 1909-1934.
Cultivar name presumed registered 1953; name established and accepted.

'**Roihuvuori R-71**', *S. vulgaris*
Origin not known pre-2018 ; S III
Photo seen from Hongiston Nursery by Mari Ranki and Timo Saarimaa in 2020 ILS Lilac Photo Database.
Cultivar name not established.

'**Rokoko**', *S. vulgaris* (not Makedonskaya)
Kārkliņš 2003; D II/V
under evaluation at Latvia State Institute of Fruit Growing, Dobele
Photo on Jorgovani/Lilacs 2015 DVD.
Name: Latvian for rococo.
Cultivar name not established.

'**Rokoko**', *S. vulgaris* (not Kārkliņš)
'Рококо'
Makedonskaya 2016; D V
Statutory registration with the State Inspection for testing and protection of plant varieties of the Republic of Belarus; inventor's certificate № 0005725(Belarus), registered 2016. Makedonskaya N.V. Breeding Lilacs in Belarus Yesterday. TODAY: Materials of International scientific-practical conference "INTERNATIONAL SYRINGA 2018", Russia. Moscow: Moscow State University 2018. pp 36-40. Natalya Makedonskaya. Syringa Belarus. – Lilacs. Quarterly Journal of the

International Lilac Society. 2019. VOL. 50 · NUM. 1 PP.21-25.
Cultivar name registered; name established and accepted.

'Roland Mills', *S. vulgaris*
Klager 1930; S VII
Wister, Lilacs for America, 57 [1942], 40 [1953]
Cultivar name presumed registered 1953; name established and accepted.
Nota bene: Plants in cultivation under the name 'Roland Mills' may not be true to name; in Anon., ILS Newsletter 14(4):3-4 [1988] 'Roland Mills' is listed as D V.; Fiala, Lilacs, 200 [1988] lists 'Roland Mills' also as D V and as syn. of 'R. M. Mills'.
Likely named for the grandson of Hulga Klager, Roland Robert Mills.

'Romance', *S. vulgaris*
Havemeyer & Eaton 1954; S V
Lilac Land Cat. [1954]; Wister, Arnoldia 23(4):82 [1963] - name only; Niedz, ILS Newsletter 1(4):8 [1972]; Eickhorst, ILS Lilac Newsletter 4(1):4-5 [1978]; Photo on Jorgovani/Lilacs 2015 DVD.
Cultivar name registered 1963; name established and accepted.

'Romeo', *S.* (Villosae Group), *S.* ×*prestoniae*
Preston 1938; S V
syn. - Preston No. 26.05.23
Davis, Rep. Dom. Hort., Progress Report 1934-1948, 148-149 [1950]; Wister, Lilacs for America, 58, 64 [1942], 40, 48 [1953]; Buckley, Arboretum Notes 16:23 [1961] - as planted in 1938; Photo on Jorgovani/Lilacs 2015 DVD.
Named for the Son to Montague in Shakespear's *Romeo and Juliet*.
Cultivar name presumed registered 1953; name established and accepted.

'Romona' - see 'Ramona'.

'Ronsard', *S. vulgaris*
Lemoine 1912; S III
syn. - 'President Ronsard', 'Ropsard'
Lemoine, Cat. No. 182, 39 [1912]; McKelvey, The Lilac, 375 [1928]; Wister, Lilacs for America, 58 [1942], 39, 40 [1953]; Photo on Jorgovani/Lilacs 2015 DVD.
Named (probably) for Pierre de Ronsard, 1524-1585, French poet.
Cultivar name presumed registered 1953; name established and accepted.

'Roosa', *S. vulgaris*
Origin not known pre-2018; S V
Photo seen from Hongiston Nursery by Mari Ranki and timo Sarimaa in 2020 ILS Lilac Photo Database.
Cultivar name not established.

'Roosi', *S. vulgaris*
Vaigla pre-2001; S V/IV (II-IV per Semenov)
listed on http://aed.rapina.ee/sirelid.htm [seen 5 Nov. 2005]; I. Semenov, Lilacs 48(2):65 [2019].
Cultivar name not established.

'Rosace', *S. vulgaris*
Lemoine 1932; D IV
Lemoine, Cat. No. 210, 24 [1936]; Wister, Lilacs for America, 57 [1942], 40 [1953]; Photo on Jorgovani/Lilacs 2015 DVD.
Name: French for rosette.
Cultivar name presumed registered 1953; name established and accepted.

'Rosalie', *S. vulgaris*
origin not known ? ?
Reported in cultivation in Morden Arb. trials - name only.

'Rosalind', *S.* (Villosae Group), *S.* ×*prestoniae*
Preston pre-1928; S V-I
syn. - Preston No. 20-14-233
{*S. villosa* subsp. *villosa* × *S. komarowii* subsp. *reflexa*}
Macoun, Rep. Dom. Hort. 1928, 57 [1930]; Wister, Lilacs for America, 64 [1942]; 48 [1953] - not in cultivation, no plants distributed
Named for the Daughter to the Banished Duke in Shakespeare's *As You Like It*.
Cultivar name not established and accepted; probably extinct.

'Rosea', *S. emodi*
origin not known pre-1974; ? ?
syn. - perhaps *S. emodi* var. *rosea* Cornu, which is included in *S. villosa* subsp. *villosa* Vahl
Reported in Plant Research Inst. collection, Ottawa, Canada
Cultivar name not established.

'Rosea', *S. josikaea*
origin not known pre-1908; S IV
syn. - *josikaea rosea*
McKelvey, The Lilac, 61, 100 [1928] - perhaps a pale form of *S.* ×*henryi*; Wister, Lilacs for America, 50, 58 [1942], 32, 41 [1953] - as S V, perhaps the same as 'Eximia' (*josikaea*)
Cultivar name not established.

'Rosea', *S. tomentella* subsp. *tomentella*
Hillier 1948; S V
syn. - *tomentella rosea*
Hillier, Trees and Shrubs, 136 [1950]; Wister, Lilacs for America, 42 [1953]
Cultivar name presumed registered 1953; name established and accepted.

Rosea, (*S. villosa* subsp. *villosa*) - see *S. villosa* subsp. *villosa* Vahl
probably *S. villosa* subsp. *villosa* var. *rosea* C.K. Schneider
origin not known pre-1928; S I
McKelvey, The Lilac, 82, 90 [1928]; Wister, Lilacs for America, 60 [1942], 43 [1953].

'Rosea', *S. vulgaris*
   International Exhibition, 1876, US Centennial Commission, Volume 11, p. 310 - name only; McKelvey, The Lilac, 375 [1928].
   Cultivar name not established.

'Rosea', *S. tomentella* subsp. *yunnanensis*
   Hillier ca 1946; S V
   Wister, Lilacs for America, 57, 60 [1942], 40,44 [1953]; Hilliers' Manual of Trees & Shrubs, p. 391, 573 [1971]; Photo on Jorgovani/Lilacs 2015 DVD.
   Cultivar name presumed registered 1953; name established and accepted.

'Rosea carnea', *S. vulgaris*
   origin not known pre-1880; ? V
   common name: rose carné
   A. Leroy, Cat., 47 [1851]; McKelvey, The Lilac, 375 [1928].
   Cultivar name not established.

'Rosea Grandiflora', *S. vulgaris*
   origin not known pre-1851; S VI
   syn. - see McKelvey [1928]
   common name: Rose Grand
   A. Leroy, Cat., 47 [1851]; Stand. Pl. Names, 487 [1923] - as Rose Grand; McKelvey, The Lilac, 375-376 [1928] - S or D, confused name; Wister, Lilacs for America, 58 [1942] - as D V; Wister, Lilacs for America, 41 [1953] - as D VI; Photo on Jorgovani/Lilacs 2015 DVD and photos on ILS 2019 Photo Database confirm is single.
   Cultivar name not established.

Rose à Grandes Fleurs - see 'Rosea Grandiflora'.

Rose Grand - see 'Rosea Grandiflora'.

ROSE INFERNO
   listed in Auction Results, Lilacs - Quart. Jour. 47(2):137
   This is *Rosa* 'Inferno', not a lilac.

ROSENROT - see 'Maiden's Blush', Skinner 1966, S V
   appeared as such in catalogs of Rosskamp nurseries, Germany, and in their KIRCHER COLLECTION®, a selection of cultivars of the former Konrad Kircher nursery.
   Kircher Baumschulen, Germany, applied for the ROSENROT trademark for marketing plants of 'Maiden's Blush'; the application was rejected by the Bundessortenamt on grounds that Rosenrot is an adjective (color) in spite of the fact that it is also the name of a fairytale character. For the same reason Rosenrot would be rejected as a cultivar name (ICNCP 2009 Recommendation 21G).

ROSE PINK, *S. vulgaris*
   Case; S V
   Heard Gardens, lilac price list [March 15, 1979]; Vrugtman, AABGA Bull. 17(3):69 [1983]
   Probably a cognomen;
   Cultivar name not established.

'Rosie', *S. ×hyacinthiflora*
   Schoustra 2017; D V
   {selected from unnamed seedling progeny originated by the late Ralph Moore}
   part of BEACH PARTY™ series; see also 'Snowy'
   Cultivar name established and accepted.

'Rosiflora', *S. emodi*
   origin not known pre-1974; ? ?
   Reported in Plant Research Inst. collection, Ottawa, Canada
   Cultivar name not established.

Rossa, *S. villosa* subsp. *villosa*
   Peterson, Lilacs 16(1):25 [1987]; erroneous listing, Peterson in litt., Peterson to Vrugtman [May 26, 2006].
   Not a cultivar name.

Rothomagensis - see *S. ×chinensis*.

'Rouen', *S. chinensis*
   origin not known pre-1887; S VII
   Stand. Pl. Names, 487 [1923] - as Rouen; McKelvey, The Lilac, 376 [1928] - perhaps a misnamed rootstock. However, seen in "Syringa Cultivar Catalog" (2019) p. 450 by Nalalia Savenko.
   Cultivar name not established. Possibly a cognomen, see "Rouen lilac".

Rouen lilac - see *S. ×chinensis* Schmidt ex Willd.

ROUENENSIS - see: *S. ×chinensis*
   Fiala, Lilacs, Pl. 83 centre right [1988] - shown in the picture is a *S. ×chinensis*
   rejected name that does not apply to any plant, clone or cultivar.

Rouge de Marly, Rouge de Marley - see **Marlyensis**.

'Rouge de Trianon', *S. vulgaris*
   Briot pre-1858; S VI
   syn. - 'De Trianon', 'Rubra Trianoniana', 'Trianoniana', var. *rubra Trianoniana* Hortorum
   Hérincq, Hort. Français, 66 [1858]; Ellwanger & Barry, Cat., [1892]; McKelvey, The Lilac, 376-378 [1928]; Wister, Lilacs for America, 58 [1942], 41 [1953]; Photo on Jorgovani/Lilacs 2015 DVD.
   Name: In French and Spanish, the word trianon suggests a special place, pleasant surroundings, beauty and balance.
   Cultivar name presumed registered 1953; name established and accepted.

Rouge ponctué - see **Rubra Insignis**.

'Rouge Royal', *S. vulgaris*
   origin not known pre-1839; S VI
   Oudin, Cat., 1 [1839]; McKelvey, The Lilac, 378 [1928].

'Rowancroft Pink', *S. ×hyacinthiflora*
   Blacklock ca 1963; D V
   Wister, Arnoldia 23(4):82 [1963] - name only;

Rowancroft Gardens, Cat. No. 17, 31 [ca 1963] - as S V; Photo on Jorgovani/Lilacs 2015 DVD.
Cultivar name registered 1963; name established and accepted.
Nota bene: Although 'Rowancroft Pink' was described as having single, pink flowers, plants received by Royal Botanical Gardens in 1963 from Rowancroft Gardens (RBG# 63811) have double, pink flowers. Propagules of this cultivar have been distributed to Ottawa Research Station and Select Plus nursery, Canada; Kircher Collection, Germany; Main Botanical Garden, Moscow, Russian Federation.

Royal Blue - see '**Coerulea Superba**'.

'**Royal Crown**', *S.* (Villosae Group)
Fiala 1985; S IV
{*S. tomentella* subsp. *sweginzowii* × (*S. tomentella* subsp. *sweginzowii* × *S. tomentella* subsp. *tomentella*)}
Fiala, Lilacs, 224 [1988]
Cultivar name established and accepted.

'**Royal Purple**', *S.* ×*hyacinthiflora*
Skinner 1966; D VII
Wister, Arnoldia 26(3):14 [1966]; Wister, Lilac Registrations (mimeogr. list), 4 [n.d.; ca 1968]; Pringle, Baileya 21(3):107 [1981]; Photo on Jorgovani/Lilacs 2015 DVD.
Cultivar name registered 1966; name established and accepted.

'**Royalty**', *S.* (Villosae Group), *S.* ×*josiflexa* (possibly *S.* ×*prestoniae*)
Preston & Leslie 1936; S VII
syn. - 'Royalthy'
{parentage not known}
Wister, Lilacs for America, 58, 64 [1942], 41, 48 [1953] - as ×*josiflexa*; Wister, Lilac Registrations (mimeogr. list), 4 [n.d.; ca 1967] - as ×*prestoniae*; Buckley, Greenhouse-Garden-Grass 8(3):2 [Fall 1969] - as ×*josiflexa*; Wister & Oppe, Arnoldia 31(3):123 [1971] - questioned whether ×*josiflexa* or ×*prestoniae*; Cumming, Ann. Rep. Ornam. Pl. Breeders 1973, 7 [1973] - as ×*josiflexa*; Cumming, Agric. Canada Public. 1628, 17, fig. 18 [1977] - introduced in 1936; Photo on Jorgovani/Lilacs 2015 DVD.
Cultivar name presumed registered 1953; name established and accepted.
Nota bene: *S.* (Villosae Group) 'Royalty' has been designated nomenclatural standard for the Villosae Group (see Villosae Group).

Roza Moskvy – see '**Minkarl**'

'**Różana Młodość**', *S. vulgaris*
Karpow-Lipski 1960; S V
syn - 'Rozana Mlodosc'
Wister & Oppe, Arnoldia 31(3):126 [1971] - as 'Rozana Mlodosc'
Name: Polish for Rozana youth.
Cultivar name registered 1970; name established and accepted.

Roze, *S. vulgaris* - see: 'D-Dream'
Note: This trade designation may have been applied also to other pink selections in the Dutch nursery trade, see:
http://www.budgetplant.nl/gewone-sering-syringa-vulgaris-roze
http://www.infokaarten.nl/syringa-vulgaris-roze/

'**Rozovaya Dymka**', *S. villosa* subsp. *wolfii*
'Розовая Дымка'
Pshennikova 2006; S V
Registered with the State Commission of the Russian Federation for Testing and Protection of Selection Achievements, No. 9358788, 2006; Certificate of authorship No. 45063. Pshennikova, L.M. 2007, Lilacs, cultivated in the Botanical Garden-Institute FEB RAS, p. 18; Photo on Jorgovani/Lilacs 2015 DVD.
Name: Russian for pink haze or pink smoke.
Cultivar name registered, established and accepted.

'**Rozovaya Piramida**', *S. vulgaris*
'Розовая Пирамида'
Dyagilev & Degtev 2020, D V
(Международная научная конференция "Syringa L.: коллекции, выращивание, использование") "International Scientific Conference "Syringa L.: collections, cultivation, using" / Collection of Scientific Articles of Botanical Institute named after V.L. Komarov, Botanical Garden of Peter the Great BIN RAS. - St. Petersburg. -2020.- pp.23-27 (in Russian).
Russian for Pink Pyramid.
Cultivar name established and accepted.

'**Rozovaya Radost**", *S. vulgaris*
'Розовая Радость'
Mel'nik 1977, S IV-V
{'Mechta' × OP}
Syn. 'Manshuk'
Rubanik, V. G. et al., Siren' - Syringa L., publishing house "Kaĭnar", Alma-Ata [1977] p 53, - in Russian; Rubtzov et al. 1980. Vidy i sorta sireni, kul'tiviruemye v SSSR. Kiev; Naukova Dumka. – in Russian; Holetich, C.D. 1982. Lilac species and cultivars in cultivation in USSR. Lilacs 11(2):1-38. - translation of Rubtzov et al. 1982.
Name: Russian for pink joy.
Cultivar name established and accepted.

'**Rozovoe Oblako**', *S. vulgaris*
'Розовое Облако'
Rubtzov & Zhogoleva 1956; S IV-V
{'Ruhm von Horstenstein' × ? }
Rubtzov et al. 1980. Vidy i sorta sireni, kul'tiviruemye v SSSR. Kiev; Naukova Dumka. – in Russian; Holetich, C.D. 1982. Lilac species and cultivars in cultivation in USSR. Lilacs 11(2):1-38. - translation of Rubtzov et al. 1982.
Name: Russian for pink cloud.
Cultivar name established and accepted.

Rubella - see '**Rubella Plena**'.

'Rubella Plena', *S. vulgaris*
Lemoine 1881; D VI
syn. - 'Rubella', *Rubella floreplena*
common name: Double Rubella
Lemoine, Cat. No. 87, 3 [1881]; Stand. Pl. Names, 486, 488 [1923] - as Double Rubella; McKelvey, The Lilac, 378-379 [1928]; Wister, Lilacs for America, 58 [1942], 41 [1953]; Photo on Jorgovani/Lilacs 2015 DVD.
Cultivar name presumed registered 1953; name established and accepted.

Rubra (Loddiges) - see **'Saugeana'** (*S. ×chinensis*)
McKelvey, The Lilac, 421-425 [1928].

'Rubra', *S.* (Villosae Group), *S. ×josiflexa*
Origin not known; S VI
syn. - *S. ×josiflexa rubra*
Wister, Lilacs for America, 58 [1942], 32, 41 [1953]
Cultivar name not established, questionable name.

'Rubra', *S. josikaea*
origin not known pre-1885; S VI
syn. - 'Flore Rubra', *S. josikaea rubra*
common name: Red Hungarian
Stand. Pl. Names, 264 [1923] - as Red Hungarian; McKelvey, The Lilac, 61-62 [1928] - probably a color variant; Wister, Lilacs for America, 50, 58 [1942], 32, 41 [1953]
Cultivar name presumed registered 1953; name established and accepted.

'Rubra', *S. ×persica*
Poscharsky 1908; S VI
syn. - *S. persica rubra*
common name: Red Persian
Niemetz, Mitt. Deutsch. DenDr Ges. 17:191 [1908]; Stand. Pl. Names, 264, 487 [1923] - as Red Persian; McKelvey, The Lilac, 467 [1928]; Wister, Lilacs for America, 56, 58 [1942], 38, 41 [1953]; Photo on Jorgovani/Lilacs 2015 DVD.
Cultivar name presumed registered 1953; name established and accepted.

Rubra, *S. vulgaris* - see **'Charles X'**.

'Rubra', *S. vulgaris*
International Exhibition, 1876, US Centennial Commission, Volume 11, p. 310 - name only.
Cultivar name not established.

'Rubra Coerulea', *S. vulgaris*
origin not known pre-1851; S III
A. Leroy, Cat., 47 [1851]; McKelvey, The Lilac, 379 [1928].

Rubra de Marley - see **'Marlyensis'**.

'Rubra Foliis Variegatis', *S. vulgaris*
origin unknown; pre-1851; S VI *
A. Leroy, Cat., 47 [1851]; McKelvey, The Lilac, 379 [1928] - a doubtful plant.

'Rubra Grandiflora', *S. vulgaris*
origin not known pre-1846; S VI
Oudin, Cat., 17 [1846]; McKelvey, The Lilac, 379 [1928] - confused name.

'Rubra Insignis', *S. vulgaris*
origin not known pre-1852; S VII
syn. - 'Insignis Rubra', 'Rouge Ponctué'; perhaps identical with 'Rouge de Trianon'
common name: Red Guide
A. Leroy, Cat., 58 [1852]; Ellwanger & Barry, Cat., [1892]; Stand. Pl. Names, 487, 488 [1923]; - as Red Guide; McKelvey, The Lilac, 379-380 [1928] - confused name; Wister, Lilacs for America, 58 [1942], 41 [1953]; Photo on Jorgovani/Lilacs 2015 DVD.
Cultivar name presumed registered 1953; name established and accepted.
Nota bene: Plants in cultivation are mostly not true to name.

'Rubra Major', *S. villosa* subsp. *villosa*
origin not known pre-1908; S VI
syn. - *persica rubra major*
Wister, Lilacs for America, 56 [1942], 38 [1953]
Cultivar name presumed registered 1953; name established and accepted.

Rubra Major, *S. vulgaris* - see **'Charles X'**.

'Rubra Major Foliis Aureo Variegatis', *S. vulgaris*
origin not known pre-1872; S VI *
syn. - *S. vulgaris rubra major foliis aureo variegatis*
{mutation of 'Charles X'}
Baudriller, Cat. No. 43, 143 [1880]; McKelvey, The Lilac, 276 [1928].

'Rubra Plena', *S. vulgaris*
origin not known pre-1868; D VI
A. Leroy, Cat., 100 [1868]; McKelvey, The Lilac, 380 [1928].

'Rubra Purpurea', *S. vulgaris*
origin not known pre-1880; S VII
Baudriller, Cat. No. 43, 143 [1880]; McKelvey, The Lilac, 381 [1928]

Rubra Trianoniana, *S. vulgaris* - see **'Rouge de Trianon'**.

'Rubro-coerulea', *S. oblata* subsp. *oblata*
origin not known pre-1903; S VII
syn. - *S. oblata* var. *typica* f. *rubro-coerulea* Lingelsheim
Beissner et al, Handbuch der Laubholz-Benennung [1903]; McKelvey, The Lilac, 192 [1928]

'Ruby', *S. vulgaris*
Klager 1920; S VII
Wister, Lilacs for America, 58 [1942], 41 [1953]
Cultivar name presumed registered 1953;
Cultivar not reported in cultivation.

'Ruby Cole', *S. ×hyacinthiflora*
Peterson; S V
{'Anna Shiach' × 'Serene'}

Peterson, Lilacs - Quart. Jour. 16(1):24 [1987] - name only
Cultivar name not established.

'Ruhm von Horstenstein', *S. vulgaris*
Wilke 1928; S VI
{possibly 'Andenken an Ludwig Späth' × 'Charles X', but more likely a chance seedling}
syn. - 'Glory of Horstenstein', 'Ruhm Van Horsenstein', 'Ruhm von Horsenstein', 'Ruhn von Horenstein', Rнuм von (trade designation used for cut flowers of this cultivar)
Anon., Gartenflora [April 1928] - ill.; Tilk, Möllers Deutsche Gärtner-Zeitung 1928(9):102 - in German; Anon., Gartenwelt 32:132 [1928]; Abt. Züchtung u. Anerkennung, Reichsverb. deutsch. Gartenb., Blumen- und Zierpflanzenbau, Heft 2, [6.2.1929] - approved forcing cultivar, in German; Späth, Späth-Buch, 305 [1930]; Wister, Lilacs for America, 58 [1942], 41 [1953]; Meyer, Flieder, 57 [1952]; Photo on Jorgovani/Lilacs 2015 DVD.
Named for Horstenstein, a section of Berlin-Marienfelde, Germany, location of the Horstensteiner Baumschulen, 1847- ca 1950.
Cultivar name presumed registered 1953; name established and accepted.
Forcing cultivar in the Netherlands and Germany.

'Rus'', *S. vulgaris*
'Русь'
Vekhov 1952; S V
syn. - 'Rusj'
Magazine "Tsvetovodstvo" ("Floriculture") No. 7, 1977, p. 11
Rubtzov et al. 1980. Vidy i sorta sireni, kul'tiviruemye v SSSR. Kiev; Naukova Dumka. – in Russian; Holetich, C.D. 1982. Lilac species and cultivars in cultivation in USSR. Lilacs 11(2):1-38. - translation of Rubtzov et al. 1982; Photo on Jorgovani/Lilacs 2015 DVD.
Cultivar name established and accepted.

'Russkiï Sever', *S. vulgaris*
'Русский север'
Aladin, S., Aladina, O., and Polyakova, T. 2014; D I
{'Miss Ellen Willmott' × 'Tat'yana Polyakova'}
Садовник (Gardener) magazine 04 (140)/2017 :18-25; Вестник АППМ (Catalog in Vestnik APPM (Planting material association) magazine) 1/2018: 59-72 (in Russian).
Named for the Russian North.
Cultivar name established and accepted.

'Russkie Sezony', *S. vulgaris*
'Русские сезоны'
Aladin, S., Aladina, O., Polyakova, T., and, Aladina, A. 2017; S IV
Statutory registration, Russia, State Register and Plant Patent No. 80054/8058584 (2019)
{'Alice Eastwood' × OP}
IX International Scientific Conference (IX Международная научная конференция "Цветоводство: история, теория, практика") " Floriculture: history, theory, practice", St. Petersburg, Botanical Garden of Peter the Great BIN RAS, September 7-13, 2019: (in Russian); II All-Russian scientific-practical conference with international participation (II Всероссийская научно-практическая конференция с международным участием) " Botanical Gardens in the XXI Century: Biodiversity Conservation, Development Strategy and Innovative Solutions Belgorod, Botanical Garden of NRU "BelSU", September 23-26, 2019; in oral presentation only.
Named for Russian Seasons (Saisons Russes) of Sergei Pavlovich Dyagilev (Сергей Павлович Дягилев), who introduced the world to Russian music, ballet, painting, theater (1908–1914).
Cultivar name established and accepted.

'Russkaya Krasavitsa', *S. vulgaris*
'Русская Красавица'
Stashkevich pre-1974; S I
syn. - 'Russkaya Krasavista', 'Russkaya Krasavitsa'
Gromov, Lilacs - Proceedings 2(4):16 [1974]; Fiala, Lilacs, 213 [1988] - as 'Russkaya Krasavista'.
Name: Russian for Russian beauty.
Cultivar name established and accepted.

'Russkaya Pesnya', *S. vulgaris*
'Русская Песня'
Vekhov 1952; D II
{'Maréchal Lannes' × ?}
syn. - 'Russkaya Pesnya'
Magazine "Tsvetovodstvo" ("Floriculture") No. 7, 1977, p. 10. Rubtzov et al. 1980. Vidy i sorta sireni, kul'tiviruemye v SSSR. Kiev; Naukova Dumka. – in Russian; Holetich, C.D. 1982. Lilac species and cultivars in cultivation in USSR. Lilacs 11(2):1-38. - translation of Rubtzov et al. 1982; Photo on Jorgovani/Lilacs 2015 DVD.
Name: Russian for Russian song.
Cultivar name established and accepted.

'Russkiï Suvenir', *S. vulgaris*
'Русский Сувенир'
Potutova; S VII
syn. - 'Ruskij Souvenir'
Rubtzov et al. 1980. Vidy i sorta sireni, kul'tiviruemye v SSSR. Kiev; Naukova Dumka. – in Russian; Holetich, C.D. 1982. Lilac species and cultivars in cultivation in USSR. Lilacs 11(2):1-38. - translation of Rubtzov et al. 1982.
Name: Russian for Russian souvenir.
Cultivar name established and accepted.

'Rustica', *S. vulgaris*
Lemoine 1950; D IV
Lemoine, Cat No. 221, 3 [1950]; Wister, Lilacs for America, 41 [1953]; Photo on Jorgovani/Lilacs 2015 DVD.

Cultivar name presumed registered 1953; name established and accepted.

'Rutilant', *S.* (Villosae Group), *S.* ×*nanceiana*
Lemoine 1931; S VII
syn. - ×*henryi* 'Rutilant'
Lemoine, Cat. No. 207, 25 [1933] - as *S.* ×*henryi* 'Rutilant'; Wister, Lilacs for America, 58 [1942], 41 [1953]; Photo on Jorgovani/Lilacs 2015 DVD.
Cultivar name presumed registered 1953; name established and accepted.

'R. W. Mills', *S. vulgaris*
Klager 1928; D V
Cooley, Cat., 7 [1928] - as double, deep pink; McKelvey, The Lilac, 561 [1928]; Wister, Lilacs for America, 58 [1942] - as D IV; Wister, Lilacs for America, 41 [1953] - as S V; Rogers, Tentative International Register, 67 [1976] - as S V; Anon., ILS Newsletter 14(4):3-4 [1988] - as single, dark purple (?). Fiala, Lilacs, 200 [1988] - misspelled 'R. M. Mills', not identical to 'Roland Mills'.
Named for Roy Wilson Mills (aka Rody Mills) (1871-1946), son-in-law of Hulga Klager and husband of her daughter Elizabeth.
Cultivar name presumed registered 1953; name established and accepted.

'Ryabchik', *S. vulgaris*
'Рябчик'
Kravchenko 1970; D IV-VI
{'Congo' × 'Mme Lemoine'}
Kravchenko L. Culture of lilacs in Uzbekistan. Publishing house "Uzbekistan", Tashkent, 1970 p. 13,14.
Name: Russian for motley.
Cultivar name established and accepted.

'Sacrament', *S. vulgaris*
Fiala 1985; S I
{'Rochester' × 'Primrose'}
Fiala, Lilacs, 223 [1988]; Photo on Jorgovani/Lilacs 2015 DVD.
Cultivar name established and accepted.

'Saima', *S. vulgaris*
Vaigla 1952; S VII (IV/VI per Semenov)
{'Andenken an Ludwig Späth' × ? }
Kivistik, Maakodu 1997(5):22-23 (ill.) [1997] - in Estonian; I. Semenov, Lilacs 48(2):65 [2019].
Cultivar name established and accepted.

Saint . . . - also: St. . . .

'Saint-Georges de Beauce' - see **'Ville de Saint-Georges'**.

'Saint Jerzy Popieluszko', *S. vulgaris*
Fiala 1985; S VI
syn. - 'St Jerzy Popieluszko'
{'Prodige' × 'Rochester'}
Fiala, Lilacs, 103 & 223 [1988]; Photo on Jorgovani/Lilacs 2015 DVD.
Named for Jerzy Alfons Popieluszko, 1947-1984, priest of the archdiocese of Warszawa, Poland; activist, murdered at Włocławek. Although not yet proclaimed a saint, the Vatican started the process in 1997 which has lead to the beatification of Father Popieluszko in 2010.
Cultivar name established and accepted.

'Salavat Yulaev', *S. vulgaris*
'Салават Юлаев'
Sakharova 1973; D VII/II
syn. - Sakharova No. 1642, 'Salavat Julaev'
{'Mme Lemoine' × 'Congo'}
Sakharova, Introduktsiya i selektsiya dekorativnykh rastenii v Bashkirii, 31 [1973] - in Russian; Rubtzov et al. 1980. Vidy i sorta sireni, kul'tiviruemye v SSSR. Kiev; Naukova Dumka. – in Russian; Holetich, C.D. 1982. Lilac species and cultivars in cultivation in USSR. Lilacs 11(2):1-38. - translation of Rubtzov et al. 1982; Photo on Jorgovani/Lilacs 2015 DVD.
Named for Salavat Yulaev, 1754-1800, poet and hero of the Bashkir peasant revolt, 1773-1775, Bashkortostan, Russian Federation.
Cultivar name established and accepted.

'Salvifolia', *S. villosa* subsp. *villosa*
origin not known pre-1836; ? ?
Loddiges, Cat., 67 [1836]; McKelvey, The Lilac, 468 [1928]
Cultivar name not established.

'Samal', *S. vulgaris*
'Самал'
Mel'nik, Rubanik & Dyagilev pre 1994, D V
Pikaleva, Lilacs - Quart. Jour. 23(4):88 [1994]
(Международная научная конференция "Syringa L.: коллекции, выращивание, использование")
"International Scientific Conference "Syringa L.: collections, cultivation, using" / Collection of Scientific Articles of Botanical Institute named after V.L. Komarov, Botanical Garden of Peter the Great BIN RAS. - St. Petersburg. -2020.- pp.23-27 (in Russian).
Named for the prestigious Samal district of the city of Almaty, Kazakhstan.
It is also a woman's name and can mean cool breeze.
Cultivar name established and accepted.

'Samanta', *S. vulgaris*
Kārkliņš 2003; S VII
(no information; listed by T. Poliakova, 2014)
Photo on Jorgovani/Lilacs 2015 DVD.
Name: A woman's name.
Cultivar name not established.

'San', *S. villosa* subsp. *wolfii*
originator not known ca 1995; S V
{selected from *S. villosa* subsp. *wolfii* seedlings grown from seed collected 1972 at Sulak-san and Odae-san, Korea}
L. Molberg, Gartneryrket 12/1998:23; in litt. O. B. Hansen in litt. to F. Vrugtman, March 15, 2000
Name: San is Korean for mountain.
Cultivar name established and accepted.

'Sandy Nye', *S. vulgaris*
Peterson 2003; D V
{'Beth' × OP}
In private collection (KA) in USA per email to Registrar 10-4-19.
Named for a family friend of the developer.
Cultivar name not established.

Sangeana, *S.* ×*chinensis*
reported in cultivation at Morden Arb. trials - name only probably misspelling of 'Saugeana'.

'Sanguinea', *S. vulgaris*
Ellwanger & Barry 1868; S VI
Ellwanger & Barry, Cat. No. 2, 43 [1867]; McKelvey, The Lilac, 381 [1928]; Wister, Lilacs for America, 58 [1942], 41 [1953]
Cultivar name presumed registered 1953; name established and accepted.

'Saniya', *S. vulgaris*
'Сания'
Sagitova; D III
Kazakh magazine "Tsvetochnui Dom", 2008, #1 'Iz otechestvennoi sekllektsii, Rodomiz Kazakhstana', page 8 – Цветочный Дом, 2008, No.1, «Из отечественной селекции. Родомиз Казахстана", стр.8.
Named for Saniya, the younger sister of the originator.
Cultivar name established and accepted.

'Santa', *S. vulgaris*
Kārkliņš 2003; S II/V
Strautiņa & Kaufmane, Dobeles ceriņi, pp. 13-14 [2011]; Semënov, I., and S. Strautina, Lilacs 42(2):53-55, ill. [2013]; Photo on Jorgovani/Lilacs 2015 DVD.
Cultivar name established and accepted.

'Sapun-Gora', *S. vulgaris*
'Сапун-Гора'
Klimenko, V. 1955; S II
Rub*t*zov et al. 1980. Vidy i sorta sireni, kul'tiviruemye v SSSR. Kiev; Naukova Dumka. – in Russian; Holetich, C.D. 1982. Lilac species and cultivars in cultivation in USSR. Lilacs 11(2):1-38. - translation of Rub*t*zov et al. 1982.
Named for Sapun Gora Mountain, site of the May 1944, World War II liberation battle of Sevastopol, Crimea, Ukraine.
Cultivar name established and accepted.

'Sarah Sands', *S. vulgaris*
Havemeyer 1943; S VII
Wister, Lilacs for America, 58 [1942], 41 [1953]; Kammerer, Morton Arb. Bull. Pop. Info. 36(6):27-29 [1961]; Niedz, ILS Newsletter 1(4):7-8 [1972] - as {'L'Oncle Tom' × 'Negro'} (?); Eickhorst, ILS Lilac Newsletter 4(1):4-5 [1978]; Lilacs - Quart. Jour. 20(4): back cover ill. [1991]; Photo on Jorgovani/Lilacs 2015 DVD.
Named for Sarah Sands, sister of Katherine Aymar Sands Havemeyer.

Cultivar name presumed registered 1953; name established and accepted.

'Sara's Reflections of Passion', *S.* ×*hyacinthiflora*
Moro, F. 2013; D III & I
{'Pocahontas' × ?}
Lilacs - Quart. Jour. 42(3):85 & 86 (photo) [2013]; in lit. Moro to Vrugtman July 13, 2013
Named for Sara Moro [1966-] after a Yanni song that makes her think of Colby.
Cultivar name established and accepted.

Sargentiana (*S. sargentiana* C.K. Schneid.) - see *S. komarowii* subsp. *komarowii* C.K. Schneid.

'Sārtais Viesis', *S. vulgaris*
Upītis ca 1970; S V/II
Kalniņš, L., Ceriņu jaunšķirnes Dobelē, Dārs un drava 1986 (12):13-15 - in Latvian; in litt. S. Strautiņa to F. Vrugtman [22 Jan. 2008] - ca 1970, S V/II; Photo on Jorgovani/Lilacs 2015 DVD.
Name: Latvian for pink guest.
Cultivar name established and accepted.

Sass seedling, *S. vulgaris*
origin not known ? ?
Anon., Lilacs - Proceedings 13(1):23 [1984]
Cognomen, not a cultivar name.

'Satin Cloud', *S. vulgaris*
Fiala 1985; S I
{'Rochester' × 'Elsie Lenore'}
Fiala, Lilacs, 92 & 223 [1988]
Cultivar name established and accepted.

'Saturnale', *S. vulgaris*
Lemoine 1916; S III
syn. - 'Saturneale'
Lemoine, Cat. No. 190, 25 [1916]; McKelvey, The Lilac, 381 [1928]; Wister, Lilacs for America, 58 [1942], 41 [1953]
Named for Saturnale, Roman god of agriculture.
Cultivar name presumed registered 1953; name established and accepted.

'Sauerbrey', *S. vulgaris*
Towson ca 1936; D V
Towson Nurs., Cat., 83 [1938]; Wister, Lilacs for America, 22 [1942], 41 [1953]
Cultivar name presumed registered 1953;
Cultivar not reported in cultivation.

'Saugeana', *S.* ×*chinensis*
Saugé ca 1820; S V-VII
syn. - many; see McKelvey [1928]
common name: Purple Chinese
Anon., Revue horticole 1:81-82 [1829], as Lilas Saugé; Baudriller, Cat. No. 43, 141 [1880]; Rehder, in Bailey, Stand. Cycl. Hort. 6:3301 [1917]; Stand. Pl. Names, 264 [1923] - as Purple Chinese; McKelvey, The Lilac, 421-425 [1928]; Wister, Lilacs for America, 58 [1942], 41 [1953];

Photo on Jorgovani/Lilacs 2015 DVD.
Named for the originator, Pierre Saugé, 1757-1835, florist, 1807-1835, at 13 rue de la Santé, Paris, France. Most likely named by Jacques Varin, head of the Jardin des plantes at Rouen, the garden where *S. ×chinensis* originated.
Cultivar name presumed registered 1953; name established and accepted.

'Sauget alba', *S. vulgaris*
origin not known pre-1937; ? ?
Wister, Lilacs for America, 37, 58 [1942] - as doubtful name
Cultivar name not established, not recorded in cultivation in 1953.

'**Savonarole**', *S. vulgaris*
Lemoine 1935; D III
syn. - 'Savanarole'
Lemoine, Cat. No. 210, 23 [1936]; Wister, Lilacs for America, 58 [1942], 41 [1953]; Photo on Jorgovani/Lilacs 2015 DVD.
Named for Giralamo Savonarole, 1452-1498, Florentine reformer.
Cultivar name presumed registered 1953; name established and accepted.

'Savoyer', *S. vulgaris*
origin not known pre-1953; ? ?
Wister, Lilacs for America, 41 [1953] - grown in Holland
Named (perhaps) for the royal family of Italy.
Cultivar name not established.

SCENT AND SENSIBILITY™ PINK - see '**SMSXPM**'.

SCENTARA™ DOUBLE BLUE - see '**SMNSHBBL**'.

'**Schermerhornii**', *S. vulgaris*
probably Parsons pre-1875; S V
common name: Schermerhorn
Parsons, Cat., 50 [1889]; Dunbar, Gard. Mag. 1:233 [1905]; McKelvey, The Lilac, 381 [1928]; Stand. Pl. Names, 617 [1942] - as Schermerhorn; Wister, Lilacs for America, 58 [1942], 41 [1953] - erroneously as 'Schermerhorn'; Photo on Jorgovani/Lilacs 2015 DVD.
Named, perhaps, for Simon Jacob Schermerhorn, 1827-1901, farmer, politician and congressman, Rotterdam, New York, USA.
Cultivar name presumed registered 1953; name established and accepted.

Schkolnitsa - see '**Shkol'nitsa**'.

SCHNEEKÖNIGIN® - see '**Sovetskaya Arktika**'.

'**Schneelavine**', *S. vulgaris*
origin not known pre-1875; S I/V
syn. - 'Schneelawine'
Transon, Cat., 50 [1875]; McKelvey, The Lilac, 381-382, 563 [1928]; Wister, Lilacs for America, 58 [1942], 41 [1953]
Cultivar name presumed registered 1953; name established and accepted.

SCHNEEWEISSCHEN™ - see '**Mount Baker**'.

Scholokhov - see '**Sholokhov**'.

'**Schoharie**', *S. vulgaris*
Lape; S-D II
{'Kapriz' × ? }
Vrugtman, AABGA Bull. 17(3):68 [1984]
Named for Schoharie County, New York, USA.
Cultivar name registered 1982;
Cultivar not reported in cultivation.

'**SCHolirofrag**', *S. ×hyacinthiflora*
Schoustra 2020; S IV
{unnamed seedling x 'Snowy'}
PP 32085 August 18, 2020
Flower upper RHS N74C color; bud color RHS N74B
Cultivar name registered by statute. Name established and accepted.

SCHÖNER VON FRANKFURT - trade designation for '**Hermann Eilers**'.

SCHÖNE VON MOSKAU - trade designation for '**Krasavitsa Moskvy**'.

'Schöne von Stuttgart', *S.*
no information; D VII
Seen 21 January 2018 <http://www.piccoplant.de/en/assortment/lilacs>
Name: German for beauty from Stuttgart
Cultivar name not established.

'**Scipion Cochet**', *S. vulgaris*
Cochet pre-1872; S VII
Dauvesse, Cat. No. 36, 46 [1872]; McKelvey, The Lilac, 382 [1928]; Wister, Lilacs for America, 58 [1942], 41 [1953]; Photo on Jorgovani/Lilacs 2015 DVD.
Named for Scipion Cochet, 1833-1896, younger son of the originator.
Cultivar name presumed registered 1953; name established and accepted.

'**Scotia**', *S. ×hyacinthiflora*
Scott pre-1942; S V
Wister, Lilacs for America, 58 [1942], 41 [1953]; Photo on Jorgovani/Lilacs 2015 DVD.
Cultivar name presumed registered 1953; name established and accepted.

'Sculptured Ivory', *S. vulgaris*
Fiala 1985; S I
{'Rochester' × 'Primrose'}
Fiala, Lilacs, 92, 223 [1988]; Photo on Jorgovani/Lilacs 2015 DVD.
Cultivar name established and accepted.

'Seafoam', *S. vulgaris*
Fiala 1985; D I
{'Rochester' × unnamed octoploid (?) seedling}
Fiala, Lilacs, 223 [1988]
Cultivar name established and accepted.

'Sea Storm', *S. vulgaris*
    Fiala 1984; S III
    {'Flora 1953' × 'Mrs A. Belmont'}
    Fiala, Lilacs, 96, 98, 223 [1988] - p. 96 lists erroneous parentage
    Cultivar name established and accepted.

Seedling 1001 or One-thousand-and-one, *S. vulgaris*
    Berdeen; D VI
    {'Paul Thirion' × ? }
    Niedz, in litt. to Vrugtman [Apr.5/1976]; Vrugtman, AABGA Bulletin 17(3):69 [1983]; King & Coggeshall, Lilacs - Quart. Jour. 27(2):49-50 [1998] - name only
    Originator's code or cognomen, not a cultivar name.

Select, *S. pubescens* subsp. *patula*
    de Belder; ? ?
    Belgische Dendrologie 1994, p. 191; in litt. X. Misonne to D. De Meyere, [January 12, 2004]
    breeder's designation or cognomen, not a cultivar name.

'Selma Margaretten', *S. vulgaris*
    Margaretten; S III
    {'Mme Lemoine' × ? }
    reported in cultivation at Royal Botanical Gardens, Ontario, Canada; Photo on Jorgovani/Lilacs 2015 DVD.
    Cultivar name established and accepted.

'Semiplena', *S. villosa* subsp. *villosa*
    origin not known pre-1915; ? ?
    Schelle, Mitt. D. Dendrol. Ges. 24:208 [1915]; McKelvey, The Lilac, 468 [1928]
    Cultivar name not established.

'Semiplena', *S. villosa* subsp. *villosa*
    origin not known pre-1895; S-D V
    McKelvey, The Lilac, 97 [1928] - confused name
    Cultivar name not established.

'Semiplena', *S. vulgaris*
    origin not known pre-1851; S-D I
    syn. - 'Alba Semipleno', semi-plena
    International Exhibition, 1876, US Centennial Commission, Volume 11, p. 310 - name only; McKelvey, The Lilac, 382 [1928] - confused name
    Cultivar name not established.

'**Sénateur Volland**', *S. vulgaris*
    Lemoine 1887; D VI
    syn. - 'Senateur Volland', 'Senator Volland'
    Lemoine, Cat. No. 107, 8 [1887]; McKelvey, The Lilac, 382-383 [1928]; Wister, Lilacs for America, 58 [1942], 41 [1953]; Photo on Jorgovani/Lilacs 2015 DVD.
    Cultivar name presumed registered 1953; name established and accepted.

'**Senkōhanabi**', *S. pubescens* subsp. *pubescens*
    '線香花火'
    Ihara 2004; S VII
    {*S. pubescens* subsp. *pubescens* 'Palibin' × *S. pubescens* subsp. *pubescens* 'Palibin'}
    syn. - seedling no. 20040520001#5.
    (Vrugtman, Cultivated Plant Diversity ... 2017)
    Name: Japanese for sparkler.
    Cultivar name registered 2017; name established and accepted.

Sensācija - see 'Paarsteigums'
    name used in error by Kalva, V., Ceriņi (Lilac), 165-166 [1980].

'**Sensation**', *S. vulgaris*
    Eveleens Maarse 1938; S VII & I
    {mutation of 'Hugo de Vries'; periclinal chimera}
    syn. - 'Sensācija' (not 'Paarsteigums')
    Wister, Lilacs for America, 41 [1953]; Eveleens Maarse, Dendron 1(1):11 [1954]; Eveleens Maarse, US Pl. Pat. No. 1242 [Jan. 19, 1954]; Pearson, Landscape Trades, 52-53 [1992]; Photo on Jorgovani/Lilacs 2015 DVD.
    Name: Referring to being a sensation, since it was the first bicolor lilac ever selected.
    Awards: First Class Certificate 1938 (KMTP).
    Cultivar name presumed registered 1953; name established and accepted.
    Forcing cultivar in the Netherlands.
    NOTE: When 'Sensation' is propagated by way of meristem cuttings (micropropagation) a small percentage of the plants produced will have rather unattractive off-white florets. These are not sports, mutations or reversions; these are plants where the pigment-free cells, which appear white, form the upper layer of cells of the florets. Despite being rather unattractive plants, they are sometimes marketed as Sensation Sport, Sport of Sensation, Sensation White Reversion, Sensation Picot, etc.

Sensation White Reversion, *S. vulgaris*
    Origin not known; S I
    Weston Nurseries Cat. 2006, 39
    Selector's designation or cognomen, not a cultivar name.

'Sentinel', *S. pubescens* subsp. *microphylla*
    Fiala 1984; S V-VI
    {'Hers' × 'George Eastman'}
    Fiala, Lilacs, 104, 224 [1988]
    Cultivar name established and accepted.

'Serdtse Danko' *S. vulgaris*
    'Сердце Данко'
    Kolesnikov pre-1960; S VII
    {parentage not known}
    T. Polyakova, 2018, Мастер Сиреневой Кисти (Master of the Lilac Brush), p. 109 - photo only. Seen 5/27/20 as Facebook post from Lomonosov Botanical Garden of the Moscow State University.
    Name: Russion for Danko's heart.
    Cultivar name established and accepted.

'Serebristyĭ Landysh', *S. vulgaris*
Серебристый Ландыш
Potutova 1971; D I
Photo on Jorgovani/Lilacs 2015 DVD.
Russian for Silvery Lily of the Valley.

'Serebryanyĭ Vek', *S. vulgaris*
'Серебряный век'
Aladin, S., Aladina, O., Polyakova, T., and Aladina, A. 2014; D III-IV
{elite form 11-94' × OP}
Садовник (Gardener) magazine 04 (140)/2017 :18-25; Вестник АППМ (Catalog in Vestnik APPM (Planting material association) magazine) 1/2018: 59-72 (in Russian).
Named for the Silver Age in Russian art, music, poetry and theater in the early XXth century.
Cultivar name established and accepted.

'Serene', *S. vulgaris*
Havemeyer & Eaton 1954; S V-III
Wister, Lilacs for America, 41 [1953]; Lilac Land, Cat. [1954]; Niedz, ILS Newsletter 1(4):7-8 [1972]; Eickhorst, ILS Lilac Newsletter 4(1):4-5 [1978]; Anon., Lilacs - Quart. Jour. 30(1): back cover [2001]; Photo on Jorgovani/Lilacs 2015 DVD.
Cultivar name presumed registered 1953; name established and accepted.

'Serezha', *S. vulgaris*
'Серёжа'
Sagitova, S VII
Varietal denomination registered 1994, No. 12, State Register of Selected Achievements in Republic of Kazakhstan;
Cultivar name established and accepted.
Photo on Jorgovani/Lilacs 2015 DVD.

'Sergeĭ Rakhmaninov', *S. vulgaris*
'Сергей Рахманинов'
Aladin, S., Aladina, O., Polyakova, T., and Aladina, A. 2014; S IV-III
{elite form 11-112H × 'Rus"}
Садовник (Gardener) magazine 04 (140)/2017 :18-25; Вестник АППМ (Catalog in Vestnik APPM (Planting material association) magazine) 1/2018: 59-72 (in Russian);
Named for Sergei Vasilievich Rakhmaninov (Сергей Васильевич Рахманинов), 1873-1943, outstanding Russian composer, pianist and conductor.
Cultivar name established and accepted.

'Sergeĭ Vladimirskiĭ', *S. vulgaris*
'Сергей Владимирский'
Aladin, S., Aladina, O., Polyakova, T., and Aladina, A. 2018; S IV
{'Gilbert' × OP}
IX International Scientific Conference (IX Международная научная конференция "Цветоводство: история, теория, практика") " Floriculture: history, theory, practice", St. Petersburg, Botanical Garden of Peter the Great BIN RAS, September 7-13, 2019 (in Russian).
Named for Sergei Nikolaevich Vladimirskii (Сергей Николаевич Владимирский), 1951-2006, Russian multi-instrumentalist, philologist, teacher, composer, singer, artist, collector of musical instruments.
Cultivar name established and accepted.

'Serotina', *S. vulgaris*
origin not known pre-1880; ? ?
syn. - 'Tardiva'
Baudriller, Cat. No. 43, 143 [1880]; McKelvey, The Lilac, 387 [1928] - as identical to 'Tardiva', but priority not established
Cultivar name not established.

'Sesquicentennial', *S. vulgaris*
Fenicchia 1988; S II
syn. - R418 RAF333
{'Rochester' × 'Glory'}
Hoepfl & Rogers, Lilac Newsletter 14(7):6 [1988]; Fiala, Lilacs, 95 [1988] - as S IV; Vrugtman, HortScience 24(3):435 [1989]; Lilacs - Quart. Jour. 26(4):front cover ill. [1997]; K. Millham, Lilacs - Quart. Jour. 42(2):62 & ill. 70 [2013]; Photo on Jorgovani/Lilacs 2015 DVD.
Named for the 150th anniversary, 1971, of the establishment of Monroe County, New York, USA.
Cultivar name registered 1988; name established and accepted.

'Sevastopol'', *S. vulgaris*
'Севастополь'
Aladin, S., Aladina, O., and Polyakova, T. and Aladina, A. 2016; D I
{'Grace Orthwaite' × OP}
Садовник (Gardener) magazine, 05 (141)/2017 :16-22; Вестник АППМ (Catalog in Vestnik APPM (Planting material association) magazine) 1/2018: 59-72 (in Russian).
Named for the hero city of Sevastopol on the Crimean Peninsula on the Black Sea.
Cultivar name established and accepted.

'Sevastopol'skiĭ Val's', *S. vulgaris*'
'Севастопольский Вальс'
Klimenko, V. 1955; S IV
{'Mme Casimir Périer' × 'Andenken an Ludwig Späth'}
syn. - 'Sevastopol'skij Val's', 'Sevastopol'skiĭ' Salyut' (*)
*book T.Polyakova, N. Dvoryak 'Victory Lilac', Belgorod, 2020 page 45
Rubtzov et al. 1980. Vidy i sorta sireni, kul'tiviruemye v SSSR. Kiev; Naukova Dumka. – in Russian; Holetich, C.D. 1982. Lilac species and cultivars in cultivation in USSR. Lilacs 11(2):1-38. - translation of Rubtzov et al. 1982.
Named after a popular song written in 1955 by composer K. Listyev and poet G. Rublev in honor of the

10th anniversary of the Victory in World War II.
Cultivar name established and accepted.

'Severnaya Pal'mira' (North Palmyra), *S. vulgaris*
'Северная Пальмира'
Aladin, S., Aladina, O., Polyakova, T., and Aladina, A. 2019; D III
{'Katherine Havemeyer' × OP}
(Международная научная конференция "Syringa L.: коллекции, выращивание, использование")
"International Scientific Conference "Syringa L.: collections, cultivation, using" / Collection of Scientific Articles of Botanical Institute named after V.L. Komarov, Botanical Garden of Peter the Great BIN RAS. - St. Petersburg. -2020.- pp.3-7 (in Russian); Photo exhibition of all varieties of the creative breeding group "Russian Lilac" at the Festival "Lilac February", St. Petersburg, Botanical Garden of Peter the Great BIN RAS, February 22-24, 2020.
This is the poetic name of St. Petersburg.
Cultivar name established and accepted.

'Shantelle', *S.* (Villosae Group), *S. ×prestoniae*
Bron pre-2002; S VII
{reportedly propagated from a witches'-broom on 'Royalty' caused by phytoplasmas}
distributed also by Bailey Nursery, St Paul, MN, USA, but discontinued.
Cultivar name not established.
Nota bene: The presence of phytoplasma in plants of 'Charisma', a similar cultivar also propagated from a witches'-broom on 'Royalty', has been confirmed (in litt. D. Thompson to F. Vrugtman, December 8, 2003).
Vrugtman 2005, Lilacs - Quart. Jour. 34(4):106.

'Shaura', *S. vulgaris*
'Шаура'
Sakharova 1973; S VI
syn. - Sakharova No. 1775
{'Andenken an Ludwig Späth' × 'Capitaine Baltet'}
Sakharova, Introduktsiya i selektsiya dekorativnykh rastenii v Bashkirii, 32 [1978] - in Russian
Named for Shaura, opera by the Bashkir composer Zagir Garipovich Ismagilov, Ufa, Bashkortostan, Russian Federation.
Cultivar name established and accepted.

SHAU TING HSIEN, *S. pubescens* subsp. *pubescens*
S VII
{Frank N. Meyer No. 695 collected in China in 1908; Arnold Arboretum No. 6623}
USDA-ARS GRIN database, PI No. 23032; McKelvey, The Lilac, 170 [1928]
probably a common name, not a cultivar name.

Shelagh, *S.*
Chapman ?, ? ?
Chapman, Lilacs - Quart. Jour. 38(3):83[2009] - name only
Cultivar name not established.

'Sheremetev', *S. ×hyacinthiflora*
'Шереметев'
Mikhaĭlov & Rybakina 2002; S IV
{'Kosmos' × 'Esther Staley'}
Chapman, Lilacs - Quart. Jour. 32(1):17-18 [2003] - translated from N. L. Mikhaĭlov in Tsvetovodstvo, May-June issue (in Russian); http://home.onego.ru/~otsoppe/enciclop/kustar/syring_s.html (July 26, 2003)
Named for the Earl Sheremetev who created the exquisite gardens at Ostankino in the 18th century.
Cultivar name established and accepted.

'Sheridan', *S.*
(species affiliation not known)origin not known ? ?
reported in cultivation by Ole Heide at Thisted, Denmark.
Cultivar name not established.

'Shimmering Sea', *S. vulgaris*
Fiala 1984; S III
{'Elsie Lenore' × 'Rochester'}
Fiala, Lilacs, 223 [1988]
Cultivar name established and accepted.

'Shiryu', *S.*
origin not known 1968, S III/VII
Sakata Seed Inc. Cat. autumn 1968, p. 14
Cultivar name established and accepted.

'Shishi', *S. pubescens* subsp. *pubescens*
'紫史'
Ihara 2018; S VII
{*S. pubescens* subsp. *pubescens* 'Palibin' seedling 20040520001#8 × *S. pubescens* subsp. *pubescens* 'Hoshikuzu' seedling 2011S1128007#3}
registered 17 November 2018 by Hideo Ihara Tokiwa 450-1, Minamiku, Sapporo, Hokkaido, 005 - 0863 Japan.
Frequent multipetaling.
Named for the title of the book of the Tales of Genji written by Murasaki Shikibu.
Cultivar name registered 2018; name established and accepted.

'Shishkin Les', *S. vulgaris*
'Шишкин лес'
Aladin, S., Aladina, O., and Polyakova, T. and Aladina, A. 2016; S IV
{elite form 11-112' × 'Rus"}
Named for the village of Shishkin Les, on the bank of the Pakhra River, where once was a school of the Timiryazev Academy.The name means Cone Forest or Evergreen Forest.

'Shkol'nitsa', *S. vulgaris*
'Школьница'
Shtan'ko & Mikhaĭlov 1956; S III-IV
syn. - 'Schkolnitsa', 'Shkol'nica'
{'Prince de Beauvau' × ? }
Gromov et al., Siren', 79 [1974] - in Russian; Rubtzov et al. 1980. Vidy i sorta sireni, kul'tiviruemye v SSSR. Kiev;

Naukova Dumka. – in Russian; Holetich, C.D. 1982. Lilac species and cultivars in cultivation in USSR. Lilacs 11(2):1-38. - translation of Rubtzov et al. 1982.
Name: Russian for schoolgirl; named for Mikhaïlov's elder daughter who entered first grade of secondary school in the year the cultivar was named.
Cultivar name established and accepted.

'Sholokhov', *S. vulgaris*
 'Шолохов'
 Kolesnikov pre-1961; S IV-V
 syn. - Kolesnikov No. 061, 'M. Scholochov', 'Scholokhov', 'Sholokhov', 'Sholokov'
 {'Alphonse Lavallée' × 'Kolesnikov No. 504'}
 Gromov, Lilacs - Proceedings 2(4):16 [1974]; Rubtzov et al. 1980. Vidy i sorta sireni, kul'tiviruemye v SSSR. Kiev; Naukova Dumka. – in Russian; Holetich, C.D. 1982. Lilac species and cultivars in cultivation in USSR. Lilacs 11(2):1-38. - translation of Rubtzov et al. 1982.
 Named for Mikhaïl Aleksandrovich Sholokhov, 1905-1984, Russian journalist and writer ("And Quiet Flows the Don", "Virgin Soil Upturned"), winner of the Nobel Prize in Literature 1965.
 Cultivar name established and accepted.

'Sholpan', *S. vulgaris*
 'Шолпан'
 Mel'nik, Rubanik & Dyagilev 1989, D III/IV
 {'President Grévy' × OP} (seedling 86)
 Dyagilev, Lilacs - Quart. Jour. 22(1):20 [1993]; Pikaleva, Lilacs - Quart. Jour. 23(4):88 [1994]
 This is a woman's name in Kazakhstan and means morning star.
 Cultivar name established and accepted.

'Siberian', *S.* (species affiliation not known)
 origin not known pre-1874; ? ?
 Windsor Nurseries, Cat. [1874]
 Cultivar name not established; probably extinct.

Siberian lilac, *S.* (species not known) Origin not known; S VI
 Notcutt, Cat., 49 [1934] - described as a red flowering species.
 Common name, not cultivar name.

'Siberica', *S.* ×*chinensis*
 Origin not known; S ?
 Stand. Pl. Names, 617 [1942] - as Sibirica, name only; Wister, Lilacs for America, 37, 58 [1942] - "Many *S. chinensis* cultivars were grafted on *S. vulgaris*, and suckers from the stock have crowded out the true cultivars."; perhaps a Loddiges specimen of the mid 19th century - in litt. Colin Chapman to F. Vrugtman [Jan. 22, 2008]
 Cultivar name not established; not recorded in cultivation in 1953.

'Sibirica', *S. vulgaris*
 origin not known pre-1836; S VII
 Loddiges, Cat., 67 [1836] - name only; McKelvey, The Lilac, 383 [1928]; Anon., Lilacs - Quart. Jour. 17(1):22 [1988] - in cult. at Rochester Parks, NY.
 Cultivar name not established.

'Sibirica Alba', *S.* ×*chinensis*
 Origin not known; S I
 Elwanger & Barry, Cat., [1892] - described as vigorous grower, foliage small and narrow, flowers white with a bluish tint.
 Cultivar name not established; not recorded in cultivation in 1953.

'Siebold', *S. vulgaris*
 Lemoine 1906; D I
 Lemoine, Cat. No. 164, 8 [1906]; McKelvey, The Lilac, 384 [1928]; Wister, Lilacs for America, 58 [1942], 41 [1953]; Photo on Jorgovani/Lilacs 2015 DVD.
 Named for Philip Franz von Siebold, 1796-1866, German physician and botanist.
 Cultivar name presumed registered 1953; name established and accepted.

'Sierra Blue', not a *Syringa*
 Lammerts May 26, 2002
 Wister, Lilac Registrations (mimeogr. list), 4 [n.d.; ca 1968] - this is a cultivar of *Ceanothus* L or California lilac, not a *Syringa*.
 Erroneous registration.

'Sierra Snow', *S.* ×*hyacinthiflora*
 Lammerts 1963; S I
 Lammerts, US Pl. Pat. No. 2,744 [May 30, 1967] - parentage information incomplete; Wister, Lilac Registration (mimeogr. list), 5 [appr. 1967] - as *S. vulgaris* L. × *S. laciniata* Mill.; Photo on Jorgovani/Lilacs 2015 DVD.
 Cultivar name registered 1967; name established and accepted.
 Nota bene: Since this cultivar appears to be of 'Lavender Lady' ancestry; see also: Pringle, Lilacs - Quart. Jour. 24(4):97-99 [1995]; and Vrugtman, HortScience 31(3):328 [1996]

SIGNATURE™ - see 'Sigzam'.

'Sigzam', *S. reticulata* subsp. *reticulata*
 Zampini 1999; S I
 marketed in North America as SIGNATURE™
 Lake County Nursery, Inc., Cat., 5 [1999] - name only, as *S. japonica* 'Sigzam', in litt. J. Zampini to F. Vrugtman [Apr. 08, 2004] - similar to 'Ivory Silk' but thyrses globose instead of pyramidal, bronze autumn color.
 Cultivar name established and accepted.

'Si Ji Lan', *S.*
 Zang & Fan 1989; S III-VII/VI
 {*S. pubescens* subsp. *pubescens* × *S. pubescens* subsp. *microphylla*}
 syn. - 'Si Gi Lan', 'Sijilan', 'Si Ji-Lan', 'Si Jilan'
 Acta Horticulturae 404:63-67 [1995]; Vrugtman,

HortScience 33(4):588-589 [1998] - as 'Sijilan'; Anon., Beijing Bot. Garden 2006:24 - as *S. meyeri* 'Si Ji Lan'; Photo on Jorgovani/Lilacs 2015 DVD.
Cultivar name registered 1997; name established and accepted.

'Silja', *S. vulgaris*
Vaigla 1969; D II/V (IV/I per Semenov)
{'Mrs Edward Harding' × ? }
Kivistik, Maakodu 1997(5):22-23 (ill.) [1997]; I. Semenov, Lilacs 48(2):64,65,58 (photo) [2019].
Cultivar name established and accepted.

'Silver King', *S. vulgaris*
Lemke 1941; S III
Wister, Lilacs for America, 58 [1942], 41 [1953]; Vrugtman, Lilacs - Proceedings 12(1):21 [1983]; Lilacs - Quart. Jour. 24(1): front cover ill. [1995]; Chapman, Lilacs - Quart. Jour. 31(2):35-36 & front cover ill. [2002]; Holetich, Lilacs - Quart. Jour. 31(4):89 & back cover ill. [2002]; Photo on Jorgovani/Lilacs 2015 DVD.
Cultivar name presumed registered 1953; name established and accepted.

'Silvia', *S.* (Villosae Group), *S. ×prestoniae*
Preston 1928; S V
syn. - Preston No. 20-14-99, 'Sylvia', *josikaea* 'Silvia', *josikaea* 'Sylvia'
{*S. villosa* subsp. *villosa* × *S. komarowii* subsp. *reflexa*}
Macoun, Rep. Dom. Hort. 1928, 57 [1930] - name only; Wister, Lilacs for America, 58, 64 [1942], 41, 48 [1953]; Monrovia Nurs., Wholesale Cat., 82 [1970]; Photo on Jorgovani/Lilacs 2015 DVD.
Named for the Daughter to the Duke of Milan in Shakespeare's *Two Gentlemen of Verona*.
Cultivar name presumed registered 1953; name established and accepted.

'Silvi Vrait', *S. vulgaris*
Vaigla pre-2001; D V-I
listed on http://aed.rapina.ee/sirelid.htm [seen 5 Nov. 2005]; I. Semenov, Lilacs 48(2):65 [2019].
Cultivar name not established.

'Simfonija', *S. vulgaris*
Kārkliņš 2003; D II
Photo on Jorgovani/Lilacs 2015 DVD.
Name: Latvian for symphony.
Cultivar name not established.

'Simpātija', *S. vulgaris*
Kārkliņš 2003; S VII/II
under evaluation at Latvia State Institute of Fruit Growing, Dobele
Photo on Jorgovani/Lilacs 2015 DVD.
Name: Latvian for sympathy.
Cultivar name not established.

Sinai, Sinai Hell Lila, Sinai hell-lila and Sinai Lila - see **'Hermann Eilers'**.

'Sineglazka', *S. vulgaris*
'Синеглазка'
Makedonskaya, 2018; S III
{open pollinated seedling}
Statutory registration with the State Inspection for testing and protection of plant varieties of the Republic of Belarus. Makedonskaya N. 'Assortment of lilac varieties for landscaping cities and towns of Belarus' pp 85-89 "International Scientific Conference "Syringa L.: collections, cultivation, using" / Collection of Scientific Articles of Botanical Institute named after V.L. Komarov, Botanical Garden of Peter the Great BIN RAS. - St. Petersburg. -2020 (in Russian)
Name: Russian for girl with blue eyes.
Cultivar name established and accepted.

'Sinen′kiĭ Skromnyĭ Platochek', *S. vulgaris*
'Синенький Скромный Платочек'
Aladin, S., Polyakova, T., Okuneva, I., and Akimova, S. 2011; S III
{parentage not known}
Vestnik Tzvetovoda No. 9(149):22-26 [May 2010]; Registered with the State Commission of the Russian Federation for Testing and Protection of Selection Achievements, No. 8853121, 2011; Питомник-частный сад (Pitomnik i chastnyi sad; Nursery and private garden) 3/2015:14-22 (in Russian); Садовник (Gardener) magazine 04 (140)/2017 :18-25; ; Приусадебное хозяйство (Annex to the magazine Homestead farming: "Flowers in the garden and at home. Brushes and paints") 08/2015: 5-14; Вестник АППМ (Catalog in Vestnik APPM (Planting material association) 1/2018: 59-72 (in Russian); Photo on Jorgovani/Lilacs 2015 DVD.
Named for the most popular Russian song of the Second World War: "Modest little blue head-scarf".
Cultivar name registered, established and accepted.

'Sinensis alba', *S. vulgaris*
International Exhibition, 1876, US Centennial Commission, Volume 11, p. 310 - name only. (possibly: *S. ×chinensis* 'Alba')
Cultivar name not established.

'Sir Alvin', *S. vulgaris*
Klager; S V
Anon., ILS Newsletter 14(4):3-4 [1988]
Cultivar name not established.

'Sirenevaya Piramida', *S. vulgaris*
'Сиреневая Пирамида'
Potutova 1971; S VII
syn. - 'Sirenevaja Piramida'
Rubtzov et al. 1980. Vidy i sorta sireni, kul'tiviruemye v SSSR. Kiev; Naukova Dumka. – in Russian; Holetich, C.D. 1982. Lilac species and cultivars in cultivation in USSR. Lilacs 11(2):1-38. - translation of Rubtzov et al. 1982.
Name: Russian for lilac pyramid.
Cultivar name established and accepted.

'Sirenevoe Schast'e', *S. vulgaris*
'Сиреневое счастье'
Aladin, S., Aladina, O., and Polyakova, T. 2014; S IV
{'Me<u>ch</u>ta' × OP}
Садовник (Gardener) magazine 04 (140)/2017 :18-25; Вестник АППМ (Catalog in Vestnik APPM (Planting material association) magazine) 1/2018: 59-72 (in Russian).
Name: Russian for lilac happiness – with reference to Rachmaninov's song, Op. 21, No. 5, Lilacs: "In life, only one happiness was destined for me to discover, and that happiness lives in the lilacs; in the green boughs, in the fragrant blooms, my unworthy happiness blossoms..."
Cultivar name established and accepted.

'Sirenevyĭ Kaskad', *S. vulgaris*
'Сиреневый Каскад'
Klimenko, V. & Z., & Grigor'ev 1955; S IV
syn. - 'Sirenvyj Kaskad'
{'Mme Casimir Périer' × 'Andenken an Ludwig Späth'}
Rubtzov et al. 1980. Vidy i sorta sireni, kul'tiviruemye v SSSR. Kiev; Naukova Dumka. – in Russian; Holetich, C.D. 1982. Lilac species and cultivars in cultivation in USSR. Lilacs 11(2):1-38. - translation of Rub<u>tz</u>ov et al. 1982.
Name: Russian for lilac cascade.
Cultivar name established and accepted.

'Sirenevyĭ Tuman', *S. vulgaris*
'Сиреневый Туман'
Strekalov pre-2010; ? ?
Vestnik <u>Ts</u>vetovoda May 09 (149) 2010, p. 25 - name only
Named for the song "Sirenevyĭ Tuman" (Purple Haze) of the mid 1980s.
Cultivar name not established

Sister Justena - see '**Sister Justina**'.

'**Sister Justina**', *S.* ×*hyacinthiflora*
Skinner 1956; S I
syn. - 'Sister Justena'
Wister, Lilacs for America, 41 [1953]; Skinner's Nurs., Cat., 13 [1956]; Skinner, Hort. Horizons, 50, 81, Pl.27, 108 [1966]; Fiala, 90, 92, 205, Pl. 45 [1988] - as 'Sister Justena'; Lilacs - Quart. Jour. 21(1): front cover ill. [1992]; Photo on Jorgovani/Lilacs 2015 DVD.
Cultivar name presumed registered 1953; name established and accepted.

'**Skinneri**', *S.*
Skinner 1947; S I
syn. - *S. skinneri* Hort.
{*S. pubescens* subsp. *patula* × *S. pubescens* subsp. *pubescens*}
Skinner's Nurs., Cat., 12 [1947] - as *S. skinneri*; Woody Plant Register AAN, No. 64 [1949]; Wister, Lilacs for America, 41 [1953]; Photo on Jorgovani/Lilacs 2015 DVD.
Named for Frank Leith Skinner, 1882-1967, Canadian nurseryman.
Cultivar name presumed registered 1953; name established and accepted.

skinneri Hort. - see '**Skinneri**'.

'Skromnitsa', *S. vulgaris*
'Скромница'
Mikhaĭlov & Rybakina 2002; S V-I
{'Alenu<u>sh</u>ka' × 'Pascal'}
Chapman, Lilacs - Quart. Jour. 32(1):17-18 [2003] - translated from N. L. Mikhaĭlov in <u>Ts</u>vetovodstvo, May-June issue (in Russian); http://home.onego.ru/~otsoppe/enciclop/kustar/syring_s.html (July 26, 2003); Photo on Jorgovani/Lilacs 2015 DVD.
Name: Russian for modest.
Cultivar name established and accepted.

'**Slater's Elegance**', *S. vulgaris*
Slater 1964; S I
{'Agincourt Beauty' × unnamed white seedling}
J.C. Wister, Alphabetical List, 1968 addition - name only, as 'Slaters Elegance' [1968]; Landscape Canada 10(7):19 [1973]; registered with COPF in 1973; Slater, US Pl. Pat. No. 3695 [May 15, 1975] - statutory registration; Rogers, O.M., Tentative International Register - name only, as 'Slaters Elegance', p. 69 [1976]; Sheridan Nurs., Cat., 56 [1983]; Lilacs - Quart. Jour. 21(1): back cover ill. [1992]; Photo on Jorgovani/Lilacs 2015 DVD; L. Gregory to F. Vrugtman in lit 3 July 2017, flower bud color Green-White Group 157D (RHS Color Chart 1966), florets White-Group 155B.
Cultivar name established, accepted and registered.

Slater's Irene - see '**Mrs Irene Slater**'.

'Slava', *S. vulgaris*
de Belder; S I
{'Rochester' seedling × ? }
X. Missone, Belgische Dendrologie 1994, p. 191 - name only; in litt. X. Misonne to D. De Meyere, [January 12, 2004] - probably extinct.
RHS Certificate of Preliminary Commendation, May 18, 1987.
Named for a relative of Jelena De Belder.
Cultivar name not established; not reported in cultivation.

'Slava Stalinu' – renamed after 1956 by originator to '**Zarya Kommunizma**'.

'Slavin', *S. komarowii* subsp. *reflexa*
Slavin & Fiala pre-1988; S V
syn. - Park No. Slavin #1
Fiala, Lilacs, p.71, Pl. 50 [1988] - selection and name proposed by J. L. Fiala
Cultivar name not established; not reported in cultivation.

'Sleeping Beauty', *S.*
Moro, F. 2001; S V

{'Josée' × ?}
F. Moro, Cat. Suppl. flyer [2001] - dwarf, re-blooming, reddish fall foliage; Giguère & Moro, Les Lilas, p. 304 [2005]; Photo on Jorgovani/Lilacs 2015 DVD.
Cultivar name established and accepted.

S. L. Wheeler - see 'Lawrence Wheeler'.

'Smaidoshais Laiks', *S. vulgaris*
Upītis ca 1970; S II
Kalniņš, L., Ceriņu jaunšķirnes Dobelē, Dārs un drava 1986(12):13-15 - in Latvian; Strautiņa, S., Ceriņu un jasmīnu avīze. LA, R., p. 62 [2002] - in Latvian
Name: Latvian for smiley time.
Cultivar name established and accepted.

'Small Blue', *S. vulgaris*
origin not known ? ?
Anon., Lilacs - Proceedings 17(1):27 [1988] - name only.
Cultivar name not established.

'Smaragd', *S. josikaea*
Schmidt 1991; S VII*
Schmidt, Gábor, & Imre Tóth, editors. 2000. Fajtaismertető a Dísznövénytermesztési és Dendrológiai Tanszék közreműködésével nemesített és honosított díszfákról díszcserjékről. Budapest; Szent István Egyetem, Kertészettudományi Kar; page 31; see also G. Schmidt <www.magyardisznoveny.hu/files/specifikus_fajta.pdf> p. 45 [2009]; Photo on Jorgovani/Lilacs 2015 DVD.
Named for the gemstone smaragd or emerald, a rich green variety of beryl.
Cultivar name established and accepted.

'Smile Kaho', *S. pubescens* subsp. *pubescens*
Ihara 2003; S VII
{*S. pubescens* subsp. *pubescens* 'Palibin' × *S. pubescens* subsp. *pubescens* 'Palibin'} Seedling number 20040520001#7.
(Vrugtman, Cultivated Plant Diversity ... 2017)
Named for Kaho Ihara second daughter of the originator.
Cultivar name registered 2015, name established and accepted.

S. M. Kirov — In Memoriam - see 'Pamyat' o S. M. Kirove'.

'SMNJRPI', *S*, (Pubescentes Series)
Wood 2017; S V
syn. - marketed in the US as Bloomerang® Dwarf Pink, trademark No. 3655456, registered 14 July 2009
{JosRebloom × ?}
http://springmeadownursery.com/plants_details.php?id=81660
USPP 29802; Canadian Plant Breeders' Rights applied for
Cultivar name established and accepted.

'SMNJRPU', *S*. (Pubescentes Series)
Wood 2013; S VII
syn. - marketed in the US as Bloomerang® Dwarf Purple, trademark No. 3655456, registered 14 July 2009
{JosRebloom × ?}
https://www.provenwinners.com/plants/syringa/bloomerang-dwarf-purple-reblooming-lilac-syringa-x
USPP 29831, 13 November 2018, statutory registration; Canadian Plant Breeders' Rights applied for
Cultivar name established and accepted.

'SMNSDTP', *S*. (Pubescentes Series)
Wood 2019; S VII
{Miss Kim × ?}
Spring Meadow Nursery (Grand Haven, MI USA)
Proven Winners Catalog 2020
Syn. – marketed in the USA as Baby Kim®, PPAF, CBRAF
Cultivar name established and accepted.

'SMNSHBBL', *S.* ×*hyacinthiflora*
Wood 2017; D III
{unnamed advance selection × ?} from mixed seed ×*hyacinthiflora* treated with gamma radiation
syn. - marketed in the US as Scentara™ Double Blue, trademark No. 87585826, registered 28 August 2017
USPP 29801 November 6, 2018; Canadian Plant Breeders' Rights applied for
http://springmeadownursery.com/plants_details.php?id=78470

'SMNSHSO', *S.* ×*hyacinthiflora*
Wood 2018; S VII
{parentage not given} from mixed seed ×*hyacinthiflora* treated with gamma radiation
Flower color RHS 85A, bud color RHS N79D
syn. - marketed in the US as Scentara Pura™
USPP 31119 November 26, 2019; Canadian Plant Breeders' Rights applied for
https://springmeadownursery.com/plantfinder/scentara-pura-78500

'SMNSYPRZ1', *S*. (Pubescentes Series)
Wood 2007; S VII
syn. - marketed in the US as Rhythm & Bloom®, trademark No. 4884895, registered 12 January 2016
{*S.* 'Josée' × ?}
US Plant Patent 26,927 (12 July 2016); statutory registration.
Canadian Plant Breeders' Rights applied for as SMSYPRZ1, 10 August 2014, No. 14-8396
Cultivar name established and accepted.

'SMSDTL', *S. pubescens* subsp. *patula*
Wood 2018; S VII
syn. - marketed in the US as Little Darling®, trademark No. ??, registered ??
USPP applied for
https://www.monrovia.com/plant-catalog/plants/6505/little-darling-lilac/
Cultivar name established and accepted.

Smokey-Grey, *S. vulgaris*
  Havemeyer; ? ?
  in litt. June 6, 1968, J. H. Alexander Sr to J. C. Wister - as unnamed selection; Eickhorst, ILS Lilac Newsletter 4(1):4-5 [1978]
  Breeder's designation or cognomen, not a cultivar name.

SMSCPM, *S.* - see: '**SMSXPM**', *S.*
  Note: Listed erroneously by Oregon Pride Nurseries, Inc. http://www.oregonpridenurseries.com/index.cfm/fuseaction/plants.plantDetail/plant_id/211/index.htm as Scent And Sensibility™ Pink lilac.
  Also listed by COPF, Plants with Restricted Propagation, October 2013, p. 14:
  http://www.copf.org/auwa/pdf/October%202013%20Restricted%20Plants.pdf
  This appears to be a typing error; should be 'SMSXPM' - in lit. Tim Wood to Vrugtman August 30, 2016.

'SMSDML3', *S. pubescens* subsp. *patula*
  Wood 2012; S VII-I
  syn. - marketed in the US and Canada as Purple Be Dazzled™ (trademark No. 85739152, registered 26 September 2012, but abandoned 2013-07-25)
  {*S. pubescens* subsp. *patula* 'De Belder' seedling × ? }
  Listed by Sheridan Nurseries 2016
  <http://www.sheridannurseries.com/plant_product_view?SH0687>
  Canadian Plant Breeders' Rights applied for 10 Sept. 2012, No. 12-7740, but withdrawn 17 March 2014.
  <www.inspection.gc.ca/english/plaveg/pbrpov/cropreport/lil/app00008944e.shtml>
  Cultivar name established and accepted.

'SMSJBP7', *S.* (Pubescentes Series)
  Wood 2010; S VII
  syn. - marketed in the US as Bloomerang® Dark Purple (trademark No. 3655456, registered 14 July 2009); also marketed as Jo Big Purple and Jo Big Pur by Rangedala Plantskola, Sweden.
  {*S.* 'Penda' × ? }
  Spring Meadow Nursery, Flowering Shrubs Spring Meadow Nursery, Inc. Starter Plants Catalog and Shrub Reference 2012-2013, pp. 1-3, 9, 17 and 69; (in print Vrugtman, Jour. Cult. Plant Diversity ... 2018)
  2014 Green Thumb Award from Direct Gardening Association USA.
  US Plant Patent 26,549 (29 March 2016); Canadian Plant Breeders' Rights No. 5076, effective 2015-06-30 to 2035-06-30.
  Cultivar name registered 2016, name established and accepted; statutory registration.

'SMSMPRZ1', *S.*
  Wood 2016; S IV
  syn. - marketed in the US as Rhythm & Bloom™
  (Trademark registered 12 January 2016, Registration No. 4884895)
  (Vrugtman, Cultivated Plant Diversity ... 2017)
  US Plant Patent No. 26,927 (12 July 2016); statutory registration.
  Cultivar name registered 2016, name accepted and established.

'SMSXPM', *S.* (Pubescentes Series)
  Wood 2007; S V
  {*S.* 'Josée' × 'Red Pixie'}
  syn. - marketed in the US as Scent And Sensibility™ Pink (trademark No. 85954899 registered 2013-06-13, but abandoned 2014-06-24.
  Spring Meadow Nursery, Flowering Shrubs Spring Meadow Nursery, Inc., Starter Plants Catalog and Shrub Reference 2012-2013, pp. 1-3, 9, 17 and 70; (in print Vrugtman, Jour. Cult. Plant Diversity ... 2018).
  US Plant Patent 26,548 (29 March 2016); Canadian Plant Breeders' Rights No. 5077, effective 2015-06-30 to 2035-06-30.
  <www.inspection.gc.ca/english/plaveg/pbrpov/cropreport/lil/app00008905e.shtml>
  Cultivar name registered 2016, name established and accepted; statutory registration.

'SMSYPRZ1' - see '**SMNSYPRZ1**'.

'Snezhinka', *S. vulgaris*
  'Снежинка'
  Kolesnikov; ? I
  syn. - 'Snezhinka'
  Gromov, A., Siren', 85 [1963] - name only; Fiala, Lilacs, p. 213 [1988] - name only
  Name: Russian for snowflake or snowball.
  Cultivar name not established.

'Snezhnyĭ Kom', *S. vulgaris*
  'Снежный Ком'
  Mel'nik, Rubanik & Dyagilev 1967; S I
  syn. - 'Snezhnii Kom', seedling No. 97
  {'Vestale' × OP}
  Rubanik, V. G. et al., Siren' - Syringa L., publishing house "Kaĭnar", Alma-Ata [1977] p 57, - in Russian;
  Rubanik, V. G. et al., Siren' - *Syringa* L., 70 [1977] - in Russian; Dyagilev, Lilacs - Quart. Jour. 22(1):20 [1993]; Pikaleva, Lilacs - Quart. Jour. 23(4):88 [1994]; Photo on Jorgovani/Lilacs 2015 DVD.
  Name: Russian for snowball.
  Cultivar name established and accepted.

Snowcap™ - see 'Elliott'.

'Snow Cap', *S. vulgaris*
  Fiala 1985; S I
  {'Rochester' × 'Professor Robert B. Clark'}
  Fiala, Lilacs, 223 [1988]; Photo on Jorgovani/Lilacs 2015 DVD.
  Cultivar name established and accepted.

Snowdance™ - see '**Bailnce**'.

'Snowdrift', *S.* (Villosae Group), *S.* ×*prestoniae*
Fiala 1983; S I
{(*S.* ×*prestoniae* × *S.* ×*josiflexa*) × *S.* ×*prestoniae*}
Fiala, Lilacs, 92, 224 [1988] - as a mixtoploid (?), conflicting dates of introduction
Cultivar name established and accepted.

'Snowflake', *S. vulgaris*
Havemeyer & Eaton; S I
Wister, Lilac Registration 1965 (mimeogr. list), 4 [ca 1968]; Eickhorst, ILS Lilac Newsletter 4(1):4-5 [1978]; Photo on Jorgovani/Lilacs 2015 DVD.
Cultivar name registered in 1965; name established and accepted.

'Snow Princess', *S. vulgaris*
Fiala 1984; D I
{'Rochester' × 'Mother Louise'}
Fiala, Lilacs, 223 [1988]
Cultivar name established and accepted.

Snow Shower, *S. vulgaris*
Sass, H.E. pre-1953; S I
syn. - 'Snow Showers'
Wister, Lilacs for America, 41 [1953]; Photo on Jorgovani/Lilacs 2015 DVD.
Cultivar name presumed registered 1953; name established and accepted.

'Snowstorm', *S. pubescens* subsp. *pubescens*
Moro, F. 1998; S I
{*S. pubescens* subsp. *pubescens* 'Palibin' × ? }
Select Plus, Cat. 2000 - as 'Snowwhite'; Giguère & Moro, Les Lilas, p. 293 [2005] - as V; F. Moro, in litt. February 21, 2008 - as S I
Cultivar name established and accepted.

Snow White, *S. vulgaris*
Oliemans 1958; D I
{mutation of 'Mme Florent Stepman'}
Wister, Arnoldia 23(4):83 [1963]; Bunnik/Stapel, in litt. January 3, 2000; Cornelis van Dam, in litt. - very limited production for forcing only
Awards: Certificate of Merit 1956 (KMTP).
Cultivar name registered 1963; name established and accepted.

'Snowy', *S.* ×*hyacinthiflora*
Schoustra 2008; S I
{'Lavender Lady' × ?}
part of BEACH PARTY™ series; see also 'Rosie'
Cultivar name established and accepted.

'Sobra', *S. vulgaris*
Rankin; D IV
{parentage not known}
Wister, Arnoldia 23(4):83 [1963]; Photo on Jorgovani/Lilacs 2015 DVD.
Cultivar name registered 1963; name established and accepted.

'Solomon Margaretten', *S. vulgaris*
Margaretten; D IV & I
{'Mme Lemoine' × ? }
Macore Co. Inc. photo library [Nov.28 1999] http://www.macore.com/photolib.htm; reported in cultivation at Royal Botanical Gardens, Ontario, Canada
Cultivar name established and accepted.

'Solov'inyĭ Sad' *S. vulgaris*
'Соловьиный Сад'
Aladin, S., Aladina, O., Polyakova, T., and Aladina, A. 2015; D IV
{'Anabel' × OP}
(Международная научная конференция "Syringa L.: коллекции, выращивание, использование") "International Scientific Conference "Syringa L.: collections, cultivation, using" / Collection of Scientific Articles of Botanical Institute named after V.L. Komarov, Botanical Garden of Peter the Great BIN RAS. - St. Petersburg. -2020.- pp. 7-13 (in Russian); Photo exhibition of all varieties of the creative breeding group "Russian Lilac" at the Festival "Lilac February", St. Petersburg, Botanical Garden of Peter the Great BIN RAS, February 22-24, 2020.
Name: Russian for Nightingale Garden
Cultivar name established and accepted.

'Sonia Colfax', *S. vulgaris*
Havemeyer; S I
Wister, Lilacs for America, 58 [1942], 41 [1953]; Eickhorst, ILS Lilac Newsletter 4(1):4-5 [1978]
Cultivar name presumed registered 1953; name established and accepted.

'Sonnet', *S. vulgaris*
Fiala 1983; S IV
{'Mrs A. Belmont' × 'Flora 1953'}
Fiala, Lilacs, 95, 223 [1988]; Photo on Jorgovani/Lilacs 2015 DVD.
Cultivar name established and accepted.

'Sorok Let Komsomola', *S. vulgaris*
'Сорок Лет Комсомола'
Kolesnikov 1959; S IV
syn. - Kolesnikov No. 176, '40 Let VLKSM', '40 Liet VLKSM'
{(Kolesnikov No. 105 × 'Congo') × 'Alphonse Lavallée'}
Gromov, A., Siren', 103 [1963]; Howard & Brizicky, AABGA Quart. Newsl. No. 64, 17-21 [1965]; Bilov et al., Siren', 75 [1974] - in Russian; Gromov, Lilacs - Proceedings 2(4):17 [1974]; Rubtzov et al. 1980. Vidy i sorta sireni, kul'tiviruemye v SSSR. Kiev; Naukova Dumka. – in Russian; Holetich, C.D. 1982. Lilac species and cultivars in cultivation in USSR. Lilacs 11(2):1-38. - translation of Rubtzov et al. 1982; Photo on Jorgovani/Lilacs 2015 DVD.
Named for the 40th anniversary of the LYCLSU (Leninist Young Communist League of the Soviet Union).
Cultivar name established and accepted.

Soumerki - see '**Sumerki**'.

Souv. . . . - see also: Souvenir . . .

Souv. de Ludwig Spaeth, Souv. of Ludwig Spaeth - see '**Andenken an Ludwig Späth**'.

Souvenir . . . - see also Souv . . . .

'**Souvenir d'Alice Harding**', *S. vulgaris*
Lemoine 1938; D I
syn. - 'Alice Harding', 'Souv. D'Alice Harding'
Lemoine, Cat. No. 212, 22 [1938]; Wister, Lilacs for America, 58 [1942], 41 [1953]; Photo on Jorgovani/Lilacs 2015 DVD.
Named for Alice Howard Harding (Mrs Edward Harding), x -1938, American amateur horticulturist and author.
Cultivar name presumed registered 1953; name established and accepted.

'**Souvenir de A. J. Klettenberg**', *S. vulgaris*
Klettenberg 1937; D VI
Wister, Lilacs for America, 41 [1953]
Cultivar name presumed registered 1953; name established and accepted.

'**Souvenir de Billiard**', *S. vulgaris*
Billiard 1875; ? ?
syn. - 'Souv. de Billiard'
Burbridge, Cultivated Plants, 408 [1877]; McKelvey, The Lilac, 561 [1928]; Wister, Lilacs for America, 37, 58 [1942], 41 [1953]
Cultivar name presumed registered 1953;
Cultivar not reported in cultivation.

'**Souvenir de Claudius Graindorge**', *S. vulgaris*
Klettenberg 1930; S V
syn. - 'Souv. de Claudius Graindorge'
Klettenberg, Cat., 18 [1930]; Wister, Lilacs for America, 37, 58 [1942] - as S V; Wister, Lilacs for America, 41 [1953] - name only; Photo on Jorgovani/Lilacs 2015 DVD.
Named for Claude Graindorge, 1891-1914, one of two sons of Henry Graindorge killed in battle during World War One; Henry Graindorge, 1862-1943, was a grower of forced lilacs near Paris, France.
Cultivar name presumed registered 1953; name established and accepted.

'**Souvenir de Florent Stepman**', *S. vulgaris*
Klettenberg 1934; S VI
syn. - 'Souv. de Florent Stepman'
Klettenberg, Cat., 21 [1934]; Wister, Lilacs for America, 41 [1953]
Named for Grégoire Léopold Florent Stepman, 1856-1915, nurseryman and florist (Stepman-Demessemaeker), Anderlecht and Molenbeek-Sint-Jean, Bruxelles, Belgium.
Cultivar name presumed registered 1953; name established and accepted.

'**Souvenir de François Nagels**', *S. vulgaris*
Klettenberg 1937; S VI
syn. - 'Souv. de François Nagels'
Wister, Lilacs for America, 41 [1953]
Cultivar name presumed registered 1953; name established and accepted.

'**Souvenir de Gaspard Callot**', *S. vulgaris*
origin not known; D VII
syn. - 'Dr Gaspard Callot', 'Souv. de Gaspard Callot'
common name: Gaspard Callot
Stand. Pl. Names, 615 [1942] - as Gaspard Callot; Wister, Lilacs for America, 37, 58 [1942] - as D VI; Wister, Lilacs for America, 28, 41 [1953]; Photo on Jorgovani/Lilacs 2015 DVD.
Named for Gaspard Callot, 1866 - x.
Cultivar name presumed registered 1953; name established and accepted.

'**Souvenir de Georges Truffaut**', *S. vulgaris*
Lemoine 1953; D VI
syn. - 'Souv. de Georges Truffaut'
Lemoine, Cat. No. 225, 3 [1954]; Wister, Lilacs for America, 41 [1953]
Named for George Truffaut, 1872-1945, French horticulturist, founder of the Company George Truffaut, 1897, at Vineuil, and founder of Jardinage, the first review of horticulture, 1911.
Cultivar name presumed registered 1953; name established and accepted.

'**Souvenir de Gérard op't Eynde**', *S. vulgaris*
Klettenberg 1930; S IV
syn. - 'Souv. de Gérard op't Eynde'
Klettenberg, Cat., 18 [1930]; Wister, Lilacs for America, 41 [1953]
Cultivar name presumed registered 1953; name established and accepted.

'**Souvenir de Gustave Graindorge**', *S. vulgaris*
Klettenberg 1930; S VII
syn. - 'Souv. de Gustave Graindorge'
Klettenberg, Cat., 18 [1930]; Wister, Lilacs for America, 37, 58 [1942], 41 [1953]
Named for Gustave Graindorge, 1893-1917, one of two sons of Henry Graindorge killed in battle during World War One; Henry Graindorge, 1862-1943, was a grower of forced lilacs near Paris, France.
Cultivar name presumed registered 1953; name established and accepted.

'**Souvenir de Henri Simon**', *S. vulgaris*
Simon pre-1920; S III
syn. - 'Souv. de Henri Simon', 'Souv. de Henry Simon'
Turbat, Cat. [1912]; McKelvey, The Lilac, 384 [1928]; Wister, Lilacs for America, 58 [1942], 41 [1953]; Photo on Jorgovani/Lilacs 2015 DVD.
Cultivar name presumed registered 1953; name established and accepted.

'**Souvenir de Louis Chasset**', *S. vulgaris*
　　Lemoine 1953; S VI
　　syn. - 'Souv. de Louis Chasset', 'Souvenir de Luis Chasset'
　　Named for Louis Chasset, 1873-1950, French horticulturist and writer ("Manuel d'arboriculture fruitière", 1941).
　　Lemoine, Cat., No. 228, 3 [1957]
　　Cultivar name presumed registered 1953; name established and accepted.

'**Souvenir de L. Thibaut**', *S. vulgaris*
　　Lemoine 1893; D V
　　syn. - 'Souvenir de Louis Thibaut', 'Souvenir de Thibault'
　　common name: Thibaut
　　Lemoine, Cat. No. 125, 9 [1893]; Stand. Pl. Names, 488 [1923] - as Thibaut; McKelvey, The Lilac, 384 [1928]; Wister, Lilacs for America, 58 [1942], 41 [1953]; Photo on Jorgovani/Lilacs 2015 DVD.
　　Named for Louis Thibaut, 1817-1892, French horticulturist, partner of Doyen Keteleer.
　　Cultivar name presumed registered 1953; name established and accepted.

Souvenir de Ludwig Spaeth - see '**Andenken an Ludwig Späth**'.

'**Souvenir de Mevrouw Dr Kenis**', *S. vulgaris*
　　Nelen 1936; S II
　　syn. - 'Mevrouw Dr Kenis', 'Mrs Edmond Kenis', 'Souv. de Mevr. Dr Kenis', 'Souv. de Mme Edmond Kenis', 'Souvenir de Mme Edmond Kenis'
　　Lombarts, Cat., 54 [1950]; Wister, Lilacs for America, 41 [1953]; Photo on Jorgovani/Lilacs 2015 DVD.
　　Cultivar name presumed registered 1953; name established and accepted.

Souvenir de Mme Edmond Kenis - see '**Souvenir de Mevrouw Dr Kenis**'.

'Souvenir de Mme Léon Kenis', *S. vulgaris*
　　Kenis 1936; ? ?
　　Belgische Dendrologie 1994, p. 191
　　Cultivar name not established.

'Souvenir de Mme Louis Gielis', *S. vulgaris*
　　Gielis 1950; S I
　　syn. - 'Louis S I Gillis', 'Mme Louis Gialis', 'Souv. de Mme Louis Gielis'
　　Wister, Lilacs for America, 42 [1953] - name only; Vrugtman, Lilacs -Quart. Jour. 32(4):149 [2003] - as S I
　　Cultivar name not established.

Souvenir de Rothpletz - see '**Stadtgärtner Rothpletz**'.

'**Souvenir de Simone**', *S. vulgaris*
　　Bruchet pre-1923; D I
　　Turbat, Cat., 76 [1923]; McKelvey, The Lilac, 385 [1928]; Wister, Lilacs for America, 58 [1942], 42 [1953]; Photo on Jorgovani/Lilacs 2015 DVD.
　　Cultivar name presumed registered 1953; name established and accepted.

'**Souvenir de Slock**', *S. vulgaris*
　　Slock pre-1913; S IV
　　Wister, Lilacs for America, 42 [1953]
　　Cultivar name presumed registered 1953; name established and accepted.

'Souvenir de Spa', *S. vulgaris*
　　origin not known pre-1893; ? ?
　　Martinet, Jardin 7:104 [1893]; McKelvey, The Lilac, 385 [1928]
　　Cultivar name not established.

Souvorovets - see 'Suvoro<u>vets</u>'.

'Sovetska<u>ya</u> Arktika', *S. vulgaris*
　　'Советская Арктика'
　　Kolesnikov 1955; D I
　　syn. - Kolesnikov No. 300, 'Sovetskaja Arktika', 'Sovjetskaia Arktika', 'Souvietskaia Arctica'
　　marketed in the USA as Russian Arctic; marketed in Europe as Schneekönigin®
　　(No. 307071529; G. & J. Rosskamp, part of the KC Kircher Collection™)
　　{'Mme Lemoine' × ('Sniez<u>h</u>inka' × 'Mme Casimir Périer')}
　　Gromov, A., Siren', 69 [1963]; Gromov, Lilacs - Proceedings 2(4):18 [1974]; Rub<u>tz</u>ov et al. 1980. Vidy i sorta sireni, kul'tiviruemye v SSSR. Kiev; Naukova Dumka. – in Russian; Holetich, C.D. 1982. Lilac species and cultivars in cultivation in USSR. Lilacs 11(2):1-38. - translation of Rub<u>tz</u>ov et al. 1982; Photo on Jorgovani/Lilacs 2015 DVD.
　　Named for the Soviet arctic.
　　Cultivar name established and accepted.

'So<u>yuz</u>-Apollon', *S. vulgaris*
　　'Союз-Аполлон'
　　Klimenko, V.; ? ?
　　syn. - 'Sojuz-Apollon'
　　Rub<u>tz</u>ov et al. 1980. Vidy i sorta sireni, kul'tiviruemye v SSSR. Kiev; Naukova Dumka. – in Russian; Holetich, C.D. 1982. Lilac species and cultivars in cultivation in USSR. Lilacs 11(2):1-38. - translation of Rub<u>tz</u>ov et al. 1982.
　　Named for the USA-USSR cooperative Apollo-Soyuz spaceflight project, 1975.
　　Cultivar name not established.

'Speciosa', *S. vulgaris*
　　origin not known pre-1857; S ?
　　Ellwanger & Barry, Cat., No. 2 [1857]; International Exhibition, 1876, US Centennial Commission, Volume 11, p. 310 - name only; McKelvey, The Lilac, 385 [1928] - as doubtful name; Wister, Lilacs for America, 58 [142], 42 [1953]
　　Cultivar name not established; doubtful name

'Spectabilis', *S. vulgaris*
　　origin not known pre-1845; ? ?
　　syn. - 'Remarquable'
　　Oudin, Cat. [1845]; McKelvey, The Lilac, 385-386 [1928]

- confused name; Photo on Jorgovani/Lilacs 2015 DVD.
Cultivar name not established.

'Spectabilis', *S. vulgaris*
origin not known pre-1876; S IV
International Exhibition, 1876, US Centennial Commission, Volume 11, p. 310 - name only; Wister, Lilacs for America, 37, 58 [1942]; Anon., Lilacs - Proceedings 17(1):22 [1988] - recorded as having been planted in 1892, name only
Cultivar name not established.

'Spellbinder', *S.* (Villosae Group)
Fiala 1968; S V
{*S. komarowii* subsp. *komarowii* × *S. villosa* subsp. *wolfii*}
Fiala, Lilacs, 7, 101, 224, Pl. 56 [1988] - as *S.* ×*clarkiana* J.L.Fiala (hybrid name not validly published), and induced tetraploid (?)
Cultivar name established and accepted.

'Splendor', *S.* ×*hyacinthiflora*
Clarke 1948; D VII
syn. - 'Purple Splendour'
{unnamed double seedling × ? }
AAN reg'n card No. 518; Clarke, Wholes. Cat., 18 [1948] - as *S. vulgaris*; Clarke, US Pl. Pat. No. 837 [May 17, 1949] - as *S. vulgaris*; Wister, Lilacs for America, 42 [1953] - as "Early Hybrid of giraldi"; Photo on Jorgovani/Lilacs 2015 DVD.
Cultivar name presumed registered 1953; name established and accepted.

'Spokane', *S.*
Ballreich 1995; D V
syn. - #3-203
{*S. vulgaris* 'Tita' × *S.* ×*hyacinthiflora* 'Mary Short'}
Ballreich, Lilacs - Quart. Jour. 28(4):91-92 [1999] - name only, as *vulgaris*; Peterschick, Lilacs - Quart. Jour. 31(3):73 [2002] - as double pink; M. Prager, The Spokesman-Review, D7 [April 25, 2003]; E. Kelcoyne, Lilacs - Quart. Jour. 32(3):112 [2003]; Vrugtman, HortScience 39(6):1524 [2004]; Munts, The Spokesman-Review Sect. D1, pp. 1 & 8 [April 22, 2005]; Photo on Jorgovani/Lilacs 2015 DVD.
Named for the city of Spokane, Washington State, USA.
Cultivar name registered 2003, name established and accepted.

SPORT OF EDMOND BOSSIER (sic.), *S. vulgaris*
Hohman pre-1949; S II-VII
most likely refers to a sport of 'Edmond Boissier'
Kingsville Nurseries, Cat., 71 [n.d.; rec'd stamp Jan. 1949]
Not a cultivar name.

SPORT OF SENSATION, *S. vulgaris*
RBG, Hamilton; S I
syn. - RBG no. 71560, see also SENSATION SPORT
{mutation of *S. vulgaris* 'Sensation'}
Peterson, Lilacs-Proceedings 16(1):22 [1987] - as Sensation Sport, name only; in litt. Holetich to Vrugtman, Mar. 08, 2007; Photo on Jorgovani/Lilacs 2015 DVD.
Selector's designation orr cognomen, not a cultivar name.

'Spring Dawn', *S.* ×*hyacinthiflora*
Clarke 1960; S III
Clarke, Cat., 41 [1959]; Wister, Arnoldia 23(4):83 [1963]
Cultivar name registered 1963; name established and accepted.

'Spring Glory', *S.* ×*hyacinthiflora*
Clarke 1958 (not Spaargaren); S V
Wister, Arnoldia 23(4):83 [1963]
Awards: Certificate of Merit 1957 (KMTP).
Cultivar name registered 1963;
Cultivar not reported in cultivation.

'Spring Glory', *S. vulgaris*
Spaargaren 1957 (not Clarke); S V
Wister, Arnoldia 23(4):83 [1963]
Cultivar name registered 1963;
Cultivar not reported in cultivation.

Spring in Descanso - see **Descanso Spring**.

'Spring Parade', *S. vulgaris*
Fiala 1984; S IV
{'Rochester' × unnamed seedling}
Fiala, Lilacs, 223 [1988]; Photo on Jorgovani/Lilacs 2015 DVD.
Cultivar name established and accepted.

'Spring Song', *S.* (species affiliation not known)
origin not known 1979; S V
Little Lake Nursery, Cat., inside back cover [1980]
Cultivar name not established.

'Spring Sonnet', *S.* ×*hyacinthiflora*
Sobeck; S IV
Wister, Arnoldia 26(3):13 [1966].
Cultivar name registered 1966; name established and accepted.
Nota bene: Since this cultivar appears to be of 'Lavender Lady' ancestry see also: Pringle, Lilacs - Quart. Jour. 24(4):97-99 [1995]; and Vrugtman, HortScience 31(3):328 [1996]

'Springtime', *S.* (Villosae Group)
Fiala 1968; S V
{(*S. tomentella* subsp. *sweginzowii* × *S. tomentella* subsp. *tomentella*) × *S. villosa* subsp. *wolfii*)}
Fiala, Lilacs, 7, 102, 224 [1988] - as *S.* ×*fialiana* R.B. Clark (hybrid name not validly published)
Cultivar name established and accepted.

'Square Deal', *S. vulgaris*
Hoepfl 1995; D VII/II
syn. - FC 09

{'Flower City' × ? }
Hoepfl, Lilacs - Quart. Jour. 36(2):74-75 and front & back cover photos [2007] - background information only; (Vrugtman, Cultivated Plant Diversity ... 2017)
Named for the campaign slogan of Theodore Roosevelt, US president 1901-1909.
Cultivar name registered 2016; name established and accepted.

St. . . . - see also: Saint . . .

'Stadtgärtner Rothpletz', *S. vulgaris*
Froebel 1905; S VII
syn. - 'Gloire de Rothpletz', 'Souvenir de Rothpletz', 'Stadtgärtner Rodpeltz'
common name: Stadtgartner Rothpletz
Froebel, Cat. No. 134, 2 [1905] - probably S; Wister, National Hort. Mag. 6(1):14 [1927]; McKelvey, The Lilac, 386 [1928] - no clear description; Stand. Pl. Names, 617 [1942] - as Stadtgartner Rothpletz, double florets; Wister, Lilacs for America, 58 [1942], 42 [1953] - as D VII; Meyer, Flieder, 62-63 [1952] - as S; Vrugtman, Lilac Newsletter 6(3):3 [1980]
Named for Mr Rothpletz, "city gardener" of Zürich, Switzerland, ca 1910.
Cultivar name not established; no clear description available.
Nota bene: Plants cultivated in North America under the name of 'Stadtgartner Rothpletz' appear to be all double-flowered and are not true-to-name.

'Stalingrad', *S. vulgaris*
Aladin, S., Aladina, O., Polyakova, T., and Aladina, A. 2017; S VI-IV
{elite form 8-356 × OP}
IX International Scientific Conference (IX Международная научная конференция "Цветоводство: история, теория, практика") " Floriculture: history, theory, practice", St. Petersburg, Botanical Garden of Peter the Great BIN RAS, September 7-13, 2019 (in Russian); Photo by Tatiana Polyakova Database published in Vestnic (Gardener's Herald) 5/22/2016/
Named for the heroic Russian city Stalingrad whose defense was a turning point in the World War II.
Cultivar name established and accepted.

'Stamm 12', *S. vulgaris*
Löbner 1929.
Meyer, Flieder, 76 [1952]; Krüssmann, Die Baumschule, 2nd ed., pp. 454-460 [1954] - seed provenance for rootstock production selected at the Versuchsanstalt Friesdorf, Bonn, Germany
Cultivar name not established; perhaps extinct.

'Stanisław Moniuszko', *S. vulgaris*
Karpow-Lipski 1971; S II-VI
{'Mikołaj Karpow-Lipski' × ? }
Anon., Lista odmian roślin ozdobnych 1971, 17; varietal denomination registered COBORU 1971; Lista..1973, 25; Lista . . . 1980, 153 - in Polish; Lilak Pospolity - COBO Informator 8/78 [1976], statutory registration; Photo on Jorgovani/Lilacs 2015 DVD.
Named for Stanisław Moniuszko, 1819-1872, Polish composer.
Cultivar name registered; name established and accepted.

'Staraya Moskva', *S. vulgaris*
'Старая Москва'
Aladin, S., Aladina, O., Polyakova, T., and, Aladina, A. 2015; S II
{'Cavour' × 'Monge'}
Садовник (Gardener) magazine 04 (140)/2017 :18-25; Вестник АППМ (Catalog in Vestnik APPM (Planting material association) magazine) 1/2018: 59-72 (in Russian).
Name: Russian for old Moscow.
Cultivar name established and accepted.

'Starlight', *S. vulgaris*
Fiala, (not Polin); S I
{'Rochester' × 'Primrose'}
Fiala, Lilacs, 223 (1988)
Cultivar name not established; rejected name.

'Starlight', *S. vulgaris*
Polin (not Fiala); D II
Wister & Oppe, Arnoldia 31(3):123 [1971]
Cultivar name registered 1970;
Cultivar not reported in cultivation.

'Starry Skies', *S.* (species affiliation not known)
origin not known 2004; D V
Anon., Lilacs - Quart. Jour. 33(1):11 [2004]
Cultivar name not established.

'Steencruysii', *S.*
(species affiliation uncertain)
origin not known pre-1855; S VII
syn. - 'Steencruys', 'Steencruysi', 'Steenkruyssii'
Dauvesse, Cat. No. 20, 24 [1855] - name only; Ellwanger & Barry, Cat. No. 2, 42 [1867]; McKelvey, The Lilac, 465, 515-516 [1928]; Rehder, Bibliogr., 568b [1949]; Wister, Lilacs for America, 59 [1942], 42 [1953].
Cultivar name presumed registered 1953; name established and accepted.
Nota bene: S. ×chinensis 'Steencruysii' is listed as being in cultivation at Monroe County Parks, Rochester, New York, in 1988. It was obtained in 1892 as *S. vulgaris* Steencruysi from Parsons Nursery, Flushing, NY, who listed it as having "dark reddish-purple flowers" (S VII). Lit. ref.: Parsons Nursery catalog, 1890, p. 50; Wister, J. C., Lilacs for America 1953, p. 42; Lilacs-Proceedings 17(1):19 [1988]; in lit, K. Millham to F. Vrugtman [May 20, 2004] - RHS Color Chart between 77B and C, fading to 76C.

'Stefan Makowiecki', *S. vulgaris*
Karpow-Lipski 1958; S VI-VII
syn. - Siewka nr 145

Karpow-Lipski, Arboretum Kórnickie 3:104 [1958]; varietal denomination registered COBORU 1971; Wister & Oppe, Arnoldia 31(3):126 [1971] - as S VI; Anon., Lista odmian roślin ozdobnych 1971, 17 & Lista..1973, 25
Named for Stefan Makowiecki, 1860-1949, Polish horticulturist, dendrologist and author.
Cultivar name registered 1970; name established and accepted.

'Stephanie Rowe', *S. vulgaris*
Berdeen 1979; S V
syn. - 'Stephie Rowe'
Fiala, Lilacs, 100, 217 [1988] - only as "pink"; King & Coggeshall, Lilacs - Quart. Jour. 27(2):49-50 [1998] - name only; Vrugtman, Lilacs -Quart. Jour. 32(4):149 [2003] - as S V
Cultivar name established and accepted.

Stepman - see '**Mme Florent Stepman**'.

'Stepman Max', *S. vulgaris*
origin not known pre-1952; ? I
Wister, Lilacs for America, 42 [1953]
Cultivar name not established.

STERNTALER™ - see Primrose (Holden).

St. Jerzy Popieluszko - see 'Saint Jerzy Popieluszko'.

'**St Joan**', *S. vulgaris*
Blacklock ca 1957; D I
syn. - 'Saint Joan'
Rowancroft Gardens, Cat. No. 15, 30 [n.d.; ca 1957]; Wister, Arnoldia 23(4):82 [1963] - erroneously as 'Saint Joan'; Photo on Jorgovani/Lilacs 2015 DVD.
Named for a St Joan (there are about 22 saints by the name of Joan).
Cultivar name registered 1963; name established and accepted.

'**St Margaret**', *S. vulgaris*
Blacklock ca 1957; D I
syn. - 'Saint Margaret', 'Saint Margareth', 'Frau Holle' marketed in Germany as FRAU HOLLE™ (#3070701510; G. & J Rosskamp)
Rowancroft Gardens, Cat. No. 15, 30 [n.d.; ca 1957]; Wister, Arnoldia 23(4):82 [1963] - erroneously as 'Saint Margaret'; Photo on Jorgovani/Lilacs 2015 DVD.
Named for a St Margaret (there are about 28 saints by the name of Margaret).
Cultivar name registered 1963; name established and accepted.

'Stolovaya', *S. vulgaris*
'Столовая'
Michurin; ? VII
Achievements I. V. Michurin vol.1, p.160 [date ?]; Rubtzov et al. 1980. Vidy i sorta sireni, kul'tiviruemye v SSSR. Kiev; Naukova Dumka. – in Russian; Holetich, C.D. 1982. Lilac species and cultivars in cultivation in USSR. Lilacs 11(2):1-38. - translation of Rubtzov et al.
1982 - earliest cultivar selection made in Russia, does not exceed 35 cm in height.
Name: Russian for canteen.
Cultivar name not established; extinct.

'Streflexa', *S. villosa* subsp. *villosa*
Origin not known; S V
Kingsville Nurseries, Noteworthy Flowering Trees and Shrubs for the Home Landscape, 67 [n.d.; ca Jan. 1949]
Cultivar name not established.

'**Stropkey Variegated**', *S. josikaea*
Stropkey; S V *
{open-pollinated seedling}
Stropkey, US Pl. Pat. No. 2204 [Dec. 25, 1962]; Wister & Oppe, Arnoldia 31(3):123 [1971]; in lit. Paul Stropkey to Mark DeBard, July 19, 2017, 'Stropkey Variegated' is still extant at their nursery.
Cultivar name registered 1970; name established and accepted.

'Subjosikaea', *S.* (species affiliation uncertain)
origin not known pre-1942; ? ?
syn. - *henryi subjosikaea*
Wister, Lilacs for America, 59 [1942], 42 [1953]
Cultivar name not established.

SUGAR PLUM FAIRY™ - see '**Bailsugar**'.

'Sultan', *S. vulgaris*
Origin not known pre-2016; S IV
<http://www.esveld.nl/zoeken.php?zoekterm=syringa&product=planten&pagina=6>
seen 8 Feb. 2017
Cultivar name not established.

'Sulte', *S.* (Villosae Group), *S. ×josiflexa*
origin not known pre-1936; S IV
syn. - *S. rothomagensis* 'Sulte', *villosa sulte*
Wister, Lilacs for America, 59 [1942], 42 [1953] - as doubtful name, *S. villosa* selection, or identical to 'Lutèce'; Howell Nurseries, Price List, 27 [1943]; Wyman, Arnoldia 8(7):34 [1948] - as *S. ×chinensis* cultivar; Vrugtman, Lilac Newsletter 6(7):4-5 [1980]; Anon., Lilacs - Quart. Jour. 21(4):106 [1992] - as *S. vulgaris* cultivar
Named (perhaps) for Benjamin Sulte, 1841-1923, French-Canadian poet, journalist, critic, historian and author of the 8 volume "Histoire des Canadiens-Français", 1882/85.
Cultivar name not established.

'Sumerki', *S. vulgaris* (not Kolesnikov)
Sagitova; S VII
no information
Cultivar name not established.

'**Sumerki**', *S. vulgaris*
'Сумерки'
Kolesnikov 1954; S II

syn. - Kolesnikov No. 104, 'Soumerki', 'Sumierki'
{'Pasteur' × Kolesnikov No. 401}
Howard, Arnoldia 19(6-7):31-35 [1959]; Gromov, A., Siren', 105 [1963]; Howard & Brizicky, AABGA Quart. Newsl. No. 64, 17-21 [1965]; Wister & Oppe, Arnoldia 31(3):125 [1971] - erroneously as S ? and 'Sumierki'; Gromov, Lilacs - Proceedings 2(4):17 [1974]; Rubtzov et al. 1980. Vidy i sorta sireni, kul'tiviruemye v SSSR. Kiev; Naukova Dumka – in Russian; Holetich, C.D. 1982. Lilac species and cultivars in cultivation in USSR. Lilacs 11(2):1-38. - translation of Rubtzov et al. 1982; Photo on Jorgovani/Lilacs 2015 DVD.
Named (perhaps) for the poem Sumerki (twilight), 1836, by Fyodor Ivanovich Tyutchev (or Tiutchev), 1803-1873; Tyutchev is regarded as one of the three greatest Russian poets of the 19th century.
Cultivar name registered 1970; name established and accepted.

Sumierki - see **'Sumerki'**.

'Summer Beauty', *S.* ×*henryi*
origin not known ? ?
Chapman, Lilacs - Quart. Jour. 26(2):46 [1997] - name only; NPPG listing, Plant Finder Reference Library 1998/99 CD-ROM
Cultivar name not established.

SUMMER CHARM™ - see **'DTR 124'**.

'Summer Skies', *S.* ×*hyacinthiflora*
Clarke 1948 (not Fiala); S VI
{'Mme F. Morel' × ? }
Clarke, Cat. 16:9 [1948]; Woody Plant Register, AAN, No. 142 [1949]; Wister, Lilacs for America, 42 [1953]; Photo on Jorgovani/Lilacs 2015 DVD.
Cultivar name presumed registered 1953; name established and accepted.

Summer Skies, Fiala (not Clarke) - see **'Sunrise'**.

'Summer Snow', *S. reticulata*
Schichtel 1980; S I
{*S. reticulata* seedling selection}
Schichtel's Nursery, New York Price Guide, 17 [1991]; Gressley, Lilacs - Quart. Jour. 29(3):84-85 [2000].
Cultivar name established and accepted.

'Summer Storm', *S. reticulata*
Robinson, Kelly 2013; S I
US Plant Patent applied for; Application #20130291238 PDF <https://www.freshpatents.com/account/pdf/display.php?app=20130291238> <http://www.google.com/patents/US20130291238> <www.faqs.org/patents/app/20130291238>; PP 32085
Cultivar name registered by statute, name established and accepted.

'Summer White', *S.* (Villosae Group), *S.* ×*henryi*
Lape 1975; S I
{parentage not known}
syn. - 'White Summer', 'White Summers'
Lape, Lilacs - Proceedings 5(2):inside back cover [July 1977] - as *S. komarowii* seedling; Vrugtman, Lilacs - Proceedings 6(1):16 [1978] - as 'White Summer'; Vrugtman, Lilacs - Proceedings 7(1):36 [1979] - correction to 'Summer White'; Vrugtman, AABGA Bull. 13(4):106 [1979]; Photo on Jorgovani/Lilacs 2015 DVD.
Cultivar name registered 1976; name established and accepted.

'Sun and Moon', *S.* (Villosae Group)
Nelson, Stephen 2011; S I*
{*S. villosa* subsp. *wolfii* × ? } pollen parent possibly *S. villosa* subsp. *villosa*, but definitely not *S. emodi*.
Nelson, S., Lilacs - Quart. Jour. 41(1):16-17, ill. [2012]; Vrugtman, Hanburyana 7:26-27 [2013].
Cultivar name registered 2011; name established and accepted.

'SunDak', *S. pekinensis*
Herman 1996; S I (155D, RHS Color Chart 1995 and Mini Color Chart 2005).
Marketed in the USA as COPPER CURLS®, trademark No. 3,105,783 [June 20, 2006].Redlin, Herman & Chaput; HortScience 42(1):170-171 [February 2007]
United States Plant Patent No. 16,570 [May 23, 2006]; statutory registration.
Cultivar name established and accepted.

'Sunny', *S. vulgaris*
Hughes; S I
{parentage not known}
Named for the pale-yellow color of its petals.
Cultivar not established.

'Sunol', *S. vulgaris*
Clarke 1936; D III
renamed French cultivar; probably 'Alphonse Lavallée'
Clarke, Cat., 12 [1937]; Wister, Lilacs for America, 59 [1942], 42 [1953]
Cultivar name not established.

'Sunrise', *S.* (Villosae Group)
Fiala 1968; S V
syn. - 'Summer Skies', Fiala, not Clarke
{(*S. tomentella* subsp. *sweginzowii* × *S. tomentella* subsp. *tomentella*) × *S. villosa* subsp. *wolfii*)}
Fiala, Lilacs, 224 [1988] - as *S.* ×*fialiana* R.B. Clark (name not validly published)
Cultivar name established and accepted.

'Sunset', *S.* ×*hyacinthiflora*
Clarke 1949; D VI
syn. - ELFENKÖNIG
marketed in Germany as ELFENKÖNIG™ (No. 399487832; K. Kircher)
{unnamed double seedling × ? }
AAN reg'n card No. 519; Clarke, Cat. 16:9 [1949]; Clarke, US Pl. Pat. No. 937 [June 13, 1950] - as S.

vulgaris; Wister, Lilacs for America, 42 [1953] - as "Early Hybrid of giraldi"; Anon., Lilacs - Quart. Jour. 33(1):11 [2004]; Photo on Jorgovani/Lilacs 2015 DVD.
Named for the Pacific Coast Magazine "Sunset".
Cultivar name presumed registered 1953; name established and accepted.

'Superba', *S. emodi*
origin not known pre-1963; ? ?
Hortus III, 1090 [1976]; reported in Morden Arb. Trials [1979]
Cultivar name not established.

'**Superba**', *S. pubescens* subsp. *microphylla*
Cassegrain 1933; S V
syn. - *microphylla superba* Cassegrain; see also 'Daphne' (*S. microphylla*)
common - littleleaf lilac
Grandes Roseraies, Cat., 2 [1933]; Wister, Lilacs for America, 53, 59 [1942], 35, 42 [1953]; Boom, Jaarb. Ned. Dendrol. Ver. 20:114 [1957]; Poor & Brewster, Plants that merit attention 2:253 [1996] - as: "Introduced in 1910 by William Purdom"; this has not been substantiated; Photo on Jorgovani/Lilacs 2015 DVD.
Awards: Certificate of Merit 1955 (KMTP); RHS Award of Merit 1957; RHS Award of Garden Merit 1993.
Cultivar name presumed registered 1953; name established and accepted.

'**Superba**', *S. oblata* subsp. *dilatata*
Upton 1951; S VI
syn. - *oblata dilatata superba*
Wister, Lilacs for America, 37 [1953]
Cultivar name presumed registered 1953; name established and accepted.

'**Superba**', *S. tomentella* subsp. *sweginzowii*
Lemoine 1915; S V
syn. - 'Superbum', *sweginzowii* var. *superba*
common name: Turner
Anon., Gard. Chron., ser. 3, 64:27, fig. 11 [1918]; Stand. Pl. Names, 488 [1923] - as Turner; Lemoine, Cat. No. 189, 23 [1925]; McKelvey, The Lilac, 127-128 [1928] - prob. identical to the nominate species; Boerner, Mitt. Deutsch. Dendr. Ges. 44:52 [1932] - as var. *superba*; Rehder, Bibl. Cultivation Trees and Shrubs, 565 [1949] - as syn. of *S. sweginzowii*; Wister, Lilacs for America, 59 [1942], 42 [1953]; Photo on Jorgovani/Lilacs 2015 DVD.
Awards: RHS Award of Merit 1918.
Cultivar name presumed registered 1953; name established and accepted.

'Superba', *S. tomentella* subsp. *tomentella*
origin not known pre-1974; ? ?
syn. - *tomentella superba*
Cultivar name not established.

Superba, *S. villosa* subsp. *villosa*
Alexander Sr 1969; S IV-V
syn. - *villosa superba*
{*S. villosa* subsp. *villosa* seedling selection}
Wister, Arbor. Bot. Gard. Bull. 1(2):20 [1967] - name only; Alexander Sr, Cat. sheets, Late Blooming Lilacs, 4 [n.d.; rec'd March 1969]
Cultivar name not established; name registered 1967, but epithet rejected (Latinized form);
Cultivar not reported in cultivation.

Superba Alfi, *S.*
no informaton; S V ?
seen 21 January 2018 <http://www.piccoplant.de/en/assortment/lilacs>
epithet rejected (Latinized form).

'**Susan B. Anthony**', *S. vulgaris*
Dunbar 1923; S VI
syn. - Dunbar no. 271
{parentage not known}
McKelvey, The Lilac, 387 [1928]; Wister, Lilacs for America, 59 [1942], 42 [1953].
Although originally described as being a single, plants reported in cultivation appear to be double, Vrugtman, Lilacs - Quart. Jour. 38(2):65 [2009]; D. McCown, Lilacs - Quart. Jour. 41(4):124 [2012].
Named for Susan Brownell Anthony, 1820-1906, American social reformer and women's suffrage leader.
Cultivar name presumed registered 1953; name established and accepted.
Nota bene: Plants under this name with double florets are not true to name.

'**Susanna**', *S. vulgaris*
Klager 1928; S I
Wister, Lilacs for America, 59 [1942], 42 [1953]; Fiala, Lilacs, 21-Q (line drawing) [1988]
Cultivar name presumed registered 1953; name established and accepted.

'**Suvorovets**', *S. vulgaris* (or ×*hyacinthiflora* ?)
'Суворовец'
Stashkevich pre-1970; S VII
Pikaleva, Lilacs - Quart. Jour. 23(4):88 [1994]; Photo on Jorgovani/Lilacs 2015 DVD.
Name: A Souvorovets is a cadet at one of the Suvorov Military High Schools, Russia.
Cultivar name established and accepted.

'**Suyunshi**', *S. vulgaris*
'Сююнши'
Sagitova 1991; S VII
varietal denomination registered 1991, No. 5518, State Register of Selected Achievements in USSR;
Named for a sculpture in Karaganda, Kazakhstan.
Cultivar name established and accepted.

'Svensk Rapsodi', *S.*
Origin unknown before 2019; S III
{'Rochester' × ?}
Photo by Ole Heide in Denmark seen in ILS 2020 Photo DVD.
Name: in Danish means Swedish Rhapsody.
Cultivar name not established.

'Svityazanka', *S. vulgaris*
 'Свитязанка'
 Smol'skiĭ & Bibikova 1964; S VII
 syn. - 'Svitjazanka', 'Svityazanka'
 {'Hyazinthenflieder' × 'Réaumur'}
 Rubtzov et al. 1980. Vidy i sorta sireni, kul'tiviruemye v SSSR. Kiev; Naukova Dumka. – in Russian; Holetich, C.D. 1982. Lilac species and cultivars in cultivation in USSR. Lilacs 11(2):1-38. - translation of Rubtzov et al. 1982; Semenov, Igor, Lilacs - Quart. Jour. 43(3):85-87 [2014]; Photo on Jorgovani/Lilacs 2015 DVD.
 Named for the poem "Svityazanka" by Polish poet Adam Mickiewicz (see also 'Adam Mickiewicz').
 Cultivar name established and accepted.

'Svyatoslav Rikhter', *S. vulgaris*
 'Святослав Рихтер'
 Aladin, S., Aladina, O., Polyakova, T., and Aladina. A. 2014 D VII-IV
 {'Président Grévy' × OP}
 seen 19 March 2015 <http://allaboutlilacs.com/2015/03/19/>; Садовник (Gardener) magazine 04 (140)/2017:18-25; Вестник АППМ (Catalog in Vestnik APPM (Planting material association) magazine) 1/2018: 59-72 (in Russian).
 Named for Svyatoslav Teofilovich Rikhter (Святослав Теофилович Рихтер), 1915-1997, one of the foremost Russian pianists of the 20th century.
 Cultivar name established and accepted.

'S. V. Lavrov', *S. vulgaris*
 'С. В. Лавров'
 Lavrov; D IV
 syn. - 'Lavrov', 'Lovrov'
 Bilov et al., Siren', 74 [1974] - in Russian; Rubtzov et al. 1980. Vidy i sorta sireni, kul'tiviruemye v SSSR. Kiev; Naukova Dumka. – in Russian; Holetich, C.D. 1982. Lilac species and cultivars in cultivation in USSR. Lilacs 11(2):1-38. - translation of Rubtzov et al. 1982; Photo on Jorgovani/Lilacs 2015 DVD.
 Named after horticulturist Sergey Lavrov from Kharkov, Ukraine.
 Cultivar name established and accepted.

'Swanee', *S.* (Villosae Group), *S.* ×*prestoniae*
 Preston & Leslie 1936; S I
 {parentage not known}
 Wister, Lilacs for America, 59, 64 [1942] - as S I; Wister, Lilacs for America, 42 [1953] - as S V; Cumming, Agric. Canada Public. 1628, 17 [1977] - introduced in 1936; Photo on Jorgovani/Lilacs 2015 DVD.
 Cultivar name presumed registered 1953; name established and accepted.

'Swansdown', *S. vulgaris*
 Fiala 1984; S I
 {'Rochester' × 'Atheline Wilbur'}
 Fiala, Lilacs, 91, 224 [1988]
 Cultivar name established and accepted.

'Swarthmore', *S.* ×*hyacinthiflora*
 Skinner 1954; D IV
 Wister, Lilacs for America, 42 [1953]; Skinner, Hort. Horizons, 50, 80, Pl. 24, 108 [1966]; Photo on Jorgovani/Lilacs 2015 DVD.
 Named, probably, for the town of Swarthmore, Saskatchewan, Canada, the hometown of John Lloyd, a pioneer nurseryman of the early 20th century.
 Cultivar name presumed registered 1953; name established and accepted.

'Sweet Charity', *S.* ×*hyacinthiflora*
 Lammerts 1953; S VII
 {(Lammerts C112 × 'Lamartine' seedling) × (Lammerts 42-109-4 × ?)}
 Lammerts, US Pl. Pat. No. 3892 [May 25, 1976]; Vrugtman, Lilacs 6(1):16 [1978]; Vrugtman, AABGA Bull.13(4):107 [1979]; Photo on Jorgovani/Lilacs 2015 DVD.
 Cultivar name registered 1976; name established and accepted.
 Nota bene: Since this cultivar appears to be of 'Lavender Lady' ancestry; see also: Pringle, Lilacs - Quart. Jour. 24(4):97-99 [1995]; and Vrugtman, HortScience 31(3):328 [1996].

'Sweetheart', *S.* ×*hyacinthiflora*
 Clarke 1953; D VI
 syn. - 'SweetHeart'
 {*S.* ×*hyacinthiflora* 'Alice Eastwood' × ? }
 Clarke, US Pl. Pat. No. 1128 [Sept. 16, 1952] - as S. vulgaris; Wister, Lilacs for America, 42 [1953] - as S. vulgaris; Clarke, Cat., 34 [1954] - as s. vulgaris; Fiala, Lilacs, 58, 104, 206, 258 [1988]; Lilacs - Quart. Jour. 24(2): front cover ill. [1995]; in litt., Holetich to Vrugtman, correction of color determination to D I & VI, 29 March 2015; Photo on Jorgovani/Lilacs 2015 DVD.
 Cultivar name presumed registered 1953; name established and accepted.

'Sweet Moments', *S.*
 Moro, F. 2016; ? ?
 {parentage not listed}
 <http://www.spi.8m.com/>, name only, no description, photo (S V?)
 Cultivar name not established.

'Sweet Refrain', *S.* ×*hyacinthiflora*
 Franklin, M.L.; D V
 {parentage not known}
 Wister & Oppe, Arnoldia 31(3):123 [1971] - as D III and *S. vulgaris*, but ×*hyacinthiflora* according to the originator; Vrugtman, Lilacs - Quart. Jour. 23(3):75 [1994]; (Perhaps in the collection at the Minnesota Landscape Arboretum; Tim McCauley)
 Cultivar name registered 1970, name established and accepted.

SWEET TREAT™ - see 'Greswt' (*S. pubescens* subsp. *patula*).

sweginzowii albida - see '**Albida**' (Villosae Group).

sweginzowii densiflora - see '**Densiflora**' (*S. tomentella* subsp. *sweginzowii*).

sweginzowii superba - see '**Superba**' (*S. tomentella* subsp. *sweginzowii*).

'**Sylvan Beauty**', *S.* ×*hyacinthiflora*
Sobeck; S V
syn. - 'Sylvan's Beauty'
Wister, Arnoldia 26(3):13 [1966]; Photo on Jorgovani/Lilacs 2015 DVD.
Cultivar name registered 1966; name established and accepted.
Nota bene: Since this cultivar appears to be of 'Lavender Lady' ancestry; see also: Pringle, Lilacs - Quart. Jour. 24(4):97-99 [1995]; and Vrugtman, HortScience 31(3):328 [1996]

Sylvia - see '**Silvia**'.

'**Syrenprinsessen**', *S. vulgaris*
Heide 1995; S? II/V to V ?
syn. - Lilac Princess'
<www.heidesplanteskole.dk/Syrenprinsessen.htm> seen September 25, 2011
Ole Heide photo seen in 2020 ILS DVD
Cultivar name not established.

'**Syurpriz**', *S. vulgaris*
'Сюрприз'
Dyagilev 1992; S V
{'Volcan' × OP}
Name: Russian for surprise
Cultivar name not established.

SYV180, *S. villosa* subsp. *villosa*
origin not known pre-1990; S V-I
{parentage not known; open pollinated}
USDA-ARS GRIN database, PI No. 540443; historical record only
Not a cultivar name; probably a cognomen.

'**T-34**', *S. vulgaris*
Aladin, S., Aladina, O., Polyakova, T., and, Aladina, A. 2015; S IV
{'Flora 53' × OP}.
IX International Scientific Conference (IX Международная научная конференция "Цветоводство: история, теория, практика") " Floriculture: history, theory, practice", St. Petersburg, Botanical Garden of Peter the Great BIN RAS, September 7-13, 2019:........ (in Russian); II All-Russian scientific-practical conference with international participation (II Всероссийская научно-практическая конференция с международным участием) " Botanical Gardens in the XXI Century: Biodiversity Conservation, Development Strategy and Innovative Solutions Belgorod, Botanical Garden of NRU "BelSU", September 23-26, 2019; pp.141-145 (in Russian).
Named for the famous Russian tank the T-34, one of the symbols of World War II.
Cultivar name established and accepted.

Tadeiszko - see '**Tadeusz Kościuszko**'.

'**Tadeush**', *S. vulgaris*
'Тадеуш'
Sagitova 1991; S VI
varietal denomination registered 1991, No. 5517, State Register of Selected Achievements in USSR;
Named for the husband of the originator.
Cultivar name established and accepted.

'**Tadeusz Kościuszko**', *S. vulgaris*
Karpow-Lipski 1958; D IV
syn. - Siewka nr 14, 'Tadeiszko'
Karpow-Lipski, Arboretum Kórnickie 3:105, 108 (1958); Wister & Oppe, Arnoldia 31(3):126 (1971) - erroneously as 'Tadeiszko', D VI; Vrugtman, HortScience 25(6):618 [1990]
Named for Tadeusz Andrezei Bonawentura Kościuszko, 1746-1817, Polish soldier, patriot and national hero.
Cultivar name registered 1970; name established and accepted.

'**Taff's Treasure**', *S.* ×*persica*
Taffler pre-1999; S VII *
Monksilver Nursery, Cat. No. 10, 72 [1999] - "new leaves are strongly pink-tinged and then variably suffused with fine white spotting".
Named by Stephen Taffler, 1922-2005, horticulturist and author, Berkhamsted, Herfordshire, England.
Cultivar name established and accepted.

'**Taglioni**', *S. vulgaris*
Lemoine 1905; D I
Lemoine, Cat. No. 161, 30 [1905]; McKelvey, The Lilac, 387 [1928]; Wister, Nat. Hort. Mag. 6(1):14 [1927]; Wister, Lilacs for America, 59 [1943], 42 [1953]; Photo on Jorgovani/Lilacs 2015 DVD.
Named for Marie Taglioni, Countess des Voisins, 1804-1884, Italian ballerina.
Cultivar name presumed registered 1953; name established and accepted.

'**Talisman**', *S. vulgaris*
Fiala 1984; S VI
{'Sarah Sands' × 'Rochester'}
Fiala, Lilacs, 103, 224 [1988]
Cultivar name established and accepted.

Tamara - see '**Tamora**'.

'**Tamara Kolesnikova**', *S. vulgaris*
'Тамара Колесникова'
Kolesnikov; D IV-V
syn. - Kolesnikov No. 32
Gromov, A., Siren', 74-75 [1963]; Rubtzov et al. 1980. Vidy i sorta sireni, kul'tiviruemye v SSSR. Kiev; Naukova Dumka. – in Russian; Holetich, C.D. 1982. Lilac species

and cultivars in cultivation in USSR. Lilacs 11(2):1-38. - translation of Ru<u>tz</u>ov et al. 1982; Polyakova, 2010, Istori<u>ya</u> Russkoĭ Sireni, p. 128.
Named for Tamara Kolesnikova, daughter of the originator.
Cultivar name established and accepted.

'Tammelan Kaunotar', *S.* (Villosae Group)
Viksten pre-1990; S I
{*S. josikaea* × ? }
Name: Finnish for Tammela's beauty.
Cultivar name established and accepted.

'Tamora', *S.* (Villosae Group), *S.* ×*prestoniae*
Preston; ? ?
{*S. villosa* subsp. *villosa* × *S. komarowii* subsp. *reflexa*}
syn. - Preston No. 20-14-124, 'Tamara'
Macoun, Rep. Dom. Hort. 1928, 57 [1930] - name only; Wister, Lilacs for America, 64 [1942]; 48 [1953] - as 'Tamara', not in cultivation, no plants distributed
Named for the queen of the Goths in Shakespeare's *Titus Andronicus*.
Cultivar name not established, probably extinct.

'Tane<u>ch</u>ka', *S. vulgaris*
'Танечка'
Smol'skiĭ & Bibikova 1964; S III-V
syn. - 'Tanetshka'
{'Hyazinthenflieder' × 'Réaumur'}
Rub<u>tz</u>ov et al. 1980. Vidy i sorta sireni, kul'tiviruemye v SSSR. Kiev; Naukova Dumka. – in Russian; Holetich, C.D. 1982. Lilac species and cultivars in cultivation in USSR. Lilacs 11(2):1-38. - translation of Ru<u>tz</u>ov et al. 1982; Semenov, Igor, Lilacs - Quart.Jour. 43(3):85-87 [2014]. Per Makedonska<u>ya</u> and Okuneva in Lilacs 46(1):23, Bibikova labeled as unpromising, excluded from collection, last flowered 1972, now extinct.
Named for the daughter of Veronika Fedorovna Bibikova.
Cultivar name established and accepted.

'Tanika's', *Syringa pubescens* subsp. *patula*
Moro 2009; S I
{'Excellens' × ? }
Vrugtman, Hanburyana 7:30-31 [2013].
Named for Tanika, a friend of the Moro family in Airlie Beach, Australia.
Cultivar name registered 2012; name established and accepted.

'Tankist', *S. vulgaris*
'Танкист'
Sta<u>sh</u>kevi<u>ch</u> pre-1967; D V
syn. - 'Tamkist', Tankman
Gromov, Lilacs - Proceedings 2(4):16 [1974] - name only; Fiala, Lilacs, 215, 263 [1988] - name only, as 'Tamkist' in index; Alexander, Arnoldia 56(1):28 [1996] - as Tankman, D V; Photo on Jorgovani/Lilacs 2015 DVD.
Name: Russian for tankman. The originator was a Soviet army colonel, professor at the tank academy in Moscow.
Cultivar name established and accepted.

Tankman - see 'Tankist'.

'Tapani', *S.* (Villosae-Group)
Katainen ?; S VI
personal communication, K. Kolkka to F. Vrugtman, 30 March 2009
Cultivar name not established.

'Taras Bul'ba', *S. vulgaris*
'Тарас Бульба'
Rub<u>tz</u>ov, <u>Zh</u>ogoleva, L<u>ya</u>punova & ? Gorb 1956; D IV
syn. - 'Taras Bulba', 'Taras Buljba'
{'Léon Gambetta' × ? }
Bilov et al., Siren', 75 [1974] - in Russian; Rub<u>tz</u>ov et al. 1980. Vidy i sorta sireni, kul'tiviruemye v SSSR. Kiev; Naukova Dumka. – in Russian; Holetich, C.D. 1982. Lilac species and cultivars in cultivation in USSR. Lilacs 11(2):1-38. - translation of Rub<u>tz</u>ov et al. 1982; Photo on Jorgovani/Lilacs 2015 DVD.
Named for the hero in the novel "Taras Bul'ba", by Nikolaĭ Vasil'evich Gogol, 1809-1852, considered to be the finest epic in Russian literature. (Not to be confused with Taurus Bulba, a Walt Disney cartoon character in the *Darkwing Duck* series!).
Cultivar name established and accepted.

'Tardiva', *S. vulgaris*
origin not known pre-1880; ? ?
syn. - 'Serotina'
Noisette, Man. Gen. Pl 3:410 [1880]; McKelvey, The Lilac, 387 [1928] - identical to 'Serotina', but priority not established
Cultivar name not established.

'Tat'<u>ya</u>na Pol<u>ya</u>kova', *S. vulgaris*
'Татьяна Полякова'
Aladin, S., Arkhangelskiĭ, V., and Aladina, O. 2010; S I
{'Jan van Tol' × OP}
Registered with the State Commission of the Russian Federation for Testing and Protection of Selection Achievements, No. 8853117, 2011; Lilacs Quart. Journ. 40(2):42 [2011] - name only; Питомник-частный сад (Pitomnik i chastnyi sad; Nursery and private garden) 2/2013:24-34 (in Russian); Вестник АППМ (Catalog in Vestnik APPM (Planting material association) magazine) 1/2018: 59-72 (in Russian); Photo on Jorgovani/Lilacs 2015 DVD.
Named for Tatyana Polyakova (Татьяна Владимировна Полякова), Regional Vice President for Russia and Asia of the International Lilac Society, Moscow, Russia; contemporary Russian lilac breeder member of the creative breeding group "Russian Lilac", journalist, originator of the projects "Moscow is a City of Lilacs" and "Lilac of Victory", author of articles and books "The Time of Lilacs" and "The History of Russian Lilacs".
Cultivar name registered, established and accepted.

'Tat'<u>ya</u>nin Den'', *S. vulgaris*
'Татьянин День'

Chub, Dvortsova & Kiris 2013, S I/V
Chub, Dvortsova & Kiris, Lilacs - Quart. Jour. 46(4):150-152 [2017] - spelling errors in the transliteration
Name: Russian for Tatiana Day, a Russian religious holiday observed on 25 January according to the Gregorian calendar, January 12 according to the Julian; it is named after Saint Tatiana, a Christian martyr in 3rd century Rome during the reign of Emperor Alexander Severus; Saint Tatiana is the patron saint of students. Statutory registration, Russia, State Register No. ??? (Jan 2020).
Cultivar name established and accepted.

Tausendschön, *S. oblata* subsp. *dilatata*
origin of selection not known ca 2000; S V
trademark applied for by Kircher Baumschulen, Germany, for marketing plants of *S. oblata* subsp. *dilatata* (Nakai) P.S. Green & M. C. Chang, but rejected on grounds that Tausendschön is the German common name for *Bellis perennis*).
In its online 2008-2009 pricelist Rosskamp Nursery, Wiefelstede, Germany, offers *Syringa oblata* 'Tausendschön' as a cultivar; it is described as single, pink, very strongly fragrant; this may or may not be a clone. <www.baumschule-rosskamp.de/sortiment.pdf> [seen 25 Dec. 2008].

'Taylor Mitchell', *S. vulgaris*
Moro, F. 2010; S V-IV
{'White Lace' × ?}
Vrugtman, Hanburyana 7:30 [2013].
Named for Taylor Mitchell, which was the stage name of Taylor Josephine Stephanie Luciow, 1990 - 2009, Canadian folk singer and songwriter.
Cultivar name registered 2012; name established and accepted.

'Teet', *S.*
Mägi pre-2018; S III/IV
Semenov, I., Lilacs 48(2):68,69 (photo) [2019].
Cultivar name not established.

Teevzeme - see 'Tēvzeme'

'Telimena', *S.* (Villosae Group), *S.* ×*prestoniae*
Bugała pre-1970; S V
syn. - 'Telemena', 'Telemina'
Bugała, Arboretum Kórnickie 15:61-70 [1970]; Wister & Oppe, Arnoldia 31(3):123 [1971]; Bugała, Lilacs - Quart. Jour. 24(4):90-91 [1995]; Photo on Jorgovani/Lilacs 2015 DVD.
Cultivar name registered 1970; name established and accepted.

'Tëmnaya Noch', *S. vulgaris*
'Тёмная ночь'
Aladin, S., Aladina, O., Polyakova, T. 2015; S II
{elite seedling 09-217H × 'Violetta'}
Садовник (Gardener) magazine, 05 (141)/2017 :16-22; Вестник АППМ (Catalog in Vestnik APPM (Planting material association) magazine) 1/2018: 59-72 (in Russian).
Name: Russian for dark night.
Cultivar name established and accepted.

Temptation, *S. vulgaris*
Peart 2005; S V
{sport of 'Jessie Gardner'}
[propagules distributed in 2005 for micropropagation and evaluation]
Cultivar name not established and accepted.

'Tev Jaunība', *S. vulgaris*
Upītis ca 1970; S II
Kalniņš, L., Ceriņu jaunšķirnes Dobelē, Dārs un drava 1986(12):13-15 - in Latvian; in litt. S. Strautiņa to F. Vrugtman [22 Jan. 2008] - ca 1970, S II.
Name: Latvian for youth.
Cultivar name established and accepted. Probably no longer in cultivation.

'Tēvzeme', *S. vulgaris*
Upītis 1965; S I
syn. - Upītis No. 3846
Kalniņš, L., Ceriņu jaunšķirnes Dobelē, Dārs un drava 1986(12):13-15 - in Latvian; Strautiņa, S. 1992. Ceriņi Dārzs un Drava. No. 6, pp.12-13; in litt. S. Strautiņa to F. Vrugtman [21 Dec. 2007] - 1965, S I; Photo on Jorgovani/Lilacs 2015 DVD.
Name: Latvian for fatherland.
Cultivar name established and accepted.

'The Bride', *S.* ×*hyacinthiflora*
Skinner 1961; S I
Wister, Arnoldia 23(4):83 [1963]; Skinner, Hort. Horizons, 50, 108 [1966]; Photo on Jorgovani/Lilacs 2015 DVD.
Cultivar name registered 1963; name established and accepted.

The Cheat - see '**Kapriz**'.

'Theodore Roosevelt', *S.*
(species affiliation not known)
origin not known ? ?
see also 'President Theodore Roosevelt'
Reported in cultivation in Prairie Regional Trials, pre-1990.
Cultivar name not established.

'Theo Holetich', *S. vulgaris*
Margaretten; S VI
{'Mme Lemoine' × ? }
reported in cultivation at Royal Botanical Gardens, Ontario, Canada
Named for Mrs C. D. (Theo) Holetich, Hamilton, Ontario, Canada.
Cultivar name established and accepted.

'The Queen', *S. vulgaris*
origin not known probably pre-1912; S I
reported by Colin Chapman, U.K.; personal

communication, in litt. Chapman to Vrugtman, Oct. 26, 2008.
Cultivar name not established.

'Theresa', *S.*
Mägi pre-2018; S VII
Semenov, I., Lilacs 48(2):71,70 (photo) [2019].
Cultivar name not established.

Thibaut - see '**Souvenir de L. Thibaut**'.

'**Thomas A. Edison**', *S. vulgaris*
Dunbar 1922; S VII
syn. - Dunbar no. 230
{'Aline Mocqueris' × ? }
Dunbar, Florists Exch., 831 [Sept. 22, 1923]; McKelvey, The Lilac, 387 [1928]; Wister, Lilacs for America, 59 [1942], 42 [1953]
Named for Thomas Alva Edison, 1847-1931, American inventor and physicist.
Cultivar name presumed registered 1953; name established and accepted.

'**Thomas Jefferson**', *S. vulgaris*
Dunbar 1922; S V
syn. - Dunbar no. 228
{parentage not known}
Dunbar, Florists Exch., 831 [Sept. 22, 1923]; McKelvey, The Lilac, 388 [1928]; Wister, Lilacs for America, 59 [1942], 42 [1953]; Photo on Jorgovani/Lilacs 2015 DVD.
Named for Thomas Jefferson, 1743-1826, 3rd president of the USA.
Cultivar name presumed registered 1953; name established and accepted.

THUMBELINA™ - see 'Bailina'.

'**Thunberg**', *S. vulgaris*
Lemoine 1913; D IV
Lemoine, Cat. No. 185, 40 [1913]; McKelvey, The Lilac, 388 [1928]; Wister, Lilacs for America, 59 [1942], 42 [1953]; Photo on Jorgovani/Lilacs 2015 DVD.
Named for Carl Per Thunberg, 1743-1828, Swedish botanist.
Cultivar name presumed registered 1953; name established and accepted.

'Thunderbolt', *S. vulgaris*
Fiala 1985; S VII
{'Prodige' × 'Rochester'}
Fiala, Lilacs, 224 [1988]
Cultivar name established and accepted.

Ti Amo Sara, ?
Moro, F. ?; ? ?
Name only, in lit. F. Moro to Vrugtman, 10 Apr. 2015.
Cultivar name not established.

'Tiffany Blue', *S. vulgaris*
Fiala 1984; S III
{'True Blue' × 'Mrs A. Belmont'}
Fiala, Lilacs, 96, 98, 224, Pl. 1 [1988]
Cultivar name established and accepted.

'Tigernan' - see 'Tong Yong'.

Tigerstedtii - see *S. tomentella* subsp. *sweginzowii* Koehne & Lingels.

'Tihiĭ Don', *S. vulgaris*
'Тихий Дон'
Kolesnikov no date; ? ?
Polyakova, 2010, Istoriya Russkoĭ Sireni, p. 43; name only.
Named for the 1934 novel *Tihiĭ Don* (Quietly Flows the Don) by Michail Aleksandrovich Sholokhov, 1905-1984.
Cultivar name not established.

'**Tiina**', *S. vulgaris*
Vaigla 1969; S V (VI-V per Semenov)
{parentage not known}
Vrugtman, HortScience 26(5):477 [1991]; Kivistik, Maakodu 1997(5):22-23 [1997] - in Estonian; I. Semenov, Lilacs 48(2):62,65 [2019].
Cultivar name registered 1990; name established and accepted.

'Tiit Rondla', *S. vulgaris*
Mägi pre-2018; S III/IV
Semenov, I., Lilacs 48(2):68,66 (photo) [2019].
Cultivar name not established.

'Tiiu', *S. vulgaris*
Mägi pre-2017 ; S VII
Photo taken in Estonia by Mägi seen on 2020 ILS Photo Database.
Cultivar name not established.

'Tikhaya Obitel', *S. vulgaris*
'Тихая обитель'
Aladin, S., Aladina, O., and Polyakova, T. 2016; S III
{elite form 8-304 × OP}
Садовник (Gardener) magazine 04 (140)/2017 :18-25; Вестник АППМ (Catalog in Vestnik APPM (Planting material association) magazine) 1/2018: 59-72 (in Russian).
Name: Russian for quiet abode.
Cultivar name established and accepted.

Tikshanaas Prieks - see '**Ēsibas Prieks**'.

'**Timandra**', *S.* (Villosae Group), *S.* ×*prestoniae*
Preston 1928; S VI
syn. - Preston No. 20-14-111
{*S. villosa* subsp. *villosa* × *S. komarowii* subsp. *reflexa*}
Macoun, Rep. Dom. Hort. 1928, 57 [1930] - name only; Wister, Lilacs for America, 59, 64 [1942], 42, 48 [1953]
Named for the Mistress to Alcibiades in Shakespeare's *Timon of Athens*.
Cultivar name presumed registered 1953; name established and accepted.

Timbuctoo - see 'Tombouctou'.

'Timiryazevka', *S. vulgaris*
'Тимирязевка'
Aladin, S., Aladina, O., Polyakova, T., and Aladina A. 2015; D IV
{elite form 07-98-35 × OP}
Вестник АППМ (Catalog in Vestnik APPM (Planting material association) magazine) 1/2018: 59-72 (in Russian).
Named for the Timiryazev Agricultural Academy, Moscow, one of the oldest agrarian educational institutions in Russia, founded in 1865.
Cultivar name established and accepted.

Tinkerbelle™ - see '**Bailbelle**'.

Tiny Dancer™ - see 'Elsdancer', *S. vulgaris*

'Tiny One', *S. vulgaris*
Klager (?); S V
Anon., ILS Newsletter 14(4):3-4 [1988]; Stenlund, Lilacs - Quart. Jour. 20(2):41 [1991]; Chapman, Lilacs - Quart. Jour. 32(1):18 [2003]
Cultivar name established and accepted.

'Tishina', *S. vulgaris*
'Тишина'
Aladin, S., Aladina, O., Polyakova, T., and Aladina, A. 2017; S V
{'Stefan Makowiecki' × OP}
IX International Scientific Conference (IX Международная научная конференция "Цветоводство: история, теория, практика") " Floriculture: history, theory, practice", St. Petersburg, Botanical Garden of Peter the Great BIN RAS, September 7-13, 2019 (in Russian)
Name: Russian for silence.
Cultivar name established and accepted.

'Tita', *S. vulgaris*
Margaretten; D V
{'Mme Lemoine' × ? }
Peterson, Lilacs - Proceedings 16(1):22 [1987] - name only; Gressley, Lilacs - Quart. Jour. 18(3):74 [1989] - name only; Photo on Jorgovani/Lilacs 2015 DVD.
Named for the wife of the originator.
Cultivar name established and accepted.

'Titania', *S.* (Villosae Group), *S.* ×*prestoniae*
Preston 1928; S VII
syn. - Preton No. 20-14-115
{*S. villosa* subsp. *villosa* × *S. komarowii* subsp. *reflexa*}
Macoun, Rep. Dom. Hort. 1928, 57 [1930] - name only; Wister, Lilacs for America, 59, 64 [1942], 42, 48 [1953]; Photo on Jorgovani/Lilacs 2015 DVD.
Named for the queen of the Fairies in Shakespeare's *Midsummer Night's Dream*.
Cultivar name presumed registered 1953; name established and accepted.

'Tit Tat Toe', *S. vulgaris*
Havemeyer & Eaton; S VI-VII
syn. - 'Tic Tac To'
Wister & Oppe, Arnoldia 31(3):123 [1971]; Niedz, ILS Proceedings 1(4):8 [1972] - as "blend of light purples"
Cultivar name registered 1970; name established and accepted.

'Tjeu', *S. reticulata*
origin not known; S I
<www.esveld.nl/wetenschappelijk.php?letter=s&group=syringa&ppagina=4> seen Nov. 23, 2011 - no descriptive information.
Cultivar name not established.

'Tobias', *S.*
no information; D V ?
seen 21 January 2018 <http://www.piccoplant.de/en/assortment/lilacs>
Cultivar name not established.

'Todmorden', *S. vulgaris*
Scott pre-1942; S V
Wister, Lilacs for America, 59 [1942], 42 [1953]; Photo on Jorgovani/Lilacs 2015 DVD.
Cultivar name presumed registered 1953; name established and accepted.

'Tombouctou', *S. vulgaris*
Lemoine 1910; S VII
common name: Timbuctoo
Lemoine, Cat. No. 176, 31 [1910]; Stand. Pl. Names, 488 [1923] - as Timbuctoo; McKelvey, The Lilac, 388 [1928]; Wister, Lilacs for America, 59 [1942], 42 [1953]; Photo on Jorgovani/Lilacs 2015 DVD.
Named for the town in the Gao region of northern Mali, West Africa, centre of Muslim learning.
Cultivar name presumed registered 1953; name established and accepted.

tomentella aurea - see '**Kum Bum**'.

tomentella rosea - see '**Rosea**' (*S. tomentella* subsp. *tomentella*).

tomentella superba - see 'Superba' (*S. tomentella* subsp. *tomentella*).

Toms Double Blue, *S.*
Origin not known; D III
listed by Kilcoyne Lilac Farm <www.kilcoynelilacfarm.com/flowers.html> seen August 2009
Probably not a cultivar name.

'Tom Taylor', *S.* ×*hyacinthiflora*
Skinner 1962; D VII
Wister, Arnoldia 23(4):83 [1963]; Skinner, Hort. Horizons, 50, 108 [1966]; Photo on Jorgovani/Lilacs 2015 DVD.
Cultivar name registered 1963; name established and accepted.

'Tong Yong', *S.* (Villosae Group)
   Fiala 1987; S II
   syn. - 'Tigernan'
   {*S. tomentella* subsp. *sweginzowii* × (*S. tomentella* subsp. *yunnanensis* × *S.* ×*prestoniae* 'Isabella')}
   Fiala, Lilacs, 224, Pl. 52 [1988]
   Named (probably) for Tong Yong, the port-city at the southern tip of Korea known for its laquer-ware.
   Cultivar name established and accepted.

'Topaz', *S. vulgaris*
   'Топаз'
   Zhogoleva 1976; S II
   syn. - 'Topas'
   {'Andenken an Ludwig Späth' × ?}
   Rubtzov et al. 1980. Vidy i sorta sireni, kul'tiviruemye v SSSR. Kiev; Naukova Dumka. – in Russian; Holetich, C.D. 1982. Lilac species and cultivars in cultivation in USSR. Lilacs 11(2):1-38. - translation of Rubtzov et al. 1982; Photo on Jorgovani/Lilacs 2015 DVD.
   Name: Russian for topaz.
   Cultivar name established and accepted.

'Top Gun', *S. villosa* subsp. *wolfii*
   Zwijnenburg 2000; S VII
   {seedling of *S. villosa* subsp. *wolfii*}
   in lit. Peter Zwijnenburg to Marco Hoffman 29 October 2009 - more vigorous and more floriferous than its parent plants; http://plantago.nl/plantindex/plant/BO/S/1/syringa-wolfii-top-gun/390751.html (seen 26 November 2016)
   Cultivar name established and accepted.

'Topsvoorts Giant', *S. vulgaris*
   Eveleens Maarse 1953; ? ?
   Topsvoort New Lilac Introduction, Fa. W. Topsvoort, flyer [ca 1953] - name only; existence not confirmed by Vaste Keurings Commissie, Roelofarendsveen, July 26, 2007
   Cultivar name not established; not reported in cultivation.

'Touch of Spring', *S.* ×*hyacinthiflora*
   Fiala 1982; S II
   {parentage not known}
   Fiala, Lilacs, 94 [1988]
   Cultivar name established and accepted.

'Tougen', *S. oblata*
   '桃源'
   origin not known; S III
   reported in the trade in Japan; reported in collection at Sapporo.
   Photo by Hideo Ihara on 2020 ILS Lilac Photo Database.
   Cultivar name not established.

Tour d'Avergne - see '**La Tour d'Auvergne**'.

'**Tournefort**', *S. vulgaris*
   Lemoine 1887; D II
   Lemoine, Cat. No. 107, 13 [1887]; McKelvey, The Lilac, 388-389 [1928]; Wister, Lilacs for America, 59 [1942], 42 [1953]; Photo on Jorgovani/Lilacs 2015 DVD.
   Named for Joseph Pitton de Tournefort, 1656-1708, French botanist and professor at the Jardin des Plantes in Paris.
   Cultivar name presumed registered 1953; name established and accepted.

'**Toussaint-Louverture**', *S. vulgaris*
   Lemoine 1898; S VII
   syn. - 'Taoussaint l'Ouverture', 'Toussaint L'Ouverture', 'Toussaint-l'Ouverture'
   Lemoine, Cat. No. 140, 19 [1898]; McKelvey, The Lilac, 389 [1928]; Wister, Lilacs for America, 59 [1942], 42 [1953]; Photo on Jorgovani/Lilacs 2015 DVD.
   Named for Pierre Dominique Toussaint L'Ouverture, 1746-1803, Haitian revolutionary leader born of African slave parents.
   Cultivar name presumed registered 1953; name established and accepted.

'**Towson Beauty**', *S. vulgaris*
   Towson 1938; D V
   Towson Nurs., Cat., 83 [1938]; Wister, Lilacs for America, 59 [1942], 42 [1953]
   Cultivar name presumed registered 1953; name established and accepted.

'Transon', *S.* ×*chinensis*
   origin not known ? ?
   listed in Morden Arb. Trials [1989].

'**Treesje Topsvoort**', *S. vulgaris*
   Eveleens Maarse 1948; S IV
   {'Maréchal Foch' × 'Hugo de Vries'}
   Wister, Lilacs for America, 42 [1953]; Eveleens Maarse, Dendron 1(1):12 [1954]; Photo on Jorgovani/Lilacs 2015 DVD.
   Awards: Certificate of Merit 1948 (KMTP); Certificate First Class 1953 (KMTP).
   Cultivar name presumed registered 1953; name established and accepted.

Trianon, Trianoniana - see '**Rouge de Trianon**'.

'**Triomphe de Moulins**', *S. vulgaris*
   origin not known pre-1880; S IV
   Transon, Cat., 67 [1880]; McKelvey, The Lilac, 389 [1928]; Wister, Lilacs for America, 59 [1942], 42 [1953]; Photo on Jorgovani/Lilacs 2015 DVD.
   Cultivar name presumed registered 1953; name established and accepted.

'**Triomphe d'Orléans**', *S. vulgaris*
   Berniau 1854; S VI
   syn. - 'Aurelianensis', 'Triomph d'Orleans', 'Triomphe d'Orleans', 'Triumphe d'Orleans', *S. vulgaris triumphum Aureliae*
   Carrière, Rev. Hort., 363 [1852]; McKelvey, The Lilac, 389-390 [1928]; Wister, Lilacs for America, 59 [1942] - as

S IV; Wister, Lilacs for America, 42 [1953]; Photo on Jorgovani/Lilacs 2015 DVD.
Cultivar name presumed registered 1953; name established and accepted.

'Triste Barbaro', *S. vulgaris*
origin not known pre-1938; S VII
Wister, Lilacs for America, 37, 59 [1942]; 42 [1953]; Anon., Woody Pl. Morton Arb., 386 [1990]; Photo on Jorgovani/Lilacs 2015 DVD.
Cultivar name presumed registered 1953; name established and accepted.

Triumphe d'Orleans - see **'Triomphe d'Orléans'**.

'Triunfo de Santa Ines', *S. vulgaris*
Santa Ines pre-1912; D IV
Criadero de Árboles de "Santa Ines", Catálogo Jeneral No. 5, 356 [año 24 = 1912]; McKelvey, The Lilac, 390 [1928].
Probably extinct.

'True Blue', *S. vulgaris*
Havemeyer pre-1942; S II
Wister, Lilacs for America, 59 [1942] - as S III, 42 [1953]; Niedz, ILS Proceedings 1(4):8 [1972]; Eickhorst, ILS Lilac Newsletter 4(1):4-5 [1978]; Photo on Jorgovani/Lilacs 2015 DVD.
Cultivar name presumed registered 1953; name established and accepted.

'True Pink', *S. vulgaris*
Klager; S V
Anon., Lilac Newsletter 14(4):3 [1988]
Cultivar name not established.

'Tsarskosel'skaya', *S. vulgaris*
'Царскосельская'
Aladin, S., Aladina, O., Polyakova, N., and Aladina, A. 2016; D IV & III
{'Zhemchuzhina' × OP}
Садовник (Gardener) magazine 04 (140)/2017 :18-25; Вестник АППМ (Catalog in Vestnik APPM (Planting material association) magazine) 1/2018: 59-72 (in Russian); II All-Russian scientific-practical conference with international participation (II Всероссийская научно-практическая конференция с международным участием) « Botanical Gardens in the XXI Century: Biodiversity Conservation, Development Strategy and Innovative Solutions Belgorod, Botanical Garden of NRU «BelSU», September 23-26, 2019; pp.141-145 (in Russian).
Named for the palace, park and museum in Tsarskoye Selo, Pushkin, St Petersburg.
Cultivar name established and accepted.

'Tsvetnoĭ Bul'var' (Flower Boulevard), *S. vulgaris*
'Цветной Бульвар'
Aladin, S., Aladina, O., Polyakova, T., and Aladina, A. 2012; D IV-V
{'Anabel' × OP}
(Международная научная конференция "Syringa L.: коллекции, выращивание, использование") "International Scientific Conference "Syringa L.: collections, cultivation, using" / Collection of Scientific Articles of Botanical Institute named after V.L. Komarov, Botanical Garden of Peter the Great BIN RAS. - St. Petersburg. -2020.- pp.3-7 (in Russian); Photo exhibition of all varieties of the creative breeding group "Russian Lilac" at the Festival "Lilac February", St. Petersburg, Botanical Garden of Peter the Great BIN RAS, February 22-24, 2020.
Named for the old, beautiful, beloved by Muscovites, Flower Boulevard, which got its name in the 19th century from the Flower Market.
Cultivar name established and accepted.

'TTT', *S. vulgaris*
Upītis 1970; S VII/II
syn. - Upītis No. 3138
{parentage not known}
Kalniņš, Ceriņu jaunšķirnes Dobelē, Dārs un drava 1986 (12):13-15 - in Latvian; Strautiņa, S. 1992. Ceriņi Dārzs un Drava. No. 6, pp.12-13; Vrugtman, HortScience 31(3):328 [1996]; Strautiņa, S. 2002. Ceriņu un jasmīnu avīze. LA, R., p. 62; in litt. S. Strautiņa to F. Vrugtman [21 Dec. 2007] - 1970, S VII/II; Semenov, Igor, Lilacs - Quart. Jour. 44(2):49, ill. 53 [2015] - as V; Photo on Jorgovani/Lilacs 2015 DVD.
Named for Tramm-Trolleybus-Trust of Riga, the famous Soviet woman's basketball team. Between 1960-1980 it was champion of Europe 20 times.
Cultivar name registered 1995; name established and accepted.

'Tuesday', *S. vulgaris*
Hoepfl 1991; D VII-II
syn. - FC 07
{'Flower City' × ? }
Hoepfl, Lilacs - Quart. Jour. 36(2):74-75 [2007] - background information only; Millham, Lilacs - Quart. Jour. 42(4):130 & photo 132 [2013] - reference to FC 07; Millham, Lilacs - Quart. Jour. 43(2):52 [2014] - as D VII/II; Hoepfl, Lilacs - Quart. Jour. 43(3):90 & photo 91 [2014] - Hose-in-hose double florets; (Vrugtman, Cultivated Plant Diversity ... 2017)
Name: According to the sign of the Zodiac the planet Mars rules over Aries and Scorpio and is associated with Tuesday; these are the astrological signs of Marcia and Bob Hoepfl, the originator.
Cultivar name registered 2014; name established and accepted.

'Turenne', *S. vulgaris*
Lemoine 1916; S VII
Lemoine, Cat. No. 190, 25 [1916]; McKelvey, The Lilac, 390 [1928]; Wister, Lilacs for America, 59 [1942], 42

[1953]; Photo on Jorgovani/Lilacs 2015 DVD.
Named for Henri de La Tour d'Auvergne, Vicomte de Turenne, 1611-1675, Marshal of France.
Cultivar name presumed registered 1953; name established and accepted.

'Turgot', *S.* ×*hyacinthiflora*
Lemoine 1920; S V
Lemoine, Cat. No. 194, 18 [1921]; McKelvey, The Lilac, 199 [1928]; Wister, Lilacs for America, 59 [1942], 42 [1953]; Photo on Jorgovani/Lilacs 2015 DVD.
Named for Anne Robert Jacques Turgot, 1727-1781, French jurist, statesman and economist.
Cultivar name presumed registered 1953; name established and accepted.

'Turmalin', *S. vulgaris*
'Турмалин'
Aladin, S., Polyakova, T., Aladina, O., and Aladina, A. 2015; S VII & V
{'Gortyenziya' × OP}
(Международная научная конференция "Syringa L.: коллекции, выращивание, использование") "International Scientific Conference "Syringa L.: collections, cultivation, using" / Collection of Scientific Articles of Botanical Institute named after V.L. Komarov, Botanical Garden of Peter the Great BIN RAS. - St. Petersburg. -2020.- pp.3-7 (in Russian); Photo exhibition of all varieties of the creative breeding group "Russian Lilac" at the Festival "Lilac February", St. Petersburg, Botanical Garden of Peter the Great BIN RAS, February 22-24, 2020.
Thanks to the contrasting combination of reddish-purple flowers and shades, the inflorescences of this cultivar resemble the precious gemstone tourmaline.
Cultivar name established and accepted.

TWILIGHT - see '**Sumerki**'.

'**Two Star General**', *S. vulgaris*
Rankin; D IV
{parentage not known}
Wister, Arnoldia 23(4):83 [1963]
 cultivar name registered 1963; probably extinct.

'Ukraina', *S. vulgaris*
'Украина'
Zhogoleva 1974; S IV-V
{'Réaumur' × ? }
Rubtzov et al. 1980. Vidy i sorta sireni, kul'tiviruemye v SSSR. Kiev; Naukova Dumka. – in Russian; Holetich, C.D. 1982. Lilac species and cultivars in cultivation in USSR. Lilacs 11(2):1-38. - translation of Rubtzov et al. 1982; Photo on Jorgovani/Lilacs 2015 DVD.
Named for the Ukraine.
Cultivar name established and accepted.

'Ulrich Brunner', *S. vulgaris*
origin not known pre-1906; D ?
Bellair, Rev. Hort., 321 [1906]; McKelvey, The Lilac, 390 [1928]
Named perhaps for the Swiss rosarian Ulrich Brünner [no dates], Lausanne, Switzerland.
Cultivar name not established.

Ultra Lavender, *S. vulgaris*
origin not known pre-1982; D II-VII
{parentage not known}
Peterson, Lilacs - Proceedings 16(1):23 [1987] - name only; in litt. Max Peterson to F. Vrugtman [Jun.06/2002], plant received from Donald Egolf ca 1982, florets semi-double
Cultivar name not established.

UNA WHITE, (Villosae Group), *S.*
origin not known pre-1958; S I
reported at Cherry Hill Nurseries, Inc.
Cognomen; probably originally as UNH WHITE, a University of New Hampshire selection.

Uncle Tom - see '**L'Oncle Tom**'.

UNH DWARF, *S. pubescens* subsp. *patula*
Rogers pre-1980s; S I
Syn – 'Owen Rogers'
Syringa Plus Lilac Collectors List 2010, p. 1 – measuring only 3ft × 3ft after 30 years;
perhaps useful in future hybridizing to achieve dwarfing.
Seen 2019 on website: https://www.hopespringsnursery.com/collections/lilacs-a-z?page=3
Cognomen for a University of New Hampshire selection.

undulatifolia, *S. tomentella* subsp. *yunnanensis*, f. (forma)
Gorb 1975; S ?
bud mutation selected as a cultivar
Gorb 1989 Сирени на Украина, p. 61; listed by Heide Planteskole
Cultivar name not established; after 1958 cultivar names in Latin form are not established.

'Upīša bērns', *S. vulgaris*
origin not known pre-2018; S VI
Syn. – 'Ŭpēta Bērks'
Photo taken at Dobele, Latvia with ID plate by Natalia Savenko, in 2020 ILS Lilac Photo Database.

Upiisha Velte - see '**Kristīne Baltpurviņa**'.
Kalniņš, L., Ceriņu jaunšķirnes Dobelē, Dārs un drava 1986(12):13-15 - in Latvian; Strautiņa, S., Ceriņu un jasmīnu avīze. LA, R., p. 62 [2002] - in Latvian; in litt. S. Strautiņa to F. Vrugtman [22 Jan. 2008] - synonym of 'Kristīne Baltpurviņa'.

Uralensis or *uralensis*
Pringle, Lilacs 7(1):50-67 [1979] - as invalid name.

'Urmas', *S. vulgaris*
Mägi pre-2017; S VII
Photo from Estonia by Mägi seen in 2020 ILS Lilac Photo Database.
Cultivar name not established.

'**Ursula**', *S.* (Villosae Group), *S.* ×*prestoniae*
   Preston 1928; S V
   syn. - Preston No. 20-14-214
   {*S. villosa* subsp. *villosa* × *S. komarowii* subsp. *reflexa*}
   Macoun, Rep. Dom. Hort. 1928, 57 [1930]; Wister, Lilacs for America, 59, 64 [1942], 42, 48 [1953]; Photo on Jorgovani/Lilacs 2015 DVD.
   Named for the Attendant on Hero in Shakespeare's *Much Ado About Nothing*.
   Cultivar name presumed registered 1953; name established and accepted.

'Uspekh', *S. vulgaris*
   'Успех'
   Smol'skiĭ & Bibikova 1964; S I
   {'Hyazinthenflieder' × 'Marie Legraye'}
   Pikaleva, Lilacs - Quart. Jour. 23(4):88 [1994] - name only; in litt. Igor Semenov to Vrugtman 13 August 2014; Makedonskaya, Natal'ya. 2016. Results of an Introduction *Syringa L.* species in the Central Botanical Garden NAS prospects of their use. In: Floriculture; History, Theory, Practice. Proceedings of the VII International Scientific Conference (May 24-26, 2016, Minsk, Belarus), Minsk "Konfido", p. 160-161.
   Name: Russian for success.
   Cultivar name established and accepted.

'Utro Moskvy', *S. vulgaris*
   'Утро Москвы'
   Kolesnikov 1938; D IV-V
   syn. - Kolesnikov No. 77
   {'Emile Lemoine' × 'Mme Lemoine'}
   Kolesnikov, Lilac, 26 [1955]; Howard, Arnoldia 19(6-7):31-35 [1959]; Gromov, A., Siren', 78 [1963]; Howard & Brizicky, AABGA Quart. Newsl. No. 64, 17-21 [1965]; Bilov et al., Siren', 76 [1974] - in Russian; Rubtzov et al. 1980. Vidy i sorta sireni, kul'tiviruemye v SSSR. Kiev; Naukova Dumka. – in Russian; Holetich, C.D. 1982. Lilac species and cultivars in cultivation in USSR. Lilacs 11(2):1-38. - translation of Rubtzov et al. 1982; Photo on Jorgovani/Lilacs 2015 DVD.
   Name: Russian for morning in Moscow.
   Cultivar name established and accepted.

'Utro Rossii', *S. vulgaris*
   'Утро России'
   Vekhov 1952; D II
   Magazine "Tsvetovodstvo" ("Floriculture") No. 7, 1977, p. 11
   Rubtzov et al. 1980. Vidy i sorta sireni, kul'tiviruemye v SSSR. Kiev 1952 p. 96; Naukova Dumka. – in Russian; Holetich, C.D. 1982. Lilac species and cultivars in cultivation in USSR. Lilacs 11(2):1-38. - translation of Rubtzov et al. 1982; Photo on Jorgovani/Lilacs 2015 DVD.
   Name: Russian for Russian morning.
   Cultivar name established and accepted.

'**Uvertyura**', *S. vulgaris*
   'Увертюра'
   Grigorieva, V. & Grichachina, T pre-1985; S III
   Sdlg No. 509
   Registered by the USSR State Committee for Inventions and Discoveries in the State Register of Breeding Achievements of the USSR No. 8507848, 1985. Certificate № 4567
   Magazine "Tsvetovodstvo" ("Floriculture") No. 3, 1988, p. 13
   information provided by Elena Olegovna Kuzmina, chief agronomist of the Control and Seed Experimental Station (KCOC) in 1978 - 1993.
   Name: Russian of overture.
   Cultivar name established and accepted; name registered.

'Uzcītīgais Dunkers', *S. vulgaris*
   Upītis 1969; D VII
   syn. - 'Uzcitigais Dunkers'
   Kalniņš, L., Ceriņu jaunšķirnes Dobelē, Dārs un drava 1986(12):13-15 - in Latvian; Strautiņa, S. 1992. Ceriņi Dārzs un Drava. No. 6, pp.12-13; in litt. S. Strautiņa to F. Vrugtman [21 Dec. 2007] - 1969, D VII; Semenov, Igor, Lilacs - Quart. Jour. 44(2):49,ill. 54 [2015]; Photo on Jorgovani/Lilacs 2015 DVD.
   Name: Latvian for diligent dunkers.
   Cultivar name established and accepted.

'**Vaiga**', *S.* ×*hyacinthiflora*
   Vaigla 1970; S V (V-I per Semenov)
   {'Esther Staley' × ? }
   Vrugtman, HortScience 26(5):476 [1991]; Kivistik, Maakodu 1997(5):22-23 [1997] - in Estonian; I. Semenov, Lilacs 48(2):62,65,63 (photo) [2019].
   Named for the originator's younger daughter.
   Cultivar name registered 1990; name established and accepted.

'Vaigla Valge', *S. vulgaris*
   Vaigla pre-2001; D I
   {'Silja' × ? }
   listed on http://aed.rapina.ee/sirelid.htm [seen 5 Nov. 2005]; I. Semenov, Lilacs 48(2):64,65 [2019].
   Cultivar name established and accepted.

'Valaam', *S. vulgaris*
   'Валаам'
   Aladin, Aladina A., Aladin O., and Polyakova T. 2015; S IV
   {'Cavour' × 'Madame Charles Souchet'}
   Named for the island and village of Valaam, located in the northern part of Ladoga Lake, Karelia, Russia.
   Cultivar name established and accepted.

'Valdek', *S.*
   Mägi pre-2018; S VII
   Semenov, I., Lilacs 48(2):68 [2019].
   Cultivar name not established.

'Valentina', *S. vulgaris*
   origin not known pre-1846; ? ?
   Baumann, Cat., 15 [1846]; McKelvey, The Lilac, 390-391 [1928] - possibly misnomer for 'Valetteana'
   Cultivar name not established.

'Valentina Dvortsova', *S. vulgaris*
　'Валентина Дворцова'
　Kiris, Uromova and Rudaya ca 2008; S V/IV to IV
　{'Bogdan Khmel'nitskii' × ?}
　registration pending with the State Register of Breeding Achievements
　Named for Valentina Dvortsova, Candidate of Biological Science, rose specialist, head of ornamental perennials working group for 40 years of Moscow State University Botanical Garden, author of books and articles.

'Valentina Grizodubova', *S. vulgaris*
　'Валентина Гризодубова'
　Kolesnikov 1946; D V
　Bilov et al., Siren', 36 [1974] - in Russian; Rubtzov et al. 1980. Vidy i sorta sireni, kul'tiviruemye v SSSR. Kiev; Naukova Dumka. – in Russian; Holetich, C.D. 1982. Lilac species and cultivars in cultivation in USSR. Lilacs 11(2):1-38. - translation of Rubtzov et al. 1982; Photo on Jorgovani/Lilacs 2015 DVD.
　Named for Valentina Grizodubova, 1910-1993, Russian aviatress; in 1938 Grizodubova, Raskova and Osipenko set a world record with a non-stop flight from Moscow to Siberia (see also Osipenko and Raskova).
　Cultivar name established and accepted.

'Valentina Tereshkova', *S. vulgaris*
　'Валентина Терешкова'
　Kravchenko; D V
　{'Congo' × 'Lamarck'}
　Kravchenko L. Culture of lilacs in Uzbekistan. Publishing house "Uzbekistan", Tashkent, 1970 p. 12
　Rubtzov et al. 1980. Vidy i sorta sireni, kul'tiviruemye v SSSR. Kiev; Naukova Dumka. – in Russian; Holetich, C.D. 1982. Lilac species and cultivars in cultivation in USSR. Lilacs 11(2):1-38. - translation of Rubtzov et al. 1982.
　Named for Valentina Tereshkova, 1937- x, Russian cosmonaut, the first woman to travel in space.
　Cultivar name established and accepted.

'Valentin Serov', *S. vulgaris*
　'Валентин Серов'
　Aladin, S., Aladina, O., Polyakova, T. and Aladina, A. 2015; D IV-III
　Statutory registration, Russia, State Register and Plant Patent No. 80050/8058580 (2019)
　{elite form 08-202H× 'Olya'}
　Садовник (Gardener) magazine 04 (140)/2017 :18-25; Вестник АППМ (Catalog in Vestnik APPM (Planting material association) magazine) 1/2018: 59-72 (in Russian); II All-Russian scientific-practical conference with international participation (II Всероссийская научно-практическая конференция с международным участием) « Botanical Gardens in the XXI Century: Biodiversity Conservation, Development Strategy and Innovative Solutions Belgorod, Botanical Garden of NRU «BelSU», September 23-26, 2019; pp.141-145 (in Russian).
　Named for Valentin Aleksandrovich Serov (Валентин Александрович Серов), 1865-1911, Russian painter and graphic artist.
　Cultivar name established and accepted.

'Valeria', *S.* (Villosae Group), *S. ×prestoniae*
　Preston 1928; S II
　syn. - Preston No. 20-14-149
　{*S. villosa* subsp. *villosa* × *S. komarowii* subsp. *reflexa*}
　Macoun, Rep. Dom. Hort. 1928, 58 [1930] - name only; Macoun, Rep. Dom. Hort. 1930, 68 [1931]; Wister, Lilacs for America, 59, 64 [1942], 42, 48 [1953]; Photo on Jorgovani/Lilacs 2015 DVD.
　Named for the Friend to Virgilia in Shakespeare's *Coriolanus*.
　Cultivar name presumed registered 1953; name established and accepted.

'Valetteana', *S. vulgaris*
　origin not known pre-1845; S VII
　syn. - 'Valentiana', 'Valettiana', 'Valleteana', 'Valletiana', 'Valletteana', etc.
　common name: Valette
　Oudin, Cat., 6 [1845]; Stand. Pl. Names, 488 [1923] - as Vallette; McKelvey, The Lilac, 391 [1928] - as S ? , poorly defined cultivar;
　Cultivar name presumed registered 1953, but identity questionable.
　Nota bene: Wister, Lilacs for America, 59 [1942], 42 [1953] - as D IV, refers to plants grown in North America; Photo on Jorgovani/Lilacs 2015 DVD - as D II-V.

'Valkyrja', *S. villosa* subsp. *wolfii*
　origin not known pre-1965; S V
　{seedling of *S. villosa* subsp. *wolfii*}
　http://www.kjarr.is/?page_id=353
　Cultivar of Iceland origin
　Cultivar name established and accepted.

'Valter', *S. vulgaris*
　Mägi pre-2017; S VII
　Photo in Estonia by Mägi seen on 2020 ILS Lilac Photo Database.
　Cultivar name not established.

Van Aerschott - see **'Mons. van Aerschot'**.

'Van Eaton', *S. vulgaris*
　Klager; S VII
　Anon., ILS Newsletter 14(4):3-4 [1988]
　Cultivar name established and accepted.

Van Houttei - see **'Louis van Houtte'**.

'Van Loveland', *S. vulgaris*
　Lape; D VII
　{'Kapriz' × ? }
　Vrugtman, AABGA Bull. 17(3):68 [1984]

Named for Van Loveland [no dates], banker, a friend of the originator.
Cultivar name registered 1984;
Cultivar not reported in cultivation.

'Van Plitz', S.
(species affiliation not known)
origin not known pre-1999; ? ?
syn. - see also 'Von Plitz'
common - red lilac
Macore Co. Inc. photo library [Nov.28, 1999] http://www.macore.com/photolib.htm
Cultivar name not established.

Van's Purple, S. vulgaris
Vander Zalm pre-2000; S VII
syn. - lilac # 102, Van's Dwarf Purple
{open pollinated F2 seedling from irradiated seed of unknown origin; the same irradiated seed lot also gave rise to 'Prairie Petite' or lilac # 103}
Mitsch Nursery, Cat. [1996] - as Van's Purple; Gasshouse Works, [Mar.27, 2001]; Van's Inc. Nurs. [June 12, 2001] http://www.lilac-King.com - as Van's Dwarf Purple
Cognomen, not cultivar name.

'Variegata', S. emodi
origin not known pre-1877; S I *
syn. - 'Aureovariegata', 'Aureo-variegata', *emodi variegata*
Ottolander, Sieboldia 3:376 [1877]; McKelvey, The Lilac, 26 [1928]; Wister, Lilacs for America, 44, 47 [1942], 25, 59 [1953]; Boom, Jaarb. Ned. DenDr Ver. 20:113 [1955]; Photo on Jorgovani/Lilacs 2015 DVD.
Cultivar name presumed registered 1953; name established and accepted.

Variegata, S. ×hyacinthiflora
origin not known ? ?
Select Plus N, Cat. [2000] - name only
Not a cultivar name; probably a cognomen.

'Variegata', S. ×prestoniae
Origin not known pre-2019; S V
Seen in 2019 personal email to Registrar as a 2015 picture taken in the Netherlands by Ronald Houtman.
Cultivar name not established.

'Variegata', S. vulgaris
origin not known pre-1826; S III *
Miller (Bristol Nursery), Cat., 14 [1826]; International Exhibition, 1876, US Centennial Commission, Volume 11, p. 310 - name only; McKelvey, The Lilac, 391-392 [1928] - confused background, probably not a single clone
Cultivar name not established.

'Variegata', S. villosa subsp. *wolfii*
origin not known; S VI *
reported by J. C. Wister; no lit. ref.
Cultivar name not established.

Variegated, S. vulgaris
origin not known; D IV *
Northwest Rose Growers Inc. listing [seen Apr.28/99]
Not a cultivar name; probably a cognomen.

Variegated Double, S. vulgaris
origin not known; D ? *
RHS Plant Finder / PFRL CD-ROM 1996/97; no other lit. ref.
Not a cultivar name; probably a cognomen.

Varin - see S. ×chinensis.

varina duplex Lemoine - see '**Duplex**' (S. ×chinensis).

varina 'La Lorraine' - see '**La Lorraine**' (S. ×chinensis).

varina 'le Progrès' - see '**Le Progrès**' (S. ×chinensis).

varina saugeana - see '**Saugeana**' (S. ×chinensis).

'Värtön Valkea', S. (Villosae Group), S. ×henryi
origin not known; S. I.
Kolkka, Sorbifolia 37(1):33-34, Fig. 5 [2006] - name only
Cultivar name not established.

'Vasaras Svētki', S. vulgaris
Upītis 1965; S II
Kalniņš, L., Ceriņu jaunšķirnes Dobelē, Dārs un drava 1986(12):13-15 - in Latvian; Strautiņa S. 1992. Ceriņi Dārzs un Drava. No. 6, pp.12-13; in litt. S. Strautina to F. Vrugtman [21 Dec. 2007] - 1965, S II.
Name: Latvian for summer festival.
Cultivar name established and accepted.

'Vasiliĭ Tërkin', S. vulgaris
'Василий Тёркин'
Aladin, S., Aladina, O., and Polyakova, T. 2014; D IV-V
{elite form 8-76 × elite form 10-51}
Приусадебное хозяйство (Annex to the magazine Homestead farming: "Flowers in the garden and at home. Brushes and paints") 08/2015: 5-14; Садовник (Gardener) magazine, 05 (141)/2017 :16-22; Вестник АППМ (Catalog in Vestnik APPM (Planting material association) magazine) 1/2018: 59-72 (in Russian).
Named for the epic poem Vasilii Terkin by Aleksander Tvardovsky, written during WWII.
Cultivar name established and accepted.

'Vauban', S. ×hyacinthiflora
Lemoine 1913; D V
syn. - *praecox* 'Vauban', *praecox pl.* 'Vauban'
Lemoine, Cat. No. 185, 41 [1913]; McKelvey, The Lilac, 199-200 [1928]; Wister, Lilacs for America, 59 [1942], 43 [1953]; Photo on Jorgovani/Lilacs 2015 DVD.
Named for Sébastien le Prestre de Vauban, 1633-1707, French military engineer, marshal of France, 1703.
Cultivar name presumed registered 1953; name established and accepted.

Veberöd, *S. vulgaris* f. *alba*
    a white-flowered lilac propagated from seed, suitable for hedges (in litt Björn Aldén to F. Vrugtman, Nov. 10, 2007); see also ICNCP Article 2.13, Ex. 11.Name: Veberöd is the name of the locality where the seed is collected (in litt Kimmo Kolkka to F. Vrugtman, Dec. 13, 2007)
    Cultivar name established and accepted.

'Ve<u>ch</u>ernnii Vladivostok', *S.* ×*hyacinthiflora*
    'Вечерний Владивосток'
    P<u>sh</u>ennikova 2006; S II-VII
    Registered with the State Commission of the Russian Federation for Testing and Protection of Selection Achievements, No. 9358839, 2006; P<u>sh</u>ennikova, L.M. 2007.
    Lilacs, cultivated in the Botanical Garden-Institute FEB RAS, Wladivostok; p. 39-40; Photo on Jorgovani/Lilacs 2015 DVD.
    Name: Russian for evening in Vladivostok.
    Cultivar name registered, established and accepted.

'Ve<u>ch</u>ernii Zvon', *S. vulgaris*
    'Вечерний Звон'
    Aladin, S., Arkhangel'skii, V., Polyakova, T., and Aladina, O. 2011; S V
    {'Gortenziya' × OP}
    Registered with the State Commission of the Russian Federation for Testing and Protection of Selection Achievements, No. 8853120, 2011; Питомник-частный сад (Pitomnik i chastnyi sad; Nursery and private garden) 1/2013:26-29 (in Russian); Вестник АППМ (Catalog in Vestnik APPM (Planting material association) magazine) 1/2018: 59-72 (in Russian); in litt. Holetich to Vrugtman 16 Oct. 2013; Photo on Jorgovani/Lilacs 2015 DVD.
    Садовник (Gardener) magazine 04 (140)/2017 :18-25;
    Name: Russian for evening bell or evening call.
    Cultivar name registered, established, and accepted.

'Ve<u>ch</u>ernyaya Moskva', *S. vulgaris*
    'Вечерняя Москва'
    Aladin, S., Arkhangel'skii, V., Polyakova, T., and Aladina, O. 2011; D III-IV
    {'Président Grévy' × OP}
    Registered with the State Commission of the Russian Federation for Testing and Protection of Selection Achievements, No. 8853115, 2011; Lilacs Quart. Journ. 40(2):42 [2011] - name only; Питомник-частный сад (Pitomnik I chastnyi sad; Nursery and private garden) 2/2013:24-34 (in Russian); Вестник АППМ (Catalog in Vestnik APPM (Planting material association) magazine) 1/2018: 59-72 (in Russian); Photo on Jorgovani/Lilacs 2015 DVD.
    Name: Russian for evening Moscow.
    Cultivar name registered, established and accepted.
    Cultivar suitable for forcing.

'Veera', *S.* (Villosae Group), *S.* ×*josiflexa*
    Peteri 1980s; S VII-V
    syn. - 'Alvatar'
    Pihlajaniemi, J. Appl. Bot. and Food Quality 79:107-116 [2005] - name only; Found near Rovaniemi, near the arctic circle; reported in cultivation at Elit-plantstation, Laukaa, Finland, 2005 (personal communication Kimmo Kolkka to F. Vrugtman, Feb.05/05); <http://www.smts.fi/MTP%20julkaisu%202004/posterit04/Siuruainen.pdf> as 'Alvatar' name only, seen Dec. 6, 2006; synonym 'Alvatar', (personal communication Kimmo Kolkka to F. Vrugtman, Feb.17/07); MTT (Agrifood Research Finland) cat. Varmennetun taimituotannon emokasvihinnasto vuonna 2010, p. 53.
    Cultivar name established and accepted.

'Veiksme', *S. vulgaris*
    Kārkliņš 2003; D V-VII
    in cultivation at the Latvian State Institute of Fruit-Growing, Dobele; Photo on Jorgovani/Lilacs 2015 DVD.
    Name - Latvian for success.
    Cultivar name established and accepted.

'Vek', *S.*
    (species affiliation not known)
    'Век'
    Mi<u>kh</u>aĭlov & Rybakina 2002; D IV
    {parentage not known}
    Chapman, Lilacs - Quart. Jour. 32(1):17-18 [2003] - translated from N. L. Mi<u>kh</u>aĭlov in <u>Ts</u>vetovodstvo, May-June issue (in Russian); http://home.onego.ru/~otsoppe/enciclop/kustar/syring_s.html (July 26, 2003); Photo on Jorgovani/Lilacs 2015 DVD.
    Name: Russian for century.
    Cultivar name established and accepted.

'Velika<u>ya</u> Pobeda', *S. vulgaris*
    'Великая Победа'
    Kolesnikov & Mironovich 1986; D IV/III
    Novikov & Pikaleva, Lilacs - Quart. Jour. 23(4):91 [1994]; Registered with the State Commission of the Russian Federation for Testing and Protection of Selection Achievements, No. 8803390, 1998; Polyakova, 2010, Istori<u>ya</u> Russkoĭ Sireni, p. 74; Photo on Jorgovani/Lilacs 2015 DVD.
    Name: Russian for a great victory.
    Cultivar name established and accepted.

velutina excellens - see **'Excellens'** (*S. pubescens* subsp. *patula*).

'Velutina Korea' - see *S. pubescens* subsp. *patula*.

venusta (var.), *S. villosa* subsp. *villosa*
    no information; S IV-V
    listed by Fa C. Esveld, Boskoop, NL
    http://www.esveld.nl/zoekstrucen/lstlila/zoeklila0000006.html [February 8, 2004]
    Probably not a valid name.

'Vera Khoruzhaya', *S. vulgaris*
'Вера Хоружая'
Smol'skiĭ & Bibikova 1964; S IV-V
syn. - 'Vera Khorujaja', 'Vera Khorujaya', 'Vera Khoruzhya', 'Vera Khoruzhaja'
{'Mme Abel Chatenay' × 'Réaumur'}
Bilov et al., Siren', 36 [1974] - in Russian; Rubtzov et al. 1980. Vidy i sorta sireni, kul'tiviruemye v SSSR. Kiev; Naukova Dumka. – in Russian; Holetich, C.D. 1982. Lilac species and cultivars in cultivation in USSR. Lilacs 11(2):1-38. - translation of Rubtzov et al. 1982; Semenov, Igor, Lilacs -Quart. Jour. 43(3):85-87 & photo 87 [2014]; Photo on Jorgovani/Lilacs 2015 DVD.
Named for Vera Khoruzhaya (Weronika Karczewska), 1903-1942, who worked for the underground resistance during WW II and died in Vitebsk prison; Hero of the Soviet Union.
Cultivar name established and accepted.

'Verdugo's Pride', *S. ×hyacinthiflora*
Sobeck; S V
Wister, Arnoldia 26(3):13 [1966].
Named for the Verdugo Hills, California, USA.
Cultivar name registered 1966; name established and accepted.
Nota bene: Since this cultivar appears to be of 'Lavender Lady' ancestry see also: Pringle, Lilacs - Quart. Jour. 24(4):97-99 [1995]; and Vrugtman, HortScience 31(3):328 [1996].

'Vergissmeinnicht', *S. vulgaris*
Späth 1887; S IV/III
{chance seedling of unknown parentage}
Späth, Cat. No. 69, 4 [1887]; McKelvey, The Lilac, 392-393 [1928]; Späth, Späth-Buch, 110, 305 [1930]; Wister, Lilacs for America, 59 [1942], 43 [1953] - as S III; Photo on Jorgovani/Lilacs 2015 DVD.
Name: German for forget-me-not.
Cultivar name presumed registered 1953; name established and accepted.

Versailles - see '**Versaliensis**'.

'Versaliensis', *S. vulgaris*
origin not known pre-1857; S VII
syn. - versaillensis, 'Versailles'; see also 'Gloire de Versailles'
common name: Versailles
Oudin, Cat. No. 79, 8 [ca 1857]; Stand. Pl. Names, 488 [1923] - as Versailles; McKelvey, The Lilac, 393 [1928]; Wister, Lilacs for America, 59 [1942], 43 [1953] - as S VI; Photo on Jorgovani/Lilacs 2015 DVD.
Cultivar name presumed registered 1953; name established and accepted.

'Verschaffeltii', *S. vulgaris*
origin not known pre-1865; S IV
syn. - 'Verschaffelt'; see also 'Ambroise Verschaffelt'
A. Leroy, Cat., 100 [1865]; McKelvey, The Lilac, 393-394 [1928]; Wister, Lilacs for America, 60 [1942], 43 [1953]; Photo on Jorgovani/Lilacs 2015 DVD.
Named for one of the Verschaffelts, nurserymen, breeders of azaleas, Gent, Belgium; Ambroise Verschaffelt, 1825-1886, was the founder of "L'Illustration Horticole" (1854-1896).
Cultivar name presumed registered 1953; name established and accepted.

'Versicolor', *S. vulgaris*
origin not known ? ?
Kirchner, Arb. Muscav., 496 [1864]; McKelvey The Lilac, 394 [1928]
Cultivar name not established.

'Vesenniĭ Motiv'; *S. vulgaris*
'Весенний Мотив'
Mel'nik, Rubanik & Dyagilev 1989; D V/IV
Dyagilev, Lilacs - Quart. Jour. 22(1):20 [1993]; Pikaleva, Lilacs - Quart. Jour. 23(4):88 [1994]
Name: Russian for spring motive.
Cultivar name established and accepted.

'Vesennyaya Krasa', *S. vulgaris*
'Весенняя Краса'
Klimenko, V. 1955; S II-IV
syn. - 'Vesennjaja Krasa'
Rubtzov et al. 1980. Vidy i sorta sireni, kul'tiviruemye v SSSR. Kiev; Naukova Dumka. – in Russian; Holetich, C.D. 1982. Lilac species and cultivars in cultivation in USSR. Lilacs 11(2):1-38. - translation of Rubtzov et al. 1982.
Name: Russian for spring beauty.
Cultivar name established and accepted.

'Vesna 1942 Goda', *S. vulgaris*
'Весна 1942 Года'
Kolesnikov; D VII
syn. - 'Vesna', 'Vesna 1942 g.'
Rubtzov et al. 1980. Vidy i sorta sireni, kul'tiviruemye v SSSR. Kiev; Naukova Dumka. – in Russian; Holetich, C.D. 1982. Lilac species and cultivars in cultivation in USSR. Lilacs 11(2):1-38. - translation of Rubtzov et al. 1982; Photo on Jorgovani/Lilacs 2015 DVD.
Name: Russian for spring of year 1942
Cultivar name established and accepted.

'Vesnovka', *S. vulgaris*
'Весновка'
Sagitova & Dzevitski; D IV
{parentage not known}
Named for a river in the Almaty region of Kazakhstan.
Cultivar name not established.

'Vesper', *S. vulgaris*
Fleming 1979; S VII/II
{parentage not known}
Vrugtman, AABGA Bull. 15(3):71 [1981]; Photo on Jorgovani/Lilacs 2015 DVD.
Cultivar name registered 1980; name established and accepted.

'Vesper Song', *S.* ×*hyacinthiflora*
    Fiala 1981; S II
    {'Pocahontas' × 'Maréchal Foch'}
    Fiala, Lilacs, 224 [1988] - erroneously listed as 'Eventide'; Knight Hollow Nursery, 1998 Cultured cutting and liner descriptive list; Photo on Jorgovani/Lilacs 2015 DVD.
    Cultivar name established and accepted.

'Vestale', *S. vulgaris*
    Lemoine 1910; S I
    syn. - 'La Vestale', 'Vestal', 'Vestalin'
    Lemoine, Cat. No. 176, 7 [1910]; McKelvey, The Lilac, 394 [1928]; Wister, Lilacs for America, 60 [1942], 43 [1953]; Photo on Jorgovani/Lilacs 2015 DVD.
    Name: French for virgin.
    Awards: RHS Award of Garden Merit 1931 & 1993.
    Cultivar name presumed registered 1953; name established and accepted.

'Vēstule Solveigai', *S. vulgaris*
    Upītis 1968; S VI
    syn. - 'Veestule Solveigai', 'Vestule Solveigai'
    {parentage not known}
    Kalva, V., Ceriņi, 165-166 [1980]; Rubtzov et al. 1980. Vidy i sorta sireni, kul'tiviruemye v SSSR. Kiev; Naukova Dumka. – in Russian; Holetich, C.D. 1982. Lilac species and cultivars in cultivation in USSR. Lilacs 11(2):1-38. - translation of Rubtzov et al. 1982; Kalniņš, Ceriņu jaunšķirnes Dobelē, Dārs un drava 1986 (12):13-15 - in Latvian; Strautiņa, S. 1992. Ceriņi Dārzs un Drava. No. 6, pp.12-13; Vrugtman, HortScience 31(3):328 [1996]; in litt. S. Strautiņa to F. Vrugtman [21 Dec. 2007] - 1968, S VI
    Name: Latvian for letter to Solveig.
    Cultivar name registered 1995; name established and accepted.

'Vésuve', *S. vulgaris*
    Lemoine 1916; S VII
    syn. - 'Vesuve'
    Lemoine, Cat. No. 190, 25 [1916]; McKelvey, The Lilac, 394-395 [1928]; Wister, Lilacs for America, 60 [1942], 43 [1953]
    Named for the volcano near Naples, Italy.
    Cultivar name presumed registered 1953; name established and accepted.

'Vetka Mira', *S. vulgaris*
    'Ветка мира"
    Kolesnikov 1952; D I
    Syn. – 'Belaya Vetka'
    Polyakova, "Master of the Lilac Inflorescence", "Penta", Moscow 2018 page 57
    Pikaleva, Lilacs - Quart. Jour. 23(4):84 [1994]; Photo on Jorgovani/Lilacs 2015 DVD.
    Name: Russian for white branch or peace branch.
    Cultivar name established and accepted.

'Victor', *S. vulgaris*
    origin not known pre-1955; S II
    Anon., Lilacs - Proceedings 12(1):17 [1984] - name only; reported in cultivation at Univ. of Wisconsin Arb., received from Brand Peony Farm in 1955; no lit ref.
    Cultivar name not established.

'Victore Harrington', *S. vulgaris*
    origin not known pre-1953; ? ?
    Wister, Lilacs for America, 43 [1953]
    Cultivar name not established.

'Victoria', *S. vulgaris*
    origin not known pre-1865; S VI
    Anon., Wochenschr. Ver. Beförd. Gartenb. Preuss. 8:88 [1865] & 12:43 [1869]; McKelvey, The Lilac, 395 [1928] - descriptions vary.

'Victorie', *S. vulgaris*
    Tulp pre-1952; S I
    syn. - President F. D. Roosevelt
    {mutation of 'Mme Florent Stepman'; very similar to 'Margaretha'}
    Wister, Lilacs for America, 43 [1953]; Eveleens Maarse, Dendron 1(1):13 [1954]; Bunnik/Stapel, in litt. January 3, 2000 - almost identical to 'Margartetha', never taken in production for forcing; Cornelis van Dam, in litt. January 11, 2000 - sold as garden lilac.
    Awards: Certificate of Merit 1952; First Class Certificate 1953 (KMTP).
    Cultivar name presumed registered 1953; name established and accepted.

'Victor Lemoine', *S. vulgaris*
    Lemoine 1906; D IV
    Lemoine, Cat. No. 164, 8 [1906]; McKelvey, The Lilac, 395 [1928]; Wister, Lilacs for America, 60 [1942], 43 [1953]; Photo on Jorgovani/Lilacs 2015 DVD.
    Named for Pierre Louis Victor Lemoine 1823-1911, horticulturist and principal of V. Lemoine & Fils, pepinières, Nancy, France.
    Cultivar name presumed registered 1953; name established and accepted.

'Victory', *S. vulgaris*
    Sass, H.E.; S V
    Anon., Lilacs - Quart. Jour. 33(1):11 [2004]
    Cultivar name established and accepted.

'Vidzemes Debesis', *S. vulgaris*
    Upītis 1965; S II/III
    syn. - Upītis No. 62-7, 'Vidzemes Debess'
    Kalva, V., Ceriņi, 165-166 [1980] - in Latvian; Kalniņš, L., Ceriņu jaunšķirnes Dobelē, Dārs un drava 1986(12):13-15 - in Latvian; Strautiņa, S. 1992. Ceriņi Dārzs un Drava. No. 6, pp.12-13; Strautiņa, S. 2002. Ceriņu un jasmīnu avīze. LA., R., p. 62; in litt. S. Strautiņa to F. Vrugtman [21 Dec. 2007] - 1965, S II/III; Semenov, Igor, Lilacs - Quart. Jour. 44(2):49-50, ill. 55 [2015] - as V/II turning III; Photo on Jorgovani/Lilacs 2015 DVD.
    Name: Latvian for sky of Vidzeme cloud, a region of Latvia.
    Cultivar name established and accepted.

Viger - see **'Président Viger'**.

Villa Nova, *S. josikaea*
origin not known pre-1970; S II ?
Palsson, Garðyrkjuritið 78:13 [1998] in Icelandic; in litt.
Dora Jakobsdottir to F. Vrugtman [Jun.01/00]
Probably a cognomen for an unknown cultivar.

'Villars', *S. ×hyacinthiflora*
Lemoine 1920; S IV
syn. - 'Viliars', 'Villers'
Lemoine, Cat. No. 194, 18 [1920]; McKelvey, The Lilac, 200 [1928]; Wister, Lilacs for America, 60 [1942], 43 [1953]
Named for Dominique Villars, 1745-1814, French botanist.
Cultivar name presumed registered 1953; name established and accepted.

'Ville de Berne', *S. vulgaris*
origin not known pre-1953; ? ?
Wister, Lilacs for America, 43 [1953]
Cultivar name not established.

'Ville de Liège', *S. vulgaris*
Klettenberg 1926; S V
Wister, Lilacs for America, 43 [1953]
Cultivar name presumed registered 1953; name established and accepted.

'Ville de Limoges', *S. vulgaris*
origin not known pre-1889; S V
syn. - 'Ville d'Imoges'
common name: Ville de Limoges
Parsons, Cat., 50 [1889] - as Ville d'Imoges, name only; Stand. Pl. Names, 488 [1923] - as Ville de Limoges; McKelvey, The Lilac, 395 [1928]; Wister, Lilacs for America, 37, 60 [1942] - as S IV; Photo on Jorgovani/Lilacs 2015 DVD.
Cultivar name presumed registered 1953; name established and accepted.

'Ville de Lyon', *S. vulgaris*
origin not known pre-1953; D VII-VI
syn. - 'Ville de Lyons'
Wister, Lilacs for America, 43 [1953]; Barbier & Cie, Cat., 16 [Aut. 1962]
Cultivar name presumed registered 1953; name established and accepted.

'Ville de Namur', *S. vulgaris*
Klettenberg 1937; S V
Wister, Lilacs for America, 43 [1953]
Cultivar name presumed registered 1953; name established and accepted.

'Ville de Saint-Georges', *S. vulgaris*
Moro, F. 2008; D I
{'Excellent' × ? }
Fouquet, Lilacs - Quart. Jour. 41(1):21 [2012] - name only; F. Moro, Lilacs - Quart. Jour. 41(2):55 [2012] - erroneously as 'Saint-Georges de Beauce'.
Named for Ville de Saint-Georges, Beauce Region, Quebec, Canada.
Cultivar name registered 2012; name established and accepted.

'Ville de Troyes', *S. vulgaris*
Baltet pre-1868; S VII
Bonard, Hort. Français, 31 [1868]; McKelvey, The Lilac, 395-396 [1928]; Wister, Lilacs for America, 60 [1942], 43 [1953]; Photo on Jorgovani/Lilacs 2015 DVD.
Cultivar name presumed registered 1953; name established and accepted.

Ville d'Imoges - see **'Ville de Limoges'**.

villosa alba - see '**Alba**' (*villosa* subsp. *villosa*).

villosa aurea, Villosa Aurea - see '**Aurea**' (*S. villosa* subsp. *villosa*).

villosa bretschneideri - see **'Dr Bretschneider'**.

Villosae Group, *S.*
Hoffman 2003
S. Villosae Group is based on the botanical series *Villosae* C.K. Schneider.
S. 'Royalty' has been designated nomenclatural standard for the Villosae Group.
The suggested way of writing cultivar names is: *Genus* (Group) 'Cultivar', e.g. *Syringa* (Villosae Group) 'Royalty'. Users have the choice of leaving out he Group part, e.g. *Syringa* 'Royalty'.
Hoffman, M.H.A., *Syringa* Villosae Groep, sortimentsonderzoek en keuringsrapport. Dendroflora 39:104-119 (2002) (in Dutch, summaries in English and German) [September 2003]; Hoffman, M.H.A., Lilacs-Quart. Jour. 33(1):25-27 [2004]; Vrugtman & M.H.A. Hoffman, HortScience 39(6):1524 [2004].
Cultivar group name registered in 2003, name established and accepted.

villosa rosea - see Rosea (*S. villosa* subsp. *villosa*).

villosa sulte - see 'Sulte'

villosa superba - see Superba (*S. villosa* subsp. *villosa*).

villosa venusta, *S.*
Origin not known; S IV
Fa. C. Esveld, on-line Cat [January 26, 2004] - as a botanical taxon http://www.esveld.nl/zoekstruc/lstlila/zoeklila0040005.html

'Vintage Wine', *S. vulgaris*
Mezitt, E. 1970s; S VI
{'Sensation' × ? }
Weston Nurseries, Cat., 135 [1998]; <www.westonnurseries.com/plantname/Syringa-vulgaris-Vintage-Wine>
Cultivar name established and accepted.

'Viola', *S.* (Villosae Group), *S.* ×*prestoniae*
Preston 1928; S VII
syn. - Preston No. 20-14-180
{*S. villosa* subsp. *villosa* × *S. komarowii* subsp. *reflexa*}
Macoun, Rep. Dom. Hort. 1928, 58 [1930]; Wister, Lilacs for America, 60 [1942] - name only; 43 [1953] - name only
Named for Viola, who is in love with the Duke of Illyria in Shakespeare's *Twelfth Night*.
Cultivar name presumed registered 1953; name established and accepted.

violacea - see *S. vulgaris* var. *violacea* Aiton - included in *S. vulgaris* L.

Violacea - see **'Marlyensis'** (*S. vulgaris*).

'Violacea Foliis Variegatis', *S. vulgaris*
origin not known pre-1880; S II *
Baudriller, Cat. No. 43, 144 [1880]; McKelvey, The Lilac, 396 [1928]
Cultivar name not established; probably extinct.

'Violacea Plena', *S. vulgaris*
origin not known pre-1864; D II
syn. - *violacea flore pleno*
Baudriller, Cat. No. 43, 144 [1880]; McKelvey, The Lilac, 396 [1928] - descriptions vary
Name not established.

'Violacea Purpurea', *S. vulgaris*
origin not known pre-1885; S VII
probably identical to 'Marlyensis'
Dieck, Haupt-Cat. Zöschen, 79 [1885]; McKelvey, The Lilac, 396 [1928]
Cultivar name not established.

'Violacea Purpurea Plena', *S. vulgaris*
origin not known pre-1880; D VI
Baudriller, Cat. No. 43, 144 [1880]; McKelvey, The Lilac, 396 [1928]
Cultivar name not established.

'Violet Fizz', *S. pubescens* subsp. *pubescens*
Ihara 2012; S VII
syn. - seedling no. 2011S1128006#2.
{*S. pubescens* subsp. *pubescens* 'Hoshikuzu' × *S. pubescens* subsp. *pubescens* seedling no. 20040520001#8}
(Vrugtman, Cultivated Plant Diversity ... 2017)
Named for the Violet Fizz Cocktail.
Cultivar name registered 2017; name established and accepted.

'Violet Glory', *S. vulgaris*
Castle 1969; S II
Wister & Oppe, Arnoldia 31(3):123 [1971]; Photo on Jorgovani/Lilacs 2015 DVD.
Cultivar name registered 1970; name established and accepted.

'Violetta', *S. vulgaris*
Lemoine 1916; D II
Lemoine, Cat. No. 190 [1916]; McKelvey, The Lilac, 396-397 [1928]; Wister, Lilacs for America, 60 [1942], 43 [1953]; Photo on Jorgovani/Lilacs 2015 DVD.
Named for the heroine of Duma's "La Dame aux Camelias" and Verdi's opera "La Traviata".
Cultivar name presumed registered 1953; name established and accepted.

Violet Uprising™ - see **'JN Upright Select'**.

'Virgilia', *S.* (Villosae Group), *S.* ×*prestoniae*
Preston 1928; S VI
syn. - Preston No. 20-14-211
{*S. villosa* subsp. *villosa* × *S. komarowii* subsp. *reflexa*}
Macoun, Rep. Dom. Hort. 1928, 58 [1930]; Wister, Lilacs for America, 60, 64 [1942], 43, 48 [1953]; Photo on Jorgovani/Lilacs 2015 DVD.
Named for the Wife to *Coriolanus* in Shakespeare's *Coriolanus*.
Cultivar name presumed registered 1953; name established and accepted.

Virgin, Virginal, Virginalis, Virginalis Alba - see **'Alba Virginalis'**.

'Virginia Becker', *S. vulgaris*
Becker 1947; S V
{'Hugo Koster' × ? }
Wister, Lilacs for America, 43 [1953]; Photo on Jorgovani/Lilacs 2015 DVD.
Cultivar name presumed registered 1953; name established and accepted.

'Virginité', *S. vulgaris*
Lemoine 1888; D V
syn. - 'Virginite'
Lemoine, Cat. No. 110, 10 [1888]; Ellwanger & Barry, Cat., [1892]; McKelvey, The Lilac, 397 [1928]; Wister, Lilacs for America, 60 [1942], 43 [1953]; Photo on Jorgovani/Lilacs 2015 DVD.
Cultivar name presumed registered 1953; name established and accepted.

Virgin White - see: **'Geraldine Smith'**.

'Vīrietis Labākajos Gados', *S. vulgaris*
Upītis ca 1970; S VII/II
Kalniņš, L., Ceriņu jaunšķirnes Dobelē, Dārs un drava 1986(12):13-15 - in Latvian; in litt. S. Strautiņa to F. Vrugtman [22 Jan. 2008] - ca 1970, S VII/II.
Name: Latvian for the man in the best years.
Cultivar name established and accepted.

Virtual Violet™ - see: **'BailBridget'**.

'Viscountess Willingdon', *S.* ×*hyacinthiflora*
Preston 1932; S IV
syn. - 'Vicountess Willingdon', 'Viscountess Willington'
Wister, Lilacs for America, 43 [1953]; Photo on Jorgovani/Lilacs 2015 DVD.
Named for Lady Marie Adelaide Brassey (Lady

Willingdon), 1875-1960, wife of Viscount Willingdon, Governor General of Canada, 1926-1931, patron of the Ottawa Horticultural Society.
Cultivar name presumed registered 1953; name established and accepted.

'Vita', *S. vulgaris*
Upītis 1970; D II
Kalniņš, L., Ceriņu jaunšķirnes Dobelē, Dārs un drava 1986(12):13-15 - in Latvian; Strautiņa, S. 2002. Ceriņu un jasmīnu avīze. LA, R., p. 62; in litt. S. Strautiņa to F. Vrugtman [21 Dec. 2007] - 1970, D II; Photo on Jorgovani/Lilacs 2015 DVD.
Cultivar name established and accepted.

'Vitālais Sebris', *S. vulgaris*
Upītis 1970; D VII/V
Kalniņš, L., Ceriņu jaunšķirnes Dobelē, Dārs un drava 1986(12):13-15 - in Latvian; Strautiņa, S. 1992. Ceriņi Dārzs un Drava. No. 6, pp.12-13; in litt. S. Strautiņa to F. Vrugtman [21 Dec. 2007] - 1970, D VII/V
Named for the Latvian actor Karlis Sebris, 1914-2009, a close friend of the originator.
Cultivar name established and accepted.

'Vivian Christenson', *S.* (Villosae Group), *S.* ×*prestoniae*
Alexander Sr; S V
{parentage not known}
Wister & Oppe, Arnoldia 31(3):123 [1971]
Cultivar name name registered 1970;
Cultivar not reported in cultivation.

'Viviand-Morel', *S. vulgaris*
Lemoine 1902; D IV
syn. - 'Viviande Morel', 'Viviand Morel', 'Viviane Morel'
Lemoine, Cat. No. 152, 8 [1902]; McKelvey, The Lilac, 397 [1928]; Wister, Lilacs for America, 60 [1942], 43 [1953]; Photo on Jorgovani/Lilacs 2015 DVD.
Named for Joseph Victor Viviand-Morel, 1843-1915, French botanist.
Cultivar name presumed registered 1953; name established and accepted.

'Vivian Evans', *S. vulgaris*
Klager & Case pre-1953; S IV
Wister, Lilacs for America, 43 [1953]; Photo on Jorgovani/Lilacs 2015 DVD.
Cultivar name presumed registered 1953; name established and accepted.

'Vizija', *S. vulgaris*
Kārkliņš (not Upītis) 2003; D V/VII/II
under evaluation at Latvia State Institute of Fruit Growing, Dobele
Photo on Jorgovani/Lilacs 2015 DVD.
Name: Latvian for vision.
Cultivar name not established; rejected name.

'Vīzija', *S. vulgaris*
Upītis (not Kārkliņš) ca 1970; S II
Kalniņš, L., Ceriņu jaunšķirnes Dobelē, Dārs un drava 1986(12):13-15 - in Latvian; in litt. S. Strautiņa to F. Vrugtman [22 Jan. 2008] - ca 1970, S II.
Name: Latvian for vision.
Cultivar name established and accepted. Probably no longer in cultivation.

'V. L. Wing', *S. vulgaris*
Klager; S VII
Wister, Lilacs for America, 60 [1942], 43 [1953]
Cultivar name presumed registered 1953;
Cultivar not reported in cultivation.

'Vladimir Arkhangel'skiĭ', *S. vulgaris*
'Владимир Архангельский'
Aladin, S., Aladina, O., Polyakova, T., and , Aladina, A. 2016; D IV-III
{'Ami Schott' × elite seedling 12-331}
Садовник (Gardener) magazine 04 (140)/2017 :18-25; Вестник АППМ (Catalog in Vestnik APPM (Planting material association) magazine) 1/2018: 59-72 (in Russian).
Named for Vladimir Arkhangel'skii (Владимир Николаевич Архангельский) [1956-2011], nurseryman (Flora nursery), Russian collector and lilac breeder, Moscow, Russia.
Cultivar name established and accepted.

'Vladimir Vysotskiĭ', *S. vulgaris*
'Владимир Высоцкий'
Dyagilev& Degtev 2020; S I
(Международная научная конференция "Syringa L.: коллекции, выращивание, использование")
"International Scientific Conference "Syringa L.: collections, cultivation, using" / Collection of Scientific Articles of Botanical Institute named after V.L. Komarov, Botanical Garden of Peter the Great BIN RAS. - St. Petersburg. -2020.- pp.23-27 (in Russian).
Named for Vladimir Semyonovich Vysotsky (1938-1990), a Soviet singer-songwriter, poet, and actor.
Cultivar name established and accepted.

'Vnuchka Lenochka', *S. vulgaris*
'Внучка Леночка'
Kolesnikov 1946; S V
Rubtzov et al. 1980. Vidy i sorta sireni, kul'tiviruemye v SSSR. Kiev; Naukova Dumka. – in Russian; Holetich, C.D. 1982. Lilac species and cultivars in cultivation in USSR. Lilacs 11(2):1-38. - translation of Rubtzov et al. 1982.
Name: Russian for granddaughter Lenochka.
Cultivar name established and accepted.

'Voci', 'Voycie', 'La Voicie' - see **Lavoisier**.

'Volcan', *S. vulgaris*
Lemoine 1899; S VII
syn. - 'Vulcan'
Lemoine, Cat No. 143, 24 [1899]; McKelvey, The Lilac, 397-398 [1928]; Wister, Lilacs for America, 60 [1942], 43 [1953]; Photo on Jorgovani/Lilacs 2015 DVD.
Named for the Roman god of fire and metallurgy.

Cultivar name presumed registered 1953; name established and accepted.

'Volkhonka', *S. vulgaris*
'Волхонка'
Aladin, S., Aladina, O., Polyakova, T., and Aladina, A. 2017; S IV
{'Glory' × OP}
(Международная научная конференция "Syringa L.: коллекции, выращивание, использование") "International Scientific Conference "*Syringa* L.: collections, cultivation, using" / Collection of Scientific Articles of Botanical Institute named after V.L. Komarov, Botanical Garden of Peter the Great BIN RAS. - St. Petersburg. -2020.- pp.3-7 (in Russian); Photo exhibition of all varieties of the creative breeding group "Russian Lilac" at the Festival "Lilac February", St. Petersburg, Botanical Garden of Peter the Great BIN RAS, February 22-24, 2020.
Named for the old Moscow street, stretching from the Kremlin southwest to the Cathedral of Christ the Savior, famous area of museums and art galleries near the Moscow river.
Cultivar name established and accepted.

'Vologodskie Kruzheva', *S. vulgaris*
'Вологодские кружева'
Aladin, S., Aladina, O., Polyakova, T., and, Aladina, A. 2016; D I
{'Rochester' × OP}
Садовник (Gardener) magazine 04 (140)/2017 :18-25; Вестник АППМ (Catalog in Vestnik APPM (Planting material association) magazine) 1/2018: 59-72 (in Russian).
Named for the lace of the Vologda region of Russia.
Cultivar name established and accepted.

'Volshebstvo Maya', *S.*
'Волшебство Мая'
Semenyuk 2015; S V
Registered with the State Commission of the Russian Federation for Testing and Protection of Selection Achievements, No. 8456462, 2016, and registered patent No. 8762, valid until 31 December 20146.
Russian for magic of May.
Cultivar name registered, establisjed and accepted.

'Volumnia', *S.* (Villosae Group), *S.* ×*prestoniae*
Preston date not known; ? ?
E. von Bayer, Canadian Horticultural History 1(3):174 (1987); original source not provided - name only
Named for Volumnia, Mother to Caius Marcus *Coriolanus* in Shakespeare's *Coriolanus*.
Cultivar name not established and accepted; not know in cultivation.

Von Oberschott - see '**Mons. Van Aerschott**'.

'Von Plitz', *S. vulgaris*
origin not known; ? VII
syn. - see also 'Van Plitz'
Stenlund, Lilacs - Quart. Jour. 20(2):41 [1991].
Cultivar name not established.

'**Voorzitter Buskermolen**', *S. vulgaris*
Spaargaren 1954; S II
Marchal, Jaarverslag Proefstation Aalsmeer, 120 [1954]; Tuinbouwgids 1955, 712 [1955]; Wister, Arnoldia 23(4):83 [1963]
Named for Gerardus Buskermolen, 1891-1983, prominent Aalsmeer grower and chairman of the board of the Proefstation voor de Bloemisterij, 1931-1958.
Awards: Certificate of Merit 1954 (KMTP).
Cultivar name registered 1963; name established and accepted.

'**Voorzitter Dix**', *S. vulgaris*
Eveleens Maarse 1950; S VI
{'Ambassadeur' × 'Maréchal Foch'}
Wister, Lilacs for America, 43 [1953]; Eveleens Maarse, Dendron 1(1):12 [1954]; Photo on Jorgovani/Lilacs 2015 DVD.
Awards: Certificate of Merit 1950 (KMTP); First Class Certificate 1953 (KMTP).
Cultivar name presumed registered 1953; name established and accepted.

'Vospominanie o Pavlovske', *S. vulgaris*
'Воспоминание о Павловске'
Aladin, S., Aladina, O., Polyakova, T., and, Aladina, A. 2016; D IV/V
{'Violetta' × OP}
Садовник (Gardener) magazine 04 (140)/2017 :18-25; Вестник АППМ (Catalog in Vestnik APPM (Planting material association) magazine) 1/2018: 59-72 (in Russian).
Named for the municipality of Pavlovsk, part of the UNESCO World Heritage Site St Petersburg, Russia.
Cultivar name established and accepted.

Vulcan - see '**Volcan**'.

vulgaris alba - see *S. vulgaris* var. *alba* Weston.

vulgaris elevatus dimicatio - see '**Géant des Batailles**'.

vulgaris flore pleno - see '**Violacea Plena**'.

vulgaris nana - see '**Mount Domogled**'.

vulgaris nigricans - see '**Nigricans**'.

vulgaris notgeriana - see '**Prince Notger**'.

vulgaris purpurea - see *S. vulgaris* var. *purpurea* Weston.

vulgaris rubra major foliis aureao variegatis - see '**Rubra Major Foliis Aureo Variegatis**'.

vulgaris serotina - see '**Tardiva**'.

vulgaris triumphum Aureliae - see '**Triomphe d'Orléans**'.

vulgaris var. *purpurea* Weston - see '**Marlyensis**' (?)

vulgaris vershaffeltii - see '**Verschaffeltii**'.

vulgaris violacea - see *S. vulgaris* var. *violacea* Aiton - included in *S. vulgaris* var. *purpurea* Weston.

'Waddal', 'Waddel' or 'Waddle', *S. vulgaris*
Klager; D I
confused name - see also 'Weddle', Klager 1928 - D VI
Anon., ILS Newsletter 14(4):3-4 [1988] - as D I; Stenlund, Lilacs - Quart. Jour. 20(2):41 [1991] - as 'Weddle'; Macore Co. Inc. photo library [Nov.28, 1999] http://www.macore.com/photolib.htm - as 'Waddle'
Cultivar name not established.

'Waines-Pink', *S.* ×*hyacinthiflora*
Waines; S V
Seen at UC Riverside, California USA; photograph by Natalia Savenko 5/2018.
Not a cultivar name. May be a cognomen, nickname, or breedr's temporary name.

'Waldeck-Rousseau', *S. vulgaris*
Lemoine 1904; D V
syn. - 'Waldeck Rousseau'
Lemoine, Cat. No. 158, 8 [1904]; McKelvey, The Lilac, 398 [1928]; Wister, Lilacs for America, 60 [1942], 43 [1953]; Photo on Jorgovani/Lilacs 2015 DVD.
Named for Pierre Marie René Ernst Waldeck-Rousseau, 1846-1904, French premier, 1899-1902.
Cultivar name presumed registered 1953; name established and accepted.

'Walter Oakes', *S.* ×*hyacinthiflora*
Fiala (not Margaretten); S V
{'Maiden's Blush' × 'Flora 1953'}
Fiala in litt. [3 Nov. 1987], no lit. ref.
Named for Walter Warren Oakes, 1928-2005, accountant, bank manager and auditor, Dixfield, Maine, USA; founding member of the International Lilac Society.
Cultivar name not established.

'Walter Oakes', *S. vulgaris*
Margaretten (not Fiala); D III
{'Mme Lemoine' × ? }
Named for Walter Warren Oakes, 1928-2005, accountant, bank manager and auditor, Dixfield, Maine, USA; founding member of the International Lilac Society.
Cultivar name not established; not reported in cultivation.

Walter's Pink, *S. vulgaris*
Berdeen 1987; S V
Peterson, Lilacs - Proceedings 16(1):23 [1987] - name only; King & Coggeshall, Lilacs - Quart. Jour. 27(2):49-50 [1998] - name only
Named for a friend of the originator from Dixfield, Maine.
Originators code, not a cultivar name.

'Wan Hua Zi', *S. oblata*
Zang & Fan 1984; S VII
syn. - 'Wan Hua-zi', 'Wanhuazi'
{*S. oblata* × ? }
Zang Shuying et al., Pap. Celebration 30th Anniv. Beijing Bot. Gard. Acad. Sinica [1985]; Vrugtman, HortScience 32(4):587-588 [1997] - as 'Wan Hua-zi'; Anon., Beijing Bot. Garden 2006:24 - as 'Wan Hua Zi'; Photo on Jorgovani/Lilacs 2015 DVD.
Cultivar name registered 1996; name established and accepted.

'Washington', *S. vulgaris*
origin not known pre-1867; ? VII
Ellwanger & Barry, Cat. No. 2, 43 [1867]; McKelvey, The Lilac, 398 [1928]
Cultivar name not established.

'Watagashi', *S.* (Pubescentes Series)
'綿菓子'
Ihara 2012; S VII
syn. - seedling no. 2011S1128004#2.
{*S.* 'MORjos 060F' × *S.* 'MORjos 060F'}
(Vrugtman, Cultivated Plant Diversity ... 2017)
Name: Japanese for cotton candy.
Cultivar name registered 2017; name established and accepted.

WATER TOWER® or WATERTOWER® - see 'Morton'.

'Wedding Bells', *S. vulgaris*
Moro, F. 2013; S V
{'Firmament' × ?}
Lilacs - Quart. Jour. 42(3):85 & 87 (photo) [2013]; in lit. Moro to Vrugtman July 13,2013
Cultivar name established and accepted.

'Weddle', *S. vulgaris*
Klager 1928; D VI
syn. - 'Wedle'
not: 'Waddal', 'Waddel' or 'Waddle', Klager - D I
Wister, Lilacs for America, 60 [1942] - as D IV; Wister, Lilacs for America, 44 [1953]; Photo on Jorgovani/Lilacs 2015 DVD.
Cultivar name presumed registered 1953; name established and accepted.

'Wedgwood Blue', *S. vulgaris*
Fiala 1981; S III
syn. - 'Wedgewood Blue', 'Wedgwood', WEDGWOOD (trade designation used for cut flowers of this cultivar)
{'Rochester' × 'Mrs A. Belmont'}
Fiala, Lilacs, 98, 224 [1988]; Knight Hollow Nursery, 1998 Cultured cutting and liner descriptive list; American Nurseryman 190(5) [1999]; Photo on Jorgovani/Lilacs 2015 DVD.
Named for the characteristic blue color used by Josiah Wedgwood, 1730-1795, English potter and designer, whose son John Wedgwood, 1766-1844, was one of the

seven founding members of the Horticultural Society of London, 1804, the present day Royal Horticultural Society.
Cultivar name established and accepted.
Forcing cultivar in the Netherlands.

'Wee Lassie', *S.* ×*hyacinthiflora*
Morey; ? ?
in litt.
Cultivar name not established; not reported in cultivation.

WEEPER, *S. pekinensis*
origin not known; S I
{*S. pekinensis* 'Pendula' × ? }
Peterson, Lilacs - Proceedings 16(1):25 [1987] - name only
Cognomen, not a cultivar name.

Weeping, Weeping Peking, weeping Peking lilac - see '**Pendula**' (*S. pekinensis*).

Weisser Traum - see 'Engler Weisser Traum'.

W. E. Marshall - see '**Mrs W. E. Marshall**'.

Wentworth - 'Governor Wentworth'.

'**Westend**', *S. vulgaris*
Spaargaren 1956; S I
Wister, Arnoldia 23(4):83 [1963]
Named for the Westend, the Aalsmeer neighborhood renowned for its production of forced lilacs.
Awards: Certificate of Merit 1956 (KMTP).
Cultivar name registered 1963; name established and accepted.

'Weston's Rainbow', *S. vulgaris*
Mezitt, R.W. 1997; S II*
syn. - SPRING RAINBOW
{seedling of unknown parentage}
floret color 86D (Violet Group; RHS Color Charts 1966)
Cultivar name established and accepted.

'WFH2', *S. pekinensis*
Hendricks 2015; S I
syn. - Marketed in the USA as GREAT WALL™ lilac
http://klynnurseries.com/product/syringa-pekinensis-great-wall/
(US Plant Patent applied for)
Cultivar name established and accepted.

'Wheatly Pink', *S.* (species affiliation not known)
origin not known ? V
{sport of ? }
Anon., Lilacs - Quart. Jour. 21(4):93 [1992].

WHIM - see '**Kapriz**'
Brizicky, AABGA Quart. Newsletter No. 64, 22 [Oct. 1965].

White Angel - see 'Angel White'.

White Chinese lilac or *S.* ×*chinensis* f. *alba* - see 'Correlata'.
Stand. Pl. Names, 264, 488 [1923] - White Chinese.

'White Cloud', *S.* (species affiliation not known)
origin not known; D I
in cultivation at Descanso Gardens per photo by Natalia Savenko 2018.
Cultivar name not established.

WHITE DREAM - see 'Engler Weisser Traum'.

'White Elf', *S. vulgaris*
Fiala (?); ? ?
{'Rochester' × ? }
Lilacs, Fiala, 115, 224 (?) [1988] - name only
Cultivar name not established.

'White Giant', *S. vulgaris*
Eveleens Maarse 1953; ? I
Topsvoort New Lilac Introduction, Fa. W. Topsvoort, flyer [n.d.; ca1953] - name only; existence not confirmed by Vaste Keurings Commissie, Roelofarendsveen, July 26, 2007
Cultivar name not established; not reported in cultivation.

'**White Hyacinth**', *S.* ×*hyacinthiflora*
Clarke 1948 (not Skinner); S I
{unnamed double × ? }
Clarke, Cat. 16:9 [1949]; Woody Plant Register, AAN, No. 141 [1949]; Wister, Lilacs for America, 44 [1953]; Photo on Jorgovani/Lilacs 2015 DVD.
Cultivar name presumed registered 1953; name established and accepted.

'White Hyacinth', *S.* ×*hyacinthiflora*
Skinner (not Clarke); ? I
{*S. vulgaris* × *S. oblata* subsp. *dilatata*}
Skinner, Hort. Horizons, 50 [1966]
Cultivar name not established; name rejected; not introduced.

'White Lace', *S. vulgaris*
Rankin 1964; S I
{parentage not known}
Fiala, Lilacs, 208 [1988] - as "small florets, but very heavy bloomer"; Photo on Jorgovani/Lilacs 2015 DVD.
Cultivar name established and accepted.

'White Long Fellow', *S. vulgaris*
Rankin; S I
syn. - 'Longfellow', 'Long Fellow'; 'White Longfellow'
{parentage not known}
Lilacs, Fiala, 208 [1988]; Lilacs - Quart. Jour. 20(2):34 [1991] - as 'Long Fellow'; Photo on Jorgovani/Lilacs 2015 DVD.
Cultivar name established and accepted.

White Marly - see '**Marlyensis Pallida**'.

White Nodding - see '**Alba**' (*S. komarowii* subsp. *reflexa*).

white Noesette lilac - see '**Noisettiana Alba**'.

White Persian lilac - see *S.* ×*persica* var. *alba* Weston
Stand. Pl. Names, 264, 488 [1923] - as White Persian lilac.

'White Primrose', *S. vulgaris*
origin not known; S I
{'Primrose' mutation}
United Information Systems Inc., DataScape Botanical Index, 107 [1994] - name only; Beaver Creek Nurs., Wholesale Cat., 39 [Spr. 1994]; Klehm Nurs., Wholesale Cat. [Fall 1994]
Cultivar name not established.
Nota bene: Since 'Primrose' is a mutation of the single, white 'Marie Legraye' it appears likely that 'White Primrose' is similar, if not identical, to 'Marie Legraye'. No information on a comparison of these two cultivars has been reported.

'**White Sands**', *S. vulgaris*
Gardner 1971; S I
Wister & Oppe, Arnoldia 31(3):123 [1971]
Cultivar name registered 1970;
Cultivar not reported in cultivation.

'White Sire', *S. vulgaris*
Heeren 2007; S I
{mutation of 'Mme Florent Stepman'}
http://www.plantscope.nl/pls/pscprdaut/psc_htm_utils.psc_startframeset?pnTalId=1 [seen March 11, 2007] - as RHS Color Chart 999D or pure white
Cultivar name established and accepted.
Forcing cultivar in the Netherlands since 2007 (only by Fa Heeren).

'White Spires', *S. vulgaris*
origin not known pre-1982; S I
Peterson, Lilacs - Proceedings 16(1):23 [1987] - name only
Cultivar name not established.

'**White Spring**', *S.* ×*hyacinthiflora*
Sobeck; S I
Wister, Arnoldia 26(3):13 [1966].
Cultivar name registered 1966; name established and accepted.
Nota bene: Since this cultivar appears to be of 'Lavender Lady' ancestry see also: Pringle, Lilacs - Quart. Jour. 24(4):97-99 [1995]; and Vrugtman, HortScience 31(3):328 [1996]

White Summer - see '**Summer White**'.

'**White Superior**', *S. vulgaris*
Eveleens Maarse 1953; S I
{'G. J. Baardse' × 'Excellent'}
Wister, Lilacs for America, 44 [1953]; Tuinbouwgids, 440 [1954]
Awards: Certificate of Merit 1953 (KMTP).
Cultivar name presumed registered 1953; name established and accepted.

'White Supreme', *S. vulgaris*
Castle; ? I
perhaps misspelling of 'White Surprise'
Fiala, Lilacs, 207 [1988]
Cultivar name not established.

'**White Surprise**', *S. vulgaris*
Blacklock ca 1964; D I
Wister, Arnoldia 23(4):83 [1963]; Rowancroft Gardens, Cat. No. 18, 32 [n.d., ca 1964]
Cultivar name registered 1963; name established and accepted.

'**White Swan**', *S. vulgaris*
Havemeyer pre-1942; S I
Wister, Lilacs for America, 60 [1942], 44 [1953]; Lilac Land, Cat. [1954]; Niedz, ILS Newsletter 1(4):7-8 [1972] - perhaps identical to 'Mont Blanc'; Eickhorst, ILS Lilac Newsletter 4(1):4-5 [1978]; Photo on Jorgovani/Lilacs 2015 DVD.
Cultivar name presumed registered 1953; name established and accepted.

'White Wonder', *S. vulgaris*
Bunnik (2007?); S I
{sport of ?}
Patricia Boon, Een wonder van een sering. De Telegraaf, T25, 17 April 2005
Cultivar name not established.

'**Wild Fire**', *S. oblata* subsp. *dilatata*
Fiala 1984; S IV
syn. - 'Wildfire'
{*S. oblata* subsp. *dilatata* selection for autumn color}
Fiala, Lilacs, 62, 224, Pl. 2 [1988] - as 'Wild Fire' and 'Wildfire'; Photo on Jorgovani/Lilacs 2015 DVD.
Cultivar name established and accepted.

Wild River Double Lilac - see '**Nadezhda**'.

Wilhelm Robinson - see '**William Robinson**'.

'Willamette', *S. reticulata*
origin not known; S I
marketed in the USA as Ivory Pillar™
Carleton Plants, Cat. [2000]. Picture by Natalia Savenko in 2017 at Royal Botanical Gardens, Hamilton, Ontario, Canada.
Cultivar name not established.

'**William C. Barry**', *S. vulgaris*
Dunbar 1917; S IV
syn. - Dunbar no. 227, 'Willam C. Berry', 'Wm. C. Barry'
{'Marlyensis Pallida' × ? }
Dunbar, Horticulture 26:35 [1917]; Wister, Nat. Hort. Mag. 6(1):1-16 [1927]; McKelvey, The Lilac, 398 [1928]; Wister, Lilacs for America, 60 [1942], 43 [1953]; Photo on Jorgovani/Lilacs 2015 DVD.
Named for William C. Barry [1847-1916], horticulturist, elder son of Patrick Barry and last proprietor [1906-

1916] of the nursery of Ellwanger & Barry, Rochester, New York.
Cultivar name presumed registered 1953; name established and accepted.

'William Edwin Armstrong', S. vulgaris
Dodds pre-2002, S VII
in cultivation at RBG 2002-0251 for evaluation
Cultivar name not established.

'William Emerson', S. vulgari
Margaretten; D IV
{'Mme Lemoine' × ?}
Not reported in cultivation
Cultivar name not established.

'**William H. Judd**', S. ×diversifolia
Sax & Skinner; S I
syn. - 'Judd'
{S. pinnatifolia × S. oblata subsp. oblata; grown from seed received from the Arnold Arboretum, resulting from the cross made by Dr Karl Sax in 1929}
Anderson and Rehder, J. Arnold Arb. 16:362-363 [1935]; Woody Plant Register, AAN, No. 76 [1949]; Wister, Lilacs for America, 44 [1953]; Pringle, Baileya 21(3):101-103 [1981], (4):198 [1982]; Fiala, Lilacs, 54, 62 [1988] - cross erroneously credited to Skinner; Photo on Jorgovani/Lilacs 2015 DVD.
Named for William H. Judd, 1888-1946, American horticulturist, plant propagator, 1913-1946, at the Arnold Arboretum, Jamaica Plain, Massachusetts, USA.
Cultivar name registered in 1953; name established and accepted.

William K. Mills - see '**Wm. K. Mills**'.

'**William Robinson**', S. vulgaris
Lemoine 1899; D IV
syn. - 'William Robertson', 'Wilhelm Robinson', 'Wm. Robinson'
Lemoine, Cat. No. 143, 10 [1899]; McKelvey, The Lilac, 398-399 [1928]; Wister, Lilacs for America, 60 [1942] - as D VI; Wister, Lilacs for America, 43 [1953]; Photo on Jorgovani/Lilacs 2015 DVD.
Named for William Robinson, 1838-1935, British horticulturist and author.
Cultivar name presumed registered 1953; name established and accepted.

William Robertson - see '**William Robinson**'.

William's S. vulgaris
Origin not known pre-1800; S ?
Catalog of Plants &c. &c. in the Dublin Society's Botanic Garden, at Glasnevin, p. 10 [1800] - name only
Cultivar name not established; probably extinct.

'**William S. Riley**', S. vulgaris
Dunbar 1922; S VI
syn. - Dunbar no. 219, 'Wm. S. Riley'
{'Président Massart' × ?}
Wister, Nat. Hort. Mag. 6(1):1-16 [1927] - as S IV; McKelvey, The Lilac, 399 [1928]; Wister, Lilacs for America, 60 [1942] - as S IV; Wister, Lilacs for America, 43 [1953]; Photo on Jorgovani/Lilacs 2015 DVD.
Named for William S. Riley [no dates], commissioner of parks, Rochester, New York, USA.
Cultivar name presumed registered 1953;
Cultivar name established and accepted.

'**Will Rogers**', S. vulgaris
Klager; S VII
Wister, Lilacs for America, 60 [1942], 44 [1953]
Cultivar name presumed registered 1953; not reported in cultivation

'Windsong', S. vulgaris
Fiala 1984; S V
syn. - 'Wind Song'
{'Rochester' × 'Elsie Lenore'}
Fiala, Lilacs, 224 [1988]; Chapman, Lilacs - Quart. Jour. 29(3):69 and front cover [2000]; Photo on Jorgovani/Lilacs 2015 DVD.
Cultivar name established and accepted.

'Winner's Circle', S. vulgaris
Fiala 1985; D VI
{'Rochester' × 'Mrs W. E. Marshall'}
Fiala, Lilacs, 224 [1988]
Cultivar name established and accepted.

'Winter Sky', S. vulgaris
Moro, F. 2013; D III
{'Paul Thirion' × ?}
Lilacs - Quart. Jour. 42(3):85 & 86 (photo) [2013]
Cultivar name established and accepted.

'Wittbold Variegated', S. vulgaris
Block 1960s?; S IV *
reported in Lumley collection; in litt., Block
Cultivar name not established.

'Wittbrod variegated', S. vulgaris
origin not known ? ? *
syn. - perhaps identical to 'Wittbold Variegated'
Anon., Lilacs - Proceedings 13(1):23 [1984] - name only

Witte - see 'Hortulanus Witte'.

Wm. C. Barry - see '**William C. Barry**'.

'**Wm. K. Mills**', S. vulgaris
Klager 1930; S VII
syn. - 'William K. Mills', 'W. K. Mills'
Common name: Billy Mills
Cooley, Cat., 7 [1930]; Wister, Lilacs for America, 44, 60 [1942], 25, 44 [1953]; Photo on Jorgovani/Lilacs 2015 DVD.
Named for Hulda Klager's grandson, William Klager Mills, son of her daughter Elizabeth.
Cultivar name established and accepted; name presumed registered 1953.

Wm. Robinson - see '**William Robinson**'.

Wolfii Pink, *S. villosa* subsp. *wolfii*
origin not known pre-1996; S V
reported in cultivation at Univ. Utrecht Bot. Garden.
Cognomen; not a cultivar name.

Wolf lilac - see *S. villosa* subsp. *wolfii* C.K. Schneider.

'**Wonderblue**', *S. vulgaris*
Fiala 1989; S III
syn. - 'Little Boy Blue', 'Wonder Blue'
{'Tiffany Blue' × 'Rochester'}
Vrugtman, HortScience 24(3):435 [1989] & 29(9):972 [1994]; Clark., Lilacs, Quart. Jour. 18:4, 42 [1989]; Ameri-Hort Research, descriptive list [n.d., ca 1990] - as 'Little Boy Blue'; Knight Hollow Nursery, 1998 Cultured cutting and liner descriptive list - as 'Little Boy Blue'; Photo on Jorgovani/Lilacs 2015 DVD.
Cultivar name registered 1988; name established and accepted.

'**Wonderland**', *S. pubescens* subsp. *patula*
Moro, F. 2009; S I
{'Excellens' × ? }
Vrugtman, Hanburyana 7:31 [2013]
Named for Alice's Adventures in Wonderland, the 1865 novel by C. L. Dodgson under the pseudonym Lewis Carroll.
Cultivar name registered 2012; name established and accepted.

'**Woodland**', *S. vulgaris*
Klager 1930; S VII
syn. - 'City of Woodland'
Cooley, Cat., 7 [1930]; Wister, Lilacs for America, 45, 60 [1942], 26, 44 [1953]; Anon., ILS Newsletter 14(4):3-4 [1988] - as 'City of Woodland'
Cultivar name presumed registered 1953; name established and accepted.

'**Woodland Blue**', *S. vulgaris*
Hancock 1967; S III
{parentage not known}
Wister & Oppe, Arnoldia 31(3):123 [1971]; Woodland Nursery, Cat., 16 [n.d.; 1973]; Photo on Jorgovani/Lilacs 2015 DVD.
Named for Woodland Nursery, Mississauga, Ontario, Canada.
Cultivar name registered 1970; name established and accepted.

'**Woodland Violet**', *S. vulgaris*
Sass, H.E. pre-1953; S VII
Wister, Lilacs for America, 44 [1953]; Photo on Jorgovani/Lilacs 2015 DVD.
Cultivar name presumed registered 1953; name established and accepted.

'**W. T. Lee**', *S. vulgaris*
Schloen 1962; D V
Wister, Arnoldia 23(4):83 [1963] - in error as S III; Ellesmere Nurs., Cat. [1966]; Photo on Jorgovani/Lilacs 2015 DVD.
Cultivar name registered 1963; name established and accepted.

'**W. T. Macoun**', *S.* (Villosae Group), *S.* ×*prestoniae*
Preston 1927; S V
syn. - Preston No. 20-14-51
{*S. villosa* subsp. *villosa* × *S. komarowii* subsp. *reflexa*}
McKelvey, The Lilac, 112, t. 39 [1928]; Macoun, Rep. Dom. Hort. 1928, 55 [1930]; Wister, Lilacs for America, 60, 64 [1942], 44, 48 [1953]; Photo on Jorgovani/Lilacs 2015 DVD.
One of the original two *S.* ×*prestoniae* McKelvey cultivars selected, named and described by McKelvey; see also 'Isabella'.
Named for William Tyrrell Macoun, 1869-1933, Dominion Horticulturist, 1911-1932, Ottawa, Canada.
Cultivar name presumed registered 1953; name established and accepted.

W. W. Smith, *S. vulgaris*
Gundersen, Brooklyn Bot. Gard. Record 30(3):200 [1941] - erroneous listing;
Cultivar does not exist, in litt. D. K. Ryniec to F. Vrugtman, 21 Sept. 1989

'**Xiang Xue**', *S.* ×*hyacinthiflora*
Zang & Fan 1984; D I
syn. - 'Xiang xue', 'Xiangxue', 'Xiung Xue e'
{*S. oblata* Lindl. × *S. vulgaris* L. 'Alba-plena'}
Zang & Fan, Pl. Introd. Acclimatization 3:117-121 [1983] - in Chinese; Zang, Fan & Li, Acta Horticulturae 404:63-67 [1995]; Yoshikawa, Kyoto Engei (Kyoto Horticulture), 84:21-23 [?] - in Japanese; Vrugtman, HortScience 32 (4):588 [1997]; Anon., Beijing Bot. Garden 2006:24, ill.; Photo on Jorgovani/Lilacs 2015 DVD.
Cultivar name registered 1996; name established and accepted.

'Ýalta', *S. vulgaris*
'Ялта'
Kostetskiĭ pre-1948; S VII-II
in lit. Tatyana Polyakova to Vrugtman (23 June 2015); in cultivation at Nikita Botanical Garden, 'Lilacs', volume 45 (4) Fall 2016 "Breeding in the Crimea" by Vera Zykova
Named for the port city of Yalta, Crimea, Ukraine.
Cultivar name not yet established.

'Yaltinska͟ya Prelest"; *S. vulgaris*
'Яалтинская Прелестъ'
Klimenko, V.& Z., & Grigor'ev 1955; S VII
syn. - 'Jaltinskaja Prelest"
{'Andenken an Ludwig Späth' × 'Jeanne d'Arc'}
Rubtzov et al. 1980. Vidy i sorta sireni, kul'tiviruemye v SSSR. Kiev; Naukova Dumka. – in Russian; Holetich, C.D.

1982. Lilac species and cultivars in cultivation in USSR. Lilacs 11(2):1-38. - translation of Rub<u>t</u>zov et al. 1982.
Name: Russian for the beauty of Yalta.
Cultivar name established and accepted.

'Yankee Doodle', *S. vulgaris*
Fiala 1985; S VII
{'Prodige' × 'Rochester'}
Fiala, Lilacs, 224 [1988]; Anon, Falconskeape 2(3):4 [Autumn 1989] - erroneously as {'Protege' × 'Rochester'}; Anon., Ameri-Hort Research, descriptive list [n.d., ca 1990] - erroneously as {'Protege' × 'Rochester'}; Photo on Jorgovani/Lilacs 2015 DVD.
Named for a popular song of the American Revolution era, 1770-1782.
Cultivar name established and accepted.

'<u>Y</u>auza', *S. vulgaris*
'Яуза'
Aladin, S., Aladina, O., Polyakova, T., and Aladina, A. 2014; S IV
{'Glory'× OP}
(Международная научная конференция "Syringa L.: коллекции, выращивание, использование")
"International Scientific Conference "Syringa L.: collections, cultivation, using" / Collection of Scientific Articles of Botanical Institute named after V.L. Komarov, Botanical Garden of Peter the Great BIN RAS. - St. Petersburg. -2020.- pp.3-7 (in Russian); Photo exhibition of all varieties of the creative breeding group "Russian Lilac" at the Festival "Lilac February", St. Petersburg, Botanical Garden of Peter the Great BIN RAS, February 22-24, 2020.
Named for the Yauza River, the "connecting river", one of the symbols of Moscow. Within the city, more than fifty bridges connect its shores.
Cultivar name established and accepted.

'Yellow Curiosity', *S. vulgaris*
origin not known pre-1940; S I
perhaps identical to 'Primrose'
Wister, Lilacs for America, 44 [1953]
Cultivar name not established.

'Yellow Fragrance', *S. pekinensis*
origin not known; S I
listed in on-line catalog by Pier Luigi Priola, Azienda Agricola Priola, Via delle Acquette, 4, 31100, Treviso, Italy, as: "fiori ricadenti- terreno:normale ben drenato- esp.:sm - fiore:giallo crema-" 'Yellow Fragance' (sic). <http://www.priola.it/it/dept_2176.html> [Dec. 10, 2004]; Dirr, Manual of woody landscape plants, 6th ed., p. 1106 [2009], presumably from Northern China, introduced 1881, name only.
Cultivar name not established.

Yellowleaf, *S.* ×*emodi*
origin not known pre-1942; ? ? *
Stand. Pl. Names, 617 [1942].
Cultivar name not established.

'Yellowspot', *S.* ×*emodi*
origin not known pre-1942; ? ? *
Stand. Pl. Names, 617 [1942].
Cultivar name not established.

Yellow Wonder - see '**Primrose**'.

Yi Guan, *S.* (perhaps *pubescens* subsp. *microphylla*)
origin not known pre-2008
Vrugtman & Cui, Lilacs 41(3):98-99(2012)
Cultivar name not established.

'Yong Ling', *S.* (Villosae Group)
Fiala 1985; S II
{*S. tomentella* subsp. *sweginzowii* × (*S. tomentella* subsp. *yunnanensis* × *S.* ×*prestoniae* 'Isabella')}
in litt. Fiala 3 Nov. 1987
Named (probably) for Yong Ling, the Ming tomb of emperor Long Qing, 1567-1572, Beijing, China.
Cultivar name not established.

'Yubile<u>ĭ</u>naya', *S. vulgaris*
'Юбилейная'
Krav<u>c</u>henko (not Sagitova) (not Shtan'ko & Mikhaĭlov) 1970; S IV-III
{'Andenken an Ludwig Späth' × OP }
Krav<u>c</u>henko L. Culture of lilacs in Uzbekistan. Publishing house "Uzbekistan", Tashkent, 1970 p. 9,10.
Name: Russian for jubilee edition or anniversary.
Cultivar name established and accepted.

'Yubile<u>ĭ</u>naya', *S. vulgaris*
'Юбилейная'
Sagitova; ? ?
no information
Name: Russian for jubilee edition or anniversary.
Cultivar name not established.

'Yubile<u>ĭ</u>naya', *S. vulgaris*
'Юбилейная'
Shtan'ko & Mi<u>kh</u>aĭlov 1956; S IV-V (not Sagitova)
syn. - 'Jubileinaja', 'Jubilejnana', 'Yubileinaya'
{'Congo' × ? }
Bilov et al., Siren', 84 [1974] - in Russian; Rub<u>t</u>zov et al. 1980. Vidy i sorta sireni, kul'tiviruemye v SSSR. Kiev; Naukova Dumka. – in Russian; Holetich, C.D. 1982. Lilac species and cultivars in cultivation in USSR. Lilacs 11(2):1-38. - translation of Rub<u>t</u>zov et al. 1982.
Name: Russian for jubilee edition or anniversary.
Cultivar name established and accepted.

'**Yuki-usagi**', *S. pubescens* subsp. *pubescens*
'雪兎'
Ihara 2004; S VII
syn. - seedling no. 20040520001#11.
{*S. pubescens* subsp. *pubescens* 'Palibin' × *S. pubescens* subsp. *pubescens* 'Palibin'}
(Vrugtman, Cultivated Plant Diversity ... 2017)
Name: Japanese for snow rabbit.
Cultivar name registered 2017; name established and accepted.

yunnanensis var. *rosea* - see '**Rosea**' (*S. tomentella* subsp. *yunnanensis*).

Yunnan lilac - see *S. tomentella* subsp. *yunnanensis* Franch.

'Yunost', *S. vulgaris*
  'Юность'
  Kravchenko (not Vekhov) 1970; D IV
  {'Lamartine' × 'Belle de Nancy'}
  Kravchenko L. Culture of lilacs in Uzbekistan. Publishing house "Uzbekistan", Tashkent, 1970 p. 16, 17.
  Name: Russian for youth.
  Cultivar name established and accepted.

'Yunost', *S. vulgaris*
  'Юность'
  Vekhov 1952; S IV-V
  syn. - 'Junost'
  Magazine "Tsvetovodstvo" ("Floriculture") No. 7, 1977, p. 11
  Rubtzov et al. 1980. Vidy i sorta sireni, kul'tiviruemye v SSSR. Kiev; Naukova Dumka. – in Russian; Holetich, C.D. 1982. Lilac species and cultivars in cultivation in USSR. Lilacs 11(2):1-35. - translation of Rubtzov et al. 1982.
  Name: Russian for youth.
  Cultivar name established and accepted.

'Yuriï Gagarin', *S. vulgaris*
  'Юрий Гагарин'
  Kravchenko D.V. 1970; D V
  syn. - 'Jurij Gargarin'
  {'Marie Legraye' × 'Lamarck'}
  Kravchenko L. Culture of lilacs in Uzbekistan. Publishing house "Uzbekistan", Tashkent, 1970 p. 14
  Rubtzov et al. 1980. Vidy i sorta sireni, kul'tiviruemye v SSSR. Kiev; Naukova Dumka. – in Russian; Holetich, C.D. 1982. Lilac species and cultivars in cultivation in USSR. Lilacs 11(2):1-38. - translation of Rubtzov et al. 1982.
  Named for Yuriï Gagarin, 1934-1968, Soviet cosmonaut.
  Cultivar name established and accepted.

'Yuzhanka', *S. vulgaris*
  'Южанка'
  Klimenko, V. 1955; S VII-VI
  syn. - 'Juzhanka'
  Rubtzov et al. 1980. Vidy i sorta sireni, kul'tiviruemye v SSSR. Kiev; Naukova Dumka. – in Russian; Holetich, C.D. 1982. Lilac species and cultivars in cultivation in USSR. Lilacs 11(2):1-38. - translation of Rubtzov et al. 1982.
  Russian for a woman who lives in the south region of the country.
  Cultivar name established and accepted.

'Yuzhnyï Krest', *S. vulgaris*
  'Южный Крест'
  Zalivsky pre-1959, S VII/IV
  {parentage not known}
  Poliakova to Vrugtman, June 23, 2018.
  Name: Russian for Southern Cross.
  Cultivar name not established; more information & publication required.

'Yuzhnaya Noch', *S. vulgaris*
  'Южная Ночь'
  Dyagilev (not Klimenko, V.) 1992; S III
  {'Obmanshchitsa' × OP}
  Dyagilev, Lilacs - Quart. Jour. 22(1):19 [1993]
  Name: Russian for southern night.
  Cultivar name not established.

'Yuzhnaya Noch', *S. vulgaris*
  'Южная Ночь'
  Klimenko, V. (not Dyagilev) 1955; S II
  syn. - 'Juzhnaja Noch'
  Rubtzov et al. 1980. Vidy i sorta sireni, kul'tiviruemye v SSSR. Kiev; Naukova Dumka. – in Russian; Holetich, C.D. 1982. Lilac species and cultivars in cultivation in USSR. Lilacs 11(2):1-38. - translation of Rubtzov et al. 1982.
  Name: Russian for southern night.
  Cultivar name established and accepted.

zaailing (seedling), *S.*
  origin not known ? ?
  (species affiliation not known)
  {parentage not known}
  Anon., Boskoop Research Stn 1994
  Cognomen, not a cultivar name.

Zaailing Spijk 1, *S. vulgaris*
  Botanical Gardens Wageningen; ? ?
  {parentage not known}
  Bot. G. Wageningen, Cat. 1996, 88
  Cognomen, not a cultivar name.

Zabel, Zabeli - see '**H. Zabel**'.

'Zagadka', *S. vulgaris*
  'Загадка'
  Sagitova; ? ?
  no information
  Name: Russian for riddle.
  Cultivar name not established.

'Zaiga', *S. vulgaris*
  Upītis ca 1970; D II
  Kalniņš, L., Ceriņu jaunšķirnes Dobelē, Dārs un drava 1986(12):13-15 - in Latvian; in litt. S. Strautiņa to F. Vrugtman [22 Jan. 2008] - ca 1970, D II.
  Name: Latvian feminine given name.
  Cultivar name established and accepted. Probably no longer in cultivation.

'Zailiïskaya', *S. vulgaris* - see '**Antonina Mel'nik**'

'Zarnitsa', *S. vulgaris*
  'Зарница'
  Aladin, S., Aladina, O., and Polyakova, T. 2014; S V
  {'Vecherniï Zvon' × OP}

Приусадебное хозяйство (Annex to the magazine Homestead farming: "Flowers in the garden and at home. Brushes and paints") 08/2015: 5-14; Садовник (Gardener) magazine, 05 (141)/2017 :16-22; Вестник АППМ (Catalog in Vestnik APPM (Planting material association) magazine) 1/2018: 59-72 (in Russian).
Name: Russian for summer lightning.
Cultivar name established and accepted.

'Zarya', *S. vulgaris* [rejected epithet; see 'Zarya', Vekhov]
'Заря'
Sagitova & Dzevitski; S VI-V
{open pollinated seedling of 'Necker'}
Name: Russian for dawn.
Cultivar name not established.

'Zarya', *S. vulgaris*
'Заря'
Vekhov 1952; D VII
syn. - 'Zaria', 'Zarja'
Rubtzov et al. 1980. Vidy i sorta sireni, kul'tiviruemye v SSSR. Kiev; Naukova Dumka. – in Russian; Holetich, C.D. 1982. Lilac species and cultivars in cultivation in USSR. Lilacs 11(2):1-38. - translation of Rubtzov et al. 1982; Photo on Jorgovani/Lilacs 2015 DVD.
Name: Russian for dawn (not to be confused with 'Dawn', Havemeyer; or 'Dawn', Klager)
Cultivar name established and accepted.

'Zarya Kommunizma', *S. vulgaris*
'Заря Коммунизма'
Kolesnikov 1951; S VI-VII
syn. - Kolesnikov No. 153, 'Zaria Kommunizma', 'Zarja Kommunizma', 'Slava Stalinu'
marketed in the USA as Dawn of Communism
{(Kolesnikov No. 110 × 'Andenken an Ludwig Späth') × Kolesnikov No. 105}
Howard, Arnoldia 19(6-7):31-35 [1959]; Gromov, Siren', 99, 101 [1963]; Howard & Brizicky, AABGA Quart. Newsl. No. 64, 17-21 [1965]; Wister & Oppe, Arnoldia 31(3):125 [1971] - as S VII; Rubtzov et al. 1980. Vidy i sorta sireni, kul'tiviruemye v SSSR. Kiev; Naukova Dumka. – in Russian; Holetich, C.D. 1982. Lilac species and cultivars in cultivation in USSR. Lilacs 11(2):1-38. - translation of Rubtzov et al. 1982; Photo on Jorgovani/Lilacs 2015 DVD.
Name: Russian for dawn of communism.
Cultivar name registered 1970; name established and accepted.

'Zashchitnikam Bresta', *S. vulgaris*
'Защитникам Бреста'
Smol'skiĭ & Bibikova 1964; D I
syn. - 'Zashchitnikam Bresta'
{'Mme Abel Chatenay' × 'Réaumur'}
Rubtzov et al. 1980. Vidy i sorta sireni, kul'tiviruemye v SSSR. Kiev; Naukova Dumka. – in Russian; Holetich, C.D. 1982. Lilac species and cultivars in cultivation in USSR. Lilacs 11(2):1-38. - translation of Rubtzov et al. 1982; Semenov, Igor, Lilacs - Quart. Jour. 43(3):85-87 [2014]; Photo on Jorgovani/Lilacs 2015 DVD.
Named for the defenders of Brest, Защитникам Бреста, Belarus, during WW II.
Cultivar name established and accepted.

'Zashchitnikam Leningrada', *S. vulgaris*
'Защитникам Ленинграда'
Aladin, S., Aladina, O., Polyakova, T., and Aladina, A. 2015; D VI
{'Rowancroft Pink' × OP}
(Международная научная конференция "Syringa L.: коллекции, выращивание, использование") "International Scientific Conference "Syringa L.: collections, cultivation, using" / Collection of Scientific Articles of Botanical Institute named after V.L. Komarov, Botanical Garden of Peter the Great BIN RAS. - St. Petersburg. -2020.- pp.3-7 (in Russian); Photo exhibition of all varieties of the creative breeding group "Russian Lilac" at the Festival "Lilac February", St. Petersburg, Botanical Garden of Peter the Great BIN RAS, February 22-24, 2020.
Named for the lifting of the siege of the city of Leningrad and dedicated to the defenders and liberators of the city during the Second World War.
Cultivar name established and accepted.

'Zashchitnkam Moskvy', *S. vulgaris*
'Защитникам Москвы'
Kolesnikov, Mironovich 1986, D VII
{parentage not known}
T. Polyakova , 2018, Мастер Сиреневой Кисти (Master of the Lilac Brush), p. 66
Registered with the State Commission of the Russian Federation for Testing and Protection of Selection Achievements, No. 8803560, 1998; Polyakova , 2010, Istoriya Russkoĭ Sireni, p. 85 - not a synonym of 'Pamyat' o S. M. Kirove'; Photo on Jorgovani/Lilacs 2015 DVD.
Named for the defenders of Moscow during WW II.
Cultivar name established and accepted.

Zaya Kosmodem' Yanskaya - see 'Zoya Kosmodem'yanskaya'.

'Zemgaliete', *S. vulgaris*
Upītis 1989; S IV
Photographed with identifying sign at Dobele, Latvia May 2018 by Natalia Savenko.
Cultivar name not established.

'Zemzariene', *S. vulgaris*
Upītis pre-1976; S VII-II
Semenov, Igor, Lilacs - Quart. Jour. 44(2):48, ill. 52 [2015]; Photo on Jorgovani/Lilacs 2015 DVD.
Name: Latvian for Zemzaris' wife.
Cultivar name established and accepted.

'Ženja', *S. vulgaris*
Upītis pre-1970; S V-VII
photo on Lilacs/Jorgovani DVD, 2nd ed. 2015; in cultivation at the Latvian State Institute of Fruit-Growing, Dobele; in litt. Igor Semenov to C. Holetich 16

March 2015; Photo on Jorgovani/Lilacs 2015 DVD.
Name: short form of Eugeni; named for a secretary of the originator.
Cultivar name not established.

'Zhang Zhiming', *S. pekinensis*
Zhang Zhiming 2004; S I
distributed in North America as Beijing Gold™
registered by Chicagoland Grows
Song Sparrow Nursery, Cat. 52 [2004]; Kim, Lilacs 38(4):132-133 [2009].
Distinguishing characteristics include unique primrose-yellow flowers, attractive, cinnamon-colored bark, and yellow-golden autumn color of foliage.
This selection was introduced to the USA through the North America China Plant Exploration Consortium (NACPEC) and named at the Morton Arboretum.
<http://www.chicagolandgrows.org/downloads/beijing_gold.pdf>
Photo on Jorgovani/Lilacs 2015 DVD.
Named for the originator, Zhang Zhiming, 1938- x, (Mr) professor of horticulture; worked at Beijing Botanical Garden, Institute of Botany, Chinese Academy of Sciences 1962-1998; deputy director of Beijing Botanical Garden 1986-1990; director of Beijing Botanical Garden 1990-1995; PR China.
Cultivar name established and accepted.

'Zhdi Menya', *S. vulgaris*
'Жди меня'
Aladin, S., Aladina, O., Polyokova, T, and Aladina A. 2014; D IV-V
Statutory registration, Russia, State Register and Plant Patent No. 80053/8058583 (2019)
{'Mikhaïlo Lomonosov' × 'Blanche Sweet'}
Питомник-частный сад (Pitomnik i chastnyi sad; Nursery and private garden) 3/2015:14-22 (in Russian); Приусадебное хозяйство (Annex to the magazine Homestead farming: "Flowers in the garden and at home. Brushes and paints") 08/2015: 5-14; Садовник (Gardener) magazine, 05 (141)/2017 :16-22; Вестник АППМ (Catalog in Vestnik APPM (Planting material association) magazine) 1/2018: 59-72 (in Russian); II All-Russian scientific-practical conference with international participation (II Всероссийская научно-практическая конференция с международным участием) " Botanical Gardens in the XXI Century: Biodiversity Conservation, Development Strategy and Innovative Solutions Belgorod, Botanical Garden of NRU "BelSU", September 23-26, 2019; pp.141-145 (in Russian).
Named for Zhdi Menya (Wait for Me), the poem by Konstantin Simonov (Константин Михайлович Симонов), 1915-1979, Russian war poet, novelist and playwright.
Cultivar name established and accepted.

'Zhemchug', *S. vulgaris*
'Жемчуг'
Dyagilev; ? ?
Pikaleva, Lilacs - Quart. Jour. 23(4):89 [1994]
Name: Russian for pearl.
Cultivar name not established.

'Zhemchuzhina', *S. vulgaris*
'Жемчужина'
Smol'skiĭ & Bibikova 1994; D V
syn. - 'Zhemchuzina', 'Zhemjuzhina'
Pikaleva, Lilacs - Quart. Jour. 23(4):89 [1994] - as D I; Chapman, Lilacs - Quart. Jour. 25(4):98 [1996] and 30(1):5-6 & front cover [2001] - as D V; Anon., Lilacs - Quart. Jour. 33(1):11 [2004]; Semenov, Igor, Lilacs -Quart. Jour. 43(3):85-87 & photo inside back cover [2014]; in litt. Semenov toVrugtman 13 August 2014.
Name: Russian for pearl.
Cultivar name established and accepted.

Zhmurka - see 'Chmurka'.

'Zhuravlik Origami', *S. vulgaris*
'Журавлик Оригами'
Aladin, S., Polyakova, T., and Aladina, O. 2016; S I
{'Lebedushka' × OP}
Садовник (Gardener) magazine 04 (140)/2017 :18-25; Вестник АППМ (Catalog in Vestnik APPM (Planting material association) magazine) 1/2018: 59-72 (in Russian).
Name: Russian for crane origami.
Cultivar name established and accepted.

'Zilacite', *S. vulgaris*
Kārkliņš 2003; S VII
Photo from Dobele, Latvia by Natalia Savenko on 2020 ILS Photo Database.
Cultivar name not established.

'Zilais Kalns', *S. vulgaris*
Upītis 1970; S VII/II
syn. - 'Zilaiskalns'
Kalniņš, L., Ceriņu jaunšķirnes Dobelē, Dārs un drava 1986(12):13-15 - in Latvian; Strautiņa, S. 1992. Ceriņi Dārzs un Drava. No. 6, pp.12-13; in litt. S. Strautiņa to F. Vrugtman [21 Dec. 2007] - 1970, VII/II; Photo on Jorgovani/Lilacs 2015 DVD.
Name: Latvian for blue mountain.
Cultivar name established and accepted.

'Zilgma', *S. vulgaris*
Upītis; ? ?
Kalniņš, L., Ceriņu jaunšķirnes Dobelē, Dārs un drava 1986(12):13-15 - in Latvian
Cultivar name not established.

'Zirka Travnya', *S. vulgaris*
'Зирка Травня'
origin unknown; D III-IV
syn. - 'Zirka Travnja', 'Zirka Travnya'
Bilov et al., Siren', 46 [1974] - in Russian; Rubtzov et al. 1980. Vidy i sorta sireni, kul'tiviruemye v SSSR. Kiev; Naukova Dumka. – in Russian; Holetich, C.D. 1982.

Lilac species and cultivars in cultivation in USSR. Lilacs 11(2):1-38. - translation of Rubtzov et al. 1982; Photo on Jorgovani/Lilacs 2015 DVD.
Name: Ukrainian for star of May.
Cultivar name established and accepted.

'Zixia', *S.* ×*hyacinthiflora*
Chen, Jinyoung 2006; D II
{*Syringa* × *hyacinthiflora* 'Pocahontas' and *S. oblata* subsp. *oblata* var. *alba*}
Chen, Jinyoung, et al. 2015. (Chinese Botanical Garden) 18:??; (Vrugtman, Cultivated Plant Diversity ... 2017).
Named for the fairy Zixia, a character in A Chinese Odyssey, Part One: Pandora's Box (1995).
Cultivar name registered 2016, name established and accepted.

'Ziyu', *S.* ×*hyacinthiflora*
Chen, Jinyoung 2006; D II-I
{*Syringa* × *hyacinthiflora* 'Pocahontas' and *S. oblata* subsp. *oblata* var. *alba*}
Chen, Jinyoung, et al. 2015. (Chinese Botanical Garden) 18:??; (Vrugtman, Cultivated Plant Diversity ... 2017).
Named for Ziyu (or ZiYu ?), the mythical swordsman, one of the characters in the Feng Shen Ji, Chronicles of the Gods Order.
Cultivar name registered 2016, name established and accepted.

'Zi Yun', *S.* ×*hyacinthiflora*
Zang & Fan 1984; D II
syn. - 'Zi Un', 'Zi yun'
{*S. oblata* × *S. vulgaris* L. 'Alba-plena'}
Zang & Fan, Pl. Introd. Acclimatization 3:117-121 [1983] - in Chinese; Zang, Fan & Li, Acta Horticulturae 404:63-67 [1995]; Yoshikawa, Kyoto Engei (Kyoto Horticulture), 84:21-23 [?] - in Japanese; Vrugtman, HortScience 32 (4):588 [1997]; Anon., Beijing Bot. Garden 2006:24; Photo on Jorgovani/Lilacs 2015 DVD.
Cultivar name registered 1996; name established and accepted.

'Znamya Lenina', *S. vulgaris*
'Знамя Ленина'
Kolesnikov pre-1936; S VII-IV
syn. - Kolesnikov No. 039, 'Znamia Lenian', 'Znamia Lenina', 'Znamja Lenina', 'Znamya Lenina', 'Znamya Lenyna'
marketed in the USA as BANNER OF LENIN
{('Congo' × Kolesnikov No. 110) × ('Congo' × Kolesnikov No. 105)}
Howard, Arnoldia 19(6-7):31-35 [1959]; Gromov, Siren', 103 [1963]; Howard & Brizicky, AABGA Quart. Newsl. No. 64, 17-21 [1965]; Wister & Oppe, Arnoldia 31(3):125 [1971] - as S ?; Gromov, Lilacs - Proceedings 2(4):17 [1974]; Rubtzov et al. 1980. Vidy i sorta sireni, kul'tiviruemye v SSSR. Kiev; Naukova Dumka. – in Russian; Holetich, C.D. 1982. Lilac species and cultivars in cultivation in USSR. Lilacs 11(2):1-38. - translation of Rubtzov et al. 1982; Lilacs - Proceedings 17(1): back cover ill. [1988]; Lilacs - Quart. Jour. 25(4): front cover ill. [1996]; Photo on Jorgovani/Lilacs 2015 DVD.
Name: Russian for banner of Lenin, or standard of Lenin.
Cultivar name registered 1970; name established and accepted.

'Znamya Perestroĭki', *S. vulgaris*
'Знамя Перестройки'
Dyagilev pre-1993; S V
Dyagilev, Lilacs - Quart. Jour. 22(1):19 [1993]; Pikaleva, Lilacs - Quart. Jour. 23(4):89 [1994]
Name: Russian for banner of restructuring.
Cultivar name not established.

'Zolotoĭ Amur', *S. villosa* subsp. *villosa*
'Золотой Амур'
Kuklina and Firsov 2008; S V *
{*S. villosa* subsp. *villosa* seedling, grown from seed collected from cultivated plants at the town of Svobodny, Amur Oblast, Russian Federation, [N 1983-15], received March 1982}
G.A. Firsov, Lilacs - Quart. Jour. 47(2):81-86 [2018] - originated at the Botanical Garden of the V L Komarov Botanical Institute RAS (BIN), at Aptekarsky Island, St Petersburg, Russian Federation; Registered with the State Commission of the Russian Federation for Testing and Protection of Selection Achievements, No. 9154026, 2010.
Name: Russian for the golden Amur.
Cultivar name established and accepted.

ZORIE - trade designation used for cut flowers of *S. vulgaris* 'Belorusskie Zori'.

'Zor'ka Venera', *S. vulgaris*
'Зорька Венера'
Smol'skiĭ & Bibikova 1964; S VII
{'Hyazinthenflieder' × 'Réaumur'}
Rubtzov et al. 1980. Vidy i sorta sireni, kul'tiviruemye v SSSR. Kiev; Naukova Dumka. – in Russian; Holetich, C.D. 1982. Lilac species and cultivars in cultivation in USSR. Lilacs 11(2):1-38. - translation of Rubtzov et al. 1982; Semenov, Igor, Lilacs - Quart. Jour. 43(3):85-87 & photo inside front cover [2014]; Photo on Jorgovani/Lilacs 2015 DVD.
Name: Russian for virgin Mary star.
Cultivar name established and accepted.

'Zoya Kosmodem'yanskaya', *S. vulgaris*
'Зоя Космодемьянская'
Kolesnikov 1943; S III-IV
syn. - 'Zaya Kosmodem' Yanskaya', 'Zoya Kosmodem'janskaja', 'Zoya Kosmodemyanskaya'
Kolesnikov, Lilac, 26 [1955]; Howard, Arnoldia 19(6-7):31-35 [1959]; AABGA Quart. Newsl. No. 64, 17-21 [1965]; Rubtzov et al. 1980. Vidy i sorta sireni, kul'tiviruemye v SSSR. Kiev; Naukova Dumka. – in Russian; Holetich, C.D. 1982. Lilac species and cultivars in cultivation in USSR. Lilacs 11(2):1-38. - translation of Rubtzov et al. 1982; Fiala, Lilacs, 214 [1988] - as 'Zaya Kosmodem' Yanskaya'; Photo on Jorgovani/Lilacs 2015 DVD.

Named for Zoya Anatolyevna Kosmodem'yanskaya, 1923-1941, Soviet partisan and Hero of the Soviet Union.
Cultivar name established and accepted.

zugentzii, S.
no information available, no literature reference listed as a S. species by Esveld nursery, Boskoop, Netherlands </www.esveld.nl/~laur/index.php?lan=eng&s=plant&q=product_group&g=Syringa&cp=heesters&p=7> [Feb. 8, 2009] and Arboretum Waasland <http://users.telenet.be/saswerkers/arboretum%20Waasland/CAT2007LO.pdf> [Feb. 8, 2009].

'Zukunft', *S. vulgaris*
Rottert pre-1930; D IV
Späth, Späth-Buch, 308 [1930] - as D IV; Meyer, Flieder, 55 [1952] - as D IV; Wister, Lilacs for America, 37, 60 [1942] - as S VII; Wister, Lilacs for America, 44 [1953] - as S IV
Name: German for future.
Cultivar name presumed registered 1953; name established and accepted.
Nota bene: Plants cultivated in North America under the name of 'Zukunft' appear all to be single-flowered and therefore not true to name.

'Zulu', *S. vulgaris*
Havemeyer pre-1942; S VII
Wister, Lilacs for America, 60 [1942], 44 [1953]; Lilac Land 1954 cat. - as D VII; Eickhorst, ILS Lilac Newsletter 4(1):4-5 [1978]; Oakes, ILS Lilac Newsletter 12(4):7 [1986] - 'Zulu' is single, not double; Photo on Jorgovani/Lilacs 2015 DVD.
Cultivar name presumed registered 1953; name established and accepted.

'Zviozdochka Kieva', *S. vulgaris*
'Звёздочка Киева'
probably Rubtzov & Zhogoleva; pre-1963; D I
Gromov, A., Siren', 70 [1963]
Name: Russian for little star of Kiev.
Cultivar name not established.